FEMINISM
AND
TRADITION
IN
AESTHETICS

FEMINISM
AND
TRADITION
IN
AESTHETICS

EDITED BY
PEGGY ZEGLIN BRAND
AND
CAROLYN KORSMEYER

THE PENNSYLVANIA STATE UNIVERSITY PRESS
UNIVERSITY PARK, PENNSYLVANIA

Library of Congress Cataloging-in-Publication Data

Feminism and tradition in aesthetics / edited by Peggy Zeglin Brand and Carolyn
   Korsmeyer.
       p.   cm.
   Includes bibliographical references (p.   ) and index.
   ISBN 0-271-01340-0 (cloth : acid-free paper)—
   ISBN 0-271-01341-9 (paper : acid-free paper)
   1. Aesthetics.   2. Feminist theory.   3. Feminism and the arts.
I. Brand, Peg. II. Korsmeyer, Carolyn.
HQ1219.F45   1995
305.42—dc20   94-13667
                                                  CIP

Chapters 1, 3, 5, 7, 9, 12, 15, 16, 17, 18, and 20 were previously published as a special
issue of the *Journal of Aesthetics and Art Criticism,* Vol. 48, No. 4 (Fall 1990), copyright
1990 by The American Society for Aesthetics, and are reproduced here by permission
of the Society.

Published by The Pennsylvania State University Press,
University Park, PA 16802-1003

It is the policy of The Pennsylvania State University Press to use acid-free paper for
the first printing of all clothbound books. Publications on uncoated stock satisfy the
minimum requirements of American National Standard for Information Sciences—
Permanence of Paper for Printed Library Materials, ANSI Z39.48–1984.

Contents

List of Illustrations

Foreword

Arthur C. Danto

When feminism in its modern form arose in the late 1960s, it did so as a political movement and as an intellectual one, and it was inevitable, in view of their profession, that academic women should be affected by both aspects at once. Politically, feminism drew attention to, and sought to undermine, the institutionally grounded invidiousness of gender, in terms of the unequal distribution of rewards and of burdens across gender lines, and the suddenly unacceptable way in which the life-projects of individuals were systematically thwarted or enhanced on the mere basis of sexual bimorphism and the biology of reproduction. It seemed immediately unjust that women, merely because they were women, should be excluded from avenues of fulfillment to which men, merely because they were men, took themselves to have a natural right of access. These perceptions, and the imperatives of political action they entailed, were shared by academic feminists with their sisters elsewhere in society. And because what they were frustrated and oppressed by was grounded in institutions that had to be changed if their lives were to be changed, political feminism was almost certainly the most subversive of the liberationist movements of the period, largely because gender cuts across all the other disabling divisions of society, and because once the grip of institutions was weakened or broken in the case of women, everyone must in some way be affected. As for academic women themselves, they could not see it inscribed in the very nature of things that access, promotion, and reward in the institutions through which they had chosen to define their lives, should in any way turn upon gender, and the kinds of reasons colleges and universities gave for gender-based differentials seemed increasingly unacceptable and even outrageous. These reasons in fact were forms of myth that served the purpose of keeping women "in their place"—and out of the places to which they aspired.

The transperception of reasons as but disguised myths was facilitated by a number of theoretical ideas that merged together with feminism in this period, and to which, in a great many of the traditional academic disciplines, feminism, as an intellectual movement, bound itself in a nearly chemical sense. This set of ideas, imported mainly from France, had the most monumental impact on the academic mentality, and it seemed in many ways to underwrite political feminism, and to explain how it was possible through academic labor—through a newly defined scholarship—to make a political and not merely an intellectual contribution. There was to begin with the detachment of texts from their authors in such a way as to render textual criticism an autonomous exercise, in which authorial intention was irrelevant and considerations of historical truth diminished in their relevance. Then there was the thought, advanced in a number of stunning writings by Michel Foucault, that all texts were to be understood as driven by political subtexts, and as serving entrenched powers, whatever the texts themselves might on their surface appear to be saying. And then there was the strategy of deconstruction, associated primarily with the thought of Jacques Derrida, which offered methods of reading texts in such a way as to penetrate to the covert agendas the texts promote. These intoxicating ideas were salted and seasoned with novel readings of Freud and of Marx, and attached themselves to certain abstract ideals of social revolution for which any disenfranchised body, not merely the traditional working class, might serve as the vehicle. These various strands of thought became constituted as "theory," and "theory" yielded up to those who accepted its authority the confidence that in the very act of textual deconstruction, they were advancing the *political* aims of feminism, as well as of the various other liberationist movements to which feminism was inevitably allied. Quite possibly they were right. Theory really did encourage the questioning of authority, and rested on the belief, almost a paraphrase of an ancient teaching of the Sophist Thrasymacus, that truth was what was in the interest of the ruling gender—or class, or race—to believe. And this relativism, allied with the anti-authoritarianism of theory, may very well have spread beyond the walls of the classroom, and helped feminists in their battles against the inequalities of everyday life.

Now the major enabling texts of theory came out of an intellectual tradition that was by no means shared by those academics in America upon whom theory had so immense an impact. All its main figures were trained in philosophy, and carried as part of their intellectual equipment the exacting knowledge of philosophy the French system demands of those who are to teach it. And it is fair to say that though Foucault's *Les mots et les choses* was a best-seller in France in the late 1960s, and though Derrida and Barthes were Parisian celebrities, their impact on the Continent was altogether different from that which their writings had in the text-oriented departments of American colleges and universities, whose members had not been especially trained to deal with philosophical ideas. There is nothing, for example, in the traditional disciplines of literary scholarship, or in the practices of close reading required of those who undertake advanced studies in literature, to equip them to handle texts that enter with the authority of philosophy, having been cast in the intoxicatingly obscure language that became the verbal vestment of theory as a form of writing. There were, so to speak, no defenses against it, with the result that the division between those who came of academic age in the pre-theory period, and those whose education came from the texts of theory, was all but total. The originating texts of political as well as of intellectual feminism, preeminently Simone de Beauvoir's *Le deuxième sexe,* could have been easily assimilated to pre-theory academic minds, and indeed have been used to support political action of the direct sort, agitating for equal opportunities and affirmative action, and the dismantling of barriers to women's aspirations. It was the bonding of feminism to theory that made academic work seem like political work, so that reading Jane Austen as subversive was itself an act of subversion in the larger struggle of the sex. In academic departments other than those that were text-driven, in science and in law and in engineering, political feminism made inroads on its own, without attaching itself to a body of texts understood as transformative of the disciplines. To be sure, the term "deconstruction," and something of its spirit, caught on, in part perhaps, because it harmonized with the spirit of the times. And some of the tenets of theory were certainly invoked by scholars outside the textual disciplines. But it was these disciplines, mainly, that sustained the impact and underwent the greatest transformation through internalizing theory's main attitudes and ideas. It was primarily the central humanistic disciplines of literature and the arts where the impact was felt. And it has been, by and large, the text-driven disciplines that have tended to make the news that has elicited shrieks from the conservative press, with proposals for the revision of the canon, and the insistence upon what the media refer to as political correctness.

Philosophers very early in the movement committed themselves to political feminism, and indeed some of the original feminist theorizing was done by philosophers, almost all of whom were women. But theorizing, in their case, had relatively little to do with theory, as this evolved in the humanities and to a lesser extent in the social sciences. Philosophers, however strong their feminist credentials, have by and large been cool to the claims of theory. Something in professional philosophical education rendered this discipline an inhospitable site for the novel strains of thought before which, for example, literature departments crumpled. In part this was a matter of the language:

Anglo-American philosophy has aspired to a certain ideal of clarity, in which terms are defined with almost painful exactitude, and theses formulated with a nearly logical precision. And in part the traditional training in logic and in logical analysis has fortified philosophers against theory's almost systematic excesses. And while there is beyond question a body of historical texts all philosophers are required to be familiar with, these are hardly canonical in any damaging sense of the term: rather, part of philosophical education consists in criticizing these texts, in finding logical gaps and inferential flaws. The "canonical" texts of philosophy constitute a kind of gymnasium for the development of philosophical muscles, rather than a repository of disenabling truths. Beyond question the traditional philosophers had unenlightened things to say about women. But it would be difficult to see the philosophies, under deconstruction, as merely devices for enhancing the status of men. To teach them that way would dissolve their value in the philosophical curriculum. So philosophers today have a kind of continuity with their tradition quite different from what is sought in departments of theory. And this continuity in part is finally because philosophers do not merely do scholarship on the texts of philosophy. They are expected to do philosophy themselves. Poets, similarly, might have a very different relationship to the canons of literature than literary scholars do. Within the humanistic division, philosophy stands rather apart.

Certain themes, endemic to theory, are naturally going to be resisted by philosophers, however feminist. The topic of intention, authorial or otherwise, has for example been canvased since the early 1950s, with the publication of Wittgenstein's *Philosophical Investigations,* and the subsequent appearance of Elizabeth Anscombe's brilliant *Intention.* It is widely accepted by philosophers that there is some connection, not readily analyzed, between action and intention, and that this connection implies something for the philosophy of mind. At the very least, aware of the systematic embedding of intention with a large complex of concepts, philosophers would be circumspect in cutting intention out of consideration in the analysis of action. There are, as Anscombe was among the first to demonstrate, descriptions of actions under which they are not intentional—descriptions under which, as she would say, the question of reasons does not arise. But the central descriptions are those that connect action and intention together, and it is far from plain that the other descriptions have the importance for literature required by theory. Inevitably, texts can be described in ways having nothing to do with intentions, nor, accordingly, with the author's knowledge of what was being done and the reasons for doing it. But the descriptions under which texts are intentional may also be the ones under which they are literature.

Similarly, relativism is not simply something to be accepted flatly. Not even Richard Rorty, who has been the philosopher theorists find most congenial, has denied that there are facts or that facts are real, only that truth is not something independent of human beings. By this, however, he means something not quite so exciting as it sounds: he means that "truth" is a property of sentences, and only human beings make sentences. But it hardly follows that in making sentences that are true, they somehow make them true; that is something that happens from the direction of the world. The issues of truth are thus left sufficiently intact that the further issue of relativism is not foreclosed. Relativism, like skepticism, is a constant topic of philosophical debate, but hardly a tenet of philosophical dogma, and in contrast with theory, philosophers are not ready to throw truth overboard as a condition for liberation. Philosophical criticism is rarely deconstructive in tone or in effect. It rather gives philosophers credit for wishing their theses to withstand critiques and to be able to overcome difficulties. The targets of criticism are typically treated as the critics' peers.

It is in this spirit, in which for the most part feminist philosophers have participated, that they have taken on questions felt to be of immediate interest to feminism: issues of language, of sexuality, of embodiment, of justice and equality, and of values. A corpus of serious philosophical literature has been emerging along these and other fronts, in which the methods of criticism and analysis have been powerful and exact instruments in the clarification of the issues that affect women's lives and thought—and the lives and thoughts of men as well. There remain, of course, questions of a profound philosophical nature, left over when the issues of equality and justice are resolved, that seek to overlap the differences of gender. These have to do with the extent to which the self itself is gendered, and the degree to which gender may be said to inflect our most profound relationships to and connections with one another and with the world. There is an as yet underdeveloped feminist philosophy of knowledge, of mind, of self, and of metaphysics. And it is hard not to speculate upon the possibility that gender might inflect everything, to the point where men and women might be said to live different worlds. Living different worlds need not entail—indeed, ought not to entail—discriminations in the common world. But it infuses the topic of the meaning of having a world in ways as yet hardly understood.

Aesthetics is a very good area in which to extend feminist considerations, in part because philosophers will be addressing the very objects—"textual objects"—addressed by theory. But also because works of art have a philosophical complexity that enables analysis of them to serve as models for the analysis of the larger complexes of lived life: issues of value, of subjectivity, of content, of meaning, and of embodiment that resonate throughout the domains of philosophical reflection. This volume is a pioneering work, and of the utmost importance not for feminism alone, but for aesthetics itself, which must benefit greatly through the ventilation of the topics feminists have made salient. Peg Brand and Carolyn Korsmeyer are exemplary philosophers and creative aestheticians, feminist thinkers, and intellectual crusaders. They have assembled in this sparkling collection some of the most instructive texts in the contemporary philosophy of art, demonstrating that feminism is neither a restricted topic nor solely of interest to a restricted audience. I am honored to have been asked to contribute this foreword.

Acknowledgments

This project was first undertaken as a special issue of the *Journal of Aesthetics and Art Criticism*. For their help and encouragement during the time that the special issue was produced and thereafter as it developed into a book, we would like to thank the late John Fisher, editor of the *Journal of Aesthetics and Art Criticism* until 1988, Donald Crawford, editor of the journal from 1988 to 1993, Arthur C. Danto, president of the American Society for Aesthetics from 1989 to 1991, and Roger Shiner, secretary-treasurer of the American Society for Aesthetics. We would also like to thank Laurie Shrage and Mary Bittner Wiseman for their helpful reviews of the manuscript. We are grateful to Nancy Spero for her generosity in allowing us to reproduce her artwork on the cover.

Introduction:
Aesthetics and Its Traditions

Peggy Zeglin Brand and Carolyn Korsmeyer

Any entry into the lists of scholarship takes its place among the received and developing ideas of its time. Feminist scholarship has a particular obligation to be reflective about this and to situate itself in the furiously changing history of challenges, questionings, and deconstructions of traditional systems of understanding that have taken place over the last quarter century. Approaches to the study of women and of gender, to the differences represented by gender, sexual desires, and racial, ethnic, and national identities, have moved so very rapidly that it is difficult even for the diligent reader to keep informed. At the same time feminist methodologies, assumptions, and insights have developed unevenly, such that what is common presumption in one field of study may be perplexingly nonstandard even to feminists in another.

Some of the diversity of feminist scholarship proceeds from expectable differences of opinions about subjects under investigation, such as the role of biology in the formation of gender or the independence of female cultural traditions, to mention just two long-standing themes of debate. At other times, this diversity is entangled in one of the most notable reforms of research that feminism has fostered: the tremendous growth of scholarship that trades methodologies across disciplines. From the early days of their endeavors, feminist scholars have rightly perceived that barriers to thorough understanding of issues concerning women, sex, gender, patriarchy, and social diversity are constituted by traditions of inquiry themselves that proscribe what is considered legitimate research within recognized disciplinary frameworks. The blurring of conventional academic divisions of study has dramatically enhanced the advancement of feminist scholarship.

Sometimes, however, what is proclaimed as interdisciplinary scholarship not only rejects and supplants but also forgets or ignores what have been staple issues of inquiry. Reflection on this phenomenon focuses attention on the complexities of traditions and their overthrow. The essays collected in *Feminism and Tradition in Aesthetics* shed light on the tenacity—sometimes tyrannical, sometimes useful—of various traditions in philosophies of the arts and theories of aesthetics. What cultural and intellectual frameworks inform our thinking about perception, beauty, art, and culture? And how have these influenced and been perpetuated by scholarly writing in aesthetics and philosophy of art? The essays collected herein are contributions by scholars in several disciplines, but they all address directly or implicitly aspects of the philosophical tradition. In what follows we speculate about the particular and idiosyncratic development of feminism in philosophical aesthetics; we seek to clarify its traditions and to indicate both how these traditions have resisted feminist inroads and how they afford important territory for feminist analyses.

In the 1990s there is already much well-known feminist scholarship in the arts, especially in literature and literary theory, art history and criticism, and film studies. The field of philosophy too has seen the development of a body of feminist thinking, particularly in the areas of philosophy of science and ethics. The philosophical subdiscipline of aesthetics, on the other hand, has only just begun to develop a feminist presence. One need only look at the syllabus for a standard introductory course or review the recommended reading list for a Ph.D. comprehensive exam in aesthetics to realize that the appearance of feminist scholarship is infrequent, if present at all.[1] In light of twenty-five years of rich and stimulating feminist thought on the arts—feminist challenges applicable to the foundations of philosophical aesthetics—we ask, "Why, in the 1990s, are feminist writings still rare?"

The same question arises when one considers journal publication. The first special issue of an academic philosophy journal in English devoted to feminism was *The Monist* 57, no. 1 (January 1973). Later the same year *Philosophical Forum* published another special issue. Shortly thereafter the journal *Ethics* began publishing feminist pieces, and even the *Journal of Philosophy* and other mainstream journals have had their occasional feminist pieces over the last decades. In short, while still a distinctly maverick voice, feminism has been heard in philosophy for quite some time.

It comes as a surprise to learn, therefore, that the *Journal of Aesthetics and Art Criticism* did not have any feminist presence whatsoever until 1990 with the publication of the special issue that became the basis for this collection (48, no. 4 [Fall 1990]). Conversely, the journal of feminist philosophy, *Hypatia*, saw few entries in aesthetics until the publication of its own special issue on the subject, also in 1990 (5, no. 2 [Summer 1990]).[2] This phenomenon is even more perplexing if one bears in mind that the cognate disciplines of aesthetics, such as literary theory, art history, and film studies, have been among the academic vanguard of feminism since the early 1970s. This peculiar absence of feminism from the area of philosophy that—at first glance—looks to be among the most obvious for the entry of feminist scholarship deserves some comment. The following speculations hazard some answers as to why this has been the case.

Within the field of philosophy, aesthetics comprises a rather small area. The professional society devoted to the field is an interdisciplinary society, though the majority of its members are philosophers.[3] Quite a few of these are also participants in other philosophical fields, notably philosophy of science, ethics, philosophy of law, metaphysics, epistemology, and various areas in the history of philosophy. In short, philosophers who work in aesthetics are well connected to other areas of philosophy, as well as to related disciplines such as musicology, art history and criticism, and literature.

The converse, however, is not the case. While a philosopher interested in aesthetics is expected to be familiar with other areas of the field such as ethics, epistemology, logic, or metaphysics, practitioners in these latter fields may consider themselves quite well educated without knowing even a smattering of aesthetic theory. (Even in 1951, John Passmore lamented this fact, wondering whether [mere] philistinism was to blame.)[4] Aesthetics and feminist philosophy thus share an unenviable parallel: their scholars must know the work of others, though the others feel no reciprocal need to learn about either aesthetics or feminism. Therefore, to a degree the absence of feminist perspectives from aesthetics has been occasioned by bad intellectual habits.

If these disciplinary ruts were the only factors to consider, the matter would be merely of interest for sociology of knowledge, (or if one is feeling cynical, sociology of the academy). But there are also matters of considerable substance involved that concern basic presumptions about beauty, value, and art, in short, about the "tradition" to which this volume refers. Considering these factors requires an excursion into the issues that lie at the heart of the discipline.

Traditions of Aesthetics

In the longer version of its name, this field is known as "aesthetics and philosophy of art." Aesthetic theories are often principally about art, but the two component terms actually point in different if overlapping directions. "Aesthetics" is the more recent area of study, having developed in early modern European theory. It pertains to theories of perception that are interested in discovering the nature of the apprehension of beauty and other perceptual qualities of intrinsic value. The objects of aesthetic perception may or may not be works of art. As the philosophers of the eighteenth century whose founding interest is credited with the generation of the modern discipline observed, nature and mathematics could provide examples of aesthetic objects just as well as art. The chief goal of classic aesthetic theory is to investigate the bases for shared taste and perception of value. (A fuller discussion of these issues is presented in the preface to Part I.)

"Philosophy of art," like so many areas of philosophy, has been around since Plato. It concerns itself with the nature of creativity and of art objects, their value and social role, and their power to form character and convey knowledge. If beauty or other aesthetic qualities are held to be the presiding values for art, then theories of beauty become part of philosophy of art. And insofar as art theorists analyze perception, then the two areas of "aesthetics" and "philosophy of art" converge. (Because this is frequently the case in the modern period, the term "aesthetics" is often used as shorthand for the entire area of study.) Interest in perception and appreciation of works of art generates theories of the nature of interpretation and criticism and the ascription of meaning to cultural products. In this latter dimension aesthetics overlaps—in scope if not method—with critical studies of the arts.

In what is perhaps the most obvious sense, tradition for all these areas of aesthetics consists of so-called classics or canonical texts in the field and may be discovered by looking at required reading in university programs.[5] While the content of instructional texts varies, there is considerable de facto agreement about what constitutes the staple readings of the field. Teaching anthologies typically include entries from Plato, Aristotle, Hume, and Kant in their historical sections, and often also include selections from writers such as Hegel, Schopenhauer, Nietzsche, Heidegger. These texts are generally familiar to scholars in other areas of philosophy and in the arts-related disciplines and are customarily acknowledged as of formative importance (and thus "canonical") for general intellectual history. When it comes to entries that deal with problems of contemporary aesthetics, the standard pieces shift character to much narrower disciplinary considerations. Some names remain widely familiar, especially those recent writers who are influential across disciplines such as Ricoeur, Foucault, or Derrida. But many others are new to all but those already practicing in aesthetics: names such as Bullough, Stolnitz, Sibley, Kennick, Weitz, Beardsley, that have been staple entries in aesthetics for decades and grow out of the ambient traditions of Anglo-American analytic philosophy.

The "tradition" within and against which feminist perspectives are developed in the essays collected here is thus best considered in the plural. It is impossible to discern clean categories within cultural history, but our purposes are served by distinguishing two aspects of tradition: the most familiar and general tradition of Western philosophy that has shaped modern consciousness about art in a wide sweep of disciplines;[6] and the more recent philosophical precedents that have influenced aesthetics.[7] Both of these connect with critical traditions regarding the interpretation and ascription of meaning to cultural products. Here we devote the most attention to the twentieth-century methods and approaches practiced in American philosophy; they form the principal backdrop for the variety of views that come to be united in this volume.

Historical Traditions of Western Aesthetics

The greatest theoretical continuity within the Western tradition in aesthetics extends only since the eighteenth century, although roots of modern ideas go deep and have parallels as far back as classical antiquity. Any tradition that traces its roots as far back as Plato is going to contain considerable variety, not to mention contrariety. The concept of art has not been a stable one; indeed, the idea of "fine art" is itself a product of early modern European intellectual history.[8] But even shearing off the older history of philosophy of art, there have been so many varieties of theory in the last several hundred years that even the modern traditions contain irreconcilable theories of art and aesthetic value. Some of their differences are signaled by the several "isms" of the field, such as the formalisms of Kant, Bell, and Hanslick; the idealisms of Hegel, Schopenhauer, and Croce; the expressionisms of Collingwood, Tolstoy, and Kandinsky. These categories are not exhaustive, their terms of description are not always univocal, and their memberships overlap and shift, depending upon the aspect of art or theory under attention. Moreover, while in some respects the frequent entry of a thinker in a teaching text indicates an importance credited to his (or occasionally her) theory,[9] some of their voices are entered as oddities or examples of extremist views and have not had the same influence over theory formation as the weight of their names would suggest. (Such is the case with Tolstoy and Dewey, for example, both of whom depart from the conventional assignment of high importance to the fine arts and recommend an overthrow of traditional aesthetic values.)[10]

Even among those who have exerted long influence over the formation of theory, there is considerable disagreement on such questions as the essential nature of art, the nature of creativity, and the character of the experience of beauty and other aesthetic values. Generalization, therefore, must proceed cautiously. Bearing these caveats in mind, we may yet step back and notice that the vast majority of these theories share two presumptions. They capture not only aspects of philosophical theories of art and aesthetics, but also the ideas about art that hold sway in the popular imagination and are thus broadly influential over the ways we thought and still think about the place of art in our lives.

First of all, it is rarely questioned that art's value transcends cultural differences and is a source of timeless and everlasting value. This ideal lies behind many popular cultural establishments, such as the notion that museums and libraries are important public institutions that guard the culture of the past for present and future generations. It subtends appeals to the value of liberal education in the humanities. And statements manifesting this value are present in theories that are otherwise vastly different. One could hardly find more divergent philosophical sensibilities than those of Hume and Heidegger, yet Hume observes that "The same Homer, who pleased at Athens and Rome two thousand years ago, is still admired at Paris and at London. All the changes of climate, government, religion, and language, have not been able to obscure his glory."[11] And Heidegger credits the timelessness of great art as providing a glimpse of Truth (the "unconcealedness of being").[12] Any created object of such a character must be the product of an unusual sensibility, and thus the artist who is capable of providing us with Art is often credited with Genius. Kant called genius the talent that "gives the rule to art," and Schopenhauer places art and the artist in fully reverent terms when he states that Art is the work of genius, which "repeats the eternal Ideas apprehended through pure contemplation, the essential and abiding element in all the phenomena of the world."[13]

Several of the authors of these scattered references express certain ideas of European Romanticism, though in their views about the special insight of the artist and the lasting value of art they echo ideas both more ancient and more modern. That theorists who differ on so many points should agree on the universal value of art indicates the depth of this presumption about the nature and character of art. Of course, that a vast array of thinkers should credit art with lasting importance is hardly surprising and not on the face of it particularly sinister. However, the collateral ideas that are invoked to explain the timeless value of art are ones that have come in for sharp critique from feminists. The brief quotes above indicate, for example, that the value of art is linked with the special mind of artists, and thus these theories give rise to a picture of the artistic Genius, a figure deeply inflected with masculine properties both historically and conceptually.[14] (Several of the essays in this volume continue discussion of the links between the concept of genius, the value of art, and the corollary evaluation of art by women; see Chapters 4, 12, and 13.)

There is a second common presumption underlying the broad sweep of intellectual history that constitutes this tradition. This pertains to the nature of appreciation of art and stipulates the state of mind that characterizes the apprehension of beauty, sublimity, and artistic greatness. It is held that the state of aesthetic contemplation is a principal instance of intrinsic value; it takes one out of one's own self-concerns and peculiarities and into a state of mind that may be shared by any other human being. Thus it affords an escape from the individual ego and unites all who experience it in a common appreciation, transhistorical and transcultural.

This assumption is less widespread in the history of philosophy and art theory than is the former, but it is very strong in theory from the eighteenth century well into our own time. Perhaps it finds its purest expression in Kant's "Analytic of the Beautiful," where free beauty is characterized as disinterested pleasure taken in representation. Or in Schopenhauer's articulation of aesthetic attention as a will-less state where the sense of self is lost and one is no longer bound by time and place. It finds its way into artwriting in Clive Bell's description of the appreciation of "significant form." In less extreme forms we find a host of views that typify aesthetic contemplation as a state of mind that distances the perceiver from ordinary, mundane aspects of life.[15] And the very term "aesthetic" qualities, referring to the presentational qualities of an object apart from its instrumental, economic, or political characteristics, represents continuation of the idea that aesthetic value occupies its own domain, separable from aspects of practical life.[16]

Both these tenets about art and aesthetic value rely on a presumption that is under fire from several directions at the present time: namely, that art and aesthetic attention are both in some sense universal. By "universal" it is asserted that art and aesthetic value possess at least ideally the same value for everyone, that they bind people together in experience. These two broad theses have been challenged repeatedly in the latter part of this century, both by feminists and postmodernists, and earlier by followers of Wittgenstein. Postmodernism's challenge is especially acute on the issue of the universality of aesthetic appreciation. It questions the notion of common subjectivity and hence undermines what is strongest about theories that delimit a distinct area of aesthetic consciousness: their demonstration of a common human faculty that binds all together and permits transcendence of cultural barriers.

Feminists, especially those who study critical disciplines such as literary and film theory, have developed critiques of the broad Western tradition that are by now becoming familiar: that the universal subject is historically situated (masculine, patriarchal, imperialistic); and that the concept of fine or high art, along with the notion of artistic genius, is exclusionary both historically and conceptually. Several of the essays in this volume advance such critiques of modern European philosophical aesthetics, especially those in Part I. The essays in Part II continue feminist critiques of theories of aesthetic appreciation by considering the alternative theories of the gaze as illuminating modes of understanding the apprehension of visual art. (This challenge is discussed more fully in the preface to Part II.)

It is less well known that the history of analytic aesthetics has contained parallel objections to systematic theories of the arts and of aesthetic appreciation—objections that, while not feminist in character, provide more congenial company for feminist thinking than is ordinarily expected in philosophy. While at present many feminists regard analytic philosophy as a stultifying predecessor and look to European philosophy and its psychoanalytic cousins for the richer theoretical tools by which to understand gender, culture, and historical contingency, the early analytic turn was reacting to certain concerns that feminists share, notably skepticism about essentialism. The recent history of aesthetics and philosophy of art in this tradition is the subject we turn to next. The character and history of analytic aesthetics helps further to explain the late arrival of feminism to the scene.

Analytic Aesthetics

In certain respects philosophers of the analytic school continued the older traditions of aesthetics. For example, the tenet that aesthetic value and aesthetic qualities require definition in contrast to moral and practical properties remained strong in this school of thought. Thus continuity with the eighteenth-century theories of taste mentioned above is especially evident.[17] But in other dramatic respects analytic philosophy broke radically with its precursor traditions, particularly those speculative philosophies of the nineteenth and early twentieth centuries that offered systematic theories of art embedded in metaphysical constructs. Hegelian and post-Hegelian idealist theories such as those of Benedetto Croce came under fire, although the general complaint eventually was directed to any aesthetic theory that attempted a systematic, essentialist definition of art.

Thus in the 1940s and 1950s, philosophers developed their own idiosyncratic sense of "tradition" in which "tradition" came to mean "pre-analytic," that is, works by authors predating Bertrand Russell, G. E. Moore, and others writing in the early years of this century who turned away from the speculative Idealist systems that at the time were models of philosophical methodology. In terms of aesthetics, this notion of tradition congealed in mid-century with the hindsight of theorists heavily influenced by Wittgenstein, who were dissatisfied with the essentialism, romanticism, idealism, and what they perceived to be the endemic vagueness of their predecessors. Thus in 1958 William E. Kennick began his essay "Does Traditional Aesthetics Rest On a Mistake?" by stipulating, in no uncertain terms, what he meant by "traditional aesthetics": "By 'traditional aesthetics' I mean that familiar philosophical discipline which concerns itself with trying to answer such questions as the following: What is Art? What is Beauty? What is the Aesthetic Experience? What is the Creative Act? What are the criteria of Aesthetic Judgment and Taste? What is the function of Criticism?"[18]

In 1948 W. B. Gallie had laid out "The Function of Philosophical Aesthetics" in an attack on the essentialist doctrines of Croce and Collingwood. He not only called for an "informed skepticism" about all generalities concerning art, he also turned an analytic eye to art-critical literature, urging careful rewriting of obscure and logically faulty criticism, pegging Wordsworth as his prime example.[19] That same year, Arnold Isenberg delivered an address to the American Society for Aesthetics, later published under the title, "Critical Communication," in which he called for a similar redirection of energies.[20] In its very title, John Passmore's "The Dreariness of Aesthetics" (1951) could not have been clearer in expressing the growing sentiment to abandon all work on definitions of art, beauty, aesthetic experience, and the underlying principles common to all "good" works of art. Five years later Morris Weitz published "The Role of Theory in Aesthetics," in which he argued against "any attempt to state the defining properties of art," sounding the death knell for "traditional" theory: "theory—in the requisite classical sense—is *never* forthcoming in aesthetics," he proclaimed.[21]

Thus the period during and just after World War II witnessed a prolific number of writings in analytic aesthetics, coinciding with the shift of the center of the artworld from Paris to New York, the rise of abstract expressionism with its attendant critic-devotees, and, interestingly enough, the formation and growth of the fledgling interdisciplinary group, the American Society for Aesthetics. Writing decades later, Richard Shusterman reconstructed the way philosophers must have felt at the time, namely, that analytic aesthetics came along just in time to "clarify" the "murky confusion" of the tradition.[22] According to Shusterman, analytic aesthetics recommended a threefold assault upon tradition—anti-essentialism, metacriticism (seeking to clarify art criticism), and adoption of the paradigmatic methodology of scientific inquiry. One would surmise that this promoted some antagonism between philosophers who saw aesthetics as metacriticism and critics who saw no need or use for philosophers. As aestheticians invaded the domain of criticism, offering to "rewrite" critical copy they found faulty and obscure, it comes as no surprise to find, at least within the publications of the ASA's journal, that the number of nonphilosophers' contributions consistently diminished throughout its fifty-year history.[23] It is evident that the feminist scholarship that emerged from disciplines such as art history and literary theory in the early 1970s would not be welcomed by this particular legacy of the analytic tradition.

And yet, ironically, the impetus behind the initial feminist critiques of art history in the 1970s shares a certain orientation with analytic aesthetics of mid-century, specifically its skepticism about the univocity of "art" and its call to examine closely the way critical language actually functions, rather than to rely on hortatory prescriptions about how great art ought to be enjoyed. Linda Nochlin's ground-breaking essay of 1971, "Why Have There Been No Great Women Artists?" launched an entire movement centered on women's involvement in the arts.[24] In her review of the systematic exclusion of female artists from teaching studios and other realms of art instruction, Nochlin also suggested that because of its history, the traditional idea of fine art (and attendant concepts such as genius) may continue to overlook the creative products customarily undertaken by women.

Such analyses of the concept of art also contributed to the early questioning of the "canon" and of the standards that have chosen its membership. Feminist scholarship has unearthed women artists, writers, and musicians of the past that were oftentimes well known, amply commissioned, and self-supporting in their day but were subsequently omitted from the canon of "greats" in the written histories of art.[25] These studies prompted skepticism about the "canon" of great art, leading feminists in the direction of more theoretical and abstract pursuits such as deconstructive analyses of the underlying assumptions of critical standards. A "new art history" was taking hold, emphasizing the "work of art itself as a piece of history" as opposed to the traditional focus on "the development and achievement of period styles, the history or sequence of works."[26]

In their studies of the language of art history and criticism, feminist scholars began to explore the concepts of "greatness" and "genius" and why women never succeeded in acquiring either accolade. As with earlier anti-essentialism, definitions of "art" were rejected. To feminists, they were seen as limiting and oppressive: privileging "high" art over low, "fine" art over craft, men's art over women's. Early on, enthusiasm ran high that something like a female nature was discernible and that a woman's art or a feminine sensibility could be discovered.[27] It was overturned by another strain of anti-essentialism that focused not only on gender differences but differences within gender of nationality, race, class. The entire foundation of interpretation and evaluation came undone as feminists, in rejecting the conventional meanings assigned canonical works and texts, also questioned the obviousness of the intrinsic merits of Great Art. Thus, the first collection of feminist art-historical essays, *Feminism and Art History: Questioning the Litany,* sought to distinguish itself from catalogues and monographs by examining "Western art history and the extent to which it has been distorted, in every major period, by sexual bias."[28] Similarly, Rozsika Parker and Griselda Pollock's ground-breaking work, *Old Mistresses: Women, Art and Ideology* sought to establish strategies to subvert and collapse stereotypes of women and their art by means of analyzing women's historical and ideological position within the world of art production.[29] Over less than twenty years, feminist critiques have broadened in scope to combine historical reclamation, linguistic analysis, sociological explanation, and philosophical questioning of the underlying assumptions of the traditions of a variety of fields.[30]

While analytic aesthetics and feminist art history share a disposition to criticize the staple concepts of theories of art, it is still the differences between these movements that are the most striking. Sharing as they may a skeptical and particularist method, they diverge profoundly in content and in the scope of questions considered important to pursue. Subjects mentioning women and gender have been very difficult to insert into analytic philosophy generally, for the simple reason that no such topics were considered "philosophical." Some portion of the philosophical literature of the twentieth century is mindful of the nature of philosophy itself, taking pains to distinguish this field from psychology, sociology, or criticism. Part of the early resistance of analytic philosophy to the advent of feminist perspectives in scholarship stemmed from the belief that subjects that specify gender digress into another discipline, one that deals in empirical data but not the abstract theorizing that marks philosophy. For similar reasons, philosophers have avoided the political dimension of art. Hence part of the charge of feminism to analytic aesthetics is that philosophers still neglect the cultural and historical context of a work of art, such as the gender, race, class, and particular historical situation of the artist and her audience. Happily, the era of erecting strict boundaries for legitimate philosophical inquiry has largely passed, although its lingering influence accounts in part for the late entry of feminism into philosophical aesthetics. One can see a general discomfort regarding the limitations of scope of legitimate subject matter in recent reflections on the state of aesthetics in general and analytic aesthetics in particular.[31]

It is important to note that despite early enthusiasms to the contrary, not all philosophers found (or continue to find) analytic aesthetics to be a panacea for critical and philosophical ills. The cyclical process of criticizing and replacing old ways with the new was bound to result in the new itself becoming old. Thus philosophers critical of analytic aesthetics have adopted yet another, more inclusive meaning of the term "tradition." For the authors in the 1980s and 1990s, "tradition" not only includes the pre-analytic, speculative, and Idealist traditions, but also the body of analytic writings that dominated American philosophy mid-century.

The 1987 special issue of the *Journal of Aesthetics and Art Criticism* provides a retrospective look at the past decades of analytic aesthetics and speculations about its future. The mood it conveys is quite different from that of earlier years. Somber and speculative, it brings to light the concerns and rumblings building for several years over the influx of "other" modes of thinking in aesthetics, including the deconstructive styles of poststructuralism. Shusterman's introduction to the issue suggests that the future of analytic aesthetics is in doubt. As he puts it, the pressing issue is whether analytic aesthetics "needs an epitaph and (if it does) what should there be inscribed."[32] For some, the prospect of a postanalytic period (or worse yet, as Shusterman adds, a postphilosophical era) was sobering. For others, it was a welcome relief.

Anita Silvers asks the question this way: "Has Analysis Made Aesthetics Clear?"[33] Referring to the original goals of Arnold Isenberg, W. B. Gallie, and Margaret Macdonald, she concludes that analytic aesthetics actually *added* to the dreariness cited by Passmore in 1951 by calling for too strict a revision of art-critical language and argument forms at the expense of fulfilling their function: to make art more accessible and appreciated. Praising the more recent theories of Arthur Danto and Nelson Goodman (discussed below) as exemplars of Isenberg's recommendation "to integrate insightful commentary on art with rigorous philosophical argument," Silvers encourages a return to a discussion of art objects to ground and advance theoretical concerns. To Marx Wartofsky, analytic aesthetics only succumbed to dreariness when put in a "derivative" or "dependent posture," that is, of relying upon previous analysis for its raison d'être. His suggestion for infusing new life into the profession? Again, a return to the arts.[34] What emerges from a number of authors is a sense that, in spite of intentions to attend more closely to actual works of art, analytic philosophers became isolated from the world of art and too self-absorbed. (Roger Scruton, writing elsewhere, castigated aesthetics and philosophy in general, for retreating from artistic and literary culture, thereby abandoning it to the deconstructionists, and for adopting "the rigour—or *rigor mortis*—of semantic analysis.")[35]

These authors record what Joseph Margolis calls "a kind of increasing suicidal neglect of the leading themes of cultural life," in spite of attempts by Arthur Danto and George Dickie to come to grips with the most provocative art of the twentieth century.[36] Margolis has resisted the insularity of analytic aesthetics and suggests that the field can be resuscitated by accommodating all forms of critique, including Continental philosophy ("the historicist, hermeneutic, the preformational, structuralist and poststructuralist, the deconstructive, the genealogical, the praxical") and, specifically, feminism.[37]

Analytic approaches in aesthetics as described earlier and as the subject of this recent critical reflection saw their glory days in mid-century. In the 1960s aesthetics as practiced by analytic philosophers began to shift its orientation, at first gradually, then with increasing rapidity in the 1970s and 1980s. A noteworthy catalyst for this shift was the publication in 1965 of Nelson Goodman's *Languages of Art*. Goodman's previous work had been in metaphysics and philosophy of science, not aesthetics, and thus perhaps he felt more carefree with regard to the standard questions framing philosophy of art. His book bypassed issues of the nature of artworks and the character of the aesthetic, concentrating rather on symbol systems and the logical relations between different kinds of symbols and their objects. The previous year Arthur Danto published his influential essay "The Artworld," which argued against anti-essentialism and made legitimate again the exploration of the concept of art, replacing appeal to shared exhibited properties with relational properties situating artworks in cultural space and historical contexts.[38] These ideas were further developed in *The Transfiguration of the Commonplace* (1981) and put into practice in Danto's art criticism.[39] (Interestingly, this attention to symbols and to the relation of art to cultural contexts returns philosophy of art to its earliest problematic: the nature of mimesis.)[40]

Goodman, Danto, and Margolis are but three of the major theorists who have fostered a change in aesthetic theorizing toward the historical contexts in which art takes form and achieves meaning. The current approaches to art and culture that typify present-day aesthetics are potentially rich for the development of feminist perspectives, for they place attention to cultural frameworks and their historical contingencies at the heart of philosophies of art. They dispense once and for all with the stubborn analytic claim that descriptors of social diversity derail philosophy into sociology. Therefore in a general way they are ineluctably (if not explicitly) politicized; as such they invite close inspection of the practices of institutions, especially their selection practices (whether patriarchal, class-based, colonialist).

In spite of this potential, however, attention to feminism or to gender is still not a significant presence in contextualist theories, even those that are otherwise iconoclastic about time-honored dichotomies such as the distinction between fine art and craft and "high" or "low" art. Perhaps the cold hand of the earlier legacies of philosophy still touches the discipline. Then, too, the new contextualist theories, in returning to classic questions about the distinguishing attributes of art, have been more interested in discovering why and how an object becomes a recognized artwork than in investigating what is not so recognized or what has been shouldered out of the limelight. The task remains for feminists to cultivate this project as they explore useful intersections between the advances made in (post-)analytic aesthetics and recent strategies of feminist theorizing.

Interpretive Frameworks: The Ascription of Meaning to Art

The self-reflective nature of recent analytical writing, such as that of Danto and Margolis, opens the door to exploring issues of gender and other sociopolitical aspects of art by highlighting the importance of the historical context of a work of art. Concurrent with this broadening of outlook in philosophy, feminism has already undergone several phases of self-reflection. A constant reassessment of artistic practices and interpretive approaches has fostered attention to what it means to analyze art in its fullest, broadest context. Although at times its character and tone might appear unrecognizable to those unschooled in its ways, analysis has always been part of feminist theorizing.[41] Its central purpose is a moving away from the entrenched, dominant, and limiting tenets of "patriarchal aesthetics," which permits only some predetermined aspects of a work to be considered contextually relevant, toward a strategy of less constrained attention to a variety of facets, determined by the historical moment and particular character of an experience.[42] Thus feminism and philosophy share an interest in the question of how the nature and boundaries of art are shaped by context.

Thus far we have discussed matters that pertain to the philosophical traditions of aesthetics, especially theories of the nature of art and of aesthetic perception. We have said little directly regarding related disciplines and theories of interpretation or viewer and reader response; thus we have not engaged the literature of theoretical criticism that has had such an influential feminist presence. Here we shall not even attempt to summarize this massive field; we refer readers to the bibliographies at the end of each of the five parts of the text. We shall, however, briefly discuss two issues that not only bear on the common question of defining the parameters of contextual relevance, but also confront staple elements of the philosophic tradition discussed above: the philosophy of mind employed by theories of the viewing subject, and the methods by which aesthetically relevant properties of art are to be determined.

Classic theories of aesthetic perception that were developed in eighteenth-century philosophy were based upon a certain view of perception and of the mind. They presumed that the human mind should be considered in its basic components as a kind of generic subjectivity, operating similarly in all fully functioning rational creatures. These philosophies—well aware that judgments of taste (assessments of artistic quality and value) often vary noticeably by individual, historical period, and culture—were bent upon articulating the bases for aesthetic pleasures that transcended these "incidental" differences. This articulation was made possible by the assumption that pure aesthetic pleasure (often taken in formal relations or nature, objects of attention less reliant on cultural fluency than complex works of art) is a basic capacity of the human perceptive faculty. And this assumption is only possible if one first assumes that beneath their contingent differences all minds are essentially similar.

This model of the mind and of conscious experience has not been noticeably useful to feminists, whose interests focus on understanding the development of gendered points of view and understanding the diverse positions of the masculine and the feminine in culture. Thus neither the generic consciousness of earlier European philosophy, nor its theoretical orientation to formal aesthetic pleasure has suited the aims of recent feminist theory. More complex models of consciousness have been needed, suited to understanding the subtle and devious pleasures of representation. One of the most fruitful models of mind available for this task has its roots in Freud's psychoanalytic theory and its Lacanian modifications.[43] (Within the Anglo-American tradition, psychoanalysis has not been widely embraced by philosophers writing in aesthetics.)[44] Feminists have adapted psychoanalytic insights in order to formulate theories more sensitive to gender and social position than either Enlightenment philosophy or Anglo-American philosophy has provided. This body of scholarship has yielded not only schools of reading and interpretation, but also a theoretical tool that has been widely employed in feminist understandings of art: theories of the gaze. Supplanting older notions of aesthetic perception, theories of the gaze analyze the pleasure to be found in representation by bringing to light the consciousness of the culturally prescribed viewer: a male of dominant social standing. Theories that employ the notion of the male gaze are one manifestation of widespread suspicion of the older notion of a universal subject, and of assumptions of the transparency of the mind, such that one can know from introspection the nature of aesthetic pleasure. (In this volume, discussions of psychoanalytically informed feminism may be found in Chapters 5 and 6; modifications or challenges to psychoanalytic approaches are presented in Chapters 15 and 16.)

Psychoanalysis is not the only recent theoretical movement to challenge traditional approaches to the appreciation and interpretation of art. Indeed, the vigorous effort on the part of feminists to situate artworks in their historical context and to read their changing meaning for contemporary audiences confronts an old analytic question: What qualities actually "belong" to the work itself? In our discussion of the broad philosophical tradition, we noted two presumptions shared by most participant theorists: that the value of art is timeless and transhistorical, and that the apprehension of aesthetic qualities removes the perceiver from his or her particular and contingent situation. A certain approach to critical interpretation and evaluation of art is bound together with these two theses, namely, that whatever value art has, it possesses autonomously. The aesthetic qualities of art are thus available for appreciation without reliance on knowledge of anything outside the work of art itself. In an extreme form this view was enacted by the New Criticism of the 1940s and 1950s. Its most famous statement in aesthetics was made in 1946 with the publication of "The Intentional Fallacy" by Monroe Beardsley and W. K. Wimsatt, which objected to the relevance of what they called "nonaesthetic" historical and contextual data, that is, data *external* to a work of art.[45] Critics of this view have hewn away at it for some time, but the question central to their claim—What are the parameters to legitimate artistic interpretation?—is as relevant as ever.

Indeed, feminist criticism and art history have given this question new life, as scholars reinterpret the historical record and the legacy of artworks and as they assess both the treatment of women in art and the type of art produced by women. (See Chapters 12–14.) Virtually all feminist interpretive strategies give rise to the philosophical question of whether and how the gender of artists—as well as their other socially marked identities—are to count as properties of works of art and to be recognized as aesthetically relevant. (See also Chapter 9 for a discussion of feminist frameworks as schemata for interpretation.) But the role such factors play in ascribing meaning to art is not always clear; hence the need for extending the dialogue between philosophy and feminist art theory.

Feminism and philosophy are fortunately situated at a moment of intersecting interests that provides opportunities for transdisciplinary scholarship on common theoretical questions. Though feminists are hesitant to prescribe any monolithic, unified feminist aesthetic, they are determined to maximize and extend discussions of the role of gender in cultural production. (Chapter 19 argues against *an* autonomous aesthetic while still emphasizing *the* aesthetic.) Some envision feminist theory relocated more centrally within aesthetic inquiry; others worry about the incompatibility of feminism with long-standing analytic and Continental philosophical concerns. (See Chapters 17, 18, and 20.) Others seek more linguistic analysis and the study of intertextuality, pursuing strategies that cope with texts the meanings of which are determined by context but the context of which can change without limits.[46] Still others prefer a sociological approach, emphasizing the social history of the discipline of aesthetics and the ways it has influenced the production and reception of objects deemed art.[47] Recalling Alpers's characterization of the "new art history" in 1977, which brought attention to the "work of art itself as a piece of history," these suggestive frameworks redirect concentration toward an emphasis on the actual practice of encountering and confronting art, in keeping with the reflective criticism of recent philosophical aesthetics.

Each of the parts that organize this volume is preceded by a short preface that reviews the issues the essays address, expanding upon the topics of "tradition" that we have introduced here. The majority of our contributors have their academic roots in philosophy; one is a psychoanalytic theorist, and others work in the critical disciplines of art, music, and literature. Two are both scholars and practicing artists. Adrian Piper, philosopher and graphic/conceptual artist, and Trinh T. Minh-ha, literary scholar, composer, and filmmaker, represent ways in which feminist perspectives on aesthetic value may be enacted in the practices of art. We hope that these multidisciplinary approaches will both advance the growing work of feminism in aesthetics and prompt writers in other fields to consider some of the issues as they are treated herein.

We have stressed here the departure from tradition fostered by feminist perspectives; in doing so we have focused on the ways these essays review the past. But it will be obvious that they equally well preview the future. We hope that the philosophical slant of this book will contribute to the development of transdisciplinary thinking about art theory, concepts relevant to aesthetics, and feminism. We urge more disciplinary dialogue among feminists in philosophy in order to link insights from other areas with philosophies of the arts. Topics in aesthetics can be usefully informed by recent feminist advances made in philosophy of science, epistemology, ethics, and political theory: for instance, challenges to traditional theories of rationality in which the disinterested, disembodied Cartesian knower is replaced by a conception of the knowing subject "as situated, as engaged and as a part of a community" parallel feminist deconstructions of aesthetic perception.[48] Similarly, challenges to traditional moral theory's notion of an independent, impartial moral agent who is replaced by a model of moral thinking based on relationships, with moral actions arising out of responsibilities and affiliations rather than duties or rights, could be brought to bear on the aesthetic assessment of the moral and political value of art. Might this cast a different light on the traditionally valued Romantic notion of the independent (male) genius? How would the feminist notion of an "ethics of care" affect the interpretation and evaluation of woman's crafts, for example, quilts? political activist art? How does the evaluation of women's art mesh with traditional political theory, which bifurcates the public and private realms? How is the status of women in the worlds of art further complicated by issues of race, class, culture, and sexual identities?[49] And more reflexively, how does philosophy enter into the web of determinants concerning how we think about art? The essays gathered here begin to investigate the traditions of aesthetics and to determine the power of theoretical frameworks themselves to invite or constrain recognition of artists and cultures.

Notes

1. Of the many existing anthologies recently published, only three contain entries on feminism: John W. Bender and H. Gene Blocker, eds., *Contemporary Philosophy of Art: Readings in Analytic Aesthetics* (New York: Prentice-Hall, 1993); Stephen David Ross, ed., *Art and Its Significance*, 2d ed. (Albany: State University of New York Press, 1987); and Patricia Werhane, ed. *Philosophical Issues in Art* (New York: Prentice-Hall, 1984). The selection of essays for teaching collections has come in for earlier criticism. In 1973 Mary Mothersill complained that "the same essays appear in each new anthology" (introduction, *Aesthetics and the Theory of Criticism: Selected Essays of Arnold Isenberg* (Chicago: University of Chicago Press), xix–xx.

2. Feminist interest in the body and norms for female beauty have prompted steady attention in this journal. *Hypatia*, moreover, has published a number of articles devoted to or influenced by French feminism, including a special issue edited by Nancy Fraser and Sandra Bartky (3, no. 3 [Winter 1989]). This type of theory is particularly sensitive to style and to modes of presentation

of ideas and thus is at least tangentially relevant to aesthetics even when the subject under discussion is something else.

3. On the occasion of its fiftieth anniversary, Lydia Goehr documents the membership of the American Society for Aesthetics and the authorship of articles in its main publication, the *Journal of Aesthetics and Art Criticism*: see "The Institutionalization of a Discipline: A Retrospective of *The Journal of Aesthetics and Art Criticism* and the American Society for Aesthetics, 1939–1992," *JAAC* 51, no. 2 (Spring 1993). Members of the ASA numbered 957 in 1992 (as compared to approximately 7000 members of the American Philosophical Association). Overall, 46 percent of the articles in the *JAAC* written between 1941 and 1991 were by philosophers; however, between 1941 and 1951, 35 percent were written by philosophers whereas between 1981 and 1991, philosophers authored 70 percent.

4. John Passmore, "The Dreariness of Aesthetics," *Mind* 60 (1951). This essay is reprinted in William Elton, ed., *Aesthetics and Language* (Oxford: Basil Blackwell, 1954), and in Francis J. Coleman, ed., *Aesthetics: Contemporary Studies in Aesthetics* (New York: McGraw-Hill, 1968).

5. With the advent of the J. Paul Getty funding in the form of the DBAE (Discipline-Based Art Education), which includes the multiple disciplines of studio art, art criticism, art history and aesthetics, philosophical issues have been introduced into the K–12 curriculum in certain areas of the country. The readings in aesthetics in those curricula replicate standard "canonical" texts, thereby educating future generations to be more philosophically astute in their discussions of art, though no broader in outlook than their predecessors.

6. There are cultural precedents in Asia, Africa, and elsewhere in which philosophies reflect the inseparability of the arts from other aspects of life, precedents that have provided models for some feminist scholars. Renée Lorraine, whose essay "A History of Music" appears in this volume, is one such scholar. See also her "A Gynecentric Aesthetic," in *Aesthetics in Feminist Perspective*, ed. H. Hein and C. Korsmeyer (Bloomington: Indiana University Press, 1993). As a rule these non-Western traditions have not played much of a role in the United States either in aesthetics or in philosophy generally.

7. Both the long and the recent intellectual traditions have ignored consideration of sex and gender in their theorizing. But while feminism is beginning to establish an increasingly well known critique of the former, Anglo-American traditions have been largely neglected until very recently. More feminist work has been done on analytic epistemology and philosophy of science. For some specific treatments of this method, see Jane Duran, *Toward a Feminist Epistemology* (Savage, Md.: Rowman and Littlefield, 1991) and Lynn Hankinson Nelson, *Who Knows: From Quine to Feminist Empiricism* (Philadelphia: Temple University Press, 1990).

8. See Paul Osker Kristeller, "The Modern System of the Arts," *Journal of the History of Ideas* 12–13 (1951–52), widely reprinted; and L. Lipking, *The Ordering of the Arts in Eighteenth-Century England* (Princeton: Princeton University Press, 1970) for discussions of the development of the idea of the fine arts in the early modern period.

9. There were several women active in the early days of analytic aesthetics, including Margaret Macdonald, Helen Knight, Katherine Gilbert (coauthor with Helmut Kuhn of *A History of Aesthetics* [Bloomington: Indiana University Press, rev. ed. 1953]), and Isabel Creed Hungerland. Gilbert and Hungerland each served two-year terms as president of the ASA, in 1946 and 1965 respectively. The content of their scholarship did not deviate significantly from the general concerns of the male-dominated group. Probably the best-known book in aesthetics by a woman is Susanne Langer's *Feeling and Form* (1953).

10. Some feminists have found in pragmatism a neglected American tradition that is congenial to feminism. See the special issue of *Hypatia*, edited by Charlene Haddock Siegfried, devoted to feminism and pragmatism (8, no. 2 [Spring 1993]). A recent appreciation of Dewey also can be found in Richard Shusterman's *Pragmatist Aesthetics* (Oxford: Basil Blackwell, 1992).

11. David Hume, "Of the Standard of Taste" (1757), in *Aesthetics: A Critical Anthology*, ed. G. Dickie, R. Sclafani, and R. Roblin (New York: St. Martin's Press, 1977), 596.

12. See "The Origin of the Work of Art," in *Art and Its Significance*, ed. Stephen David Ross (Albany: State University of New York Press, 2d ed., 1987).

13. Arthur Schopenhauer, *The World As Will and Representation*, 2 vols., trans. E. F. J. Payne (New York: Dover, 1969; first published 1859), 1:184.

14. See, for example, Christine Battersby, *Gender and Genius* (London: Women's Press; Bloomington: Indiana University Press, 1989); and Whitney Chadwick, *Women, Art, and Society* (London: Thames and Hudson, 1990).

15. See Kant, *The Critique of Judgment* (1790), especially the "First Moment of Beauty;" Schopenhauer, *The World as Will and Representation* (1819); Clive Bell, *Art* (1914); and Edward Bullough, " 'Psychical Distance' as a Factor in Art and an Aesthetic Principle" (1912), widely reprinted, including in Dickie, Sclafani, and Roblin, eds., *Aesthetics: A Critical Anthology*.

16. More recent theories of the aesthetic may be found in Jerome Stolnitz, *Aesthetics and Philosophy of Art Criticism* (Boston: Houghton Mifflin, 1960) and Frank Sibley, "Aesthetic Concepts," *Philosophical Review* 68, no. 4 (1959), and widely reprinted.

17. This continuity is explored by Jerome Stolnitz, "On the Origins of Aesthetic Disinterestedness," *Journal of Aesthetics and Art Criticism* (Winter 1961), widely reprinted, including in Dickie, Sclafani, and Roblin, eds., *Aesthetics: A Critical Anthology*.

18. William E. Kennick, "Does Traditional Aesthetics Rest on a Mistake?" *Mind* 67 (1958), reprinted in Francis J. Coleman, ed., *Aesthetics: Contemporary Studies in Aesthetics* (New York: McGraw-Hill, 1968), 411.

19. W. B. Gallie, "The Function of Philosophical Aesthetics," *Mind* 57 (1948), reprinted in Coleman, ed., *Aesthetics*.

20. Arnold Isenberg, "Critical Communication," *Philosophical Review* 58 (1949), widely reprinted. Isenberg also wrote an unpublished report to the Rockefeller Foundation in 1950 titled, "Analytical Philosophy and the Study of Art," only portions of which are published in *Aesthetics and the Theory of Criticism: Selected Essays of Arnold Isenberg* (Chicago: University of Chicago Press, 1973). A detailed account of Isenberg's work in its historical context is provided by Anita Silvers, "Letting the Sunshine In: Has Analysis Made Aesthetics Clear?" originally published in *Journal of Aesthetics and Art Criticism* 46 (1987) and reprinted in Bender and Blocker, eds., *Contemporary Philosophy of Art*.

21. Morris Weitz, "The Role of Theory in Aesthetics," *Journal of Aesthetics and Art Criticism* 15 (1956), widely reprinted.

22. See Richard Shusterman's introduction to *Analytic Aesthetics* (New York: Basil Blackwell, 1989), 1–19. A portion of these essays was originally published in a special issue of the *Journal of Aesthetics and Art Criticism* 46 (1987).

23. Lydia Goehr charts these decreasing numbers (see note 3 above.) The speculation offered here is ours.

24. Linda Nochlin's essay originally appeared in *Art News* 69 (January 1971) and is reprinted in her *Women, Art, and Power and Other Essays* (New York: Harper and Row, 1988).

25. The show "Women Artists: 1550–1950" and its accompanying catalogue brought to light works by women that were attributed to male artists, forgotten in museum basements, and obscured by the preponderance of "masterpieces" that hogged the limelight. See Ann Sutherland Harris and Linda Nochlin, *Women Artists: 1550–1950* (Los Angeles: Los Angeles County Museum of Art, 1976). References are too numerous to name in the brief description of the feminist movement offered here, but there are several synopses that might be helpful: Norma Broude and Mary D. Garrard, eds. *Feminism and Art History: Questioning the Litany* (New York: Harper and Row, 1982); Thalia Gouma-Peterson and Patricia Mathews, "The Feminist Critique of Art History," *Art Bulletin* 69 (September 1987): 326–57; Toril Moi, *Sexual/Textual Politics: Feminist Literary Theory* (New York: Methuen, 1985 and several reprints); and Norma Broude and Mary D. Garrard, eds., *The Expanding Discourse: Feminism and Art History* (New York: HarperCollins, 1992). See also the bibliographies provided within each of the five parts of this volume.

26. Svetlana Alpers, "Is Art History?" *Daedelus* 106, no. 3 (Summer 1977).

27. A feminine aesthetic was under discussion in Germany in the early years of the women's movement. Essays from the late 1970s and early 1980s became available in translation in Gisela Ecker, ed., *Feminist Aesthetics* (Boston: Beacon, 1985).

28. Broude and Garrard, eds., *Feminism and Art History*, 1.

29. Rozsika Parker and Griselda Pollock, *Old Mistresses: Women, Art, and Ideology* (New York: Pantheon, 1981).

30. For an overview of this development in the history of visual arts, see Norma Broude and Mary D. Garrard's introduction to *The Expanding Discourse: Feminism and Art History.*

31. In addition to the special issue on analytic aesthetics mentioned above, two recent issues of the *Journal of Aesthetics and Art Criticism* provide reflection on the state of the discipline. See the fiftieth-year commemorative volume mentioned above, and the volume dedicated to "Philosophy and the Histories of the Arts" (51, no. 3 [Summer 1993]), ed. Donald W. Crawford. Other sources include Bender and Blocker's *Contemporary Philosophy of Art*, and the thorough and well-written *Definitions of Art* by Stephen Davies (Ithaca: Cornell University Press, 1991).

32. Shusterman, *JAAC* 46 (1987): 115. It is interesting to note that the first essay in this issue is a portion of Arnold Isenberg's "Analytical Philosophy and the Study of Art: A Report to the Rockefeller Foundation" (1950).

33. Silvers, "Letting the Sunshine In."

34. Marx Wartofsky, "The Liveliness of Aesthetics," *Journal of Aesthetics and Art Criticism* 46 (1987). Nicholas Wolterstorff concurs in "Philosophy of Art After Analysis and Romanticism" in the same issue.

35. Roger Scruton, "Modern Philosophy and the Neglect of Aesthetics," *Times Literary Supplement* (5 June 1987).

36. Joseph Margolis, "The Eclipse and Recovery of Analytic Aesthetics," in Shusterman, ed., *Analytic Aesthetics.* See also "Exorcising the Dreariness of Aesthetics," *Journal of Aesthetics and Art Criticism* 51, no. 2 (Spring 1993): 133–40.

37. Margolis, "Eclipse and Recovery," 35–36. See also his essay in this volume.

38. See also George Dickie's institutional theory in *Art and Aesthetics: An Institutional Analysis* (Ithaca: Cornell University Press, 1974), and Joseph Margolis's theory of cultural emergence, *Art and Philosophy* (Brighton, Sussex: Harvester, 1980).

39. Arthur C. Danto, "The Artworld," *Journal of Philosophy* 61, no. 19 (1964); *The Transfiguration of the Commonplace* (Cambridge: Harvard University Press, 1981). In addition to his philosophical work, Danto writes a column on art for *The Nation.* Some of his collected essays on art may be found in *Encounters and Reflections* (New York: Farrar, Straus, and Giroux, 1990) and *The State of the Art* (New York: Prentice-Hall, 1987).

40. See, for example, Kendall Walton, *Mimesis and Make-Believe* (Cambridge: Harvard University Press, 1990).

41. French feminist writers like Hélène Cixous, Luce Irigaray, and Julia Kristeva are sometimes considered inaccessible and as a result have been widely ignored by American philosophers. This is true in spite of works such as Irigaray's analysis of the history of Western philosophy in *Speculum de l'autre Femme (Speculum of the Other Woman)* (Paris: Minuit, 1977).

42. Toril Moi presents a cogent overview of both the Anglo-American and French strands of feminist literary theory and how they relate to "patriarchal aesthetics" in *Sexual/Textual Politics.* See also K. K. Ruthven, *Feminist Literary Studies: An Introduction* (Cambridge: Cambridge University Press, 1984) and Rita Felski, *Beyond Feminist Aesthetics* (Cambridge: Harvard University Press, 1989).

43. Freud and Lacan have influenced both French feminism and feminist critics such as Jane Gallop, Shoshana Felman, and Gayatri Spivak. An overview of French thinkers can be found in Elaine Marks and Isabelle de Courtivron, eds., *New French Feminisms* (Brighton, Sussex:

Harvester, 1980). The influence of these on American theory is discussed in Hester Eisenstein and Alice Jardine, eds., *The Future of Difference* (Boston: G. K. Hall, 1980).

French philosophy and feminism is discussed in Jeffner Allen and Iris Marion Young, eds., *The Thinking Muse: Feminism and Modern French Philosophy* (Bloomington: Indiana University Press, 1989).

44. A noteworthy exception is Richard Wollheim; see his *Painting as an Art* (Princeton: Princeton University Press, 1987).

45. W. K. Wimsatt, Jr., and Monroe C. Beardsley, "The Intentional Fallacy," in *The Verbal Icon* (Lexington: University of Kentucky Press, 1954), reprinted in Joseph Margolis, *Philosophy Looks at the Arts*, 3d ed. (Philadelphia: Temple University Press, 1987).

46. This is Toril Moi's recommendation in *Sexual/Textual Politics*, as influenced by Kristeva and Derrida.

47. See Janet Wolff, *Aesthetics and the Sociology of Art*, 2d ed. (Ann Arbor: University of Michigan Press, 1993). This work invites comparison to Dickie's institutional analysis of art.

48. See Nancy Tuana's comments on the challenge of feminism for philosophy in *Woman and the History of Philosophy* (New York: Paragon House, 1992).

49. Elizabeth V. Spelman, *Inessential Woman: Problems of Exclusion in Feminist Thought* (Boston: Beacon, 1988).

I

Gender and Eighteenth-Century Aesthetic Theory: New Readings of Traditional Theories of Taste, Beauty, and Sublimity

The modern discipline of aesthetics began to take shape in the early eighteenth century in Europe; during this period several concepts basic to theories of perception and appreciation were developed, including the notion of the aesthetic itself, and the paired ideas of the beautiful and the sublime. The essays in this part explore the formative years of aesthetics and the degrees to which gender enters into the formulation of theories about taste, beauty, and sublimity.

Prior to this time value qualities such as beauty and goodness tended to be interpreted as objective qualities actually possessed by objects of appreciation. The experience of (what was later known as) aesthetic enjoyment was understood to be a rational enjoyment brought about when the mind grasps a truth presented in harmonious or imaginative pattern. The rise of empiricism occasioned a sharp rise of subjectivism in the analysis of value qualities. "Beauty" was seen to refer not to the perception of a quality in an object, but rather to the fact that a perceiver was experiencing pleasure.

This new understanding of the nature of value qualities engendered a host of questions that theories had to address. The pleasure identified with beauty, for example, had to be distinguished from other types of pleasures, notably sensual pleasures and the satisfaction of desires. In so distinguishing beauty-pleasure from other values, the notion of "aesthetic" appreciation was born. Aesthetic enjoyment is pleasure in the presentation of an object to perception, without concern for its moral value or practical use, or even its cognitive meaning.

These stipulations delineating the realm of the aesthetic were necessary in order to retain the possibility of standards for aesthetic value. Few philosophers were willing to conclude that the subjective pleasure of beauty is simply relative to the individual. The tension set up between the subjectivity of pleasure and the universal validity of judgments about value focused philosophical attention on what is called the "problem of taste." As Hume put the question, How can beauty be a subjective pleasure, and yet some judgments of beauty be clearly superior to others? Or as Kant put it, How can a judgment of taste still be both universal and necessary?

Philosophies of taste rely heavily on assumptions about common human nature or common mental faculties to reconcile subjective pleasure with universally valid aesthetic judgments. Thus they invest a great deal in the claim that all of "us" are constituted similarly, so that our subjective responses to nature and art are similar. Thus these "subjectivist" theories are emphatically not "relativist," because they maintain that the bases of subjective responses are common to all human perceivers.

Feminist scholars have discovered that a great many of the claims that philosophers have made on behalf of common human nature are modeled covertly on a view of ideal masculine characteristics, which in turn are articulated by contrast with a subsidiary set of traits ascribed to females. Thus many fundamental theoretical concepts that purport to refer universally to all mankind are in fact "gendered" concepts.

Gendered concepts are the focus of Carolyn Korsmeyer's study of Hume's analysis of critical judgments and his famous standard of taste. She examines the methods that Hume articulates to solve the problem of taste and questions the soundness of his reliance on the common constitution of human nature. Exploring his writings to discover the patterns of his ideas about women and femininity, she argues that Hume's philosophy—and, insofar as his is a model, any philosophy of universal human nature—is unstable and riddled with tension regarding the position of females. Thus his standard of taste is cast into doubt by the instability of the concept of human nature on which so much of his philosophy relies.

As philosophers considered the various objects of aesthetic pleasure with increasing exactitude, it became evident that beauty was but one of a number of types of distinct pleasures. Values to be found in the pleasurable experience both of nature and of art included not only the beautiful, but also the picturesque, the comic, the grotesque. The most important concept that sits alongside beauty in philosophical treatises of the time is the sublime. While beauty was delimited as bounded, contained, harmonious, controlled, the sublime referred to the awesome experience of boundless power, especially to be found in regions of vast and even terrifying nature.

The concepts of the beautiful and the sublime are quite evidently linked to ideas of gender as well as pleasure. Paul Mattick surveys several eighteenth-century theories in his consideration of the development of the idea of fine art, specifically the arts of painting and poetry. He argues that gender is deeply involved in the articulation of the notions of the beautiful and the sublime, and he examines influential authors such as Kant and Burke to demonstrate how beauty is feminized while sublimity is ascribed masculine traits. Mattick places the development of gendered aesthetic concepts in the context of social and political changes in eighteenth-century England and France. He traces the development of ideas of beauty and sublimity to traditional debates over painting and poetry, in which we can see painting demoted to the passive realm of femininity and poetry exalted as the imaginative, unbounded sublime accessible to masculine imagination. As painting regains its status in the nineteenth century, he argues, it is by entering the realm of the sublime and assuming the heroic stature of the masculine.

Essays by Timothy Gould and Christine Battersby focus on Kant's concept of the sublime. Gould examines the Kantian sublime for positive lessons adaptable for feminist purposes, pointing out that if the sublime is a "masculine" notion, it cannot be so in the same sense that real males are supposed to be masculine. The experience of sublimity requires a degree of passivity and openness, he points out, and thus "beautiful" and "sublime" are less easily aligned with "feminine" and "masculine" than might appear. Gould considers contemporary feminist scholarship, particularly that of Eve Kosofsky Sedgwick, to explore the difficulty with expressing an experience of the sublime, which he suspects is a necessary completion of that experience.

The connection between genius and the sublime is the focus of Christine Battersby's essay. She notes that while feminists have been open to the idea of an alternative feminist ethics, they have been more resistant to developing a feminist aesthetic. While Battersby believes that an alternative concept of the aesthetic is both important and available in history in the work of certain women writers, she argues that the influential distinctions that Kant draws in his articulation of the aesthetic are maladaptive for feminist purposes. Kant elevated pure form to the core of aesthetic pleasure, and Battersby argues that form is itself a masculine concept (compared to the "matter" of femininity). She urges examining the work of past women artists—she provides an example of a German poet—for clues to a woman-centered aesthetic and notion of the sublime. Her essay both promotes this mission of feminist scholarship and reveals the complex dimensions of gender inflection that characterize influential philosophies such as Kant's.

These essays not only offer analyses of specific theories and problems in the history of aesthetics, they also raise general questions about the outcome of feminist perspectives and theoretical traditions: What, if anything, may be retained from tradition when its gender bias is revealed? How reparable are concepts such as sublimity? How ineluctable is the presence of gender in such ideas?

1

Beautiful and Sublime: "Gender Totemism" in the Constitution of Art

Paul Mattick, Jr.

A striking feature of a number of central texts of eighteenth-century aesthetics is the use of descriptive terms associated at the time with masculine and feminine characters to classify art objects and types of such objects. What is to be made of this? Does the metaphorical application of gender stereotypes to the domain of art simply reflect the *mentalité* of a sexist society? Viewing gender-classification systems along the lines of Lévi-Strauss's analysis of totemism, Judith Shapiro has observed that the qualities a society—such as our own—may think of as distinguishing women and men "belong to a web of metaphors that have, in fact, to do with many things other than gender *per se*. The opposition between male and female serves as a source of symbolism for a diversity of cultural domains; at the same time, gender differences them-selves are defined through categories of the economy, the polity—in brief, of the wider social universe in which they are located."[1] This social universe includes the arts. Is it not possible that the arts are one sphere in which gender has been defined for modern culture, just as gender classification may, beyond providing an external system of terms for the categorization of artworks, be deeply involved with the very idea of the fine arts?

I

Artworks have long been described in gender terms, as when Vitruvius described the Doric order as appropriate to honor the "virile strength" of masculine gods and assigned the delicate, ornamented Corinthian to female deities. Such terminology acquired a new, systematic character with the beginning of aesthetics as a literary subject in the eighteenth century. This subject could hardly have made an earlier appearance, as it was at this time that the idea of the fine arts as a widely accepted classification of certain practices and institutions came into existence in Europe and, consequently, the Americas. Although its origin can be traced to the later Middle Ages and especially to the Italian Renaissance, it is only since the late eighteenth century that the notion has been taken for granted (in Paul Oskar Kristeller's words) "that the five 'major arts' constitute an area all by themselves, clearly separated by common characteristics from the crafts, the sciences, and other human activities."[2] The development of this notion, of course, reflected not the recognition of hitherto overlooked properties shared by the fine arts, but an actual transformation of the social place and significance of writing, painting and sculpture, music, dance, and architecture. This involved, centrally, their increasing autonomy as practices with respect to earlier religious and political functions. New social institutions—the academy, the museum, the public concert—were created around them, in turn transforming them. Furthermore, we are dealing here with an extremely complex historical moment, in which an accelerating emergence of capitalism produced in social, political, economic, and cultural relations both a continuous series of upheavals and a desire for principles, practical and theoretical, able to impose order on this alternatively or simultaneously exhilarating and terrifying experience.[3]

The prime representative in aesthetic theory of this character of the age is to be seen in the rise to prominence of the category of the sublime, after its introduction into the language of criticism at the end of the seventeenth century. This category was quickly appropriated from its original use in stylistics to serve as a signifier of the transgression of boundaries, of the overwhelming effect of vastness and power, with irresistible impact on the emotions of the audience. By the time of the publication of Burke's *Philosophical Enquiry into the Origin of Our Ideas of the Sublime and Beautiful* (1759), its sister concept had also come to be defined in terms of the emotions awakened by a natural phenomenon or work of art, rather than in terms of properties (classically, harmony and proportion) of the thing itself. I say "sister concept," because Burke differentiates the beautiful from the sublime in terms clearly identifying these with the feminine and masculine poles of the gender system; and in this he only states more explicitly than usual the consensus of his period.

The features Burke lists as characterizing objects experienced as beautiful are such as would still today likely be typed as "feminine": smallness, smoothness, curviness, delicacy, cleanliness, soft coloration, lack of resistance, quietness.[4] Similarly, the properties of objects said to induce the sensation of sublimity are conventionally "masculine" ones—vastness, roughness, jaggedness, heaviness, strong coloration, hardness, loudness. These sets of characteristics are associated, respectively, with the emotions of love and fear, which for Burke are responses to weakness and to strength. Thus, criticizing the view that some formal "perfection" of an object is the cause of our experience of it as beautiful, he states that beauty, "where it is highest in the female sex, almost always carries with it an idea of weakness and imperfection. Women are very sensible of this; for which reason, they learn to lisp, to totter in their walk, to counterfeit weakness and even sickness. In all this, they are guided by nature. Beauty in distress is the most affecting beauty."[5]

The sublime, in contrast, causes not love but admiration. It "always dwells on great objects" while the beautiful is found in "small ones, and pleasing; we submit to what we admire, but we love what submits to us." Sublimity is to be found, for example, in "the authority of a father," which "hinders us from having that entire love for him that we have for our mothers, where the parental authority is almost melted down into the mother's fondness and indulgence" (*Philosophical Enquiry*, 110, 113, 111). Fundamentally, the source of the sublime is to be found in "whatever is fitted in any sort to excite the ideas of pain and danger, that is to say, whatever is in any sort terrible, or is conversant about terrible objects, or operates in a manner analogous to terror"—at any rate, "at certain distances" from danger, when fear gives way to the delightful frisson of an aesthetic experience.[6]

There is thus a deeper significance to the dual grouping of properties than simple sexual difference. For Burke, the distinction between terror and love, evoked by the two groups of properties, corresponds to the division of the human passions under the two familiar headings of pain and pleasure. And the experiences classed under these headings "may be reduced very nearly to these two heads, *self-preservation* and *society;* to the ends of one or the other of which all our passions are calculated to answer." The former, "the most powerful of all the passions," are those "which are conversant about the preservation of the individual" (38). The latter in its turn has two subdivisions:

"1. the society of the *sexes,* which answers the purpose of propagation"; and, second, "the more *general society,* which we have with men and with other animals." The root cause of the pleasures derived from "the society of the sexes" is that of orgasm, a pleasure "of a lively character, rapturous and violent, and confessedly the highest pleasure of sense" (40). While coupling gives pleasure, deprivation of it gives no great pain; this frees us from obsession with orgasm, and allows us, as rational creatures, to integrate sexual pleasure into our social existence generally. This takes the concrete form—or so Burke appears to suggest—of our choice of a single partner, in our feeling for whom sexual passion is connected with and heightened by "the idea of some *social* qualities." This "mixed passion" is love, and its general object "is the *beauty* of the *sex,*" just as "men . . . are attached to particulars by personal *beauty*" (42).

There is a slippage in Burke's language here that seems unconscious: from "man" as subject of analysis to "men." Even though the passage continues with the observation that "women and men, and not only they, but . . . other animals give us a sense of joy and pleasure in beholding them," the "we" is the masculine "we" who "love what submits to us" (43). This is made clearer in a later passage, where Burke describes the object of sexual love as "the beauty of women" while that of its extension into love for "the great society with man and all other animals" is beauty *tout court,* "a name I shall apply to all such qualities in things as induce in us a sense of affection and tenderness" (51).

The complexly coded nature of these aesthetic concepts is not peculiar to Burke;[7] it is, for instance, visible even in the highly abstract versions of them that Kant creates in his Third Critique. In his account, the beautiful is our experience of the harmony of the imagination—fed by the senses—with the understanding; the sublime, with its disparity between the imagination and the reason, allows us to feel our non-natural power, our freedom from physical determinism. This suggests the common association of the female with nature and the male with the humanly created, which we will investigate below in other forms. But the image of woman as incarnation of sociality, seen not only as the ground of civilization and higher pleasures but also as representative of the domestic sphere from which the male must venture forth to do great deeds, is to be found here as well. While Kant conceives the sense of freedom connected with the sublime fundamentally as an intimation of our moral nature, its incarnation as a human type is "the warrior" for whom even "a fully civilized society" retains a "superior esteem." Though the hero must embody the virtues of peace as well as those of war, in a comparison between "the statesman" (incarnating the social virtues) and "the general, . . . an aesthetic judgment decides in favor of the general." For "war has something sublime about it."[8]

II

Burke's association of sociality and sexuality was no novelty. Pope's *Essay on Man* (1734), for instance, sees the latter as the very foundation and principle of the former: with humanity as with all creatures, he explains in Epistle III,

> Each loves itself, but not itself alone,
> Each sex desires alike, till two are one.
> Nor ends the pleasure with the fierce embrace;
> They love themselves, a third time in their race.

Generation leads to social complexity:

> A longer care man's helpless kind demands;
> That longer care contracts more lasting bands:
> Reflection, reason, still the ties improve,
> At once extend the interest, and the love.

Pope imagines no conflict between self-preservation and the social passions: both God and Nature bid "self-love and social be the same." He equally seems to experience no difficulty in leaping from finding the source of "mutual happiness" in "mutual wants" to discovering the principle of political order in the rule of the father over his family:

> The same which in a sire the sons obeyed,
> A prince the father of a people made.

In Rousseau's version of the story, the birth of society as by-product of sexual passion leads to a fall of man from the state of freedom in which he was born to the chains he lives in now. While "man's first sentiment was that of his own existence; his first concern was that of his preservation," things changed radically with the gradual formation of family groups.

> The first developments of the heart were the effect of a new situation
> that united the husbands and wives, fathers and children in one

> common habitation. The habit of living together gave rise to the
> sweetest sentiments known to men: conjugal love and paternal love.
> . . . [I]t was then that the first difference was established in the
> lifestyle of the two sexes. . . . Women became more sedentary and
> grew accustomed to watch over the hut and the children, while the
> man went to seek their common subsistence.[9]

In this situation male competition for women leads to the birth of *amour-propre*—"this is the source of emulation, rivalries, and jealousy"[10]—contrasted by Rousseau with "the gentle and affectionate passions born of self-love," which "is always good and always in conformity with order." It is after the birth of *amour-propre* "that man finds himself outside of nature and sets himself in contradiction with himself" (*Emile*, 214, 213). Sociality is thus double-edged. While it makes possible a higher, self-conscious moral state, perhaps to be achieved in the future, it also means the loss of the primal innocent freedom of the individual in the state of nature.

Given sociality's roots in sexuality, regeneration demands, as Rousseau explains in *Emile*, among other things the correct ordering of relations between the sexes. According to Rousseau, the two sexes are, given the institution of society, radically different: "One ought to be active and strong, the other passive and weak." Woman "is made to please and to be subjugated," while man's "merit is in his power; he pleases by the sole fact of his strength. This is not the law of love" (358). Indeed it is not; it is the law of terror, for what have we here but the figures of the beautiful and the sublime?

Only "a strange depravity of judgment," insists Rousseau, could think it appropriate for men and women to behave as equals in the expression of sexual desire:

> how can one fail to see that if reserve did not impose on one sex [the
> female] the moderation which nature imposes on the other, the result
> would soon be the ruin of both, and mankind would perish by the
> means established for preserving it? If there were some unfortunate
> region on earth where philosophy had introduced this practice—
> especially in hot countries, where more women are born than men—
> men would be tyrannized by women. . . . [Men] would finally be their
> victims and would see themselves dragged to death without ever
> being able to defend themselves. (*Emile*, 358–59)

Instead of tempting men to physical destruction by endless intercourse, women must be encouraged to take their natural place at the center of the family, as bearers, sucklers, and caretakers of children. In this position they are mediators between nature and culture. But just as procreation and the pleasing of men are the chief functions of women, so the cultural realm is preeminently man's. "The quest for abstract and speculative truths, principles, and axioms in the sciences, for everything that tends to generalize ideas, is not within the competence of women. All their studies ought to be related to practice. . . . [All] the reflections of women ought to be directed to the study of men or to the pleasing kinds of knowledge that have only taste as their aim; for, as regards work of genius, they are out of the reach of women" (*Emile*, 386). Given mankind's emergence from the state of nature, which has led to the birth of gender distinction, culture must take clear precedence over nature. The reintegration of the two principles, now set in opposition, requires patriarchy, so that woman's "first and most important quality" is "gentleness."[11]

Despite the dissimilarity between their accounts of social experience, the common elements in Rousseau's account of relations between the sexes and Burke's theory of the sublime and beautiful should be apparent. At work here is more than an association of the beautiful with the pleasurable subservience assigned to women, and of the sublime with the dominating power of the male. We enter more deeply into this complex of ideas when we compare Rousseau's assignment of female and male to the poles of nature and culture with Burke's explanation of the superior power of poetry compared to painting as due to the artificial, nonmimetic character of poetry's medium, language, in contrast with the natural character of the painted sign. Painting, when it reaches for the higher power of the sublime, must imitate the techniques of poetry (Burke, *Philosophical Enquiry*, 62). The heights of art—the territory of genius, one might say (though Burke doesn't speak of it this way)—are reserved for the male principle.

III

The contrast of natural with artificial signs is fundamental also to Lessing's argument, in the *Laocoön*, about "the limits of painting and poetry." The former makes use of the natural signs of "figures and colors in space" to "imitate physical beauty." In contrast, speech, the poet's medium, consists of "arbitrary signs."[12] This means that poetry cannot very successfully imitate physical beauty; whatever the skill of Ariosto's word-portrait of Alcina, "What good is all this erudition and insight to us his readers who want to have the picture of a beautiful woman, who want to feel something of the soft excitement of the blood which accompanies the actual sight of beauty?"[13] The special dignity of poetry lies elsewhere, in its appeal to the reader's or listener's imagination, which must create an image not from "sensuous impressions" but "from weak and wavering descriptions of arbitrary signs."[14]

From this difference between two types of sign Lessing draws his central conclusion:

> If it is true that painting employs in its imitations quite other means or signs than poetry employs, the former—that is to say, figures and colors in space—but the latter articulate sounds in time; as, unquestionably, [!] the signs used must have a definite relation to the thing signified, it follows that signs arranged together side by side can express only subjects which, or the various parts of which, exist thus side by side, whilst signs which succeed each other can express only subjects which, or the various parts of which, succeed one another. . . . Consequently, bodies with their visible properties form the proper subjects of painting . . . [and] actions form the proper subjects of poetry. (99)

The presence here of the gender categories we have been examining is clear in the opposition of the body as aesthetic object, passive and still—the exemplar of the beautiful—to action, source of the experience of the sublime.

Despite Lessing's insistence on the radical separation of powers between poetry and painting, history painters as well as poets reached for the sublime; their work characteristically involved the conceptual materials on which Lessing drew. To take a well-known example, the first commentators on David's *Oath of the Horatii* (1785) stressed the artist's "departures from accepted practice, his defiance of rules and tradition. . . . Gorsas [*Promenades de Crites au Sallon de l'année 1785*] suggests that the 'sublime' expression of Horatius 'would have escaped any other but M. David.' "[15] The *Horatii*, along with *The Lictors returning to Brutus the Bodies of his Sons* (1789) and other pictures of this period, were sublime works in the classical (Longinian) sense of treating noble subjects, in a manner calculated not to attract the taste for decorative prettiness but, through the idealizing of natural forms, to inspire the viewer to high and profound thoughts. They were also sublime in the newer, Burkean, sense of presenting images of fearsome moments, expressive of the artist's powerful imagination and inspiring strong feeling in the spectator. It is in accord with the gendered character of this sublime that a review of the 1789 Salon described the *Brutus* as "male, severe, terrifying";[16] the pictures themselves reveal this aspect of the aesthetic categories.

Both the *Horatii* and the *Brutus* picture the conflict between the claims of the national polity and those of familial love, and are structured in terms of male and female embodiments of these claims. The former places the Roman father in the center; his sons face him on the left, their taut bodies testifying to the strength of their resolve to use the power of death he holds out to them in the shape of three swords. At the right sit three women—one of them a sister of the men the Horatii are setting out to kill, another a sister of the Roman triplets, pledged in marriage to one of their opponents—with their children. Though the picture is strongly divided by the three open spaces that frame the figures, the twofold division of its subject between masculine and feminine is equally pronounced. The central action is indeed the transmission of power from father to sons, who at the same moment abandon their marriage-formed family alliances. To this moment the group of women is linked only by implication: their grief reflects the fact that they are faced with loss no matter who wins the coming fight. Everything is stronger on the men's side than in the women's: the color of their clothing, the shadows behind them, and their tense, muscled bodies in contrast with the soft, smooth skin of the women, who seem not agitated by despair but sunk in a deep, sleeplike passivity.[17]

The *Brutus* reverses the distribution of action between the sexes. Here the father sits brooding as the bodies of his sons, executed at his orders for treason, are carried in, while the women of the house rise in anguish, gesturing toward the bier. The women are experiencing horror and fear (one has fainted and one hides her face), but they themselves are beautiful, objects of pity. They are brightly illuminated, made for the sense of sight, while Brutus sits in obscurity, awesome, strong, interiorizing his grief rather than acting it out in womanly rhetoric. The women here are not the female citizens of Sparta whom Rousseau held up as models, happy to lose their sons for the military good of the city, but Brutus is the citizen who "was neither Caius nor Lucius; he was a Roman."[18]

Lessing's view of natural signs implies that neither historical art nor allegorical painting can exemplify the best of that art, "because they can be understood only by means of their additional arbitrary signs." Such pictures, that is, are fully comprehensible only to someone who knows the classical legend or who is able from emblematic signs to recognize their subjects. Lessing thus makes an argument against illustration, the production of images whose comprehension requires an accompanying text. It is an early form of argument in favor of what would later be thought of as the autonomy of art, criticizing the use of painting in religious ritual as "an outward compulsion" on the work of the creative artist, forced to look "more to the significant than to the beautiful" (*Laocoön*, 133, 87).

This conception reappears in the contrast made in Kant's *Critique of Judgment* between "paintings properly so called" and "those intended to *teach* us, e.g., history or natural science." Visual images ideally are "there merely to be looked at, using ideas to entertain the imagination in free play, and occupying the aesthetic power of judgment without a determinate purpose."[19] Kant, of course, develops this conception far beyond Lessing's version, to the idea of visual beauty as exemplified by pure forms that "represent nothing, no object under a determinate concept, and are free beauties." Lest we be misled by Kant's language, which for us points toward "high art" nonrepresentational painting, it is important to remember that for him "painting" included "the decoration of rooms with tapestries, bric-a-brac, and all the beautiful furnishings whose sole function is to be *looked at,* as well as the art of dressing carefully" and "a room with all sorts of ornaments (including even ladies' attire)" (*Critique of Judgment,* 77). For Kant as for Lessing, among the arts "*poetry* holds the highest rank," because it leads us beyond the world of sensory appearance to the "supersensible" and so "fortifies the mind" (*Critique of Judgment,* 196). Painting lies farther from sublimity, which "cannot be contained in any sensible form but concerns only ideas of reason," and indeed, "perhaps the most sublime passage in the Jewish Law is the commandment: Thou shalt not make unto thee any graven image, or any likeness of any thing that is in heaven or on earth, or under the earth, etc" (*Critique of Judgment,* 135).

The rejection of pictorial imagery by the "people of the book" is echoed in a further dimension of Lessing's separation of the literary from the visual, beyond the attack on illustration and symbolism: a critique of realism (probably in particular of the Dutch-inspired genre painting dear at the time to German burghers). While language is the medium of *truth,* painting's speciality is, as we have seen, the "imitation of beautiful bodies." Although freedom of speech is a necessity for the sciences, therefore, restrictions should be placed on the arts, whose ultimate purpose is to give pleasure. This becomes an argument against realism in painting. Language is free to represent the ugly and the laughable, precisely because it is not an imitative art; whereas a picture of an ugly object is itself ugly, a poetic description of an ugly scene need not be, and can be used "as an ingredient in order to produce or intensify certain mixed states of feeling with which [the poet] must entertain us in default of feelings purely pleasurable."[20] In visual art, truth must be sacrificed in the interest of visual harmony which is its essence; the wise Greeks saw that "this veiling was a sacrifice which the artist offered to Beauty" (*Laocoön*, 65).

The gendered character of the antithesis between truth and beauty is apparent; we need only remember the differing educational programs prescribed by Rousseau to Emile and to his Sophie, or Kant's advice, in the *Observations on the Feeling of the Sublime and Beautiful* (1763), that "deep meditation and long-sustained reflection are noble but difficult, and do not well befit a person in whom unconstrained charms should show nothing else than a beautiful nature."[21] Joseph Wright's *Experiment with the Air-Pump* of 1768 (painted, thus, two years after the publication of *Laocoön;* Fig. 1.1), while far from expressing a Kantian disdain for women, provides an illustration of the relation of truth to beauty. This may be seen in the contrast between the

Fig. 1.1.   Joseph Wright of Derby, *Experiment with an Air Pump*. Tate Gallery, London

apprehension and distress of the two girls and the eager participation in the experiment of the boy who, understanding that the bird, apparently destroyed, will soon be revived, lowers the cage to which the beautiful creature will be returned. The light that shines full on the girls makes them into aesthetic objects for the picture's viewer, from which the man with his protective arm around them points upward to the sight of the unfortunate cockatoo, a thing of beauty here transformed into an object of rational investigation. The other men in the room are absorbed, each in his own way, in the experiment, except for the male of the couple to the left who, gazing into his betrothed's eyes, in spirit has left his fellows to join her in domestic bliss.[22]

Truth is difficult and so painful, and thus opposed to the pleasure served by art. This gives truth an aesthetic character of its own: the scientific attitude involves the unflinching contemplation of *ugliness,* while the voice of the artist faced with a "misshapen" reality should wonder, according to Lessing, "Who will wish to paint you, when no one wishes to see you?" Unfortunately, Lessing continues, many modern artists do wish to paint the ugly, seeking to imitate all of Nature, who "herself at all times sacrifices beauty to higher purposes" (*Laocoön,* 63, 66). In this way, "Art in these later days has been assigned far wider boundaries than the ancients allowed" (66).

The confusion of artistic modes—the mixing of literary and visual genres—is possible, because painting can suggest action, as poetry can suggest the experience of physical beauty, but Burke and Lessing held it to be essential, if both forms are to achieve their highest possibilities, to keep each within its allotted domain. Furthermore, separation here is also hierarchy. For Burke, as we saw, while "poetry and rhetoric do not succeed in exact description as well as painting does," they "are more capable of making deep and lively impressions than any other arts, and even than nature itself in very many cases" (*Philosophical Enquiry,* 172, 173). Lessing decried the modern critics' tendency to ignore this hierarchy of genre power as a mode of aesthetic violence: "Now they force poetry into the narrower bounds of painting; and again, they propose to painting to fill the whole wide sphere of poetry" (*Laocoön,* 59).

Such expressions can be described as a revival of the Renaissance *paragone* in the form of writers' defense of literature against the threat to its preeminence posed by the rising social significance of painting. But, given the charge of gender carried by the concepts of painting and poetry, as the arts of the beautiful and the sublime, it is not hard to read the passages in Lessing and Burke protesting incursions by the visual arts into the domain of poetry also as analogues in art theory to the anxiety about female transgression into the sphere of the male given expression in Rousseau's strictures on female morals and education.

IV

Rousseau's fear of the potential consequences of woman's insatiable sexual appetites, while reflecting preoccupations peculiar to him, exemplified a conception of woman widely shared in Europe at least since the later Middle Ages. In Natalie Zemon Davis's words, "the female sex was thought the disorderly one par excellence in early modern Europe," where her genius for social disorder was associated with a propensity for sexual insatiability.[23] Though such ideas are certainly to be found in premodern society, the accelerated development of a secular, urban culture and national state formation from the fourteenth century on seems to have brought with it a "sharp turn toward misogyny." This accompanied a redefinition of male and female gender roles integral to modernization, notably involving an important loss of power by upper-status women and the redefinition of woman's sphere as a domestic one in a restructured patriarchal household.[24]

These developments intensified in the course of the seventeenth century. By the eighteenth century married women had lost most of their earlier legal, economic, and political rights. The transformation of gender relations did not happen without resistance on the part of women, of which one important manifestation was the rise of various sorts of feminist literature from the fourteenth century on. Given the role of the patriarchal family as model for the social order as a whole (visible, to take two examples, in the conception of the king as "father of his country" and in the very name of the new science of political "oeconomy") it is not surprising that "the relation of the wife—of the potentially disorderly woman—to her husband was especially useful for expressing the relation of all subordinates to their superiors."[25] It could, that is, be used to figure both the hierarchical order required for social health, and the threat to or actual disruption of that order. Female insubordination to the new gender relations, whether in the name of earlier rights or in that of utopian aspirations, served as an emblem of the conflict between higher and lower orders ineluctably produced by the development of capitalist social relations.

The association of woman with social disorder was more than symbolic; from the seventeenth century on we find women "telling off priests and pastors, being central actors in grain and bread riots in town and country, and participating in tax revolts and other rural disturbances."[26] But during the same period—and well into the nineteenth century—we also find male rioters and resisters to oppression dressing as women or taking women's names. And we cannot be surprised when we discover these gender characters reappearing, on a more abstract level of representation, in the use in political discourse of the aesthetic categories of the beautiful and sublime.

V

Burke makes the connection between aesthetic and political categories clear in the *Philosophical Enquiry* itself, listing as exemplars of the sublime not just stern fatherhood but "those despotic governments, which are founded on the passions of men, and principally on the passion of fear," who "keep their chief as much as may be from the public eye," thus creating the effect of obscurity basic to the sublime. And in praising Milton's poetry for the sublimity of its images, he mentions as themes "the ruin of monarchs, and the revolutions of kingdoms" (*Philosophical Enquiry*, 59, 62).

In Burke's description of the French Revolution, we find the gendered character of the categories of beautiful and sublime demonstrated by the very failure of the women of Paris to play their allotted role. The queen of France indeed exemplifies the beautiful—lovely, passive, weak, she arouses Burke's pity as she is forced by the "swinish multitude" to flee her palace. Such a scene, one would expect, would have its sublime aspect: here is that ruin of monarchs whose description Burke praised in Milton. But in fact this experience seemed so frightful as to lie outside the bounds of artistic representation, which must be a cause of delight even in its horror.[27] The overthrow of an actual monarch, and that in a series of acts with serious repercussions for the stability of the British political and social system, could not be kept within the frame of aesthetic experience. After all, for terror to produce delight it must "not press too close"; as Kant was to echo this, "we must find ourselves safe in order to feel this exciting liking" that is the experience of the sublime.[28] And one manifestation of the passing of the scene of the overthrow of the French monarchy beyond the bounds of aesthetic contemplation is the role played in it by women; the king and queen are led from their palace "amidst the horrid yells, and shrilling screams, and frantic dances, and infamous contumelies, and all the unutterable abominations of the furies of hell, in the abused shape of the vilest of women."[29]

In this picture of the revolutionary mob we can recognize the modern European association of the female—and in particular the woman of the lower classes—with the danger of social disorder. This is here carried to its ultimate point: an attack on the king himself, the paternal keystone of political order. The violation of the queen, embodiment of beauty, is equally terrible, not only in itself but because it mirrors the refusal by the women of the mob to accept their place in the social cosmos. They inspire Burke with horror by their negation of womanly beauty, but this horror is not one that can lead to delight and the sublime. The women of the mob are by social nature ugly—"swinish" and "vile."[30] Their action spells the abolition of the social differentiation both exemplified and symbolized by the male privilege implicated in the category system of sublime and beautiful.

This radical undermining of the aesthetic system might be called the Female Sublime or—from the dominant point of view—the Bad Sublime. The whole cast of aesthetic characters can be seen at play in Mozart's *Magic Flute* (1791). Sarastro, of course, incarnates the sublime: mysterious, deep-voiced, his is the fatherly power whose victory over rebellious femininity the opera celebrates as the triumph of the light of reason over darkness. The Queen of the Night, risen against him, seeks to seduce the young Tamino with her daughter's beauty, as an ally against her husband. Inevitably, social harmony (modeled by that of music) is reestablished: under Sarastro's dominion, Tamino and Pamina take their places as domestic master and wife, while the Queen (with her black ally) is "demolished, extinguished, defeated."[31] But Mozart's genius—concretely, his responsiveness to the needs of opera and the demands of singers—makes him give her the great, wild "revenge" aria, in which she achieves true sublimity, if only before her end.

In the treatment of the female sublime by a radical woman the inherent categorical conflict becomes more interestingly apparent. Mary Wollstonecraft's *Vindication of the Rights of Woman* (1792) is an explicit attempt "to convince the world that the poisoned source of female vices and follies," as well as their oppression by men, "has been the sensual homage paid to beauty." She contrasts "beauty of features" or "a pretty woman, as an object of desire" with "a fine woman, who inspires more sublime emotions by displaying intellectual beauty." The juncture of aesthetics and politics is as clear here as in the writings of Burke, her antagonist. Wollstonecraft's enemies are "tyrants of every denomination, from the weak king to the weak father of a family"; she wishes to move "the civilized women of the present century" who, "with a few exceptions, are only anxious to inspire love, when they ought to cherish a nobler ambition, and by their abilities and virtues exact respect."[32]

Wollstonecraft's argument is based on a set of reversals of the standard treatment of the beautiful and sublime. For her it is the sacrifice of "strength of body and mind . . . to libertine notions of beauty" with the goal of establishing themselves in the world by marriage that makes "mere animals" of women (83). Having compared "beautiful" women to animals (and children), Wollstonecraft reverses a fundamental archetype of beauty and sublimity by comparing degraded womankind to military men who, like women, "become a prey to prejudices, and taking all their opinions on credit, . . . blindly submit to authority." Soldiers too are "attentive to their persons, fond of dancing, crowded rooms, adventures, and ridicule" (106). And, finally, Wollstonecraft holds that, like soldiers, monarchs and aristocrats generally cannot be considered exemplars of sublimity, for "[b]irth, riches, and every extrinsic advantage that exalt a man above his fellows, without any mental exertion, sink him in reality below them" (131).

Where, then, are heroes to be found? In her basic reversal, Wollstonecraft calls on women to exemplify the sublimity absent from patriarchal society. "It is time to effect a revolution in female manners—time to restore to them their lost dignity—and make them, as a part of the human species, labour by reforming themselves to reform the world" (132). By the overthrow at once of the divine right of husbands and the divine right of kings, a corrupt social order, in which "wealth and female softness equally tend to debase mankind" (140) will be abolished. Beauty may be, as Burke proclaimed, the virtue of subordinates, but if the great end of human beings is "to unfold their own faculties, and acquire the dignity of conscious virtue" (109), then the beautiful must be recognized as itself an image of distorted and deformed nature, whose true shape is visible only in the sublime.

Sublimity for Wollstonecraft remains a masculine attribute, although one that males themselves have lost. Taken up by women, it is desexualized, as her ideal woman seems to be a widowed mother, the embodiment of republican virtue in a world without men: "she subdues every wayward passion to fulfill the double duty of being the father as well as the mother of her children. Raised to heroism by misfortunes, she represses the first faint dawning of a natural inclination, before it ripens into love, and in the bloom of life forgets her sex" (138). The categories are strained to the breaking point in the effort to figure a radical alteration of society.

Wollstonecraft's critique of beauty as degraded state is confirmed by the evidence of turn-of-the-century history painting. In general, woman, if beautiful, is passive, grief-stricken, asleep, or dead. Woman represented as active and powerful reflects the fear voiced by Burke and Rousseau: she is a witch, or killer of children or husband (Medea, Clytemnestra, Phaedra). The former type appears over and over in the nineteenth century in such guises as Juliet, Ophelia, or harem girl. The latter type—the Bad Sublime—takes fin-de-siècle form as Salome, sphinx, and vampire (she makes a notable twentieth-century entrance among the Demoiselles d'Avignon).

That these were not the only possibilities is demonstrated by Delacroix's *Liberty Leading the People,* in which we have the transformation of the Burkean mob of the "vilest of women" into a revolutionary avatar of Mary Wollstonecraft's feminine sublime. Gun in one hand, tricolor in the other, her bare breasts demonstrating her continued sexual presence, she appears at the barricade not as destroyer of order but as incarnation of a new order in which the bourgeois and laboring classes will create a common destiny. Republican men here stand with her, not against her. Perhaps it is not just the difference between France and Britain but the actuality of revolution—the picture was made in 1830—that saved her from restriction to sublime widowhood and allowed her the sexuality of the "woman of the people" crowned as Liberty in 1789.[33] But of course the new order was a chimera, and this image had no immediate successor.

VI

In 1805 Goethe could still write that "To make the transition from the world of letters, and even from the highest manifestations of words and language, namely poetry and rhetoric, to the visual arts, is difficult and well-nigh impossible: for between them lies an enormous gulf which only a special natural aptitude can bridge."[34] On the other hand, in 1795 Schiller demanded that "the plastic arts . . . must become sheer form," though only because "it is an inevitable and natural consequence of their approach to perfection that the various arts, without any displacement of their objective frontiers, tend to become ever more like each other in their effect upon the psyche." In any and every art, "subject-matter . . . always has a limiting effect upon the spirit, and it is only from form that true aesthetic freedom can be looked for."[35] To say this is to abandon the claims of such as Lessing and Burke for the superiority of poetry over painting. But this is achieved only insofar as the "feminine" nature of the visual arts, as clearly defined images of beautiful bodies, is abandoned, as in Delacroix's claim that painting and music are "above thought" and hence superior to literature precisely "through their very vagueness."[36] By freeing itself from clarity of image, and moving in the direction of "abstraction," painting moves in the direction of sublimity, or masculinity.

The goals of art—literary and visual—were radically reformulated in the later nineteenth century, with the rise of realism. At this time, music continued to be the home of the Romanticism into which the ideal of sublimity had metamorphosed. Thus music also took the place of poetry as the exemplary art; as Carl Dahlhaus says, "music increased its influence because it was almost alone in bearing the burden of providing an alternative to the realities of the world following the Industrial Revolution."[37] Central to at least one important line of the "modernist" painting that the twentieth century brought, however, has been a tendency for the demands of mimesis to be overwhelmed by the reduction of the image to the elements of line, pictorial space, and color, and its reconstruction as a product of the painter's activity. While theorists of abstract art invert Lessing's critique of history painting to make pure form a carrier of spiritual truth, the categories employed are descendants of those we have examined here.

Barnett Newman is notable for explicitly calling on the categories of the beautiful and the sublime for the statement of a modernist program:

> The failure of European art to achieve the sublime is due to [the] blind desire to exist inside the reality of sensation (the object world . . .) and to build an art within the framework of pure plasticity (the Greek ideal of beauty. . .). In other words, modern art, caught without a sublime content, was incapable of creating a new sublime image. . . . [S]ome of us . . . are finding the answer, by completely denying that art has any connection with the problem of beauty. . . . We are reasserting man's natural desire for the exalted.

It is hardly surprising when Newman, seeking an ancestry for his art in that of the original inhabitants of the American Northwest, finds it in "an abstract symbolic art . . . not to be confused with the geometric designs of its decorative arts, which were a separate realm practiced by the women of the tribes. The serious art of these tribes, practiced by the men, took the form of a highly abstract concept."[38] In the preeminence it gives the sublime over the beautiful and in the gender associations of the terms, Newman's conception is more continuous with tradition than he suspected.

In modernist formalism so-called content is identified, as by Lessing, with the literary; so-called form is then free to represent higher, or deeper, universal structures of meaning and expression. The body of nature is abandoned as inessential; the spirit or soul of nature is identified with the creative act of the artist (I am thinking of Pollock's pronouncement: "I am nature"). We have here a radical transformation of the late eighteenth-century aesthetics I have been discussing. But its materials are still the gendered constructs of that aesthetic, according to which it is only by taking form in the activity of the heroic male that art could claim to embody both the supposedly elemental, natural force of self-love and the highest development of universal civilization.[39]

Notes

1. Judith Schapiro, "Gender Totemism," manuscript (1986), 2.

2. Paul Oskar Kristeller, "The Modern System of the Arts," chap. 9 in his *Renaissance Thought II* (New York: Harper Torchbook, 1965), 165.

3. On the place of aesthetics in this historical complex, see the essays in Paul Mattick, ed., *Eighteenth-Century Aesthetics and the Reconstruction of Art* (Cambridge: Cambridge University Press, 1993), in particular (on gender in aesthetics) Elizabeth Bohls, "Disinterestedness and the Denial of the Particular: Locke, Adam Smith, and the Subject of Aesthetics."

4. Interestingly enough, "beauty" is a development from Latin *bellum*, which replaced *pulchrum* during the Renaissance. This derives from *bonellum*, a diminutive of *bonum* applied originally only to women and children. See Wladislaw Tatarkiewicz, *A History of Six Ideas* (The Hague: Nijhoff, 1980), 121.

5. Edmund Burke, *A Philosophical Enquiry into the Origin of Our Ideas of the Sublime and the Beautiful*, ed. J. T. Boulton (Notre Dame: University of Notre Dame Press, 1968), 110.

6. Ibid., 39, 40; see also 46: "for terror is a passion which always produces delight when it does not press too close."

7. Had Burke himself not unequivocally identified the sublime as masculine in nature, we could cite John Cleland's description of "the essential object of enjoyment," as seen through the eyes of Fanny Hill: "Its prodigious size made me shrink again; yet I could not, without pleasure, behold, and even ventur'd to feel, such a length, such a breadth of animated ivory! . . . then the broad and bluish-casted incarnate of the head, and blue serpentines of its veins, altogether composed the most striking assemblage of figure and colours in nature. In short, it stood an object of terror and delight" (*Memoirs of a Woman of Pleasure* [New York: Putnam, 1963], 85). To this may be compared not only Kant's discovery of the sublime in the *monstrous* and the *colossal*, but also his analysis of our feeling of the sublime as "a pleasure . . . produced by the feeling of a momentary inhibition of the vital forces followed immediately by an outpouring of them that is all the stronger" (Kant, *Critique of Judgment*, trans. Werner Pluhar [Indianapolis: Hackett, 1987], 109, 98).

8. Immanuel Kant, *Critique of Judgment* [1790], trans. W. S. Pluhar (Indianapolis: Hackett, 1987), 121, 122.

9. Jean-Jacques Rousseau, "Discourse on the Origin of Inequality" [1754], in *On the Social Contract*, trans. D. A. Cress (Indianapolis: Hackett: 1983), 140, 142–43.

10. Jean-Jacques Rousseau, *Emile, or On Education* [1762], trans. A. Bloom (New York: Basic Books, 1979), 214.

11. Hence a proper education for females must incorporate "habitual restraint," which will produce "a docility which women need all their lives, since they never cease to be subjected either to a man or to the judgements of men and they are never permitted to put themselves above these judgements" (*Emile*, 370).

12. G. E. Lessing, *Laocoön, or On the Limits of Painting and Poetry* [1766], trans. W. A. Steel, in H. B. Nisbet, ed., *German Aesthetic and Literary Criticism: Winckelmann, Lessing, Hamann, Herder, Schiller, Goethe* (Cambridge: Cambridge University Press, 1985), 99, 114, 105.

13. Ibid., 116–17. In his important letter to Nicolai of 26 May 1769, Lessing clarifies his position: ". . . it is not true that painting uses only natural signs, just as it is not true that poetry uses only arbitrary signs. But one thing is certain: the more painting departs from natural signs, or employs natural and arbitrary signs mixed together, the further it departs from its true perfection; just as conversely poetry draws all the closer to its true perfection, the closer it makes its arbitrary signs approach the natural"—i.e., in drama, which represents speech, culture as human nature in action (133).

14. Ibid., 91; the passage contrasts a painter working after nature with one inspired by nature poetry.

15. T. E. Crow, *Painters and Public Life in Eighteenth-Century Paris* (New Haven: Yale University Press, 1985), 216–17.

16. J. L. David, letters to Wicar, in R. L. Herbert, *David, Voltaire, Brutus, and the French Revolution: an essay in art and politics* (New York: Viking, 1973), 123, 124; review in *Mercure de France* 1 (24 October 1789), in Herbert, *David,* 126. See the reviews in the *Journal de Paris* and the *Supplément aux remarques sur les ouvrages éxposés au Salon,* translated in Herbert, 126, 127, which state (respectively) that in this work "history belongs in the same manner to painter and to poet" and that David's "production is more of a great poet than of a painter."

17. That this is not simply a modern commentator's projection of the categories of beautiful and sublime on David's picture can be seen from Tischbein's contemporary description: "Determination, courage, strength, reverence for the gods, love of freedom and of the fatherland show themselves in the men; in the women inconsolable dejection, weak and numb collapse, tenderness for the spouse, the bridegroom, the children, the brothers; in the children playful innocence and naivete"; see J. H. W. Tischbein, "Letters from Rome," *Der teutsche Merkur* (February 1786), trans. in E. G. Holt, ed. *The Triumph of Art for the Public, 1785–1848* (Princeton: Princeton University Press, 1983), 19. Other contemporary accounts make the same point.

18. Rousseau, *Emile*, 40. Grimm's account of the 1789 Salon noted the familiar duality: "This austere figure [Brutus], isolated and as it were enshrouded in shadows, forms an admirable contrast with this group of women, illuminated with a light that is rather bright, but gentle and tranquil" (trans. in R. Herbert, *David,* 128). A gender-structured contrast similar to that made in David's two paintings on Roman themes can be identified also in his *Death of Socrates* and *Paris and Helen,* produced in 1787 and 1789, respectively, but apparently intended for presentation as a contrasting pair. The first represents the sublime theme of the death of a hero of intellectual and patriotic virtue; the second a depiction of sexual desire, pursued at whatever cost to national or personal honor.

19. Immanuel Kant, *Critique of Judgment* [1790], trans. W. S. Pluhar (Indianapolis: Hackett, 1987), 193.

20. Ibid.; and see 86, "to the poet alone belongs the art of depicting with negative traits, and by mixing them with positive to bring two images into one."

21. Immanuel Kant, *Observations on the Feeling of the Sublime and Beautiful,* trans. John T. Goldthwait (Berkeley and Los Angeles: University of California Press, 1960), 78. "A woman is embarrassed little that she does not possess certain high insights, that she is timid, and not fit for serious employments, and so forth; she is beautiful and captivates, and that is enough. On the other hand, she demands all these qualities in a man, and the sublimity of her soul shows itself

only in that she knows to treasure these noble qualities so far as they are found in him." He, meanwhile, "by [her] fine figure, merry naivete, and charming friendliness . . . is sufficiently repaid for the lack of book learning and for other deficiencies that he must supply by his own talents" (93–94).

22. For a different take on gender in Wright's painting, see David Solkin, "ReWrighting Shaftesbury: The Air Pump and the Limits of Commercial Humanism," in John Barrell, ed., *Painting and the Politics of Culture: New Essays on British Art, 1700–1850* (Oxford: Oxford University Press, 1992), esp. 93–95.

Thomas Eakin's *The Gross Clinic* (1875) demonstrates the longevity of the themes of Wright's painting. Here the bird as object of experimentation is replaced by the human body as a field for dissection; the scientific passion of the medical men contrasts sharply with the inability of the one woman in the scene to face the truth before her: like the older girl in the *Experiment*, she hides her face. Dr. Gross, like the scientist in Wright's picture, is a hero of modern times; successor to the warriors of old, he embodies what a hundred years before was called the sublime. This is not to say that times do not change. Eakins's *Agnew Clinic*, painted fourteen years later, features a woman who has herself entered the territory of the sublime: the assisting nurse, present not for aesthetic enjoyment, but as participant in men's work.

23. Natalie Zemon Davis, "Women on Top," in *Society and Culture in Early Modern France* (Stanford: Stanford University Press, 1975), 124–25. In the eighteenth century this tradition takes the form of "an archetypal conception of woman as a sexually insatiable creature when her desire is aroused . . . one of the major sexual myths traceable in many medical handbooks, and certainly underlying much eighteenth-century fiction": see Paul-Gabriel Bouce, "Some Sexual Beliefs and Myths in Eighteenth-Century Britain," in P.-G. Bouce, ed., *Sexuality in Eighteenth-Century Britain* (Manchester: Manchester University Press, 1982), 28–46; quotation is 41–42.

24. Joan Kelly, "Early Feminist Theory and the *Querelle des Femmes*, 1400–1789," in *Women, History, and Theory* (Chicago: University of Chicago Press, 1984), 70.

25. Davis, "Women," 127.

26. Ibid., 146.

27. See the passage quoted by Ronald Paulson in his interesting discussion: "The condition of France at this moment was so frightful and horrible, that if a painter wished to portray a description of hell, he could not find so terrible a model, or a subject so pregnant with horror, and fit for his purpose. Milton, with all that genius which enabled him to excel in descriptions of this nature, would have been ashamed to have presented to his readers such a hell as France now has . . . ; he would have thought his design revolting to the most unlimited imagination, and his colouring overcharged beyond all allowance for the license even of poetical painting"; speech in Commons, 11 April 1794, cited in Paulson, *Representations of Revolution (1789–1820)* (New Haven: Yale University Press, 1983), 66.

28. Burke, *Enquiry*, 46; Kant, *Critique of Judgment*, 121.

29. Burke, *Reflections on the Revolution in France* [1790], ed. J. G. A. Pocock (Indianapolis: Hackett, 1987), 63.

30. It is a complaint of Burke's that the mob's action expresses a scheme of things in which "a king is but a man; a queen is but a woman; a woman is but an animal; and an animal not of the highest order" (*Reflections*, 67)—that is, queen and woman of the "swinish multitude" are equalized.

31. "Zerschmettert, zernichtet ist unsere Macht, / Wir alle gesturzet in ewige Nacht."

32. Mary Wollstonecraft, *Vindication of the Rights of Woman*, ed. M. B. Kramnick (Harmondsworth, Middlesex: Penguin, 1975), 134, 87, 79.

33. See the related mythology sketched by Hugo in reporting the June Days of 1848 in his *Choses Vues*: "At that moment a young woman appeared on the crest of the barricade, a young woman, beautiful, dishevelled, terrifying. This woman, who was a public whore, pulled her dress

up to the waist and cried to the guardsmen, in that dreadful brothel language that one is always obliged to translate: 'Cowards! Fire, if you dare, at the belly of a woman!' . . . It's a hideous thing, this heroism of abjection, when all that weakness contains of strength bursts out." Victor Hugo, *Oeuvres complètes* (Paris, 1955) 31:365–66; cited by Neil Hertz, "Medusa's Head: Male Hysteria under Political Pressure," in *Representations* 4 (1983), 29.

34. J. W. von Goethe, *Winckelmann*, trans. H. B. Nisbet, in H. B. Nisbet, ed., *German Aesthetic and Literary Criticism*, 243.

35. Friedrich Schiller, *On the Aesthetic Education of Man* [1795], trans. E. M. Wilkinson and L. A. Willoughby (Oxford: Clarendon Press, 1967), 155.

36. *The Journal of Eugène Delacroix*, trans. W. Pach (New York: Grove, 1961), 61.

37. Carl Dahlhaus, *Between Romanticism and Modernism* (Berkeley and Los Angeles: University of California Press, 1980), 8.

38. Barnett Newman, "The Sublime is Now" (1948), in *Selected Writings and Interviews*, ed. John P. O'Neill (New York: Knopf, 1990), 173; "The Painting of Tamayo and Gottlieb" (1945), in ibid., 75.

39. I am grateful for comments on earlier forms of this essay by Rochelle Feinstein, Nancy Fraser, Claire L'Enfant, Sidney Tillim, and Alan Wallach.

2
Gendered Concepts and Hume's Standard of Taste

Carolyn Korsmeyer

Hume introduces his *Treatise of Human Nature* with a remark that summarizes his entire approach to philosophical investigation: " 'Tis evident, that all the sciences have a relation, greater or less, to human nature; and that however wide any of them may seem to run from it, they still return back by one passage or another."[1] Thus his examinations of knowledge, of ethics, of politics, and—of particular interest for this essay—of art and taste, are all grounded on an understanding of human nature. Indeed, a trust in the common constitution of human nature permits Hume to admit considerable degrees of disagreement on matters of taste, without worrying that he has forfeited the grounds for a common standard of critical judgments.

Feminist scholarship has awakened us to the suspicion that such reliance on "common human nature" renders philosophical concepts not neutral and universal, as Hume believed, but heavily inflected by models of ideal masculinity that inform discussions of human nature. One purpose of this essay is to extend this line of thought by elucidating the idea of gendered concepts. By this phrase I refer to concepts that, lacking any obvious reference to males or females, or to masculinity or femininity, nevertheless are formulated in such a way that their neutral quality and universal applicability are questionable. Here I pursue this suspicion by examining Hume's famous standard of taste.

Examination of gendered concepts not only casts doubt on the scope and operation of such a standard; it reveals the peculiarly unstable position of the idea of "female" in concepts of the "human."

The so-called problem of taste was a thorny issue for eighteenth-century theoreticians. Most granted the premise that "beauty" and like terms of aesthetic value signify, not qualities in beautiful objects, but pleasures aroused in perceivers. Since the experience of pleasure appears to be relative to the perceiver, this subjectivist analysis of beauty made the search for a standard of taste both difficult and urgent. On the one hand, good taste appeared to be very unevenly distributed; on the other, it was held to be a universal value with shared standards for quality. Reconciling these apparent contraries was the task of philosophers, who recognized two routes open for stabilizing taste disparities: they could argue that human nature is so similarly formed in all that our pleasure reactions are also basically the same, in spite of some apparent diversity. And they could discover a common denominator in all the objects of beauty, thus finding some objective property that could be identified as the correlate of aesthetic pleasure. Many thinkers of the time pursued both courses. Hume chose only the latter route, and since he puts all his faith in common human nature, his theory is ideal for analyzing presumptions of universality in the operations of aesthetic judgment and the extent to which this enterprise contains biases of both gender and culture.

Hume's most famous writing on taste appears in the essay "Of the Standard of Taste" (1757). The essay opens with the observation that every voice is united in praising basic aesthetic principles, a fact confirming the presence of a universal standard for taste. Yet immediately Hume notes that when we come to particular judgments, agreement is displaced by diversity of opinion as to how general principles apply.[2] On the one hand, he continues, it is clear that wherever there is pleasure there is beauty; yet it is equally obvious that some judgments are superior to others. As he puts it, "To seek the real beauty, or real deformity, is as fruitless an enquiry, as to pretend to ascertain the real sweet or real bitter . . . and the proverb has justly determined it to be fruitless to dispute concerning tastes." Yet at the same time, "Whoever would assert an equality of genius and elegance between Olgilby and Milton, or Bunyan and Addison, would be thought to defend no less an extravagance, than if he had maintained a molehill to be as high as Teneriffe, or a pond as extensive as the ocean."[3]

How to resolve this apparent conundrum? Hume's answer is to bypass examination of the objects of aesthetic judgment and concentrate on the judge and the process by which judgments of taste are made. The result is the endorsement of the judgment of good critics throughout the ages, whose opinions converge as art passes the test of time and remains appreciated thoughout history. He recommends that we should emulate the taste of persons whose good judgment is already recognized, since by following their example we shall refine and develop our own tastes according to tested criteria of artistic judgment.

Though he has been castigated by critics and sympathizers alike for a conservative endorsement of canons of art (surprising from a philosopher labeled in his own day as a dangerous skeptic), this reliance on consensus of informed critics is philosophically a wily move. Being convinced that not all aesthetic pleasures are equally worthy, and also skeptical that the objective world provides any discoverable property causally related to pleasure, Hume concludes that the only way to explain a standard of taste is to refer it to those who, as a matter of fact, are the taste-setters.[4]

The taste of a good critic, though founded on natural dispositions, must be cultivated, and the means of cultivation are—in theory—available to any person of sufficient leisure to pursue them. The foundation for critical judgment is a natural delicacy of taste. Hume describes this as a condition where "the organs are so fine, as to allow nothing to escape them; and at the same time so exact as to perceive every ingredient in the composition."[5] In addition, critical acuity requires experience and practice; initial exposure to art is inevitably confusing. In order to learn to rank objects as to their beauty and artistry, the critic must learn to make comparisons of objects, and in so doing should endeavor to form judgments with a mind free from prejudice. This ability is particularly important if judgments are to form a standard of taste valid for different times and different cultures, and not just reflect the conventional preferences of a particular society.[6] The generally useful characteristic of good sense regulates the interference of prejudice and other factors that skew judgments of artistic quality. Pursuit of these five routes to taste—delicacy of sentiment, practice, comparative judgment, freedom from prejudice, and good sense—produces a person who readily and reliably perceives the qualities in objects that all of us have a basic natural disposition to enjoy.

At the same time that he relies upon common human nature to defend universal values and standards, Hume recognizes that there is considerable variety in the ways in which those values are manifest. Preferences for one poetic form over another, for a particular style of music, even for variant codes of conduct, may be accommodated within the general standards for taste and good living that Hume believed obtain for all human creatures. Because Hume permits a degree of variety and disagreement among equally sound judgments, if any approaches to taste are successfully universalist without being arbitrary, his should be among them.

The standard of taste thus developed is not a set of criteria or principles, but a kind of person or group of people; it is a pragmatic standard that focuses upon the process of discerning aesthetic merit. How successful is this approach as a standard of taste? Is Hume really invoking commonalities of human nature, such that the standard of taste functions universally? Or is he mistaking culturally specific properties such as education, class, gender, and nationality for the properties ideally attributable to us all? I choose gender as the principal lens for exploring these questions because Hume made sufficiently complex remarks about gender to construct a pattern of his thought on the subject. In fact, I shall argue that gender has a particularly deep place in theories such as Hume's that employ arguments assuming universal human nature.

As is the case with many philosophers, Hume's direct comments about sex differences and women are scattered and apparently unsystematic. They are also complicated and open to divergent interpretations. Apparent inconsistency, as we shall see, is less a symptom of bad reasoning in the case of gendered concepts, than of the complexity of the philosophical role of the concept "female" and its kin. We must reconstruct Hume's analysis of gender before sorting through its relevance for the establishment of standards of taste.

Hume enjoys a small reputation for being accommodating to the idea of sex equality.[7] To a certain extent this is merited. Paging through Hume's writings on morals and manners, one can find a number of passages where women's equality is suggested or where their qualities are particularly praised. His personal sociability emerges in much of this writing, and he praises societies that foster *friendship* among men and women. Hume was alert to the distortions that society contributes to our understanding not only of what is right and proper, but also what is "natural." (One of his objections to social contract theory, for example, is that it focuses exclusively on adult males in the notional state of nature.)[8] He was aware that we have often mistaken customary relations between the sexes for the dictates of nature, and insofar as he incorporates observations like this into his writing he anticipates the liberal feminism of Wollstonecraft and Mill. However, at the same time that Hume evinces progressive sentiments about women, males and females play very different roles in the formulation of the basic concept of human nature, and these differences undermine the very foundation of his philosophical goals.

Because Hume denies that moral virtues are founded on any objective relations, he frees his philosophy from the task of explaining any stable, unchanging codes of behavior that would fix present social disparities in the roles of men and women. Hume discovers two distinct foundations for moral behavior: natural sentiments and social utility. As he proceeds though analyses of commonly named virtues, he argues that if there were no *social use* for certain "artificial" virtues, there would be no reason to recommend them at all.[9] Such is the context in which he discusses chastity.

While sexual self-discipline is commendable for both men and women, Hume considers chastity primarily a female virtue. (In fact, sexual abstinence in men counts as one of the "monkish virtues" Hume scorns.)[10] There is, however, no pretense that women's innate nature requires any particular kind of sexual conduct. If chastity is a moral trait, it is so only because it describes behavior that fits into a social pattern that maximizes utility. This discussion of female chastity is both iconoclastic and conservative, however; after puncturing the idea that there is any intrinsic merit to chastity, Hume repeats the bromide that the reason chastity is important for social utility is that children promiscuously conceived would be deprived of known paternity and stable families. He goes on to acknowledge that, logically, chastity ought only to apply to women who can bear children. This logic is overridden, however, by the worry that the evident fun of older women would be dangerous for the younger, who might unduly advance the time of their own release from the constraints of this virtue.[11] Thus chastity for all females remains socially desirable. Although much of this discussion takes an ironic tone that mocks the gravity that often attends discussions of chastity, later in the *Enquiry* Hume betrays an interesting anxiety about the difficulty of keeping track of a woman's virtue. "A female has so many opportunities of secretly indulging these appetites, that nothing can give us security but her absolute modesty and reserve; and where a breach is once made, it can scarcely ever be fully repaired."[12] Thus, having briefly opened the possibility that women's sexual behavior is not governed by laws that limit their freedom any more than men's, Hume quickly closes it by finding sufficient social utility in preserving norms of chastity.

Hume's considerable interest in the relations of the sexes is also pursued in his discussions of manners and marriage customs. His judgments about exotic sexual customs and moral development are often presented with a tone of address that complicates their meaning. Thus not only the substance but also the style of Hume's discussion of relations between the sexes pertains to the way that gender permeates his work. Hume famously reveled in the company of ladies, engaging with them in intellectual conversation and friendship. Some were aristocrats, some were friends of humbler background; all were "modest," having good manners and a sense of propriety. (Of course, what was deemed proper varied hugely in Hume's own experience. His friend Mme de Boufflers could have lovers both for her own entertainment and for sustaining and improving her social rank; a servant fallen into sexual labor became a prostitute, a situation for which Hume evidently had scant sympathy.)[13] Though Hume personally did not seem to think women lacked intellectual capacity—and his company in the salons of France and the drawing rooms of England would have borne this out—the fact was that no matter how accomplished, women remained for him in a different social category from men. As a result, Hume adopts a pervasive tone of gallantry when addressing women or even sometimes when discussing gender in his essays. Gallantry in fact is both a style and a natural virtue, and as such provides an illuminating angle on human nature and gender.

For example, gallantry is a social corrective for what Hume refers to now and again as the "natural" superiority of men over women. Just what constitutes this superiority is never explored very thoroughly, but it seems to stem from commonplace and vague observations about greater physical strength. In a just society, Hume remarks, natural male superiority must be *corrected* to bring the sexes into more equal status. "As nature has given *man* the superiority above *woman*, by endowing him with greater strength both of mind and body; it is his part to alleviate that superiority, as much as possible, by the generosity of his behaviour, and by a studied deference and complaisance for all her inclinations and opinions."[14] There is nothing of particular social utility to be preserved in the subordination of women, so social practices ought to equalize gender roles.

While barbarian nations make slaves of their women, Hume observes, those of civilized Europe have gentler means: "But the male sex, among a polite people, discover their authority in a more generous, though not a less evident manner; by civility, by respect, by complaisance, and, in a word, by gallantry."[15] Pursuing the implications of this statement, we may define gallantry as the gentle art of consolidating authority by treating with tactful solicitude one's gender inferiors.

Despite the fact that this disposition emerges among "polite" peoples, Hume stresses that gallantry is a "natural" sentiment. The term "natural" is, as ever, fraught with multiple meanings; but labeling gallantry "natural" places this conduct in the company of that fundamental natural virtue that makes Hume's ethics so warmhearted and kindly: benevolence. As a natural sentiment, gallantry is refined but not created by civilization. A central agent in that refinement, moreover, is the softening influence of a woman.

"What better school for manners, than the company of virtuous women; where the mutual endeavor to please must insensibly polish the mind, where the example of the female softness and modesty must communicate itself to their admirers, and where the delicacy of that sex puts every one on his guard, lest he give offense by any breach of decency."[16]

Thus women are both the object of gallant good manners and the fund of development for those manners. (Similarly, as we shall see, they are both the object of taste and its judgments, and a source of development of good taste.) Natural gallantry leads men to relinquish their position of superiority to allow women an honored social place; and women, cultivated and refined because of that deference (for only *modest* and *virtuous* women can serve in this way), foster still further the development and honing of fine manners.

Gallantry is sufficiently out of fashion now as to appear simply obnoxious in many circles, though of course nothing could have been further from the effect of this style or this sentiment in Hume's time.[17] However, no matter how it is appreciated, when gallantry is a norm of conduct, it not only puts its object on a different standing from the bestower of gallant behavior, but, because its purpose is amelioratory, it blinds one to the effects of this practice. This partially accounts for the fact that Hume, ordinarily careful to guard against inconsistency, could assert the equality of the sexes in certain contexts, call it into question in others, and treat females as actually outside the realm of general humanity in still others.

For in spite of an often inclusive use of the term "man," Hume on several occasions alludes to females as though they stand outside the domain of interest he investigates: human nature. Much of the time this is implicit: the social roles and activities that he discusses (with the obvious exception of love and marriage)—eloquence, politics, etc.—are public affairs that in his time excluded women so thoroughly that their absence was unremarkable. But sometimes the exclusion is dramatically explicit, as when women are considered the objects of an attention that reveals some truth of the human nature of the subject attending. Frequently this emerges when women are considered the objects of judgments of taste. Women are ranked alongside works of art in this passage from the *Treatise* discussing the conversion of pleasure into pain through repetition: "But when the fair sex, or music, or good cheer, or any thing, that naturally ought to be agreeable, becomes indifferent, it easily produces the opposite affection."[18]

Women play a similar role as the objects of some passion of "human" nature, as when Hume speculates on the effects of climate on national character. Temperate climate is the most conducive to accomplishment, he surmises, because passion is high enough to fuel ambition, yet not so high as to keep one in a frenzy of sexual desire: "the people, in very temperate climates, are the most likely to attain all sorts of improvement; their blood not being so inflamed as to render them jealous, and yet being warm enough to make them set a due value on the charms and endowments of the fair sex."[19]

The antecedents of "they" in this passage oscillate wildly. "People" sounds generic, and certainly all people of particular areas live in the same climates. Yet the objects of "their" passion turn out to be some portion of "them" whose own objects of passion are unnamed. Similar confusion of referents is evident in scattered passages passim, as for example in the essay "Of Dignity or Meanness in Human Nature," where in the space of only two lines *"our sex,"* referring quite obviously to men (to whose good looks is contrasted the beauty of women), gives way to a mention of *"our species."*[20] Women flicker in and out of inclusion in the first-person plural, and since the discussion is human nature itself, women are from time to time thrust to the very rim of that category.

Like virtually all writers, Hume used the term "man" loosely and uncritically, and while sometimes he clearly construes it inclusively, the intended scope of much of this usage is simply unclear. I suspect that most of the time Hume intended its use generically in a vague sort of way, while having as his model a man rather like himself. This is the most typical use of the generic masculine, and I shall have more to say about it later. But Hume was not merely unthinking about the implications of this language, and from time to time he finds it necessary to stipulate that he indeed does mean *everybody*. The contexts for such emphases are those where he might have anticipated that his readers would exempt women from the general assertion. The most remarkable instance concerns sexual drives, where Hume is led to insist, "there is in all men, both male and female, a desire and power of generation, more active than is ever universally exerted."[21] In a long footnote to the essay that contains this passage, Hume explores the relationship between pairs of terms he calls "correlatives." Consideration of correlative concepts illuminates the problems of generalization in which Hume welters. He writes: "It is an universal observation, which we may form upon language, that where two related parts of a whole bear any proportion to each other, in numbers, rank or consideration, there are always correlative terms invented, which answer to both the pairs, and express their mutual relation. . . . Thus *man* and *woman, master* and *servant, father* and *son, prince* and *subject, stranger* and *citizen,* are correlative terms."[22] But lest we presume such relations are fixed, he continues: "Languages differ very much with regard to the particular words where this distinction obtains; and may thence afford very strong inferences, concerning the manners and customs of different nations."

It would be nice to discover here the idea that any imbalance in gender correlates is attributable merely to culture. However, not only does Hume not pursue this possibility, he elsewhere asserts the superiority of the male correlate in such a way that it appears virtually impossible to challenge. The locus is the long "Dissertation on the Passions," where Hume engages in an analytical catalogue of human characteristics and feelings, explaining them all according to the fact that they afford pleasure. The subject is pride—a good trait in Hume's view when it stops short of conceit—and the objects of which we are proud or even vain. "We" (says Hume, brother of Lord Home of Ninewells) are proud of ancient families, and particularly proud if our line of descent proceeds unbroken through the male line.[23] He explains the source of this sentiment: "It is an obvious quality of human nature, that the imagination naturally turns to whatever is important and considerable; and where two objects are presented, a small and a great, it usually leaves the former, and dwells entirely on the latter. This is the reason, why children commonly bear their father's name, and are esteemed to be of a nobler or meaner birth, according to *his* family."[24] Hume is clear that this habit of evaluation has nothing to do with the merits of the individuals in question: "And though the mother should be possessed of superior qualities to the father, as often happens, the *general rule* prevails, notwithstanding the exception."[25]

When the exception proves the rule so stubbornly, it is clear that it is principally the conceptual framework itself that holds the masculine correlate superior. That is, the abstract category "male" remains dominant, even when most members of that class are inferior to the members of the correlative female class. This rigidity of systemic thinking imports gendered concepts into seemingly neutral terrain. Indeed, the material for this very point is present in Hume's own analysis of abstract ideas. Hume notes in the *Treatise* that an "abstract" idea is always experienced as an idea of an *individual* thing. "Abstract ideas are therefore in themselves individual, however they may become general in their representation. The image in the mind is only that of a particular object, tho' the application of it in our reasoning be the same, as if it were universal."[26] No matter how wide our experience, and how carefully we collect diverse qualities of real individuals to represent their class, the abstract ideas we form to represent *all* are always manifest in an image of a representative *individual*. Individual differences are blurred as the mind relates particulars according to their relations of *resemblance*. Hume himself trusts the similar constitution of human nature and does not anticipate the dangers lurking in the observation: "If ideas be particular in their nature, and at the same time finite in their number, 'tis only by custom they can become general in their representation, and contain an infinite number of other ideas under them."[27] These cautions he asserts about the formation of abstract ideas go far to explain the difficulties a reader has in determining the scope of the vexing generic term "man." There is an abiding tension in his discussions of gender between basic common nature and the channels societies impose on manners. At the same time that Hume analyzes sex inequality as inutile cultural distortion of natural relations, he also retains disparity between male and female in his treatment of fundamental human nature.

How do these observations regarding women bear upon Hume's general philosophy of human nature and on his attempt to establish the foundations for uniform normative standards? It is now pretty clear that Hume's philosophy viewed women in a way that, however amiable and graceful, ranked them in one way or another secondary or adjunct to men. Can we, however, uproot eighteenth-century prejudices and retain Hume's standard of taste, in much the way that essentially democratic legislation can extend rights to a larger population? To anticipate my conclusion, there is a degree to which I think we, in rather obvious ways, *can* do so. But this will turn out to be the least philosophically interesting discovery about uniform standards and gendered concepts. For to do so would be to look at gender only as it refers to individuals who use a standard, and not also as it penetrates the concept of the standards themselves.

As we have seen, the establishment of criteria for artistic merit proceeds according to the accumulation of the judgments of good critics whose conclusions are reaffirmed by generations over time. One of the requirements of the good critic is *delicacy* of taste. And Hume notes repeatedly that females excel in this dimension.[28] It is a dangerous trait to overindulge, however, because of its closeness to delicacy of passions (at which females also excel), which is not a good moral characteristic, being more histrionic than sensible. The other characteristics of a good critic—good sense, lack of prejudice, discernment in comparisons, and practice—are even more cultivable than delicacy. Theoretically, nothing at all rules out anyone from participating in the standard of taste so far.[29]

Furthermore, the standard of taste accommodates a wide variety of irreconcilable preferences. The grounds Hume notes for these are "the different humours of particular men" and "the particular manners and opinions of our age and country. The general principles of taste are uniform in human nature. . . . But where there is such a diversity in the internal frame or external situation as is entirely blameless on both sides, and leaves no room to give one the preference above the other; in that case a certain degree of diversity in judgment is unavoidable, and we seek in vain for a standard, by which we can reconcile the contrary sentiments."[30]

Differences of taste that emerge from such contingencies neither undermine the existence of standards nor require a ranking of preferences. Since Hume explicitly allows diversity of taste within the operation of a universal standard of taste, might we add gender to factors like age and nationality, to account without prejudice for differences of taste, when they occur? This issue is not addressed, though collateral comments raise serious doubts that this can be done, raising again the unstable position that females have within the idea of mankind.

When Hume respects difference, he does so not with terms he elsewhere calls "correlatives," but with examples where no superiority may be presumed: the young man who prefers Ovid over Tacitus is neither inferior nor superior to the man of mature taste. But "male" and "female" are correlative pairs, as we have seen, and the disparity of quality assigned them is evident in the language of criticism. "Feminine" might correlate with "masculine" when describing tastes or artistic styles, but in point of fact the correlative term Hume almost always uses with "masculine" is the perjorative *"effeminate."*[31]

Could the standard of taste be established in part through contributions of "feminine" judgments? The question opens up a gap in the text. Good critics have basic points of agreement, all of which satisfy traditional standards of style. Good female critics concur in these judgments—as a matter of fact they often do. But can they as women be the *arbiters* of the standard of taste? That is, are they included in that body of good critics that constitutes the standard of taste itself? There are two reasons to be doubtful that this is the case.

There is first of all a powerful social disparity to be reckoned with in women's abilities to cultivate taste. Hume is high in his praise of modest and virtuous women, who are the civilizing influences that promote taste generally. But such women face a problem in launching their careers as good critics, for retaining one's modesty and virtue requires a certain *limitation* on experience, and breadth of experience is another necessary prerequisite for the development of good taste. (Even if the requirement of experience is interpreted to refer only to experience of art, there are limits of decency in the worlds of art that prevent a virtuous woman's adventures into immodest taste. Perhaps this is another instance, like chastity, where the overriding utility of limited feminine experience argues for lesser freedom for women.) Moreover, were women to lose these feminine virtues, they would also lose what limited standing they have as taste-setters. Once this is noticed, it is also evident why a tone of leisure and class privilege pervades discussions of writings on taste. Modesty and virtue also suggest limitations on the activities, both domestic and public, that one can engage in to earn a wage. Taking a male perspective, we can see that the refining influence of modest and virtuous women is going to be reaped only by those men who are in a position to fraternize with such women.[32]

It may be argued that this consideration is an artifact of eighteenth-century bourgeois manners, expungible from Hume's basic philosophy. However, let me offer further support for the claim that women of good taste are those who find amenable a standard set outside of their own distinctive participation. It is straying from the standard of taste, but I think into relevant territory, to note two passages where Hume does address the union of male and female and the cancellation of their differences: the subject is marriage.

The fascinating essay "Of Polygamy and Divorces" opens with observations about the various forms of marriage, referring to them all as contracts between equals. The equality is more asserted than demonstrated, however, as wives are invariably spoken of as commodities to be parceled out to available husbands, no matter which sex is in the majority because of warfare, shipwreck, or whatever circumstance renders a shortage of partners. Despite an initial liberality about forms of marriage, Hume goes on to argue against polygamy for reasons that are a combination of a preference for European monogamy over the exotic practices of the Turkish seraglio, and egalitarian arguments concluding that utilitarian good is never served by social practices that do not foster friendship between the sexes. The sovereignty of the male, states Hume, "is a real usurpation, and destroys that nearness of rank, not to say equality, which nature has established between the sexes."[33]

Monogamy having been defended, the subject turns to divorce. Human nature loves liberty, effuses Hume, and any permanent constraint in its way leads not to increased conjugal loyalty, but to aversion and deceit. In fact, Hume outlines reasons to approve the possibility of divorce as a freedom from bondage and unhappiness with so much eloquence that one is surprised to discover he ends with thudding arguments *against* freedom from the ties of marriage. (As if in anticipation of this observation, he remarks: "But what is man but a heap of contradictions!")[34] Some of these reasons are familiar ones concerning the responsibility for children when a marriage ends, but the fervor of argument concentrates on a union of man and wife that is so thorough in a good marriage that there is no longer any dissension to prompt divorce.

"Nothing is more dangerous than to unite two persons so closely in all their interests and concerns, as man and wife, without rendering the union entire and total."[35]

Here is another suggestive passage. The essay "Of Love and Marriage" concocts a variation on Aristophanes' myth of sexual attraction in the *Symposium*. In Hume's version of the story the restless search for one's missing counterpart explains not only desire but also marriage. He has Jupiter decreeing that marriage between male and female shall only take place where that union is utter and complete. As he puts it, in the reunited androgyne, "The seam is scarce perceived that joins the two beings; but both of them combine to form one perfect and happy creature."[36] (Unlike Plato, Hume leaves no scope for the union of two halves of the same sex.)

In this ideal union, it would be the female who discards whatever differences she has with her husband and adopts his preferences as her own. Supporting this extrapolation is Hume's own observation in the *Treatise* about the weakening of children's ties to their mother upon her second marriage.[37] So strong is a woman's identity with her husband, that when she marries again, her children's chain of associated ideas, formerly from themselves to her back to themselves again, is now drawn from themselves to her and to her husband, lingering there because of her new ties and obligations to him. Only with difficulty does the imagination return to the children; thus the relation of children to mother is actually weakened, since she has become a different social person with her new set of family ties.

What I import from these passages to an understanding of normative standards and the accommodation of difference is this: there is something systematic and dangerous for sexual difference in this philosophy, *if* that difference is to be given the kind of notice that other differences such as those of age, nationality, or even personal preference are accorded. And I speculate that this has to do with the conceptual depth of gender as well as the unstable position that the idea of femaleness occupies in the concept of human nature. This means that when attention to *differences* among people is directed to *gender* differences, honoring them undermines the project of analyzing human nature. When Hume countenances differences of taste, the model judges he considers are all appropriate *subjects* whose perceptions and judgments form part of the continuum from which standards of taste and comprehension of utilitarian values emerge. But females are frequently considered as the "objects" of perceptions and judgments—perceptions and judgments that are used to draw conclusions about human nature. So if we grant any important standing to judgments that issue from some "female point of view," we shift out of the normal subject position and risk the loss of confidence that there are general standards or norms left at all.

That is one part of the picture. We also have to remember that Hume frequently refers to women as the catalysts of refinement in taste and morals. This puts females (though still not in a subject position) in the center of the spectrum of judgments from which standards emerge. I hypothesize that in such cases, Hume is positing the *union* of minds and values that he rather hyperbolically stresses when he discusses marriage. Male and female are ideal critics when they do *not* diverge in taste. Whatever diversity they systematically manifest sunders his foundation for universal human nature, if that diversity is treated as philosophically significant.

If this is the case, then the diversity that Hume does countenance is of necessity a superficial sort. Hume appears to embrace much variation and disagreement on normative matters without undermining the discovery of basic standards for judgment. The sorts of differences he mentions, however, are typically of three sorts: age, culture, and personal preference. The first is something we all pass through, and thus differences in age are ones that any individual might experience in the course of a lifetime. The standard remains steady, since we ("we") all go through these various stages. The second, culture, is an explanation for variety of taste that does not founder on the idea of uniform human nature, because differences in education and culture are major and obvious ways to *account* for difference. These differences are variations on a theme, and the basic theme is still stable. The third source of disagreement in taste, idiosyncratic personal preference, is not one that Hume dwells on, nor is it one he apparently took very seriously, philosophically speaking. I see it as a residue category that acknowledges the mysteries of pleasures when their sources cannot be accounted for. Gender differences pose a deeper problem.

If Hume were both to acknowledge philosophically the gender differences he subscribes to, and rely as heavily on uniform human nature as he does to stabilize differences of taste and valuation, the result would be a concept of "human nature" that is so obviously riven with difference as to recommend abandonment of the pretense to any uniform constitution in human nature at all. With a philosophy like Hume's, gender differences cannot be brought into the light and pursued systematically, without sacrificing the basis for the root philosophical enterprise. Gendered concepts depend for their operation on the subtle shifts possible from their hidden positions.

In this philosophy gendered concepts like the standard of taste are a symptom of ideas of femaleness that oscillate in their proximity to and distance from the paradigmatic human. Thus it is not correct to say that women are ignored by Hume's philosophy, such that his conclusions apply only to males, indeed, only to eighteenth-century, genteel, male Europeans. It is clear that women are not only intentionally included within the scope of his ideas of human nature, but also that in some respects female presence is accommodated as easily as male. On the other hand *and* at the same time, the concept of human nature proceeds from a point of view that shifts women from the position of participating subject to that of objects to be considered in philosophical deliberations about "human nature," so frequently arrived at by a combination of introspection and social analysis. It is in doing the former that the female reader undergoes the split of consciousness that simultaneously makes her a participant in the analysis and an object of the analysis, puts her with the other humans in the center of things, and with other females at the edge. I have used the metaphor of *oscillation* to capture this phenomenon, because it connotes a continuous, repeating movement from one point to another. Gendered concepts are oscillating concepts in that the ideas of the female and the feminine that they covertly employ, move back and forth from center to periphery in relation to the focus of analysis, occupying unstable and therefore ceaselessly moving positions.

Philosophies like Hume's are probably no more riven with the complexities of identity and unstable subject positions than our own current ways of thinking; indeed, the various places assigned women in this theory are familiar. Moreover, the oscillating position of ideas of the female in philosophical concepts also complicates the discovery of a stable perspective from which to pursue feminist analyses. The standard of taste cannot be dismissed as a masculinist artifact. Nor, as we have seen, is it easily patched up. I prefer to view it as one more proving ground for discovering how tangled is the concept of human nature, as well as how complex is the whole discussion of uniformity in standards and norms. For if concepts like taste are gendered, they are also the operational tools that drive philosophizing; as such they have to be repaired while in use as we explore how many of the presumptions of universality we wish to discard or retain, and what is gained and sacrificed along the way.

Notes

1. [1888], ed. L. A. Selby-Bigge (London: Oxford University Press, 1973), xv.
2. Typically Hume sets up a philosophical problem by calling to the reader's attention opposing

propositions, both of which have some commonsense credibility. Donald W. Livingston gives extended consideration to this approach in *Hume's Philosophy of Common Life* (Chicago: University of Chicago Press, 1984); see especially chap. 2.

3. Hume, "Of the Standard of Taste," in *Essays Moral, Political, and Literary*, by David Hume, 2 vols., ed. T. H. Green and T. H. Grose (London: Longmans, Green, 1898) 1:269.

4. I have argued that the best candidate for a correlative objective property is the relational property of utility in "Hume and the Standard of Taste," *JAAC* 35, no. 2 (Winter 1976): 201–15.

5. "Of the Standard of Taste," 1:273.

6. Hume and many others of his time saw in historical and social differences the sources of disruption for naturally uniform taste. But it is doubtful that social privilege was regarded as an actual prerequisite to taste. Instructive here is the highly popular novel *Pamela*, published in 1740, whose virtuous heroine moves from the position of servant girl to aristocrat's wife, but whose natural taste shines through even in her days of service, and additionally provides a signal of her inviolable virtue. Samuel Richardson, *Pamela* (New York: Everyman's Library, 1962); see especially Lady Davers's letter, 2:33–34.

However, see below and note 32 for further consideration of class and taste.

7. The most articulate feminist defender of Hume is Annette Baier. See her "Hume: The Reflective Women's Epistemologist?" in *A Mind of One's Own*, ed. Louise M. Anthony and Charlotte Witt (Boulder, Colo.: Westview, 1993); "Hume, the Women's Moral Theorist?" in *Women and Moral Theory*, ed. Eva Feder Kittay and Diana T. Meyers (Totowa, N.J.: Rowman and Littlefield, 1987); "Good Men's Women: Hume on Chastity and Trust," *Hume Studies* 5, no. 1 (1979): 1–19. See also John V. Price, *The Ironic Hume* (Austin: University of Texas Press, 1965).

For a contrasting view see Christine Battersby, "An Enquiry Concerning the Humean Woman," *Philosophy* 56, no. 217 (July 1981): 303–12; and the brief but interesting comments of Michele Le Doeuff in *Hipparchia's Choice*, trans. Trista Selous (Oxford: Blackwell, 1991).

8. See the essays "Of the Origin of Government," in *Essays*, ed. Green and Grose, vol. 1, esp. 113; and "Of the Original Social Contract," in *Essays*, eds. Green and Grose, vol. 1, esp. 451. See also *Treatise* III, ii, esp. 493.

9. Hume does not draw a firm line dividing natural from artificial virtues, since appreciation of social utility also comes to us naturally in the confirmation of useful actions by sentiments. "Mankind is an inventive species; and where an invention is obvious and absolutely necessary, it may as properly be said to be natural as any thing that proceeds immediately from original principles, without the intervention of thought or reflexion" (*Treatise*, 484).

10. *An Enquiry Concerning the Principles of Morals*, in *Essays*, ed. Green and Grose, 2:246.

11. Ibid., 2:199.

12. Ibid., 2:222.

13. See Letter 104 in *New Letters of David Hume*, ed. Raymond Klibansky and Ernest Mossner (Oxford: Clarendon Press, 1954), 191.

14. "Of the Rise and Progress of the Arts and Sciences," in *Essays*, ed. Green and Grose, 1:193.

15. Ibid.

16. Ibid., 1:194.

17. It is a mark of how complicated it is to evaluate the manners of another time that "condescension" formerly could describe a good character trait, indicating the generous attention of one of superior rank to an inferior. See Mr. Collins's references to Lady Catherine de Burgh in *Pride and Prejudice*.

Jerome Christensen discusses Hume's gallantry in his *Practicing Enlightenment: Hume and the Formation of a Literary Career* (Madison: University of Wisconsin Press, 1987), chap. 4.

18. *Treatise*, 424. See also remarks on Fontinelle in "The Sceptic."

19. "Of National Characters," in *Essays*, ed. Green and Grose, 1:258. See also "A Dissertation

on the Passions," in *Essays,* ed. Green and Grose, 2:163, concerning "a person" and "his mistress."

20. "On the Dignity or Meanness of Human Nature," in *Essays,* ed. Green and Grose, 1:154.

21. "Of the Populousness of Ancient Nations," in *Essays,* ed. Green and Grose, 1:383–84.

22. Ibid., 1:389.

23. "A Dissertation on the Passions," in *Essays,* ed. Green and Grose, 2:150. This section elaborates the argument presented in *Treatise* II, part I, sect. ix.

24. Ibid., 2:150–51. Cf. Pamela's husband's argument to Lady Davers, that in marrying a servant girl, he has the power to elevate her rank; whereas an aristocratic woman marrying a common man descends to his rank.

25. Ibid., 2:151.

26. *Treatise,* 20.

27. Ibid., 24; see also 34.

28. "Of the Delicacy of Taste and Passion," in *Essays,* ed. Green and Grose, vol. 1.

29. "Of Eloquence," in *Essays,* ed. Green and Grose, vol. 1.

30. "Of the Standard of Taste," 1:280–81.

31. "Rise and Progress," 1:183; "Of Refinement in the Arts," in *Essays,* ed. Green and Grose, 1:304.

32. See also Richard Shusterman, "Of the Scandal of Taste: Social Privilege as Nature in the Aesthetic Theories of Hume and Kant," *Philosophical Forum* 20 (1989): 211–29.

33. "Of Polygamy and Divorces," in *Essays,* ed. Green and Grose, 1:234.

34. Ibid., 1:238.

35. Ibid., 1:239.

36. "Of Love and Marriage," in *Essays,* Green and Grose, 2:388. This is one of the essays Hume later withdrew from republication. See the comments by Green and Grose in *Essays,* 1:43–44.

37. *Treatise* II, ii, sect. iv. One can view these comments as a logical extension of the doctrine of coverture.

3
Intensity and Its Audiences: Toward a Feminist Perspective on the Kantian Sublime

Timothy Gould

How does one stand to behold the sublime?
                    —Wallace Stevens, "The American Sublime"

It is because her appetite for immediacy is so huge that she feels so
powerfully the impossibility of directing it at a listener—even at a reader.
Her hunger for direct language turns into a sense of knowledge, a
suppurating consciousness of possessing something dangerous to those
about her. This is the precise breeding ground of the unspeakable. The
unspeakable is willed—it has not, that is to say, a pre-existent content
that is itself already unspeakable—but its gratuitousness is grounded in, is
rendered visible in the colors of, the individual obsession and the obsession
of the age.
                    —Eve Kosofsky Sedgwick on Lucy Snowe in *Villette*[1]

The goal of this essay is to begin a reassessment of Kant's aesthetics and
specifically his account of the sublime. This reassessment is intended to
demonstrate its indebtedness to some recent feminist critics of philosophy and
literature. Somewhat artificially, I will characterize the criticism in question as
containing two categories or directions of investigation. The first sort is aimed
at the unmasking of gender prejudice and ideology in the standpoint or
conceptual framework of writers such as Burke and Kant.[2] The second sort of
criticism is less familiar and harder to characterize, but it can be located
among the works of literary critics who make use of recent poststructuralist
philosophy and psychoanalysis. Terms like "poststructuralist" are often used
to cover a multitude of texts. The focus of the later sections of this essay is a
narrower segment of such writing, including principally the work of Eve
Kosofsky Sedgwick, along with that of Neil Hertz, Frances Ferguson, Joshua
Wilner, and Naomi Schor.[3] Although many poststructuralist currents are
beginning to circulate through the precincts of English-speaking philosophical

aesthetics, the strands of thought represented by these writers have remained largely unknown. (Schor's book is probably the most likely to be familiar to American philosophers.) And while a single essay cannot do justice to the complexity of these writers, it remains a secondary aim of my essay to encourage aestheticians and feminists to encounter this body of work for themselves.

I begin by offering a selective summary of the elements of experience and philosophical theory that go into Kant's account of the sublime. I then outline the first type of criticism of Kant's aesthetics and raise questions about this version of the masculinist orientation of the sublime. Without disputing the idea that there is something right—and importantly right—about the ideological critique of Kant's orientation, I attempt to nudge the discussion of Kant in another direction. This leads me to invoke Sedgwick's accounts of the sublime, especially as she unearths its outlines and details in writers like Charlotte Brontë and Emily Dickinson. Sedgwick's account makes a theme out of the affinity between the experiences of the sublime and of the various degrees of the inexpressible. Finally, I use Sedgwick's investigations to motivate a discussion of some features in Kant's account of the sublime.

My general interpretive suggestion is this: Kant teaches us that the experience of the sublime requires a certain "preparation" or "culture." Otherwise we experience, for instance, a repulsion or a shrinking back from the sublime and not the alternation between repulsion and attraction that constitutes the fullest experience of the sublime. Sedgwick's work suggests that just as the experience of the sublime requires a kind of preparation, so it requires a kind of completion or aftermath. And if there is no suitable region—whether natural or social or aesthetic—in which this experience can be expressed and hence fulfilled, the aftermath is likely to be both aesthetically and humanly difficult. Given what Kant says about the experience of those who lack the necessary "preparation" for the sublime, we might go so far as to characterize the deprivation that Sedgwick speaks of as a transformation or deformation of the experience and not merely as a contingent or purely personal fact about the person having the experience. Such a thought need not lead us to abandon all thought of our aesthetic judgments as grounded in a transcendental principle. But it might lead us to a greater appreciation of the historical conditions within which the hope for such a principle was formed. After all, neither the hope for the transcendental ground of communicability nor the particular empirical acts of communication in question must necessarily be thought of as themselves immune to historical pressures and changes.

My contention is that the terms of Sedgwick's analyses—and, of course, the writers that her terms illuminate—will clarify these further aspects of the sublime and overcome the obstacles to its communication. It is my further hope that the critical turns in this reading of Kant will prove useful to feminist critics and to other readers of Kant. Whether or not this hope is fulfilled, the material I am introducing into the discussion would seem to possess some immediate pertinence to a feminist investigation of aesthetics. For it is noteworthy that among Sedgwick's primary subjects are women writing in the aftermath of the great projects of the philosophical Enlightenment, of political revolution, and of literary Romanticism. In this historical moment, some women of the middle classes were absorbing the fact that the achievements of the eighteenth century had often excluded their own aspirations.[4] Or else they discovered that their aspirations had been included in ways that transformed them almost beyond recognition, transformations that made those very aspirations into vehicles of constraint and isolation. Sedgwick's work operates at a level where an increasing material comfort was not only consistent with a traumatic deprivation of the human need of expression but may actually have worked to exacerbate this deprivation. That for some women these deprivations were involved in an astonishing access of insight and productivity should not make the circumstances seem any the less shameful.

The Kantian Sublime: An Introduction

When Kant first began to write about the sublime[5] he was taking on a field of critical investigation and an episode in the history of taste that was already five or six decades old. The sublime was the name given to a region of experience where the mind takes pleasure in powerful natural forces and in tremendous vistas. The experience of the sublime was (and often still is) bounded by wonder, awe, and dread. The paradox of the pleasurable terrors and exhilarations of nature became linked in aesthetic reflection to the paradoxical effects of epic and tragic poetry. The resultant sixty or seventy years of intense focus on the issues of the sublime can be regarded as a kind of historical transition from the fading authority of nature as the scene of God's voice to the rising power of nature as a source of Romantic writing. As early as Addison's *Spectator* essay, theoreticians of the sublime were uncertain about whether the sublime satisfies the mind's eagerness for an image of freedom and power *external* to itself or whether it represents the mind turning inward on itself and relishing the immensity of its own imaginative appetites.[6]

The writings of Edmund Burke signaled a new stage of sophistication in accounting for workings of the imagination in the experience of the sublime. He emphasized the covertness of the mind's responses to the sublime, and he outlined its capacity for turning inward and aggrandizing itself in the experience of the sublime. The mind, Burke argued, acquires a peculiar sense of seriousness deriving from a (real or imagined) danger against which it also knows itself to be protected. Burke is thus not only among the first psychologists of the sublime; he is also its first demystifier.[7]

Kant honored Burke's theoretical advances even while he wished to rescue from Burke's empiricism a transcendental necessity within our feelings for the sublime and the beautiful.[8] (For Kant, such a rescue operation was far from merely theoretical.) Not surprisingly, Kant tried to reconceive the by then fairly traditional characterizations of the "inner" and "outer" locations of the sublime. Kant's model locates the sublime as an inner response to an outer occasion—an inner response that provides us with a perspective on our "elevated" destiny, our true "sublimity." From the perspective of the sublime experience, the sublimity (the actual elevation or *being* elevated [*Erhabenheit*]) of our moral autonomy could be both glimpsed and fortified.[9]

For Kant the element of initial or recurrent pain in the sublime has less to do with the Burkean "danger" than with a movement of self-deprivation on the part of the imagination. The mind feels the inadequacy of its efforts to imagine the ideas (e.g., of God and of freedom) as represented in nature. Of course, such an inadequacy only shows up in a mind that is striving to make nature into such a representation or, in Kant's terms, striving to use nature as a "schema" for representing the ideas of reason (124 [265]). Kant thinks that every human mind is capable of these ideas of reason because each of us is capable of the moral law. But he does not think that every mind is equally "prepared" for the effort to *find* these ideas represented in nature. Hence, the experience of the sublime is not, for Kant, as widely available as the experience of the beautiful. In abiding by this sense of inadequacy, the imagination "by its own action" deprives itself of its full freedom and shows us its capacity for obedience to a kind of law that is beyond its habitual employment (129 [269]). The imagination thus points beyond itself, and the mind as a whole receives—somewhat mysteriously—a greater scope and energy than it previously possessed.

The Sublime: Some Uses and Abuses

Given the theoretical and experiential emphasis on the power and grandeur of the sublime, it is perhaps not surprising that accounts of the sublime became entangled with masculinist ideology and sensibility. And, given the centrality of the sublime in the rise of eighteenth-century aesthetics, it is perhaps also not surprising that the feminist critiques of philosophy should have singled out the sublime as a major target for criticism.[10] Accounts of the sublime constitute an especially vivid instance of a tendency in philosophy to set up certain experiences—characterized in male-inflected terms—as universally valid norms for the character and judgment of all human beings.

The process is sometimes said to go like this: First, certain objects or experiences are characterized in more or less overtly "masculine" terms (in the case of the sublime, terms such as "powerful," "active," "threatening," "dominating," "masterful," "warlike," and so forth). Second, the capacity for having certain experiences is given a systematic form and a central place in the philosopher's vision of the aesthetic, cultural, and moral education of humanity. Third, women are "discovered" to have either no capacity or only a deficient capacity for undergoing this set of experiences. Fourth, the (male) philosopher therefore feels justified in concluding that women are less capable of developing into full-fledged human beings in these crucial aesthetic and moral dimensions.

Such a pattern of "argument" was not invented by eighteenth-century aestheticians, and, of course, the pattern has not ceased to have its proponents.[11] The main outlines of this pattern can be found in Burke and at least in the pre-critical Kant, most egregiously in the third section of *Observations on the Beautiful and the Sublime*.[12] I am suggesting, however, that we need to ask some further questions about the implications that we are to draw from this pattern. If we dwell on the pattern too exclusively, we are likely to miss something about Kant's aesthetics. Perhaps more important, we may miss a chance to retrieve for aesthetics some of the very aspects of human need and feeling that Kant himself is commonly supposed to have neglected or distorted.

It should be noted that there are now writers who would deny that any of Kant's projects can be rescued from the taint of patriarchy or from the cauldron in which bourgeois aesthetic ideology was brewed.[13] There is not enough room here to give these charges the answer they deserve, but I do want to say a word or two about some tendencies that seem inherent in this type of critique. Perhaps Kant helped to create intellectual tendencies that served the needs of nineteenth- and twentieth-century aesthetic ideologies.

(This might well be true of what I take to be certain influential misinterpretations of "disinterestedness" and the so-called autonomy of art.) But Kant is also the principal philosophical thinker who demanded a place for the idea that human freedom is an end in itself, requiring no religious or political purposes to legitimize it. Perhaps this idea will prove to be ultimately—or humanly—untenable. But the idea seems too important for the theories and practices of human liberation to jettison merely on the grounds that it is subject to abuse.

Of course, liberating ideas can be perverted by later ideologies, and they may well contain some of the seeds of their own perversion. But since virtually any idea is susceptible to being thus tainted by ideology and mystification, we are left with the task of sorting out what we can still use of the past from what is no longer usable. The reason for such an effort is not mere piety toward the past. Overcoming our tendency to distort and flatten the past in the name of a less oppressive future may help us approach a more specific problem in the critical work of the present. For the tendency to reduce a philosopher to the ideologies that he or she participates in is likely to leave us more or less in the dark about a question that still seems crucial: How does any thinker ever make an advance toward the overcoming of the mystifications that surround us? Unless we imagine that we are somehow less liable than Kant to be deceived by ideology and mystification, then the connection between Kant's philosophical criticism and its ideological matrices ought to remain of more than academic interest to us.

Another issue that needs sorting through has to do with our ability to appreciate the ways in which past generations of women writers were responding to issues and materials that they first encountered at the hands of men. Let us assume that the theories and discourses of the sublime were initially the province of male writers, and assume further that the accounts they gave of this experience were marked by the masculine perspectives within which the accounts were arrived at. A couple of points are still worth making. First, that the initial mapping or modeling of the experience was carried out from a male perspective does not mean that the experience is somehow preeminently the property of men. To the extent that Burke and Kant thought otherwise, we can show that they were wrong. Second, when later generations of women writers (from Gothic to George Eliot) turned to the topics of "the Sublime," these topics took on different colors and were turned to different narrative and figurative uses. Nevertheless, the changes and discontinuities will not show up clearly—or perhaps not show up at all—apart from an understanding of the later writers' points of departure within the themes and figures of the (male-inflected) sublime.

It is possible—and sometimes necessary—to remind ourselves, that the later women writers are often responding to issues and materials that are recognizably continuous with the eighteenth-century sublime. These issues and materials of human feeling and expression may have been exploited by eighteenth-century male consciousness, but they were not created by it. And if "the Sublime" as an episode in the history of taste was, in the first instance, a creature largely of male consciousness, that was scarcely the end of the story. To dismiss the male-inflected eighteenth-century maps of the sublime because of their vivid display of the tensions of patriarchal consciousness is, at least potentially, to cut ourselves off from a dimension of the power and originality of the next two generations of women writers.

A Tension in the Paternal Sublime

I want to cite one place where Burke and Kant offer us an instructive tension in their accounts. Let us look again at the tendency to characterize the sublime objects as "active," "powerful," "forceful," and so forth. Suppose we grant that these terms carry with them certain conventional and historical associations with masculine activity—or, more exactly, with paternal power. [14] Suppose that we grant further that Burke and the pre-critical Kant are inclined to exploit the masculine drift within their characterizations of the objects of the sublime experience. [15] And suppose, finally, that Burke and Kant were also sometimes inclined to characterize the human male as especially capable of experiencing the sublime. [16] But at this stage, we are in a position to see that these thinkers have introduced a tension into this particular gendering of the sublime. For the *object* provoking the sublime experience cannot be characterized as masculine in the *same* sense or fashion in which the *subject* of the sublime experience is characterized as masculine.

This is not primarily a point about the logic of their positions. It is perhaps possible that Burke or Kant could have found ways of removing the tension; for instance, by characterizing the masculinity of the sublime event as other than the masculinity of the sublime spectator. My point is that to have removed the tensions would have been to remove something significant about the experience that they were trying to account for. (As far as we can tell, neither of them tried to remove this tension.)

There is a larger point to be made here. For Kant, at least, the experiences of the sublime involve an initial passivity in the subject's relation to the sublime object. This passivity (which the imagination to some extent imposes on itself) is then found to grant us at least emotional access to a heightened sense of our capacity for independent activity. The access that the sublime grants us to our capacity for activity in the truest sense does not guarantee that we will fulfill the promise of autonomy. (For Kant, nothing can guarantee this). But it does give us at least a kind of route by which we might move from the elevating and sublime experiences that open the perspectives of freedom to the actual exercise of our freedom. Whether we make this leap or not, Kant has rendered the relation between "activity" and "passivity" significantly more problematic than he found it. And this ought to have been especially true for any simplistic equation of masculinity and activity. Whether or to what degree, Kant recognized[17] that his work had rendered any such equation problematic, the accounts in the *Critique of Judgment* tend to emphasize exactly the confounding of active and passive that is so disruptive to canonically male forms of consciousness.

A contrasting analogy might be useful: the fact of relatively sedentary men watching the activities of physically powerful men (who are frequently characterized as embodiments of quasi-natural forces)—moreover watching these activities from a position of safety—remains central to the masculine side of American bourgeois, petit bourgeois, and working-class culture. Let us even suppose that there is a certain continuity between the eighteenth-century concern with the masculine or the paternal sublime and the relation of many American men to football, boxing, racing cars, and various items of lethal weaponry. Putting moral and political questions aside for the moment, what is missing from the modern versions of male spectatorship is precisely the Kantian shift toward an emphasis on the significance of the spectator's judgment. Of course, various claims are made about the spiritual benefits of loyalty to particular teams or particular cars. And there are beer commercials promoting a sense of masculine camaraderie that is linked to sports and is, apparently, otherwise unavailable to American men.[18] In my experience, however, no theorist sympathetic to the modern male spectator has gone so far as to claim that the true sublimity of football is to be sought in "the mind of the judging subject." But this is roughly what Kant does claim about the sublime, or at least about the ultimate point or destination of the experience of the sublime.[19]

Someone might wish to respond by suggesting that the Kantian shift is different only by a degree of emphasis. The modern celebrations of (male) spectatorship stop short of examining its inherent passivity (perhaps especially its passivity in relation to more active and more powerful men). Nevertheless (so the argument might go) Kant is engaged in a related evasion; namely, that of converting the passive spectator into something ultimately more significant and even, in a sense, more active.

One need not deny that Kant was capable of exploiting his own account in an ideologically motivated fashion, as long as we bear in mind three further features in Kant's account of the spectator's situation. First, Kant's particular conversion of the spectator into something more than a spectator cannot occur without to some extent challenging the simplistic picture of the masculine-as-active (whether overtly or not). Second, the movement of conversion, as we shall see, leaves residual difficulties, both about the "preparation" required for such a conversion of the spectator and about his or her need of further expression. (I shall be arguing in the last section that Kant's description of the experience of the sublime at the very least leaves open the possibility that the experience remains in some sense incomplete until further mental activity and expression have occurred.) Third, the recovery of a mode of activity on the part of the judging subject is not primarily enacted as a successful "recuperation," in the poststructuralist sense of a compensation whose deficiencies are covered over by some further ideological mystification. The human imagination (and not just the male imagination) must renounce certain connections or identifications with nature in order to claim its heritage of sublimity and its consequent heightened capacity for moral action. Hence, to the extent that the self-definition of the eighteenth-century male depended on certain relations to nature (e.g., as an object of knowledge, conquest, domination, or technological mastery), this self-definition is at least partially undermined by Kant's critical philosophy. It is not just that the spectator of the sublime is the true home of the sublime, and that certain kinds of activity are not as sublime as men had thought. In Kant's account, every action and even every apparently great deed turns out to be passive, if it is not commanded by the moral law or encouraged by some relation to the free play of certain spontaneous activities of the mind.

One may attack these conceptions of morality and of beauty on other grounds. But one should not miss the tendency of these conceptions to subvert conventional eighteenth- (or twentieth-) century pictures of the masculine "activity" that lurks in Kant's idea of the sublimity of moral action. This idea of moral action as having to overcome false (and often masculine) pictures of what genuine activity amounts to is closely tied to the role of the sublime in his aesthetics.[20]

Sedgwick on the Sublime and the Untellable

Some of the criticisms that I have examined in the first part of this paper have shared a willingness to reduce the complexity of the relations between the subjects and the objects of aesthetic experience. Applied to Kant's aesthetics this seems to be especially ironic, since it is here that Kant took the greatest pains to reinstate the complexities and indeed the legitimacy of our subjective responses to nature. It would be unfortunate if this side of Kant's work were slighted or missed entirely in the general move to denounce the "rationalist" or "universalist" aspects of his vision of human freedom and its aesthetic requirements. This brings me to the second type of feminist critic and to the second part of my topic. Here we shall discover a feminist criticism that might render Kant's account at once more complex and more responsive to the various situations in which our feelings seek expression.[21]

Though the work of Eve Kosofsky Sedgwick only infrequently addresses philosophical texts directly, I think her work is of great importance to current aesthetics. I want now to follow out some of her clues about the location of the sublime in relation to regions of the unspeakable and the unutterable. It is, of course, no secret that the experience of the sublime is bound up in certain issues of the limits of representation. It would certainly be worth exploring the relationship between the ways in which Kant characterizes the sublime as bound up in the "inadequacy of nature" to represent or to exhibit ideas of reason (124 [265]).[22] I shall use Sedgwick's analyses as a means of isolating a somewhat different sort of "unrepresentability" and a different sense of the inexpressibility of certain aspects of the experience of the sublime.

Crudely and provisionally, here is an account of one strand of Sedgwick's work: she focuses attention on the various rifts that may be created between the one who experiences the sublime and those other human beings who might otherwise have been the natural audience for her account of her experience. I follow Sedgwick in thinking that the very intensity of the experience of the sublime contains in it the wish to communicate that experience to others. Taken together, the intensity and the wish can generate a need for expression that is itself too intense for the normal channels of human expressiveness and of ordinary communication. One version of such blockage goes like this:[23] "The hunger for direct language" becomes greater than the wish to express any particular feeling. Indeed, in some cases, the need for expression itself becomes the content of the state of mind (and body) that is seeking expression. But this is very likely to make any specific expression all but impossible. The experience of this need for expression abolishes—or appears to abolish—any place "outside" the subject, in which an audience for her feelings might exist. The very intensity of the need refuses to allow the kind of distance that ordinary human beings require, if they are to be the audience for our expressions of feeling. (Despite the renewed emphasis on the importance of sympathy and the "sharing" of experiences, we still do not possess much work on the social and epistemological conditions within which the "good listener" can exist.)

Now suppose we think of someone having such experiences, while living in the social situation of a middle-class woman in the first half of the nineteenth century. I am thinking here (not exhaustively) of an existence surrounded by the genteel encouragement to expand your capacities for self-expression and cultivation, but only so far; encouragement to speak your mind, but only on certain topics; encouragement to learn certain things about the life of the mind, but never to think of yourself as contributing to that life; encouragement to have certain delicate feelings, but never to exceed a certain point of decorum, never to display the wrong kind of intensity, and never to aspire to certain regions of exhilaration.

Suppose we add to this sphere of an all-too-discouraging encouragement (sometimes politely called the "socialization" of women), an intimation of someone who possesses what Virginia Woolf called "the heat and violence of a poet's heart when caught and tangled in a woman's body."[24] This seems a likely formula for producing the kind of freighted and desperate explorations and experiments in expression that Sedgwick is investigating. And indeed in one direction, the sense of suffocation that is produced by the failure of so intense a drive to expression lends itself to the imagery of the Gothic, with its live burials and other uncanny terms of isolation. (Sedgwick has been justly acclaimed for her efforts to understand the Gothic as something other than a projection of a merely "psychological" condition or as an episode of taste possessing merely historical interest.) In another direction, this drive to expression—at once self-inhibited and self-sustaining—becomes embodied in radically new forms of poetry and fiction. Such writing transcends distinctions between Romantic and modern (and all the more so between the modern and the so-called postmodern). And such writing equally transcends distinctions between experimentation with artistic forms of expression and the experienced violence of an author's (or character's) efforts to create a kind of rift between her consciousness and ours.[25]

For Sedgwick, it is the creation or invention of such rifts that are among the most aesthetically shocking and humanly violent accomplishments of Brontë and Dickinson. Indeed, on her account, these rifts are the means by which these writers unleash their capacity for a genuine sublime of art—or, as she puts it, they manage to free up the "impersonal authorial energy of the true sublime."[26] Kant says very little about the sublime of art, hardly more than that such a sublime must be "confined to the conditions that [art] must meet in order to be in harmony with nature" (sect. 23, p. 98 [245]).[27] Sedgwick's account provides one way of thinking about one of the most persistent issues concerning the Kantian sublime within the realm of art. For it can seem as if the audience of an artwork is, generally speaking, *too* safe to be subjected to the alternation of terror and attraction that is required for the sublime experience to take place. In Sedgwick's account, Brontë creates a rift between audience and narrator, far greater than the merely conventional distance between novel and reader. She then provides the means by which this distance can be all the more vividly and painfully apprehended, if not quite entirely overcome.

Such discoveries about the relation of the formal means of artistic expression to the narrow circumstances in which a human existence must seek expression are often described as some combination of the "psychological" and the "formal." But such descriptions are inclined to miss both the intensity and the confusion of the intersection between these realms, and the realms themselves are anything but clearly understood. Such descriptions also miss the ways in which such intersections of the formal and the psychological are not merely the special concern of a certain individual called perhaps "a writer" (or called perhaps, from another angle, a "madwoman in the attic.")[28] These intersections and these perplexities are representative of perplexities in us, which we may only rarely find the resources and the willingness to fathom.

Some Implications of Sedgwick's Account for the Kantian Sublime

Sedgwick's account seems to me to have implications beyond the terms that it proposes for itself and its subjects. It helps our understanding of the sublime and of other intensities in human experience. It points to an ordinarily less visible edge of our need for expression. And it gives us a chance to think about the circumstances that form the obstacles as well as the means for both human and artistic expression. I would like to open up a few further lines of communication between her work and the work of philosophers concerned with aesthetics.

As I suggested at the beginning, Sedgwick teaches us to pay attention to the aftermaths of our experience as well as to its prerequisites. More exactly, she teaches us to think about the connection between "having" certain experiences and being able—and being allowed—to express them and to talk about them in an appropriately receptive setting. As we have seen, Kant suggests that a certain "culture" is a necessary "preparation" for experiencing the sublime (sect. 29, p. 124 [265]). Sedgwick's account suggests that certain human beings in the grip of their experience of sublimity will also experience a need for expression that, for various reasons, is likely to go unmet. One may lack the empirical company that permits such expressions, or one may feel that the possibility of expression is lacking, or one may even come to speak (or write) and act in ways that undermine that possibility. Under those circumstances, the experience of the sublime will be modified or even deformed. These modified versions of the sublime can be cognitively and aesthetically revealing, and they can be the spur to a fantastic artistic inventiveness (though these advances are likely to contain significant human costs).

I would like to go a little further and describe the possibility of communication or expression as in a certain sense the completion of the experience of the sublime, as Kant describes a certain kind of education as the appropriate preparation for this experience. I recognize that there is an asymmetry in this formulation that renders it unclear and somewhat paradoxical. It is as if I am trying to describe as a prerequisite of the experience a possibility that occurs only after "the experience itself" has already taken place. Some of the air of paradox might vanish if we could get a more adequate picture of what I have been calling "the experience of the sublime." Already in Kant's account, it is notoriously difficult to separate the act of judgment from the experience of aesthetic pleasure, and this difficulty makes it hard to characterize the temporal "feel" of a Kantian aesthetic pleasure.[29] In any event, the experience of the sublime will certainly be hard to describe on any model that takes the flow of experience to be, so to speak, one-directional. In fact, Kant's sublime should be problematic for those empiricist accounts that see the subject as the passive recipient of experiences from the "outside," as well as for those more recent accounts that see the subject as constructing its experiences (and its own selfhood) from the materials provided by an essentially passive world. To think of the communication of an experience as a kind of completion of the experience will entail further modifications of our sense of what an experience is. But I think that these modifications and disruptions will turn out to be continuous with those entailed by Kant's account. My sense that the experience of the sublime requires a kind of completion as well as a preparation is still largely on the level of an intuition. But I can at least say a little more about how we might work with this intuition.

The claim that the various expressive aftermaths of the experience of the sublime are to be conceived as part of that experience is not intended as an empirical prediction about how people will in fact experience the sublime. Nor is it intended as an invitation to reclassify certain experiences as, for instance, not really of the sublime but merely somehow marginally related to the sublime. It is intended rather to provide a kind of perspective on a whole range of experiences and of the associated possibilities and impossibilities of communication and expression. The perspective can only be shown to have validity by the critical and philosophical work that it enables. The range is intended, for instance, to include the work of the writers that Sedgwick has discussed. But it is also intended to include the work of writers who are otherwise as different as, for instance, Sylvia Plath, Toni Morrison, and Samuel Beckett. Since I cannot prove the relevance either of my intuition or of the perspective that I would like to develop out of this intuition, I shall try at least to exemplify its importance in relation to a few other aspects of the sublime.

If the possibility of expressing the sublime is as integral a part of the experience as I am taking it to be, then I suspect that its effects will be wide-ranging. This is because, whatever one's external possibilities of communication and expression may be—whatever empirical aesthetic company one keeps—there are *already* reasons internal to the experience of the sublime that make this experience hard to express. Two of the reasons were mentioned at the beginning, and I shall now conclude this essay by articulating some features of these "internal" obstacles to the expression of the sublime and on their possible connection to the (comparatively) external difficulties of expression that we have been considering.

First, there is a kind of uncertainty or oscillation about the location of (the experience of) the sublime. (This uncertainty is related to what I characterized earlier as an "undermining" of the conventional masculinity of the sublime.) Our experience of the sublime has two poles, one of them pointing toward natural objects (or events) and one of them pointing toward a heightened activity within the mind of the judging subject. I am suggesting that it is a significant feature of the sublime, and of the judgment or experience of sublimity, that we are not always able to locate its characteristic heightening of our feelings. We may, as Kant insists, seek the sublime most "properly"—

most appropriately—in the "judging subject." But, as Paul Guyer has convincingly demonstrated, we cannot dispense with the natural object that provokes or instigates the sublime.[30]

Thus our analysis of the sublime may set up a relatively stable model: first, we are aware of the natural object or event that provokes our experience of the sublime, and then comes the recognition that the true or authentic sublimity resides in us. At any given moment, however, our experience of the sublime may very well be in transition from one pole of the experience to the other. It seems to me that the analysis of the sublime (as anchored in the judging subject but still occasioned by something in nature) can enable self-perceptions that end up by becoming part of the experience itself. If I seek the sublime in my own mind, considered as a judging subject, surely this is not merely a piece of analysis that I can keep at arm's length from my experience of the sublime. This perception and this seeking become part of my experience of the sublime that provoked them. And this effort to understand my self as contributing to the sublimity of the experience will enter into the difficulties of expressing that experience. (These difficulties seem to me analogous to the difficulties confronting Lucy Snowe in Sedgwick's account.)

Second, aesthetic judgment, though invariably characterized by Kant as containing a transcendental principle or moment, also apparently contains the material for various empirical employments. In section 41, Kant describes a possible use for the judgment of taste as furthering our ability to "communicate our feeling to everyone else," hence as furthering the satisfaction of what he calls a "natural inclination." Kant is clearly aware of the need and the wish to communicate our feelings. He discusses it under the heading of "the empirical interest in the beautiful" and he characterizes it as "something that everyone's natural inclination demands" (p. 163 [297]). Moreover, he connects this need to our "fitness and propensity" for society, or what he calls "sociability" (163 [296]). Kant never explicitly discusses this sort of empirical interest as explicitly occasioned by the sublime. But he does isolate what he characterizes as the common, "natural inclination" to communicate our feeling to everyone else. There is no obvious reason why this should not apply to our feeling for the sublime.[31]

What kind of aesthetic and personal costs would there be for human beings trapped in circumstances that denied any likelihood of fulfillment to such natural human inclinations? Kant is pretty explicit about our relation to beauty in a state of isolation:

> Someone abandoned on some desolate island would not, just for himself, adorn either his hut or himself; nor would he look for flowers,

let alone grow them, to adorn himself with them. Only in society does it occur to him to be, not merely a human being, but one who is refined in his own way [*nicht bloß Mensch, sondern auch nach seiner Art feiner Mensch zu sein*]. (This is the beginning of civilization.) For we judge someone refined if he has the inclination and the skill to communicate his pleasure to others, and if he is not satisfied with an object unless he can feel his liking for it in community with others. (p. 164 [297])

It looks as though Kant is suggesting that, although the judgment of beauty might exist in some rudimentary form in a state of isolation, human beings would do nothing to cultivate it—or, indeed, to cultivate themselves. On Kant's account, isolation seems to prevent us not so much from *having* the capacities for beauty or for human expression but from *caring* about those capacities. There is more than a hint that such capacities can continue to exist only by being developed. And without at least the presence of the possibility of the accord of other human beings, no one would care enough to develop those capacities within himself or herself.

Now it seems to me that if there were an empirical interest in communicating our sense of the sublime, the stakes would be at least as high. Instead of thinking of someone abandoned on some actual, desert island, let us think of someone like Lucy Snowe. Sedgwick's account of *Villette* teaches us, among other things, that the desolation *within* society has its greatest effect on us not only at the moment of greatest deprivation but often at the moment when it looks as if rescue—or company—might actually be at hand. On Kant's account, isolation seems to prevent us from caring about beautiful adornments or other refinements of human expression; on Sedgwick's account, the experience of the sublime may itself prove isolating. And it is likely to make us care so much about the possibility of human expression that we are swamped by the specific occasions in which the possibility is uncertainly realized.

Moreover, under the conditions of an isolation that cannot be known to be permanent and irremediable—which might provide a kind of relief—the pain and perplexity of the sublime would become acute. Under such conditions, who can afford the knowledge of the sublime? Who could survive its promise of community and communication, in the midst of an isolation whose sources cannot be traced either to society's exclusions of you or to your withdrawal from society?

Kant may have wished to claim that our access to a transcendental ground for such judgments is sufficient to sustain us in our continuing aesthetic education and practices (as he would certainly wish to claim that it was enough to legitimize our judgments of the beautiful and the sublime). But would he have been right about this? Is it quite human to think that we can live on so slim a promise of future accord and community, surrounded by the disappointments and even disasters of our actual efforts at communication? At such a moment, we may wish to turn to another writer whose version of the sublime is rendered thematic in Sedgwick's account:[32]

> The soul's Superior instants
> Occur to her—alone—
> When friend—and Earth's occasion
> Have infinite withdrawn—
>
> Or She—Herself—ascended
> To too remote a Height
> For lower Recognition
> Than her Omnipotent—

This is indeed a version of a sublime past "Earth's occasion," which is also, to say the least, beyond any specific interest in some piece of nature, which might have occasioned the experience of the soul's "height." Dickinson is not merely finding some outer "correlative" for an inner feeling of elevation. Her poem charts a geography that transcends our capacity to recognize anything spatial. And the poem takes its speaker beyond anything other than the soul's autonomous power over herself. (I must at least mention Dickinson's hint that this autonomy is all but identical to the soul's capacity to recognize herself, dispensing with intermediaries.) Here is the Kantian sublime, without the instigation of nature—but also without much possibility of being communicated to an audience. To congratulate Dickinson on achieving these heights would be beside the point, and not merely because she wouldn't be listening. The harder question to ask is, Where are we located when we attempt to recognize her achievement? Or, in the words of the epigraph from Wallace Stevens, How do we stand to behold her sublime?

These questions may seem to end up taking us beyond the realm of aesthetics and into questions about what sustains us, in the press of our own circumstances and in the knowledge that our capacities for creative withdrawal are somewhat less than those of Emily Dickinson, Charlotte Brontë, or, for that matter, Immanuel Kant. But I hope to have suggested that such questioning at least begins in a region that admits of systematic study. Moreover, this region ought to be of interest to those who are looking for connections between eighteenth-century aesthetics and the broader issues of isolation and expression, as these issues have been formulated by a feminist criticism.

Notes

1. *The Coherence of Gothic Conventions* (New York: Methuen Press, 1986), 138. For their encouragement and for their suggestions about earlier versions of this essay, I want to thank Mary Devereaux, Karen Hanson, Christine Korsgaard, Paul Mattick, Barbara Packer, Eve Sedgwick, Garrett Stewart, Kathleen Whalen, and Joshua Wilner. My work on this material was supported by a grant from the National Endowment for the Humanities.

2. See Paul Mattick, Jr., "Beautiful and Sublime: 'Gender Totemism' in the Constitution of Art," Chapter 1, this volume. Some of my thoughts about these topics were presented as a response to a shorter version of Mattick's paper, which was delivered at a panel on feminist aesthetics at the 1988 meeting of the American Society for Aesthetics. See also my "Engendering Aesthetics: Sublimity, Sublimation, and Misogyny in Burke and Kant," in *Aesthetics, Politics, and Hermeneutics,* ed. Gerald Bruns and Stephen Watson (Albany: State University of New York Press, forthcoming). Gary Shapiro and Martha Woodmansee encouraged my first tentative efforts to present the core of this material at the 1988 meeting of the International Association for Philosphy and Literature. Robin Schott's *Cognition and Eros: A Critique of the Kantian Paradigm* (Boston: Beacon, 1988) presents many of the fundamental moves of this sort of critique, most often in their Frankfort variations. Mary Wiseman and Barbara Freeman supplied suggestions and encouragement.

3. See especially Sedgwick, *The Coherence of Gothic Conventions.* Thanks to Sedgwick, I was able to consult an early unpublished essay entitled "Emily Dickinson's Sublime" and a typescript of her *Epistemology of the Closet* (Berkeley and Los Angeles: University of California Press, 1990). Also relevant is her *Between Men: English Literature and Male Homosocial Desire.* See also Neil Hertz, *The End of the Line: Essays on Psychoanalysis and the Sublime* (New York: Columbia University Press, 1985). Hertz's work shares a region of concern and procedure with Sedgwick's. Moreover, since Hertz explicitly addresses Kant's *Critique of Judgment,* his work has more than once provided me with a bridge between the language of Kant's analyses and the characteristic sublimities of Romanticism. On the specific questions of gender and sublimity see Hertz, *End,* chapter 5 and the afterword; and Joshua Wilner, "The Stewed Muse of Prose," *Modern Language Notes* 104 (1989): 1085–98. Wilner and Sedgwick both implicitly characterize De Quincey (and behind him Coleridge) as a place where the concerns of German idealism could have been thematically transmitted to a writer like Charlotte Brontë. See also Naomi Schor's *Reading in Detail: Aesthetics and the Feminine* (New York: Methuen, 1987) and Frances Ferguson's *Solitude and the Sublime: The Aesthetics of Individualism* (New York: Methuen, 1987).

4. This is also a period in which writing became conceivable as a socially acceptable and economically feasible activity. See Virginia Woolf, *A Room of One's Own* [1929] (New York: Harcourt Brace and World, 1957), 68: "The extreme activity of mind which showed itself in the later eighteenth century among women . . . was founded on the solid fact that women could make money by writing. Money dignifies what is frivolous if unpaid for. . . . [A] change came about which, if I were rewriting history, I should describe more fully and think of greater importance than the Crusades or the Wars of the Roses. The middle class woman began to write." Woolf goes

on to link *Villette* and *Middlemarch,* among others, to the existence of these eighteenth-century "forerunners." This period is, of course, in many ways not over.

5. In his pre-critical *Observations Concerning the Feeling of the Beautiful and the Sublime* [1757], trans. John T. Goldthwait (Berkeley and Los Angeles: University of California Press, 1960).

6. See Joseph Addison, *The Spectator,* 23 June 1712, reprinted in *The Spectator in Four Volumes,* ed. Gregory Smith (New York: Dutton, Everyman's Library, 1907; reset, 1945; repr. 1973), 279ff.

7. Burke, *A Philosophical Enquiry into the Origin of Our Ideas of the Beautiful and the Sublime* ed. J. T. Bolton (Notre Dame: University of Notre Dame Press, 1968), sect. 17, pp. 50–51. The double movement of the mind in Burke's version of the sublime (outward to the seriousness and danger of the occasion, inward to a kind of self-aggrandizement) is very close to a kind of imaginative bad faith or duplicity. This may well be one of the reasons why Burke's version of the sublime has been so appealing to contemporary literary theoreticians, since the doubleness or duplicity of the sublime has been taken by some literary critics to illuminate the intricate evasions at the heart of a literary imagination.

8. See *Critique of Judgment,* trans. Werner S. Pluhar (Indianapolis: Hackett, 1987), 125–26 [266 in the Academy edition; *Gesammelte Schriften,* 29 vols. (Berlin: Preussische Akademie der Wissenschaften, 1900–1985)].

9. This is a somewhat controversial reading. In particular, I have stabilized a distinction between *die Erhabene* (the sublime), "which resides in the judging subject" and *die Erhabenheit,* which is how we experience the elevation of our autonomously practical reason. There is thus a double transition, from the so-called sublime in nature to the authentic, internal sublime response, the capacity for which in turn points toward the true sublimity of our moral destiny. So far as I know, these terminological possibilities have not been exploited in the literature. And there are occasions in which Kant does not abide by the neatness of the distinction between "the elevating" (the aesthetic sublime) and the "elevated" (the sublimity of our moral autonomy, which is revealed by the aesthetic sublime), the inner destiny of human beings. I discuss these issues at greater length in the larger project to which this essay belongs.

10. Indeed, it is one of the ironies of our recent philosophical history that the critique of sublime seems to have reemerged as a theme almost as early as the renewed interest in the sublime itself. Prior to the 1980s, there seems to have been little philosophical interest in the sublime, at least for several decades. We have to go back four or five decades to find much mention in Anglo-American circles of the importance of the sublime in eighteenth-century aesthetics. To my mind, at least, a significant by-product of the feminist critique of the sublime has been to make its topics and its conceptual territory more available for study. Such a consequence is not unique to this part of our cultural and philosophical history and I believe it constitutes a major confirmation of the value and fruitfulness of feminist critique and investigation.

11. One of the first thinkers to diagnose this pattern seems to have been Mary Wollstonecraft in her *Vindication of the Rights of Women* (1792). See, for instance, the passages reprinted in *The Norton Anthology of Literature by Women,* ed. Sandra M. Gilbert and Susan Gubar (New York: Norton, 1985), 142–43 and passim.

12. Trans. John T. Goldthwait (Berkeley and Los Angeles: University of California Press, 1960). One quotation may serve to indicate the flavor of the chapter: "The virtue of a woman is a beautiful virtue. That of the male sex should be a noble virtue. Women will avoid the wicked not because it is unright, but because it is ugly; and virtuous actions mean to them such as are morally beautiful. Nothing of duty, nothing of compulsion, nothing of obligation! Woman is intolerant of all commands and all morose constraint" (81). Though paternalistic, this is not an entirely negative thing to say. It would be interesting to compare such thoughts to the work of Carol Gilligan, Nell Noddings, and other writers who present gender-based contrasts between ethical sensibilities. It

would also be interesting to compare Kant's pre-critical thoughts on these matters with the development of his moral thought in the Third Critique and in later work. Paul Guyer has pointed out to me the existence of a Schillerian strain in Kant's later work, a strain that conceives of a greater role for feeling in the moral life. We might conceive of this line of thought as partially anticipated in distorted form in some of Kant's paternalistic reflections on women.

13. Apart from various feminist critiques of the idea of universality or "disinterestedness" in ethics or aesthetics, Terry Eagleton and Pierre Bourdieu have argued for what they take to be the class origins of the very idea of taste. Most such accounts seem to be working with a very crude and un-Kantian notion of "disinterestedness." Specifically, they seem to underrate the significance of the fact that part of Kant's contrast is between my disinterest in the object— conceived as my capacity to make something of the representation of the object "within myself"—and my interest in the object conceived as "the respect in which I depend on the object's existence" (46 [205]). Nothing much is clear about this distinction. And, beyond the usual Kantian obscurity about the object and its representations, what seems especially unclear is the supposed connection between this aspect of "disinterestedness" and any ordinary sense of impartiality—a connection that Kant and his critics seem to be equally convinced of.

14. In my experience, the most convincing recent accounts suggest that the sublime occurs in the first instance not as masculine power *tout court* but as paternal power. That is what makes the experience of the sublime so suitable a successor to the experience of God's power and anger. See especially Hertz, *End,* chaps. 1 and 3. Teresa de Lauretis remarked upon a related set of theoretical issues about conceptualizing power in a seminar conducted at the School of Criticism and Theory, held in Hanover, New Hampshire, July 1991. These issues go beyond the scope of this essay.

15. This is not to deny that traces of the pre-critical views survive in the Third Critique. But I remain, to say the least, unconvinced by the effort to reduce the force of the Third Critque to the impact of a few passages (such as the oft-cited passage about the sublimity of the warrior).

16. See Mattick, "Beautiful and Sublime," for extensive identifications of such masculinist language and inclination. See also my "Engendering Aesthetics," 7–9, for a depiction of Burke's slide into a specifically male vantage point on the objects of aesthetic experience.

17. Kant, of course, insists on the connection between the sublime or "the elevated" (*das Erhabene*) and the subject's corresponding "elevation." In sect. 28, p. 121 [262], he suggests that nature is called sublime *because* it elevates (*erhebt*) the imagination.

18. On the other hand, there are advertisements for jeans and cars that suggest that such camaraderie is more or less overtly linked to social class and taste.

19. Kant is often attacked for making too much of the spectator's relation to the arts. Nietzsche goes so far as to accuse him of "unconsciously introduc[ing] the spectator into the concept 'beautiful' " (*Genealogy of Morals,* Third Essay, sect. 6). This accusation becomes part of Nietzsche's larger accusation that Kant has "emasculated" and "effeminized" aesthetics, in part by the very notion of disinterestedness. However partial a criticism this remark turns out to be in relation to the beautiful, Nietzsche here at least seems to be quite indifferent to Kant's entire discussion of the sublime. There is nothing "unconscious" about the way Kant characterizes the spectator's mind ("the judging subject") as the ultimate location of the sublime. Kathleen Whalen has reminded me that some of Ted Cohen's essays on baseball constitute an aesthetics of spectatorship possessing at least a quasi-Kantian emphasis. Cohen's analyses, however, do not emphasize the spectator at the expense of the activity and, accordingly, they seem more attuned to the beauties of a sport, conceived as a kind of "symbol" of the possibilities of human freedom.

20. On heteronomy as passivity, see *Foundations of the Metaphysic of Morals,* trans. L. W. Beck (New York: Bobbs-Merril, 1959) 77 and *CJ,* sect. 40. On the relation of sublimity and morality, see the conclusion to the Second Critique concerning the starry heavens and the moral law. But the idea of moral awakening as a sublime moment runs throughout the book, especially

in the discussion of the moral incentive. I am indebted to Christine Korsgaard for a timely reminder about this connection. The role of false pictures of the active and the passive in philosophical and literary accounts of freedom and of originality is a central topic of my forthcoming book on Kant's aesthetics and its Romantic and Gothic aftermaths.

21. Those who have been most fruitfully influenced by poststructuralist thought are often excessively casual about the details of philosophical arguments and texts. For instance, Naomi Schor's otherwise fascinating book *Reading in Detail: Aesthetics and the Feminine* begins by dismissing the entire issue of what she calls "methodology": "[A]ll literary methodologies, all critical theories and histories of critical theory serve to validate idiosyncratic relationships to the text. Unless the poetician or hermeneut be mad, however, the laws she abstracts from her personal storehouse of myths and the interpretations she translates from the hieroglyphs of her unconscious will encounter in other readers recognition and response" (6–7).

22. The sublime is also bound up with "the inadequacy of the imagination" for representing or exhibiting ideas, for example, the idea of certain wholes (109 [252]). Jean-François Lyotard has put forward an extended idea of the sublime as involved in a much wider range of efforts to represent the unrepresentable; see his *Peregrinations; Law, Form, and Event* (New York: Columbia University Press, 1988), 40–43 and passim. In response to this genre of analysis, Paul Guyer has reminded us that, although the sublime involves something that cannot be represented, we are nevertheless capable of saying quite clearly and quite precisely what it is that cannot be represented; see his *Kant and The Experience of Freedom* (Cambridge: Cambridge University Press, 1993). This essay is exploring the sublime not so much as an experience of what cannot be represented, but the sublime as an experience that is hard to represent or express—hard, that is, for the one that is having it. Lyotard and other theorists have tended to assimilate all of these dimensions to the single dimension of "an experience of unrepresentability."

23. This account refers in part to the passage quoted in the second epigraph to this essay.

24. Virginia Woolf, *Room*, 50. This phrase is part of her imagining the figure she calls "Shakespeare's sister." In the light of Sedgwick's work, we should consider Woolf's later comments about Jane Austen and the Brontës, 77–78.

25. I am here primarily summarizing her analysis of Lucy Snowe, the narrating character of *Villette*. Part of Sedgwick's complex and powerful reading—which needs to be studied in detail—is centered on Lucy's capacity for a sometimes willful silence and the connection of this capacity to Brontë's ability to present her own various versions of the sublime.

26. *Gothic Conventions*, 153.

27. This subordination of the sublime of art to the sublime of nature has been sometimes reported as if Kant thought that art was incapable of the sublime.

28. See Susan Gubar and Sandra Gilbert, *The Madwoman in the Attic* (New Haven: Yale University Press, 1979). The title signifies a particular historical way of conceiving the fate of women writers, of female creativity, and indeed of feminine sensibility, held in certain kinds of "domestic" confinement, especially in the nineteenth century.

29. Indeed, perhaps some of the difficulties in determining the precedence of "feeling" and "judgment" in Kant's account might diminish if we had a greater appreciation of the difficulties in expressing either the judgment or the feeling in all their temporal and "phenomenological" complexity. Much of the oddness of Schiller's procedures to Anglo-American ears may stem from his presupposing a temporal or developmental complexity of human experiences that sounds to us like the merest of psychological guesswork.

30. Paul Guyer, "Kant's Distinction Between the Beautiful and the Sublime," *Review of Metaphysics* 35 (1982): 753–83.

31. Here is a possible reason: Kant thought that experiencing the sublime requires a "greater culture" of the cognitive faculties (and especially of reason); therefore the experience of the sublime is rarer than the experience of the beautiful (sect. 29, p. 124 [264]). Accordingly, Kant

may also have thought that we have less inclination to communicate this experience, since we might reasonably conclude that the possible audience for our expressions of the sublime is more restricted.

But Kant's suggestion about the relative rarity of the experience of the sublime may be false. And even if the experience is rare, the lesson I am imputing to him may not be the lesson we are inclined to draw: our stake in wishing to communicate the sublime might well be increased by our sense of its rarity.

32. See *Gothic Conventions*, 131–36. The poem, which is quoted here in full, may be found in *The Complete Works of Emily Dickinson*, ed. Thomas H. Johnson (Boston: Little, Brown, 1960), no. 306.

4

Stages on Kant's Way: Aesthetics, Morality, and the Gendered Sublime

Christine Battersby

For the eighteenth-century Scots, "moral philosophy" encompassed both ethical and aesthetical enquiries, and the French *philosophes* also moved easily between the two realms. It was only really with Kant[1] that the distinction between ethical and aesthetic attitudes to the world was sharpened. But this division would work to the disadvantage of women who frequently found themselves entirely excluded from the ethical sphere, or granted a different—inferior—form of moral consciousness. Thus, Freud remarks: "I cannot evade the notion (though I hesitate to give it expression) that for women the level of what is ethically normal is different from what it is in men. Their super-ego is never so inexorable, so impersonal, so independent of its emotional origins as we require it to be in men."[2]

For Freud, female "character-traits" include showing "less sense of justice than men," being "less ready to submit to the great exigencies of life," and being "more often influenced in their judgements by feelings of affection or hostility." These prejudices of 1925 are prefigured in Kant's views, expressed most clearly in an early work of 1764. There we are told that women do not distinguish between good and bad actions on the basis of a moral sense, but by means of aesthetic taste:

The virtue of a woman is a *beautiful virtue*. That of the male sex should be a *noble virtue*. Women will avoid the wicked not because it is unright, but because it is ugly; and virtuous actions mean to them such as are morally beautiful. Nothing of duty, nothing of compulsion, nothing of obligation! . . . I hardly believe that the fair sex is capable of principles, and I hope by that not to offend, for these are also extremely rare in the male. (*O*, 81 [2:231–32])

Women have traditionally been confined to the stage of consciousness that post-Kantian philosophers termed the "aesthetic." As Judge William put it in Kierkegaard's *Stages on Life's Way,* "A feminine soul does not have and should not have reflection the way a man does"; rather "in her immediacy, woman is essentially esthetic."[3] It is, therefore, ironic that although the present-day opponents of feminism have been able to grasp that there might be a place for feminist ethics or feminist political theory within the discipline of philosophy, there is much more hostility to the notion of feminist aesthetics. Nor is it only from outside feminism that such opposition has originated. One of the most important feminist art historians, Griselda Pollock, has argued that feminists should "stop merely juggling the aesthetic criteria for appreciating art" and "reject all of this evaluative criticism."[4] In literary criticism there has also been too quick a move to neutral ground "beyond" feminist aesthetics.[5] Whereas feminists emerging from the Marxist and socialist traditions have wanted to legitimize value judgments in ethics and politics, feminist aesthetics has been regarded as necessarily ahistorical and essentialist in approach, as conservative, or, at best, confused.[6]

This hostility to a feminist aesthetics is produced, at least in part, by the acceptance of an idea that Kant developed in his later work: the *Critique of Judgment* (1790). There Kant argued—in a way that he did not in the 1764 essay—that a truly aesthetic value judgement must be "disinterested"; it must abstract from all use value and material value, and concentrate solely on the object or artwork considered as form. I shall here address the question of whether or not feminist philosophers should accept Kantian markers for the boundary between the aesthetic and nonaesthetic realms. I shall look at the way gender operates at the point in Kant's philosophy at which the aesthetic and ethical attitudes intersect: in the experience of the sublime. As we shall see, the later developments within the Kantian system mean that women fit comfortably neither side of the aesthetic/ethical divide and, indeed, fall outside personhood altogether.

Those who have addressed the question of gender in Kant's philosophy have looked primarily at that other boundary: between the moral and the political. What has been explored is the tension that exists between Kant's moral notion of freedom (as a requirement to respect all rational beings), and his political conception of freedom, which would limit the rights of citizenship to those adult males who are their "own masters."[7] Susan Mendus has argued that the paradoxicality of Kant's position on women cannot simply be explained away by reference to more general fault lines that run across the Kantian system: described variously by Kant's commentators as being "between conservatism and radicalism; idealism and pragmatism, rationalism and empiricism." Instead, Kant's comments on female nature in *Anthropology* (1798) are read by Mendus as "merely ludicrous," a result of "prejudice" and "bigotry" that could come only from a lack of experience of women.[8]

It is, however, important to recognize that Kant's comments on women are in a sense a compromise between conservatism and radicalism. And we can understand this point most clearly by focusing on that other boundary: the sublime. Kant's aesthetic theories also both reflect and resist the revolutionary: registering the radical breakdowns in gender categories that occurred toward the end of the eighteenth century, but also providing new rationalizations for an ancient sexual conservatism.

In *Gender and Genius,* I showed how notions of sex difference were fundamentally revised during the so-called Enlightenment period, as both Christianity and Aristotelianism lost their authority. Emotion, strong imagination, wildness, and powerful sexual appetite—characteristics previously despised and associated with females—were revalued when located in the bodies of an elite of males.[9] Male geniuses were promoted as "sublime" and godlike creators, while women found themselves confined to the (distinctly inferior) category of the "beautiful" by the new aesthetic vocabularies and gender distinctions that came into play during this period. Instinct, madness, the primitive, and the capricious remained "feminine" characteristics and were admired (in psychically androgynous males); but they were no longer thought of as specifically *female* characteristics. During the Renaissance, it had been woman who was represented as the sexually greedy partner. But by the mid-nineteenth century, the ideal bourgeois woman was an "angel in the house," totally lacking in sexual appetite. During the transitional phase of the Enlightenment, woman was increasingly deprived of sisterhood with the wild and threatening aspects of nature. "Beauty" linked women with delicacy, gentleness, softness, tenderness, and charm.

During the late eighteenth century unimproved nature gained a male face, as it became more admired. Mary Wollstonecraft—one of the writers most enthralled by the "sublime"—was not being simply eccentric when she referred to the "Father of nature."[10] The "sublime" was often explicitly, and nearly always implicitly, gendered as male. Thus, in his influential *A Philosophical Enquiry into the Origin of our Ideas of the Sublime and Beautiful* (1757), Edmund Burke seems to have deliberately adopted the language of sexual power to explain the psychological thrill that comes from the sublime. The latter is exemplified by kings and commanders discharging their terrible strength and destroying all obstacles in their paths, as well as by the grandeur of the Alps.[11] By contrast, the "beautiful"—small, smooth, delicate, and graceful—is claimed to be what men (= males) love in the opposite sex (*Enquiry*, 42–43, 112ff.). In much of the aesthetic literature of the period, the sublime is described as a natural force that overpowers and overwhelms the spectator by a kind of mental rape.

The spectator was passive, but so was the genius himself. Since art (even poetry, music, and tragedy) was conceptualized as an essentially mimetic activity, the genius remained little more than a privileged spectator of the sublime. Shakespeare, for example, was presented as the archetypal "natural" genius who produced his works as painlessly, as effortlessly, and as automatically as a bird on a bough in a forest produces its song. He was sublime because his subject matter was sublime: blasted heaths, ghosts, storms, shipwrecks, and terrible passions. Shakespeare was a lawless, wild "child of nature" who broke all the rules of neoclassical drama, and who was nonetheless still (mysteriously) awe-inspiring. Shakespeare was a "primitive": untutored; artless; producing his works in a blank ecstasy of imaginative and passionate inspiration; merely imitating the strong emotions that nature induced in him.

The Romantics switched the emphasis away from the reactions of a passive spectator to the actions of the artistic producer. In particular, they abandoned the notion that a sublime artwork simply overwhelms the mind of the audience with the refracted thrills of nature. However, they continued to describe that producer in language that suggested the genius retained elements of the old passivity. In the passive/active state of "intellectual intuition," the Romantic genius was provided with privileged access to the sublime and to the infinite power of nature. Indeed, the Romantics inherited from the pre-Romantics a taste for "nature" in its most savage and unimproved mode: for primeval and desolate landscapes, untouched by agriculture and untamed by gardening. Gaunt mountains, thunder and lightning, the immensity of the ocean—all remained "sublime" and were contrasted with the delicacy and "beauty" of the tranquil and cultivated valleys.¹² None of the passivity—and "femininity"—of that contact with the sublime rendered the archetypal genius female, however. Though like a woman, he was not a woman.

Kant's pre-critical essay, *Observations on the Feeling on the Beautiful and the Sublime* (1764), and his *Critique of Judgment* (1790) are positioned at this pre-Romantic and Romantic divide. *Observations* is a straightforwardly pre-Romantic text; but the Third Critique builds on the epistemological groundwork of Kant's earlier *Critique of Pure Reason* (1781) and reverses previous ontological dependencies by making nature dependent on man. This is Kant's so-called Copernican revolution, which was so important for the German Romantics and for Coleridge. There are, however, constancies, as well as change, in Kant's position, and one of the constancies is the duty Kant imposes on women not to render themselves sublime.

The differentiation between the characteristics considered "beautiful" (and typical of ideal females) and characteristics designated "sublime" (and typical of a male cultural elite) became a dominant topic in eighteenth-century "moral" philosophy. Into this tradition of theorizing sex differences Kant's *Observations* neatly fits:

> The fair sex has just as much understanding as the male, but it is a *beautiful understanding,* whereas ours should be a *deep understanding,* an expression which signifies identity with the sublime.
>
> To the beauty of all actions belongs above all the mark that they display facility, and appear to be accomplished without painful toil. On the other hand, strivings and surmounted difficulties arouse admiration and belong to the sublime. Deep meditation and a long-sustained reflection are noble but difficult, and do not well befit a person in whom unconstrained charms should show nothing else than a beautiful nature. Laborious learning or a painful pondering, even if a woman should greatly succeed in it, destroy the merits that are proper to her sex. (*O*, p. 78 [2:229])

It is the difficult, the challenging, and the overcoming of obstacles that Kant most values; these are characteristics identified with the "sublime," and restricted to male human beings. Although Kant goes on to indicate that some (few) women are capable of the sublime, he judges this to be unnatural and "disgusting" (*ekelhaft*) (*O*, 83 [2:233]). "A woman who has a head full of Greek" or who indulges in arguments about mechanics "might as well even have a beard" (*O*, 78 [2:229–30]). Her knowledge makes her ugly: makes her unable to carry out her aesthetic duties of being charming, being beautiful, and appealing to the sexual appetites of the males—thereby helping nature to propagate the race. There is thus a difference in this early work between Kant's claim about women's moral capacities—that women just do not happen to be able to follow moral principles—and his aesthetical claim that women should never attempt the sublime. In this early Kantian work we are already in a Kierkegaardian mode: facility, ease (and hence immediacy) are aesthetic duties for women. The question that raises itself for the aesthetic/ethical boundary is not, therefore, simply to do with Kant's "factual" errors about female nature, but about the duty that Kant imposes on women to remain in the immediate, and to leave their powers of reason undeveloped.

In Kant's later writings women continue to have a duty to remain outside the sublime, even though the gendering of human excellence disrupts and disturbs the whole of his critical system. Kant could not avoid these stresses, since he was revolutionary enough to accept the new anti-Aristotelian accounts of human excellence and also revolutionary enough to refuse the traditional Christian accounts that made goodness and beauty absolutes, dependent solely on God for their universal validity. But Kant was also conservative enough to have retained the older accounts of female nature: his women have a lust to dominate, have sexual appetites as strong as those of the men, and have strong emotions and instincts that must be governed and harnessed. Kant's woman is not in herself beautiful or in harmony with man's ends and purposes as a social creature. Woman—like Nature—has to be reconstructed in accordance with man's will and man's imagination. Thus in the *Anthropology* Kant would claim that in primitive societies woman is no more than a domestic animal, a *Hausthier* (*A*, 168 [7:304]). It is only civilization that has rendered her a tender, delicate, domestic, nurturing—'beautiful'—companion for the male.

In *Religion Within the Limits of Reason Alone* (1793) Kant divides the determining forces of human behavior into three main types: (1) animality/ *Thierheit* (instinctual drives, passions etc); (2) humanity/*Menschheit* (the ability to judge, reason, and posit ends for action based on a comparison between the self and others); and (3) personality/*Persönlichkeit* (the capacity to act in accordance with the dictates of reason and the will).[13] Reading Kant's remarks about women in the *Anthropology* and elsewhere in the light of this division it becomes clear that for Kant women are both fully animal and fully human, but he sees no need for them to develop the potential for personality. Thus, if we compare Kant's essay "An Answer to the Question: 'What is Enlightenment?'" with his approval of women (of whatever age) remaining in tutelage, we see that "Enlightenment" (defined as freedom from tutelage) is for Kant an inappropriate goal for women. Within the public sphere, husbands (or other males) are required to act as women's guardians. [14]

In a Kantian society it is the task of the males—particularly husbands—to discipline the anarchic forces implicit in female nature. Far from being bizarre and eccentric prejudices "almost wholly uncluttered by any actual experience," as Mendus supposes (35), Kant's views in the *Anthropology* show that he has interpreted his experience of women through the older stereotypes of female nature still in play during the eighteenth century. Rousseau is the most obvious influence; but the reader attuned to Enlightenment rhetoric can also find persistent echoes of Hume and the whole *Spectator* tradition of domesticating women into becoming suitable wives for male citizens who are their "own masters." [15]

In the Kantian universe it is the individual person who legislates moral and aesthetic values through his own will and through the play of his faculties. By the time he writes his critical philosophy, however, Kant is taking a stand against empiricism (with its emphasis on passivity, sensibility, and affectivity), as well as against the *Sturm und Drang* accounts that made the male subject as arbitrary, capricious, and irrational a creature as a Renaissance female. Thus, Kant's later, critical writings continued to have a strongly charged sexual subtext. Kant was attempting to return to the older notions of maleness that were uncontaminated by the newly revalued passions and irrationality. To this end, he adopted a kind of radical conservatism that was recognized as having revolutionary implications by his contemporaries. Thus Goethe praised Kant for his "immortal service" of having "brought us all back from that effeminacy in which we were wallowing." [16] To understand this "immortal service" more fully it will be necessary to summarize Kant's account of the differences between the beautiful and the sublime in the *Critique of Judgment*. This will help us understand how Kant's position had changed since *Observations,* and how he manipulated the transcendental ego—apparently gender-neutral, in that it is no more than a logical construct—to fit onto the body of a human male.

In the pre-critical *Observations* woman was among the paradigm examples of the "beautiful." In the Third Critique, by contrast, it is objects in nature that have become the paradigm, and a special analysis is required to explain how the term "beautiful" can be applied to human beings at all. Kant's examples of the sublime in the Third Critique have also changed so as to place less emphasis on (male, European) humans and more on natural objects. However, great military commanders and geniuses still count as sublime—along with bold, overhanging, and threatening rocks; clouds piled up in the sky; great waterfalls; storm-ridden seas; earthquakes and volcanoes (*CJ*, sect. 28, pp. 100–102 [5:260–63]). All of these would also have qualified as "sublime" in *Observations;* but Kant no longer describes the sublime as a passive response to the overwhelming, the powerful, the massive, and the colossal.[17] In the *Critique* it is not objects in nature that are *in themselves* sublime or beautiful; rather, these are qualities read on to nature by human beings (*CJ*, sect. 1, p. 37; sect. 26, p. 95 [5:203, 256]).

In *Observations* Kant could see no transcendent element in the human response to beauty. It was all just a matter of *Reiz*—normally translated as "charm" but better rendered as "attraction"— and Kant quite specifically made sexual attraction the underlying *Reiz* (*O*, 86ff. [2:235ff.]). In the *Critique of Judgment,* on the other hand, beauty has a transcendent element: it is consistent with attraction (including sexual attraction), but a response is aesthetic insofar as the experiencing subject abstracts from all *Reiz*—and hence from all use value and material value—and concentrates solely on the form of the object. The pure aesthetic reaction is "disinterested." And, since such a pure response will not generate the peculiar feeling of the sublime, the latter can never be as purely aesthetic as the appreciation of beauty (*CJ*, sect. 13, p. 59; sect. 14, p. 62 [5:223, 226]).

The pleasure in the beautiful comes from the mind's creation of a (phenomenal) reality that seems purposively designed to accord with human capacities (*CJ*, sect. 10, pp. 54ff. [5:219ff.]). Beauty—and this will include an appreciation of *Frauenzimmern* (a rather derogatory term for women that takes their shape or "frame" as their most salient characteristic)—involves pleasure in constructing and forming nature in such a way that it seems nonthreatening. The sublime, by contrast, involves registering nature as a noumenal, superhuman, nonconstructed infinity: it involves *Rührung* (usually translated as "emotion," but better rendered as "psychic disturbance" or "turbulence"). The sublime involves an enjoyment of the threatening: an awareness of danger, an attitude of respect (*Achtung*) for that which could overwhelm the ego (*CJ*, sect. 27, pp. 96ff. [5:257ff.]).

The appreciation of the sublime is the negation of fear: it requires both an appreciation of the terribleness of the object surveyed and a (simultaneous) transcendence of terror (*CJ*, sect. 28, pp. 99–100 [5:260–61]). For Kant such pleasures are closed off to all except the "moral man" who has been educated into confidence in the power of his own ego over nature (*CJ*, sect. 29, pp. 104ff. [5:264ff.]). According to Kant, this will exclude those who have been taken over by the spirit of trade (*Handelsgeist*), by base self-interest (*Eigennutz*), softness (*Weichlichkeit*) and cowardice (*Feigheit*) (*CJ*, sect. 28, p. 102

[5:263]). A "tender [*weich*] though weak [*schwach*] soul" (that is, an ideal woman) could never have the right attitude of mind; but the non-ideal woman would also be unlikely to qualify. Kant is scathing about all cringing, ingratiating, abject creatures who have no confidence in their own strengths, and about those who are only concerned with mental ease and pleasure. Such attitudes are not even compatible, Kant says, with the (still distinctly second-rate) category of the beautiful (*CJ*, sect. 29, pp. 113–14 [5:273–74]).

Kant's analysis of the sublime is thus intimately connected with his (gendered) notion of personality. A man proves his superior moral excellence by his ability to experience the sublime. And it is significant to note in this context that *Achtung*—the attitude of respect that is an integral part of the experience of the sublime—is also a key term in Kant's moral philosophy. It is that feeling (which is not strictly a feeling) that accompanies the adoption of the universal law (and hence that is required in our dealings with other persons).[18] Through his analysis of the sublime Kant escapes from his previously deontological system of ethics into aretaics. He redraws the gender divide in the Third Critique by returning to Greek notions of warrior virtues. War, we are told, is both sublime and more likely than long periods of peace to produce men capable of experiencing the sublime (*CJ*, sect. 28, p. 102 [5:262–63]).

As in the *Observations,* Kant does not make it a logical impossibility for a woman to thrill to the sublime; but there is no inference that women should be educated into the kinds of courage and self-confidence that would enable them to rise above fear. On the contrary, Kant claims in the *Anthropology* that it is important for women to be timorous in the face of physical danger. Since the future of the human race is in the hands—or, rather, the womb—of women, to ensure the continuance of the species women should be concerned with their own physical safety (*A*, 169 [7:306]). But this is an important rider to the Kantian system, because such feelings will debar women from developing *Achtung:* that reverential attitude necessary for experiencing the sublime; for acting in accordance with universal duty; for imaginative access to the noumenal realm, and hence for visionary insights of a religious nature. Kant's women are thus not incapable of becoming "persons" in the full sense that Kant outlines in his *Religion,* but have no duty to do so. On the contrary, although Kant's women count as "humans," their duty is to remain also akin to his instinct-driven "animals."

Kant concludes this point in the *Anthropology* not by demanding that women's weakness should be corrected by women themselves, but instead by requiring males to act as the protectors of women. Since Kant then goes on immediately to make reference to a kind of "cultivated propriety" that masquerades as true (duty-based) virtue, we can be sure that Kant had recognized the implications of this gendering of human excellence. Here, in the context of thinking about women and children, Kant condones actions motivated by feeling as integral to human culture and refinement.

Kant's comments on gender show him registering the importance of emotion to bodily and species survival; but only to one-half of the human race. Since it is clearly unsatisfactory for him to have devised a "universal duty" that excludes women, Kant's system of morality requires major revision. In this context, however, it is worth noting that Kant makes some useful points about the different attitudes that are open to those educated into bodily transcendence and those encouraged to respect their bodily desires and emotions. We could allow that, in our society, models of virtue and personhood are indeed gendered—or that the experience of the "sublime" might indeed be different for women—without, in any way, endorsing Kant's conservative conclusions about female nature.

If, in our society, a typically "female" response to the infinite and over-whelming involves immanence, rather than transcendence, it would disappear from literary histories that use Kantian markers to demarcate the contours of that contact with the unrepresentable that constitutes the sublime. This seems to be what has gone wrong with Timothy Gould's attempt to develop "a feminist perspective on the Kantian sublime" elsewhere in this volume. He simply accepts that "the experience of the sublime was initially the province of male writers."[19] And the same is true of Patricia Yaeger's recent account of the "feminine" or "pre-Oedipal" sublime, since she supposes these genres limited to "recent decades."[20]

The poetry of Karoline von Günderode (1780–1806) and the prose of her friend, Bettina von Arnim (née Bettine Brentano, 1785–1859), effectively show that such critics are viewing history through eyes that take the male writer as both norm and ideal. Günderode was immersed in the philosophy of Kant, Schelling, and Novalis, and used her mystical poetry and dramas to appropriate the sublime for female writers—a point not lost on Bettina who tried in her novel *Die Günderode* (1840) to position Karoline in her life and tragic suicide as the epitome of the female sublime.[21] My translation of Günderode's "Once I lived a sweet life" in the appendix to this essay illustrates how much is lost by erasing this female past.

Kant has often been attacked for leaving no room at all for emotion and for sexuality in his moral and aesthetic theory. Günderode's ability to negotiate the Kantian sublime indicates that such blanket dismissals of Kant as rationalis-tic are too simplistic. She manipulates the Kantian sublime so as to counterpoise "male" positions of transcendence (up in the heavens) by an emotional interpenetration with the earth (which she describes as a womb).[22] To understand how such reversals might be possible within a Kantian frame, it is necessary to refute a number of charges commonly leveled against Kant by recent feminist philosophers.

Robin May Schott, for example, has criticized Kant for portraying "the ideal man as a highly disciplined, apathetic creature who values pain above pleasure, whose greatest enjoyment consists in the relaxation following work, and who finds no place for love in his life."[23] But this criticism rests on a simple misunderstanding of Kant's praise of "apathy": a state of mind that Kant is careful to explain did not for the Stoics involve indifference to emotion, but which instead involved the transcendence of emotion.[24] Similarly when Schott criticizes Kant for delineating emotion as "an intoxicant which one has to sleep off" and passion as putting the self "in chains," she registers Kant's distinction between an affect (*Affekt*) and a passion (*Leidenschaft*), but without apparently grasping that Kant graded emotions (such as anger) above passions (such as hatred). Emotions are affects, says Kant, that come before reflection and can therefore be transcended once reason comes into play. Much worse are passions—"*appetite* grown into permanent inclination"—which exist alongside reason and are indulged with a "calmness" that "leaves room for reflection." Passion is condemned as a vice; emotion, by contrast, is "childish" and "weak" but, since it is natural, is not in itself morally evil.[25]

What is wrong with Kant's account of emotion and of sexuality from a feminist point of view is not simply that he downgrades so-called feminine characteristics of mind, as Schott's analysis would suggest; but rather, that he tries to reestablish the old (Aristotelian) sexual polarities that bind rationality, creativity, and the highest moral duties to the bodies of an elite of males. Kant implicitly lines up all women on the side of "weakness." Women either cannot—or should not—transcend fear. Males should ideally transcend fear, and only the (male) human being who has reached these lofty heights can be said to represent the universal—and make valid judgments of taste—or to be fully moral.

Similar remarks apply to Kant's comments on sexual desire. Schott suggests that Kant has a hostility toward sex analogous to that of the Christian mystics. She claims that Kant is so reluctant to mention the sexual act that he uses nineteen different Latin phrases on one page, rather than discuss it in his own tongue (*Cognition*, 113). But in the *Lectures on Ethics*, Kant's Latin phrases serve to make more explicit his detailed catalogue and grading—in German—of the variety of sexual perversions. Kant's text continues the German "natural law" tradition of finding justifications for social order that do not rest simply on divine law. Thus, Kant's assertion that masturbation, male homosexuality, lesbianism, and intercourse with animals are vices more heinous than incest is established on the basis of an appeal to reason, not to God or simply to instinctive repulsion.[26]

In the same series of *Lectures* Kant argues against those who promote the "mortification of the flesh." Bodies require discipline; but "discipline can be of one of two kinds: we may have to strengthen the body, or we may have to weaken it." The "fanatical and monkish" virtues of starving and wasting the flesh are compared unfavourably with those of Diogenes. "We must harden our body as Diogenes did" (158). It is probable that Kant did not know that Diogenes was famous for his acts of public masturbation (Kant's most terrible vice), as well as for living simply in his barrel. Nevertheless, Diogenes is a most interesting choice of hero. Kant suggests here—as he will also argue in his *Religion*—that it is not man's animal nature as such that is evil, but rather the failure of a man to harden himself (and it is surely a *him*self) into a person.[27]

Can male sexuality be controlled? And how about female sexuality? These are the questions that require urgent answers once the traditional Aristotelian and Christian answers have been rejected. Kant speculates that the origin of evil in society comes from the fact that males mature sexually in their midteens, but cannot (on average) afford to get married until their mid-twenties.[28] It is not that Kant's ideal male lacks desire, as Schott suggests, but that he transcends and controls desire. He also controls and governs female sexuality, even though charm (*Reiz*, and hence sexual attractiveness) is still registered in the *Anthropology* as integral to female nature (*A*, 169 [7:305]).

Sarah Kofman has some interesting observations to make on Kant's attitude to male desire. Nonetheless, although her critique is a good deal more subtle than that of Schott, her psychoanalytical reading of Kant depoliticizes his attempts to reestablish the links between human excellence and maleness. Kofman analyzes a passage in the Third Critique where Kant claims: "Perhaps nothing more sublime was ever said and no sublimer thought ever expressed than the famous inscription on the Temple of Isis (Mother Nature): 'I am all that is and that was and that shall be, and no mortal hath lifted my veil' " (*CJ*, sect. 49, p. 160n. [5:315n.]). The veiling of Mother Nature in this passage is interpreted as a fear of castration: the veil concealing the lack of the penis.[29] And this fetishistic fear is read as both an aspect of Kant's warped sexuality and also as typical of the underlying misogyny of Enlightenment man's "re-spect" for women. But reading Kant's allusion in a more historically specific way, we see that it is one of the many places in his critical writings where Kant's apparently radical "Copernican revolution" is used to buttress traditional gender hierarchies.

As I have already indicated, for the pre-Romantics the sublime in nature has a distinctly masculine persona, and Kant himself seemed to endorse this position in his *Observations*. In the Third Critique, however, Kant keeps all the standard examples of the sublime in nature—referring to Burke with evident approval—but also deprives raw nature of the masculine face descried by Burke, and that Mary Wollstonecraft had gone so far as to personify as the "Father of nature." For Kant, by contrast, nature is a mother. She is the undisclosed (and forever undiscoverable) reality: the infinity of possibilities that entice and beckon the transcendental imagination that fashions Nature as an inexhaustible whole.

This regendering of the sublime in nature as feminine sparked a kind of dialogue between Kant and his contemporaries. The issue was the proper relation (or distance) between true maleness and nature, and what constitutes a passive relation to matter. In an essay that appeared one year after Kant's *Critique of Judgment*, Schiller reused the image of a veiled Isis, suggesting that the Egyptians once had direct access to "sublime" truths about "the unity of God and the refutation of paganism." Although we are told that the key to these mysteries is lost, Schiller also indicates that particular symbols and rituals were passed down to Moses by Egyptian priests who had access to the inner sanctum of the temples of Isis and Serapis.

> At the base of an old statue of Isis one read the words: "I am what there is." And on a pyramid at Sais the remarkable ancient inscription was found: "I am all, what is, what was, what shall be; no mortal has lifted my veil." No one was permitted to enter the temple of Serapis who did not bear on his chest or forehead the name Joa—or I-ha-ho—a name resembling in sound the Hebraic Jehova and probably also having the same meaning.[30]

Those who were initiated into these mysteries were called "beholders [*Anschauer*] or Epoptes" because the discovery of this hidden truth "can be compared to a passage from darkness to light, and perhaps also because they really and truly looked at the newly discovered truths in sensuous images." In Egypt "the first revelation" made to the young initiate into the mysteries of the temple was Joa's name: "He is alone and to himself and to him alone all things owe their existence" (120).

For Schiller, nature and its creator seem to collapse into each other, and are alternatively female (Isis) then male (Joa). But the beholders of the sublime—those who seek the truth and seek to follow Moses in linking the ancient mysteries of Eleusis and Samothrace with those of "the Brotherhood of Freemasons"—are male. Indeed, for Schiller it is no more than a contingent (historical) fact that no male now is sublime enough to negotiate the way out of the darkness of the cave of Platonic illusion, to see the truth in sensuous images—and remain sane. He thus, in principle, allows access to a noumenal realm that is not constructed by man's transcendental imagination, and (taking a cue from Plato's discussion of divine madness in *Phaedrus*) romanticizes the hierophant who had the audacity to uncover one of the mysteries and "was said to have suddenly gone mad" (120–21).

This scenario reappears four years later in Schiller's poem "The Veiled Image at Sais." Behind the veil is "the truth"; but the "oracle" has decreed that truth has to reveal herself and cannot be gained by any mortal who actively wills that knowledge. Schiller's young, daring novice will not, however, respect Isis, and takes her by force:

> "Let there be under it what may. I'll raise
> This veil"—He shouts out loud—"and I shall see!"
> Shall see!
> Shouts back sarcastic'ly an echo.
> He speaks it and then raises up the veil.
> What, you may ask, saw he beneath it?
> I do not know. The priests they found him there
> By the next day, unconscious and so pale
> He lay prone at the statue's pedestal.
> What he had seen and what he learned
> He never said. The gladness of his life
> Had left his side for ever
> And to an early grave took him despair.[31]

Resisting the temptation to read this poem psychoanalytically, I shall instead position it as a contribution to a philosophical debate about access to the noumenal, and hence about intellectual intuition and a kind of (male) passivity. In his critical writings, Kant had reserved the capacity of intellectual intuition for unknowable—but not unthinkable—superhuman beings (including God). Schiller, by contrast, does not deny man (males) the capacity to see what is hidden behind the veil of appearances; he only denies that there are now males strong enough—sublime enough—to actively seek the truth in the manner of Moses. Unless the male is passive, and is simply granted a vision of the truth behind the veil—by a kind of neo-Platonic inspiration—Nature will punish him.

For Schiller, access to the sublime involves passivity and activity, along with a *male* viewing position that is linked to the transcendental imagination. Indeed, the latter seems to be presupposed in all the permutations on this theme by male artists at this time. Thus, Mozart's *Magic Flute* (1791) involves ceremonies of initiation into the temple of Isis via a symbolization of the "brotherly" rites of Masonry. Female Masons existed in separate Lodges, but were assigned a position of inferior insight by both the libretto and score of Mozart's opera. As Renée Lorraine explains, masculine and feminine principles are yoked together in the opera, but in ways that privilege male adepts and patrilineal traditions and downgrade their female counterparts.[32]

Although less misogynistic, similar themes can be detected in "The Novices at Sais," a story Novalis started in 1798. Via his hero Hyacinth, Novalis identifies with the feminine: lifting the veil of the goddess at Sais and finding truth in the form of Roseblossom, the girl he loves. Since the rose was the symbol of female initiation into the rites of Masonry, and was also an important symbol in the libretto of the *Magic Flute,* there are both Masonic and Mozartian echoes to the far-off music that accompanies the climax of initiation for Novalis's young male novice.[33] Novalis echoes Schiller, but reverses the implications, since his elite male novice is permitted to "raise the veil" without punishment or madness.

Novalis allies "truth" with "woman"; but we should not be misled into thinking that Novalis's celebration of the feminine involves a fundamental abandonment of the links between maleness and sublimity. A fragment not included in the story emphasizes this point: "One succeeded—he raised the veil of the goddess at Sais—But what did he see? he saw—miracle of miracles—himself."[34] Hyacinth's discovery of his own self and his union with his female counterpart, Roseblossom, can act as parallels in the different versions of the story, since Novalis's hero retains his identity as a male who simply appropriates the feminine as the object of his own (male) quest. Novalis might seek to transcend normal (masculine, reason-based) access to the truth that is hidden behind the veil of appearances, but femininity and passivity are not his starting-point. Rather, Novalis presents us with a hero, male enough (sublime enough) to take nature by force, to seek out the noumenal, and be rewarded with the double blessing of finding his true self and attaining a mystical union with his beloved. It is the supra-rational (but sane) male who achieves sublimity, not the female.

In *Gender and Genius* I explored the androgyny of the *male* Romantic genius, with a *male* body and a counteractive "feminine" side. This allowed a variety of male alliances with the sublime—all of which negotiated femininity, but erased (as no more than an echo) the female writers who were contemporaneously expressing their own experiences of the demonic and numinous. Karoline von Günderode's metaphoric imagery privileged the female who lifts the "holy veil" of Isis–Nature; but Karoline's voice was not heard—even though Bettina von Arnim attempted to amplify the sound by emphasizing the symbolic dimensions of Karoline's dagger through her heart. For both Karoline and Bettina a woman could be sublime; but only by embracing tragedy and renouncing her own identity within the sphere of the domestic and the "femininity" of the beautiful.[35] The female sublime was not silenced but was pushed behind a veil of logical impossibility through which no sound could penetrate. Thus, the question of whether a man was male enough/sublime enough/genius enough to lift Isis's veil became a trope of Romantic and post-Romantic writing. Even Hitler would claim in *Mein Kampf* to have "lifted a corner of nature's gigantic veil."[36]

Kant himself refused to feminize the male. Thus, when he returns to the figure of a veiled Isis in 1796 in "On a Newly Arisen Superior Tone in Philosophy"—also discussed by Kofman—it is in the context of allying himself more nearly to Aristotle than to the neo-Platonists. The essay starts with a dig at Masonic tradition, and moves on to contrast Aristotelian "labor" (*Arbeit*) with the lazy mysticism of recent neo-Platonists whose philosophy prioritizes ease, passivity, inspiration, and intellectual intuition for a fanciful elite.[37] It is not a veiled Isis, nor "metaphysical sublimation" that "emasculates" reason, says Kant (with astonishing explicitness). Emasculation (*Entmannung*) comes from a false relation to the real: from claiming that the veil of Isis is thin enough for us to be able to sense what is beneath.[38] The veiled Isis must remain as inexhaustible labor (the sublime), and not be allied with that which is given as determinate (beauty). The sublime demands a reason that is male: unemasculated by an apparently penetrative act of intellectual intuition that merely signifies a passive and dependent relationship to matter.

Nature, and the moral law, with which Isis is here allied, are regulative ideas that cannot be exhausted by any particular experience—not even by the sum of experiences. Those "mighty men who claim to have seized the goddess by the train of her veils and overpowered her" are simply giving themselves airs.[39] The truly mighty men acknowledge and kneel before "the veiled goddess . . . that is the moral law in us in its invulnerable majesty." They "hear her voice" and "understand her commandments," but they recognize the impossibility of discovering "whether she comes from man and originates in the all-powerfulness of his own reason, or if she emanates from some other powerful being whose nature is unknown to him."[40] Nature must be constructed in such a way that is consistent with its invention by man, the lawgiver; but it is also consistent with the laws of a supersensible (and unknowable) God who brought it into existence.

Nature/matter/the law/*what* is created are personified as female. The divine—or semidivine—formative force that creates Nature is not "emasculated" by this act of creation, but only by a failure to regulate distance between man and matter. Kant's claim that the purest moral and aesthetic judgments are concerned only with "form" (a priori, and a good thing) and not with "matter" (a potentially entrapping empirical thing) in effect reestablished the ancient Greek links between "form" and "maleness" and "matter" and "femaleness." Feminists have every reason to be suspicious of such a linkage. Since Kant's delineation of the subject areas of ethics and aesthetics rests on this distinction, feminists will also need to ask a much more radical question: of whether we should accept, revise, or altogether reject this Kantian divide.

I hope this initial exploration of the "sublime"—the place at which Kantian borders seem to break down—will help feminists understand that it is a mistake to collapse into a monolithic model of "fetishistic fear," the variety of ways that the female has been downgraded in aesthetic, ethical, and metaphysical thought since the Enlightenment. Romanticism grew out of Kantianism, and I therefore find it easy to resist the reading of Kant as simple defender of reason (and hence as emotionally and imaginatively paralyzed) that is currently fashionable amongst those feminists and postmoderists who lump Kant with other "Enlightenment" thinkers. This is not the Kant that I have been influenced by—and whom I also oppose. There are gaps in the Kantian system, gaps occupied by the "unrepresentable": by emotion, sexual desire, and even by a powerful feminine "Isis" as the construct (and limits of) the imagination. It was in these gaps that Romanticism flowered and in which women Romantics drew breath.

But none of this makes the Kantian universe a space in which I, as a feminist philosopher, can move freely. The "feminine" principle idealized by the Romantics is not a feminist starting-point. And neither is Kant's refusal to rape Isis as the Mother of Nature. Much feminist philosophy has evolved along lines that Margolis has identified as a "psychoanalytically informed hermeneutics of suspicion"; but for me this is not enough.[41] Use of methods derived from any of Ricoeur's three "masters of suspicion" (who include Marx and Nietzsche, as well as Freud) might bring a useful skepticism to philosophical texts, and expose *inter alia* the hidden gender-assumptions of both their truth claims and the rhetoric they employ.[42] But such techniques cannot solve the philosophical problems that remain once the finger of suspicion has been pointed—not least, because the thought of all three "masters" took male bodies, minds, and life experiences as both ideal and norm. And the same is true of those more recent "masters" of suspicion: Derrida, Foucault, Habermas, and Lyotard.

I do not see why I should assent to Margolis's dismissal: "Of course, feminism may invent new such strategies [for opposing ontological invariance or cognitive transparency], but those strategies could never remain feminist." Margolis is prepared to allow that feminist philosophy has now moved beyond "a first confused phase of an exploratory sort"; but he condemns me to a fate of negativity, of forever acting out of skepticism and suspicion. Is that all that feminist philosophy has to offer? I'm afraid my own suspicions are directed to the eagerness with which he elides a "post-post-structuralist aesthetics" with a "post-feminist aesthetics," and looks forward to the latter! (see page 428).

My own feminist philosophy asks, by contrast, what a woman-centered philosophy would be like. It asks, for example, how to think through the form/matter distinction, space, time, personhood—and the sublime—in ways that prioritize female life patterns, not the "feminine" Otherness mythologized and embraced by so many post-Kantian philosophers. It's not an easy task. And, since I would claim that there is no "outside" to language or to ideology (only competing languages and ideologies that together constitute a heteronomous whole), I would insist that one of the primary ways to transform the present lies in the possibility of a radical encounter with the past. Distinctively female traditions of argument and art have been written out of history, and continue to be erased by monolithic theories of "phallogocentric" discourse or of closed "periods" of time, such as "the Enlightenment" or "modernism." History has been defined using parameters taken from a few privileged (male) writers and artists. Some, at least, of the productions of these past generations of women remain, however. Opening ourselves up to this impossible past also transforms the way we perceive women speaking/writing/creating now.[43]

Appendix: Karoline von Günderode's "Einstens lebt ich süsses Leben"

Einstens lebt ich süsses Leben,
denn mir war, als sey ich plötzlich

nur ein duftiges Gewölke.
Über mir war nichts zu schauen
als ein tiefes blaues Meer
und ich schiffte auf den Woogen
dieses Meeres leicht umher.
Lustig in des Himmels Lüften
gaukelt ich den ganzen Tag,
lagerte dann froh und gaukelnd
hin mich um den Rand der Erde,
als sie sich der Sonne Armen
dampfend und voll Glut entriss,
sich zu baden in nächtlicher Kühle,
sich zu erlaben im Abendwind.
Da umarmte mich die Sonne,
von des Scheidens Weh ergriffen,
und die schönen hellen Strahlen
liebten all und küssten mich.
Farbige Lichter
stiegen hernieder,
hüpfend und spielend,
wiegend auf Lüften
duftige Glieder.
Ihre Gewande
Purpur und Golden
und wie des Feuers
tiefere Gluthen.
Aber sie wurden
blässer und blässer,
bleicher die Wangen,
sterbend die Augen.
Plötzlich verschwanden
mir die Gespielen,
und als ich traurend
nach ihnen blickte,
sah ich den grossen
eilenden Schatten,
der sie verfolgte,
sie zu erhaschen.
Tief noch im Westen

sah ich den goldnen
Saum der Gewänder.
Da erhub ich kleine Schwingen,
flatterte bald hie bald dort hin,
freute mich des leichten Lebens,
ruhend in dem klaren Aether.
Sah jetzt in dem heilig tiefen
unnennbaren Raum der Himmel
wunderseltsame Gebilde
und Gestalten sich bewegen.
Ewige Götter
sassen auf Thronen
glänzender Sterne,
schauten einander
seelig und lächelnd.
Tönende Schilde,
klingende Speere
huben gewaltige,
streitende Helden;
Vor ihnen flohen
gewaltige Thiere,
andre umwanden
in breiten Ringen
Erde und Himmel,
selbst sich verfolgend
ewig im Kreise.
Blühend voll Anmuth
unter den Rohen
stand ein Jungfrau,
Alle beherrschend.
Liebliche Kinder
spielten in mitten
giftiger Schlangen.—
Hin zu den Kindern
wollt ich nun flattern,
mit ihnen spielen
und auch der Jungfrau
Sohle dann küssen.
Und es hielt ein tiefes Sehnen

in mir selber mich gefangen.
Und mir war, als hab ich einstens
mich von einem süssen Leibe
los gerissen, und nun blute
erst die Wunde alter Schmerzen.
Und ich wandte mich zur Erde,
wie sie süss im trunknen Schlafe
sich im Arm des Himmels wiegte.
Leis erklungen nun die Sterne,
nicht die schöne Braut zu weken,
und des Himmels Lüfte spielten
leise um die zarte Brust.
Da ward mir, als sey ich entsprungen
dem innersten Leben der Mutter,
und habe getaumelt
in den Räumen des Aethers,
ein irrendes Kind.
Ich musste weinen,
rinnend in Thränen
sank ich hinab zu dem
Schoosse der Mutter.
Farbige Kelche
duftender Blumen
fassten die Thränen,
und ich durchdrang sie,
alle die Kelche,
rieselte Abwärts
hin durch die Blumen,
tiefer und tiefer,
bis zu dem Schoosse
hin, der verhüllten
Quelle des Lebens.

"Once I lived a Sweet Life"

Once I lived a sweet life
for it was as if I had suddenly become
but an airy cloud.

Above me I could observe nothing
except a deep blue sea
and I navigated easily around
on the waves of this sea.
Merrily I fluttered in the breezes
of heaven the whole day long,
then lay down happy and fluttering
at the edge of the earth
as, steaming and blazing,
she tore herself from the arms of the sun,
to bathe in the cool of the night,
to refresh herself in the evening wind.
Gripped by the sadness of parting,
the sun's arms went round me then,
and the beautiful, bright rays
loved all and kissed me.
Coloured lights
came spilling down,
skipping and playing,
airy partners
waving in the breezes.
Their garments
purple and golden,
like the deepest blaze
of fire itself.
But they became
fainter and fainter,
paler the cheeks,
extinguished the eyes.
Suddenly my playfellows
completely disappeared,
and as I looked
sadly after them,
I saw the great
hurrying shadow
who followed them,
to snatch them up.
Deep in the West
I still saw the golden

hem of their garments.
Then, flapping slightly, I rose upwards,
flitting first here and then there,
enjoying the lightness of life,
resting in the clear aether.
And in the deep, holy
unnameable space of the heavens
I saw strange and wondrous shapes
and figures that moved.
Eternal gods
sat on thrones
of glittering stars,
looked one at another,
blissful and laughing.
Ringing shields,
clanging spears
were borne by
powerful, warring heroes;
and running before them
were powerful beasts,
others moved
round earth and heaven
in broad bands,
following each other
in eternal circles.
Radiant with grace
a virgin stood
amongst this fierceness,
controlling all.
Lovable children
played amidst
poisonous snakes.—
I wanted to flit over
to the children,
to play with them
and then kiss
the virgin's feet.
And I was caught up in
a deep longing within myself.

And it was as if once I had
torn myself away from a sweet body,
and now for the first time
the wounds of this ancient agony bled.
And I turned towards the earth
as, sweet in drunken sleep,
she rocked in the arm of heaven.
The stars were tinkling softly
so as not to wake the beautiful bride,
and the breezes of heaven played
softly over her tender breast.
Then it was as if I had sprung out
of the innermost life of the mother,
and had reeled forth
into the aetherial spaces
like a child gone astray.
I had to cry,
dripping with tears
I sank down
into the lap of the mother.
Coloured calyxes
fragrant flowers
caught the tears,
and I permeated them,
all the calyxes,
trickled backwards
through the flowers,
deeper and deeper,
right down to the shoots,
to the hidden place
from which life springs.

                    (Trans. Christine Battersby)[44]

Notes

1. Relevant volume and page numbers in *Kants Gesammelte Schriften*, 29 vols. (Berlin: Preussische Akademie der Wissenschaften, 1900–1985) are recorded within brackets. In-text

references to Immanuel Kant's works are abbreviated as follows: A = *Anthropology from a Pragmatic Point of View* [1798], trans. Mary J. Gregor (The Hague: Nijhoff, 1974); CJ = *Critique of Judgment* [1790], trans. J. H. Bernard (New York: Hafner, 1951); O = *Observations on the Feeling of the Beautiful and Sublime* [1764], trans. John T. Goldthwait (Berkeley and Los Angeles: University of California Press, 1960).

2. Sigmund Freud, "Some psychical consequences of the anatomical distinction between the sexes," in *Pelican Freud Library 7: On Sexuality* [1925], trans. James Strachey (1925; Harmondsworth, Middlesex: Penguin, 1977), 342.

3. Søren Kierkegaard, "Some Reflections on Marriage," in *Stages on Life's Way* [1845] ed. and trans. Howard V. Hong and E. H. Hong (Princeton: Princeton University Press, 1988), 166.

4. Griselda Pollock, *Vision and Difference* (London: Routledge, 1988), 26. For a more detailed critique of such positions, see C. Battersby, "Situating the Aesthetic: A Feminist Defence," in *Thinking Art*, ed. Andrew Benjamin and P. Osborne (London: Institute of Contemporary Arts, ICA documents no. 10, 1991), 31–43.

5. See, for example, Rita Felski, *Beyond Feminist Aesthetics* (London: Hutchinson Radius, 1989).

6. For signs of change see, however, additions to the 2d edition of Janet Wolff, *Aesthetics and the Sociology of Art* (London: Macmillan, 1993).

7. I. Kant, *On the Old Saw: That May Be Right in Theory But It Won't Work in Practice* [1793], trans. E. B. Ashton (Philadelphia: University of Pennsylvania Press, 1974), 59 [8:291]).

8. Susan Mendus, "Kant: "An Honest But Narrow-Minded Bourgeois?" in *Women in Western Political Philosophy*, ed. Ellen Kennedy and S. Mendus (Brighton: Harvester, 1987), 22, 38–39, 35.

9. C. Battersby, *Gender and Genius: Towards a Feminist Aesthetics* (London: Women's Press, 1989; Indiana University Press, 1990).

10. Mary Wollstonecraft, "The Cave of Fancy," in *Posthumous Works* [1787] (Clifton, N.J.: Augustus M. Kelley, 1972), 2:107.

11. Edmund Burke, *A Philosophical Enquiry into the Origin of our Ideas of the Sublime and Beautiful* [1757], ed. James T. Boulton (Oxford: Basil Blackwell, 1987), 64ff.

12. Later in the eighteenth century, the "picturesque" was developed as an intermediate category, designed to fit between the Burkean beautiful and the sublime. Its gender logic—and the problem it poses for feminists seeking to reclaim the sublime—is analyzed by C. Battersby, "Gender and the Picturesque: Recording Ruins in the Landscape of Patriarchy" in *Public Bodies/ Private States*, ed. Jane Brettle and S. Rice (Manchester: Manchester University Press, 1994).

13. I. Kant, *Religion Within the Limits of Reason Alone* [1793], trans. Theodore M. Greene and H. H. Hudson (New York: Harper Torchbooks, 1960), 21ff. [6:26ff.]

14. Compare Kant's essay "An Answer to the Question 'What is Enlightenment?' " in *Kant on History* [1784], ed. Lewis White Beck (Indianapolis: Bobbs-Merrill, 1963), 3-10 [8:35–42] with *Anthropology*, 79–80 [7:209].

15. For Hume on gender, see C. Battersby, "An Enquiry Concerning the Humean Woman," *Philosophy* 56 (1981): 303–12; also *Gender and Genius* for the *Spectator*, etc.

16. Goethe's letter to Chancellor von Müller (29 April 1818), quoted in Ernst Cassirer, *Kant's Life and Thought* [1918], trans. James Haden (New Haven: Yale University Press, 1981), 270. Cassirer obviously agrees with Goethe's sentiments, since he praises effusively Kant's "completely virile way of thinking" and his opposition to "the effeminacy and over-softness that he saw in control all around him."

17. For a list of sublime objects in *Observations*, see 47–50 [2:208–10].

18. I. Kant, *Critique of Practical Reason* [1788], trans. T. K. Abbott (London: Longmans, 1909), 167–70 [5:75–78]. Also *Foundations of the Metaphysics of Morals* [1785], trans. Lewis White Beck (Indianapolis: Library of Liberal Arts, 1959), 17n.–18n. [4:401n.]. Kant had clearly

changed his mind to some extent about *Achtung* between the Second and Third Critiques, since in the cited passage from the Second Critique Kant also insists that respect is only accorded to persons, and not to objects.

19. Timothy Gould, "Intensity and its Audiences," Chapter 3 of this volume.

20. See Patricia Yaeger, "Toward a Female Sublime," in *Gender and Theory*, ed. Linda Kauffman (Oxford: Basil Blackwell, 1989), 191ff. A more extended critique of Yaeger is included in C. Battersby, "Unblocking the Oedipal: Karoline von Günderode and the Female Sublime," in *Political Gender: Texts and Contexts*, ed. S. Ledger, Josephine McDonagh, and J. Spencer (Hemel Hempstead: Harvester Wheatsheaf, 1994).

21. Bettina von Arnim's *Die Günderode* was a work of fiction, but was based on actual letters between her and Karoline von Günderode (also spelled Günderrode). As such, it was an exact counterpart to the earlier Goethe's *Letters to a Child* (1835) in which Bettina situated Goethe as the paradigm (sublime) genius. Christa Wolf also semifictionalizes Günderode in her 1979 novel *Kein Ort. Nirgends (No Place on Earth)*. Wolf has also edited and written on Günderode in *Der Schatten eines Traumes* (1979), and in her edition of Bettine von Arnim, *Die Günderode* (1983).

22. For a more detailed analysis of Günderode's sublime, see my "Unblocking the Oedipal."

23. Robin May Schott, *Cognition and Eros: A Critique of the Kantian Paradigm* (Boston: Beacon, 1988), 109.

24. *Metaphysical Elements of Ethics*, printed with Abbott's trans. of *Critique of Practical Reason* (1797; op. cit.), sect. 17, pp. 319–20 [6:sect. 16, pp. 408–9]. Abbott's translation is weak at this point, and perhaps contributes to leading Schott astray.

25. Schott, 105–6; Kant, ibid., sect. 16, p. 319 [6:sect. 15, pp. 407–8]. As well as feminist critiques of Kant, there are feminist defenses of his position that are also far too extreme. I certainly would not support Ursula Pia Jauch's reading of Kant as "a feminist 'avant la lettre'" in her *Immanuel Kant zur Geschlechterdifferenz* (Vienna: Passagen, 1988).

26. Kant, *Lectures on Ethics* [1775–81], trans. Louis Infield (collated 1930; New York: Harper and Row, 1963), 169–71.

27. *Religion*, 30–31 [6:34–36].

28. "Conjectural Beginning of Human History," in *Kant on History* (1786; op. cit.), 61 and n. 2 [8:116 and n.]

29. Sarah Kofman, from *Le Respect des Femmes*, trans. as "The Economy of Respect: Kant and Respect for Women," in *Social Research* 49 (1982): 383–404.

30. Friedrich von Schiller, "Die Sendung Moses," *Thalia* [1791] trans. in Kristin Pfefferkorn, *Novalis: A Romantic's Theory of Language and Poetry* (New Haven: Yale University Press, 1988), 120.

31. Schiller, "Das verschleierte Bild zu Sais," *Die Horen* [1795], in Pfefferkorn, 125–26.

32. See Renée Lorraine, "A History of Music," Chapter 7, this volume.

33. See plate 9 (a woman's Masonic Apron, decorated with roses) and "Commentaries on the Plates," in Jacques Chailley, *The Magic Flute, Masonic Opera*, trans. Herbert Weinstock (New York, Knopf, 1971; London: Gollancz, 1972).

34. Novalis (Georg Friedrich Philipp von Hardenberg), *Vermischte Fragmente* III, ii, 584, no. 250 in Pfefferkorn, 126, 220. Fragment relating to "Die Lehrlinge zu Sais." My discussion of Isis is greatly indebted to Pfefferkorn, although some of the gender and philosophical context given here complicates Pfefferkorn's thesis.

35. Margarete Lazarowicz has noted that the metaphor of Nature as a veiled Isis anchors Günderode's use of mythological imagery. See her *Karoline von Günderrode: Porträt einer Fremden* (Frankfurt: Peter Lang, 1986), n. 108 and pp. 168ff. For Günderode, the veil of Nature is "thick" (as it is for Kant); but, unlike Kant, she indicates that it can be lifted by those few whose lives are "undivided" in their surrender to the power of the virgin Isis. The priestess of Apollo is made the paradigm example of one who has raised the "holy veil," and who is taken over

by the sublime, which uses her as its mouthpiece. Karoline thus goes beyond Novalis both in privileging the female initiate into the sublime and in suggesting—via her portrait of Cassandra in her drama *Magic and Destiny* (1805)—that such a surrender would produce tragedy in a woman's life by placing her outside the realm of the domestic.

36. Adolf Hitler, *Mein Kampf* (Boston, 1943), 287; quoted in Susan Griffin, *Pornography and Silence* (London: Women's Press, 1981), 168.

37. "On a Newly Arisen Superior Tone in Philosophy," in *Raising the Tone of Philosophy* [1796], trans. and ed. Peter Fenves (Baltimore: Johns Hopkins University Press, 1993), 51ff. [8:389ff.]. Fenves's translation has only recently appeared; I am therefore grateful to my colleague Tony Phelan for allowing me access to the first draft of his own translation of "Von einem neuerdings erhobenen vornehmen Ton in der Philosophie."

38. Ibid., 64ff. [8:399ff.].

39. Ibid., 66n. [8:401n.], amended translation.

40. Ibid., 71 [8:405], amended translation.

41. Joseph Margolis, "Reconciling Analytic and Feminist Philosophy and Aesthetics," Chapter 18, this volume. Margolis also includes other forms of suspicion as feminist.

42. Introduction to Paul Ricoeur, *Hermeneutics and the Human Sciences*, ed. and trans. John B. Thompson (Cambridge: Cambridge University Press, 1981), 6.

43. Preliminary versions of this paper have been presented at the Universities of Amsterdam, Southampton, and Warwick and the British Society for Eighteenth Century Studies in London. I am grateful to participants for comments that extended the range of my analysis.

44. Permission to reprint my translation, which first appeared in *Political Gender: Texts and Contexts* (ed. S. Ledger, Josephine McDonagh, and J. Spencer [Hemel Hempstead: Harvester Wheatsheaf, 1994]), has been granted by Paramount Publishing International, Hemel Hempstead, Herts., England.

SELECT BIBLIOGRAPHY TO PART I

Battersby, Christine. *Gender and Genius: Towards a Feminist Aesthetics.* London: The Women's Press, 1989. Bloomington: Indiana University Press, 1990.

Bordo, Susan. *The Flight to Objectivity: Essays on Cartesianism and Culture.* Albany: State University of New York Press, 1987.

Broude, Norma. *Impressionism: A Feminist Reading: The Gendering of Art, Science and Nature in the Nineteenth Century.* New York: Rizzoli, 1991.

Burke, Edmund. *A Philosophical Enquiry into the Origin of our Ideas of the Sublime and the Beautiful.* Edited by J. T. Boulton. Notre Dame: University of Notre Dame Press, 1968. (Originally published 1757)

Crowther, Paul. *The Kantian Sublime: From Morality to Art.* Oxford: Clarendon Press, 1989.

Diehl, Joan Feit. *Women Poets and the American Sublime.* Bloomington: Indiana University Press, 1990.

Duncan, Carol. *The Aesthetics of Power: Essays in the Critical History of Art.* Cambridge: Cambridge University Press, 1993.

Gutwirth, Madelyn. *The Twilight of the Goddesses: Women and Representation in the French Revolutionary Era.* New Brunswick: Rutgers University Press, 1992.

Guyer, Paul. *Kant and the Claims of Taste.* Cambridge: Harvard University Press, 1979.

Hume, David. "Of the Standard of Taste" (1757). In *Essays Moral, Political, and Literary*, edited by T. H. Greene and T. H. Grose. London: Longmans, Green, 1875.

Jones, Vivien, ed. *Women in the Eighteenth Century: Constructions of Femininity.* London: Routledge, 1990.

Jordanova, L. J. *Sexual Visions: Images of Gender in Science and Medicine Between the Eighteenth and Twentieth Centuries.* New York: Harvester Wheatsheaf, 1989.

Kant, Immanuel. *Critique of Judgment.* Translated by Warner Pluhar. Indianapolis: Hackett, 1987. (Originally published 1790)

———. *Observations on the Feeling of the Beautiful and Sublime.* Translated by J. T. Goldthwait. Berkeley and Los Angeles: University of California Press, 1960. (Originally published 1764)

Keener, Frederick M., and Susan E. Lorsch, eds. *Eighteenth-Century Women and the Arts.* New York: Greenwood, 1988.

Kneller, Jane. "Discipline and Silence: Women and Imagination in Kant's Theory of Taste." In *Aesthetics in Feminist Perspective*, edited by Hilde Hein and Carolyn Korsmeyer. Bloomington: Indiana University Press, 1993.

Kristeller, Paul Osker. "The Modern System of the Arts." In *Renaissance Thought, II*, New York: Harper Torchbook, 1965.

Lipking, L. *The Ordering of the Arts in Eighteenth-Century England.* Princeton: Princeton University Press, 1970.

Mattick, Paul, Jr. *Eighteenth-Century Aesthetics and the Reconstruction of Art.* Cambridge: Cambridge University Press, 1993.

Moller, Anne K. *Romanticism and Gender.* New York: Routledge, 1993.

Monk, S. H. *The Sublime: A Study of Critical Theories in XVIIIth Century England.* Ann Arbor: University of Michigan Press, 1960.

Schor, Naomi. *Reading in Detail: Aesthetics and the Feminine.* New York: Methuen, 1987.

Schott, Robin. *Cognition and Eros: A Critique of the Kantian Paradigm.* Boston: Beacon, 1988.

Spencer, Samia I., ed. *French Women and the Age of Enlightenment.* Bloomington: Indiana University Press, 1992.

Wiseman, Mary Bittner. "Beautiful Exiles." In *Aesthetics in Feminist Perspective,* edited by Hilde Hein and Carolyn Korsmeyer. Bloomington: Indiana University Press, 1993.

II

Aesthetic Responses:
Subjective Differences
and the
Challenge to
Traditional Theories
of Appreciation

The philosophies discussed in Part I set in place a tradition of positing a generic observer who stands for anyone and everyone. The analysis of the response or pleasure of this subject provided a way to understand the nature of aesthetic judgments and how, despite their subjectivity, they were amenable to general theorizing. What began in the eighteenth century as an explicit defense of standards of taste grounded on an understanding of common human nature was retained in the tradition in the form of this neutral figure, whose historical time, place, social class, gender, nationality, or individual traits were held to be irrelevant to the experience of aesthetic quality.

As moral and aesthetic theories were increasingly separated in the late eighteenth and nineteenth centuries, philosophers spent considerable time distinguishing the appreciation of aesthetic objects from other kinds of evaluation. They were intent on articulating the nature of this particular type of apprehension of value; thus many theories define aesthetic appreciation negatively, in terms of what it is *not*. It is not, for example, moral approval, political or religious agreement, or instrumental or pragmatic appreciation. Aesthetic merit is intrinsic value par excellence, esteemed for its own sake alone and not for any further advantage it might occasion. In its extreme form, pure aesthetic attention was characterized as a state of mind akin to contemplation, in which individual identity is virtually insignificant and the perceiver loses himself in the object of attention.

This construal of appreciation has had a powerful influence over the development of modernist aesthetics. An early theorist of this century, Edward Bullough, summed up much thinking on the subject by referring to aesthetic attention with the metaphor of "psychical distance." He emphasized the disengagement of the appreciative spectator from the subject matter of art, ensuring that true appreciation was dispassionate. The related movement of formalism in visual art enhanced this detachment. In Clive Bell's extreme version of formalist theory, the only aesthetically relevant values of painting are formal qualities of composition, all else being interfering elements of mere illustration.

Even in the more compromised and qualified forms that the aesthetic took in the later part of this century, the aesthetic qualities of art were given primacy over all others in evaluating the importance and value of a work of art. And the ideal viewer of art was still characterized as a generic type—the perceiver—whose actual identity is virtually irrelevant to understanding the process of aesthetic appreciation.

The contrast between the notion of a contemplative, universal subject who appreciates art, and feminist analyses of the phenomena of appreciation, could hardly be more dramatic. Feminist skepticism about the validity of a generic, universal subject casts suspicion on the basic presumptions of traditional theories of aesthetic appreciation. Moreover, analyses of the objects of appreciation—works of art themselves—reveal further grounds for disbelieving that the nature of appreciation is disinterested and contemplative. Just who is the ideal critical observer supposed to be, feminists query, given that so much art—for example, painting in the European tradition—poses female figures as the object of aesthetic contemplation? This question is just one of many that begins to dispel the mask of disinterestedness describing aesthetic pleasure.

If studies of the objects of appreciation raise questions about traditions of aesthetic contemplation, the challenge to theories of the universal subject is even greater. Feminist theories of mind employ models for perception and interpretation that are hardly compatible with older ideas about generic perceivers and aesthetic value. They are deeply indebted to psychoanalysis and related traditions, for they are interested in discovering the nature and origin of gender. Early feminism in the United States assumed an egalitarian view of human nature, such that observable gender differences in behavior and social roles could be thoroughly explained by differing socialization for boys and girls. However, further consideration of the complexities and intransigence of gender differences soon rendered inadequate this sort of descriptive account. While Freud and other psychoanalytic schools received feminist criticism for their bias toward understanding the male psyche, they have also been widely adapted to explore the formation of gender in character and consciousness because of the complex model of the mind they offer. Rather than a unitary consciousness similar in all perceivers, psychoanalytic models approach subjectivity as self-consciousness that develops according to differing psychosocial and sexual forces. Thus they provide a methodology that promises a systematic understanding of gender in culture and art.

The visual arts have provided grounds for one of the most powerful tools of feminist psychoanalytic approaches: theories of "the gaze" and interpretations of the position of the viewer of the art of dominant Euro-American culture. In the essay that opens this section, Mary Devereaux explains the idea of the "male gaze." This term refers to the cultural construction of an ideal observer of art, who, far from being a generic perceiver, is in fact occupying a heterosexual, masculine, culturally dominant viewing position—even when the actual person viewing art is not a member of this group. Devereaux explores how theories of the viewing subject have developed among feminist film theorists and considers the incommensurability of this approach with some of the staple ingredients of standard philosophical aesthetics. She concludes by suggesting several additional routes for feminists to explore in their critiques and revisions of aesthetics.

White feminists began to disrupt the unitary viewing subject with their use of theories of the gaze, but they ran the danger of supplanting assumptions about a gender-neutral audience with their uniform treatment of all women. Analyses of female figures in art that appeal to the male gaze may overlook the particularities of the kinds of females so posed, and consideration of women's self-conscious appreciative responses may ignore differences among women perceivers. This line of thought is pursued by bell hooks, who discusses the experience of appreciating films as a black American woman. She begins by noting the power of looking and the particular prohibitions against looking that obtained for black Americans during slavery and thereafter; looking directly at a person was, and for children still is, considered insolent. She explores "the oppositional gaze"—the view that develops when those who are oppressed look in spite of the restriction on them not to do so. She speculates that the person who exercises the oppositional gaze is in a better position than most to discover how different concepts of womanhood are constructed by art.

Throughout much of the tradition we are discussing, theories of the perception of art have been chiefly modeled on visual perception. The sense most discussed is vision, and the art forms that most frequently demonstrate theory are the visual arts of painting and film. But obviously not all art forms appeal to the sense of vision, and Renée Lorraine shifts our attention to another source of aesthetic pleasure: music. Theories of the gaze claim that much art constructs the position of the perceiver, leading everyone to adopt a masculine viewing position. Something similar may be discovered in listening to certain kinds of music. Lorraine takes a sweeping look at the history of music from ancient Mediterranean cultures, through early Christian church music, eighteenth- and nineteenth-century European opera, and finally rock and roll. Not only what the music represents—for example, in the stories of opera—but its very form is the subject of her analysis. Like the theorists of the gaze, she is interested in understanding the conflictual pleasures of a feminist appreciating art forms that, she argues, represent a suppression of female traditions and perpetuate stereotypic ideas about womanhood.

These examinations of film and music discuss several of the many ways feminists have developed critical analyses of different art forms. They provide material for further refinement of feminist critiques of the notional universal subject of aesthetic appreciation. In so doing, they raise questions about analysis of aesthetic pleasure: How many and what kinds of social differences are involved in the appreciation of art? Does a multitude of subjectivities negate both the notion of a universal standard for appreciation and any notion of intrinsic value? If all value becomes "instrumental," how does one assess or appreciate it? Can anything like an "aesthetic appreciation" be retained or salvaged from the "tradition"?

5

Oppressive Texts, Resisting Readers, and the Gendered Spectator: The "New" Aesthetics

Mary Devereaux

At the heart of recent feminist theorizing about art is the claim that various forms of representation—painting, photography, film—assume a "male gaze." The notion of the gaze has both a literal and a figurative component. Narrowly construed, it refers to actual looking. Broadly, or more metaphorically, it refers to a way of thinking about, and acting in, the world.

In literal terms, the gaze is male when men do the looking. Men look both as spectators and as characters within works. In figurative terms, to say that the gaze is male refers to a way of seeing that takes women as its object. In this broad sense, the gaze is male whenever it directs itself at, and takes pleasure in, women, where women function as erotic objects. Many feminists claim that most art, most of the time, places women in this position. In Laura Mulvey's words, man is the bearer of the gaze, woman its object.[1]

Feminist theorists, like many other theorists, take as basic the tenet that no vision, not even artistic vision, is neutral vision. All vision is colored by the "spectacles" through which we see the world. The notion that all seeing is "a way of seeing" contrasts sharply with the traditional realist assumption that observation can be cleanly separated from interpretation, at least under certain ideally specified conditions. In part, feminist theorists can be understood as reiterating a familiar, but still important, objection to the naive notion of the innocent eye. As E. H. Gombrich convincingly argues, observation is never innocent: "Whenever we receive a visual impression, we react by docketing it, filing it, grouping it in one way or another, even if the impression is only that of an inkblot or a fingerprint. . . . [T]he postulate of an unbiased eye demands the impossible."[2] Observation is always conditioned by perspective and expectation.

Yet, feminist claims that our representations inscribe a male gaze involve more than a denial of the eye's innocence. They involve asserting the central role that gender plays in formulating those expectations. Feminist theorists insist, moreover, that these expectations are disproportionately affected by male needs, beliefs, and desires. Both men and women have learned to see the world through male eyes. So, for example, women throughout their lives expend enormous amounts of time and energy and money making themselves "beautiful." In undertaking this costly process, women judge themselves according to internalized standards of what is pleasing to men. As Sandra Bartky observes, adolescent girls "learn to appraise themselves as they are shortly to be appraised."[3] In this sense, the eyes are female, but the gaze is male.

Feminist theorists object to seeing the world "through male eyes." They equate the male gaze with patriarchy. The notion of patriarchy is key here. Defined as a social system structured upon the supremacy of the father and the legal dependence of wives and children, patriarchy makes women depend upon men not only for status and privilege, but for their very identity. The assumption is that this arrangement oppresses women. It also, as both feminists and nonfeminists have argued, oppresses men, although not necessarily in the same way as it oppresses women.

This oppression occurs at the symbolic as well as the material level. Women, as the first editorial of the film journal *Camera Obscura* announced, "are oppressed not only economically and politically, but also in the very forms of reasoning, signifying and symbolical exchange of our culture."[4] Thus, to take a familiar but powerful example, in English "he" functions as the unmarked term, "she" as the marked term. "His" attributes define all humanity ("mankind"); "hers" define only women. The higher priority assigned to male attributes passes unnoticed because our language, like our thinking, equates "male" gender with gender-neutral.

Art, as another form of symbolical exchange, also participates in this oppression. In both its high and low forms, feminist theorists argue, art inscribes "a masculinist discourse" that we learn to reproduce in our everyday

Fig. 5.1.   Barbara Kruger, *Untitled (Your Gaze Hits the Side of My Face)*, 1981.
Courtesy Mary Boone Gallery, New York

lives. Feminist theorists here draw on the insight that art both reflects the conditions of life and helps to establish and maintain them. The male gaze inscribed in art triggers what Elizabeth Flynn and Patrocinio Schweickart describe as a deep-seated impulse for women to adapt themselves to the male viewpoint.[5] Griselda Pollock goes further, arguing that the history of art itself is a series of representational practices that actively encourage those definitions of sexual difference that contribute to the present configuration of sexual politics and power relations.[6]

For this reason, much feminist theorizing about art is critical in tone. From its perspective, the artistic canon is androcentric, and hence, politically repressive. In Schweickart's words, "for a woman, then, books do not necessarily spell salvation."[7] Briefly summarized, the feminist critique of representation rests on the equation: the medium = male = patriarchal = oppressive.

Some will greet this equation as exaggerated, even absurd. The idea that art is political or ideologically charged contradicts the deeply held belief that art speaks to and for all human beings. Socrates' charges against the poets notwithstanding, the Western European tradition characterizes art as liberating, enlightening, uplifting. Art's effects are positive; the experiences it offers intrinsically valuable. In categorizing art with other forms of patriarchal oppression, feminist theorists reject the division of art and politics basic to Anglo-American aesthetics.

The implications of this rejection are important and far-reaching. In dividing the artworld into male and female, feminist theorists irrevocably link the production and consumption of art with issues of power and control. Outside the Anglo-American paradigm, this linkage is not new. The Marxist tradition in aesthetics has long placed the concept of power at the center of the discussion of art. Marxism's emphasis on how class and other social forces and practices enter into the reading of any text lays the groundwork for feminist investigations of how gender enters the exchange with the text.

What is original to feminism is the linkage of art with sexual politics. Issues of sexual politics lie at the center of current academic debate in English departments, film studies programs, and feminist theory groups. Philosophical aesthetics, at least in America, has been slower to notice or respond to this debate. That philosophical interest in feminist issues has lagged behind other disciplines is especially surprising given that philosophers from Plato to Nelson Goodman have been preoccupied with representation—an issue that feminism, from another direction, centrally addresses.

This lack of attention to issues transforming the discussion of art in other disciplines is frequently attributed to a difference in vocabulary. Feminist theory has its roots in Foucault and Lacan, not in Plato, Aristotle, and Kant. Confronted with talk of "mirror stages," "voyeurism," and "difference," practioners of traditional aesthetics may feel trapped by the jargon of a foreign discourse, one not bound by rules their own training insists upon. Stanley Cavell describes the experience of reading these works as involving a different set of satisfactions.[8] Whatever the promise of these satisfactions, some will maintain, it is difficult not to lose patience with contemporary writers whose texts demand the exegetical labors normally reserved for the dead and the "truly great."

On this account, feminist theories remain marginalized due both to their difficulty and unfamiliarity. But this explanation does not, I think, tell the whole story. Regular readers of the mainstream aesthetics journals have no doubt noticed the growing number of articles dealing with the latest developments in literary theory (the work of Stanley Fish, Jacques Derrida, Mikhail Bakhtin), hermeneutics (Hans-Georg Gadamer), and the philosophy of language (Donald Davidson). In each of these cases, vocabulary and methodology pose formidable challenges. Not every reader will find such challenges worth the time or effort. But clearly, in aesthetics, as in philosophy generally, difficulty alone never warrants exclusion.

The reason feminist theories of art and aesthetics have remained relatively neglected lies deeper, I think. At stake in the debate over feminism are deeply entrenched assumptions about the universal value of art and aesthetic experience. The overthrow of these assumptions—linchpins of aesthetic theory since Kant—constitutes what art historian Linda Nochlin describes as a Kuhnian paradigm shift.[9] The new paradigm is a feminist paradigm and what we face is a conceptual revolution. If I am right, then the deeper explanation for the lack of attention to feminist theories lies in the natural resistance of those suddenly faced with the overthrow of an entrenched way of thinking.

As recent developments in the philosophy of science and ethics highlight, aesthetics cannot simply "add on" feminist theories as it might add new works by Goodman, Arthur Danto, or George Dickie. To take feminism seriously involves rethinking our basic concepts and recasting the history of the discipline. And that requires more than adding women's names to the canonical list of great philosophers.

The requirement that we engage in such radical rethinking may seem burdensome and unnecessary. It is helpful to the self-esteem of women or to women who are feminists. But what of those who do not fit into either of these two categories? What, they may wonder, do they have to gain from feminist aesthetics?

In partial answer to such questions, I shall in the next section return to the notion of the male gaze. In examining this key feminist notion more carefully, I shall make clear the intrinsic interest of this approach to aesthetics and suggest why its concerns merit serious consideration. To this end, I investigate how gendered vision works in one specific representational practice: film. Film is a natural choice for such a study because it is a medium so fundamentally built around the activity of looking. It is also, not surprisingly, the medium where the male gaze has been most extensively discussed. The relationship of gender and cinematic vision is extremely complicated. A complete analysis of this topic would require several hundred pages. In what follows, I focus on two key claims: that in cinema the gaze is male, and that the cinematic text is a male text. I make clear how these claims should be understood and situate them philosophically. In confining myself to the core claims of this debate, I shall of necessity leave aside many important, but internal, issues in film theory.

Despite the extensive literature that refers to and relies upon it, the concept of the male gaze remains difficult to understand. It is so in part because, as noted above, the male gaze refers both to literal and metaphorical vision. A further difficulty in understanding the male gaze arises from the failure to distinguish three different gazes: that of filmmaker, that of the characters within the film, and that of the spectator. With each of these gazes, literal and figurative seeing interact in a variety of ways.

In the first case, that of the filmmaker, someone looks through the view-finder of a camera, someone (often the same person) looks at the rushes after the day's shooting, and someone looks at the film's final cut. This person may be male, but need not be. Women, too, make movies and have done so since the early days of the medium (e.g., Maya Deren, Dorothy Arzner, Leni Riefenstahl).

What does it mean then to say that at this level the gaze is male? It means that despite the presence of women directors and screenwriters, the institutions of filmmaking remain largely populated by men. Not all films have male authors, but whoever makes movies must work nonetheless within a system owned and operated by men. At the level of the filmmaker, then, men do not always do the looking, but they generally control who does. The male gaze is not always male, but it is always *male-dominated*.

By male-dominated, feminist theorists mean male-gendered, not simply possessed of male anatomy. A key move distinguishes sex from gender. A child is born sexed; through education and experience, it acquires gender. On this account, education and experience create the particular way of seeing that the term "the male gaze" describes. Male institutional control thus refers not to the anatomy of film-world personnel, which includes both men and women, but to the way film, however authored, contributes to the hegemony of men over women.

From a feminist point of view, this control matters because it "builds in" a preference for a particular type of film, that is, one that positions women in ways consistent with patriarchal assumptions. Movies promote a way of seeing that takes man as subject, woman as object. Simone de Beauvoir's *The Second Sex* puts the point succinctly. "Representation of the world, like the world itself, is the work of men; they describe it from their own point of view, which they confuse with absolute truth."[10] As Beauvoir explains, women, unlike men, do not learn to describe the world from their own point of view. As the "other," woman learns to submerge or renounce her subjectivity. She finds her identity in the subjectivity of the men to whom she is attached (father, husband, lover). In the eyes of men, she finds her identity as the object of men's desire. In arguing that cinema, too, assigns woman this position, feminist theorists link male control of film institutions with a patriarchal way of seeing. At this point it should be clear that in attempting to describe the literal gaze of the filmmaker, the question of whether men or women do the looking is not the issue. The real issue centers on whether, whoever stands behind the camera, a patriarchal way of seeing the world prevails. The discussion of the literal gaze thus very quickly becomes a discussion of the figurative gaze.

I do not deny the heuristic usefulness of talking about "literal" looking in film. Someone does look through the lens of the camera, and filmgoing is irrefutably a visual experience. Moreover, the medium itself offers a range of devices for representing what characters on screen themselves see, for example, the long sequences in Alfred Hitchcock's *Vertigo* in which we see what the protagonist, Scottie, sees as he follows Madeleine. A deeper and more damaging objection to the literal/figurative distinction emerges from the claim that literal seeing is always already figurative. Men—like women—do not simply look. Their looking—where and when they do it and at what—mimics a particular way of thinking about and acting in the world. So understood, seeing never escapes a *way* of seeing.

How then does the figurative way of seeing deemed "male" translate to the screen? How *are* women represented from the male point of view? And with what effect on the spectator? To answer these questions requires shifting our attention from the filmmaker's gaze to the manipulation of the gaze within film. At the textual level, feminist theorists have focused most directly on the story films of Hollywood as opposed to the international art cinema, experimental film, or documentary film. Attention to the Hollywood film arose naturally from the broad popularity and profound influence this tradition exercised on American cultural life.

Feminist theorists initially attacked the Hollywood film for its patriarchal content. Early feminist works such as Molly Haskell's *From Reverence to Rape*[11] examined how the portraits of the Good Girl, the Vamp, and the Dutiful Wife presented so forcefully in westerns, detective films, and melodramas reinforced a cultural mythology. In film after film, that mythology defined the value of women as their value to men. The good girl was a dutiful daughter who preserved herself (that is, her virginity) for the right man "to take" from her. The bad girl, in contrast, flaunts her sexuality indiscriminately, "losing" her virginity or "giving it away."

Haskell's broadly sociological approach understood movies to tell the same stories we heard outside the theater. In the movies, as in life, good girls were rewarded, bad girls punished. Any alternative point of view, one that might tell a different tale or the same tale differently, was effectively excluded. Put in the strongest terms, the charge was that the Hollywood film "belonged to patriarchy."[12] This commitment need not be intentional. Nor need it be confined to the works of male directors. Yet, as an institution, cinema, like television, was held to participate in and help perpetuate a system of social organization that assigns power and privilege by gender.

Admittedly, not all films perpetuate patriarchy. Individual films may resist this arrangement. The strong-willed heroines typically played by Katharine Hepburn, Lauren Bacall, and Bette Davis do not conform to this sterotype, nor do films such as Howard Hawks's *His Girl Friday*. As feminist critics themselves have demonstrated, the films of Hollywood evidence more variation and internal tension than a charge of monolithic patriarchy allows.

In speaking of Hollywood film as "belonging to patriarchy," something more subtle is at work than overt stereotyping. At the simplest level, Haskell and others had maintained, film reinforced women's dependence on men. As noted above, women on screen regularly won their happiness in the service of others (Griffith's Dear One, Marion as the amiable spouse in *Shane*). When they depart from societal norms, as Hepburn's high-level political reporter does in *Woman of the Year*, they are revealed to be cold-hearted and in need of "reeducation." Tess learns from her husband Sam to place work second to companionate time with spouse and the duties of parenting. Those who refuse this role, find themselves alone and lonely, as Tess learns from her Aunt Ellen. Those who opt for illicit instead of married love, end up dead (Marion in *Psycho*, Alex in *Fatal Attraction*).

Thus, as Mary Ann Doane convincingly argues, at a more complex level, the Hollywood film functions as "a recuperative strategy" designed to return the wayward woman to the fold.[13] This return operates both within the narrative and externally, in the narrative's effect on its female audience. Internally, the Hollywood narrative typically charts the course by which a woman in a nonnormative role cedes her control to a man.[14] The happy ending in which Tess returns to Sam serves externally to "recuperate" wayward members of the female audience as well. The message is that for a woman, unlike for a man, the satisfactions of solitude, work, or adventure cannot compare to those of caring for husband and children.

The classic Hollywood film reinforces this message stylistically by confining the spectator to the point of view of the narrative hero. In Tania Modleski's words, "the film spectator apparently has no choice but to identify with the male protagonist, who exerts an active, controlling gaze over a passive female object." By consistently stressing the man's point of view, the Hollywood film thus negates the female character's view.[15] Stressing the male protagonist's point of view need not involve confining us consistently to his visual field. The one well-known experiment that confined us consistently to the first-person visual field of a character, that of Marlowe (Robert Montgomery) in *The Lady in the Lake*, failed miserably to convey that character's figurative point of view. We saw what he saw, but we didn't feel what he felt. More typical narrative films, such as *The Big Sleep*, alternate between what the protagonist sees and what other characters see. Hawks gives us not only Marlowe looking at Vivian but Vivian looking at Marlowe. The gaze is thus not directly that of the protagonist.

Nevertheless, within the Hollywood film there is a long tradition of women performing for the camera. Women sing, dance, dress, and undress, all before the steady, often adoring, gaze of an implied spectator. Frequently, female performance plays a role in the plot, as when Vivian sings for Marlowe and the audience of Eddie Mars's nightclub. But whether playing fictional characters who sing and dance before an audience or not, Marlene Dietrich, Marilyn Monroe, Ingrid Bergman, and other female "stars," perform *for* the camera. As Stanley Cavell has pointed out, in photographing beautiful women, the cinema has found one of the subjects most congenial to it. But "congenial" here means the congeniality of men making films for men.

The male-controlled institutions of filmmaking thus place women on screen in a particular position. As eroticized objects, women are doubly victimized. As E. Ann Kaplan argues, the male gaze involves more than simply looking; it carries with it the threat of action and possession. This power to act and possess is not reciprocal. Women can receive and return a gaze, but they cannot act upon it.[16] To be fully operative as a mechanism of oppression, the male gaze depends upon a second condition. Not only must looking come with some "backup"—physical, economic, social—but "being looked at" must also activate some level of female narcissism. Women themselves must not be indifferent to the gaze turned upon them; they must have internalized a certain assignment of positions.[17]

It is this disequilibrium in power both inside and outside the arena of looking that makes the male gaze different from what some have called a female or gender-neutral gaze. Consider the oft-cited cases where men serve as the object of the gaze, as in the Richard Gere movies *Breathless* and *American Gigolo*. Despite the "role reversal," the degradation that women suffer in occupying the role of "looked at" is not matched by their male counterparts.

It would be useful at this point to make distinctions among objectification, aestheticization, and degradation.[18] "Objectification," as I use the term, means no more than to make someone or something the object of my gaze. There is nothing inherently oppressive about objectification understood in this way. Nor is the filmic male gaze any more objectifying than any other gaze. Aestheticization, defined here, means simply treating people or things as objects of aesthetic contemplation. There is nothing inherently oppressive about aestheticization. Both objectification and aestheticization may be degrading, but they need not be. "Degradation" is a complex notion, associated with such concepts as respect, human dignity, and worth. To degrade is to demean or debase someone, where this involves not only failing to respect, but also, in some sense, actively diminishing the value or dignity of the person. Rape, slavery, and torture provide three obvious examples of degradation.[19]

Given these distinctions, it is easy to see that male characters, like their female counterparts, may be objectified or even, as in the case of Richard Gere, aestheticized (or eroticized). And they, like women, may also be portrayed in degraded or less than fully human ways. It is with respect to actual degradation that the asymmetry between men and women reappears. In the case of women, real-life degradation often runs parallel to portrayals of degradation. Because women typically lack power offscreen, they are more likely than men to be degraded by their portrayals onscreen. Even if men are portrayed in degrading ways, their real-life power—as men—frequently shields them from actual degradation.

As I've said above, objectification and aestheticization need not be in themselves degrading. Nevertheless, feminist theorists are correct that Hollywood films reflect and encourage a cultural proclivity to treat the female body and the female self *only* as objects of aesthetic contemplation. And they are also correct in suggesting that this way of treating women *is* degrading. While, as I have argued, movie-making and movie-watching cannot be held solely responsible for the oppression of women, feminist theorists rightly emphasize the connection between how we represent our lives and lived experience itself.

In turning, finally, to the effect of the film text on its spectators, I want first to consider the means by which the gender bias of many Hollywood films remains hidden. The Hollywood film conventionally presents its telling as, to quote Beauvoir again, "absolute truth." It depends for its effect upon creating a narrative illusion. The film story must unfold transparently, as though happening before our very eyes. It is crucial to such filmmaking that it proceed without calling attention to itself as a story. In this, the stylistic conventions of Hollywood follow those of the nineteenth-century realist novel. For a film to acknowledge its status as a story or fiction admits a point of view, a place from which its story gets told. Devices such as Godard's use of stop-action and words written across the screen aim to resist narrative illusionism. They announce the film as a film, as a fiction, a construct.[20]

For many feminists, as for many Marxists, the narrative illusion central to the classic Hollywood film is politically compromised. Hollywood films are said to foster strong character identification and full absorption in the action. This absorption in turn is believed to encourage viewer passivity. At its worst, warned Max Horkheimer and Theodor Adorno, such filmmaking undermines individual autonomy. It renders its audience a "mass" easily manipulated in the interests of the status quo.

In an effort to encourage active, critically engaged spectatorship, feminist theorists often exaggerate the connection between conventional Hollywood techniques of storytelling and passive spectatorship. Passive spectatorship is not, however, restricted to Hollywood narratives, nor do all such films aim for, or achieve, such an effect (for example, Spike Lee's *Do The Right Thing*). To the extent that the average Hollywood product *does* encourage passivity, it renders *both* male and female spectators passive. Unfortunately, feminist critics often lose sight of this point.

In calling for active reading to replace this passivity, feminist critiques of the Hollywood film here parallel Brecht's critique of Aristotelian drama. Both denounce what they see as efforts to elicit the passive empathy of the spectator; both ask for art to break the narrative illusion. However, feminist theorists go beyond Brecht's analysis to examine how identification differs in male and female spectators. Gender, they rightly assert, plays a key role in eliciting the empathy and identification typical of narrative film.

The analysis of film's effects on the spectator brings us to the third and, I would argue, most important site at which the male gaze operates. In developing a theory of spectatorship, feminist theorists move beyond an initial concern with film content and style to explore the mechanisms of viewing. To the question How does film represent women? is added the question What sources of satisfaction do these representations of women offer the spectator? At what many now call its second stage, feminist film theory shifts attention from the literary-critical and sociological reading of individual films to the more broadly theoretical project of describing the unconscious mechanisms involved in watching movies.[21]

Primary among these mechanisms is voyeuristic pleasure. In this view, enormously influential among film theorists, spectators derive erotic pleasure through the opportunities for looking that the cinema affords. As Christian Metz argues in *The Imaginary Signifier* (1975), the darkened theater, the absence of the object viewed, and its inability to return the gaze all contribute to the idea that film viewing constitutes unauthorized looking.[22] From its early association with the nickelodeon, the motion picture has come to function as a metaphor for the illicit activity of the voyeur, as Alfred Hitchcock's *Rear Window* (1954) illustrates. Lest one miss the point, Hitchcock makes L. B. Jeffries—an inveterate voyeur—a photographer.[23]

The question of how film plays to our already existing desires, fantasies, and fears received one of its most influential treatments in Laura Mulvey's now-classic, "Visual Pleasure and Narrative Cinema." Mulvey begins from the premise that film reflects the psychical obsessions of the society that produces it. In making this assumption, Mulvey, like most other second-wave theorists, draws heavily on psychoanalysis, particularly Freud and Lacan. She sets out to analyze the characteristic sources of pleasure and unpleasure offered by the cinema.

Narrative cinema, by which she means narrative in the unself-conscious mode described above, provides the spectator with two sources of pleasure. First, it provides what Freud calls "scopophilic" pleasure, the pleasure of viewing another as an erotic object. As we saw above, this pleasure characteristically takes the form of looking at women. In film after film, women function both as erotic objects for characters within the movie, as Vivian does for Marlowe, and as erotic objects for the spectator in the moviehouse, as Lauren

Bacall does for us. Thus, women's presence onscreen presupposes the appreciative glance of a male spectator.

Men, in contrast, only rarely function as eroticized objects for female (or male) spectators. Men, Mulvey points out, feel uncomfortable in such a role. Neither the ruling assumptions of patriarchy "nor the psychical structures that back it up" encourage the male "to gaze at his exhibitionist like."[24] Instead, man's role is to function as the locus of narrative action. His role, onscreen as off, involves shooting the bad guys and blazing the trails. The male movie star attracts our admiration and respect by his deeds. We are encouraged to *identify with* him, to imagine ourselves doing what he does.

In Freudian terms, the male functions as an "ego-ideal," not as an object of erotic desire. The possibility of identifying with this ego-ideal offers the spectator a second, contrasting source of pleasure, that is, the pleasure of identifying with the characters projected onscreen. Since, in Mulvey's analysis, it is the male hero who makes things happen and controls them, we typically identify with him. Thus, the spectator's gaze is male in two senses, both in its direction at women as objects of erotic fascination and in its identification with the male protagonist. The division of male and female roles onscreen mimics traditional gender roles: women functioning as the passive objects of the viewer's gaze; men functioning as the active subjects' of the viewer's imagination.

In playing to our existing desires, fantasies, and fears, film also offers what Mulvey calls unpleasure. In the patriarchal unconscious, woman represents the threat of castration. This threat the Hollywood film typically meets in one of two ways. It may contain the threat posed by the mystery and fearsomeness of women by domesticating them, typically through marriage (for example, *Notorious*), or, more drastically, by killing them off (*Fatal Attraction*). Alternatively, the threat may be denied altogether by elevating the woman to the status of a fetish. In the latter case, the woman becomes reassuring instead of dangerous.[25]

To summarize, then, the male gaze refers to three interlocking forms of control. With respect to the filmmaker, it refers to male control of the practices of filmmaking. This control leads, at the level of the film text, to a product whose content and style inscribe the patriarchal unconscious of the culture at large. Lastly, these devices position us as male or female audience members to find in film a way of seeing that calms our fears and satisfies our desires.

This is a provocative account of film spectatorship. To ask who is doing the looking assumes all spectators are not similarly positioned, that is, that factors such as gender have a role to play in structuring—maybe even in constituting—what we see. Mulvey's original analysis, however, leaves the *female* spectator with no active viewing position except to identify with the male protagonist. In identifying with the women onscreen, the female spectator is assumed to align herself with the female-as-object.[26] More recent feminist theory rightly inquires how Mulvey's account explains the pleasure women derive from going to the movies. As E. Ann Kaplan has asked, is the female spectator's pleasure, like the man's, the pleasure of looking at women, the masochistic pleasure of enjoying objectification, or the sadistic pleasure of identifying with the men who oppress her?[27]

In "Afterthoughts on Visual Pleasure and Narrative Cinema," Mulvey herself proposes, more positively, that identification with the male allows the female spectator to revert, at least imaginatively, to the active independence of what Freud termed the female child's "early masculine period." In this "tomboy" phase, she takes pleasure in a freedom that correct femininity will later repress.[28]

In moving beyond the static model of active male/passive female, current theories of spectatorship acknowledge women's resistance to the position assigned to them in patriarchal culture. There remains, however, a tendency to speak of *the* female spectator as if all women shared the same aims and aspirations and came to film texts similarly equipped. To make these assumptions overlooks important differences between women of color and white women, rich and poor, feminists and nonfeminists, and different varieties of feminists.

Similarly, feminist theories of spectatorship tend to speak of *the* male spectator as though all men's gazes are male. This assertion assumes, unjustifiably, that all men are equally powerful and that they stand equally to gain from the arrangements of patriarchy. Such assumptions contradict feminism's own insistence on the relationship between power and variables such as economic standing, education, ethnic identity, sexual orientation, and so on. Thus, for example, in feminist terms, the male gaze is not only sexist but also heterosexist. Should not then an adequate theory of spectatorship also include an account of how the male gaze operates when the spectator is not heterosexual? As these objections suggest, a more fine-grained analysis of spectatorship undermines the easy identification of male viewer with "the male gaze." Moreover, the characterization of the male gaze as "totally active" is, I suggest, difficult to sustain once we move beyond the assumption that all men occupy the same position in a patriarchal social system. Whatever his real political and social power, the male spectator cannot interact with the onscreen woman. She appears, but is physically absent. Equating the male gaze with the active gaze thus ignores the passive element involved in looking at movies. Indeed, the assumed activity and control of the male spectator is at odds with the widespread notion that the Hollywood film monolithically encourages a form of passive spectatorship.

As I have made clear, the notion of the male gaze cannot simply be identified with the way men see the world. The gaze, properly understood, has undergone certain refinements. It describes a way of seeing the world that is typically male. But it is not a way of seeing confined to men nor is it the province of all men. Part of what makes feminist theories interesting and powerful is their attention to factors which affect how we see and respond to texts. Gender is one of these factors. As they evolve, however, feminist film theories, like feminist theories more generally, have increasingly recognized the necessity to move beyond a simple binary analysis of gender. In articulating the interconnections between gender and other variables, such as sexual orientation, race, and class, a feminist orientation serves to fine-tune our understanding of art and its effects upon us.

What general conclusions can we draw from this analysis of the male gaze? That film works to reinforce societal norms? That it is male? That film, like art generally, may be harmful to women? Such conclusions are now common in film studies. As noted earlier, we find similar arguments in older, more entrenched, fields such as literature and art history. As a body of theory, feminism has succeeded in placing the question of gender at the center of contemporary and literary theory. This new agenda has unsettling consequences for traditional aesthetics. It seeks not only to have us surrender certain long-standing assumptions, but to replace them with whole new ways of thinking about art and our relationship to it. I conclude therefore by sketching briefly some of these changes and raising several questions for us to consider.

First, feminist theorists ask us to replace the conception of the artwork as an autonomous object—a thing of beauty and a joy forever—with a messier conception of art. Seen in these terms, the artwork moves from an autonomous realm of value to the everyday realm of social and political praxis. It gains a history that overflows the former bounds of "art history." Who makes art and what type of art gets made depend, we learn, on the interaction of the artworld with other worlds. In drawing our attention to culture in the broadest sense, feminist theorists rely on an alternative, European view of art. In this, feminist aesthetics constitutes part of a larger movement away from "autonomous" aesthetics. Even within Anglo-American aesthetics, the old paradigm no longer holds the place it once did. Our understanding of representation, of the pleasures and powers of art, and of spectatorship have been immeasurably enriched by the expanded context in which we now look at art. Yet, in this enlarged context, how does a concept of the "aesthetic," if by that we mean the *purely* aesthetic, function? Is the discipline of aesthetics possible apart from sociology, cultural studies, identity politics?

Second, feminist theorists propose that we reexamine art's claim to speak for all of us. Does art speak in a gender-neutral voice or does it privilege some experiences and ways of seeing over others? Traditional aesthetics inherits from Aristotle belief in a universal human condition of which art, at least great art, speaks. But feminist theorists challenge the adequacy of the classic, Aristotelian model not only with respect to the Hollywood film (which some might argue is not great enough to quality as "great" art), but with respect to all art. The films of Sergei Eisenstein and Jean Renoir, like the plays of Shakespeare, all speak in "particular" voices. On the new view, the artwork, like the generic pronoun, speaks for "mankind," but mankind includes only some of us.[29]

To question art's autonomy and universality need not imply that these artworks are without value—quite the contrary—but their value may differ from what we once supposed. Nothing in feminist theory precludes ranking Henry James a more important novelist than Jane Austen or Alice Walker a greater writer than John Steinbeck. In making these evaluative rankings, feminist theorists do insist, however, that we acknowledge the criteria used in defining "important" and "great." Does "great" mean the forcefully written or the spare, the heartfelt or the coolly reasoned, the typical or the innovative? When is a text forcefully written, and who decides? Feminist theorists offer a framework from within which we may and should raise such questions. Only when we explicitly acknowledge the criteria used in making these judgments do we create space for competing criteria.

Third, in denying that artworks or the criteria we use to judge them are value-neutral, feminist theorists urge us to reconsider our relationship to established artistic traditions. The canon, still heralded by some as a reservoir for the best of human thinking, is accused of excluding and silencing women (among other groups). At the very least, a feminist perspective requires that we rethink our relationship to the artistic tradition in terms that do not assume a monolithic "we." Describing existing artistic traditions as uniformly enlightening and liberating ignores those for whom the authority of these traditions is unquestionably problematic. Thus, we must ask whether the coming-of-age stories of Holden Caulfield and David Copperfield affect adolescent girls in the same way as adolescent boys, and what significance this difference, if any, makes. Being willing to ask *who* is doing the reading forces us to question whether the pleasures of art are invariant and impervious to factors such as class, race, and gender.

Fourth, feminist theorists alter the characterization of reading or viewing as neutral activities. Like hermeneutics and reader-response theories, they seek to explain how the social and historical placement of the spectator affects the meaning derived from the text. Meaning is no longer determined exclusively by the text. Aside from emphasizing the social and historical context in which interpretation occurs, feminist theorists break new ground in demonstrating how texts themselves "assume" a particular reader through narrative and stylistic devices. The best of feminist theorizing executes this demonstration through a careful analysis of texts.

In advancing new theories of readership, however, what justifies feminist theorists in assigning "the woman reader" a central place in the analysis of texts? If it is meaningful to think in terms of "the woman reader," then why not in terms of "the lesbian reader,"[30] "the adolescent reader," "the ideal reader," "the overeducated reader"? Are all of these categories equally important, and according to what theoretical or political criteria?

Last, feminist theorists, like other poststructuralist theorists, endeavor to make the unnoticed noticed. They adopt from the Frankfurt School the belief that the informed spectator is a more critical spectator, and the critical spectator is one less likely to be victimized by the text. Calls for critical reading are unlikely to meet resistance among aestheticians. But what of claims that art may not be good for us?—at the very least, not all art and not for all of us. In adopting a *politics* of art, feminist theorists confront Anglo-American aesthetics head-on. They replace reverence for art with skepticism. They ask that we be willing to rethink what we value and the reasons we value it.

In suggesting that this challenge deserves serious consideration, I might be understood to claim that all traditional aesthetics is useless, that the accomplishments of the last century are a chimera. This is not my intent. My intent is instead to describe the cognitive dissonance that marks the current situation in aesthetics. If feminism constitutes a new paradigm, then we may wish to ponder how far the old model of aesthetics and the new are commensurable. Is traditional aesthetics contingently or necessarily associated with patriarchy? Can the "gender-neutral" aesthetics of the traditional model be reformed or must it be rejected?

Aside from these theoretical issues, feminist theory raises several practical issues. If art contributes to the disequilibrium in power between the sexes, then what should we do? Should we simply quit going to the movies? Raising such questions returns us to the Socratic tradition, which urges caution in the face of art's power. Socrates followed that warning with a call for censorship. With this suggestion, however, many feminists would not agree. Feminist theory confronts the ancient problem of art's potential for harm with two other, far more promising, strategies. Neither appears to have occurred to Socrates. I conclude therefore by looking very briefly at these solutions.

The first proposed solution is a call for a new type of art. Some feminists, Claire Johnson for example, have proposed the creation of a countercinema to compete with mainstream Hollywood cinema.[31] This strategy, like establishing public radio and television stations aims to offer an alternative to the usual fare. The suggestion that we create an alternative art might please Socrates. It would allow him to replace Homer's epics with his own, more philosophically informed, tales. This so-called revision of the canon would meet the Socratic objections to art whose content and form encouraged a weakening of the requisite moral virtues.

Creating new artistic traditions provides an alternative to the passive reception of dominant traditions. This strategy is most often described as creating a female voice or female gaze. It allows women to write their own texts, their own history. Achieving such a "female gaze" requires more than simply providing women with access to the means of filmmaking. As Diane Waldman correctly argues, women don't make better, less "patriarchal" films simply because they are women, as if women automatically had access to resources not available to the male psyche. The required transformation of film depends not upon some female essence, but upon a consciously adopted political perspective.[32]

Adopting such a perspective has resulted in interesting films by Mulvey, Sally Potter, Lizzie Borden, Barbara Hammer, and others. These films strive in a variety of ways to disrupt or rework the narrative conventions of the dominant cinema. Sally Potter's *Thriller*, for example, retells the story of *La Bohème*. In Potter's film noir version of the doomed love affair, Mimi investigates her own death. Her voice-over and the fragmented narrative through which her story unfolds resist the character identification and narrative closure typical of traditional narrative. Films such as *Thriller* critique the dominant modes of cinematic representation by privileging heterogeneity and multiplicity of meaning. In this, these films free the spectator to engage more actively with the text. Other films, such as those of Barbara Hammer, seek alternatives to the forms of cinematic pleasure provided by the glossy image of the professional photographer. The range and variety of feminist filmmaking far exceeds what I can survey here. However, these films are shown primarily in film courses and private film societies. Thus, despite their importance in providing an alternative tradition, their influence on mainstream audiences and film practices is limited.

The second feminist strategy consists in developing methods of dealing with existing texts. This strategy is variously described as re-reading, as reading against the grain, or as "re-vision." It involves active readership, where I mean reading in the broad sense to include both visual and written texts. These strategies have in common the aim of critique and reappropriation. Thus, they do what good criticism always does. But more than this, they involve learning to see through what Kuhn calls a "new pair of spectacles."[33] This new pair of spectacles provides an education not in *what* to think but *how*. Reading against the grain is a strategy designed by out-of-power groups to counterbalance the dominant textual traditions by offering alternative interpretations of works within those traditions.

Thought of in these terms, feminist theories offer a different critical perspective. They provide a means of resistance, and an alternative, to the male gaze. Admittedly, just as the male gaze involves a distinct political position, so too a feminist perspective is not, nor should it be regarded as, politically neutral.[34] Yet, as a way of seeing, it differs importantly from its male counterpart in acknowledging itself *as* a way of seeing.

The possibility of such textual strategies is politically important not only for feminists but for others concerned with "neutralizing" the effects of certain artworks or forms of art within a cultural setting committed to the protection of free speech. Reading "against the grain" offers an alternative to the passive readership that censorship assumes, and in its paternalism, encourages. As an interpretative strategy, it opens to all of us—male and female—the possibility of finding our own way through the text. For various historical and cultural reasons, feminist theorists look more optimistically than did Socrates on the capacity of each of us to find that way. Yet producing new forms of art and reading against the grain of the old will not by themselves topple the existing gender hierarchy. For that, women must also have power offscreen.

Notes

1. Laura Mulvey, "Visual Pleasure and Narrative Cinema, " in *Film Theory and Criticism*, 3d ed., ed. Gerald Mast and Marshall Cohen (New York: Oxford University Press, 1985), 803–16.

2. E. H. Gombrich, *Art and Illusion: A Study in the Psychology of Pictorial Representation* (Princeton: Princeton University Press, 1960), 297–98.

3. Sandra Bartky, "Women, Bodies and Power: A Research Agenda for Philosophy," *APA Newsletter on Philosophy and Feminism* 89 (1989): 79.

4. Robert Lapsley and Michael Westlake, *Film Theory: An Introduction* (Manchester: Manchester University Press, 1988), 23.

5. Elizabeth A. Flynn and Patrocinio P. Schweickart, eds., *Gender and Reading: Essays on Readers, Texts, and Context* (Baltimore: Johns Hopkins University Press, 1986), xix.

6. Griselda Pollock, *Vision and Difference* (New York: Routledge, 1988), 11.

7. Patrocinio Schweickart, "Toward a Feminist Theory of Reading" in *Gender and Reading*, 41.

8. Stanley Cavell, *In Quest of the Ordinary: Lines of Skepticism and Romanticism* (Chicago: University of Chicago Press, 1988), 131.

9. Linda Nochlin, *Women, Art and Power and Other Essays* (New York: Harper and Row, 1988), 146.

10. Simone de Beauvoir, *The Second Sex*, trans. and ed. H. M. Parshley (New York: Vintage, 1974), 134.

11. Molly Haskell, *From Reverence to Rape: The Treatment of Women in the Movies* (Harmondsworth, Middlesex: Penguin, 1974).

12. E. Deidre Pribram, ed., *Female Spectators: Looking at Film and Television* (New York: Verso, 1988), 1.

13. See Mary Ann Doane, *The Desire to Desire: The Woman's Film of the 1940s* (Bloomington: Indiana University Press, 1987), chap. 2.

14. Mary Beth Haralovich, cited in Annette Kuhn, *Women's Pictures: Feminism and the Cinema* (London: Routledge and Kegan Paul, 1982), 34.

15. Tania Modleski, *The Women Who Knew Too Much: Hitchcock and Feminist Theory* (New York: Methuen, 1988), 73.

16. E. Ann Kaplan, "Is the Gaze Male?" in *Women and Values: Readings in Recent Feminist Philosophy*, ed. Marilyn Pearsall (Belmont, Calif.: Wadsworth, 1986), 231.

17. The idea that women's oppression depends upon the fulfillment of both of these conditions I owe to a conversation with Tim Gould.

18. I base these distinctions on Lydia Goehr's helpful commentary on an earlier version of this paper. Her comments were presented at the American Society for Aesthetics, Eastern Division Meeting, State College, Pa., 16 March 1990.

19. In saying that acts such as rape degrade their victims, I do not mean to endorse the conventional view of women according to which rape is degrading because it destroys or damages a woman's "purity." I do, however, want to maintain that there is a sense in which rape (along with slavery and torture) is truly degrading. The notion of degradation is complicated and we are likely to have conflicting intuitions. Many of us would like to uphold the Kantian idea that human dignity is inviolable. In this view, human dignity is such that no act can diminish it. On the other hand, there is the also compelling view that certain acts are such that they do degrade and diminish persons. In this latter view, it is the potential for real degradation that makes the rapist's acts so horrible.

20. Interestingly, what is termed the "new" Hollywood cinema has adopted some of the techniques and self-conscious strategies of the international art cinema.

21. This division of feminist film theory into first and second stages can be found, for example, in Lapsley and Westlake, *Film Theory*, 25. The same division emerges less explicitly in Claire Johnson, "Women's Cinema as Counter-Cinema," in *Movies and Methods*, ed. Bill Nichols (Berkeley and Los Angeles: University of California Press, 1976), 209–15.

22. Christian Metz, from *The Imaginary Signifier, Film Theory and Criticism*, 3d ed., ed. Gerald Mast and Marshall Cohen (New York: Oxford University Press, 1985), 799–801.

23. See Modleski's chapter on *Rear Window* for a discussion of the film's critical reception.

24. Mulvey, "Visual Pleasure and Narrative Cinema," 810.

25. Ibid, 811.

26. Pribram, *Female Spectators*, 1–2.

27. Kaplan, "Is the Gaze Male?" 252.

28. Laura Mulvey, *Visual and Other Pleasures* (Bloomington: Indiana University Press, 1989), 37.

29. For a more detailed analysis of the concepts of art's autonomy and universality, see my article "The Philosophical and Political Implications of the Feminist Critique of Aesthetic Autonomy," in *Turning the Century: Feminist Theory in the 1990s*, ed. Glynis Carr, *The Bucknell Review* 36, no. 2 (Cranbury, N.J.: Associated University Presses, 1992).

30. Jean E. Kennard, "Ourself Behind Ourself: A Theory for Lesbian Readers" in *Gender and Reading*, ed. Flynn and Schweickart, 63.

31. Johnson, "Women's Cinema as Counter-Cinema."

32. Diane Waldman, "Film Theory and the Gendered Spectator: The Female or the Feminist Reader?" *Camera Obscura* 18 (1988): 81.

33. Kuhn, *Women's Pictures*, 70.

34. Ibid.

6

The Oppositional Gaze: Black Female Spectators

bell hooks

When thinking about black female spectators, I remember being punished as a child for staring, for those hard intense direct looks children would give grown-ups, looks that were seen as confrontational, as gestures of resistance, challenges to authority. The "gaze" has always been political in my life. Imagine the terror felt by the child who has come to understand through repeated punishments that one's gaze can be dangerous. The child who has learned so well to look the other way when necessary. Yet, when punished, the child is told by parents, "Look at me when I talk to you." Only, the child is afraid to look. Afraid to look, but fascinated by the gaze. There is power in looking.

Amazed the first time I read in history classes that white slaveowners (men, women, and children) punished enslaved black people for looking, I wondered how this traumatic relationship to the gaze had informed black parenting and black spectatorship. The politics of slavery, of racialized power relations, were such that the slaves were denied their right to gaze. Connecting this strategy

*This essay is reprinted with permission from bell hooks, *Black Looks: Race and Representation* (Boston: South End Press, 1992), 115–31.

of domination to that used by grown folks in southern black rural communities where I grew up, I was pained to think that there was no absolute difference between whites who had oppressed black people and ourselves. Years later, reading Michel Foucault, I thought again about these connections, about the ways power as domination reproduces itself in different locations employing similar apparatuses, strategies, and mechanisms of control. Since I knew as a child that the dominating power adults exercised over me and over my gaze was never so absolute that I did not dare to look, to sneak a peep, to stare dangerously, I knew that the slaves had looked. That all attempts to repress our/black peoples' right to gaze had produced in us an overwhelming longing to look, a rebellious desire, an oppositional gaze. By courageously looking, we defiantly declared: "Not only will I stare. I want my look to change reality." Even in the worse circumstances of domination, the ability to manipulate one's gaze in the face of structures of domination that would contain it, opens up the possibility of agency. In much of his work, Michel Foucault insists on describing domination in terms of "relations of power" as part of an effort to challenge the assumption that "power is a system of domination which controls every-thing and which leaves no room for freedom." Emphatically stating that in all relations of power "there is necessarily the possibility of resistance," he invites the critical thinker to search those margins, gaps, and locations on and through the body where agency can be found.

Stuart Hall calls for recognition of our agency as black spectators in his essay "Cultural Identity and Cinematic Representation." Speaking against the construction of white representations of blackness as totalizing, Hall says of white presence: "The error is not to conceptualize this 'presence' in terms of power, but to locate that power as wholly external to us as extrinsic force, whose influence can be thrown off like the serpent sheds its skin." What Franz Fanon reminds us, in *Black Skin, White Masks,* is how power is inside as well as outside:

> . . . the movements, the attitudes, the glances of the Other fixed me there, in the sense in which a chemical solution is fixed by a dye. I was indignant; I demanded an explanation. Nothing happened. I burst apart. Now the fragments have been put together again by another self. This "look," from—so to speak—the place of the Other, fixes us, not only in its violence, hostility and aggression, but in the ambivalence of its desire.[1]

Spaces of agency exist for black people, wherein we can both interrogate the gaze of the Other but also look back, and at one another, naming what we see.

The "gaze" has been and is a site of resistance for colonized black people globally. Subordinates in relations of power learn experientially that there is a critical gaze, one that "looks" to document, one that is oppositional. In resistance struggle, the power of the dominated to assert agency by claiming and cultivating "awareness" politicizes "looking" relations—one learns to look a certain way in order to resist.

When most black people in the United States first had the opportunity to look at film and television, they did so fully aware that mass media was a system of knowledge and power reproducing and maintaining white supremacy. To stare at the television, or mainstream movies, to engage its images, was to engage its negation of black representation. It was the oppositional black gaze that responded to these looking relations by developing independent black cinema. Black viewers of mainstream cinema and television could chart the progress of political movements for racial equality via the construction of images, and did so. Within my family's southern black working-class home, located in a racially segregated neighborhood, watching television was one way to develop critical spectatorship. Unless you went to work in the white world, across the tracks, you learned to look at white people by staring at them on the screen. Black looks, as they were constituted in the context of social movements for racial uplift, were interrogating gazes. We laughed at television shows like *Our Gang* and *Amos 'n' Andy,* at these white representations of blackness, but we also looked at them critically. Before racial integration, black viewers of movies and television experienced visual pleasure in a context where looking was also about contestation and confrontation.

Writing about black looking relations in "Black British Cinema: Spectatorship and Identity Formation in Territories," Manthia Diawara identifies the power of the spectator: "Every narration places the spectator in a position of agency; and race, class and sexual relations influence the way in which this subjecthood is filled by the spectator." Of particular concern for him are moments of "rupture" when the spectator resists "complete identification with the film's discourse."[2] These ruptures define the relation between black spectators and dominant cinema prior to racial integration. Then, one's enjoyment of a film wherein representations of blackness were stereotypically degrading and dehumanizing co-existed with a critical practice that restored presence where it was negated. Critical discussion of the film while it was in progress or at its conclusion maintained the distance between spectator and the image. Black films were also subject to critical interrogation. Since they came into being in part as a response to the failure of white-dominated cinema to represent blackness in a manner that did not reinforce white supremacy, they too were critiqued to see if images were seen as complicit with dominant cinematic practices.

Critical, interrogating black looks were mainly concerned with issues of race and racism, the way racial domination of blacks by whites overdetermined representation. They were rarely concerned with gender. As spectators, black men could repudiate the reproduction of racism in cinema and television, the negation of black presence, even as they could feel as though they were rebelling against white supremacy by daring to look, by engaging phallocentric politics of spectatorship. Given the real-life public circumstances wherein black men were murdered/lynched for looking at white womanhood, where the black male gaze was always subject to control and/or punishment by the powerful white Other, the private realm of television screens or dark theaters could unleash the repressed gaze. There they could "look" at white womanhood without a structure of domination overseeing the gaze, interpreting, and punishing. That white supremacist structure that had murdered Emmet Till after interpreting his look as violation, as "rape" of white womanhood, could not control black male responses to screen images. In their role as spectators, black men could enter an imaginative space of phallocentric power that mediated racial negation. This gendered relation to looking made the experience of the black male spectator radically different from that of the black female spectator. Major early black male independent filmmakers represented black women in their films as objects of male gaze. Whether looking through the camera or as spectators watching films, whether mainstream cinema or "race" movies such as those made by Oscar Micheaux, the black male gaze had a different scope from that of the black female.

Black women have written little about black female spectatorship, about our moviegoing practices. A growing body of film theory and criticism by black women has only begun to emerge. The prolonged silence of black women as spectators and critics was a response to absence, to cinematic negation. In "The Technology of Gender," Teresa de Lauretis, drawing on the work of Monique Wittig, calls attention to "the power of discourses to 'do violence' to people, a violence which is material and physical, although produced by abstract and scientific discourses as well as the discourses of the mass media."[3] With the possible exception of early race movies, black female spectators have had to develop looking relations within a cinematic context that constructs our presence as absence, that denies the "body" of the black female so as to perpetuate white supremacy and with it a phallocentric spectatorship where the woman to be looked at and desired is "white."

(Recent movies do not conform to this paradigm but I am turning to the past with the intent to chart the development of black female spectatorship.)

Talking with black women of all ages and classes, in different areas of the United States, about their filmic looking relations, I hear again and again ambivalent responses to cinema. Only a few of the black women I talked with remembered the pleasure of race movies, and even those who did, felt that pleasure interrupted and usurped by Hollywood. Most of the black women I talked with were adamant that they never went to movies expecting to see compelling representations of black femaleness. They were all acutely aware of cinematic racism—its violent erasure of black womanhood. In Anne Friedberg's essay "A Denial of Difference: Theories of Cinematic Identification" she stresses that "identification can only be made through recognition, and all recognition is itself an implicit confirmation of the ideology of the status quo."[4] Even when representations of black women were present in film, our bodies and being were there to serve—to enhance and maintain white womanhood as object of the phallocentric gaze.

Commenting on Hollywood's characterization of black women in *Girls on Film,* Julie Burchill describes this absent presence:

> Black women have been mothers without children (Mammies—who can ever forget the sickening spectacle of Hattie McDaniel waiting on the simpering Vivien Leigh hand and foot and enquiring like a ninny, "What's ma lamb gonna wear?") . . . Lena Horne, the first black performer signed to a long term contract with a major (MGM), looked gutless but was actually quite spirited. She seethed when Tallulah Bankhead complimented her on the paleness of her skin and the non-Negroidness of her features.[5]

When black women actresses like Lena Horne appeared in mainstream cinema most white viewers were not aware that they were looking at black females unless the film was specifically coded as being about blacks. Burchill is one of the few white women film critics who has dared to examine the intersection of race and gender in relation to the construction of the category "woman" in film as object of the phallocentric gaze. With characteristic wit she asserts: "What does it say about racial purity that the best blondes have all been brunettes (Harlow, Monroe, Bardot)? I think it says that we are not as white as we think."[6] Burchill could easily have said "we are not as white as we want to be," for clearly the obsession to have white women film stars be ultra-white was a cinematic practice that sought to maintain a distance, a separation between that image and the black female Other; it was a way to perpetuate white supremacy. Politics of race and gender were inscribed into mainstream cinematic narrative from *Birth of A Nation* on. As a seminal work, this film identified what the place and function of white womanhood would be in cinema. There was clearly no place for black women.

Remembering my past in relation to screen images of black womanhood, I wrote a short essay, "Do You Remember Sapphire?" which explored both the negation of black female representation in cinema and television and our rejection of these images. Identifying the character of "Sapphire" from *Amos 'n' Andy* as that screen representation of black femaleness I first saw in childhood, I wrote:

> She was even then backdrop, foil. She was bitch—nag. She was there to soften images of black men, to make them seem vulnerable, easygoing, funny, and unthreatening to a white audience. She was there as man in drag, as castrating bitch, as someone to be lied to, someone to be tricked, someone the white and black audience could hate. Scapegoated on all sides. *She was not us.* We laughed with the black men, with the white people. We laughed at this black woman who was not us. And we did not even long to be there on the screen. How could we long to be there when our image, visually constructed, was so ugly. We did not long to be there. We did not long for her. We did not want our construction to be this hated black female thing—foil, backdrop. Her black female image was not the body of desire. There was nothing to see. She was not us.

Grown black women had a different response to Sapphire; they identified with her frustrations and her woes. They resented the way she was mocked. They resented the way these screen images could assault black womanhood, could name us bitches, nags. And in opposition they claimed Sapphire as their own, as the symbol of that angry part of themselves white folks and black men could not even begin to understand.

Conventional representations of black women have done violence to the image. Responding to this assault, many black women spectators shut out the image, looked the other way, accorded cinema no importance in their lives. Then there were those spectators whose gaze was that of desire and complicity. Assuming a posture of subordination, they submitted to cinema's capacity to seduce and betray. They were cinematically "gaslighted." Every black woman I spoke with who was/is an ardent moviegoer, a lover of the Hollywood film, testified that to experience fully the pleasure of that cinema they had to close down critique, analysis; they had to forget racism. And mostly they did not think about sexism. What was the nature then of this adoring black female gaze—this look that could bring pleasure in the midst of negation? In her first novel, *The Bluest Eye,* Toni Morrison constructs a portrait of the black female spectator; her gaze is the masochistic look of victimization. Describing her looking relations, Miss Pauline Breedlove, a poor working woman, maid in the house of a prosperous white family, asserts:

> The onliest time I be happy seem like was when I was in the picture show. Every time I got, I went, I'd go early, before the show started. They's cut off the lights, and everything be black. Then the screen would light up, and I's move right on in them picture. White men taking such good care of they women, and they all dressed up in big clean houses with the bath tubs right in the same room with the toilet. Them pictures gave me a lot of pleasure.[7]

To experience pleasure, Miss Pauline sitting in the dark must imagine herself transformed, turned into the white woman portrayed on the screen. After watching movies, feeling the pleasure, she says, "But it made coming home hard."

We come home to ourselves. Not all black women spectators submitted to that spectacle of regression through identification. Most of the women I talked with felt that they consciously resisted identification with films—that this tension made moviegoing less than pleasurable; at times it caused pain. As one black woman put it, "I could always get pleasure from movies as long as I did not look too deep." For black female spectators who have "looked too deep" the encounter with the screen hurt. That some of us chose to stop looking was a gesture of resistance; turning away was one way to protest, to reject negation. My pleasure in the screen ended abruptly when I and my sisters first watched *Imitation of Life.* Writing about this experience in the "Sapphire" piece, I addressed the movie directly, confessing:

> I had until now forgotten you, that screen image seen in adolescence, those images that made me stop looking. It was there in *Imitation of Life,* that comfortable mammy image. There was something familiar about this hardworking black woman who loved her daughter so much, loved her in a way that hurt. Indeed, as young southern black girls watching this film, Peola's mother reminded us of the hardworking,

churchgoing, Big Mamas we knew and loved. Consequently, it was not this image that captured our gaze; we were fascinated by Peola.

Addressing her, I wrote:

> You were different. There was something scary in this image of young sexual sensual black beauty betrayed—that daughter who did not want to be confined by blackness, that "tragic mulatto" who did not want to be negated. "Just let me escape this image forever," she could have said. I will always remember that image. I remembered how we cried for her, for our unrealized desiring selves. She was tragic because there was no place in the cinema for her, no loving pictures. She too was absent image. It was better then, that we were absent, for when we were there it was humiliating, strange, sad. We cried all night for you, for the cinema that had no place for you. And like you, we stopped thinking it would one day be different.

When I returned to films as a young woman, after a long period of silence, I had developed an oppositional gaze. Not only would I not be hurt by the absence of black female presence, or the insertion of violating representation, I interrogated the work, cultivated a way to look past race and gender for aspects of content, form, language. Foreign films and U.S. independent cinema were the primary locations of my filmic looking relations, even though I also watched Hollywood films.

From "jump," black female spectators have gone to films with awareness of the way in which race and racism determined the visual construction of gender. Whether it was *Birth of A Nation* or Shirley Temple shows, we knew that white womanhood was the racialized sexual difference occupying the place of stardom in mainstream narrative film. We assumed white women knew it too. Reading Laura Mulvey's provocative essay, "Visual Pleasure and Narrative Cinema," from a standpoint that acknowledges race, one sees clearly why black women spectators not duped by mainstream cinema would develop an oppositional gaze. Placing ourselves outside that pleasure in looking, Mulvey argues, was determined by a "split between active/male and passive/female."[8] Black female spectators actively chose not to identify with the film's imaginary subject because such identification was disenabling.

Looking at films with an oppositional gaze, black women were able to critically assess the cinema's construction of white womanhood as object of phallocentric gaze and choose not to identify with either the victim or the perpetrator. Black female spectators, who refused to identify with white womanhood, who would not take on the phallocentric gaze of desire and possession, created a critical space where the binary opposition Mulvey posits of "woman as image, man as bearer of the look" was continually deconstructed. As critical spectators, black women looked from a location that disrupted, one akin to that described by Annette Kuhn in *The Power of the Image:*

> . . . the acts of analysis, of deconstruction and of reading "against the grain" offer an additional pleasure—the pleasure of resistance, of saying "no": not to "unsophisticated" enjoyment, by ourselves and others, of culturally dominant images, but to the structures of power which ask us to consume them uncritically and in highly circum-scribed ways.[9]

Mainstream feminist film criticism in no way acknowledges black female spectatorship. It does not even consider the possibility that women can construct an oppositional gaze via an understanding and awareness of the politics of race and racism. Feminist film theory rooted in an ahistorical psychoanalytic framework that privileges sexual difference actively suppresses recognition of race, reenacting and mirroring the erasure of black womanhood that occurs in films, silencing any discussion of racial difference—of racialized sexual difference. Despite feminist critical interventions aimed at deconstruct-ing the category "woman" which highlight the significance of race, many feminist film critics continue to structure their discourse as though it speaks about "woman" when in actuality it speaks only about white women. It seems ironic that the cover of the recent anthology *Feminism and Film Theory* edited by Constance Penley has a graphic that is a reproduction of the photo of white actresses Rosalind Russell and Dorothy Arzner on the 1936 set of the film *Craig's Wife* yet there is no acknowledgment in any essay in this collection that the woman "subject" under discussion is always white.[10] Even though there are photos of black women from films reproduced in the text, there is no acknowledgment of racial difference.

It would be too simplistic to interpret this failure of insight solely as a gesture of racism. Importantly, it also speaks to the problem of structuring feminist film theory around a totalizing narrative of woman as object whose image functions solely to reaffirm and reinscribe patriarchy. Mary Ann Doane addresses this issue in the essay "Remembering Women: Psychical and Historical Construction in Film Theory":

> This attachment to the figure of a degeneralizible Woman as the
> product of the apparatus indicates why, for many, feminist film
> theory seems to have reached an impasse, a certain blockage in its
> theorization. . . . In focusing upon the task of delineating in great
> detail the attributes of woman as effect of the apparatus, feminist film
> theory participates in the abstraction of women.[11]

The concept "Woman" effaces the difference between women in specific
sociohistorical contexts, between women defined precisely as historical subjects rather than as *a* psychic subject (nonsubject). Though Doane does not
focus on race, her comments speak directly to the problem of its erasure. For
it is only as one imagines "woman" in the abstract, when woman becomes
fiction or fantasy, can race not be seen as significant. Are we really to imagine
that feminist theorists writing only about images of white women, who
subsume this specific historical subject under the totalizing category "woman,"
do not "see" the whiteness of the image? It may very well be that they engage
in a process of denial that eliminates the necessity of revisioning conventional
ways of thinking about psychoanalysis as a paradigm of analysis and the need
to rethink a body of feminist film theory that is firmly rooted in a denial of the
reality that sex/sexuality may not be the primary and/or exclusive signifier of
difference. Doane's essay appears in a very recent anthology, *Psychoanalysis
and Cinema,* edited by E. Ann Kaplan, where, once again, none of the theory
presented acknowledges or discusses racial difference, with the exception of
one essay, "Not Speaking with Language, Speaking with No Language,"[12]
which problematizes notions of orientalism in its examination of Leslie Thornton's film *Adynata.* Yet in most of the essays, the theories espoused are
rendered problematic if one includes race as a category of analysis.

Constructing feminist film theory along these lines enables the production of
a discursive practice that need never theorize any aspect of black female
representation or spectatorship. Yet the existence of black women within
white supremacist culture problematizes, and makes complex, the overall
issue of female identity, representation, and spectatorship—if, as Friedberg
suggests, "identification is a process which commands the subject to be
displaced by an other; it is a procedure which breaches the separation between
self and other, and, in this way, replicates the very structure of patriarchy."[13]
If identification "demands sameness, necessitates similarity, disallows difference"—must we then surmise that many feminist film critics who are
"overidentified" with the mainstream cinematic apparatus produce theories
that replicate its totalizing agenda? Why is it that feminist film criticism,

which has most claimed the terrain of woman's identity, representation, and subjectivity as its field of analysis, remains aggressively silent on the subject of blackness and specifically representations of black womanhood? Just as mainstream cinema has historically forced aware black female spectators not to look, much feminist film criticism disallows the possibility of a theoretical dialogue that might include black women's voices. It is difficult to talk when you feel no one is listening, when you feel as though a special jargon or narrative has been created that only the chosen can understand. No wonder then that black women have for the most part confined our critical commentary on film to conversations. And it must be reiterated that this gesture is a strategy that protects us from the violence perpetuated and advocated by discourses of mass media. A new focus on issues of race and representation in the field of film theory could critically intervene on the historical repression reproduced in some arenas of contemporary critical practice, making a discursive space for discussion of black female spectatorship possible.

When I asked a black woman in her twenties, an obsessive moviegoer, why she thought we had not written about black female spectatorship, she commented: "We are afraid to talk about ourselves as spectators because we have been so abused by 'the gaze.'" An aspect of that abuse was the imposition of the assumption that black female looking relations were not important enough to theorize. Film theory as a critical "turf" in the United States has been and continues to be influenced by and reflective of white racial domination. Since feminist film criticism was initially rooted in a women's liberation movement informed by racist practices, it did not open up the discursive terrain and make it more inclusive. Recently, even those white film theorists who include an analysis of race show no interest in black female spectatorship. In her introduction to the collection of essays *Visual and Other Pleasures,* Laura Mulvey describes her initial romantic absorption in Hollywood cinema, stating:

> Although this great, previously unquestioned and unanalyzed love was put in crisis by the impact of feminism on my thought in the early 1970s, it also had an enormous influence on the development of my critical work and ideas and the debate within film culture with which I became preoccupied over the next fifteen years or so. Watched through eyes that were affected by the changing climate of consciousness, the movies lost their magic. [14]

Watching movies from a feminist perspective, Mulvey arrived at that location of disaffection that is the starting point for many black women approaching cinema within the lived harsh reality of racism. Yet her account of being a part of a film culture whose roots rest on a founding relationship of adoration and love indicates how difficult it would have been to enter that world from "jump" as a critical spectator whose gaze had been formed in opposition.

Given the context of class exploitation, and racist and sexist domination, it has only been through resistance, struggle, reading, and looking "against the grain," that black women have been able to value our process of looking enough to publicly name it. Centrally, those black female spectators who attest to the oppositionality of their gaze deconstruct theories of female spectatorship that have relied heavily on the assumption that, as Doane suggests in her essay, "Woman's Stake: Filming the Female Body," "woman can only mimic man's relation to language, that is assume a position defined by the penis-phallus as the supreme arbiter of lack."[15] Identifying with neither the phallocentric gaze nor the construction of white womanhood as lack, critical black female spectators construct a theory of looking relations where cinematic visual delight is the pleasure of interrogation. Every black woman spectator I talked to, with rare exception, spoke of being "on guard" at the movies. Talking about the way being a critical spectator of Hollywood films influenced her, black woman filmmaker Julie Dash exclaims, "I make films because I was such a spectator!" Looking at Hollywood cinema from a distance, from that critical politicized standpoint that did not want to be seduced by narratives reproducing her negation, Dash watched mainstream movies over and over again for the pleasure of deconstructing them. And of course there is that added delight if one happens, in the process of interrogation, to come across a narrative that invites the black female spectator to engage the text with no threat of violation.

Significantly, I began to write film criticism in response to the first Spike Lee movie, *She's Gotta Have It,* contesting Lee's replication of mainstream patriarchal cinematic practices that explicitly represents woman (in this instance black woman) as the object of a phallocentric gaze. Lee's investment in patriarchal filmic practices that mirror dominant patterns makes him the perfect black candidate for entrance to the Hollywood canon. His work mimics the cinematic construction of white womanhood as object, replacing her body as text on which to write male desire with the black female body. It is transference without transformation. Entering the discourse of film criticism from the politicized location of resistance, of not wanting, as a working-class black woman I interviewed stated, "to see black women in the position white women have occupied in film forever," I began to think critically about black female spectatorship.

For years I went to independent and/or foreign films where I was the only black female present in the theater. I often imagined that in every theater in the United States there was another black woman watching the same film wondering why she was the only visible black female spectator. I remember trying to share with one of my five sisters the cinema I liked so much. She was "enraged" that I brought her to a theater where she would have to read subtitles. To her it was a violation of Hollywood notions of spectatorship, of coming to the movies to be entertained. When I interviewed her to ask what had changed her mind over the years, led her to embrace this cinema, she connected it to coming to critical consciousness, saying, "I learned that there was more to looking than I had been exposed to in ordinary (Hollywood) movies." I shared that though most of the films I loved were all white, I could engage them because they did not have in their deep structure a subtext reproducing the narrative of white supremacy. Her response was to say that these films demystified "whiteness," since the lives they depicted seemed less rooted in fantasies of escape. They were, she suggested, more like "what we knew life to be, the deeper side of life as well." Always more seduced and enchanted with Hollywood cinema than I, she stressed that unaware black female spectators must "break out," no longer be imprisoned by images that enact a drama of our negation. Though she still sees Hollywood films, because "they are a major influence in the culture"—she no longer feels duped or victimized.

Talking with black female spectators, looking at written discussions either in fiction or academic essays about black women, I noted the connection made between the realm of representation in mass media and the capacity of black women to construct ourselves as subjects in daily life. The extent to which black women feel devalued, objectified, dehumanized in this society determines the scope and texture of their looking relations. Those black women whose identities were constructed in resistance, by practices that oppose the dominant order, were most inclined to develop an oppositional gaze. Now that there is a growing interest in films produced by black women and those films have become more accessible to viewers, it is possible to talk about black female spectatorship in relation to that work. So far, most discussions of black spectatorship that I have come across focus on men. In "Black Spectatorship: Problems of Identification and Resistance" Manthia Diawara suggests that "the components of 'difference' " among elements of sex, gender, and sexuality give rise to different readings of the same material, adding that these conditions produce a "resisting" spectator.[16] He focuses his critical discussion on black masculinity.

The recent publication of the anthology *The Female Gaze: Women as Viewers of Popular Culture* excited me, especially as it included an essay, "Black Looks," by Jacqui Roach and Petal Felix that attempts to address black female spectatorship.[17] The essay posed provocative questions that were not answered: Is there a black female gaze? How do black women relate to the gender politics of representation? Concluding, the authors assert that black females have "our own reality, our own history, our own gaze—one which sees the world rather differently from 'anyone else.' " Yet, they do not name/describe this experience of seeing "rather differently." The absence of definition and explanation suggests they are assuming an essentialist stance wherein it is presumed that black women, as victims of race and gender oppression, have an inherently different field of vision. Many black women do not "see differently" precisely because their perceptions of reality are so profoundly colonized, shaped by dominant ways of knowing. As Trinh T. Minh-ha points out in "Outside In, Inside Out": "Subjectivity does not merely consist of talking about oneself . . . be this talking indulgent or critical."[18]

Critical black female spectatorship emerges as a site of resistance only when individual black women actively resist the imposition of dominant ways of knowing and looking. While every black woman I talked to was aware of racism, that awareness did not automatically correspond with politicization, the development of an oppositional gaze. When it did, individual black women consciously named the process. Manthia Diawara's "resisting spectatorship" is a term that does not adequately describe the terrain of black female spectatorship. We do more than resist. We create alternative texts that are not solely reactions. As critical spectators, black women participate in a broad range of looking relations, contest, resist, revise, interrogate, and invent on multiple levels. Certainly when I watch the work of black women filmmakers Camille Billops, Kathleen Collins, Julie Dash, Ayoka Chenzira, Zeinabu Davis, I do not need to "resist" the images even as I still choose to watch their work with a critical eye.

Black female critical thinkers concerned with creating space for the construction of radical black female subjectivity, and the way cultural production informs this possibility, fully acknowledge the importance of mass media, film in particular, as a powerful site for critical intervention. Certainly Julie Dash's film *Illusions* identifies the terrain of Hollywood cinema as a space of knowledge production that has enormous power. Yet, she also creates a filmic narrative wherein the black female protagonist subversively claims that space. Inverting the "real-life" power structure, she offers the black female spectator representations that challenge stereotypical notions that place us outside the realm of filmic discursive practices. Within the film she uses the strategy of Hollywood suspense films to undermine those cinematic practices that deny black women a place in this structure. Problematizing the question of "racial" identity by depicting passing, suddenly it is the white male's capacity to gaze, define, and know that is called into question.

When Mary Ann Doane describes in "Woman's Stake: Filming the Female Body" the way in which feminist filmmaking practice can elaborate "a special syntax for a different articulation of the female body," she names a critical process that "undoes the structure of the classical narrative through an insistence upon its repressions." An eloquent description, this precisely names Dash's strategy in *Illusions,* even though the film is not unproblematic and works within certain conventions that are not successfully challenged. For example, the film does not indicate whether the character Mignon will make Hollywood films that subvert and transform the genre or whether she will simply assimilate and perpetuate the norm. Still, subversively, *Illusions* problematizes the issue of race and spectatorship. White people in the film are unable to "see" that race informs their looking relations. Though she is passing to gain access to the machinery of cultural production represented by film, Mignon continually asserts her ties to black community. The bond between her and the young black woman singer Ester Jeeter is affirmed by caring gestures of affirmation, often expressed by eye-to-eye contact, the direct unmediated gaze of recognition. Ironically, it is the desiring objectifying sexualized white male gaze that threatens to penetrate her "secrets" and disrupt her process. Metaphorically, Dash suggests the power of black women to make films will be threatened and undermined by that white male gaze that seeks to reinscribe the black female body in a narrative of voyeuristic pleasure where the only relevant opposition is male/female, and the only location for the female is as a victim. These tensions are not resolved by the narrative. It is not at all evident that Mignon will triumph over the white supremacist capitalist imperialist dominating "gaze."

Throughout *Illusions,* Mignon's power is affirmed by her contact with the younger black woman whom she nurtures and protects. It is this process of mirrored recognition that enables both black women to define their reality, apart from the reality imposed upon them by structures of domination. The shared gaze of the two women reinforces their solidarity. As the younger subject, Esther represents a potential audience for films that Mignon might produce, films wherein black females will be the narrative focus. Julie Dash's recent feature-length film *Daughters of the Dust* (see Fig. 6.1) dares to place black females at the center of its narrative. This focus caused critics (especially white males) to critique the film negatively or to express many reservations. Clearly, the impact of racism and sexism so overdetermine spectatorship—not

Fig. 6.1. Film still from *Daughters of the Dust* by Julie Dash. Courtesy Kino International Corporation, New York

only what we look at but whom we identify with—that viewers who are not black females find it hard to empathize with the central characters in the movie. They are adrift without a white presence in the film.

Another representation of black females nurturing one another via recognition of their common struggle for subjectivity is depicted in Sankofa's collective work *Passion of Remembrance.* In the film, two black women friends, Louise and Maggie, are from the onset of the narrative struggling with the issue of subjectivity, of their place in progressive black liberation movements that have been sexist. They challenge old norms and want to replace them with new understandings of the complexity of black identity, and the need for liberation struggles that address that complexity. Dressing to go to a party, Louise and Maggie claim the "gaze." Looking at one another, staring in mirrors, they appear completely focused on their encounter with black femaleness. How they see themselves is most important, not how they will be stared at by others. Dancing to the tune "Let's get Loose," they display their bodies not for a voyeuristic colonizing gaze but for that look of recognition that affirms their subjectivity—that constitutes them as spectators. Mutually empowered they eagerly leave the privatized domain to confront the public. Disrupting conventional racist and sexist stereotypical representations of black female bodies, these scenes invite the audience to look differently. They act to critically intervene and transform conventional filmic practices, changing notions of spectatorship. *Illusions, Daughters of the Dust,* and *A Passion of Remembrance* employ a deconstructive filmic practice to undermine existing grand cinematic narratives even as they retheorize subjectivity in the realm of the visual. Without providing "realistic" positive representations that emerge only as a response to the totalizing nature of existing narratives, they offer points of radical departure. Opening up a space for the assertion of a critical black female spectatorship, they do not simply offer diverse representations; they imagine new transgressive possibilities for the formulation of identity.

In this sense they make explicit a critical practice that provides us with different ways to think about black female subjectivity and black female spectatorship. Cinematically, they provide new points of recognition, embodying Stuart Hall's vision of a critical practice that acknowledges that identity is constituted "not outside but within representation," and invites us to see film "not as a second-order mirror held up to reflect what already exists, but as that form of representation which is able to constitute us as new kinds of subjects, and thereby enable us to discover who we are." It is this critical practice that enables production of feminist film theory that theorizes black female spectatorship. Looking and looking back, black women involve ourselves in a process whereby we see our history as countermemory, using it as a way to know the present and invent the future.

Notes

1. Frantz Fanon, *Black Skin, White Masks* (New York: Grove Press, 1967).

2. Manthia Diawara, "Black British Cinema: Spectatorship and Identity Formation in *Territories*," *Public Culture* 3, no. 1 (Fall 1990): 33–34.

3. Teresa de Lauretis, "The Technology of Gender," in *Technologies of Gender: Essays on Theory, Film, and Fiction* (Bloomington: Indiana University Press, 1987), 17.

4. Anne Friedberg, "A Denial of Difference: Theories of Cinematic Identification," in E. Ann Kaplan, ed., *Psychoanalysis and Cinema* (New York: Routledge, 1990), 45.

5. Julie Burchill, *Girls on Film* (New York: Pantheon Books, 1986), 98–100.

6. Ibid., 103.

7. Toni Morrison, *The Bluest Eye* (New York: Washington Square Press, 1972), 97.

8. Laura Mulvey, "Visual Pleasure and Narrative Cinema," in *Visual and Other Pleasures* (Bloomington: Indiana University Press, 1989), 19.

9. Annette Kuhn, *The Power of the Image: Essays on Representation and Sexuality* (London: Routledge & Kegan Paul, 1985), 8.

10. Constance Penley, ed., *Feminism and Film Theory* (New York: Routledge, 1988).

11. Mary Ann Doane, "Remembering Women: Psychical and Historical Construction in Film Theory," in Kaplan, *Psychoanalysis and Cinema*, 47.

12. Linda Peckham, "Not Speaking with Language, Speaking with No Language: Leslie Thornton's *Adynata*," in Kaplan, *Psychoanalysis and Cinema*, 181–87.

13. Anne Friedberg, "A Denial of Difference: Theories of Cinematic Identification," in Kaplan, *Psychoanalysis and Cinema*, 36.

14. Mulvey, *Visual and Other Pleasures*, xiii.

15. Mary Ann Doane, "Woman's Stake: Filming the Female Body," originally published in *October* 17 (Summer 1981), and in Constance Penley, ed., *Feminism and Film Theory* (New York: Routledge, 1988), 223.

16. Manthia Diawara, "Black Spectatorship: Problems of Identification and Resistance," *Screen* 29, no. 4 (1988): 66–76.

17. Jacqui Roach and Petal Felix, "Black Looks," in Lorraine Gamman and Margaret Marshment, eds., *The Female Gaze: Women as Viewers of Popular Culture* (London: Women's Press, 1988), 130–42.

18. Trinh T. Minh-ha, "Outside In, Inside Out," in Jim Pines and Paul Willemen, eds., *Questions of Third Cinema* (London: British Film Institute, 1989), 147.

7
A History of Music

Renée Lorraine

Euoi! Euoi!
—the Bacchantes

My, my, my, my . . .
—Mick Jagger

The Goddess

The Phrygians settled in ancient Anatolia (now Turkey) in the second millennium B.C.E., probably from Macedonia and Thrace, and dominated Asia Minor from the thirteenth to the seventh century B.C.E., when they were defeated by the Cimmerians. Phrygians left magnificent tombs and shrines. They were highly proficient at building and fortification techniques, at wood and ivory carving, at bronzework and metallurgy. It is said that the Phrygians invented the clasp and the art of embroidery. They were weavers of mohair, hemp, linen, and tapestry, and wove the antecedents of our Persian carpets. Their pottery was decorated with animals and birds, geometric patterns, swastikas, mazes, and lozenges. Their clothing was colorful and highly decorated with patterns and tassels. They were considered to be exceptional musicians, and were believed by the Greeks to be the inventors of the flute, the cymbals, the triangle, and the syrinx. Because they were considered to be refined and artistic, they were favored by the Greeks and Romans as slaves. But the Phrygian cap, a soft, fitted cap with a pointed crown that curls forward, became a symbol of resistance, and was worn by emancipated slaves in Greece and Rome.[1] (Later, the Phrygian cap became a symbol of emancipation in the French Revolution.)

Spinning, weaving, metallurgy, music, and dancing were all associated with the principal deity of Phrygia, the Great Goddess Kubile, Kubaba or Matar Kubile, Mother of all deities, humans and beasts, Goddess of life, death, and regeneration. Kubile was called Cybele or Cybebe by the Greeks, Kybele by the Lydians, Mater Deum Magna Ideae by the Romans, and was also worshiped in Lycia, Thrace, Syria, Phoenecia, North Africa, Spain, Gaul, Britain, and Germany. (In Rome, Cybele was also known as the Berecynthian Mother, Augusta the Great One, Alma the Nourishing One, Sanctissima the Most Holy One, and as Rhea Lobrine, Goddess of sacred caves. The Goddess is both one and many; the names of the Goddess in her various manifestations of Maiden, Mother, or Crone include Britomartis, Dictynna, Mâ, Dindymene, Hecate, Gaia, Pheraia, Artemis, Baubo, Aphaia, Ortheia, Nemesis, Demeter, Persephone, Selene, Medusa, Eleuthera, Leto, Hera, Aphrodite, Bendis, Hathor, Taeit, and Isis.[2] In some manifestations the Goddess is the earth or the universe itself, space and time and all within it, and is beyond male and female, beyond all dualities.) Kubile is a Mountain Mother or Goddess, and sometimes takes the form of a mountain. Anthropomorphic sculptures and wall carvings of Kubile show her flanked by lions or leopards, or holding a lion in her lap. (Representations of the Great Goddess flanked by lions or leopards in Anatolia date back to the sixth millennium B.C.E. The Goddess is also seen and associated with birds, serpents, or the moon. Later, the goddess in her bird form is transformed into a siren or a harpy; the serpent, also associated with Dionysus and Attis, becomes a symbol of evil; and the moon is thought to give rise to insanity, especially in women.) The Goddess and music is "an ever-recurring combination." Kubile or her attendants are often depicted with drums, double aulos, lyre, flute, syrinx, castanets, and especially cymbals and tambourine. Her attendant Maenads (mad ones) are often dancing, and it was said that the dance Kubile taught the Corybantes could cure mental illness. (In the worship of the Goddess, healing, spirituality, and the erotic are all associated with music and dancing.)

The Phrygians also worshiped Dionysus, a consort of the Goddess thought to have originated in Phrygia or Thrace. Dionysus, a nature god of vegetation and especially wine and ecstasy, is the son of Semele, a Phrygian earth goddess. (In one of his oldest forms Dionysus is the horned Dionysus Melanaigis, Dionysus of the Black Goatskin. The Dionysian dithyramb was sung and danced to the Phrygian mode and melodies.) Dionysus had many converts among women, who were said to abandon their families to join his worshipers. Among these worshipers were Maenads or (Roman) Bacchantes, a group of women who had occult powers, could charm snakes and suckle animals, and had great physical strength. (Bacchantes were sometimes referred to as "mothers." The Greeks and Romans claimed that the Bacchantes would tear to pieces any man who dared witness their ritual.) Wearing faunskins and crowns of ivy, they danced by torchlight to the rhythm of the cymbals, aulos, and drum, crying "Euoi! Euoi!" Their dance was enhanced by the consumption of spotted toadstools that induced altered states of consciousness and qualities associated with Dionysus and the Goddess herself: great strength, erotic power, visions, the gift of prophecy, the power of healing, and collectivity.

The Decline of the Goddess

When the Ionians, Acheans, and Dorians invaded Mycenea (Greece) from c. 2500 to c. 1000 B.C.E., they brought with them worship of the thunderbolt god Zeus and a patriarchal order. (The name "Zeus" derives from a word meaning "sky" or "heaven." An earlier Zeus of Crete is a young consort of the Goddess.) Unable to eradicate worship of the various aspects of the Great Goddess, they instead appropriated and subordinated them. Zeus rapes them, fathers them, marries them. The powerful Great Goddess Hera, worshiped long before Zeus, becomes his petty and jealous wife. (Jane Ellen Harrison tells us that Hera represents a matrilinear system, and that Zeus and Hera's marital difficulties show that she was "coerced, but never really subdued by an alien conqueror.")[3] The moon and snake Goddess Athena, peaceful protectress of the home and town, patroness of wisdom, arts, and skills, becomes martial and motherless, springing fully armored from the head of Zeus, representing cool reason, and siding with the gods against women. (Athena was the special protectress of spinners and weavers, but when Arachne weaves a tapestry superior to that of Athena, a tapestry with scenes critical of the gods, Athena tears it to shreds and turns Arachne into a spider.) Aphrodite, a Great Mother associated with powerful procreative energy, is now the daughter of Zeus and Dionne, is married to the vulgar fire god Hephaestus, and becomes temptress, seductress. The many-breasted Artemis, Goddess of fertile motherhood, becomes the embodiment of chastity. Pandora, the Maiden aspect of the Goddess who is giver of all gifts and abundance, becomes bringer of disease, pain, death. Zeus seduces Semele, no longer a goddess but a mortal, and becomes the father of the once fatherless Vine-Dionysus. (When Semele asks to see Zeus in his god-form, she is killed by magnitude of this presence, and fetus Dionysus is transferred to and gestates in Zeus's thigh.)

And Zeus rapes Kubile, and she gives birth to a hermaphroditic being named Agdistis, a being later castrated by Dionysus. Agdistis comes to love Attis, consort of Kubile. (Although Kubile is often presented as independent of any male demiurge, in some traditions she is accompanied by Attis, her son or lover. Like Dionysus, Adonis, Linus, and Osiris, Attis is a vegetation god who is resurrected after his death.[4] In sculpture and carvings, Attis is almost always much smaller than the Goddess, is feminine in appearance, and is often playing instruments or dancing for her or by himself. He sometimes wears a crown of poppies, pinecones, flowers, and corn ears.) When Attis becomes involved with another woman, he is driven mad by the wrath of Agdistis and castrates himself under a pine tree. (After the image and sacred stone of Kubile were transported to Rome in 204 B.C.E. from Pessinus,[5] Agdistis is equated with Kubile/Cybele, and the Goddess's high priests, called galli or "cocks," castrated themselves in the frenzy of their worship. There is no mention of such practices in the descriptions of the rites of the Goddess in Phrygia.)[6]

The Dorian invasion was followed by a cultural dark age. The Spartan Dorians, who gave first priority to their military, attempted to eradicate music, dancing, and poetry on the grounds that they gave rise to effeminacy. But gradually the Dorians advanced the worship of Apollo, and were early influences on the development of classical Greek art. (Originally, Apollo was the son of the Moon Goddess Artemis; later he became her twin, appropriated her lyre, and laid claim to her powers of prophecy, music, poetry, magic, and healing. Apollo also adopted the Muses and the Graces as his own, and slew the Serpent who guarded the shrine at Delphi, the shrine that belonged to the earth Goddess Gaia or Rhea, and confiscated the shrine's oracle for himself. Nietzsche tells us that Apollo represents light, measure, restraint, individuation. Apollonian art draws an aesthetic veil over reality, creating an ideal world of form and beauty. The Apollonian tendency is best manifested in the plastic arts, and is timeless and eternal. Dionysus, in contrast, represents the process of life, breaking down barriers and ignoring restraints, becoming one with Primordial Unity. Dionysian art embraces existence in all its darkness and horror. It is constantly changing, and takes the form of music and tragedy. Nietzsche does not mention that Dionysus was a consort of the Goddess.)[7]

Even in the late archaic age, an age of Zeus and Apollo, women continued to worship the Goddess and lament the dying god with music, lyric, and dance.

Among these are Phantasia of Memphis, Megolastrata of Sparta, Telesilla of Argos, Corinna of Boetia, Praxilla of Sicyon, and Sappho and Erinna of Lesbos in Asia Minor. Sappho (sixth century B.C.E.) was admired for her vernacular, personal songs about love ("Love shook my heart, like a wind falling on oaks on the mountain"), her intimate appeals to Aphrodite, her songs of the moon.[8] She accompanied herself with the Lydian pectis (harp), barbitos (lyre) and magadis, is said to have developed the Mixolydian mode, and used the "woman's hexameter" (reportedly developed by Phantasia and Themis) or freer meters of her own devising. There were many women's choirs in this age, women sang, played instruments and danced in religious festivals and dramas, and working women had songs for winnowing, reaping, baking, water-gathering and the mill. But gradually men took over the women's choirs and religious rituals, and women were barred from the choral dramas. (The great tragedies or "goat songs" of the classical age were associated with Dionysus, but the female characters were sung and enacted by men. In one of these dramas, Euripedes gives voice to the Bacchantes:

> When will I dance once more
> with bare feet the all-night dances
> tossing my head for joy
> in the damp air, in the dew
> as a running fawn might frisk
> for the green joy of the wide fields, . . .
> to dance for joy in the forest,
> to dance where the darkness is deepest,
>   where no man is.[9]

Socrates tells us that the Mixolydian and "intense Lydian" mode, and others similar, should be done away with; for "they are useless even to women who are to make the best of themselves, let alone to men." Their soft harmonies, he believes, give rise to drunkenness, softness, and sloth. He prefers a harmony that "would fittingly imitate the utterances and the accents of a brave man who is engaged in warfare or in any enforced business." (The Lydians were neighbors of the Phrygians and worshiped the Goddess.) Socrates prefers the instruments of Apollo to those of Marsyas, a Phrygian satyr said to have invented the syrinx, who was slain when he lost a music contest with Apollo. (And Socrates also says that the love of Aphrodite is insanity, madness, licentiousness. The right love is a sober and harmonious love of the orderly and beautiful.)

Aristotle tells us that professional musicians are vulgar, that performing music is unmanly, except when drunk or for fun. And be believes the Phrygian mode should not be allowed, "for the Phrygian harmony has the same effect among harmonies as the aulos among instruments—both are violently exciting and emotional. This is shown by poetry; for all Bacchic versification and all movement of that sort belong particularly to the aulos among the instruments, and these metres find their suitable accompaniment in melodies in the Phrygian harmony." And all agree, Aristotle continues, "that the Dorian harmony is more sedate and of a specially manly character."

Atheneus (c. 200 c.e.) tells us that the Phrygians sang "in honor of the Mountain Mother, amid the auloi," and that storax, burned as incense at the festivals of Dionysus, produces a "Phrygian odor" to those who smell it. Clement of Alexandria (c. 200 c.e.) says of tragedians and poets, "who are altogether like drunken men, let us wreathe them, if you like, with ivy, while they are performing the mad revels of the Bacchic rite, and shut them up, satyrs and frenzied rout and all." Clement derides a Scythian for "beating upon a typanum and like some priest of Cybele sounding a cymbal which hung from his neck," for "he had become unmanly among the Greeks and a teacher of the disease of effeminacy." Basil the Great of Asia Minor (330–379) recounts that Pythagoras sobered some drunken revelers by having an aulete play for them in the Dorian mode. And Boethius (c. 600 c.e.) tells us that the ancient Timotheus angered the Spartans by playing complex rhythms and harmonies, by using the chromatic genus "which is more effeminate," and by singing of the myth of the pangs of Semele. And he tells of a youth excited by the Phrygian mode who had locked himself in a room with a harlot with plans to burn down the house, and he tells how this youth's fury was reduced to a perfect state of calm when Pythagoras played a melody in an orderly, spondaic rhythm.[10]

The Fathers of the early Catholic Church revered spirit, reason, and heaven, disdained body, fleshly passion, and earth. And they associated body with woman. Philo, the first-century Jewish philosopher, was influential in identifying the female with the material, passive, corporeal, and sense-perceptible, the male with the active, rational, and incorporeal.[11] For Saint Augustine (354–430), both Adam and Eve were a compound of spirit and corporeality, and both were capable of reason. But spirit is male and corporeality female, and Eve represents body relative to Adam. Because the body must be subjugated by the spirit, woman should be subjugated by man, and man must "hate in her the corruptible and mortal conjugal connection, sexual intercourse and all that pertains to her as a wife."[12] (Augustine thought the best representative of bodily sense was the serpent. And he called Cybele a harlot mother, a mother of demons.)[13] For Leander of Seville, woman could be freed from the curse of Eve only through virginity; for the virgin "lives in manly vigor and has used virtue to give strength to her weak sex, nor has she become a slave to her body, which, by natural law, should have been subservient to a man." Saint Jerome (341–420) believed that "as long as woman is for birth and children, she is different from man as body is from soul. But when she wishes to serve Christ more than the world, then she will cease to be a woman and will be called a man." He counseled young women to remain virgins, and to be trained in the "angelic life," which "while in the body lives as though it were without flesh." Monks were warned in the fourth and fifth centuries that "the flesh of all women is fire," and to avoid the touch, the sight, the sound of women.[14] (Caroline Walker Bynum suggests that in the late Middle Ages the spiritual expressions of male and female medieval mystics were different, "and this difference has something to do with the body. Women were more apt to somatize religious experience and to write in intense bodily metaphors; women mystics were more likely than men to receive graphically physical visions of God; both men and women were inclined to attribute to women and encourage in them intense asceticisms and ecstasies.")[15]

The early Church Fathers advocated the singing of psalms, later called plainchant. Saint Basil (c. 330–379) counsels that "if somewhere one who rages like a wild beast from excessive anger falls under the spell of the psalm, he straightway departs, with the fierceness of his soul calmed by the melody. . . . A psalm is the work of the angels, the ordinance of Heaven, the incense of the Spirit." And Basil recommends the psaltery (a plucked string instrument) among instruments, which "has the origins of its harmonious rhythms above, in order that we may study to seek for those things which are on high and not be drawn down by the pleasantness of the melody to the passions of the flesh." Saint John Chrysostom (c. 337–407) tells us that "women, travelers, peasants and sailors" strive

> to lighten with a chant the labor endured in working. . . . Inasmuch as this kind of pleasure is thoroughly innate to our mind, and lest demons introducing lascivious songs should overthrow everything, God established the psalms. . . . And as swine flock together where there is a mire, but where there is aroma and incense there bees abide, so demons congregate where there are licentious chants, but where

there are spiritual ones there the grace of the Spirit descends, sanctifying mouth and mind.

John cautions that there is no need for cithara or any other instrument to accompany the psalms; "but, if you like, you may yourself become a cithara, mortifying the members of the flesh. . . . For when the flesh no longer lusts against the Spirit, but has submitted to its orders . . . then will you create a spiritual melody." Gregory of Nyssa (c. 330–c.395) suggests that the psalms can transport us to the stable, "pure" time of the Garden, and away from the "treadmill" of earth time since the Fall. (Plainchant is generally performed without meter, and was to be sung, according to Augustine, with a "fluent voice." Plainchant does not engage the body, is music of the sprit, offers a glimpse of "angelic life.")[16]

Psalm singing by women was common in the early centuries of the Christian era and was praised by Saint Jerome, Saint Augustine, Saint Zenobi, Saint Gregory of Naziana, and Saint Ambrose. But in the fourth century Church Fathers banned psalm singing by women in church. Cyril of Jerusalem (c. 315–386) writes that women should recite psalms quietly, "so that their lips move, but the ears of others do not hear." Jerome recommends that women "sing the psalms in their chambers, away from the company of men and the crowded assembly." And Isidore of Pelusium (died c. 435) determines that

> the apostles of the Lord, who wanted to put an end to idle talk in the Churches, and who were our instructors in good behavior, wisely permitted women to sing psalms there. But as every divine teaching has been turned into its opposite, so this, too, has become an occasion of sin and laxity for the majority of the people. They do not feel compunction in hearing the divine hymn, but rather misuse the sweetness of melody to arouse passion. . . . Thus it is necessary . . . that we stop these women both from singing in church, and also from loitering in the city as if they were innkeepers to Christ.[17]

(Later in the twelfth century, beautiful and innovative plainchants were composed by the visionary abbess Hildegard of Bingen, who believed that "divinity is to humanity as male is to female," and once wrote "I am wretched and more than wretched in my existence as a woman.")[18]

Religious dances comparable to pagan rituals were performed in the first three centuries of the Church by the Theraputae, the Kollyridians, the Marianites, and the Gnostics. These sects were influenced by the Goddess traditions, and their religious dancing was associated mainly with women. Saint John Chrysostom: "If neither girls nor married women may dance, then who will dance? No one.")[19] As might be expected, these practices were also condemned by the Church. Thus Saint Basil complains that women defile the shrines of martyrs at the Easter vigil:

> These licentious women . . . having cast the veils of modesty from their heads, showing contempt for God and for his angels, shamelessly in the sight of every man, shake their hair, as with wanton eye and excessive laughter they are driven madly to dance . . . they form a dancing troop in the martyr's shrines before the city, making of these holy places a workshop of their characteristic indecency; they defile the air with their harlot's songs, they defile the ground with their unclean feet.

There was particular concern expressed about dancing, singing, and instrument playing outside the Church, which was regularly deemed lascivious, pernicious, and effeminate. In a second-century description of Church ritual, Christians are distinguished from pagans in that they "pour no blood on altars in sacrificial libations / The tympanum sounds not nor does the cymbal, / Nor does the much pierced aulos with its frenzied voice, / Nor the syrinx, bearing the likeness of a crooked serpent." Clement of Alexandria complains of "maenads who perform the unholy initiatory rite of the division of the flesh," of those "defiling themselves with dancing, drunkenness and every sort of trash," of chromatic, pliant harmonies and the "erotic wailing of the aulos." Arnobius (died c. 330) laments that "lascivious souls abandon themselves to bizarre movements of the body, dancing and singing, forming rings of dancers, and ultimately raising their buttocks and hips to sway with the rippling motion of their loins." Gregory of Nazianzus (c. 329–389) offers a list of questions to ask one's soul, including "Do you desire the striking of hands upon barbitons and the way it excites? Do you want the breaking voices of pretty boys moving effeminately? And the indecent convolutions of naked maidens?" Saint Basil complains that "the more people hear lascivious and pernicious songs, which raise in their souls impure and voluptuous desires, they more they want to hear." The Fathers were especially disturbed by women singers and dancers, and it was warned that "those who delight their eyes and ears on such spectacles commit adultery." Basil tells us that a woman who plays the lyre rather than weaving "is a sorry sight for sober eyes," and a Canon of Laodicea (fourth century) declares that a "woman who dances in a tavern and who entices people through pretty singing and sweet sound, which is deceitful and full of seduction, shall, if she gives up this profession, wait forty days before she communicates; then she may receive the mysteries."[20] Little is known of this music and dance before the tenth century; songs were transmitted orally, and medieval scholars wrote little about the music itself. There are numerous reports of women singing and dancing in the late Middle Ages, and regular protests by the Church continue.[21] The dance songs of the male and female jongleurs and troubadours are notable for their woman's voice, a voice offering invitations to love, enjoy life, and resist jealous husbands: "Ha! ha! here doth come the king! eya! What a temper he doth bring! eya! Bids us dancers break our ring! eya! Lest his lady have her fling. . . . Jealousy, Haaie begone, / Go we now, go we now a dancing our own way, our own way."[22] Other songs of the goliards, jongleurs, troubadours, and trouvères, songs inscribed predominantly by males, were of spring, nature, gambling, drinking and feasting, of morality, religion and politics, but mainly of love: sensual desires, lovesickness and rejection, a lady's power. Some of these songs were misogynist, some were sexually explicit, some were respectful of a lady of high virtue, some idealized woman or the Virgin.[23] Clerics were sometimes entertained by secular musicians; and in music as in general, it is often difficult to distinguish sacred and secular in the medieval era. Yet secular music was repeatedly denounced by the Church. The music was disturbing and exciting, likely to engage the body and stimulate the bodily passions. It was rhythmic, somewhat improvisatory, moving from the Church modes toward major and minor, and often accompanied by instruments and associated with dancing.[24] And the lyrics were most likely to deal with woman: woman and love, woman and sensuality, woman and the body.

The Goddess Destroyed

Johann Josef Schikaneder's libretto to Mozart's *Die Zauberflöte* is based on a fairy tale from Asia minor entitled *Lulu, or The Magic Flute.* In *Lulu,* young prince Lulu is given a magic flute by a good fairy whose daughter has been kidnapped by an evil wizard. Lulu enchants the wizard with the flute and escapes with the daughter, and the fairy then plays the flute over the wizard's castle and reduces it to nothingness. But Schikenader and Mozart were both familiar with classical mythology and were both loyal Freemasons, and they transformed the tale to suit their philosophies. (A prominent Mason once inscribed Mozart's autograph book with a prayer to Apollo.) The good fairy becomes the dark, evil Queen of the Night, associated with the earth and the moon, a matriarch who lives in a mountain. Her terrain is rocky and wild, and she enters from and descends into the earth accompanied by thunder and lightning. She was once married to the Priest of the Sun, and she expected that her sovereignty would descend matrilineally to their daughter Pamina. But the Priest rebels by giving the Sevenfold Circle of the Sun to Sarastro, depriving the moon-Queen of her sun, and robbing her of her power. (Before he dies, the Priest tells the Queen that matters of the Sun "are not accessible to your woman's spirit. Your duty is to submit yourself completely, and your daughter also, to the direction of the Wise Men.") It is Sarastro who has Pamina abducted, but he is now no evil wizard but good, wise and noble. (The "abduction is placed in the month of springtime blossoming, of the powerful renascence under the sign of Apollo, the solar god, and under the name of Maia (Cybele), goddess of creative nature.") He takes Pamina in order to mate her with an initiate of the Sun Temple, and thus establish a patrilineal and patriarchal base for the integration of night and day. (In Masonic symbolism, day and night, sun and moon are symbols of the masculine and feminine respectively. Other Masonic dualities associated with the masculine and feminine respectively are the Egyptian deities Osiris and Isis, fire and water, gold and silver, active and passive, red and black, elucidation and discourse, bull and twins, 3 and 5. Jacques Chailly tells us that 5 is the number of the goddess Aphrodite, and represents the union of the "schizogenetic" female number 2 and the "complete" male number 3.)[25]

This initiate is Tamino, whom we first see near the Queen's circular castle battling a serpent. (In the Asian fairy tale there were lions to battle, but Schikeneder wanted lions associated with Sarastro.) The serpent is subdued and cut into three pieces by three ladies armed with silver javelins, servants of the Queen. The Queen sings plaintively to Tamino of Pamina's abduction, and vows that if he rescues her Pamina will be his. To aid him in his search, Tamino is given a magic flute that can charm and enchant animals and people, and three boys (genii) who carry the T-square, the ruler, and the compass, and represent Strength, Beauty, and Wisdom. (Later we learn that the boys are allied with the Kingdom of the Sun. Some scholars have suggested it is incongruous for the Queen and her servants to give Tamino a magic flute whose power will later be used to defeat them. But it is fitting that the healing power of music would be associated with the matriarch.) Tamino's comic sidekick Papageno, who ordinarily plays panpipes (*Waldflöten or Faunenflöten*) is given some magic bells that are later used to enchant Monostatos, whom

Sarastro employs to kidnap Pamina. (Monostatos, a moor with "a soul as black as his face," thinks only of sex, believes "white is beautiful" and wants to rape the white woman Pamina, and is later cast into darkness with the Queen. Monostatos and Papageno, the two men associated with the Queen, are weak, pathetic, easily frightened. When Papageno is told by Tamino to act like a man, he says he would rather be a girl.)

When Tamino enters Sarastro's realm, he and Pamina undergo initiation trials. (It has been suggested that these trials are not real but are trials of the inner being. The concrete realm of the Queen would thus be opposed by the spiritual realm of the Sun.) Tamino and Pamina are taken to a point between two mountains. One contains a red, fiery furnace, the other a waterfall surrounded by black clouds, thus uniting Masonic symbols of the masculine and feminine. But the feminine is maligned in various ways throughout the trials and throughout the opera. Tamino is told by Sarastro's priests not to trust women and their idle chatter, and again later to beware of woman's falsehoods and deceptions. Tamino then counsels Papageno that no credence is due women's babbling talk. Pamina is told that it is man who must guide her heart to reason, and that without his guidance woman will overstep her bounds and end in folly. A quintet consisting of Tamino, Papageno, and the three ladies sing that (unlike women), men are firm of purpose, and think before they speak. The ladies are then banished for profaning the sacred precincts of the Sun with their presence. (A Masonic constitution of 1723 limits admission to "men of good reputation" and excludes "slaves, women, and immoral or disgraced men." And the padlock Papageno wears on his mouth to help him learn not to babble like women is representative of an initiation rite for female companions in which their mouths were sealed with trowels to place them on guard against the idle chatter native to their sex.)[26] And although Pamina is initiated along with Tamino and the two will rule the Kingdom of the Sun together, the sacred marriage of sun and moon, day and night, is not a marriage of equals. It is more like the marriage of Zeus and Hera, except that unlike Hera, Pamina is "subdued by an alien conqueror." The Queen is destroyed, and Pamina and the powers of the night are appropriated and subordinated.[27]

These dynamics are powerfully enhanced by Mozart's music. The opera begins and ends in E-flat major, with the E-flat symbolizing the male principle in Masonry. The Queen sings predominantly in the minor mode, and often chromatically. Her phrases tend to be irregular, relatively long, and complex, and her vocal lines are ornate and dramatic. Her music has a strong forward thrust rhythmically, and the full orchestral accompaniment is marked by

tremolos, sfortzandos, fortepianos, crescendos, and diminuendos, and dissonant, diminished triads and seventh chords. All of this makes the music brilliant
and exciting, but unsettling; especially in her second, D-minor aria (no. 14)
there is a rhythmic, harmonic, and melodic instability that leads us to seek
resolution. The stability and resolution we crave is best found in the music of
Sarastro and his priests, who sing predominantly in C and F major. (Rita
Steblin tells us that in *Die Zauberflöte,* as in Haydn's *Creation,* C major is the
key of light, understanding, and intellectual enlightenment.)[28] Sarastro and his
priests sing diatonically, often with perfect four-bar phrases, a predominance
of winds, conventional chord progressions, simple melodies and accompani-
ments, and regular rhythms. There is little or no rhythmic or harmonic thrust,
giving the music a static quality, and a sense of peace, balance, order, and
control. (Paul Nettl describes Sarastro's music, with its "lofty arches of
melody, large intervals, serious song-like melodies reminiscent of the old
choral music, quiet simple rhythms" as "humanist.")[29]

Tamino's first aria, in E-flat major, is chromatic and ornate when he sings of
love. But as he learns the principles of the Kingdom of the Sun, his music
becomes diatonic, stately, regular. This tendency to conform musically, to
move musically from instability and darkness to clarity and light, is also evident
in the music of Pamina. In the one aria Pamina sings alone (in G minor, the
original key of the Queen) her music is minor, chromatic, dissonant, florid, and
rhythmically complex. (The postlude to this aria, an aria in which Pamina
expresses her fear that she has lost Tamino, mixes sextuple and triple meters,
probably representing Pamina's frustration and confusion.) When she sings
with men, in contrast, and especially when her initiation is complete, her music
is major and diatonic, with regular phrases and rhythms. Pamina's conversion
is best illustrated in the music for her initiation. Weak-willed and fearful, her
music is initially highly chromatic, predominantly in G minor, and with long
complex phrases, wide leaps and dissonances. Yet as she is advised and
reassured by the three boys and gradually comes to see the light, the music
moves to a simple, diatonic E-flat major. (The move from darkness to light in
the opera is captured in microcosm in the Overture. After the three opening
chords in E-flat major, the Adagio is characterized by tonal instability and a
Sturm und Drang style, while the ensuing Allegro is clear, square, and
predominantly diatonic.)

The ultimate resolution of the opera comes when the Queen and her
attendants are banished once and for all into the night. Accompanied by forte
diminished seventh chords in the orchestra and thunder and lightning on stage,
the forces of darkness cry out "Destroyed forever is our power" to the

consecutive tones of a diminished seventh, and disappear into the earth. The music gradually moves to B-flat major and then to E-flat major for the final hymn of thanks and praise to Isis and Osiris. The stage, say Schikenader's directions, is transformed into a sun. And rapt listeners and spectators have been provided with the dramatic and musical resolution they have wanted, consciously or unconsciously, ever since the first appearance of the Queen.

Women are life's music.
—Richard Wagner[30]

Wagner's *Tannhäuser* was based principally on the sixteenth-century legend of the medieval minnesinger Tanhäuser or Danhäuser, and on the legend of the song contest of minnesingers at the Wartburg. Wagner knew the Renaissance legend and various nineteenth-century versions of Tannhäuser, in which the medieval knight Tannhäuser seeks redemption from the Pope after having partaken of the sensual delights of Venus (Aphrodite), the goddess of love.[31] The Pope tells Tannhäuser that he will not be forgiven unless the dry twig or staff he holds in his hand sprouts green leaves; later the twig actually sprouts, but Tannhäuser has returned to Venus's mountain and cannot be found. (In the legend and in Wagner's opera, Venus lives in a mountain.) The Wartburg legend, which contains no mention of Tannhäuser, includes the story of the virtuous Elizabeth, daughter of the king of Hungary, who performed miracles and became a saint. Combining the two legends, Wagner's opera focuses on the tension Tannhäuser feels between his desire for Venus and his love for the chaste maiden Elizabeth. (Wagner's character of Elizabeth was also inspired by Carlo Dolci's "Madonna," which he saw at the Aussig parish church.) Though *Tannhäuser* is based mainly on German legend, however, it also reflects Wagner's avid interest in and thorough knowledge of Greek mythology. (Wagner writes at the time that "after it had overcome the raw religion of its Asiatic birth-place, built upon the nature-forces of the earth . . . the Grecian spirit, at the flowering time of its art and polity, found its fullest expression in the god Apollo, the head and national deity of the Hellenic race. It was Apollo, —he who had slain the Python, the dragon of chaos; . . . it was this Apollo who was the fulfiller of the will of Zeus upon the Grecian earth." And Wagner tells us that the story of *Lohengrin,* in which Elsa loses Lohengrin by asking him to reveal his identity, is based on the myth of Zeus and Semele. Thomas Mann has suggested, however, that in the later music drama *Tristan und Isolde,* Wagner celebrates the cult of the night: The "pronounced ascendancy of the day's 'more lovely half,' the night, is archetypally, quintessentially Romantic; in this, Romanticism is closely allied to the whole mythical complex of mother-moon cults, which have always been contrasted, since the beginnings of civilization, with sun worship, the religion of light as the male-paternal element; and it is within the general orbit of this world that Wagner's *Tristan* is firmly located.")[32]

Wagner's *Tannhäuser* begins in a womblike cavern inside the Venusberg. (Wagner originally planned to title the opera *Der Venusberg*. Wagner's conception of Venus's mountain was loosely based on the German legend of the Hörselberg, where the devil and his witches live amid flames and howls of the damned.) The Venusberg is ruled by the goddess of love, and is rife with sirens, Bacchantes, naïads, nymphs, satyrs, fauns, cupids, graces, and youths. The light is dim and rosy and the air is permeated by a blue vapor. Naïads are bathing in a lake; sirens are reclining on its banks. Venus is reclining on a couch, surrounded by cupids, and Tannhäuser kneels before her, his harp in his hand and his head on her lap. Nymphs, Bacchantes, satyrs, and fauns dance a wild dance that escalates into frenzy and induces Tannhäuser and Venus to embrace passionately. But Tannhäuser suddenly awakens as if from a dream, and sings that he is weary of continuous pleasure, misses the sunlight, longs to return to the sufferings and joys of the world of men. Venus expresses anger, then uses all of her wiles to keep Tannhäuser with her; she reminds him that with her, he is part of the divine. Yet Tannhäuser is insistent, and with condemnations and warnings, is at last allowed to leave.

Without changing his position, Tannhäuser suddenly finds himself in the bright light of day, and is touched by the sight of a shrine to the Virgin and by the song of a young shepherd. Tannhäuser's fellow minnesingers are happy to see him again, and invite him to participate in a song contest. The chaste maiden Elizabeth, whom all of the minnesingers worship from afar, is overjoyed to see him. In Tannhäuser's absence her heart was closed to joy and song, but now she looks forward to hearing Tannhäuser perform. Unfortunately for Tannhäuser, the contest songs are minnesongs, songs of love, and he cannot resist singing that none of the other minnesingers could possibly know what love is unless they have experienced the delights of Venus. The assembly reacts to this revelation with revulsion, and swords are drawn to punish Tannhäuser for his sins. But Elizabeth, though crushed, loves Tannhäuser and shields him with her body. This action by such a pure maiden is taken as a sign from heaven, and it is decided that Tannhäuser should be taken to Rome to seek forgiveness from the Pope. The Pope tells Tannhäuser forgiveness will come only when his staff sprouts, and the wretched Tannhäuser plans to return to the Venusberg. He beckons Venus with his song, and is about to melt into her arms when one of Tannhäuser's fellow minnesingers cries out the name of Elizabeth. On the very mention of Elizabeth's name, Venus and her attendants are defeated and disappear. For Elizabeth is now an angel, has prayed herself to death, has died praying to the Virgin for Tannhäuser's redemption. Tannhäuser praises Elizabeth, and amidst songs of pilgrims, dies himself; because of Elizabeth's prayers, because of Elizabeth's death, he enters eternal bliss, not the cyclical sexual bliss of Venus but the pure, stable bliss of heaven.[33] (In an earlier opera, the Flying Dutchman is also redeemed through the death of a loving and faithful woman. And Wagner writes of "a *Woman* who, of very love, shall sacrifice herself" for man. She is "the longed-for, the dreamt-of, the infinitely womanly Woman—let me out with it in one word: *the Woman of the Future.*")[34]

The music of the Venus and the Venusburg is highly chromatic. (Catherine Clément has pointed out that in Wagner, chromaticism is associated with pain, anguish, and death, but also with feminine sexuality. And because feminine sexuality is regarded as both highly attractive and odorous, wonderful and stinking, chromaticism is exciting yet stinking, suggestive of feminine stink.[35] And I remember that Boethius considered chromaticism effeminate, and that chromaticism is associated with love, pain, and death in the Italian madrigals of the late sixteenth century.) The music is beautiful, often square and in the major mode, sometimes diatonic. But melody and harmony are entangled, rhythms are irregular, and the music is spiced and intensified with diminished triads and sevenths, dissonances, deceptive cadences, tonal ambiguity, and chromatic melody and harmony.[36] (This tonal instability is also suggested in the opening music of the sirens, who first sing a sweet, radiant triad, but move to a harsh dissonance and then to a diminished seventh chord that never seems to resolve.) The music is further intensified by a predominance of third relations, moves to harmonies a third away rather than regular, stable, I–II / IV–V–I progressions. And although the music is beautiful, it seems never to achieve closure, never to rest. (Tannhäuser describes this quality of continuous beauty, continuous unrest in his song of praise to Venus in the song contest, sings of a fountain of love that rekindles desire as soon as it quenches it, that provides eternal longing and eternal bliss. And in the opening scene on the Venusberg, it is only in Tannhäuser's songs of praise that the music achieves any stability or resolution. Venus is a musical nymphomaniac, and only Tannhäuser can satisfy her desire.) Although the music of Tannhäuser himself on the Venusberg is more regular and more likely to satisfy expectations, complete resolution is found only when he leaves the Venusberg, leaves crying, "Goddess of all delights, not with thee shall my soul find its peace! My salvation lies in Mary!" The word "Mary" is accompanied by a major triad, fortissimo in the full orchestra, upon which Venus and her attendants disappear.

The music of Elizabeth, in contrast to that of Venus, is clean, square, diatonic. When Elizabeth's name is first mentioned, what has been chromatic, dissonant music suddenly resolves to a second inversion major triad, with sustained winds and harp. Her music is best exemplified by her prayer to the Virgin, a predominantly diatonic prayer in perfect four-bar phrases, with regular progressions, and accompanied by winds and brasses only (no lush strings) playing pure, clear triads. Only when Elizabeth sings of earthly longing does the melody line become predominantly chromatic: "O take me from this earth! Let me enter pure and spotless, into thy blessed kingdom! . . . if ever a sinful desire or earthly longing rose within me, I strove with untold anguish to stifle it in my heart!"[37] (Elizabeth longs to become pure spirit, and she is close to pure spirit even when on earth. Elizabeth seems only barely to have a body, has no feminine stink, no Phrygian odor. And Wagner writes that "In Tannhäuser I had yearned to flee a world of frivolous and repellent sensuousness . . . my impulse lay towards the unknown land of pure and chaste virginity." He writes at about the same time that "the most perfect human body" is "that of the male.")[38]

The final resolution of the opera comes after Venus and her Bacchantes return to reclaim Tannhäuser. Venus is calling for her lover to return to her, dancing figures are whirling around her, Tannhäuser is about to give in, and his friend Wolfram is horrified, urging Tannhäuser not to submit. At the point of greatest intensity, when Venus is singing "Come, oh come" on a diminished chord, Wolfram suddenly invokes the name of Elizabeth. Once again the name of a virgin is accompanied by a second inversion triad, fortissimo, in the full orchestra, and once again Venus is defeated and is swallowed up by the earth. Venus's blue vapors dissolve and morning dawns.[39] (This long-awaited resolution is similar to the ones when the Queen is destroyed in the *Magic Flute* and the stage is bathed in light, and when Senta dies in the *Flying Dutchman* and the stage is bathed in light, and when the highly sexual and highly chromatic Isolde dies in *Tristan and Isolde,* and when the highly sexual and highly chromatic Kundry dies in *Parsifal,* and the highly sexual, highly chromatic Carmen dies in *Carmen,* and when the highly sexual, highly chromatic Delilah and her people are destroyed in *Samson and Delilah.* And I know that these moments of resolution bring a profound release, are the most compelling moments in the operas.)

And I believe that Wagner found the feminine to be very attractive, and this is why he treats it with some of his most beautiful and exciting music. At the same time, however, he found female power and female sexuality terrifying, unsettling; this is why the beautiful and exciting music is also disturbing. Nietzsche once described his feelings for a women as *Haß-Liebe*, as hating and loving a woman at the same time.[40] Wagner clearly had feelings of *Haß-Liebe* for women as well, feelings that are evident not only in his libretti but that are reinforced by his music.[41] And this musical reinforcement is particularly powerful expressly because we are not likely to be fully conscious of it. I am disturbed (and seduced) by the sexual or powerful woman because I am disturbed (and seduced) by her sexual or powerful music. And because I want her disturbing music to be resolved, I am likely, on some level, to want the woman to be appropriated, to be defeated, to die.[42]

The Return of the God

Mick Jagger of the Rolling Stones ("the greatest rock & roll band in history") combines a persona that is fetchingly passive with music and lyrics of mastery. Jagger is slight and feminine in appearance, wears flowers in his hair, and sings of "Crushed Flowers" (poppies), and is prone to wild and frenzied dancing and ecstatic experiences. Yet his message in songs such as "Some Girls," "Stupid Girl," and "Under My Thumb," is decidedly patriarchal, exudes *Haß-Liebe*, exudes *Haß*. In "Under My Thumb," Jagger recounts his conquest of a once-dominant woman; the "girl," the "squirming dog" who once put him down is now a "sweet pet," is under his thumb. The song ends with short exhalations of breath that sound like quick thrusts and Mick saying, "Easy, baby." According to Simon Frith and Angela McRobbie, rock-music groups such as the Rolling Stones, Rod Stewart, Bruce Springsteen, and especially heavy metal such as Iron Maiden, Mötley Crüe, and Twisted Sister, are all examples of "cock rock." Cock rock performers tend to be "aggressive, dominating, boastful, and constantly seeking to remind their audience of their powers, their control." At the same time, cock rock often expresses a deep, even pathological fear of women, carrying "messages of male self-doubt and self-pity to accompany its confidence and aggression.")[43]

Yet many young women love this music, and they have idolized Jagger; while developing a course in rock music I became attracted to some of the cock music myself. Songs I particularly like by the Stones are "Let's Spend the Night Together," "Paint It Black," and "She Was Hot." All of these songs seem about to burst with energy, and they engage the body, give rise to movement and the dance. (Robert Palmer tells us that "the Stones' backbeat has long been the most resilient in rock. It makes some people shiver, but others [like the more than two million paying fans on the band's 1981 American tour alone] hear it and dance for joy. In Africa and in the African-derived cultures of the Americas, the same rhythms that Christians fear as voodoo, the Devil's work, are used by priests and shamans to heal wounds and cure sickness, to bring light and balance to diseased minds and peace and prosperity to entire communities.")[44] "Paint It Black" is about darkness and death, and has a quick, exciting beat but is in the minor mode and includes the exotic sound of the sitar. And what I like about "She Was Hot," in which "she" is so hot as to tear his clothes and pin him to the ground, are the chord progressions in the chorus. The song is in G major, but the chorus begins on a C major triad, then moves to and lingers on an E minor triad, then to a D major chord, the dominant of G, but instead of moving to G it moves to an A minor triad, then back to C for a repeat of the progression. And I realize that I love the third relations, the moves from C to e, from a to C. (And I remember how I love the third relations in Wagner's love music, and in the love songs of Richard Strauss.) And I especially like "Let's Spend the Night Together," a song that is an aggressive seduction, a subtle rape. And as the woman is seduced ("My, my, my, my"), melody and phrase seem never to rest, and a progression is played over and over that begins on the subdominant (G major), moves to the submediant (B minor) and then to the tonic (D major). Yet the tonic doesn't feel like the tonic, it feels like the dominant of G, and the progression seems never to resolve. I am reminded that music that is nonlinear and nongoal-directed and continuous has been associated with feminine sexuality, a sexuality that can be regarded as both attractive and dangerous. But here the lack of resolution is especially reflective of masculine desire and frustration. And this suggests that the resolution of the dominant-tonic "masculine" cadence is an iconic sign of the masculine climax, of masculine mastery. For there is no lack of closure in "Under My Thumb"; the song ends, with its quick breaths and its "Take it Easy, Baby," with a clear, strong resolution in the tonic, and holds the tonic chord for several measures.[45]

I come to realize that music that denigrates women is ubiquitous and continuous, and cannot be avoided completely. And yet I wouldn't want to stop listening to Gregorian chant, to Mozart, to Wagner. One reason I continue to listen is that I love the music so much. But I also continue to listen because I want to make conscious what the music has been whispering to me, I want to expose the music's hidden implications to light and air. (And in wanting to shed light I do not mean to demean darkness; for Starhawk tells us the dark is "the power of the unseen, the power that comes from within, the power of the immanent Goddess who lies coiled in the heart of every cell of every living thing, who is the spark of every nerve and the life of every breath." But when darkness is used against us, we must confront, enter, and reclaim it.)[46] Though I still love music that denigrates women, though I am still inclined to dance to misogynist music of popular culture, I hope to heal my fractured self, this self that loves music that hurts me, and to dance to the music of women, music that will help me feel good about my body and my emotions, and to dance like a Maenad, like a Bacchante.

I'm just beginning to think about these things, not having discussed them with my students, when one of my graduate students approaches me after class, a demurely dressed young woman with curly brown hair pulled back in barrettes, a young woman who has said on the first day of class that the most important thing in her life is Jesus, and she wants to know if there has been any research done on the effects of the minor mode on sexuality. She says the minor mode turns her on.

Notes

1. In fourth-century Christian art Christ is depicted in the guise of Orpheus, playing a lyre and wearing a Phrygian cap. See Count Goblet d'Alviella, *The Migration of Symbols* (New York: University Books, 1956), 89.

2. The Maiden represents potential, is independent and woman-identified; the Mother represents abundance, is giving and nurturing; the Crone represents the destruction that enables the cycle to begin again, and is wise and powerful. Patriarchal culture transformed the Maiden into an innocent virgin, the Mother into a self-sacrificing Virgin, and the Crone into a witch.

The following revelation of Isis from the *Metamorphoses* of Apuleius (second century C.E.) suggests that various Great Goddesses are One: "The Phrygians, first born of men, call me the Mother of the Gods, goddess of Pessinus; the inhabitants of Attica, Minerva of Cecrops' city [= Athens]; the Cypriots living amid the seas, Venus of Paphos; the arrow-bearing Cretans, Diana of Dictynna; the triple tongued Sicilians, Proserpina of the Styx; the original Eleusinians, Ceres of Attica, some [call me] Juno, others Bellona, some Hecate, others the One from Rhamnus." Note that the list includes Goddess as Maiden (Proserpina, Diana), Mother (Venus, Ceres, Juno), and Crone (Hecate). Quoted in M. J. Vermaseren, *Cybele and Attis* (London: Thames and Hudson, 1977), 10. According to W. K. C. Guthrie, the names of the various Cretan goddesses may once have been names for various aspects of a single Great Goddess: "The names of the Cretan heroines or nymphs Pasiphaë ('all-shining'), Ariadne ('very holy' or 'very visible'), Phaedra ('bright'), Dictynna ('she of Mount Dicte'), Britomartis (. . . 'good' or 'sweet maiden' in the Cretan tongue) . . . are all *adjectives*, and suggest that the Greeks, with their genius for concreteness and personification, may have made separate personalities out of invocations to a single great Cretan goddess or god in different capacities." (As in Phrygia, the principal deity in Crete was a Goddess.) See Guthrie, "The Religion and Mythology of the Greeks," in The *Cambridge Ancient History*, 3d ed., ed. I. E. S. Edwards, C. J. Gadd, N. G. L. Hammond, and E. Sollberger (Cambridge: Cambridge University Press, 1975), 2:part 2, p. 884. See also Marija Gimbutas, *The Language of the Goddess* (New York: Harper and Row, 1989), 316–20.

3. See Jane Ellen Harrison, *Mythology* (New York: Cooper Square, 1963), 95.

4. In some legends Attis is killed by a boar, in others he bleeds to death through self-castration. Like Dionysus, Osiris, and Orpheus, Attis appears to be a prototype for the Christ. Attis was born of a Virgin (Goddess) and was slain "to bring salvation to mankind." After his castration he was crucified on a pine tree, and was resurrected three days later. His worshipers ate his body in the form of bread. The solstitial festival of his birth was celebrated on December 21, his passion on the spring equinox of March 21. See Barbara Walker, *The Woman's Encyclopedia of Myths and Secrets* (New York: Harper and Row, 1983), pp. 77–78.

5. Her temple was in the Vatican, where St. Peter's basilica now stands, until the fourth century C.E.

6. Legends of Cybele, Agdistis, and Attis vary. On Cybele, Attis, and the Phrygians, see Herodotus, *The Histories*, trans. Henry Cary (New York: Appleton, 1899); R. D. Barnett, "Phrygia and the Peoples of Anatolia in the Iron Age," in *The Cambridge Ancient History*, 2:part 2, pp. 417–42; Vermaseren, *Cybele and Attis* and *The Legend of Attis in Greek and Roman Art* (Leiden: E. J. Brill, 1966); Sir James George Frazer, *The Golden Bough: A Study in Magic and Religion* (New York: Macmillian, 1958); Robert Graves, *The White Goddess* (New York: Noonday, 1948); Erich Neumann, *The Great Mother*, Bollingen Series 47, trans. Ralph Manheim (Princeton: Princeton University Press, 1963); and Walker, *Woman's Encyclopedia*, 201–2, 77–79. On ancient Greece and Greek mythology, see Guthrie, "The Mythology and Religion of the Greeks," and V. R. d'A. Desborough and N. G. L. Hammond, "The End of Mycenean Civilization and the Dark Age" in *The Cambridge Ancient History*, 2:part 2, pp. 851–905 and 658–712; Jane Ellen Harrison, *Prolegomena to the Study of Greek Religion* (Cambridge: Cambridge University Press, 1903, 1922) and *Themis: A Study of the Social Origins of Greek Religion* (Cambridge: Cambridge University Press, 1912); Walker, *Woman's Encyclopedia*. On the Goddess in Paleolithic and Neolithic Old Europe, see Gimbutas, *The Language of the Goddess*.

7. See Friedrich Nietzsche, *The Birth of Tragedy*, trans. William A. Haussmann (New York: Russell and Russell, 1964), and Frederick Copleston, *A History of Philosophy*, 8 vols. (New York: Image Books, 1965), 7:part 2, pp. 171–72.

8. Sappho quoted in C. M. Bowra, *Greek Lyric Poetry* (Oxford: Clarendon Press, 1961), 184, 239.

9. See Bowra, *Greek Lyric Poetry*, 176–240; Giovanni Comotti, *Music in Greek and Roman Culture*, trans. Rosaria V. Munson (Baltimore: Johns Hopkins University Press, 1989) 19–20; Sophie Drinker, *Music and Women* (New York: Coward McCann, 1948), 101–7, 135–39; and Euripides, *The Bacchae*, in *The Complete Greek Tragedies*, vol. 4, *Euripides*, ed. David Grene and Richmond Lattimore (Chicago: University of Chicago Press, 1958), 581–82.

10. Oliver Strunk, ed., *Source Readings in Music History: Antiquity and the Middle Ages* (New York: Norton, 1950, 1965), 5–9, 17–19, 50–51, 60, 82–83. On Clement and Basil, see James McKinnon, *Music in Early Christian Literature* (Cambridge: Cambridge University Press), 31, 69. See also Comotti, 128–43.

11. Margaret Miles, *Carnal Knowledge: Nakedness and Religious Meaning in the Christian West* (Boston: Beacon, 1989), 6.

12. See Rosemary Radford Ruether, "Misogynism and Virginal Feminism in the Fathers of the Church," in *Religion and Sexism: Images of Woman in the Jewish Traditions*, ed. Ruether (New York: Simon and Schuster, 1974), 156; and Martha Lee Osborne, *Woman in Western Thought* (New York: Random House, 1979), 51–53.

13. Osborne, *Woman In Western Thought,* 60, and Walker, *Woman's Encyclopedia,* 202. Walker also tells us (210) that Saint Theodore was canonized for burning down Cybele's temple at the Vatican.

14. For Leander, see Ruether, *Religion and Sexism,* 166–76; for Jerome, see Mary Daly, *The Church and the Second Sex* (New York: Harper and Row, 1968), 43; on monks, see Peter Brown, *The Body and Society: Men, Women and Sexual Renunciation in Early Christianity* (New York: Columbia University Press, 1988), 243.

15. Caroline Walker Bynum, "The Female Body and Religious Practice in the Later Middle Ages," in *Fragments for a History of the Human Body,* part 1, ed. Michel Feher with Ramona Naddaff and Nadia Tazi (New York: Urzone Books, 1989), 160–219.

16. Yet Saint Augustine expressed concern that even plainchant offers sensuous pleasure, and cautions worshipers to focus on the message and not the music. Augustine believed that music should be a matter of mathematical law and order. Later, Boethius states that "all music is reasoning and speculation," and music comes to be regarded as a science. On John, Basil, and Augustine, see Strunk, *Source Readings,* 64–70 and 73–86, and McKinnon, *Music in the Early Christian Church,* 155. On Gregory, see Brown, *The Body and Society,* 297.

Scholars disagree about the rhythmic nature of early chant. There is evidence that early chant consisted of long and short note values, while the Monks of Solesmes maintain that the tones were equal in duration, a style well established by the late Middle Ages. See Richard Hoppin, *Medieval Music* (New York: Norton, 1978), 88–90.

17. McKinnon, *Music in the Early Christian Church,* 75, 145, 61.

18. Bynum, "The Female Body," 179, and Hildegard of Bingen, *Illuminations of Hildegard of Bingen,* with commentary by Matthew Fox (Santa Fe: Bear and Company, 1985), 13. On music and women in the early Church, see also Carol Neuls-Bates, ed. *Women in Music: An Anthology of Source Readings from the Middle Ages to the Present* (New York: Harper and Row, 1982, xii, 3–20. On music in nunneries of the late Middle Ages, see Anne Bagnell Yardley, "'Ful weel she soong the service dyvyne': The Cloistered Musician in the Middle Ages," in *Women Making Music: The Western Art Tradition, 1150–1950,* ed. Jane Bowers and Judith Tick (Urbana: University of Illinois Press, 1986), 3–14.

19. Quoted in Drinker, *Music and Women,* 158.

20. McKinnon, *Music in the Early Christian Church,* 70, 26, 31, 34, 49, 73, 70, 114. On music and adultery, see Paul Henry Lang, *Music in Western Civilization* (New York: Norton, 1941), 53.

21. See Y. Rokseth, "Les Femmes musiciennes du XIIe au XIVe siécle," *Romania* 61 (1935): 464–68.

22. From "A L'entrade" (twelfth century), in *The Music of the Troubadours,* ed. Peter Wigham (Santa Barbara: Ross Erikson, 1979), 115–16.

23. From Jean de Meung's *Roman de la Rose* (1280): "Either by act, or in your hearts, you [women] all are, were, or will be tarts!" Quoted in Henry Kraus, "Eve and Mary: Conflicting Images of Medieval Woman," in *Feminism and Art History: Questioning the Litany,* ed. Norma Broude and Mary D. Garrard (New York: Harper and Row, 1982), 97. From "Friends, I'm So Sick and Tired" by Guilhem de Peitieus (1071–1127): "You see, I've developed a principle, / 'The Law of Cunt' I call it / as a man who has done well by it / and who also has come to know its sting: JUST AS OTHER THINGS DIMINISH WHEN ONE TAKES / FROM THEM / CUNT GROWS." Quoted in *The Music of the Troubadours,* 145. The lady in the more respectful songs is sometimes more ideal than real; because she is often not identified by name, and because many songs explicitly praise the Virgin Mary, it has been suggested that some of this music may fuse worship of the Virgin with expressions of sensual desire. (This eroticization of the Virgin also appears in writings of some clerics. The treatment of the Virgin and the lady in the German minnesong is more mystical, less sensual.) Rosemary Radford Ruether tells us that Mariology began to emerge in the fourth century C.E. "This new praise of Mary, as the epitome all of these images of spiritual womanhood, soon

succeeded in restoring to Mary the ancient titles of Queen of Heaven and Mother of God of the ancient Mediterranean Earth Goddess, crowning her with the moon and the stars of Isis, the turret crown of Magna Mater [Cybelle], . . . rededicating ancient temples of these Earth goddesses to Mary, and finally escorting her to the very Throne of God to take her seat beside the Jewish Ancient of Days and his son Messiah." Unlike that of the Goddess, however, Mary's body was pure and unrelated to earthly femaleness, and her idealization probably served to intensify the carnality of ordinary women. See Ruether, *Religion and Sexism*, 179. See also Maria V. Coldwell, *"Jougleresses* and *Trobairitz*: Sexual Musicians in Medieval France," in *Women Making Music*, 39–61.

24. Secular monophony is often performed in modal rhythm, with a regular beat pattern; many contemporary scholars believe the rhythms were more lax, conditioned by the texts, and varied from performance to performance. See Richard Hoppin, *Medieval Music*, 281, and Margaret Louise Switten, *The Cansos of Raimon de Miraval* (Cambridge, Mass.: Medieval Academy of America, 1985), 4–6. For ecclesiastical opposition to secular music late in the era, see Lang, *Music in Western Civilization*, 82–84. For views of the Church on women, see Eleanor Commo McLaughlin, "Equality of Souls, Inequality of Sexes: Woman in Medieval Theology," in Ruether, *Religion and Sexism*, 213–66.

25. See Jacques Chailley, *The Magic Flute: Masonic Opera*, trans. Herbert Weinstock (New York: Knopf, 1971), 86 and 103. James Frazer cites claims that Osiris originally was not a sun god but a vegetation god like Dionysus. See Frazer, *The Golden Bough*, 446–47.

26. Chailly, *The Magic Flute*, 75 and 121.

27. See William Mann, *The Operas of Mozart* (New York: Oxford University Press, 1977); H. C. Robbins Landon, *Mozart and the Masons* (New York: Thames and Hudson, 1983); Judith Eckelmeyer, "Structure as Hermeneutic Guide to *The Magic Flute*," *Musical Quarterly* 72 (1986): 51–73; and Dorothy Koenigsberger, "A New Metaphor for Mozart's Magic Flute," *European Studies Review* 5 (1975): 229–75. On Zeus and Hera, see note 3.

28. Rita Steblin, *A History of Key Characteristics in the Eighteenth and Nineteenth Centuries* (UMI Research Press: Ann Arbor, 1983), 223–26.

29. Paul Nettl, *Mozart and Masonry* (New York: Philosophical Library, 1957), 59.

30. Later Wagner writes to Matilde Maier that "One does not ask much from you women, but in the end all you do is cause us grief and pain." Quoted in Rudolph Sabor, *The Real Wagner* (London: André Deutsch, 1987), 111 and 126. Sabor is a very sympathetic biographer. After printing a letter from Wagner to his new young housekeeper (known only as "Mariechen") in which Wagner specifies that she should have her "pink panties" ready for his return home, Sabor points out that the letter was written a week after Wagner and future wife Cosima had "vowed to belong to none but one another." But Sabor cautions that "this is not a matter of fidelity or infidelity, but of needs which are normally disavowed but which Wagner blithely acknowledges." (And Cosima writes in her diary that grief is her "truest and most dependable of friends.") See Sabor, 134, 139.

31. For a discussion of Wagner's sources, see Ernest Newman, *The Wagner Operas* (New York: Knopf, 1968), 55–65.

32. Wagner, *Art Work of the Future*, vol. 1 of *Richard Wagner's Prose Works*, trans. William Ashton Ellis (New York: Broude Brothers, 1966), 32, 334–35, and Mann, *Pro and Contra Wagner*, 126–27. Wagner also tells us that his ideas about "the whole significance of the drama and of the theatre" were molded by the *Orestia* of Aeschylus, a drama that juxtaposes the light of Dike (Justice), represented by Zeus's thunderbolt, with the "tragic nightmare" of Argos, Clytemnestra's city-state. See Raymond Prior, "Language and the Credibility of Space: Wagner's Symbolic Dependence on Aeschylus," in *Wagner In Retrospect*, ed. Leroy R. Shaw, Nancy R. Cirillo, and Marion S. Miller (Amsterdam: Rodopi, 1987), 19–21.

33. It has been suggested that Venus and Elizabeth should be played by the same woman, that

together they make the complete woman. And it has been suggested that in the character of Brünnhilde, the sensual and spiritual woman are integrated. But in Wagner's swan song *Parsifal*, woman and sexual love are renounced, agape replaces eros, and agape is only for men. For woman, now Kundry, is pure sensuality: not the golden sensuality of Venus, but the sensuality of shame. Kundry's "garment is wild and looped up high; she wears a girdle of snakeskins the long ends of which hang down: her hair is black and falls in loose locks: her complexion is a deep reddish brown: her eyes are black and piercing, sometimes flashing wildly, but more often fixed in a stare like that of the dead." On Kundry, see Ernest Newman, *The Wagner Operas*, 676.

34. *Richard Wagner's Prose Works*, 1:308. On *Tannhäuser*, see Newman, *The Wagner Operas;* Barry Millington, *Wagner* (London: J. M. Dent and Sons, 1984); and Carl Dahlhaus, *Richard Wagner's Music Dramas* (Cambridge: Cambridge University Press, 1979).

35. Catherine Clément, *Opera, or the Undoing of Women*, trans. Betsy Wing, foreword by Susan McClary (Minneapolis: University of Minnesota Press, 1988), 56–67. On musical treatments of the masculine and feminine in Bizet's *Carmen*, see Susan McClary, "Sexual Politics in Classical Music," in *Feminine Endings: Music, Gender, and Sexuality* (Minneapolis: University of Minnesota Press, 1990), 53–79. See also Renée Cox, "Recovering *Jouissance:* Feminist Aesthetics and Music," in *Women and Music: A History*, ed. Karin Pendle (Bloomington: Indiana University Press, 1991).

36. The Venusberg music was revised for the Paris Opera during Wagner's *Tristan* period. Ernst Bloch called the Venusberg music a "masterpiece of lust." See Martin Gregor-Dellin, *Richard Wagner*, trans. J. Maxwell Brownjohn (San Diego: Harcourt Brace Jovanovich, 1983), 301.

37. Adorno and others believe, nevertheless, that Elizabeth has some sympathy with Tannhäuser's hedonism. See Theodor W. Adorno, *In Search of Wagner*, trans. Rodney Livingstone (London: NLB, 1981), 14.

38. *Richard Wagner's Prose Works*, 1:339 and 167. Adorno points out that for Wagner, sensual pleasure and desire are confounded with sickness, and that the "harmony" achieved in his mature work between the two main tendencies of the *Tannhäuser* period—"unrestrained sexuality and the ideal of asceticism"—is a harmony that inevitably leads to death. See Adorno, *In Search of Wagner*, 14, 92–94.

39. The unacceptable woman is now destroyed through the actions of a good woman rather than the actions of men.

40. See H. G. Schenk, *The Mind of the European Romantics* (New York: Anchor Books, 1969), 240. Psychologists tell us that male ambivalence about women, and women's ambivalence about themselves, begins early in life. The mother, in offering her breast and the warmth of her body and the music of her voice, offers the first sensual delights. And yet the mother has great power and can take the breast away or withhold the breast or leave the child alone or seem to prefer the father. And these dynamics are particularly powerful for little boys, for they, in having to develop a different gender identity than the mother, must sever their connection with her sooner and more completely than little girls. Because they want her but can no longer be part of her, they seek to possess her, to have her warmth and comfort and sensual delights for themselves alone. And because female sexuality and female power must be kept in check in order for the female to be possessed, men come to dominate and objectify women. See Dorothy Dinnerstein, *The Mermaid and the Minotaur* (New York: Harper and Row, 1976).

41. Wagner's feelings for his own mother (see note 40) were deeply ambivalent. He once wrote to her that he was "so overwhelmed by your feelings of gratitude for your glorious love for your child, which you lately showed again with such warmth and affection, that I should dearly like to write and talk of it to you in the fondest tones of a lover to his beloved. Ah, but far more than that, for is not the love of one's mother far more—far more unsullied than any other?" Elsewhere Wagner complained of his mother's "unprincipled behavior," her "propensity for distortion, misrepresentation and gossip," her stinginess, selfishness, and malice. See Gregor-Dellin, *Richard Wagner*, 23–24, 115–16.

42. Susan McClary makes this point about the opera *Carmen* in "Sexual Politics in Classical Music." I am indebted to McClary for sending me this manuscript before its publication.

The musical dynamics described in these operas are still with us in contemporary film. In Adrian Lyne's film *Fatal Attraction* (Paramount, 1987), Dan Gallagher (Michael Douglas) has an affair with flashy, sexy, independent, and successful Alex Rogers (Glenn Close), an affair that threatens his relationships with his loving and stable wife Beth (Anne Archer) and young daughter Ellen (Ellen Harrison). When Dan rejects Alex, she is disturbed, begins harassing Peter and his family, and eventually becomes homicidal, attempting to kill Beth and Dan. The music associated with wife, daughter, and home is peaceful, lyrical, and conventional, using traditional modes of melody, harmony, and structure. (This music is somewhat chromatic; it would be hokey to use purely diatonic music for these associations in 1987.) Alex's music in contrast, is almost totally unstable: there is no melody, harmony, phrase, or structure to ground the listener, only a low, dull roar, usually synthesized and initially barely audible, which increases in intensity as Alex becomes more agitated. Alex's music does not lend itself to conscious awareness, but it is nonetheless unsettling, and by the end of the movie when she attempts to stab Beth, it is extremely disturbing. The musical tension is resolved only after Alex is shot and killed by Beth, and we hear the "home and family" music as Dan is reunited with Beth and Ellen.

Essentially the same musical dynamics are presented in Walt Disney films targeted at girls and young women. In *Snow White, Sleeping Beauty, Cinderella,* and most recently *The Little Mermaid,* a sweet and passive heroine (who is neither responsible for the trouble she's in nor capable of getting herself out of it) is pitted against an antagonist who is dark, powerful, usually attractive and sexy, and always female. In stark contrast to the music associated with the heroine and her Prince, the music of the femme fatale antagonist is minor, dissonant, and unstable, and resolves only when the Prince kills or destroys her, enabling the heroine to enter the world of men. (We want the antagonist to die because she is a witch, because she uses her great and often magical power destructively. But I notice that the antagonists usually feel alienated, excluded, or afraid of abandonment. And I remember that Alex becomes destructive when she is rejected, that the Queen of the Night becomes destructive when her power is taken from her, that Kubile becomes a castrator when she is appropriated by the patriarchy, that the wise and powerful Lilith becomes destructive when she is cast out of the Garden, that the isolation of the wise and powerful Erinyes fuels their vengeance, that the wise and powerful Crone aspect of the Goddess can become self-destructive when separated from the Mother and Maiden. And I want to respect and include the Crone in others, and to integrate the Crone, Mother, and Maiden within myself.)

43. Simon Frith and Angela McRobbie, "Rock and Sexuality," *Screen Education* 29 (1979): 5. See also John Shepherd, "Music and Male Hegemony," in *Music and Society: The Politics of Composition, Performance and Reception,* ed. Richard Leppert and Susan McClary (Cambridge: Cambridge University Press, 1987), p. 164.

44. Palmer, *The Rolling Stones* (New York: Doubleday, 1983), 8. The blues rhythms spoken of here are sensual but decidedly less patriarchal than rock. On analogies between "aesthetics" in African and Goddess cultures, see Renée Cox, "A Gynecentric Aesthetic," *Hypatia: The Journal of Feminist Philosophy* 5 (1990): 43–62, reprinted in *Aesthetics in Feminist Perspective,* eds. Hilde Hein and Carolyn Korsmeyer (Bloomington: Indiana University Press, 1993), 35–52.

45. In the two most well known Stones songs about frustration, "Satisfaction" and "You Can't Always Get What You Want," the subdominant is regularly alternated with the tonic, denying the dominant-tonic cadence needed for complete resolution. "Let's Spend the Night Together" is from the album *Flowers* (London Records); "Paint It Black," "Stupid Girl" and "Under My Thumb" from *Aftermath* (RCA); and "She Was Hot" from *Under Cover* (Rolling Stones Records). Cock rock is most characteristic of Springsteen's and Jagger's work in the 1960s and 1970s. The recent "Blinded By Love" from *Steel Wheels* (Rolling Stones Records), however, shows that misogyny is

still alive and well in the Stones. For more on the Stones and rock in general, see Robert Pattison, *The Triumph of Vulgarity: Rock Music in the Mirror of Romanticism* (New York: Oxford University Press, 1987).

46. Starhawk, *Dreaming the Dark* (Boston: Beacon, 1988), xviii.

SELECT BIBLIOGRAPHY TO PART II

Bell, Clive. *Art*. London: Chatto and Windus, 1914.

Bullough, Edward. " 'Psychical Distance' as a Factor in Art and as an Aesthetic Principle." *British Journal of Psychology* 5 (1912): 87–117.

Christian, Barbara, ed. *Black Feminist Criticism: Perspectives on Black Women Writers*. New York: Pergamon, 1985.

Citron, Marcia J. *Gender and the Musical Canon*. New York: Pergamon, 1993.

Clément, Catherine. *Opera, or, the Undoing of Women*. Translated by Betsy Wing. Minneapolis: University of Minnesota Press, 1988.

Doane, Mary Ann. *The Desire to Desire: The Woman's Film of the 1940s*. Bloomington: Indiana University Press, 1987.

———. *Femmes Fatales: Feminism, Film Theory, Psychoanalysis*. New York: Routledge, 1991.

Dotterer, Ronald, and Susan Bowers, eds. *Sexuality, the Female Gaze, and the Arts*. Selinsgrove, Pa.: Susquehanna University Press, 1992.

Gallop, Jane. *Reading Lacan*. Ithaca: Cornell University Press, 1985.

Henderson, Mae Gwendolyn. "Speaking in Tongues." In *Aesthetics in Feminist Perspective*, edited by Hilde Hein and Carolyn Korsmeyer. Bloomington: Indiana University Press, 1993.

Herndon, Marcia, and Susanne Ziegler, eds. *Music, Gender, and Culture*. Wilhelmshaven: F. Noetzel, 1990.

hooks, bell. *Black Looks*. Boston: South End, 1992.

———. *Feminist Theory: from Margin to Center*. Boston: South End, 1984.

———. *Talking Back: Thinking Feminist, Thinking Black*. Boston: South End, 1989.

———. *Yearnings: Race, Gender, and Cultural Politics*. Boston: South End, 1990.

Hull, Gloria T., Patricia Bell Scott, and Barbara Smith. *All the Women are White, All the Blacks are Men, but Some of Us are Brave*. Old Westbury: Feminist Press, 1982.

Hunt, Lynn, ed. *Eroticism and the Body Politic*. Baltimore: Johns Hopkins University Press, 1991.

Kaplan, E. Ann. "Is the Gaze Male?" In *Women and Values: Readings in Recent Feminist Philosophy*, edited by Marilyn Pearsall. 2d ed. Belmont, Calif.: Wadsworth, 1993.

Kappeler, Susanne. *The Pornography of Representation*. Minneapolis: University of Minnesota Press, 1986.

Lorraine, Renée. "A Gynecentric Aesthetic." In *Aesthetics in Feminist Perspective*, edited by Hilde Hein and Carolyn Korsmeyer. Bloomington: Indiana University Press, 1993.

Lugones, Maria C., and Elizabeth V. Spelman. "Have We Got a Theory For You! Feminist Theory, Cultural Imperialism, and the Demand for 'The Woman's Voice.' " *Women's Studies International Forum* 6 (1983): 573–81.

Modleski, Tania. *Loving with a Vengeance: Mass-Produced Fantasies for Women*. New York: Methuen, 1984.

———. *The Women Who Knew Too Much: Hitchcock and Feminist Theory.* New York: Methuen, 1988.

Mulvey, Laura. *Visual and Other Pleasures.* Bloomington: Indiana University Press, 1989.

Nochlin, Linda. *Women, Art, and Power and Other Essays.* New York: Harper and Row, 1988.

Penley, Constance, ed. *Feminism and Film Theory.* New York: Routledge, 1988.

———. *The Future of an Illusion: Film, Feminism and Psychoanalysis.* Minneapolis: University of Minnesota Press, 1989.

Pollock, Griselda. *Vision and Difference: Femininity, Feminism, and the Histories of Art.* New York: Routledge, 1988.

Rose, Jacqueline. *Sexuality in the Field of Vision.* New York: Verso, 1988.

Silverman, Kaja. *The Acoustic Mirror: The Female Voice in Psychoanalysis and Cinema.* Bloomington: Indiana University Press, 1988.

Spelman, Elizabeth V. *Inessential Woman: Problems of Exclusion in Feminist Thought.* Boston: Beacon, 1988.

Wallace, Michelle. "The Problem of the Visual in Afro-American Culture." In *Aesthetics in Feminist Perspective,* edited by Hilde Hein and Carolyn Korsmeyer. Bloomington: Indiana University Press, 1993.

Wolff, Janet. *Aesthetics and the Sociology of Art.* 2d ed. Ann Arbor: University of Michigan Press, 1993.

III

Feminist Art
and the
Refusal of Aesthetic Value

Philosophers have expressed concern about the power and value of art since ancient times. Plato warned against the harmful effects of art—which he understood as a species of imitation or *mimesis*—on the irrational part of the soul. (Not subscribing to any ideas about aesthetic distance, Plato feared the power of the emotions generated by art.) The pleasures to be had from art are especially dangerous on his account, because they threaten to overwhelm the governance of the soul by reason. Aristotle took a more positive view of emotion and of the value of art, promoting tragedy as a means to gain psychological renewal, moral insight, and community cohesion.

Ancient tradition regards the value of art as bound up with its cognitive function, moral influence, and ability to bind communities together. Dominant in the modern period is the contrasting idea that art is valuable in and of itself, indeed, that its value transcends social domains and practical values. This idea was particularly strong in the "art for art's sake" movement of the nineteenth and twentieth centuries, and it lingers in the tension present in our public debates about the independence of artistic significance from social mores. Generally speaking, the experiencing of art has been historically tied to the discussion of whether it is intrinsically or instrumentally valuable, whether it is appreciated for its own sake or for other benefits it brings about, and conversely, whether arguably negative instrumental value is sufficient grounds to suppress artistic creativity.

In Part I, feminist ways of reading landmark theories of taste brought to light gender biases embedded in the foundation of the modern discipline of aesthetics. Throughout the development of this field, the notion of the aesthetic—along with its attendant concepts "aesthetic object," "aesthetic attention," and "aesthetic experience"—became the foundation for approaches to identifying objects of art and assessing their quality. Feminists have argued that criteria issuing from concepts of the aesthetic have tended to overlook many products created by women, especially those domestic crafts the practical function of which influences design. We have seen how the strategy of separating aesthetic from practical value grounds theories of art and perception; an object's use value thereby becomes either irrelevant or intrusive. Moreover, since for centuries women were not afforded the same access to artistic instruction and other opportunities of the art world, they have also not attained a major presence in the histories of the arts. These two factors combine to promote continued attention to certain kinds of created products over others.

In spite of the problems inherent with the articulation of a limited realm of aesthetic value, the concept of the aesthetic persists, as does the notion of an unbiased, expert viewer who is capable of determining the quality of art for a general audience. As we noted in Part II, the recognition of a multiplicity of differences among subjects has served to deconstruct the notion of an impartial universal subject. In contrast to this tradition, feminist modes of evaluating art build upon the ways women practically, emotionally, and personally identify with art; thus they implicitly oppose the idea of aesthetic distance.

A number of feminist artists have enacted a rejection of the notion of aesthetic value in their own creative endeavors. The notion of the "gendered spectator" from Part II is expanded here to include the gendered creator—the artist who is self-conscious about her political and social position, who makes no pretense about art transcending social conditions, and who draws attention to her "situatedness" in her work. The rejection of the traditional characterization of the aesthetic complicates the pleasures received from art, since according to the views of many feminists, practical, political, and personal factors are inseparable from the value derived from the experience of art.

As creator, the feminist artist is aware of being both a gendered subject (a perceiver of the world through feminist lenses) and a maker of objects that in turn come to be perceived and interpreted by others. This self-consciousness of subjective position pervades the acts of creating, interpreting, and evaluating, thereby blurring the traditional boundaries between them and enabling feminist art to reflect and embody an "aesthetics of resistance."

Filmmaker Trinh T. Minh-ha aptly sets the stage for exploring such issues by asking "Who is Speaking?" The seemingly innocent question captures the recent trend for women to speak out not only as artists, critics, historians, and philosophers, but also as representatives of different cultures and nationalities. In discussing her film *Surname Viet Given Name Nam,* Trinh explains how her innovative filmic techniques simultaneously deconstruct traditional documentary practice while constructing a new type of documentary based on "fictions." Women are "given a voice" to relate personal histories, but simultaneously become "representations" within a carefully constructed framework that positions them as subjects within film, community, nation, and the world. Their experiences become the bases of a multilayered, introspective challenge to entrenched gender roles, national identities, and artistic standards. As an artist speaking as interpreter of her work (she herself is interviewed), Trinh introduces modes for valuing that resist the dichotomy of aesthetic and nonaesthetic value. As she states, "the aesthetic always acts on the politics."

Given the uncharted terrain of the "new" aesthetics, how do we learn to interpret and evaluate feminist works of art more fruitfully? Elizabeth Ann Dobie discusses a variety of interpretive approaches while using the artworks and writings of Nancy Spero and Barbara Kruger. Once again, the artists enter into the process of a viewer's experience of their work. As Spero writes, "My body, my presence mediated by the mark on the paper, is no longer absent. I speak." Dobie advocates an "interweaving" of apparently incompatible feminist frameworks as a way for us to take advantage most fully of works that play critically with gender and sexual differences. In realizing that there are differences in feminist art as well as the subjective responses to it, she argues against searching for any definitively appropriate feminist interpretive approach.

Artist-philosopher Adrian Piper speaks to us *about* her art by speaking *through* it. By reading transcripts of audio monologues of two of her mixed-media installation pieces, *Four Intruders Plus Alarm Systems* and *Safe,* we are allowed to "listen in" to her explicit refusal to be judged by traditional criteria. In both works, Piper anticipates and forestalls a range of aesthetic responses by confronting the viewer with issues of racism, gender, and national identity, at the very time that the viewer is in the process of framing responses to the works. In so doing, Piper opens the door to the possibility of new ways of approaching her work, prodding the viewer to think through the process of evaluation in order to understand the politics of a "purely aesthetic" pleasure. Her counterpoint reaction to viewers experiencing *Four Intruders* attests to the risk of misinterpretation that accompanies political art.

In the final essay of the section, Peggy Zeglin Brand responds directly to one critic's attempt to devalue "activist art." Donald Kuspit's attack on the work of Piper, Kruger, and Jenny Holzer is examined within the context of both historical and idiosyncratic uses of the traditional aesthetic-nonaesthetic distinction. Brand opposes the role of critic as "commissar of the obscene," Kuspit's conception of a contemporary judge with a refined sensibility. Brand modifies the feminist "refusal" of aesthetic value by calling for a revision of the traditional distinction, and invites new voices into the discussion in order to promote the goal of devising a true multiplicity of aesthetic and artistic values.

8

"Who Is Speaking?": Of Nation, Community, and First-Person Interviews

Trinh T. Minh-ha

The following is an interview conducted by Issac Julien and Laura Mulvey after the screening of *Surname Viet Given Name Nam* at the London Film Festival, November 1989.

ISAAC JULIEN: *Apart from the title being a pun, a play on, a parody of naming a country, a nation, there seemed to be a play with documentary form in the first instance—interviewees talking as first subjects—and then this deconstruction in the middle where we saw it break down, that it was really a constructed interview, rather than something that was first person, subjective. Then the third part was really a catharsis, subjective, a number of different voices coming together, a whole breakdown, and I just wanted you to elaborate on that kind of form, because it is different from* Naked Spaces—Living is Round, *and harks a little more to* Reassemblage, *in terms of questioning documentary form, and deconstructing a number of devices.*

TRINH T. MINH-HA: You are the first viewer to talk about the naming of the country—or the attempt to name a country—and to relate that to a questioning

---

*This interview is reprinted with permission from Trinh T. Minh-ha, *Framer Framed* (New York: Routledge, 1992).

of the first-person interview in the film. It's a most perceptive reading; one that is pivotal, but that I have not yet had the opportunity to discuss, because it has not come up in the audiences' questions so far. The film, structured by multiple strategies of cultural identification, is very much about how, even and especially for insiders, the naming of their own culture (the national narrative) remains plurally unstable. Viet Nam cannot be homogenized nor subsumed into an all-embracing identity. Not only the explicit enumeration of all the names of the nation in the last third of the film recalls the different moments in its history, but the title itself, *Surname Viet Given Name Nam,* invites explanations and interpretations that differ according to gender, political affinity, and subject positioning.

This title, taken from a gendered context of recent socialist tradition in Viet Nam, suggests both a personalization of the country and a differential construction of the culture from within. It can also be read in the film's framing, as a feminist necessity to rethink the questions of community, nation, and identity, and to challenge nationalist assumptions of cultural mastery. On the one hand, *Viet* is the name of origin of the land and the ancestors of the Vietnamese people whom it is said migrated from meridional China, while *Nam* designates their further southern relocation in relation to China—whose historical domination of Viet Nam continues bitterly to mark popular memory. On the other hand, Viet Nam as a name stands for the nation's (feminine-masculine, north-south) totality; to the question "Are you married yet?" of a man who makes advances to her, an unwedded woman would *properly* imply that she is at the same time engaged and not engaged by answering, "Yes, his surname is Viet and his given name is Nam." It requires wit to reply that one is married to the state; but such wittiness speaks volume for both what it is supposed and not supposed to say on the question of gender and nationalism. And the risk incurred in this form of feminine-nationalist in/directness is, for me, the same risk taken in the simultaneous filmic construction and deconstruction of the first-person interview in documentary practice.

In the making of this film, the politics of the interview emerges fraught with uneasy questions. As you point out very clearly, the first part of the film deals with interviews that set out to be first-person witnesses to women's condition, but then as they unfold, it is also more apparent that not only their materialization borders the dialogue and the monologue; it also fundamentally raises the question "who is speaking?" Although the interviewee does address an ambiguous "you" (a "you" that is directed not only at the original interviewer and the filmmaker, but also at the English-speaking viewer, including here the Vietnamese viewer in exile), what is offered to the viewer in this part are

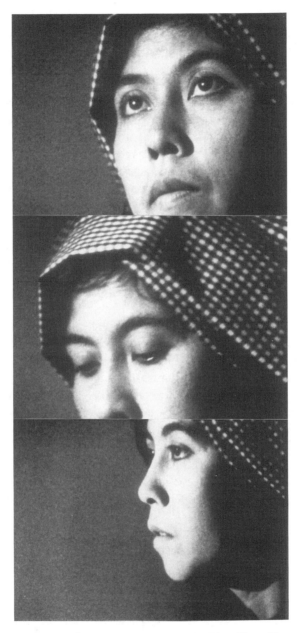

Fig. 8.1.   Film still from *Surname Viet Given Name Nam*
by Trinh T. Minh-ha. Courtesy Trinh T. Minh-ha

long socio-autobiographical criticisms whose unconventional length and use of spoken language allow each woman her own space. It is, for example, at the difficult pace of her English utterances that the story of her life is unrolled, and the film structured. Lighting, setting, framing, camera movement, shot duration, and the use of visualized words are other strategies indicative of the carefully constructed nature of the interviews. The attentive viewer is bound at one point or another to puzzle over the voice of the film. I wanted to keep the reenactment ambiguous enough in the first part so as to solicit the viewer's sense of discovery, which may grow with means other than plot, story, or message—means unique to cinema as a medium.

The interviews are made to look gradually less and less "natural" as the film advances. Only halfway through it does the staged quality of the visualized speech become more manifest: when a woman is seen pacing back and forth while she delivers her thoughts; when another woman is also seen speaking with her back to the camera in a denuded setting; or when the reflexive voice-over is heard with the synchronous voice, thinking aloud the politics of interviews. Thus, interviews that occupy a dominant role in documentary practices—in terms of authenticating information; validating the voices re-cruited for the sake of the argument the film advances (claiming however to "give voice" to the people); and legitimizing an exclusionary system of representation based on the dominant ideology of presence and authenticity—are actually sophisticated devices of fiction.

The play on the fictions of documentary is different layered throughout the film. This is conveyed to the viewer, among others, by the diverse cinematic means mentioned earlier, which became all the more perceptible in what you could call the third part of the film: when the active-reductive, more documen-tary-like editing and cinematography of the "unstaged" life activities and snatches of conversation sorely stand out in relation to those of the "staged" material offered in the first part; hence this statement by a voice-over: "By choosing the most direct and spontaneous form of voicing and documenting, I find myself closer to fiction." It is certainly nothing new to say that every documentary practice fundamentally involves elements of fiction, just as every good fiction film has a profound documentary quality to it.

IJ: *I know in my practice, and in Laura's practice as well, in using documen-tary there's always this tension if one wants to comment on the way documentary films are constructed, but then the way your subject is positioned within that text, is a problem. Then there is the extra, what I would call the burden of representation—making films about subjects that have not been given voice—that you face in relationship to trying to give that subject in some way its own voice without it being the "authentic" voice. In your film I felt these tensions. I avoided it because I didn't interview anybody, really. That was my way of dealing with it, but I know that to a certain extent that didn't work as well. I thought that your attempt was a brave one.*

T: This raises another issue that came up, on a more simple level, when I approached the women for this film. In the casting process, it was important for me to hear about their own life stories before I decided on the voices that they would be incorporating. Within the range of their personal experiences, which were sometimes worse than those they were enacting, they could drift in and out of their roles without too much pain. But in selecting them for who they are rather than simply for whom they can play, I was not so much looking for authenticity as I was interested in seeing how they would draw the line between the differing fictions of living and acting. What the film tries to set into relief is precisely the fact that whether they act or whether they are telling us about their own stories, speech is always "staged," (or "tactical," as a statement in the film says).

Direct speech does not transcend representation. To a certain extent, interviewees choose how they want to be represented in what they say as well as in the way they speak, dress, and perform their daily activities. To push the limits of self-representation a bit further, the second and even more so, the third part of the film are organized around "documented" scenes that materialize the choices the women made when, as a structural device, I asked each of them how they would like to see themselves represented, after having been put through the ordeal of incorporating other women's pain, anger, and sadness. My own role thus shifted from that of a director in the first half to that of a coordinator in the last half. Hence you move here to what you called earlier a "catharsis"—or what I myself would see as the height of "documentary" fiction: the place where the diverse fictions of representation and self-representation come together. The result in this last half is a fabric of "excess"--of scenes that were sometimes fantasized and could be judged at first sight as being gratuitously unrelated: for example, a woman is merely cooking or quietly drinking tea; another is jogging alone in a park; yet another is sitting next to a fishpond; and a fourth one is performing her Tai Ch'i or doing a public presentation on the Vietnamese dress. These are things that, in a way, embarrass me [*laughs*]—at least initially, but afterwards I understood, because they are so much a part of myself as well. They embarrass me because I have problems with forms of presentation that tend to commodify ethnicity. This was for me the case with the live exemplification of Vietnamese women's historical and customary attires (the *so dai* in its evolution). But seen in the context of this film, where women's bodies and the way they are clad constitute one of the critical threads woven through the entire texture of the work, it really adds a dimension to the critique and does not come out as just a commodification of ethnicity.

IJ: *No . . . In the beginning, where this question comes up about pleasure, where for me the beginning is very sensuous, there are the colors, the way this works to create a mood for it, I think is important.*

T: Yes. Commonly enough, I had to learn to give up much in this film and to burn all the intentions during the making process. In the reenacted interviews, we (the art director and I) were partly going after the feminist "natural look"; thus, the women involved are clad in very simple clothing, which is what they would wear in socialist Viet Nam. But in the "real-life" shooting situations where they had a choice, they would all prefer to wear makeup and to dress up with showy colors. For the viewer, especially the Western viewer, this has been misleading in terms of class, because of the habit of attributing fancy garments to the bourgeoisie and practical, if not drab clothes to the working class. Not only is such a habit itself class-defined, hence indicative of the viewer's middle-classness; it is also oblivious of circumstances and contexts. So while I was still trying to be "truthful" and to hang on to some vestiges of documentary practice in my choices as director, the women were, in fact, opening it up by insisting on what, in certain cases, is an imaginative flight from their working-class daily realities. As I state elsewhere, the legacy of dressing down in public occasions (here, on film), belongs in all probability to middle-class women who wish to ally with the cause of the working class.

IJ: *That's very interesting, because for me that's about desire, and wanting to fictionalize yourself in a particular way, because to a certain extent they realize they want to present themselves in a way that may be different from the way they may be every day. Because it's a special experience, Andy Warhol spoke about this, "15 minutes of fame." . . . Those things are unavoidable really once you start interviewing people not familiar with different technologies.*

LAURA MULVEY: *I've got a few general questions, then some specific things. The first thing is a way in which the film could be read, and judging from what I've heard you say in discussion afterward—I'm not sure if this is the way in which you intend it to be read, and that is that there is a before-and-after structure in the film. Actually, not a before-and-after, more a kind of here-and-there struc-*

*ture: the experiences women are undergoing in Viet Nam, seen or understood
through a comparison with women in the U.S. Is that a false reading?*
T: I was not so much comparing—

LM: *Would you say a kind of juxtaposition?*
T: Yes, a juxtaposition, but with no linear intent in mind, so that's why I
prefer it when you said here and there, rather than before and after, because
there is no before and after.

LM: *Yes, exactly. Because that's your point—a very beautiful point about people
thinking that there's a moment when things start, but in fact they're just a
continuum.*[1] *I think you had the sound of a train on the soundtrack . . . the
sense of something running along on its own momentum, outside the way people
may read history. I wanted to ask you about the politics of that separation—
juxtaposition—between the U.S. and Viet Nam, especially as you were talking
about the commodification of the traditional culture in the U.S., but then at the
same time the picture of Viet Nam is very much one of oppression—the state of
women in Viet Nam is one of oppression. So in some ways it's a rather bleak
picture, of sexual oppression on one side, and the commodification of sexuality
on the other side.*
T: Actually, I would also see sexual oppression happening in the context of
the United States. It's not only the commodification of ethnicity, but also the
perpetration (with refinement) of many of the oppressive concepts in traditional
Vietnamese culture. Despite its specific focus, this film is not in fact only about
Viet Nam and the Vietnamese diaspora. Certainly, some elements in the film
are more accessible to those who are familiar with the culture: nonetheless,
many viewers, especially yesterday after the screening, have come to me
individually and said that they didn't feel the film was just about Vietnamese
women, but also about themselves and about the condition of the women they
know. These viewers, mostly women of color from diverse nations, but also
white American women, recognized the experiences of the women featured as
their own. This is more important to me. When I put forth the fact that the
question of women is still very much at issue in socialist Viet Nam, I do not
see it as a problem of socialist Viet Nam alone, but as one that cuts across the
borderlines of nations and cultures. It is with this in mind that I have selected
the strategies and information advanced in the film.

The same problem exists in other socialist countries of the Third World and
in any libertarian movement. This is nothing new because feminists of color
have repeatedly been very vocal in pointing out how, within revolutionary

Fig. 8.2.   Film still from *Surname Viet Given Name Nam* by Trinh T. Minh-ha.
Courtesy Trinh T. Minh-ha

movements sexism remains a problem. One cannot simply equate left with feminist, just as the question of gender cannot be collapsed with the question of race; the differentiation of these issues has been very alive in feminist debates. The fact that one is a socialist does not mean that one is freed from patriarchal values; although of course, there can be at an institutional level, more caution and more of an effort to ameliorate the condition of women. This is not denied in the film; nonetheless that effort in Viet Nam has been reduced, for example, to texts that are written by men to be read by women in women's unions. With all these speeches on equality, what is more blatant is the fact that no women are in the political bureau. That socialist Viet Nam is still caught in the patriarchal system is nothing particular to Viet Nam. The criticism of the film is therefore not directed toward socialist Viet Nam per se; it is directed toward the condition of women—whether in socialist or capitalist context, whether back home in the nation-space or over here in the community-space. In forgetting this, I feel that the tendency is always to *obscure* the question of gender by reverting it to a question of communism versus capitalism and salvaging it in a binary system of thinking.

LM: *What I thought was very interesting was the way that the question of women came out as taking a different form in each country—the way in which I thought it was important to show the Miss Vietnam pageant, in the U.S., so you could see the Vietnamese community and traditions becoming Americanized, as well as becoming kitsch. There was one monologue I felt was perhaps the most moving and the most difficult to interpret in the context of the overall subject of the film. That was the one with the woman doctor—very beautifully filmed. The one who talks about the problems at the hospital after the liberation, the disorganization of the hospital, the husband's arrest. I found it difficult to interpret because you bring on another soundtrack, during the interview which is about the condition of being a wife in Vietnamese culture, and I became confused at that point; the text became too textured.*

T: I use that strategy more than once in the film, albeit differently each time. Aesthetically speaking, there is a moment within that passage that doesn't work for me either. That's when we hear, over the interviewee's voice, a poem read rather than sung; it's mainly a problem of distribution of dynamics that could be solved in mixing the sound. Since the aesthetic always acts on the politics, such a minor problem does influence the reception of the text. This being said, I'm glad you bring up this point, because one of the issues the film also addresses is that of translation. I am not really talking about the various meanings that one comes up with in translating, but of translation as a theoretical problem—the production of meaning, of identity, culture, and politics. The point you make reminds me of the time when I came to Paris for the International Women's Film Festival in Creteil. The translator for the festival ran up to me, and was at the same time excited, worried, and upset. She told me that it was a most challenging task to translate my film, because in many instances there are simultaneously two texts, and which one to choose! She was all worked up by that, so I said, well, you couldn't do otherwise but make a choice, and in making the choice she was very aware that translation not only determined the way the viewer would read the film; it could also not strive for mere likeness to the original without betraying the latter. Although the situation is slightly different, this is partly what I wanted to achieve myself: to problematize both the role of translation in film and the role of film as translation.

To come back to the point you made about being confused, because the two texts come at the same time—

LM: *It isn't just that they come at the same time, they seem to be also to some extent in contradiction with each other. She is talking in a sense not about her oppression as a woman, but the oppression of the southerners by the new administrative cadres.*

T: Oh yes, I see. That's a very nice reading; it also tells me that I have never seen the two as contradictory, only as supplementary. On the one hand she talks about the country, on the other she exposes the pathos of the family; and actually what appears as a representative case of a woman's and her family's distress also reads as the condition of woman in relation to the husband and the family. She was, in other words, suffering from a double cause. Although her story evolved around the deterioration of the hospital and the lack of competence of the new regime's staff, her real suffering began when her husband was taken away to a camp of reeducation. It was then that her entire perception of the working environment changed; so did her relationship with the hospital and her attitude toward her job and her children. The discovery of fear and the lonely endurance of humiliation on her side did not help the family. Finally as she told us, she quit her job and got out of that situation, simply because she decided she had nothing to lose, except some ration tickets. So I thought the two oppressions fed on one another.

LM: *I see. I think I understand more now. So what she was exemplifying was the extent to which a Vietnamese woman who is middle class and a doctor internalizes her position of wife, and identifies with her very special position of wife.*

T: Yes. But you see, the difficulty in that case was, I was not simply criticizing. Because I think it would be very abusive in such a case to be merely critical. The challenge was to present the plight critically without condemning. For someone who is in that kind of situation, it seems important to be caring at the same time as one is critical. That's something I find most difficult in working on this film. The same applies for many of the scenes of the Vietnamese community in the U.S., of which the Miss Vietnam pageant event that you mentioned is an example. How can a critique also be a compliment without being any less of a critique?

LM: *That's what I think was a bit confusing for the viewer, because I think one felt that the emotion that this woman suffered when she lost her husband, is not something that one would criticize anyone for feeling. So to what extent you were associating it with an aspect of the position of wife as subordinate to the husband, which seemed to come in on the soundtrack at a certain point, did you think so?*

T: No, even the proverb that is sung on the soundtrack at that point, simply evokes the loyalty and the sadness of the hard-working wife, who has to nourish her children while her husband is away. So once more it's not something that simply says she has submitted to her condition, but rather speaks of two sadnesses: one sadness that is proverbial and one that is historical, and the two go together. That's why even the word "criticize" here is not quite adequate, as you point out, because at the same time as one cannot condemn one can still show to what extent we—women of Viet Nam and elsewhere—are internalizing the four virtues, which are introduced and directly commented upon only later in the film, in the context of Vietnamese women in the U.S. The traditional four virtues prescribe how to behave toward one's husband and by extension toward the society. She must know how to manage the household skillfully; maintain a compliant appearance; speak properly and softly; and be faithful and respectful—all this to save the husband's face. In other words, a woman's identity is entirely defined by her demeanor toward her husband, and/or to recall the title of the film, by her adeptness at saving the nation's face.

Understanding this, how is one to look at this woman doctor? Her story is deeply moving; so are some of the proverbs and songs that tell us poignantly about the fate of women. But, the doctor carries the four virtues in her very resistance and suffering. And to a certain extent, we all do. I cannot but notice how these oppressive criteria remain imprinted in my everyday behavior. Many of us, Vietnamese women living in the U.S. and in Europe, who have access to work and individual "liberty," may laugh when we hear of the three submissions and the four virtues, but that's only because the higher we climb, the more multiply sophisticated the forms of oppression prove to be. So in looking at this doctor, or at any other women in the film, I also see myself; one cannot criticize here without getting caught in the criticism itself. This also applies to the viewers in the audience.

IJ: . . . *the way it brings us to the inside-out–outside-in dichotomy that you speak a lot about in your work. You speak about it in relation to nations—in every first world there's a third world, and vice versa. And then this is brought up again in the nexus of the problematic where you're talking about subjectivities and the way in which patriarchy has destroyed that. But I wonder if you could maybe speak a little about the way—I mean, I was very sympathetic to the film, because it's the whole thing about having ruled subjects and then the whole thing around the responsibility of the filmmaker, kind of boring questions in a sense, but they are questions that are important. This is not really different from my first question that I asked, but I mean, How does one resolve that? This may be asking for closure on this kind of discourse, because maybe its not being resolved is a good thing, but it's like the relationship in this country to documentary practice, where the burden of representation, if you're a black filmmaker or a woman filmmaker is very great still, and the grip of realism hasn't quite loosened from people's visions of seeing themselves, and I wondered what they thought when they actually saw it, because that's in the film as well.*

T: You mean the response of the women acting in the film? They did watch themselves acting on video during the rehearsal of the reenacted parts. Although one can certainly say that video doesn't quite have the same impact as that of film. They were aware of their acting, and actually, they were the ones to criticize themselves most harshly. But with regard to how they come out in the entirety of the film, none of us—including myself—really know. I started out with that limited body of interviews carried out in Viet Nam by Mai Thu Van, but the way the film developed and got "scripted" came with the making of it, and I really didn't *know* it beforehand. So when the film was shown and the women saw themselves on the large screen, I guess it was a great surprise for them. On the one hand, it has always been an odd experience to look at oneself and one's self-consciousness as spectator; they had no flattering words for themselves and tended to laugh at what they perceived as their own awkwardnesses in acting. On the other, they didn't anticipate how complex all the issues were in relation to their own role, and how powerful film could be as a medium. They were somewhat intimidated by the packed audience at the premiere of the film, and one of them told me: "we just realize now with fright that thousands of people will be seeing this film."

Of course, there are some parts that also worried them, and it has to do with the way they wanted to be represented—which brings us back to your question. I love the way you keep on asking and saying at the same time that the questions (of responsibility and of nonrepresentation) raised cannot simply be resolved, precisely because the challenge is renewed everytime one makes a film. The part the women seemed to prefer were the places where they chose how they wanted to present themselves. There is always a problem in relation to the part that they didn't choose; it was no fun to play the "ordinary" or to take on the role of a sixty-year-old woman. Some of them were even worried, as I said earlier, because if, to the outsider these reenacted interviews can be highly critical of the government in Viet Nam, to the Vietnamese viewers they are very nuanced. What is also apparent in these interviews is the fact that the women are not just aspiring for capitalism in criticizing socialism—there was none of that in their responses. On the contrary, they were saying very clearly that between two exploitations of man by man they don't know where to stand. Again, this is nothing unique to their situation in Viet Nam; especially when one takes into consideration what is happening right now in Central and Eastern Europe, where the changes the peoples are fighting for have nothing to do with any simple transfer to the ideology of the "free West." With this nuance being very much present in the interviews, as well as the questioning of the feminine lady–maid–monkey condition, the women were quite concerned about how the community would judge them. These are examples of the kind of preoccupations they had at the first viewing, but with more viewings they apparently felt proud of the work they contributed and they wanted the film to circulate in the community like the commercial videos. . . . Two of the husbands said they were very moved by the film.

LM: *How did you choose the texts that you used at the beginning? What criteria did you use?*
T: As one of the voice-overs in the film states, some of the criteria are the age, the work or the profession, the economical situation, the cultural region where the interviewee grew up, her critical ability and, sometimes, the question of personal affinity. When I first started out I was a little more "politically correct," in the sense that I was looking for a diversity of views and trying to include a wider range of professions, such as having a musician

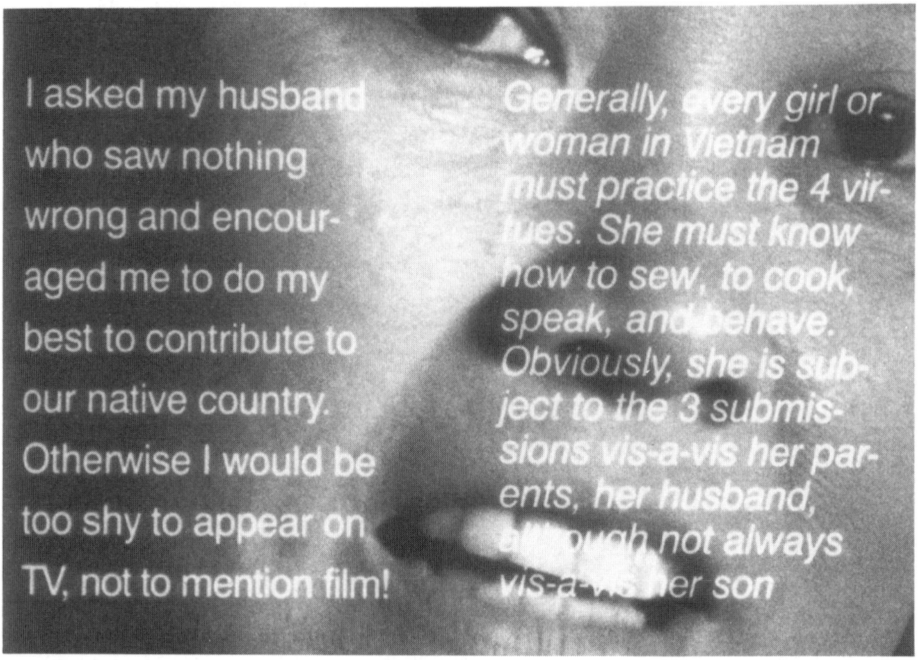

I asked my husband who saw nothing wrong and encouraged me to do my best to contribute to our native country. Otherwise I would be too shy to appear on TV, not to mention film!

Generally, every girl or woman in Vietnam must practice the 4 virtues. She must know how to sew, to cook, speak, and behave. Obviously, she is subject to the 3 submissions vis-a-vis her parents, her husband, though not always vis-a-vis her son

Fig. 8.3.   Film still from *Surname Viet Given Name Nam* by Trinh T. Minh-ha.
Courtesy Trinh T. Minh-ha

and a fishbreeder, in addition to the employee in the restaurant service for foreign embassies, the two doctors, and the health technical cadre whom you heard in the film. I chose the last three right from the start because of the scope that their stories and analyses covered. I think the fact that these women are helping other women—devoting their skill to relieving not only the physical but also the psychological pains of other women—makes them stand out as those whose interactions with women's bodies and mental health allow them to evaluate women's condition with both depth and scope.

Whether I agreed with their viewpoints or not, their stories struck me as being informed, rich, and penetrating—at once social and utterly personal. This, despite their critical denial of any intimate knowledge of their patients. Whereas some of the other interviews such as that with the fishbreeder would come out in the context of the film as being merely personal, hence reductive. Since the film was quite long, I had to cut down on the choices. The fact that the fishbreeder's account was too personal could not do justice to what she was trying to say, and it could be easily misread as some simplistic form of anticommunism. She was criticizing the system, but according to food metaphors, such as comparing the change of staple foods, from rice and fish sauce to bland potatoes, to the imposed consumption of the foreign doctrines of Marx and Lenin.

I would rather not have a representative of the manual labor class here, and maintain the integrity of the work by pursuing the links generated within the body of the diverse materials included. For example, the film also deals with the multiple appropriation and expropriation of women's bodies, and by extension, of Viet Nam as a nation—her being possessed and dispossessed at different historical moments by different outside forces. In addition to the many stories of the beloved historical heroines of Viet Nam, one epic poem occupies a pivotal role in the film: it is the popularized story of Kieu, a woman who sacrifices herself for her father and becomes a prostitute, selling her body to save his honor. All these elements tightly interact with the choice of the doctors—one from the north, one from the south, and the third being the northern health technical cadre whose ideological control over the doctors is strongly evoked in the latter's analyses.

Finally, such a choice takes into consideration regional differences to which the Vietnamese remains extremely sensitive: culturally and politically speaking, the voices of the film must represent the three regions of Viet Nam—north, south, and center. This determines not only the choices of the texts as related to the interviewee's cultural background; but also the selection of the actors, whose accents differ markedly, especially when they speak Vietnamese; and last but not least, the singing of the folk poetry.

LM: *So for example the woman that comes from the center spoke English with a voice that was accented differently from the others. . . . I missed that.*
T: It's normal. This is one aspect of language that remains inveterate and irreducibly idiomatic; I can't bring it out to the English-speaking viewer, and that's a limit of translation. For the Vietnamese, it is very evident since, by the feedback that I have had, I understand their attention is largely focused on this. As I just mentioned, such regionalist determination is also heard in the folk poetry, which was sung by one person, but in three accents, according to the context. However, if the demand for regionalism often springs from a hierarchically divisive attitude among certain members of the Vietnamese community, it can also be politicized and applied as a critical strategy. I found it very useful, for example, in trying to avoid reducing the Viet Nam reality to a binary opposition between communism and capitalism, to bring in the cultural role of the center precisely in order to decentralize the north-south duality.

Nowadays, the center part of Viet Nam does not, as in the Western sense of the term, represent power and stability. On the contrary, physically speaking, it no longer constitutes the location where the seat of the government is situated; and politically as well as culturally speaking, it stands as the unstable ground between first world and second world regulations. The central region has always been the one that remains closest to traditional culture, while the southern region adopted the modernization program of the West, and the northern region, under the influence of Russia and China, works at eliminating traditional practices considered to be "feudal and backward." So what's happening to this "tradition"—which people from all three regions keep on claiming in defining the Vietnamese identity? It is here that one realizes the potential of the center as site of resistance—not in reinstating the authority of a national patrimony, or of an essentialist identity (a mere recovery of the authentic past is in any case an "inauthentic" and unrealistic goal), but in offering an "empty," nonaligned, always-and-not-yet-occupied space where the tension between past and present is politicized, hence neither negative nor simply positive.

LM: *I've got a couple more things on the content; then we can talk about the form, because the form is so stunning. I had a problem as well with having set up the interviews—the monologues—at the beginning to show their fictionality, which I thought of not so much as a fiction but as a showing that the testimony that was being given was not coming from the people that were speaking. It was to make a separation between the actresses and the words, to show that it was not authentic subjectivity that was speaking. As a critique I felt that that became rather difficult at the end when the actresses spoke as themselves. It somehow came back to an idea of an authentic subjectivity, so that a relation appeared between the actress and the part that kind of brought back the question of authentic speech.*

T: That goes quite against what I said earlier in relation to Isaac's questions about the structural positions of the film. Of course, your reading can be just as valid, but I hope that there are enough cues in the film to engender another reading as well. I think speech is tactical, and with the unveiling not only of the fictionality of the reenacted interviews, but also the fictionality of the general nature of interviews in documentary practice, the subsequent words of the women in the "real interviews" can no longer be considered as being simply "truthful." Unmediated access to authentic reality via the interview has been questioned, so that the viewer's critical ability is solicited before the "real interviews" are introduced. These interviews in which a camera and a microphone are set up to catch the "spontaneous words" of a woman while she is having lunch, for example, are no less staged than the reenacted ones; but, now that the "staging" may be taken more for granted by the viewer, it's more hidden, concealed, because it is no longer perceptible via the mise-en-scène or the language, but more via the situating, framing, editing, and contextualizing. Furthermore, when the women spoke, they mostly "chose" how to be heard, and perhaps—

LM: *Can you give us an example?*

T: The last interview in Vietnamese with the two women who worked, one in a hydroelectric power company, and the other in a high-tech electronics company. When they were asked the question why they accepted to be on film, one replied that she had consulted her husband who encouraged her to contribute to "our native country"; and this was how she overcame her shyness to appear on film. She went on relating also how a friend of her husband teased her, saying: "Who knows, maybe you'll act so well that the Americans will notice you and you'll be a Hollywood star in the future." The other woman interviewed also considered her contribution not to be "an individual matter but one that concerns a whole community." She went on relating, similarly, her friends' reactions and how they "were taken aback when they heard I was acting the role of a sixty-year-old woman."

What stands out for me in these answers, is the fact that the women were extremely aware of both the role they played earlier in the film and the role they were assuming as they spoke "for themselves." They were clearly addressing, not the individual filmmaker, but the community and its authority. And in a way, they were also voicing their desire as actors to a cinema public. There was no such thing as catching "life on the run," or capturing the words of "truth." Clearly, one truth that did not seem to come through their "real" lines was, for example, the tremendous difficulty one of the two women had to overcome, when the time came for her to answer "on her own" and to speak as first subject. She was absolutely stuck in front of the camera and couldn't utter a single word in response to the questions. In between long uncomfort-able stretches of silence she said, "What should I say?" "How should I answer? . . . I can't talk." And typically enough, I said, just answer it the way you usually talk to me; say anything that comes through your mind. But it took her a long, long time finally to come out with speech. There is no question, really, of soliciting and reproducing the "ordinary" (or the authentic) in an "unordinary" (or inauthentic) situation. So whether it was by choice or by lack of choice (it was both), this "truth" didn't come out in the delivery; what materialized was not just "anything" that crossed the women's mind, but what they wanted the viewers to hear. It is in this sense that I find it difficult to see the last part of the film as a return to the voice of authenticity.

IJ: *It is a whole process really. I mean, your art must enter into that process with you in this kind of journey. . . . I know these questions are unresolved for myself. My practice is—since everything is fictional—to escape in fiction. And enter the realm of fantasy, then within those spaces, to try to talk about politics or representation. At the same time I'm drawn to documentary film as well because I'm interested in that kind of tension. They all have their different laws—*
T: —and different sets of problems.
LM: *Can't escape. No way out.*

IJ: *I wondered if you could talk about the use of text and image in juxtaposition, where you have the subject speaking, when in some cases they were using English, in the same way that my mother and father use English—it's half their own language and half English, so there's this kind of hybrid taking place, and then you use text as well when they talk, and when you think it might be difficult to decipher and disseminate what's being said, so I wondered if you could talk about the use of text and image in your film.*
T: Sure. Since the film tackles the problems of interviews and of translation, it cannot avoid dealing with language and with the relationship between languages. Besides deliberately using English for the interviews carried out in Viet Nam, and Vietnamese for those conducted in the States; and beside juxtaposing different instances of English as used by Vietnamese-Americans, I have also worked on the relationship between what is read, what is heard, and what is seen onscreen. The duration of the subtitles, for example, is very ideological. I think that if, in most translated films, the subtitles usually stay on as long as they technically can—often much longer than the time needed even for a slow reader—it's because translation is conceived here as part of the operation of suture that defines the classical cinematic apparatus and the technological effort it deploys to naturalize a dominant, hierarchically unified worldview.

The success of the mainstream film relies precisely on how well it can hide (its articulated artifices) in what it wishes to show. Therefore, the attempt is always to protect the unity of the subject; here to collapse, in subtitling, the activities of reading, hearing, and seeing into one single activity, as if they were all the same. What you read is what you hear, and what you hear is more often than not, what you see. My desire, on the contrary, was to "unsew" them and to present them as three distinct activities endowed with a certain degree of autonomy. Since the task of translation is more than to impart information, the viewer is made aware, in this film for example, of the gap between what is said or sung and what is read, through the minimal appearance of the burnt-in subtitles.

The necessity to free these activities from the "stickiness" of sameness can also be found in the relation between the verbal and the visual, and between writing and speech. Although differently materialized in each case, the word-image relationship in my films has always been one that refuses the use of the voice as being homogeneous to the image, and vice versa. In such a relationship, the role of an element is never simply to *serve* another—that is, to explain, to illustrate, or to objectify. For example, voice-overs need not be "fastened" to the visuals in an all-knowing mode; and the predicament of interviews lies here in their inability to solve the problem of talking heads, or to undo the fixity of synchronous sound and image—hence the name of "flat cinema" given to the talking film, and the need of a filmmaker like Marguerite Duras to break away from the habit of "screwing" (as she puts it) the voices to the mouths in realist cinema practices.

This discussion on the nonsubmissive relation between word and image leads us to the use of the text over the image in *Surname Viet*. The slight difference between the activities of reading and listening and its resulting tension is here created by the visibility of the small discrepancies between the text and the women's speeches (which are actually oral modifications of the text by the women themselves). The difference is also perceived in the fact that not only does the text not always enter at the same time as the speech, its shorter duration on the screen also makes it quasi-impossible for the viewer to hear and read at the same time without missing parts of both. The tension that the viewer experiences in trying to synchronize the two activities is, at another level, also the tension that the women experienced in reenacting a speech that has been transcribed and translated. The effort required from them is both that of transferring a written text into a spoken one, and that of delivering in a language that they have not mastered.

English as spoken by diasporic and Third World peoples has been widely treated by the media merely as a foreign language whose subtitling is a commonplace. I can't perpetrate such a hegemonic attitude, but I can't also ignore the amount of effort I require of English-speaking audiences. So as you rightly point out, I did use the text to help the viewer at moments when the women's foreign accents and articulations may start to make it difficult to follow the interview. But the texts are not presented as mere subtitles; they have a function of their own as discussed, and aesthetically speaking, they are treated as a visual superimposed on another visual. Framed and composed over and in relation to the image of the woman speaking, they often invade it in its entirety.

LM: *About the rephotography, which you've used before . . .*
T: No, I haven't used it in any other film.

LM: *So it's the first time you've used rephotography; what does it mean to you in this context? Why did you use it, and what were its resonances?*
T: There are a number of meanings possible. First, the question of time. Working in the realm of stories and popular memories, I was not interested in a linear construction of time, and I was not attempting to reconstruct any specific period of Viet Nam history. Like the reenacted interviews, the archival images are indicative of the times, the places, and the contexts to which they owe their existence. (One of the functions of the visual quotes preceding the interviews is also to date the women's accounts.) But the relations they generate among themselves as well as with the verbal texts of the film continually displace the notion of fixed time and place. Hence, the challenge is to use the very specificities of the black-and-white news footage and photographs to reach out both to a plural past and to an unspecified present and future.

An example: the 1950s footage of the north-south movement of the refugees is juxtaposed with a young woman's letter to her sister, reminiscing about the time mother and daughters spent in Guam (in 1975) while waiting to be admitted into the States. Here the focus is neither on the plight of the refugees in the '50s nor on that in the '70s; rather, what seems more important to me is the specific nature of the problems women of many times and many places have to undergo—as women. This is brought out in the remembered story, through the mother's anguish and terror of rape in experiencing *again*, "fleeing war on foot." So while the viewers follow images of refugees in the '50s with women clad quite unanimously in peasant attire and dark pants, they also hear about the mother's conviction in wearing dark clothes and persuading her daughters to do the same in the 1975 exodus "so as not to draw any attention to ourselves as women."

Another prominent example is the ending sequence of step-printed images of a group of refugees in the 1950s floating amidst the sea on a raft, seen with comments on the contemporary condition of the "boat people" and more recently yet, of the "beach people." The rephotography here stretches both the historical and the filmic time. It materializes the fragility of life, as it sets into relief the desperate and helpless character of such an escape. The insignificance of the tiny human forms on the drifting raft is seen against the vastness of the sea. But the fact that such a scene was recorded also reminds the viewer of the presence of a seer: the refugees had been spotted in the distance by a camera (and reproduced by another camera). Thus, hope is alive as long as there is a witness—or to evoke a statement in the film, as long as the witnesses themselves do not die without witnesses. In selecting the archival materials, recontextualizing and rephotographing them while acknowledging their transformations, I was, in other words, more interested in reflecting on the plight of women, of refugees, and of exile through images, than in rehashing the mediated horrors of the war and the turmoil of the subsequent fall of Saigon—which accounted for the contemporary disquieting expansion of the Vietnamese diaspora.

To come back to a word you have astutely used, rephotography displaces, and displacement causes resonance. It is extremely difficult, on a certain level, to rationalize such "resonance" without arresting it. As Pushkin would say, "poetry has to be a little stupid." But, if I am to further the discussion on another level without denying such a limit, I would add that the use of news footage and photography has its own problems in film practices—especially in documentary practices. The images have both a truth value and an error value. In other words, they are above all media memories. This is where the desire to create a different look and reading becomes a necessity. In the film, the older news photography is not only selectively reproduced, it is also deliberately reframed, de- and recomposed, rhythmized, and repeated with differences. Needless to say, media images of Viet Nam are not only ideologically loaded; they are also gender clichés. So the point is not simply to lift these news images out of their contexts so as to make them serve a new context—a feminist reading against the grain, for example, but also to make them *speak anew*.

Perhaps an example here is the very grainy black-and-white images of three women moving in slow truncated motion, right at the beginning of the film. They appear three times throughout the film, each time slightly different in their rhythms, framing, and visual legibility. The third time the viewer sees them, they are presented as they were originally shot, and with the original soundtrack, in which a male journalistic voice informs us that they were captured prisoners, whose bodies were "traditionally used by the enemy as ammunition bearers, village infiltrators and informers." A multiple approach to the same image is at times useful to cause resonance in the very modification of the material. Just as the story of Kieu has been, throughout centuries, appropriated according to the ideological need of each government, the media images of women during the war have been shot for causes in which women hardly come out as subjects—never fully witnessing, only glorified as heroines or victimized as bystanders of, spectators to, and exiles in their own history.

Notes

1. Laura is referring here to a statement in the film that says: "There is always a tendency to identify historical breaks and to say 'this begins there,' 'this ends here,' while the scene keeps on recurring, as changeable as change itself" (Trinh T. Minh-ha).

9

Interweaving Feminist Frameworks

Elizabeth Ann Dobie

One of the ways in which feminism bears an intrinsic affinity to pluralism is that it does not have, nor ought it strive for, a single voice.[1] There are different models of feminism. Each maintains certain presuppositions, addresses particular problematics, and works toward political ends. Rather than being a defect, I take this to be a positive and productive characteristic of feminist theorizing.

In a 1988 article in *Genders,* Lisa Tickner surveys three discourses of feminist theory which situate sexual difference in experiential difference, positional difference in discourse, and difference as psychoanalysis accounts for it.[2] Each perspective, emphasizing distinctive aspects of sexual difference, leads to alternative approaches to defining and explicating gender. Tickner states that an attempt to combine these three into a monolithic theory would be both monumentally difficult and undesirable.[3] While I agree with this insight, I would like to suggest that in some contexts it would be very useful, indeed preferable, to use the three perspectives in conjunction. These frameworks have much to contribute to one another and can be seen as supplements rather than as rivals.

When interpreting works of art, there are many available theoretical perspectives to which one can appeal. One factor that may influence the choice is what issues are present in the work one wishes to address.[4] In discussing the artwork of Nancy Spero, I shall illustrate how all three frameworks of sexual difference can be employed in critiquing works of art. After discussing Spero's work, I shall show how the perspectives can be theoretically compatible.

First, let me briefly comment on the aspects of difference encompassed in each perspective. Experiential difference focuses on the idea that due to the assignment of sex roles, women's and men's lives are socially structured in such a way as to provide disparate realities for each. As a result they have divergent perceptions and expectations of the world. The focus of positional difference is on the structure of language and the production of meaning through various forms of representation. Developing from a poststructuralist linguistic framework, it construes gender mainly as a semiotic category constructed relationally through "a system of difference."[5] Psychoanalysis explicates gender in terms of divergent psychological development.

Nancy Spero's work engages all three aspects of difference. Her images raise social and political questions regarding the treatment and status of women, questions of how women and men are positioned relationally in discourse, and questions of the portrayal and control of women's sexuality. The introduction to the catalogue of Spero's 1987 exhibition in London states, "Spero's exclusion from the mainstream artworld ironically reflects a more profound absence, which she has addressed through her practice as an artist and also through her leading role in political and feminist action."[6] Spero's own experience as a woman artist is an example of the absences she is addressing in her work. As a creator of images, she not only expresses her own voice in the sense of self-identity, but also articulates a space for women as represent-ers, agents, subjects. She states, "My body, my presence mediated by the mark on the paper, is no longer absent. I speak."[7]

Many of Spero's drawings take place on long scroll-like pieces of paper, some measuring more than 200 feet in length (see Figs. 9.1 and 9.2). They hang horizontally, wrapping around a room, or strips hang vertically, side by side. The representations of women are widely diverse, drawing on resources such as the Greek goddesses, Sumerian wall paintings, Egyptian hieroglyphics, and Greco-Roman art, among others. Sometimes the images are appropriated from other sources, while at times she reappropriates her own images. Many of her works include words. Image and text, appearing together, begin a new discourse.

While the format of the scroll is usually suggestive of a narrative, it does not operate as such in Spero's work. There is no linear time movement with a proper beginning and ending. Instead, the viewer may engage the drawings at any point. Moving along the scroll, one can begin to draw various associations among different sections. The viewer may choose to move in closely to read a typed script or step away to feel the overall flow of the figures on the flat and running expanse. This disruption of expected linear narration works toward altering positional meaning in discourse in two ways. First of all, the subject's position in relation to the image discourse is altered. The viewer is empowered by being able to actively engage the artwork in a method of her own choosing. She is not directed to a proper sequence of viewing. Thus, instead of being a passive observer outside of the discourse, the viewer becomes a participant within it. Second, the structure of the discourse itself is changed. Linear narrative can be taken to assume "masculine" values through its logical sequencing and movement toward closure.[8] Spero's format undermines these values by breaking the narrative structure and refusing closure for either the artist or the audience.[9]

Another way that Spero's work transforms gender meaning constructed through positioning in discourse is by making that discourse speak of women differently. In *Notes in Time on Women* (1979) we see an image of a woman reminiscent of Greco-Roman sculpture. The text within the image talks about the Greek Goddess. To the right of the image, written much like a slogan, we see "For Artemis that heals women's pain." Above the figure, is a capital "A"—not only the first letter in the name of the goddess, but also the first letter of the alphabet—the beginning of the male discourse that Spero is trying to interrupt. Text and image appear here together throughout the scroll. By using citations and historically familiar images, Spero employs the "terms" of others to create another discourse. Quotations from men about women now placed in juxtaposition to her images take on new meaning. A woman leaps in a split above Derrida's statement that, "the feminist women are men . . . feminism wants castration, even that of women."[10] Her body language laughs at the words. Successive formulations of what *they* say portray an absurdity in how women have been defined. The texts, though written boldly in typeface, are often incomplete, typed incorrectly, and difficult to read. Re-presented here, they show a lack.

While Spero speaks through creating discourse, her images are concerned with women's voices in general, which "are, for the most part, historically silenced."[11] In one sense, she examines and depicts that silencing. In another sense, she represents women with voices. Through female images brandishing phallic tongues, marginal voices are given power and meaning.

Women can speak; they can dance; they can laugh. By inverting psychoana-

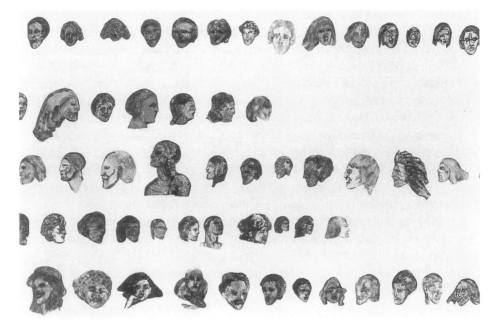

Fig. 9.1.   Nancy Spero, *Notes in Time on Women II* (detail). Courtesy Josh Baer
Gallery, New York

lytic gender dichotomies, Spero gives a new place to women in the realm of
representation. Her figures are not passive and mute; they will not submit to
a mastering gaze. They are active and engaged. Women bound through space,
jubilant, absorbed in their own activities. They are sometimes confrontive,
establishing their position as subject.[12] Or immersed in their own interchange,
they are heedless of a viewer's intrusion.

It is impossible to say unequivocally how women are represented in Spero's
images precisely because she works toward complicating the referents of
"woman." Not only do single images have many possible referents, but the
idea of woman or female is diversely portrayed. Woman is presented as actor,
as agent, as victim, as mother, as athlete, as goddess, as a sexual being.

These various images of women also illustrate a central tension in the
concept of experiential difference. On the one hand, there is a similitude of
experience which women share in virtue of being female rather than male. On
the other hand, there is a diversity of experience among women. Her
representations of females articulate an affinity of experience and yet deny

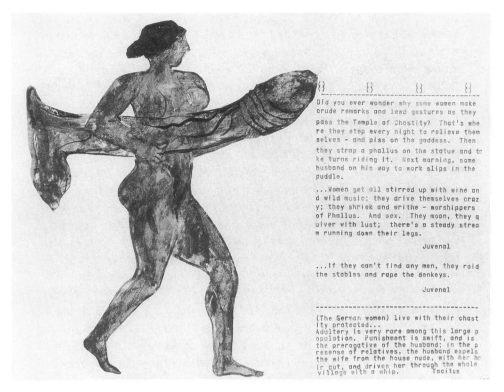

Fig. 9.2.   Nancy Spero, *Notes in Time on Women II* (detail). Courtesy Josh Baer Gallery, New York

univocity. Recognition of these two aspects are brought together in works such as *Hera Totem* (1985) in which images of women from different historical eras and diverse cultures are connected vertically on a scroll, supporting each other. While something weaves these women together, the distinctiveness of each figure suggests a plurality of unique backgrounds and viewpoints. Her female figures show a heterogeneity due to, among other things, race, nationality, economic status, and sexual preference. Still, in other works, women are presented as a group in contrast to men. *Let the Priests Tremble* (1984) announces, "Yes, we are not men, we are different." Acknowledging this difference is a positive element which is celebrated, a source of power rather than inadequacy.

The collaging technique employed in *Notes in Time on Women* (1979) and *Torture of Women* (1974–76) brings together pieces of women's actual experience. The sources of texts presented here range from newspaper articles, to reports from Amnesty International, to personal letters written by women. One aspect of these two works is to display the role of women as victim and as survivor. Here, Spero addresses the issue of domination over women exercised through both public institutions (war, torture) and those that are more personal or "private" (marriage/divorce, rape), a domination which the framework of experiential difference seeks to abolish.[13] The pain and destruction articulated in these works is a destruction not only of women's bodies but particularly of their sexuality. It suggests both a literal, physical oppression and an oppression exercised through the masculine definition and control of women's sexuality through images and myths. *Search and Destroy* (1967) shows a bomber plane (penis?) penetrating a woman lying on her back, pinned to the ground. Blood is flowing from her body (bloodshed from war? menstrual blood?). The mutilation of the woman takes place through both murder and possession which require her to be an object of his action.

Throughout her work, Spero depicts real experiences of women and what experience is like as a woman. She engages historical events, myths, textual discourses, and artistic conventions. The diversity of connotations and experiences articulated in Spero's work subverts the possibility of saying that woman is "this" and "not that." By challenging *and* celebrating differences, she undermines the traditional conceptions of gender. Her art works toward altering the position of women within discourse and their relation to it. She uses female bodies "to speculate on what is possible and to comment upon immediate events and rites of passage—political, sexual, personal."[14]

Within an experiential framework, gender is taken to reflect the divergence of experience between men and women. The categories of gender may be seen to be either biologically or socially grounded. Additionally, although "masculinity" and "femininity" may overlap and are subject to alteration by historical and social factors, they are taken to be "relatively unproblematic" categories in any given context.

Nancy Hartsock is a Marxist feminist who theorizes difference along the lines of experience. Following Marx's notion of praxis, she accepts both the claim that humans are what they do and the claim that one's epistemology is shaped by one's material life. Since women and men engage in different activities and as classes lead different material lives, they have different "lived realities" and divergent worldviews.[15]

Through the development of a feminist standpoint Hartsock provides an "epistemological tool" which can be used to critique phallocentric institutions and serve as the basis for social and political change. The availability of more than one standpoint rests on the notion of dual levels of understanding. One level is the level of appearances. Structured by the dominant viewpoint, this level defines and guides everyday social relations, interactions, and institutions. Below this level resides reality. It is on this level that the true nature of social relationships becomes evident.

Since material conditions determine epistemology, which sort of understanding one has access to depends upon the activity in which one is involved. Thus, a division of labor correlates with the two levels of understanding. Systematically divergent activities produce divergent epistemologies leading to disparate, even opposing, world views.

Hartsock claims that the basic division of labor is a sexual one.[16] By focusing on "institutionalized social practices," she explains that men are primarily concerned with production while women must be involved in both production and reproduction. This gives women's activities a "double aspect." They not only contribute to subsistence (and production) but also produce and reproduce other men and women. The types of activities they are involved in then systematically differ from those of men. Women are engaged in sensuous activity which focuses on the necessities of daily life. Continuous interaction with the material world contributes to the "special understanding" available to ruled classes and hence uniquely places women in a position to see the truth about social relations.[17] Moreover, reproductive activity allows women to experience and embrace change rather than stasis, quality rather than quantity, and a unification of mind and body: in short, a set of values more consonant with the development and flourishing of humanity than is the dominant masculine standpoint.[18]

What especially interests me about Hartsock's approach is that, in conjunction with her Marxist analysis of material conditions, she uses psychoanalysis to help explain the origin and perpetuation of the difference in feminine and masculine standpoints. She invokes the object-relations theory of Jane Flax and Nancy Chodorow to explain how it is that males and females arrive at different standpoints. The sexual division of labor requires the female both to bear and to raise children, thus leading to very different experiences of individuation for the girl and the boy. The boy must reject his mother in an effort to establish his own identity as "masculine." The girl, on the other hand, need not negate her mother since she will be the child's role model. Through the resolution of the Oedipus complex and the process of socialization, boys and girls come to have very different views of their selves. Girls may be able to have a sense of their own identity without needing to detach themselves from all others thus creating a self-in-relation, while boys begin their establishment of self by clearly breaking from an other and setting up rigid boundaries for their selves as independent beings.[19] Furthermore, since girls have a concrete role model with whom they are in contact on a day-to-day basis, they learn to value the "concrete necessities" arising from the family and home, the reproduction and contribution to subsistence that takes place there. In contrast, boys learn to reject (and thus devalue) elements of the home and to strive toward recognition in the public realm. Finally, these processes of differentiation are mirrored in the structures of institutions and society in general. How one relates to and sees the world is shaped by one's psychological development.

For a position such as Hartsock's, sex is seen as biologically given. Babies are born either male or female. From this point, psychoanalysis is taken to be an empirical account of how humans actually develop psychologically. While the psychological experience that infants and children go through establishes and reinforces the division of labor and the way women and men approach the world, the division of labor (with women bearing and raising children) perpetuates differential psychological development. The two elements thus feed into and recapitulate each other. Hartsock states, "These different (psychic) experiences both structure and are reinforced by the differing pattern of male and female activity required by the sexual division of labor, and are thereby replicated as epistemology and ontology."[20]

At first it may sound as though there is no way out of this self-perpetuating cycle, yet Hartsock does reveal a foothold. If the division of labor changes (through an extension of the feminist standpoint to the rest of society), so too the psychological development of self will change. While "masculine" and "feminine" are clearly coherent categories, they are not static ones.[21]

Hartsock's work demonstrates the compatibility of understanding difference both in terms of experience and in terms of psychoanalysis. Sex roles, coordinate with the division of labor, have created two opposing viewpoints leading to divergent perceptions and expectations of the world. Psychoanalysis supplements this account by providing the foundations of gender identification. The psychic process of development illustrates how individuals come to see their selves in relation to the world differently. In turn, the sense of self leads women and men into diverse activities. Hence psychoanalysis can elucidate how a continual difference in experience is perpetuated. Furthermore, an account of experiential difference that utilizes psychoanalysis may be more complete than one that does not. The implementation of the insights of both approaches taken together allows one to discuss and analyze aspects that would otherwise be neglected by a singular approach. As experience includes both the physical and the psychological, articulating the interplay between the two realms can give a more comprehensive analysis of differential perceptions and expectations. Psychoanalysis provides answers to questions such as why the division of labor persists, and why people accept and sustain gender categories. Additionally, it is able to explicate women's and men's motivations for making the diverse choices and decisions they do. A strategy that implements only daily physical activity would not be able to resolve these issues. Likewise, a strategy that ignores material existence would overlook elements contributing to or causing gendered societal structures that are not reducible to individual psychological development.[22] It will not always be the case that one must appeal to both perspectives, however; in some instances it will prove valuable to be able to discuss the two together in order to address a broader scope of relevant elements.

On this dual reading of difference, gender, from either aspect, is taken to provide coherent categories. As shown in Hartsock's work, Marxism and psychoanalysis converge on stable gender identities.[23] The divisibility of "masculine" and "feminine" at a societal level through distinctive viewpoints and separable activities, coincides with the psychoanalytic account of gender development.[24]

The reciprocal relation between psychoanalysis and experience is played out in a very interesting way in Spero's work. The resolution of the Oedipus complex involves the realization that females lack penises. From the boy's perspective, this may produce a feeling of superiority but also a feeling of fear of those who are different or "other." For the girl, this realization may bring about feelings of inferiority and inadequacy. The resulting situation appears in Spero's work in a manner that simultaneously mocks the ascription of values made on this basis while it portrays the very real consequences such ascriptions have had for women.

The figures of *Chorus Line I* (1985), who unabashedly present their vulvas, join with the leaping figures of *Let the Priests Tremble* (1984) in asserting, "We're going to show them our sexts! Too bad for them if they fall apart on discovering that women aren't men, that the mother doesn't have one." The seeming complicity with the psychoanalytic story is undermined by the figures' defiant indifference to men's fear. It is not women's fault if men feel this way. While these figures proudly display their sexual difference, other figures carting phalluses mock the idea that women mourn the lack of a penis.

Alternatively, the fear of women's sexuality and the need to "control" it has contributed to structuring sex roles. A quotation from Mary Jane Sherfey suggests that the subjugation of women took place through a suppression of their sexual drives which was needed in order to establish the family as the basic, stable unit of society.[25] Here again, Spero's inquiry into sex roles takes place on two levels. On the one hand, she explores how sex roles have circumscribed what is deemed proper to women in order to question any essential connection between proscribed "feminine" traits and females. On the other hand, the portrayal of "mother," for instance, acknowledges the sex role and yet reinscribes it differently. The pregnant figures move freely. Their agility suggests a desire for and contentment with their role. Even though the many-breasted Mother Goddess assumes a protective position, the figures she is poised above are those who flatly refuse to conform to stereotypical roles. Spero is able to depict the paradox of the presence of sex roles and the desire to ameliorate them.

The second approach I shall discuss is the interplay of psychoanalysis with positional difference in discourse. Both perspectives see a certain instability in gender categorization. The first perspective locates the instability within subjects who embody unconscious and bisexual drives and desires. The latter primarily situates the instability in meaning which is constructed and contingent rather than essential or foundational. The compatibility of psychoanalysis and position in discourse may be the most apparent since there is already a large body of literature which simultaneously uses both.[26]

There are two facets of position in discourse relevant to gender differences that I wish to discuss. The first is the implementation of gender terms in the sign systems themselves. Second, the relationship between speaker and subject, and speaker and audience becomes very important. If gender is defined by discourse, those who get to do the defining hold a powerful position.

In addressing the gendered structure of sign systems, Luce Irigaray and Julia Kristeva are notable examples of writers who pursue this issue through both psychoanalytic and positional discourse. In *Speculum of the Other Woman,* Irigaray undertakes an analysis of Freud.[27] The central component of Freud's theory is the penis. All explorations and definitions of sexuality are constructed in reference to this powerful signifier. Woman is the lack of penis, the negative counterpart to the man, the unresolvable engima. Irigaray's guiding insight is that this, along with Lacan's equation of the phallus with the transcendental signifier, places women outside of language and the symbolic order.[28]

By beginning with psychoanalytic discourse, Irigaray is able to extend this critique to the entirety of discourse. In *This Sex Which Is Not One,* she addresses the phallocentrism of the whole symbolic order. Reinterpreting a discourse in which "sexuality itself is at stake" reveals the "sexuality" of all discourse and its rational foundations.[29] Moreover, subjecting a text to psychoanalytic critique discloses its own structure, the law of its production. By attending to "the way the unconscious works in each philosophy . . . its syntactic laws or requirements, its imaginary configurations, its metaphoric networks, and also, of course, what it does not articulate at the level of utterance: *its silences*" are uncovered.[30] Psychoanalysis then can be an effective tool for revealing the underlying power structure of language and the positioning of the feminine and masculine within it.

Irigaray is also able to utilize her critique of psychoanalysis as a basis for altering the positions of male and female within discourse. Women are subject to the "discourse-desire-law" of the patriarchy. They are spoken of, but are not allowed to speak. In order to interrupt the masculine enterprise, women must find another voice. Her examination of psychoanalysis points to the untapped resources—the multiple sexuality of women, feminine desire repressed by the Law of the Father, the constrained gestures of women's bodies—which can serve as a well-spring for *le parler femme*. She thus provides at least one way of empowering women and allowing them to escape the patriarchal ordering of language, perhaps creating an ungendered language which would not only position men and women differently, but would give new meaning to gender categories.

Spero participates in this project. She states, "There is no way to go but for a new direction. The French feminists are talking 'L'écriture féminine,' and I am trying 'la peinture féminine.' "[31] The gestures of her female figures are not constrained. Women announce and delight in their own sexuality. They take pleasure not only in their own bodies but in one another's through embrace and touch. The figures that run and dance across the walls of *To Soar II* (1990) spill over onto the ceiling, refusing to be restricted even by a frame.[32] These images present subjects, protagonists, who do not exist for the pleasure of a male viewer. Conversely, presenting women in this provocative manner allows a new access to artworks by female viewers. A female can relate to the representations without having to occupy a masculine position nor having to identify with a passive object. By employing the "untapped resources" suggested by Irigaray, Spero transforms not only the way in which women are represented in discourse, but also the way in which female viewers engage the discourse.

When exploring gender as a semiotic category, one looks not only at the structure of language but the terms employed. A now familiar strategy is examining pair terms. For instance, in Derrida's work dichotomies that have operated throughout the history of philosophy are explored. They include being/non-being, presence/absence, essence/accident, proper/nonproper, literal/metaphorical. Part of how each word gets its meaning is its relationship to its pair term. The same type of dichotomies are at work in psychoanalysis: analyst/analysand, conscious/unconscious, male/female, unity/lack. All the dichotomies are overlaid by gender with the first terms constituting "masculine" and the latter "feminine." One aspect of Julia Kristeva's project has been to acknowledge the presence and operation of these polarities and to use them to open a new space for women's voices while at the same time undermining the unquestioned acceptance of the categories thus created. "From One Identity to An Other" deals with the interplay of the symbolic and the semiotic.[33] Again, each has a gender association. By using psychoanalytic theory, Kristeva theorizes the origin of the semiotic in instinctual drives which exist in the speaking subject prior to the constraints imposed by the symbolic order. Thus the speaking subject is capable of expressing both.[34] The semiotic, defying systemization by rules, is instantiated in rhythm, intonation, and disruption of grammatical rules, with poetry, music, and psychosis being its paradigm cases. On the other hand, scientific discourse most nearly approaches the purely symbolic. However, Kristeva illustrates how the two elements are always present within all discourse; there are no pure cases of either. It is the power of the semiotic to disrupt symbolic ordering and force theoretical reasoning "to increase its power by giving it an object beyond its limits."[35] The feminine, associated with semiotic expression, finds its voice here. Rather than inspiring a second alternative discourse, the feminine intrudes within the symbolic order, requiring it to acknowledge an element that is heterogeneous to its structure. The semiotic is outside of the symbolic order in the sense of "preceding and exceeding" meaning and originating from instinctual and maternal drives. It may best be articulated by women, Kristeva suggests, because they too are outside of the paternal order of signification. However, the ability to articulate semiotic expression, although connected with the feminine, is not necessarily limited to women. The psychoanalytic framework here provides a way to begin to dismantle the oppositional character of gender constructions in language.

Beyond the organization of language, another influential aspect determining gender positionally is the situation of the speaker. Kaja Silverman states, "Discourse always requires a speaking position (a position from which power-knowledge is exercised) and a spoken subject (a position brought into existence through the exercise of power-knowledge)."[36] Those who are speakers produce meaning in discourse. Psychoanalysis has contributed to exploring this dynamic in two respects. First of all, psychoanalysis employs similar power relations. Silverman continues, "For instance, 'analyst' indicates a speaking subject, whereas 'patient' designates a spoken subject. The analyst can occupy the position of a spoken subject in relation to himself. . . . However, the patient can never occupy the position of the speaking subject vis-à-vis the analyst, and is in fact frequently told that the analyst will decide what is significant."[37] Psychoanalysis, as a subsection of all discourse, most clearly reveals the implications of the power relation. It is precisely this recognition that has led various women artists such as Nancy Spero, Lorna Simpson, and Cindy Sherman to demand that women represent themselves.

Perhaps more important, psychoanalysis has given us the tools to undermine the authority of the producers of signs. Kristeva's "questionable-subject-in-process" constituted by the capacities for both semiotic expression and symbolic ordering mentioned above, destroys the notion of a coherent, unified subject. This harkens back to Freud's explication of the unconscious. Within each person's conscious articulation of her thoughts and desires, the unconscious is at work.[38] The recognition that a subject's intentions are not purely present to herself, has led to a rejection of the theory of interpretation that held (the true) meaning to be conveyed by authorial intentions. Instead, meaning is produced at the site of intersection between the work (text or image) and the audience. On the one hand, this has empowered the recipient, thus upsetting the hierarchical authority of the producers. On the other hand, the focus on audience has brought to light the frequency with which reception positions have been forced into masculine postures.

We have seen that Spero's work does not demand a masculine spectator nor does it allow mastery. First of all, the physical immensity of the scroll pieces won't allow one to view a work in its entirety in a single gaze. Second, there is not a fixed meaning to grasp: there is no Truth of woman here. Additionally, there is a denial of mastery by Spero herself. Fragments of texts, detached body parts, smeared images and words, physically suggest an incompleteness. Multiple connections can be made between elements within the work and to things outside of the work. What associations are made by the viewer is left as an open possibility which leads to an intertextuality.

Writers, in examining the positions of males and females in representation, have also made use of psychoanalytic theory and its attendant myths of sexuality. For example, Laura Mulvey, Peter Lehman, Naomi Schor, and Nancy Miller have written articles that explore this framework at two levels.[39] They discuss the representations of males and females within works of literature or art, examining how each either reinscribes or denies the Freudian conception of sexuality. Additionally, this critique is extended to the dynamics of reception of the work.

By critically examining the sexuality presented in representations, feminist psychoanalytic readings have exposed myths of desire and power which place men in positions of control, authority, and knowledge. The positioning of the female as a passive object, for instance, is shown not to be a description of female sexuality (what women really desire) but rather an outcome of a masculine desire for possession and mastery. Psychoanalysis provides an explanation for why these myths have been so powerful and why they persist. Situated within this theoretical context of positionality and psychoanalysis, one can expose the sexual myths constructing positions in discourse as a means to dismantling them.

The last compatability that needs to be discussed is that of experiential difference with positional difference. The most difficult problem impeding the combination of these two perspectives is that experiential difference construes gender as creating stable, sociological categories. On the other hand, positional difference shows "masculine" and "feminine" to be constructed, unstable gender categories.

Now, when dealing with Hartsock, her approach to experiential difference does take gender to create stable, sociological categories. They have this nature though in the sense of being identifiable on a societal level. Categorization of gender is linked to the type of labor in which one is engaged. The division of gender remains stable only so long as the same division of labor is perpetuated. Even on Hartsock's view, "stable" is taken within a cultural context; it does not mean constant or determinate. This notion of stability does not preclude change, future redefinition, or instability within particular sociohistorical contexts. [40]

As I see it, there are three grounding assumptions which will be necessary to coordinate these two positions. First of all, it will have to be maintained that language influences one's categories of thought. Second, since one's categories of thought influence one's experience, the position that experience is not unmediated will have to be accepted. Last, the influence of experience upon the way one thinks will have to be acknowledged. These three parts together will provide a perspective in which gender is constructed positionally and socially. As constructions, gender categories remain open to change since they are not given or in the nature of things.

It seems to me that the criticisms leveled against positional difference can be resolved by using it in conjunction with experiential difference. [41] Additionally, experiential difference benefits from the insights of positionality as it focuses on what structures our experience, namely, language.

Willard van Orman Quine makes a case in *Word and Object* that language learning and learning about the world are not two separate enterprises but occur simultaneously. One learns "facts" about the world through the acquisition of language.[42] This line of thought is developed in writers as diverse as Wilfred Sellars, Jacques Derrida, and Donald Davidson. What is found in each is a rejection of "raw" experience (the British empiricist's "sense-data" or Frege's "senses") and the claim that there is no pure given onto which language is mapped. This metaphysical position that denies the plausibility of extracting language from experience provides the foundation of meaning on which experiential and positional difference can be combined. The way language is structured must affect our perceptions of the world because the way we learn and talk about the world is through language.

On a commonsense level, there appears to be a reciprocal relation between experience and discourse. As explained previously, experiential difference maintains that the imposition of sex roles influences the way one perceives the world. While the position that one holds in discourse affects how one perceives, the existence of sex roles can influence what positions in discourse one is allowed to hold. There are two aspects of this claim, relevant to gender, that I would like to examine.

The first aspect, involving the influence of sex roles, is the experience of the artist, as a woman, within the institution of art production and reception. At the level of practice, men and women historically have played very different roles in their relations to this institution. This situation has been surveyed in detail by Linda Nochlin in her well-known essay "Why Have There Been No Great Women Artists?"[43] Inaccessibility to academic institutions, devaluation of women's intellectual and creative abilities, and expectations of women to fulfill (only) domestic duties—all contribute to their being proportionally few women included in the canon of art history.[44] These conditions stem from what sex roles have deemed proper for women. While the division may have been less contestable in the past, it still remains a problem for women artists today. Very few women artists are shown in mainstream institutions and so turn to alternative spaces to have their work shown. Alternative spaces provide valuable outlets for contemporary and "marginal" work. However, they are less accessible to (or at least are less accessed by) viewing audiences.[45] The result of this situation is that the majority of those presenting images in public arenas are male. Thus while the assignment of sex roles has had a great influence on who is admitted into the discourse (into the systems which present images), those who participate in the discourse wield a powerful influence on how sex and gender are viewed.

Alternatively, the second aspect of the relation between experience and discourse involves the way that positionality affects perceptions. One of the most obvious ways that sex and gender appear is in the representations of bodies. Female and male images are portrayed in various relations to each other, engaging in (or refraining from) diverse activities, maintaining contrasting positions relative to the viewer. The image may confront, entice, or ignore the audience. Color, form, spatial relationships, context, camera angle, or perspective—all contribute to how the figures are seen. Through its representations, the discourse of images constructs ideas of sexuality and gender. Suleiman writes, "The cultural significance of the female body is not only (not even first and foremost) that of a flesh-and-blood entity, but that of a *symbolic construct*. Everything we know about the body—certainly as regards the past, and even, it could be argued, as regards the present—exists for us in some form of discourse."[46] How we view, talk about, and read bodies is constitutive of what meanings are assigned to them.

The work of Barbara Kruger provides another example of what I have in mind here (see Figs. 5.1 and 11.4). In a recent article, Nancy Campbell has shown how Kruger's work is an attempt to change social relations through problematizing positional relations.[47] The photographs in Kruger's images are taken from commercial advertising, newspapers, and the like. These images, encountered by people every day, create subjects by telling people "who they are" and how they ought to be.[48] Thus, discursive force becomes an instrument of subjection because it produces stereotypes which are taken to be descriptive and prescriptive for actual people. It is not the stereotypes themselves which subject women, but rather the discursive force which "overdetermines" gender, stabilizing it for "real bodies involved in imaginary/ideological positions."[49]

On the one hand, Campbell maintains that Kruger's work is an effort to reveal the ideological positioning presented by discourse in order to make "acceptance of that positioning impossible."[50] On the other hand, Spero's work offers new positions within discourse. Her images struggle against subjection precisely by refusing to tell women who they are. The spectrum of images portrayed cannot be assimilated to a stable ideal. Instead, numerous possibilities are available.

The invocation of both positional difference and experiential difference is useful in talking about artists like Kruger and Spero. They recognize the effect that discursive power has on people and the necessity for "altering the subject's relation to discourse."[51] The mass media are among the more obvious examples of how discourse participates in subject construction. The media conveys messages about what we desire, how others see us, and how events are to be interpreted. In the guise of objectivity, the media presents what expectations and perceptions of the world we ought to have. This is not to suggest that people merely absorb and accept what is dictated by discourse, but rather that we are constantly confronted with and limited by systems which tell us what we are.[52]

Positional difference can share with experiential difference its aim to critique the patriarchy and end the oppression of women by men and male-dominated institutions. First of all, part of what governs these institutions is language. Second, discourse itself is a social practice and so part of the patriarchy. Positional difference is not constrained to focus on the "local" and the "textual." As shown above, it has a more general critique to make. It deals with the positions of men and women in society as constructed and influenced through discursive power, and it addresses gender within discourse itself. Both of these factors have direct relevance to ending women's oppression. Having already discussed the first point, I shall proceed to gender in language. Gendered language tends to be biased against women. It also is presumed to be neutral or objective in places where it clearly reveals a male point of view. In critiquing institutions and laws, some feminists have argued that purportedly neutral laws and rules turn out to harm women because they originate from a male point of view.[53] Thus they strive toward changing the language that governs the institutions in an effort to alter women's positions within them.

It seems apparent that gender can be seen as constructed both by the assignment of sex roles and one's position in discourse. The semiotic categories articulated through positional difference are mapped onto sociological categories. Changes in discourse or in who exercises discursive power result in altering actual positions of political power.

The artwork of Nancy Spero expresses the difficulty with presenting gender in a singular fashion. Each time the viewer is about to locate difference, the ground shifts. The multiple conceptions of difference presented in her imagery suggest the possibility of an intertexuality of feminist frameworks.[54]

Notes

1. In the use of "pluralism" here, I am referring to the view that there may be alternative critiques of artworks varying with one's theoretical framework. Accordingly, there may be more

than one correct interpretation of a single work of art or there may be interpretations that appeal to more than one theoretical framework.

2. Lisa Tickner, "Feminism, Art History, and Sexual Difference," *Genders* 3 (1988): 92–128. She borrows the distinctions from Michele Barrett. "The Concept of Difference," *Feminist Review* 26 (1987): 29–41. Tickner is interested in how concepts of difference may be used as approaches to art history. While I am not speaking directly of art history, I am concerned with the production of meaning through images, a discourse productive of knowledge, hence related to and affected by these conceptions of difference.

3. Both Tickner and Barrett believe that they are incompatible in fundamental presuppositions.

4. Among other factors that may influence the decision are one's audience and one's personal interest in the work.

5. Tickner, "Feminism, Art History, Sexual Difference," 106.

6. Iowana Blazwick, Mark Francis, and Seclan McGanagle, *Nancy Spero* (Brighton: ICA/ Fruitmarket Gallery/Foyle Arts Project, 1987), 3.

7. Nancy Spero, "Sky Goddess, Egyptian Acrobat," *Artforum International* 26 (1988): 104.

8. This describes only one type of narrative but it is a paradigmatic example of the values being undermined by Spero.

9. This issue involves both the psychoanalytic and positional frameworks. I shall return to a lengthier discussion of this point.

10. Jacques Derrida, "The Question of Style" in *The New Nietzsche*, ed. David B. Allison (New York: Dell, 1977), 182.

11. Spero, "Sky Goddess, Egyptian Acrobat," 104.

12. For example in *Rebirth of Venus* (1982) and in *Chorus Line I* (1985).

13. Tickner, "Feminism, Art History, Sexual Difference," 106. Tickner states, "It [experiential difference] relates to a theory of patriarchy which understands all women as directly and intimately oppressed by male institutions and by individual men."

14. Spero, "Sky Goddess, Egyptian Acrobat," 105.

15. Nancy C. M. Hartsock, "The Feminist Standpoint: Developing the Ground for a Specifically Feminist Historical Materialism," in *Discovering Reality*, ed. Sandra Harding and Merrill B. Hintikka (Boston: D. Reidel, 1983), 284.

16. Hartsock, "Feminist Standpoint," 289. In fact, she claims that every society has had this division and some societies have had only this one. She adds that one of the purposes of focusing on a sexual division is to ensure that the bodily aspect of existence is not forgotten or overlooked. Additionally, there still seems to be a biological difference that has yet to be overcome, namely, giving birth. While it is true that in our society it is females who give birth (this is not yet a social choice), the *way* in which this is done is not biologically given. Nor must the practice of childrearing take the form that it does at present in our society. Hartsock is quick to point out that it is unclear if this division can be said to be purely social or how much of it will turn out to be biologically given.

17. Ibid., 286.

18. It should be noted here that Hartsock states that she is talking about institutionalized roles and definitions not particular women and men. While not all women will actually have children, they "are forced to become the kinds of people who can do both (produce goods and human beings)" (ibid., 291). I take this to mean that women as a group are societally defined by their ability to give birth and contribute to subsistence in the home. Hartsock makes the further point that many typically female jobs require the same skills that mothering does, e.g., nursing, social work, and secretarial jobs (ibid., 293). Thus I take her point to be that girls are encouraged to develop skills and character traits that would prepare them to be mothers even if they never actually take on this role.

19. The only necessary element to get this project off the ground is a female primary caregiver. The values and norms attached to the resulting heterogenous selves are imposed by societal

standards. Thus the following family scenario need not be taken as an actual situation on Chodorow's account though it is important to the Marxist critique.

20. Hartsock, "Feminist Standpoint," 296.

21. Hartsock's position then does result in valuing the feminine epistemology over the masculine; however, it does not result in a separatist claim. The goal is to have all of society come to an understanding of the underlying reality by adopting the feminist standpoint.

22. Iris Marion Young, "Is Male Gender Identity the Cause of Male Domination?" in *Mothering: Essays in Feminist Theory*, ed. Joyce Trebilcot (Totowa, N.J.: Rowman and Allanheld, 1983), 129–46. Young makes the argument that while psychoanalytic theory can provide useful insights into the connection between individual gender differentiation and societal constructs of gender in terms of the pervasiveness of and investment in retaining gender meanings on a cultural level, it cannot give an explanation of the origin and existence of male *domination*. Gender differentiation processes in themselves won't explain why it is that males dominate. She states that "gender theory surely can contribute a part of the explanation of the nature and relation of social institutions, moreover. But the explanation of any institutional form, especially those relating to power and domination, requires in addition reference to the relation of institutions to one another, and an account of the material means of access, control, enforcement and autonomy that agents have within those institutions" (140).

23. Diana Meyers suggested this way of expressing their relation.

24. One of the difficulties in Hartsock's Marxist approach is that she must posit a commonality among all women. The model of an institutionalized role of women is too simplistic. The encouragement to develop nurturing skills as well as the acceptance or rejection of these skills by girls differs widely. While Hartsock is aware of this problem, she maintains that nonconformity is not "significant" until change occurs at the level of society as a whole ("Feminist Standpoint," 289).

25. Mary Jane Sherfey, M.D., *The Nature and Evolution of Female Sexuality* (New York: Random House, 1973). 142. The quotation appears in *Notes in Time on Women* (1979).

26. It will be apparent that the type of psychoanalysis discussed in this section is different from the object relations theory invoked by Hartsock.

27. Luce Irigaray, *Speculum of the Other Woman*, trans. Gillian C. Gill (Ithaca: Cornell University Press, 1986).

28. Ibid., 44, 52, 58, 60.

29. Luce Irigaray, *This Sex Which Is Not One*, trans. Catherine Porter with Carolyn Burke (Ithaca: Cornell University Press, 1985), 167–69.

30. Ibid., 75.

31. Iowana Blazwick, Mark Francis, and Seclan McGanagle, *Nancy Spero*, 5.

32. *To Soar II* (1990) is a site-specific installation created at Smith College Museum of Art, Northampton, Massachusetts.

33. Julia Kristeva, *Desire in Language*, ed. Leon S. Roudiez (New York: Columbia University Press, 1980).

34. This speaking subject has important consequences for one's position in discourse to which I shall return shortly.

35. Kristeva, *Desire in Language*, 146.

36. Kaja Silverman, "Histoire d'O: The Construction of a Female Subject" in *Pleasure and Danger*, ed. Carole S. Vance (Boston: Routledge and Kegan Paul, 1984), 320–49.

37. Ibid., 322.

38. Derrida cites Freud and the contamination of the conscious by the unconscious to question the significance of intentionality. Since the author is not an authority over himself (he cannot read off his own intentions), he cannot be an authority over the audience. See, for instance, Jacques Derrida, "Differance" in *Margins*, trans. Alan Bass (Chicago: University of Chicago Press, 1982), 1–28.

39. Laura Mulvey, "Visual Pleasure and Narrative Cinema" in *Art After Modernism: Rethinking Representation,* ed. Brian Wallis (New York: New Museum of Contemporary Art, 1984), 354–62; Peter Lehman, "In the Realm of the Senses: Desire Power, and the Representation of the Male Body," *Genders* 2 (1988): 91–110; Naomi Schor, "Female Fetishism: The Case of George Sand" and Nancy K. Miller, "Rereading as a Woman: The Body in Practice" both in *The Female Body in Western Culture,* ed, Susan Rubin Suleiman (Cambridge: Harvard University Press, 1986), 354–72.

40. There is another difficulty in supplementing positional difference with Hartsock's view of experiential difference. By positing two levels of understanding, she suggests that one group (the oppressed) have a privileged epistemological access to an objective reality. Frameworks of positional difference would deny this claim. However, this conflict is endemic to employing Hartsock's approach, not to experiential difference itself. The existence of divergent perceptions need not imply that one set is more accurate than another.

41. Tickner, "Feminism, Art History, Sexual Difference," 106, 107. The criticisms referred to are that positional difference tends to deal with the "textual" and the "local" and thus does not provide a sufficient strategy for political or social change.

42. Willard Van Orman Quine, *Word and Object* (Cambridge, Mass.: MIT Press, 1960). This thesis can be seen as part of the Kantian tradition in which knowledge is gained only through the combination of experienced "stuff" and concepts.

43. Linda Nochlin, "Why Have There Been No Great Women Artists?" in *Art and Sexual Politics,* ed. Thomas B. Hess and Elizabeth C. Baker (New York: Macmillan, 1973), 1–39.

44. See also, Suzi Gablik, "The Double Bind" in *Art and Sexual Politics,* 88–89.

45. I realize that the issue of the current museum and gallery network requires a more thorough analysis including economic, political, and historical factors. However, this project lies outside the scope of this paper. For my purposes, the observation that women do not have an equal share of exhibitions in public spaces is sufficient to make my point.

46. Susan Suleiman, "Female Body in Western Culture," 2. See also Silverman, "Histoire d'O," 325. She states, "it will be my working hypothesis that while human bodies exist prior to discourse, it is only through discourse that they arrive at the condition of being 'male' or 'female.' "

47. Nancy D. Campbell, "The Oscillating Embrace: Subjection and Interpellation in Barbara Kruger's Art," *Genders* I (1988): 57–74.

48. John Berger, *Ways of Seeing,* (London: Penguin Books, 1977). Berger offers an in-depth discussion of how images portray the way that males and females are seen and, in turn, how these images affect the way we see ourselves. He discusses how images in art and advertising construct subjects through the construction of desires, values, and beliefs.

49. Campbell, "The Oscillating Embrace," 60.

50. Ibid., 65.

51. Ibid., 60.

52. Positional difference would suggest that even the idea of there being unified subjects is constructed through discourse.

53. See Irigaray, *This Sex Which Is Not One,* and also Rosemarie Tong, *Women, Sex, and the Law* (Totowa, N.J.: Rowman and Littlefield, 1984).

54. I would like to thank Peggy Brand, Joyce Brodsky, Diana T. Meyers, and Samuel C. Wheeler III for their insightful comments and editorial assistance on an earlier draft of this paper.

10
Monologues from "Four Intruders Plus Alarm Systems" and "Safe"

Adrian Piper

[Editors' Note: *Adrian Piper is a conceptual artist whose work from the past twenty-five years has included performances, graphic art, and installation pieces. Always provocative, Piper seeks to challenge viewers' assumptions about the nature of art, aesthetic response, and modes of evaluating by creating art that involves issues of gender and race. Piper uses political art to confront viewers with emotionally charged environments that preclude our maintaining a safe, aesthetically distanced stance toward the subject matter. Being forced to confront our own prejudices, both emotionally and aesthetically, we undergo a process of change that is both cognitive (evidenced by how our interpretations of the work change and evolve) and affective (resulting in a higher level of social awareness and sensitivity). Thus, according to Piper, political art has "the potential for furnishing a forceful antidote to racism."[1]*

The following two statements consist of text written by Piper and recorded on audiotapes for two installation pieces: "Four Intruders Plus Alarm Systems" (1980) and "Safe" (1990). In the preliminary explanation to "Four Intruders Plus Alarm System," Piper describes the work and her purpose in constructing the four monologues that played on the headphones for viewers to hear. She also includes candid comments on her reaction to viewers' interaction with the work.

The second work, "Safe," is also a multimedia installation. It consists of black-and-white photographs of smiling, waving African Americans who appear to be posing for family portraits, although the text "You are safe" is superimposed across the bottom of the image. These images are hung in the corners of a room in which an aria from Johann Sebastian Bach's "Saint Matthew Passion" is heard in the background of an audiotape in which Piper's voice recites the monologue. The setting for the aria is the fulfillment of Christ's prophecy: Christ has predicted that Peter will deny him three times before the cock crows. Peter denies any knowledge of or association with Christ on three separate occasions. When the cock crows, Peter realizes what he's done and asks God's forgiveness with these words: Have mercy, Lord, on me, Regard my bitter weeping, Look at me, heart and eyes. Both weep to Thee bitterly. Have mercy, Lord!]

Four Intruders Plus Alarm Systems (September 1980)

This was the third installation I did that was concerned with ideological defenses against the comprehension of political realities and one's own involuntary (and sometimes unwilling) participation in them. Here I was concerned

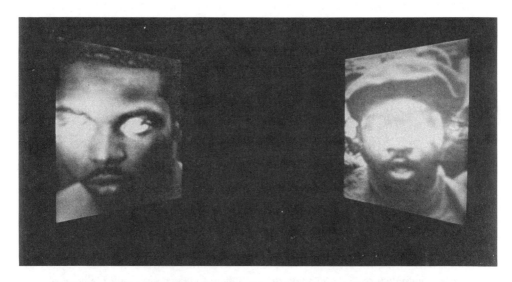

Fig. 10.1.   Adrian Piper, *Four Intruders Plus Alarm Systems.* Collection Wexner Center for the Arts, The Ohio State University, Columbus; purchased in part with funds from The National Endowment for the Arts

with articulating and isolating certain racist stereotypes of black men (aggressive, hostile, malevolent), and also a set of paradigmatic racist responses to those perceived stereotypes, among which I now include the *aestheticizing* response (avoidance or suppression of one's racist responses to blacks by simply changing the subject, just as we avoid our own gut responses to the pervasive political issues raised by art, by talking about form and color instead). There are other responses: the *appropriating* response (we know all about racial oppression because we, too, are oppressed: by our boss, our parents, or spouse [!]; the *liberal* response (of course, we wouldn't want our daughter to marry one, but only because society (not we) would make it so hard for an interracial couple, etc.); the *redneck* response (we can tell that blacks are racially inferior because, after all, they choose to live in the slums, don't they? etc.), to name just a few. I cannot, of course, describe in any way what a correct response to racism would look like; that depends too much on individuals and the particular situations in which they find themselves. I wanted to identify well-known, knee-jerk unacceptable responses—not prescribe the politically correct one. This piece merely delineates, and holds up for ridicule, what most black Americans agree are wrong (alienating, condescending, ignorant) responses. One's personal disaffection with these responses can be measured by one's ability to laugh at them, rather than defend or affirm them. The satiric funk lyrics of "Night People" suggest this reaction, but do not determine it. That depends, again, on individual viewers.

The installation consists of a small cylindrical room, painted black and excluding all external light, about 6′ in diameter and 7′ high. Four dimly lit lightboxes, 18″ by 24″ each, are hung at eye level at symmetrical intervals around the walls of the room. Each box contains a different enlarged and silk-screened photograph of an angry or hostile-looking black man, staring directly at the viewer. The only light in the room (and from the box) comes from directly behind the eyes of each image. The effect is ominous and claustrophobic. From a concealed speaker, the chorus of the song, "Night People," by War, is repeated. Beneath each lightbox is a headphone set, each transmitting one of each of the following monologues, as follows:

Monologue 1: Yes, well . . . I . . . I suppose this is . . . it's . . . it's an interesting attempt to disrupt my composure as an art viewer, the, uh, . . . the typical art viewer, if you will. But I . . . I'm not convinced that it's really that effective as art I mean, don't misunderstand me, of . . . of course I . . . I'm concerned with problems of racism and unemployment and the problems of our ghettos . . . of course trouble everyone. I think that the context is wrong for presenting this material. Certainly it's one thing to watch editorials on TV and to have this material presented in a thoroughgoing way. And somehow I just think that that's a lot more effective than trying to turn it into art, because after all, art is not social commentary. Uh, . . . it seems as though this piece is meant to shock me out of my composure, and it just doesn't succeed in doing that, because what I'm looking for when I come into a gallery is an art experience. I'm looking for an aesthetic experience; something that I can judge in terms of aesthetic standards, and this is just not that aesthetically interesting. I . . . I feel that the artist is not saying anything new, not saying anything different and creative, and politics is really just not what I'm here for. It seems to me that it's really just a gimmick to get attention, to . . . to capitalize on the latest fashion in . . . in art, which seems to be all of this political art. But frankly, I . . . I find it disappointing. I . . . I don't think that it works as art, because I really couldn't care less about racial problems when I come to a gallery. That's just not why I'm here. I expect an art experience, and that's not what I'm getting in this piece.

Monologue 2: Well, personally, I . . . I'm simply antagonized by the hostility of this piece. I . . . I have the feeling that the artist is just really distorting reality. She's . . . she's representing all blacks as completely hostile and alienated, and I just think that that's not true. These images just seem to be to be so . . . so resentful, in . . . in a way that just doesn't mesh with my reality at all. It's just not true that black people are all angry and hostile. Certainly there are those blacks—just . . . just like lots of other people—who have personal problems and angers and fears. Everyone has those things to a certain extent. And just like other people, there are some blacks that . . . that just can't contain them, and they take out that anger in lots of ways—in lots of socially unacceptable ways. But that's certainly not typical, and it's certainly not true that all blacks are like that. The only blacks who are really angry and hostile all the time . . . just people that you just can't talk to, you know, you just can't even reason with, are those blacks who just don't understand that we're trying to help them. They just don't see that we're trying to reach out to them and . . . and try and help them out of their condition. And then . . . and then those are the ones that . . . that . . . that seem to make it bad for the rest of them. Like, for example, some of my best friends are black. I know lots of black people. And I can tell you that, in fact, black people are generally not the way this artist is trying to portray them. They're just like us. You know, they have the same kinds of experiences, the same kinds of values . . . you know, the same kinds of opinions about things; some of them are Republicans, some of them are Democrats. They have the same sorts of life-styles, they have a car and a house. They . . . they're really just like us. It's just that . . . well, that . . . that they're a different color. But that . . . that doesn't make any difference, really. I mean I've . . . never had any trouble with blacks myself. I treat everybody equally, no matter what their . . . their color or their racial background. I really don't care. I mean, to me what's important is a person's personality, and how nice the person is. And I've never felt that anyone else's anger was the result of my actions. It's just not my problem, and I personally don't feel alienated from blacks at all. I feel that I have lots of good friends that are black, and . . . and we understand each other very well. We have lots in common. Well, of . . . of course, I . . . I wouldn't . . . I wouldn't advise my daughter to marry one, that's true. But it's not . . . it's not because I'm a racist. I'm really not a racist at all. As I . . . as I say, I have lots of black friends. It's . . . it's just because society makes it so difficult for an interracial couple. It's just so hard to make that kind of a marriage work and both partners just have so many pressures to contend with, that frankly I would . . . I would advise my daughter not to marry a black, just because of her own future unhappiness in an interracial marriage. But I feel that that's just a matter of what society does. It's not a matter of what I do. And I just feel as though my relation to blacks is being totally misrepresented by this piece. I feel attacked by this piece, where I don't feel attacked by blacks at all.

Monologue 3: Oh, this is . . . this is really right on. Yeah, this is . . . this is really boss, you know. Like . . . like really off the pigs, you know what I mean? Like, yeah. Yeah, I can . . . I can really get into this. I mean these, you know, these are really angry people, and . . . and like, this is to me like really socking it to the man. Yeah, really like you know, telling them, uh, them, uh, white honkies where it's at. Yeah, I mean, you know like, me personally, I . . . I'm not one of those jive white dudes. . . . I mean I can really identify, I . . . I can really get into this—you know what I mean? I mean 'cause see . . . see, I . . . I know what it's like, you know. I mean I've been really down and out myself. I mean I can . . . I can really understand black anger, because like, I'm really angry, too. I mean I've . . . I've had some real bad problems, you know. Like for example, my parents, my parents, they . . . they really bug my ass; they're really a problem, you know. And once like, when I was in college, I had this professor—that man really stomped my ass. I . . . I could . . . I could've just killed him. So like, I can really understand the black person wanting to kill someone, you know 'cause I personally, I feel like I've been ripped off by this society, too. You know, like, I mean I've . . . I've been ripped off by a lot of people, and I know what it's like to really feel angry at everybody on the street because they're just not digging where you're at, you know. I mean, they're just not getting it on at all, and they're not letting you get it on. That's what's really hard. So I, you know, like I say, more power to 'em, you know? I mean, like, off the pigs is what I say.

Monologue 4: Well, I . . . I must say this [*sigh*], this certainly doesn't bring me any closer to the uh, the so-called black experience. Personally, I . . . I find it very . . . very off-putting, all . . . all this resentment and anger, all these angry faces. You know, I . . . I feel that anger is being expressed at me for things that have nothing to do with me. It . . . it's not my responsibility. It's not my fault that things are bad for some members of this society. I didn't contribute to it and frankly, I don't want to have anything to do with it. Because to be quite honest, I . . . I don't like this. I've never had a black friend. I've found that blacks are just angry; they're difficult to get along with. They always have a chip on their shoulder, all of them. You know, you just can't have an honest, friendly conversation with them. They . . . they start out suspecting you from the very beginning. And look what a mess they've made of their environment. You know, Harlem is full of blacks, and that's their environment. And look at the way they live. It's all dirty, and slovenly, and . . . they're all immoral. And look at the way they sell their women, and they're running dope, and . . . and living on the streets. And they're ruining our public school system, they're just ruining it. So I . . . I just . . . I just think that, you know, that's just not my problem. Everyone's responsible for their own environment and their own lives, and my feeling is that, you know, they leave me alone, and I'll leave them alone. Because I don't see any reason why I should try to understand them, when they don't try to understand me, you know? If someone can't approach me with a friendly attitude and be honest with me, why should I treat that person like another human being? As far as I'm concerned, they're just all animals, you know? And if they're having a bad time, it's just due to some basic defects of character. I mean, let's face it, genes count for a lot, you know, genes are really everything. And you can't tell me that when someone just chooses to live in filth, that that's not a matter of character. They're immoral, and they're paying for it by their . . . by their misery and their poverty. And that's just not something that I can deal with. I

. . . I resent being made the focus of that kind of anger, as though somehow it was my fault.

The audience response to this piece was a revelation to me. I had used the music soundtrack as an ironical distancing device to emphasize the critical stance taken toward the stereotypical monologues. From the perspective of my experience (and, I venture to add, that of most blacks in this country), it was impossible to regard the content of the monologues as anything other than objects of ridicule, scrutiny, and self-examination. That is, I took it to be impossible to take them at face value, as expressions of the artist's advocacy of the values they voiced. Wrong. While the black audience, and some members of the white audience understood the devices used immediately, others thanked me for expressing their views so eloquently, since in fact they *did* have many black friends, but of course *wouldn't* recommend that their daughter marry one because society made it so difficult, etc., etc. This led me to a consideration of where the artist's responsibility for communicating the intended worldview to her audience ends, and whether I should have cast the material even more broadly, so that misunderstanding of its implications would have been impossible (in fact, I thought I *had* done that). I concluded that no artist with political concerns is required by a viewer's ignorance to make simplistic art, and that there is no excuse for the level of ignorance and insensitivity to racist behavior displayed by these remarks on the part of any adult American. After all, anyone who pleads ignorance of black American mores has only to pick up a copy of *Jet* or *Ebony* at his or her local supermarket checkout counter. Or call your local college's Afro-American Studies Department for a syllabus of introductory readings.

Safe (May 1990; semi-improv audio monologue for mixed-media installation)

I'm sorry, I just don't feel comfortable with this . . .

Of course I appreciate the artist's good intentions, I really do. . . . But I'm just really having a lot of trouble with this piece . . .

I feel manipulated . . . stared at . . . *laughed* at, if you want to know the truth.
. . . All these sardonic smiles! . . . It's like I'm supposed to be the butt of
some private joke. . . . I really don't see what's so funny . . .

I just can't relate to this. . . . All these faces just seem so menacing, so
unfriendly. . . . I guess it's a little too militant for me, you know? . . . really a
bit heavy-handed for my taste.

That's it, it's just too explicit . . . this is very aggressive work. . . . I really
don't need to get hit over the head with this stuff, you know . . .

Personally I think understatement would've been the way to go here . . . a
kind of subtle ambiguity, a certain *je ne sais pas quoi* is so much more effective,
really . . . whereas I feel positively assaulted by this piece!

You see, the problem is that this piece gives me no aesthetic space . . . there's
just no way you can avoid the message here . . . it leaves no room for
interpretation, for use of the imagination, for flights of fancy, you know? . . .
There's no way you can escape what the artist is trying to tell you!

Not that I want to escape anything. I already do feel completely safe with black
people, believe me, on some level I really don't even know what the problem
is. My housekeeper and I have a wonderful relationship. She's literally my
best friend, in effect, and most of the time I don't even notice that she's black!

Well, of course we do come from very different cultural environments, so
naturally there are some misunderstandings from time to time. . . . Occasional
failures of translation . . . That's to be expected . . .

Because my own ancestors are all from Norway, ultimately . . . by way of
Italy. . . . Northern Italy, of course . . . actually they're German, pure Aryan
stock, all of them . . .

But I'm all for integration, believe me. . . . Of course I support equal
opportunity and civil rights . . .

And naturally I feel terribly sorry for these poor people, who wouldn't? It's all
very sad, discrimination really is a terrible thing, it's a tragedy, of course . . .
someone should definitely do something about it, and right away! . . .

But you know my own life isn't going real well, either. . . . Appearances can
be very misleading. . . . In fact I'm a very unhappy person . . .

And besides, I don't like being guilt-tripped, and this artist is trying to guilt-
trip me about something, I can feel it! I really resent this. . . . It's so
manipulative . . .

Fig. 10.2.   Adrian Piper, *Safe #4*. Courtesy John Weber Gallery, New York

In fact this piece is really very angry . . . that's the real problem with it—it's all about the artist and her own anger! That's not what I'm here for! For someone to dump her personal problems on me! Forget it!

Well, of course she doesn't talk about her anger *explicitly,* but it's implicit in the images, really . . . you can tell by looking at the content how self-involved the piece really is . . .

Yes, well, it's very subtle, of course, it's all on a covert, understated level . . . you just have to know how to really *read* these symbols if you want to get at their true meaning. . . . But ultimately it's pretty obvious, isn't it?

Note

1. Adrian Piper, "Goodbye to Easy Listening," in *Pretend* (New York: Colorstone Printing, 1990), n.p.

11

Revising the Aesthetic-Nonaesthetic Distinction: The Aesthetic Value of Activist Art

Peggy Zeglin Brand

As feminist researchers in the 1960s and 1970s began to (re)discover forgotten female artists of the past five hundred years, the artworld responded in a variety of ways. Sometimes, it ignored the findings. At other times, it denied the status of these works of art. More prevalent, however, was the reluctant acknowledgment of such discoveries of art, accompanied by the caveat that they lacked aesthetic value. Similarly, as researchers of the 1980s undertook a similar process to (re)discover the works of minority artists or artists of color, the artworld once again responded in a narrowly circumscribed way: conceding their status as art while withholding aesthetic praise. Was this merely coincidence? Or did it reflect an ongoing trend to assess artworks that—however interesting or valuable in a nonaesthetic way—are dismissed for lack of aesthetic value? Is there some sort of philosophical tradition that serves as a basis for this trend?

This essay will explore the role that the aesthetic-nonaesthetic distinction plays in assessing activist art by women and artists of color. First, I shall review one traditional line of philosophical thought and show how it serves as the foundation for three types of reasons typically given for artworks reputed to lack aesthetic value. I develop two of the three reasons by examining recent writings opposed to the aesthetic value of activist art by well-known art critic

Donald Kuspit, pointing out his aberrant use of "obscene." Kuspit's examples of activist art—the work of Jenny Holzer, Barbara Kruger, and Adrian Piper— are presented in light of his charges. I then explore Piper's art in depth in order to outline ways of expanding the notion of aesthetic value beyond its traditional confines. Finally, I suggest moving beyond entrenched, traditional patterns of assessment and invite underrepresented voices to contribute to the emerging discussion of the multiplicity of aesthetic values.

Tradition and How It Affects Aesthetic Value

One tradition in critical and philosophical discourse on art relies upon the long-standing opposition and competition between aesthetic and nonaesthetic properties of a work. Typically, assessing such properties is sufficient for determining the aesthetic and nonaesthetic value of a work of art. This traditional "distinction" is more aptly called a "dichotomy" since the Greek *di* plus *temnein* more aptly captures the harshness of the *cutting* that results when the value of an artwork gets dissected. For it is the *whole* work of art we experience, perceive, and appreciate when it comes to making judgments about its value. We can surely analyze it into its parts—spatially, formally, temporally—but the only fair assessment of a work of art is of its totality. Anything less is either premature, partial, or uninformed.

This tradition has its roots in the eighteenth century when philosophers like Hutcheson and Shaftesbury sought to isolate the properties of an object that gave rise to a feeling of pleasure, the capacity for which was embodied in a faculty of taste or a sense of beauty. From the beginning, attempts to explain beauty focused on formal properties like uniformity in variety, smallness, and smoothness. The images under discussion, of course, were always representational. The only properties that aroused feelings of pleasure did so immediately and directly by allaying any interventionist role that practical interests might play; hence, disinterestedness became the cornerstone of the proper experience of an aesthetic object. This three-part emphasis on formal properties, disinterestedness, and pleasure was retained by Kant, Bullough, and Bell, as well as twentieth-century aesthetic-attitude theorists. It still holds strong despite attempts to the contrary, such as Dickie's "Myth of the Aesthetic Attitude" and Goodman's push for the primacy of cognitive value.[1] It should come as no surprise in assessing activist art that a tradition stressing formal properties, disinterestedness, and pleasure would not serve content-oriented, non–pleasure-producing art very well. As Bell insisted: "The representative element in a work of art may or may not be harmful, but it is always irrelevant. For to appreciate a work of art, we must bring with us nothing from life, no knowledge of its affairs and ideas, no familiarity with its emotions."[2]

Motivated by the prevailing trend of New Criticism that sought to assess a work apart from its sociohistorical context as well as recent trends in abstract art, Monroe Beardsley was most influential in reenergizing this tradition as he successively revised his theory of art from the 1950s on.[3] On his view, formal properties—unity, complexity, and intensity as revealed in a work's regional properties—play the vital role of functioning as "symptoms" of aesthetic "gratification" (a term that replaced the more problematic term "pleasure"). In one essay alone, Beardsley cited the predominance of the following terms to argue that "there *is* something peculiarly aesthetic to be found in our world or our experience":

aesthetic experience	aesthetic objects
aesthetic value	aesthetic concepts
aesthetic enjoyment	aesthetic situations
aesthetic satisfaction[4]	

According to Beardsley, the five symptoms marking the *aesthetic* character of an experience rely heavily upon relegating irrelevant (and practical) distractions to the sidelines, focusing instead on object-directedness, felt freedom, detached affect, active discovery, and "a sense of wholeness from distracting and disruptive impulses."[5] It also hints at the preference given to aesthetic value over any other value (be it cognitive, moral, or political). In a rebuttal to Goodman, he stated that cognitive value (defined by Goodman as a work's capacity to contribute to the "creation and comprehension of our worlds") is "not generally the overriding or dominant purpose of artworks."[6]

One other insight into the primacy of aesthetic value is revealed by Beardsley's antagonism to those interested in a work's moral value. In *Aesthetics and Philosophy of Art Criticism,* Beardsley concurred with the influential approach of Jerome Stolnitz, which sought to focus exclusively on a work's immediate, unmediated, aesthetic effect in *isolation* from its context, thereby relegating moral judgments to judgments about the "side effects" of a work of art. He caricatured the Moralist stance (but did not satisfactorily refute it), adding further fuel to the fire of the primacy of aesthetic value over any other value.[7] George Dickie's recent views move toward more recognition for moral/political value as one form of cognitive value, but do not take its advocacy far enough.[8] The tradition appears, at times, to be cast in stone: whatever other nonaesthetic values artworks might possess—call them cognitive, moral, or political—the tradition continually ranks them second in importance to aesthetic value.

Thus, in spite of recent improvements upon the notion of aesthetic value, activist art fares poorly by means of it when judgments are made and disseminated. The influence of the tradition on what gets exhibited, marketed, critiqued, enshrined in museums and art history texts and ultimately used as examples by aestheticians (who take their cues from the workings of the artworld as well as from dominant philosophical theories) is long-lasting and insidious. It will continue to affect the status of activist art until the notion of aesthetic value is reassessed and expanded.

What types of reasons are given by evaluators when claiming an artwork lacks aesthetic value? With respect to activist art, three types of reasons seem to emerge: (1) those that indicate an inherent lack of talent (basically ad hominem attacks), (2) those that point to the presence of or preoccupation with a message (the nonaesthetic component) that diminishes attention paid to the medium (the aesthetic component), and (3) those that express a dissatisfaction with the content—not just the presence—of the message, thereby tying the overall value of the work solely to the judgment of the work's content.

Consider the first type of reason given for a work lacking aesthetic value: a work lacks aesthetic value because the artist lacks talent. This charge, though clearly a possible charge against any artist, has been leveled more often against female artists and recently against artists of color than it has against white, male artists. Undoubtedly, the belief that women in general possessed less artistic talent on average than their male counterparts kept female artists excluded from the history of Western art until they were slowly introduced into major art history texts in the early 1980s under pressure from feminist scholars.[9] This type of strategy was extended to the devaluing of artists of color as well and lay behind the repeated practice of combining disparate types of art—for example, African and Oceanic—under the rubric "primitive" and exiling it to its own chapter in art history texts, set apart from the chronological sequence of chapters tracing development in the "real" history of art. (Asian art, Native American art, and art of the Americas were similarly segregated.) Furthermore, where the twentieth century clearly afforded more opportunities to highlight women and artists of color, they were rarely included (the exception being a token work by Georgia O'Keeffe or Jacob Lawrence).

Consider some examples of this point of view. Sofonisba Anguissola, a contemporary of Michelangelo, was characterized by a critic in 1915 as an artist who "painted with something of that tepid rose-tinted sentimentality proper to the woman-painter, then and now."[10] A similar charge was leveled in 1964 against Judith Leyster, a seventeenth-century Dutch artist: "Some women tried to emulate Frans Hals, but the vigorous brushstrokes of the master were beyond their capability, one only has to look at the works of a painter like Judith Leyster to detect the weakness of the feminine hand."[11] Charles Sterling, spokesman for the Metropolitan Museum in 1922, upon learning that a painting purchased for $200,000 and proudly dubbed "the Met's David" was possibly the work of Constance Charpentier, a student of Jacques Louis David, said: "Its poetry, literary rather than plastic, its very evident charms, and its cleverly concealed weaknesses, . . . all seem to reveal the feminine spirit."[12] Sterling's criticism reveals the crucial role that contextual information can play in assessing a work's aesthetic value. When the work was thought to have been created by David, it was considered a work with value. When the work was thought to have been created by a woman, it was a work without value. Although nothing changed visually, properties of the work that previously accounted for its high aesthetic value were immediately reassessed as properties exhibiting the artist's lack of skill. The modern version of this story is the experience of black artists whose works were considered valuable by galleries upon first viewing (in slide form) but who were subsequently turned away when they showed up in person. The more subtle form of this strategy is exemplified by galleries telling black artists in the 1980s that their works lack value.[13]

In all these cases, one strategy is repeatedly used to denigrate the skill and talent of women and artists of color. Compared to their male or white counterparts, they "naturally" came up short on talent. It is common knowledge that many women suffered at the hands of this strategy when paired with more famous and supposedly talented male artists: Camille Claudel and August Rodin, Frida Kahlo and Diego Rivera, Lee Krasner and Jackson Pollock, Elaine and Willem de Kooning, Ana Mendieta and Carl Andre, even Georgia O'Keeffe and Alfred Steiglitz (before O'Keeffe became well known). It is also known that certain women artists, for example Edmonia Lewis, who was both African American and Native American, fared much better living and working in Rome in the 1850s and 1860s than in the United States. A brief overview of the last few decades shows the meager gains made by women and artists of color in gaining recognition within the artworld.

Statistics publicized by the infamous Guerilla Girls (self-declared Conscience of the Artworld) indicate that between 1973 and 1987 the percentage of women in the Whitney Biennial—the milestone of an artist's career—never rose above 32 percent and the percentage of artworks by women acquired for permanent museum collections never rose above 14 percent. The most recent Whitney Biennial (5 March–13 June 1993) contains roughly thirty women out of eighty artists: only a slight increase to 37.5 percent.

A seven-year study completed in 1988 by Howardena Pindell (former associate curator at the Museum of Modern Art and herself an African American artist) reported 11,000 artists (African American, Asian, Hispanic, and Native American) living and working in the state of New York.[14] Fifty-four out of sixty-four galleries surveyed in the state represented mostly white artists. Thirty-nine galleries in New York City, including nearly all of the most prestigious spaces, represented *only* white artists. Not surprisingly, the problem gets replicated in museums. Given the fact that museums rely heavily upon the gallery system that chooses artists, markets them, and establishes their reputations, the representation of minority artists in major New York museums over a seven-year period ranged from either no representation at all to a mere 7 percent of the total number of artists shown.[15]

The bottom line of the "new exclusionism," as cast by Lowery Sims, current associate curator of twentieth-century art at New York's Metropolitan Museum, is money. Since works by artists of color do not sell as well in the galleries as works by whites, they are seen as poor investments. This fact lies hidden, however, beneath the surface. According to Sims, "Economic issues, therefore, are couched in diversionary issues like 'quality,' 'taste' and 'talent.' "[16] Predictably enough, defenders of the "whiteness" of the statistics deny that nonaesthetic issues like race and gender bear on their decisions. One former curator of the permanent collections at the Whitney defended his choice of artists, adamantly claiming that his decisions were based solely on aesthetic issues; "questions of race, religion, and sex were subordinated to that end."[17] Perhaps this is true, although one remains skeptical in light of the startlingly low numbers. One can envision the strictest aesthetic standards excluding *some* works by women and minorities but not the consistently high number that statistics repeatedly reveal.

A second type of reasoning used to devalue works by women and minorities is that a work of art lacks value because it contains a message (or moral). Addressing issues of gender, race, and class, these works are seen to diverge from purely aesthetic concerns into the realm of the nonaesthetic, necessarily showing less interest in the exploration and manipulation of the medium than in getting the point across. Hilton Kramer provides a classic statement of this view in critiquing a 1980 show of women's art (which he claimed reflected "no discernible standard of quality"): "This is what always occurs, of course, when art is politicized. Esthetic criteria must be subordinated to the interest of some larger cause."[18]

This kind of statement reveals the bias held by many critics, conservative and liberal alike, who—when they do value work by women or artists of color—tend to favor aesthetically "pure," nonrepresentational art like that of Louise Nevelson, Helen Frankenthaler, and Martin Puryear, over more content-oriented representational works. It also explains why art historians extol the work of "the great masters," even though such works *are* representational, many of which are religious or political. Because we are trained to look at crucifixion scenes, starving peasants, rapes, abductions, and the horrors of war disinterestedly and for the aesthetic pleasure they bring, i.e., in terms of line, color, and shape, we underplay the political or religious content that could just as easily be seen to detract from the formal properties of these works as it supposedly does in contemporary activist art. The tradition that values the aesthetic over the nonaesthetic has led critics to ignore the message of a work when it is convenient to do so (or at least suppress it in the name of aesthetic value) but then to conveniently target the content of a work when it is seen to detract from aesthetic value.

The third type of reason given for art coming up short on aesthetic value is that a work of art lacks value if its message is misguided, too strident, or simply unacceptable. It may be considered distasteful, immoral, political, politically incorrect, or even politically correct (in the pejorative sense of the term). Many feminists believe this to be the reason behind the rejection of works that celebrate women's experience or promote women's rights: works that are often categorized as propaganda. Persons of color have similar suspicions about the devaluing of works that highlight the positive aspects of race other than the predominant race. Even prior to the opening of the 1993 Whitney Biennial, one previewer complained that "too much of today's political art is utterly artless," that is, too removed from the realm of aesthetics.[19]

Consider a case of criticism from 1987 leveled against a work by African American artist Adrian Piper entitled *Cornered* (Fig. 11.1): "TALK LIKE ADRIAN PIPER'S IS REFINED AND POLITE, and full of upperclass angst, but it's about as racist as anything you can expect to hear these days."[20] An artwork that sufficiently offends a person's moral or political sensibilities can prompt a work's aesthetic value to be reduced to an assessment of its moral value (this is Beardsley's version of the Moralist's Argument from Reduction). This view, considered extremist by Beardsley, clearly departs from the traditional method of arriving at a work's aesthetic value based on formal properties, disinterestedness, and aesthetic pleasure. An artwork can be devalued simply by

Fig. 11.1.   Adrian Piper, *Cornered,* 1988. Courtesy John Weber Gallery, New York

reducing its aesthetic value to a strident and unacceptable racist (in this case, pro-black) message. This approach, which basically nullifies the aesthetic-nonaesthetic distinction by collapsing the former into the latter, has been used by critics who oppose activist art as well as by feminists who argue for it. The well-known slogan, "the personal is the political," tolerates no apolitical artwork, response, or mode of evaluating. Though there are some Moralists (and feminists) who propose the collapse of this distinction, I contend that Beardsley is right and the distinction must be preserved. There must be *some* way to capture the unique function that formal, aesthetic properties serve apart from the moral or political purposes they also serve.[21]

A less extreme view is captured by Beardsley in what he calls the Argument from Correlation, which claims that moral devaluing somehow contributes to (or correlates with) aesthetic devaluing. This view does not collapse the aesthetic-nonaesthetic distinction, but rather points to an integral, yet complicated, connection between the two types of properties. I believe Beardsley is on the right track in characterizing the relationship this way, although he abandons this approach too quickly in favor of the traditional emphasis on aesthetic properties, thereby causing him to urge an isolationist approach to a work, that is, to judge the work apart from its context. I shall pick up the thread of this approach later in advocating a retention of the aesthetic-nonaesthetic distinction, but with a concern for the moral or political value having an influence upon the aesthetic value of a work of art.

Recently, more and more critics are voicing concern over contemporary art's capacity to moralize. According to Eleanor Hartley, we are "at a moment when self-righteousness pervades the art world."[22] Donald Kuspit laments artists' attempts to rationalize their work by appealing to a right to moralize; that is, by setting universal moral standards based on one's individual code of ethics akin to Kant's categorical imperative ("act only on that maxim whereby thou canst at the same time will that it should become a universal law"). I offer an analysis of Kuspit's view in depth, since it clearly exemplifies types two and three, reasons that see activist art as lacking aesthetic value due to the presence and content of a work's message.

Only Obscene Art Has Aesthetic Value: Kuspit's Aberrant Use of "Obscene"

Kuspit's attack is studied, elaborate, and clearly reinforces the Beardsley–Stolnitz tradition. Using the highly charged label "commissar art," he claims that activist art is "inwardly bankrupt" and "no longer provocative":[23] "The moral superiority of would-be commissar art (and artist) brings in its wake tyranny and inhumanity."[24] In its place he encourages "genuinely obscene" art and encourages critics to assume a new role: one that "transcends the traditional critical goals" of description, interpretation, and evaluation. Critics are urged to move beyond criticism, to "root out and denounce what might be called the commissar factor in self-proclaimed morally concerned art" (*SN*, 111). The effect is a call for critics to become commissars themselves—commissars of the obscene. By acting as agents of the obscene, critics become empowered to dismiss the entire genre of activist art as they reject the particular moral principles embodied in individual works. In most cases, these principles promote equal, humanitarian treatment of all persons, especially the oppressed and disadvantaged. Kuspit seems to ignore these concerns, however, as he proceeds with an odd and idiosyncratic use of "obscene."

According to Kuspit, we live in the modern world with a damaged sense of self. Healing consists of one's self feeling "inwardly alive; it lost its sense of being alive in the first place because it lost contact with the obscene life within" (*SN*, 107). Art can play a role in restoring a sense of life to the self as long as it is the correct type of art: obscene art.

In the spirit of ancient philosophy, Kuspit sees a tension between the types of art that delight us and those that teach us. For him, the "opposites" of pleasure-giving and teaching in art do not mix. Simply put, art that pleases and delights the senses makes the self feel "inwardly alive"; it possesses aesthetic value and promotes healing, thereby assuring it of humanitarian value. Nonobscene art, or activist art, on the other hand, neither pleases nor delights; it fails to make the self feel inwardly alive because it is the expression of those who feel a sense of guilt at giving pleasure or delighting the senses. It is the obsession of those who believe they are healing the modern world, but who are deceived in their purpose as much as they are deceived into a sense of smug, moral superiority. Their "get-the-message art" is intended to change the world but in actuality neither moves us nor helps us heal. In fact, its "conspicuous moral influence" actually suppresses the genuinely obscene. Thus, to partake in activist art precludes the pleasure and healing a viewer of art might enjoy from obscene art. It is the fault of the artworld (critics, among others) that activist art has become mainstream; hence, Kuspit's search-and-destroy mission for the critic/commissar of the obscene.

Obscene art is genuine when it is not sanctioned or ritualized by society, when it is not idealized, glamorized or sensationalized; it is fake and inauthentic when it is accepted by society, as in the case of pornography, and when it is sensationalized, as in the fun of gambling and the glitter of Las Vegas. It is genuine when it is not "manufactured" as it was in the past by using "the excuse of a mythological theme to render a naked body or naked landscape, meaning them to be obscene" (*SN*, 108–9). It is genuine, in effect, when it is deliberate (self-conscious), vital (sparks the feeling of being inwardly alive), implicitly critical (of what is behind the scene), and most of all, uncanny. Art utilizes "freshly obscene methods" (*SN*, 110). It strikes an internal chord in the viewer without preaching, instructing, or (re-)educating.

What Kuspit seems to be saying is that obscene art moves us by its unpredictability, subtlety, and ambiguity. An unclear message is preferable to an obvious one. A thought-provoking work is better than one that does the thinking for us. Obscene art is neither didactic nor propagandistic. It resists universalizing, since its particular message is neither clear nor isolable enough to be expanded upon or generalized. The message, therefore, cannot detract from the form. Thus, obscene art escapes the two charges that lead to a loss of aesthetic value. Kuspit perpetuates the tradition by pitting aesthetic against nonaesthetic properties, giving value to the aesthetic over the nonaesthetic, and by maintaining that aesthetic value results in an experience of pleasure (or delight to the senses).

Consider his prime example: Manet's 1863 painting, *Olympia*. According to Kuspit, Manet's method is interpreted as "descriptive," "ironical," and "coolly analytic in tone." Manet is said to have "no moral opinion about the participants in the scene" but rather records what he sees before him as a "neutral observer." He does not "generalize about society as a whole." In other words, Kuspit might say, Manet provoked thought without promoting a particular message. He did not try to reeducate nor to impose his personal morality universally on others. Since the artist's attitude to the social or moral content of the work "is as important as that content itself, indeed, more important artistically," and since Manet's "moral interest is filtered through an aesthetic of ironical indifference," Kuspit concludes that "in the end, Manet's picture seems of greater aesthetic than moral interest" (*AMI*, 18). If Manet were to have made the "perverse" mistake of moralizing, he would have been utilizing art in a "fundamentally inappropriate way" (*AMI*, 19). Thus, Kuspit's reading sees Manet's work as intentionally obscene: designed to be deliberate, vital, implicitly critical, and uncanny without promoting one universalizable message.[25]

Surely this work is valuable, but given conventional usage, is it what we would ordinarily call obscene? It is difficult to see how, on Kuspit's view, "obscene" is the most appropriate term to apply to artworks that aesthetically please the senses and heal the self. Perhaps a more commonplace and less idiosyncratic meaning can be borrowed from Joel Feinberg: "Obscenity is an extreme form of offensiveness producing repugnance, shock, or disgust, though the offending materials *can* (paradoxically) be to some degree alluring at the same time."[26] According to Feinberg, works of art can be offensive for a variety of reasons: "The work might, for example, be trite, hackneyed, exploitative, imitative, cheap or vulgar, and these features might bore, anger, even disgust us."[27] Such works—also labeled "crass, bare, unveiled, rank, coarse, raw, shocking, blunt and stark"—approach the "outer limit of vulgarity."[28] On this view, obscenity is a thing or occasion to be avoided. Kuspit's approach, on the other hand, is a call for more obscenity. It yields the untenable conclusion that obscene art is both offensive and humanitarian! Though healing of the self may take place under these conditions, it seems unlikely. Offensiveness does not seem to be a good predictor of benefits, whether for individuals or humanity in general. Obscene art, as offensive art, is not humanitarian.

Furthermore, the promotion of artworks that are exciting, lively, and uncanny need not involve invoking the adjective "obscene," unless, perhaps, the aim is to titillate the viewer with exaggerated critical jargon, a critic's ploy to entice the viewer with the promise of obscenity where none really exists.[29] One might object that this is merely a dispute over terminology. Perhaps so, though Kuspit's promotion of obscene art goes beyond innovative vocabulary. In what follows, I hope to show the seriousness of the consequences of his view of art, regardless of whether nonactivist art is called obscene or not.

Nonobscene Art: Kuspit's Examples of Activist Art

Kuspit might respond to the above challenge by asking, "So, what's in a name?" He could conceivably sidestep the entire issue by claiming that the word "obscene" is not what's really at issue here; what matters is that some type of art—call it obscene or not—is still the only art that has aesthetic and humanitarian value, as opposed to activist art, which lacks it. Upon closer inspection, however, the very examples of activist art cited as lacking in value can be shown to possess aesthetic value. (Since the focus of the remainder of this essay is aesthetic value, I shall not pursue the issue of humanitarian value any further.) The examples show that Kuspit is perpetuating a version of the traditional aesthetic-nonaesthetic distinction by claiming that these works fall short of having aesthetic value, which is their *primary* value. As he applied this traditional approach to his analysis of Manet's *Olympia,* he now extends it to cover cases of activist art.

One can easily make the counterclaim to Kuspit that activist art does not lack aesthetic value simply because it combines message and medium nor because we disagree or disapprove of its message. But in order to do so, a new approach to assessing aesthetic value needs to be constructed: one that does not simply rely on the well-rehearsed approach of Beardsley or Sibley, focusing on the unity, intensity, complexity, delicacy, balance, or other aesthetic features. Kuspit's emphasis on art *delighting* and *pleasing* the senses must be dropped as well as the traditional requirement that a work be viewed disinterestedly. Because activist works of art rarely seek to cause aesthetic pleasure and can rarely be experienced disinterestedly, the traditional characterization should be seen for what it really is: limited and limiting. Upholding the distinction between aesthetic and nonaesthetic value, then, without its traditional supporting structure, means that only the tradition's focus on formal properties is retained. Let us look more closely at Kuspit's examples for new ways of determining aesthetic value along these lines.

In one sense, Kuspit casts the net too wide when he attempts to determine the scope of aesthetic value. The black paintings of Ross Bleckner are perhaps Kuspit's prime example;[30] he believes they definitively justify his stand against activist art since they are nonrepresentational and stand on their own "as essentially aesthetic art." He sees Bleckner's stipulation that they are memorials to persons with AIDS as a "defensive posture," a desperate move to "justify an art that needs no justification" (*AMI*, 21). They stand on their own merits—aesthetically—without additional contextual information that ties them to a moral or political purpose. Once tied, they lose their implicit, vital, deliberate, and uncanny nature and become explicit, nonvital, nondeliberate, and canny. Their message becomes obvious (thereby detracting from the formal properties of the work) and odious (since Kuspit objects to any message being promoted and universalized by an artist). These factors contribute to their loss of aesthetic value.

But how can this be? How can an artwork considered to have aesthetic value, come to lose it just because a viewer learns something new about it, as in this case, that it has a message? Nothing has changed visually, of course; the viewer has merely gained more knowledge about the piece. Bleckner's work, like the case of the Charpentier painting mistaken for the Met's David, is considered to lose value because of contextual information. Somehow this seems at odds with the basic (traditional) nature of aesthetic value, which depends primarily upon formal properties. Contextual information should not affect the rise and fall of aesthetic value, although it could affect some other type of value, for example, the work's monetary or political value. Thus, Kuspit's tendency to expand the parameters of aesthetic value to include contextual information goes beyond the traditional sense in order to provide a justification to devalue certain works.

But he also casts the net too narrowly, when he restricts the sense of aesthetic value to exclude works by the "self-proclaimed neo-moral realists" like Adrian Piper, Jenny Holzer, and Barbara Kruger (*AMI*, 19). Holzer's and Kruger's works are considered the result of "emulative, even identificative envy of entertainment's mass appeal and enormous social effect: the work of artists who hope to be socially accepted with aesthetically inferior art" (*AMI*, 21). To assume, however, that art that has mass appeal or attempts to influence society on a grand scale is necessarily inferior on aesthetic grounds is to confuse its effect on viewers with its cause (its internal composition). There are many examples of artworks that have had a major impact and mass appeal yet are still considered aesthetically valuable. Ironically, *Olympia* is one such work. Again, Kuspit is mistaken in thinking that contextual information— knowing that the artist aimed for mass appeal (whether successful or not)—is relevant to determining the aesthetic value of the work (though, again, it may affect other values). What, then, counts as aesthetic value in these works, that might counter Kuspit's charge that they are "aesthetically inferior art"?

Holzer is known for producing individual, legible Truisms as well as rapidly moving texts in her signature medium, the LED (light-emitting diode).[31] Her truisms ("RAISE BOYS AND GIRLS THE SAME WAY," "FATHERS OFTEN USE TOO MUCH FORCE," "YOUR OLDEST FEARS ARE THE WORST ONES") are found primarily outside gallery installations, appearing as electronic billboards in Times Square and Las Vegas, in shopping malls, airports, and printed on T-shirts. Barbara Kruger also combines image and text in a variety of mediums.[32] And like Holzer, she often displays outside the typical gallery scene—on billboards, subway stations, T-shirts, canvas shopping bags, pencils, and even rubber stamps. Most of her works are photomontages with text ("I SHOP, THEREFORE I AM," "YOUR MANIAS BECOME SCIENCE," "WHEN I HEAR THE WORD 'CULTURE' I TAKE OUT MY CHECKBOOK") consisting of black-and-white photographs (usually close-ups) of persons or fragmented images of persons on which the text is superimposed. At other times her work consists entirely of words: words printed on the floor in a gallery or words silk-screened onto vinyl panels.

The aesthetic nature of these works rests on the fact that words become the aesthetic medium as well as functioning as the nonaesthetic medium by which the message is conveyed. Thus, they can be experienced and evaluated in two ways: by aesthetic criteria alone or by criteria that seek to locate the value of the entire experience in the meaning of the words, as they are expressed by a particular person within a particular setting. The former is purely visual, looking at the text as an arrangement of formal properties *without* attending to meaning, while the latter is more cognitive, reading the text for the message being conveyed.

Consider the traditional approach, which encourages looking at formal properties and the way they affect the senses and cause aesthetic pleasure by ignoring the content of the words used. By placing her text "Lack of charisma can be . . . fatal" in two successive stages on the marquee of Caesar's Palace, Holzer provides a visual experience that partakes in, yet provides commentary upon, the glitter of the avenue. Likewise, her display of writings in *Untitled* (1989), which consisted of a 535-foot electronic sign that spiraled up the outer face of the Guggenheim Museum's parapet wall, became part of the graceful and sensual curved lines of architecture. Her most somber works, such as *Laments* (1987), place electronic signboards in a darkened room with granite sarcophagi. Sensations of death—cool, calm, and dark—are perceivable in advance of and in spite of reading the text.

In fact, if one were illiterate or if the artists used an unknown or indecipherable language, their works could still move us aesthetically. Holzer's most artificial and elaborate environments literally bombard the senses by creating intensely colorful, charged, electrified spaces. For instance, *The Last Room* (Fig. 11.2)—one of four created for the U.S. Pavilion of the Venice Biennale in 1990—contained rapidly moving text in five different languages and multiple color combinations and type styles. Described as "an assault on the senses," its hallucinatory effects clearly surpassed any message that one was able to derive, given the fast-paced movement of the text and the fact that most persons cannot understand five different languages.[33] Similarly, experiencing Kruger's work with the text in a foreign language—as in the work KEIN GEDANKE/KEIN ZWEIFEL/KEINE GUTE/KEIN VERGNÜGEN/KEIN LACHEN (NO THOUGHT/ NO DOUBT/NO GOODNESS/NO PLEASURE/NO LAUGHTER)—shows that determining its aesthetic value can clearly be independent of the content of the message for those who cannot read German. But can one really evaluate these works fairly by ignoring their message, by looking at them merely as formal exercises, by ignoring the fact that they are works by women that comment on the power structures of a world in which women fail to occupy privileged positions? I think not.

Consider the alternative approach, which looks into the meaning of these texts as statements of particular persons within a particular setting. The words, when read *as* text, are neither trivial nor soothing. In fact, they stand in harsh contrast to the delight and pleasure they bring to the senses (to use Kuspit's terms) when one experiences them merely as light, color, and in Holzer's case, movement, that is, as formal properties. Switching from one

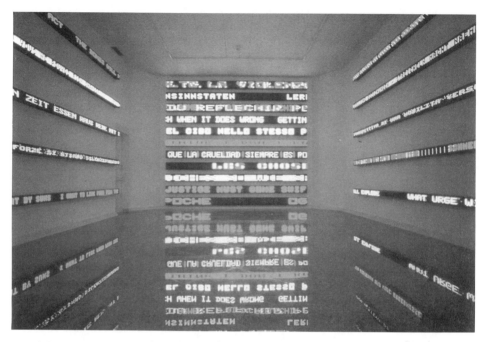

Fig. 11.2. Jenny Holzer, *Untitled (The Last Room)*. Courtesy Barbara Gladstone Gallery, New York

mode to the other (like switching from the duck to the rabbit in the famous duck-rabbit image) forces the viewer to drastically change criteria by which to judge them. Some of Holzer's strongest text, in *Untitled (The Child's Room)* (Fig. 11.3), includes ruminations on the birth of her daughter, the pain she will experience, the wrenching apart of mother and daughter that is physical at birth and then psychological as the daughter matures. The meaning of this work cannot be appreciated by simply watching light bulbs flicker on and off in aesthetically pleasing ways. A woman-centered aesthetic informs the meaning of this work: one that diverges from typical birth scenes painted by males who have rarely chosen to portray the act of birth, the pain of birth, or the separation and anxiety that follows.[34] One need only recall the numerous nativity scenes of the birth of Christ to reconstruct the backdrop to Holzer's work, scenes that place a happy, but poor family in a manger, beautiful and beatified. This backdrop, to which we are so accustomed, urges us to distinguish and appreciate nativity scenes for the aesthetic properties they express: the composition, the color, the proportions of the figures. Understanding Holzer's work, as in the case of Judy Chicago's *Birth Project*, depends

Fig. 11.3.   Jenny Holzer, *Untitled (The Child's Room)*. Courtesy Barbara Gladstone Gallery, New York

on assuming an aesthetic that does not rest on the notion of aesthetic distancing or aesthetic pleasure, both anathema to the maternal stance under scrutiny.[35]

The same holds true for Kruger. Many of her works are crucially located in a woman's point of view and express a feminist sentiment that is simply unavailable by looking at her works as black-and-white designs. It is impossible to understand a text like YOUR BODY IS A BATTLEGROUND (Fig. 11.4) superimposed upon a bisected woman's face without reflecting upon the actuality that abortion is a woman's problem but the legality of abortion rights is decided primarily by men. The treatment of women's bodies—whether they are under a woman's own control or whether they are appropriated and controlled by religion, by male artists, or by lawmakers—is essential to a feminist aesthetic. Kuspit's charge that these works are aesthetically inferior because they appeal to the masses (by this, we presume, he sometimes means masses of women) reveals his reliance on the myopic traditional approach to assessing aesthetic value and his resistance to moving beyond the tradition to incorporate new

Fig. 11.4.   Barbara Kruger, *Untitled (Your Body Is a Battleground)*, 1989.
Courtesy Mary Boone Gallery, New York

avenues of approach. His entrenched view gives us a glimpse of how a
commissar of the obscene might actually function in the artworld.

Adrian Piper: Expanding Aesthetic Values

Kuspit considers Adrian Piper's works, known for challenging the viewer on
issues of race and gender, "pseudo-intellectual" (*AMI*, 21). Though he fails to
elaborate on this charge, the most plausible reading of his criticism is that her
work, like Kruger's and Holzer's, is aesthetically inferior because it contains a
message and the message is too strong, thereby failing to be obscene (vital,
deliberate, implicit, and uncanny). It is true that Piper's methods are not

usually considered subtle, since her message—to provide "the potential for furnishing a forceful antidote to racism"—is anything but subtle.[36] In spite of acknowledging the function art *can* serve aesthetically, she readily admits that she has no interest in art that aims to increase aesthetic pleasure—what she calls "Easy Listening Art" (the art of postmodernism): "It is the art that recalls and celebrates the familiar Euroethnic history and canon of art, that reassures one with its familiar and witty strategies of form and content, that minutely refines or dilates upon those strategies in ways that serve to increase our aesthetic pleasure in recognizing and discerning minor modifications in what we have already learned."[37] Rather than rehashing artistic conventions of the past, she is more concerned with educating viewers to their long-standing prejudices—both aesthetic and nonaesthetic. Consider some examples.

An early drawing, *Self-Portrait Exaggerating My Negroid Features* (1981), is described by Lowery Sims (one of Piper's most able spokespersons) as engaging the "conflicting standards of beauty and social acceptance on the most intimate level." It confronts the viewer with the visual imagery of "black is beautiful."[38] A performance piece entitled *The Mythic Being* (1974–75), in which Piper donned a mustache and an Afro wig to masquerade as a black male, explored the additional issue of gender by which "the visual impact of blackness . . . poses not only a social threat but also an aesthetic one."[39] In both pieces, issues of race and gender are raised that the traditional approach to aesthetic value is inadequate to handle. A viewer cannot respond disinterest-edly and aesthetic pleasure is not the issue. What is at issue is assessing the aesthetic value of blackness and the beauty of blacks as it diverges from the traditional criteria of aesthetic value (disinterestedness and pleasure). As Sims aptly puts it: "Grounded as her work is in the contemplation of the black female body, it cannot—and does not—avoid raising the question of how to receive the conventions of black physicality within the canons of [white] beauty."[40]

Two works, in particular, serve to elucidate Piper's deliberate expansion of the aesthetic. (The transcripts of these two pieces appear in Chapter 10.) The first is a work from 1980 entitled *Four Intruders Plus Alarm System* (see Fig. 10.1). It is a mixed-media installation made up of four silk-screen lightboxes each measuring seven feet high that make up the interior of a small cylindrical room six feet in diameter. As one enters the room, which is painted black and excludes all external light, one encounters four 18″ by 24″ silk-screened images, hung at eye level, lit from behind. The images are representations of four hostile-looking African American males staring directly at the viewer, lit behind the eyes. The music and lyrics of "Night People," from the black musical group War, can be heard from a hidden speaker. The viewer is provided with four headphones. In each of four monologues, Piper speaks as the voice of an imaginary art viewer who responds to the work based on ideological defenses that are triggered involuntarily at the sight of a black man: "Here I was concerned to articulate and isolate certain racist stereotypes of black men (aggressive, hostile, malevolent), and also a set of paradigmatic racist responses to those perceived stereotypes."

The four responses offered here include: (1) the aestheticizing response, which ignores political content in favor of formalist concerns ("I'm looking for an aesthetic experience; something that I can judge in terms of aesthetic standards, and this is just not that aesthetically interesting"); (2) the appropriating response in which the viewer claims to be victimized by oppression as well ("I can really get into this. . . . I can really understand black anger, because, like, I'm really angry, too. . . . I've had some real bad problems, you know . . . I feel like I've been ripped off by this society, too"); (3) the liberal response, which blames racism on the rest of society ("I'm simply antagonized by the hostility of this piece. . . . I have the feeling that the artist is just really distorting reality. . . . She's representing all blacks as completely hostile and alienated, and I just think that that's not true. . . . I wouldn't advise my daughter to marry one, that's true. But it's not . . . because I'm a racist"); and (4) what Piper calls the "redneck" response ("This certainly doesn't bring me any closer to the uh, the so-called black experience. . . . I feel that anger is being expressed at me for things that have nothing to do with me. . . . I resent being made the focus of that kind of anger, as though somehow it was my fault").

A second work similar to *Four Intruders* is *Safe* (1990; see Fig. 10.2). This piece consists of a number of black-and-white photographs of African Americans, posed as in a family group portrait. This time they are smiling. In the background, one hears an aria from Bach's *Saint Matthew Passion* which is Peter's plea for mercy after his three denials of Christ. Piper again assumes the voice of art viewer in the taped monologue but instead of separating the four types of racist response by means of different tapes, they are combined on one tape. Once again she speaks for the imaginary viewer, reiterating the traditional criteria (in fact, Kuspit's criteria of implicitness and ambiguity!) for assessing aesthetic value:

> I just don't feel comfortable with this . . . I feel manipulated . . . stared at . . . *laughed* at. . . . All these sardonic smiles! . . . it's just too explicit. . . . Personally I think understatement would've been the

way to go here . . . a kind of subtle ambiguity, . . . the problem is that this piece gives me no aesthetic space . . . there's just no way you can avoid the message here . . . it leaves no room for interpretation, for use of the imagination, for flights of fancy, you know?

In both these works, Piper incorporates expected viewers' reactions *in* the work: anticipating them, questioning them, and attacking them *before* they occur. She skillfully places viewers in a Catch-22 situation of not being able to safely respond. If our initial, unpreventable gut reactions are racist, sexist, or classist in some way, she has accurately predicted them and makes them public. If we attempt to formulate less racist, sexist, or classist responses and instead opt for the safer aesthetic response, we're accused of feigning disinterestedness and searching in vain for a feeling of aesthetic pleasure. We become the object of viewing, nearly replacing the art object in importance. We are viewed by the artist as we view ourselves struggling to overcome our unacceptable reactions and undergo change. By speaking *as* viewer, Piper invests the work with a sense and recognition of her self: as African American and as a woman within a nonblack-, nonfemale-dominated (art)world. According to one critic, Piper's focus on the self is a reflection of her work in Kantian ethics as she continues to seek "a model of the self that a theory of the good society might presuppose."[41]

In setting us up in this way and in our reflection upon the manipulation of our responses, Piper uses her art to reject two of the three basic notions of traditional aesthetic value: its being rooted in a cool, detached, disinterested stance and its resulting in aesthetic pleasure or gratification of some sort. The reactions she anticipates are not aesthetic reactions but rather emotional, political, psychological, and cultural ones. Her point is that try as one might to remain neutral and distanced, one cannot avoid reacting to confrontational issues of gender or race *with* interest. For her, there is no pure aesthetic attitude one can take toward her work. The practical and the personal cannot be put on hold. The ideal experience of a work is "an interactive process" in which the viewer constructs an interpretation based on her level of political self-awareness at the time. She then comes to alter her interpretation upon reflection of this level of self-awareness, adding to a more enlightened interpretation of the work—more importantly—a less racist self. The process is therefore seen as "inherently catalytic."[42]

Thus her works separate aesthetic response from its accompanying notion of pleasure as well as from presumptions of distanced, disinterested response. Kuspit's charge that the work is pseudointellectual betrays his traditionalist tendencies to resist Piper's expansion of the term "aesthetic" into new realms of value. What Kuspit fails to appreciate—thereby denigrating her work as *pseudo*intellectual—is the extent to which Piper seeks to demarcate a separate aesthetics of color that broadens the traditional limits of the aesthetic beyond its normal confines. Issues of black versus white beauty, color (in art) as a reflection of the color of the artist and viewer, and the myth of a pure colorless, genderless aesthetic response move the boundaries of the aesthetic beyond the narrowness of disinterestedness and pleasure and into more complex arenas previously unappreciated. Feminist aesthetics, black aesthetics, ethno-aesthetics, Indian (that is, Native American) aesthetics, are instances of new terminology that seek to redefine the parameters of the aesthetic based on artworks by women and artists of color. Such extensions may be perceived as threatening to the tradition of a white male aesthetic—to be summarily ignored or dismissed—or may be perceived as a welcome and long overdue improvement. [43] In any case, they cast doubt on Kuspit's claims that activist art lacks aesthetic value simply because it seeks to convey a deliberate and explicit message.

The aesthetic value, then, of works like Kruger's, Holzer's, and Piper's is rooted in the tradition but is drastically different in character. Perhaps an analogy will help. Suppose a person has grown up eating American fast food and has acquired a taste for hamburgers, fries, and soft drinks and has no sense of savoring the nuances of flavors, no delicacy of taste. He then travels to another country, tastes the local fare, and—not surprisingly—decides it's unpalatable. He is, however, stuck in this country for months on end and has no choice but to continue sampling the regional cuisine. After some time, it becomes palatable, though not necessarily pleasurable. He begins to notice the subtlety of flavors; in effect, his taste changes from that to which he was accustomed to a new and radically different sort. For that person, there is no turning back, that is, he can no longer evaluate the food of his old eating habits in anything like the same old way. [44]

I am proposing that looking at the art of Holzer, Kruger, and Piper includes such a mind-shift of this sort and that it is difficult to discern the aesthetic value of their work because we are accustomed to looking for aesthetic value in other, very entrenched ways. We are habituated, in effect, by the way we have learned about art in the past, that is, by the numerous works of "the great masters." Repeated exposure to those works (and only those works) establishes a pattern of likes and dislikes, tastes and tolerances, that results in our developing a taste for only those items sampled so far: the Western, male-dominated history of art. (Consider how the viewing of films made by white males has similarly affected viewing audiences.)

But the artworld has much more to offer. Works of art by women and artists of color, though unfamiliar to a traditional Western taste, extend the range of our experiences beyond those we've come to know. Naturally, our first tastes are unpredictable. Our first reactions are often negative. We need to come to learn the aesthetic of such works by sampling them over and over again, by learning their ways and what unique aspects they have to offer. In some instances we may even come to value those experiences over the ones with which we grew up. We may even come to reject our old tastes in favor of the new. In any case, we can no longer view works in old ways. Exposure to new tastes inevitably impinges on our judgment of the works on which we were raised.

Sampling the artworld is *unlike* living in a foreign country, however, in that one can always retreat to one's old ways and give up the adventure of new tastes. When women artists were first introduced into art history texts, faculty often refused to teach them and retreated to the tradition they knew best. By avoiding the new and unfamiliar, they never learned to acquire a taste for them. Unlike being immersed in a foreign country, one always has the choice to return to the masters and to continue to sample the same old fare. It takes less effort to do so than to learn to value a feminist aesthetic or a black aesthetic. We need only look to the way unusual artifacts have been treated in the past to understand how they continue to be treated: for instance, the way turn-of-the-century artists like Picasso "appreciated" African artifacts. Such objects were not embraced in order to be understood for the unique values they expressed but rather were appropriated for the benefits they could bring to a burgeoning modernist movement and artists' careers.

My suggestion is that those of us trained in the tradition can only half-heartedly come to appreciate Asian art or Native American art unless we work at immersing ourselves in the aesthetic particular to the piece and continually strive to learn about it. A feminist aesthetic would attribute value to the works of Holzer, Kruger, or Piper *because* they diverge from the white, male viewpoint. Formal properties remain central to the work and one can choose to assess them in a Beardsleyan way. But there's more going on than meets the eye. These formal properties, rearranged in new and different ways, can be better understood and evaluated *as* they are informed by a feminist, black, Chicana, or Asian American aesthetic. One must come to appreciate these ways by turning away from the valuing of formal properties for their own sake and looking at them as indications of a viewpoint that seeks to restore dignity and pride in the accomplishments of artists of color and women. Thus, in expanding the traditional notion of aesthetic value beyond its usual confines, we come to have the option of many types of aesthetic values by which to evaluate more fairly the wide range of works available for us to sample.

Conclusion

I have attempted to critique Kuspit's denunciation of activist art by examining the underlying assumptions of his use of the term "aesthetic value." I have shown that expressing doubts about his endorsement of obscenity is more than just a superficial quibble over terminology; rather, it exposes modes of exclusion that masquerade as standards of aesthetic value.

Kuspit's own examples were used *against* him as counterexamples to his basic claim that only obscene art has aesthetic value. They have functioned as more than just counterexamples, however, as they point to serious flaws with any approach to art—anti-activist or otherwise—based on the traditional aesthetic-nonaesthetic distinction. In looking at the three foci of the aesthetic—its identification with formal properties, its insistence on a disinterested relationship between object and viewer, and its culminating effect of aesthetic pleasure—we find that two out of the three are not retained in a new, revised view of aesthetic value. Thus, the aesthetic need not rest on a disinterested stance and aesthetic pleasure need not result. Most important, aesthetic value need not take precedence over nonaesthetic. A revised sense of the aesthetic, on the contrary, is one that is neither narrowly circumscribed nor exclusionary.

We must become accustomed to relying upon more than one single, monolithic sense of "aesthetic" as established by the tradition. If a feminist sense of aesthetic value emerges as well as a black sense as well as a Native American sense, then so be it. Perhaps it was naive ever to think that one, universal sense of aesthetic value could ever be achieved. To the art lover worried about the proliferation of standards of aesthetic value ad infinitum, one reply is that it is inevitable that different senses will overlap and that some will become obsolete as new ones emerge. A feminist aesthetic, for instance, could encompass an aesthetic of color or class, though there are inherent difficulties in this approach that have already been enumerated.[45] These issues will need to be sorted out in the future as various types of art come to the fore and are experienced and discussed by more and more persons.

Jazz is not evaluated in the same way as Brahms. Chinese art cannot be understood by studying Western art. The films of Spike Lee enrich the dialogue begun with *Birth of a Nation* and move it in directions previously unforeseen. The novels of N. Scott Momaday, Toni Morrison, and Amy Tan spark new realms of evaluative criteria based on the importance of one's origins, an oral tradition, one's tie to the land and feelings of exclusion from the dominant race and its inherent patriarchy. The mention of all these works in the same space is not meant to conflate their differences nor to trivialize them, but rather to point to the essential need for developing informed and coherent sets of criteria for determining the values of each work. Philosophical aesthetics can help by moving away from the rigidity of the traditional aesthetic-nonaesthetic distinction and toward a revised notion (or more appropriately, notions) of aesthetic value.

Finally, to be fair to the art being evaluated, such notions ought to grow out of the context from which the art comes rather than be appropriated by those of us trained *in* the tradition. Philosophers and critics need to hear and study the voices of Holzer, Kruger, Piper, Sims, and others who seek to delineate new senses of aesthetic value. Our job is not to silence them as commissars of the obscene are charged by Kuspit to do. Our job, as persons who value the arts, is to become more open to their voices and their art, as we seek to avoid all forms of exclusionism.

Notes

1. George Dickie's essay was originally published in *American Philosophical Quarterly* 1 (1964): 56–66, and has been reprinted in a number of anthologies. Nelson Goodman's views can be found in *Languages of Art* (Indianapolis: Bobbs-Merrill, 1968) and *Ways of Worldmaking* (Indianapolis: Hackett, 1978).

2. Clive Bell, *Art* (New York: Putnam, 1958), 27. (Originally published in 1914.)

3. Monroe Beardsley, *Aesthetics: Problems in the Philosophy of Criticism* (New York: Harcourt, Brace and World, 1958). He added a postscript in 1980, prior to the second edition of 1981.

4. Monroe Beardsley, "The Aesthetic Point of View," *Contemporary Philosophic Thought* 3 (1970), reprinted in *Contemporary Philosophy of Art: Readings in Analytic Aesthetics*, ed. John W. Bender and H. Gene Blocker (Englewood Cliffs, N.J.: Prentice-Hall, 1993), 384–96.

5. Four of the five features, including the first, must be present for an experience to count as aesthetic. "In Defense of Aesthetic Value," *Proceedings and Addresses of the American Philosophical Association* 52 (1979), reprinted in Bender and Blocker, eds., *Contemporary Philosophy of Art*, 402–6.

6. Goodman, *Ways of Worldmaking*, 57–70; and Beardsley, "In Defense of Aesthetic Value," in Bender and Blocker, eds., *Contemporary Philosophy of Art*, 405.

7. As I argue in "Feminism in Context: A Role for Feminist Theory in Aesthetic Evaluation,"

Beardsley never satisfactorily defeats this less severe characterization of the Moralist position, the Argument from Correlation, which holds that Moralists grant the existence of a separate form of aesthetic value but do not make it dependent upon or correlated to moral value. See Bender and Blocker, eds., *Contemporary Philosophy of Art*, 106–21.

8. See my essay "Evaluating Art: A Feminist Case for Dickie's Matrix System," in *Institutions of Art: Reconsiderations of George Dickie's Philosophy*, ed. Robert Yanal (University Park: The Pennsylvania State University Press, 1994), 87–107.

9. There are many texts chronicling the "forgotten" history of women artists, most notably Rozsika Parker and Griselda Pollock's *Old Mistresses: Women, Art, and Ideology* (New York: Pantheon Books, 1981). See notes 10 and 12 below.

10. Ann Sutherland Harris and Linda Nochlin, *Women Artists, 1550–1950* (New York: Knopf, 1981), 107. The quote is by Claude Philips.

11. Cited in Parker and Pollock, *Old Mistresses*, 8. The quote is from an essay entitled "Women Painters," *Saturday Book* (1964):19.

12. Germaine Greer, *The Obstacle Race: The Fortunes of Women Painters and Their Work* (New York: Farrar, Straus and Giroux, 1979), 142. Greer notes that earlier evaluations considered the work to be "a perfect picture, unforgettable."

13. Patricia Failing, "Black Artists Today: A Case of Exclusion," *ARTnews* 88 (March 1989): 124–31. A postscript to this from the entertainment world is the report that MTV, in its first two years on the air, refused to air video clips by African American artists; see Daryl Chin, "Multiculturalism and Its Masks: The Art of Identity Politics," *Performing Arts Journal* 40 (January 1992): 1–15.

14. Failing, "Black Artists Today," 130.

15. Ibid. At best (the Whitney Museum of American Art), 7 percent of the artists shown from 1980 to 1987 were non-European or of non-European descent. At worst (the Guggenheim, from 1980 to 1985), no minority artists were shown. In the all-important Whitney Biennials from 1973 to 1987, only 4.4 percent were artists of color (although not even one Native American qualified in the entire time), and from 1981 to 1987 there were no one-person shows of black, Hispanic, or Native American painters or sculptors at the Whitney. The 1993 Biennial did include some Native Americans and artists of color.

16. Lowery Stokes Sims, "The New Exclusionism," *Art Papers* 12, no. 4 (July–August 1988): 37–38. The exclusionism is "new" in contrast to the exclusion of blacks in the history of art: see, for example, Albert Boime, *The Art of Exclusion: Representing Blacks in the Nineteenth Century* (Washington, D.C.: Smithsonian Institution Press, 1990); and Hugh Honour, *The Image of the Black in Western Art*, 4 vols. (Cambridge: Harvard University Press, 1989).

17. The speaker, Patterson Sims, notes, however, that "the curatorial staff was entirely white when I worked there." See Failing, "Black Artists Today."

18. Hilton Kramer, "Does Feminism Conflict with Artistic Standards?" *New York Times*, 27 January 1980, 1, 27. He continues, "The unstated implication [is], I suppose, that hard-headed critical judgment must be suspended until that heavenly day yonder when men and women achieve—in art, as in everything else—some ideal parity of talent, power and opportunity."

19. See Deborah Solomon's "The Art World Bust," *New York Times Magazine*, 28 February 1993, 32.

20. This was Barbara Barr's "Reply to Piper," in *Women Artists News* 12, no. 2 (June 1987): 6, upon hearing her talk about the 1988 work *Cornered*. Part of Piper's text is as follows: "I embody the racist's nightmare, the obscenity of miscegenation, the reminder that segregation has never been a fully functional concept, that sexual desire penetrates social and racial barriers, and reproduces itself. . . . I represent the loathsome possibility that all of you are 'tainted' by black ancestry. If someone can look and sound like me and still be black, who is safely white?"

21. One response to the feminist version of the Argument from Reduction is the challenge to

distinguish between the differing values of politically acceptable works, for instance, between a variety of quilts celebrating women's lives. Since there is no way to value one over another except by formal properties, the distinction should not be dropped.

22. Eleanor Hartley, "Cindy Sherman at Metro Pictures," *Art in America* 89, no. 9 (September 1992): 127–28. In a review of Sherman's recent work consisting of color photos of mannequin parts, masks, and assorted props, Hartley states: "In one of the most terrifying photos [*Untitled* (1992)], the mask of an old crone is attached to a legless mannequin whose torso is covered with a shield composed of the fully rounded breasts and belly of a pregnant woman. Extruding from this hybrid female's vagina is a string of brown sausages." Hartley praises Sherman as follows: "There is something brave about her willingness to grapple with some of the most unpleasant realities of the human condition. At a moment when self-righteousness pervades the art world, she opts for truths that are not sugar-coated."

23. Donald Kuspit, "Art and the Moral Imperative: Analyzing Activist Art," *New Art Examiner* (January 1991), 18–25, hereafter *AMI*.

24. Donald Kuspit, "A Sceptical Note on the Idea of the Moral Imperative in Contemporary Art," *Art Criticism* 7, no. 1 (1991): 106–12, hereafter *SN*.

25. It is important to note that Olympia stands as a paradigm of aesthetic value only when interpreted in a certain way. One would presume that Kuspit would reject a Marxist or feminist reading, as well as one that points to the difference in color between the prostitute and her maid.

26. Joel Feinberg, *The Moral Limits of the Criminal Law*, Vol. 2, *Offense to Others* (New York: Oxford University Press, 1985), 123.

27. Ibid., 120.

28. Ibid., 109.

29. Moreover, the term loses its force as Kuspit recommends not only that art be obscene, but also that criticism be bent "to its own obscene purpose" as it acknowledges "the obscenity of every canon" (*SN*, 112).

30. Though neither female nor a minority, Bleckner is vital to the discussion at hand.

31. See Michael Auping, *Jenny Holzer* (New York: Universe, 1992).

32. See Kate Linker, *Love for Sale: The Words and Pictures of Barbara Kruger* (New York: Abrams, 1990).

33. Auping, *Jenny Holzer*, 62–67. The work consisted of a medium-sized room with eleven flashing three-color LED signs, each approximately fifteen feet long and nine inches high, flanked by two walls, each supporting five horizontal three-color LED signs, twenty feet long and five inches high. Auping reports some viewers experiencing physical reactions to the piece: nausea, vertigo, and severe mood changes. "Many found it difficult to maintain their equilibrium—the intense reflection on the marble floor created the illusion of a deep hole into which the language seemed to fall infinitely away."

34. Marc Chagall's series of birth paintings is an exception to men's avoidance of this imagery.

35. Judy Chicago, *The Birth Project* (Garden City, N.Y.: Doubleday, 1985).

36. See commentary by Adrian Piper in *Pretend*, an exhibition catalogue of Piper's works (New York: Colorstone Printing, 1990).

37. Ibid. She adds, "[It] is meant to be looked at rather than seen. . . . It does not make trouble; instead it makes nice."

38. Lowery Stokes Sims, "The Mirror, The Other: The Politics of Aesthetics," *Artforum* 28 (March 1990): 111–15.

39. Ibid. See also Hilton Als, "darling," *Artforum* 29 (March 1991): 100–104.

40. Sims, "The Mirror," 115.

41. See Thomas McEvilley's review of a show of Piper's work at the Alternative Museum in *Artforum* 26 (September 1987): 128–29. In addition to being a practicing artist, Piper currently teaches philosophy at Wellesley College.

42. Piper, *Pretend,* n.p.

43. Aside from the two special issues in 1990 on feminist aesthetics in the philosophical journals, *Journal of Aesthetics and Art Criticism* and *Hypatia,* and the recent publication of Hilde Hein and Carolyn Korsmeyer, eds., *Aesthetics in Feminist Perspective* (Bloomington: Indiana University Press, 1993), philosophical aesthetics still remains relatively silent on these topics.

44. Another analogy is the person changing his diet due to a medical problem, for example, restricting salt intake over a period of time can result in a person's finding foods salty that previously tasted unsalty.

45. See, for instance, Elizabeth V. Spelman's *Inessential Woman: Problems of Exclusion in Feminist Thought* (Boston: Beacon, 1988).

SELECT BIBLIOGRAPHY TO PART III

Aristotle. "The Poetics." In *The Works of Aristotle*, edited by W. D. Ross. London: Oxford University Press, 1959.

Auping, Michael. *Jenny Holzer*. New York: Universe, 1992.

Beardsley, Monroe. "In Defense of Aesthetic Value." *Proceedings and Addresses of the American Philosophical Association* 52 (1979): 723–49.

Boime, Albert. *The Art of Exclusion: Representing Blacks in the Nineteenth Century*. Washington, D.C.: Smithsonian Institution Press, 1990.

Brand, Peggy Zeglin. "Evaluating Art: A Feminist Case for Dickie's Matrix System." In *Institutions of Art: Reconsiderations of George Dickie's Philosophy*, edited by Robert Yanal. University Park: The Pennsylvania State University Press, 1994.

———. "Feminism in Context: A Role for Feminist Theory in Aesthetic Evaluation." In *Contemporary Philosophy of Art: Readings in Analytic Aesthetics*, edited by John W. Bender and H. Gene Blocker. Englewood Cliffs, N.J.: Prentice-Hall, 1993.

Brunt, Rosalind, and Caroline Rowan, eds. *Feminism, Culture and Politics*. London: Lawrence and Wishart, 1982.

Dickie, George. *Evaluating Art*. Philadelphia: Temple University Press, 1988.

Ferguson, Russell, Cornel West, Trinh Minh-ha, and Martha Givers, eds. *Out There: Marginalization and Contemporary Culture*. New York and Cambridge: The New Museum and the MIT Press, 1990.

Gates, Henry Louis, Jr. *Loose Canons: Notes on the Culture Wars*. New York: Oxford University Press, 1992.

Greer, Germaine. *The Obstacle Race: The Fortunes of Women Painters and Their Work*. New York: Farrar, Straus and Giroux, 1979.

Hess, Thomas B., and Elizabeth C. Baker, eds. *Art and Sexual Politics*. Art News Series. New York: Collier Books, Macmillan, 1971.

Honour, Hugh. *The Image of the Black in Western Art*. Edited by Ladislas Bugner. Cambridge: Harvard University Press, 1989.

Jehlen, Myra. "Archimedes and the Paradox of Feminist Criticism." In *The Signs Reader: Women, Gender and Scholarship*, edited by Elizabeth Abel and Emily K. Abel. Chicago: University of Chicago Press, 1981.

Kauffman, Linda, ed. *Gender and Theory: Dialogues on Feminist Criticism*. New York: Basil Blackwell, 1989.

Kemal, Salim, and Ivan Gaskell, eds. *Explanation and Value in the Arts*. Cambridge Studies in Philosophy and the Arts. Cambridge: Cambridge University Press, 1993.

Lauter, Estella. *Women as Mythmakers*. Bloomington: Indiana University Press, 1984.

Linker, Kate. *Love for Sale: The Words and Pictures of Barbara Kruger*. New York: Abrams, 1990.

Lippard, Lucy R. *Mixed Blessings: New Art in a Multicultural America*. New York: Pantheon Books, 1990.

Parker, Rozsika. *The Subversive Stitch: Embroidery and the Making of the Feminine.* New York: Routledge, 1989.

———, and Griselda Pollock, eds. *Framing Feminism: Art and the Women's Movement, 1970–1985.* London: Pandora Press, 1987.

Piper, Adrian.. "The Logic of Modernism." *Flashart* 26 (January–February 1993).

———. *Pretend.* New York: Colorstone Printing, 1990.

Plato. *The Republic.* New York: Oxford University Press, 1941.

Sibley, Frank. "Aesthetic Concepts." *Philosophical Review* 67 (1959): 421–50.

Stolnitz, Jerome. *Aesthetics and Philosophy of Art Criticism.* New York: Houghton Mifflin, 1960.

Suleiman, Susan Rubin. *Subversive Intent: Gender, Politics, and the Avant-Garde.* Cambridge: Harvard University Press, 1990.

———, ed. *The Female Body in Western Culture.* Cambridge: Harvard University Press, 1986.

Trinh, T. Minh-ha. *Framer Framed.* New York: Routledge, 1992.

———. *When the Moon Waxes Red: Representation, Gender, and Cultural Politics.* New York: Routledge, 1991.

———. *Woman, Native, Other: Writing Postcoloniality and Feminism.* Bloomington: Indiana University Press, 1989.

Vance, Carole S., ed. *Pleasure and Danger.* Boston: Routledge and Kegan Paul, 1984.

Wallis, Brian, ed. *Art After Modernism: Rethinking Representation.* New York: New Museum of Contemporary Art, 1984.

IV

Feminism and the Interpretation of Artworks

Feminist theorists have examined the position of the viewing subject and the nature of appreciation and aesthetic pleasure, and many feminist artists have rejected traditional goals of art. The incompatibility of the work of some feminist artists with conventional concepts of aesthetic value was discussed in Part III. The meaning and value of canonical works of art have been reassessed by art historians, literary critics, and film theorists. These challenges have their versions in philosophy of criticism and theories of interpretation. Philosophers inquire about the conditions under which interpretive judgments are justified and artworks acquire historical significance. The five essays in this section consider various aspects of feminist revisions of the history of the arts and the interpretive methodologies employed in those revisions.

One of the central presumptions challenged by feminist revisionism is the idea that the value of artworks is contained autonomously "within" each work itself and is thereby available for appreciation by any sensitive member of the viewing, reading, or listening audience. According to this traditional approach, the successful work of art is autonomous, in the sense that discovery of its artistic/aesthetic value does not depend upon knowledge of the social context in which it was produced, of biographical information about the artist, or of any other "external" features of the work itself.

Strictly noncontextual approaches to artworks have in fact been out of fashion in critical circles for some time. (They had their heyday in the 1940s and 1950s as the so-called New Criticism adopted by literary scholars.) But questions of contextual meaning and their continued presence "in" works of art have resurfaced in contemporary scholarship. As feminists employ deconstructionist and historicist techniques to search out patterns of patriarchy in the art-historical record, opponents charge that they are imposing contemporary politics on considerations of art. Feminists have culled art and literature for evidence of patterns of women's oppression; they have exhumed the lost and neglected works of women artists and sought to establish them as having equal merit alongside canonical staples; they have reassessed the meaning of familiar works in ways that bring out the relations of gender and power manifest in image and form; they have challenged the very idea of canonicity and elevated domestic and other seldom-recognized art to a level of greater importance than it usually has.

All of this involves expanding the perimeter of relevant information that may be brought to bear on our understanding of works of art. The social contexts of art's production, including information about artists, historical circumstances, and collateral cultural artifacts, are regularly used as tools to understanding the meaning of art. Moreover, theoretical approaches of such schools as psychoanalysis, structuralism, deconstruction, and marxism are also eclectically employed by feminists.

The essays in this section provide a sampling of feminist criticism and reflections on the methodology of critical interpretation. Some authors employ one or another of these methods; some reflect upon that employment. The section opens with two philosophical analyses of feminist art history. Anita Silvers, who is interested in the phenomenon of canon formation, explores the distinction between what she designates "internal" and "external" qualities of artworks. Analyzing feminist claims about the relevance of gender to the evaluation of art, Silvers delineates ways in which the gender of the artist may or may not be considered artistically significant. She employs insights from both postmodernist and analytic philosophy in making her argument, concluding that feminists ought to resist the tendency in art-historical writing to cast the story of art as heroic narrative.

Susan Feagin also examines the philosophical foundations of feminist art history. Noting that much feminist criticism has appealed to recent Continental philosophy in search of its guiding assumptions, she inquires about the compatibility of feminist art history with traditional analytic aesthetics. She introduces a concept she calls "de facto significance," which she argues is a necessary adjustment to analytic aesthetics that would allow the insights of feminism to become incorporated into traditional philosophical aesthetics.

Both Silvers and Feagin refer to recent writing about Renaissance painting. Mary D. Garrard, an art historian, continues the attention to this period with an appreciative revision of Leonardo da Vinci. She examines his portraits of women, comparing them to more standard examples of this genre, invoking his philosophical interests and unorthodox ideas about anatomy and nature to give us a picture of a Renaissance artist unusually appreciative of women and female nature. Her essay serves as an example of feminist revisionist art history that incorporates the historical context of philosophical ideas in its reinterpretation of a familiar artist.

Literature and film are the subjects of Chapters 15 and 16. Many feminist interpretive frameworks have adapted tools of psychoanalysis to plumb the import of artworks. Some discussion of the use of psychoanalysis was included in Part II with essays that considered theories of the gaze. The uses of psychoanalytic concepts are further debated here: Ellen Handler Spitz wonders about common themes she detects in the writing of women and isolates a mythical-psychological theme that supplants the traditional focus on the Oedipus complex in psychoanalysis. Attention to mother-daughter relations in literature—which, she argues, often bear comparison with the Demeter and Persephone myth—enhances feminist understanding of literature without falling into the masculinist biases of Freud. Like Renée Lorraine's approach to music, Spitz's discussion is sympathetic to the premise that texts by women manifest a distinctively feminine imaginative world.

Noël Carroll's focus is feminist interpretation of movies. He presents a sharply critical reading of psychoanalytic film criticism, referring to some of the theories also addressed in Part II. His discussion raises questions about discerning the political import of art with the use of analytic techniques that refer to unconscious aspects of the mind, and he asserts a preference for the social analysis of movies that arose among earlier feminist critics of the 1970s. Finally, he suggests an alternative method for attaching social meaning to art, one that is available from recent analytic philosophy. In this conclusion his essay converges with the suggestion made by Susan Feagin about art history and analytic aesthetics, in that he envisions an ultimately congenial relationship between feminism and philosophical methodology of this tradition.

The issues raised here about the interpretation and attribution of meaning to art of the past and present are manifold. They encourage the reader to investigate more thoroughly various analytical methodologies—deconstructive, historicist, psychoanalytic—and they raise in new form the perennial problem of the relativity of interpretation. How determinate is the meaning to be found in a text? How many meanings can one text legitimately carry? How bound to the conditions of its production is the meaning of art? And how does one investigate the historical record for what is absent from immediate attention—the lives and consciousness of women then and now?

12

Has Her(oine's) Time Now Come?

Anita Silvers

Artemisia's Ordeal

Artemisia Gentileschi (c. 1593–1652) was well paid and highly thought of as a painter by some of the leading art patrons of the Europe of her time. In other words, in her own time she was a socially acceptable, successful artist. Yet, subsequently, the shadow of obscurity fell over her. Only about thirty paintings, from what must have been a much greater body of work, have been identified and attributed to her. Moreover, relatively little has been written about her, and only very recently has she been the subject of an extensive art-historical monograph.

In contrast, Agostino Tassi, the painter tried for raping Artemisia when she was nineteen years old, has been the subject of at least two monographs in this century.[1] Does Artemisia now lack esteem because the lines along which the story of European art has been permitted to unfold serve nonaesthetic ends, objectives prescribed by dominating male interests? Was Artemisia's art eclipsed because the narrative structure of the story of art admits heroes but rejects heroines? Such questions are typically raised in feminist or gynocriticism. What remains to be seen is whether feminists can supply answers which draw upon considerations sufficiently compelling to radically revise—indeed, to reform—the history of art.

In an extensive feminist treatment, *Artemisia Gentileschi: The Image of the Female Hero in Italian Baroque Art,* the art historian Mary Garrard introduces the question of whether Artemisia's obscurity results from sexism on the part of male scholars.[2] Because Artemisia's Caravaggist techniques are applied to show women deplorably brutalized by men or, alternatively, women triumphantly brutalizing men, Garrard hypothesizes that male art historians may be appalled by the paintings' themes. Alternatively, she suggests that males may be offended because Artemisia's violent treatments strike them as unwomanly.[3] These explanations are distinct, for the first attributes the rejection of the paintings to their subject matter, which is internal to the works, while the second proposes that a condition external to the paintings, the gender of their painter, is the source of their devaluation. If the latter explanation is adopted, we might expect to effect revisions in art-historical judgments by transforming attitudes toward attributes which are not features of artworks themselves, while the former suggests that art-historical revision requires something more, which might be thought of as a transformation of aesthetic responsiveness.

Although himself a progenitor of the type of research into social, political, and economic conditions which informs revisionist or social constructionist approaches to writing the history of art, the art historian Francis Haskell disputes Garrard's account. Noting that the brutal subjects of Artemisia's paintings are common also in works by male painters of more enduring reputation, he denies that these themes repel male scholars. But neither are Artemisia's gender or other personal characteristics or history relevant, Haskell insists. That Artemisia's rape caused her anguish is an admissible hypothesis about her, he acknowledges, but it is not thereby a fact about her art. The story of the artist is not the story of the artist's art. Haskell denies that Garrard, by telling Artemisia's admittedly poignant story, has shown her art to be sufficiently expressive to establish its lasting aesthetic value.[4] He assumes that revisionist revaluation needs something more to succeed than the transformation of social, political, or economic attitudes.

To reveal what he considers to be the banality of Artemisia's painting, Haskell tells the story of another seventeenth-century Italian artist, Artemisia's slightly younger contemporary Pietro Testa. Unlike Artemisia, Pietro failed to secure recognition as a painter, although he obtained reliable patronage for his etchings and drawings. Always melancholy, Pietro committed suicide when he was thirty-eight. In reviewing a Philadelphia Museum of Art catalogue of an exhibition of Pietro's work, Haskell comments, in the same review in which he dismisses Garrard's revaluation of Artemisia: "From this publication, Pietro Testa emerges as having possessed just those elements of originality, complexity, capacity for expressing personal suffering, and (almost) genius that, despite her great talent, were beyond the reach—or perhaps beyond the ambitions—of Gentileschi."[5]

Why should anyone suppose that telling Pietro's story of anguish and subsequent suicide is more aesthetically relevant than telling Artemisia's story of rape and subsequent anguish? Should Artemisia's work be denied elevation because her story is not like Pietro's? And in what respects is it not like Pietro's? Further examination of the review reveals that what impels Haskell's admiration most forcefully is the expressiveness of Pietro's style. He praises Pietro's work for its "hallucinating character," the "strained intensity of his treatment," and the "unusual nature of his subject matter" which makes us feel that "an individual personality of a kind . . . that was rare in seventeenth century Rome is trying to communicate to us his feelings about art and also about himself."[6] Haskell comments: "Testa seems to escape from his own century and to move straight into that excitable, 'pre-Romantic' phase of neoclassicism."[7]

Hindsight here permits Haskell to view Pietro as more influential than Artemisia on the ground that his expressive predilections prefigure a successor style. Thus, Pietro's work counts for Haskell as more exemplary, indeed (almost) as canonical, compared to Artemisia's. But is Haskell himself recounting facts about Pietro's art? Or is it instead merely a fact about the kind of art-historical story Haskell prefers to tell that art like Pietro's, but not like Artemisia's, counts as expressive? If so, is Haskell confusing the story of the artist with the story of the artist's work, the same complaint he raises against Garrard?

The answer depends in part on how features of art are to be differentiated from external conditions which may (or may not) have affected them. Do Haskell and Garrard differ primarily in regard to facts about Artemisia's work, that is, about whether or not it is expressive, or does Haskell's demurral reduce to a preference for art-historical narratives whose protagonists are male? Notice that the latter could manifest itself in a taste for stories which recount activities more usually associated with males than females, as might be so in preferring war stories to love stories. Someone who favors stories about anguish caused by failed ambition to stories about anguish caused by being raped might be more entranced by Pietro's story. In the same vein, someone unmoved or deterred by Artemisia's victimization by a rapist might be more attracted to her story if she is recast generically as having been

Fig. 12.1.   Artemisia Gentileschi, *Judith and Holofernes*. Uffizi, Florence

victimized by a dominant class. Is it a fact about her art, or only another kind of story, that Artemisia is unfairly neglected because dominant scholarly tastes prefer heroic stories?

Garrard and Haskell thus appear to diverge not only about Artemisia's art, but also about what kinds of facts about the artist should be incorporated into artwriting about the artist's art. I take the source of the seemingly intractable debate between Garrard and Haskell over Artemisia's work to be a method-ological obscurity which threatens to stall revisionist feminism. In what follows, I shall suggest that the problem lies in conflicting assumptions common to revisionism, and that its resolution lies not in deciding between masculinist and feminist theories of art but rather in clarifying a different difference, that between what is internal and what is external to artworks themselves.

Externalist revisionism grounds reform on claims that social conditions suppress certain classes of persons and, as a side effect, devalue the products of these neglected persons. Against both masculinist and feminist externalists who hold that the canon is formed and reformed as an artifact of conditions of political, social, or economic dominance, I shall argue for Garrard's and Haskell's shared *internalist* supposition that revisionist scholarship aimed at achieving canonical status for women's (or any other class of) works of art should focus on reforming the attribution of properties to works of art, not on reforming external conditions which might impede the makers of art.

But I shall trace the difficulty about whether both Garrard and Haskell confuse the stories of works of art with those of their artists to an externalist supposition they also share. Both propose to expand the canon by recharacter-izing artworks in terms of properties which link them to preceding or succeed-ing works through stories about their artists. And, as when Haskell claims Pietro as a pre-Romantic and Garrard points out Artemisia's intensification of Caravaggist techniques, both veer toward externalism by supposing that revisionist artwriting should take the form of hero(in)ic historical narrative which appeals to histories of artists as grounds for revaluing their art.

Against this latter supposition, I shall contend that for forming or reforming canons, the facts of (personal or social) history are incremental only; they cannot ground revaluation. The phenomena of art defy the predictive outcomes that would confirm the relevance of externalist historical factors. Moreover, to be canonical, a work must be appreciated as exemplary, and to be so it must have a history which casts it so, but it is not for externalist deterministic reasons that women fail to appear as hero(in)es in most of these histories. Following suggestions drawn from both analytic and postmodernist sources, I shall advise revisionist artwriters to follow Foucault's caution against conceiving of the artists whose stories are related in arts scholarship as historical persons who originated (that is, were the origins of) their art, and who, consequently, are prior to and separate from it.[8] From this perspective, it is problematic how references to properties external to works of art—properties like gender—function in the kind of artwriting crucial to canonical reform.

Feminism and Canon Reformation

One revolutionary goal of feminism is to reform the artistic canon. This program is crucial to enhancing the status of women because too few objects created by women are included among the most highly esteemed and acclaimed artistic work. As with any major movement meant to shift social and political realities, feminism manifests a variety of versions or developmental stages, and this is true both for feminist theory in general and for the application of feminist theory to the arts. Despite the differences which obtain among feminist critics and art historians of various theoretical schools, the project of canon reformation is pursued passionately by almost all of them.[9] The recasting of Artemisia as heroine is one among many efforts to make progress to this goal.

Whether the time now has come for Artemisia and other women artists of the past to assume more influence depends upon this project's being feasible. It would seem to be of a familiar type, for the histories of the arts are replete with instances in which the canon has undergone substantial change. What is rare, perhaps unique to feminism, is the attempt to root radical revision of the canon in a biological property of the artist. For how an artist's gender affects her art is not immediately self-evident.

This difficulty is not much diffused by taking the line, characteristic of feminist studies in the 1980s, that gender is not merely biological but is also a facet of social, cultural, and psychological identity, for delineating female identity in these other realms still derives from distinguishing between biologically differentiated groups. (In this connection, see also the arguments of Irene Diamond and Lee Quinby, and of Nancy Fraser and Linda Nicholson, to the effect that feminist theories such as those drawing on Marxism, semiotics, psychoanalysis, and Lacanian theory do not escape from the essentialism of natural kinds.)[10] Moreover, a feminism which divorces gender from biological difference threatens also eventually to divorce itself from women.

Given the advantage of defining feminism by reference to women in order to guarantee it as women's theory, what kind of case can this externalist approach provide for revisionist scholarship? Note first that the feminist project of canonical revision invites suspicion if it seems motivated by nothing more than the complaint that works by women artists are underrepresented in the canons of the various artistic media. Could this be just a misguided attempt to apply egalitarian or democratic principles to a realm outside their scope? There seems to be little reason to challenge the usual supposition that possession of artistic talent and the capacity to actualize it are not the sorts of things which can be expected to be subject to equitable distribution.

Usually, aesthetic theory treats artistic genius as a combination of talent and drive which occurs unpredictably in persons despite the circumstances of their group or class. While this conception may result from exaggerated romanticism, the histories of the arts do not exhibit a significant predilection for great artists to come from conditions of power rather than of subservience, wealth rather than poverty, stable rather than disrupted families, or, conversely, from conditions of subservience, poverty, or instability. That is, the facts about which artists have or have not been esteemed give reason to suspect the view that we can specify sociological conditions under which great artists more likely will occur, unless the conditions specified are already art-related, such as that of being the daughter or son of an artist.

Even a theorist like the art historian John Berger, who contends that the medium of oil painting has functioned historically as a tool to promote the concept of property, does not propose that oil painters are predominantly from the property-owning class, or for that matter, predominantly from any other economic class. Instead, Berger insists that oil painters, whether rich or poor, constitute an identifiable subservient class whose function is to create pictures which portray property-owning in a favorable light. Berger thus delineates the class relevant to his analysis by reference to features of the works its members turn out, and so his method is internalist.[11] To the extent that the feminist project of canonical reform centers on the suppression of women, identifying the relevant subservient class by reference to the gender of its members rather than to the production of art with certain distinctive properties, it differs from Berger's approach by being externalist.

Why Are There Few Great Women Artists?

Despite these observations, it is hard to cease wondering whether gender is connected to achieving artistic greatness. For by simply generalizing from the gender of those who have succeeded to this state, it seems to be predictable that women are less likely than men to create canonical works. And if predictable, then the call for explanation appears compelling, for there is something frustrating about the rarity of great women artists when artists from other suppressed classes, for instance, the powerless, the poor, and even the disabled, are relatively well represented in the Euro-centered canon.[12]

Parenthetically, regardless of why it has been so unusual for women to rise to eminence in the arts, it might be argued that the feminist program could best succeed by looking to the future and creating conditions under which women's art will flourish. This argument is advanced by Virginia Woolf in *A Room of One's Own*, and later by Linda Nochlin in "Why Have There Been No Great Women Artists?"[13] Whatever the reasons oppressive socioeconomic conditions may have affected women more deleteriously than other suppressed classes, perhaps we need not comprehend their operation fully in order to remediate. With attention, appreciation, and support, cannot women be expected to enter the arts in much larger numbers, be more freely creative, and even take greater artistic risks? When the amount of art made by women grows, it might be thought, it is a simple matter of time and statistical probability that there will be more good art made by women.

But to argue this is to confuse being highly valued with being canonical. Even if the quantity of good art by women expands dramatically, how much of it will enter the canon? Canonical works are exemplary, and so are enduring insofar as their "traces" are thought to persist in their successors. Recall that Haskell imputes this capacity to Pietro's art by deeming it "pre-Romantic." But no work can be supposed to have been a point of departure for other works unless it has a history.

Thus, when Frank Stella accounts for some aspects of his painting as successfully solving artistic problems (about the treatment of space) which are prefigured in the painting of Caravaggio, it is plausible to count Caravaggio as canonical for Stella.[14] On the other hand, Stella's art could not have influenced or been exemplary for Caravaggio, even were one to accept Stella's position that he succeeds where Caravaggio did not; accordingly it is implausible to cite resemblances between Caravaggio's and Stella's art in support of the claim that Stella's art is also canonical. Moreover, even if comparing the work of Caravaggio and Stella expands our understanding of Caravaggio's project, Stella's art alone cannot ground an interpretation of Caravaggio. Doing so requires independent art-historical and critical reasons showing that Stella's concerns were also Caravaggio's.

In general, although a newly made work may enjoy high acclaim, it seems it cannot be canonical until it has a history, has successors, and transcends its age by being reflected or referenced in some of these successors. It is the device of reiterating or referencing predecessor artworks so as to make them seem transhistorical that renders the canon conservative. Since it is so, there are likely to be ways in which it resists reformation. Now we can see how Garrard's question about whether Artemisia's gender impedes her being cast as a protagonist in art-historical narratives relates to the (lack of) enduring esteem for her art. In the absence of compelling, entrancing historical narratives about her, her work may lack a history and so may be deprived of an art-historical context which promotes it as influential, permitting it to be referenced by successors and ultimately to be regarded as canonical. *Contra* Haskell, from this perspective, the story of this artist *is* the story of the artist's art.

Feminism and the Political Reconstruction of the Canon

Is there some categorical reason why the canon promotes praising male artists making masterpieces but seems antagonistic to analogous adulation of heroines of art? We have already cast doubt on views which vaguely link canonical status with the economic, political, or social status of artworks' makers. Those argued from the absence of equitable representation of women artists in the canon to the existence of unspecified gender-directed exclusionary institutional practices. But a more plausible, more informative version of this charge might be formulated by pointing out how being esteemed as canonical depends on being thought to exert art-historical influence.

Here, it is an artwork's success in the role of historical predecessor which qualifies it as canonical, and, it might be thought, women's works have been prevented, for political, social, or economic reasons, from exerting the requisite historical influence. For instance, while Artemisia was a more renowned artist in her own time, her gender might impede her from exerting as much artistic influence as Pietro over subsequent generations. Perhaps male artists could not accept her as a role model, and male artwriters consequently saw no point in recommending attention to her work.

If being canonical means having a history, it seems prudent for feminists to focus on revising historical scholarship so as to rediscover and revalue artworks made by women in the past. This program is forward as well as backward looking, for enhancing the art-historical status of women's work may make new art by women more welcome. Arguably, what makes Haskell prefer Pietro to Artemisia are external social conditions which glorify Pietro's suffering but demean Artemisia's, and which consequently promote the attribution of expression to Pietro's art while equally resisting seeing Artemisia's as expressive. If, as in some quarters it is now fashionable to suppose, the canon is ultimately constructed for use as a tool of dominant social, political, or economic interests, future women's art may also be rejected unless revisionary feminist art-historical scholarship is sufficiently politically astute to remedy bias.[15]

Effective strategies for canon reform require understanding what forces form the canon. As feminism itself is a movement for political, social, and economic reform, it is tempting to suppose that such externalist considerations alone might be sufficiently compelling to bring about canonical change. But social constructionism, which maintains that these forces rather than aesthetic values control canon construction, overlooks important phenomena.

First, were such reductionism the complete story, one would expect the canon always to embrace the very newest works, those most likely to be informed by the dominant social, political, or economic objectives of the day. But canonical works are those which have survived the test of time and changing conditions, those which seem to us to transcend history, not those which are most topical. Were inclusion in the canon governed simply by whether works promote currently powerful self-interests, there is no function for the test of time. That is, were shifting political, social, or economic power as overwhelming as social constructionists propose, it is difficult to understand the appeal to tradition or precedent. True, proponents of this kind of reduction often propose that those in power seek validation from history, but this recommendation leaves unanswered how history could be thought to serve this purpose if it is so easily and obviously revised.

Second, an expectation raised by analyses which relativize the canon politically, socially, or economically is that the volume of canonical works representative of any socio-politico-economic period should be roughly proportional to both the period's importance and its length. That is, the influence exerted on art by any powerful sociopolitical force should be similar in extent to its influence in other domains. And one also would expect that the proportion of canonical works contributed by any such period to one artistic medium would be matched by similar proportions in other media, since sociopolitical determinants should operate equally on all media.

But neither the canon nor the histories of the arts satisfy these expectations. How much any historical period, defined social scientifically rather than culturally, contributes to the canon seems more a result of the inexplicable occurrence of figures of genius than of the explicable socio-politico-economic context. Related to this last point is another phenomenon associated with the Euro-centered canon (and with the canons of some periods in Chinese and Japanese art history): the importance of originality. Work incorporated into the canon tends to be art thought of as innovative, making an artistic breakthrough, or setting a new aesthetic direction. A deterministic socio-politico-economic dominance account makes it hard to comprehend the benefits of the innovation so admired in the European tradition, for introducing new ideas always runs the risk of challenging settled views and upsetting existing valuations. Why depart from the styles already proved effective in promoting dominant social values?

One might argue that the introduction of new styles and directions in art increases the supply of works, making it easier for newly ascendant social groups to enjoy whatever cachet owning art affords. But this explanation seems limp, as it is as compatible with simply increasing the number of works in familiar styles as with putting any premium on innovation. Indeed, popular styles or schools do generate creative industries to satisfy the market, but here as well the volume of works associated with a style or school does not seem reflected by the strength of representation of the style or school within the canon.

All these considerations resist suggestions that the forces informing canon construction can be reduced to social, political, or economic interests external to works of art themselves. Thus, shifting social, political, or economic forces are unlikely to suffice to reform the artistic canon so as to remedy the underrepresentation of women. What else is needed?

Feminism and the Explanation of the Past

If being canonical requires having a history, then reforming the canon to increase the representation of women's works appears to demand a search of the past for works eligible, but overlooked, for inclusion in the canon. But some convincing account of why women's work has been neglected should guide the search; not every previously unacknowledged piece of art is a suppressed masterpiece. Initiating the needed change invites an explanation of what in the past caused the systematic failure of those women who aspired to create art which would withstand the test of time. As we have just seen, appealing to social, political, or economic reasons to explain their exclusion seems neither to tell the whole story, nor any story sufficiently revealing to empower reform.

Presumably, for the purposes of the feminist program, an informative account must separate these causes from those which impeded unsuccessful male artists; the phenomenon to be addressed is not artistic suffering generally. It cannot be an objective of any feminist program to ensure that all persons who aspire to make great art be assured of doing so. Rather, the reasons sought are those which explain why women have been disproportionately unable to create art which is accepted as enduringly exemplary.

Moreover, to be convincing, this line of historical explanation must be able to distinguish between common and categorical exclusion from the canon, for the work of some women—for instance, Sappho and Jane Austen—is canonical. Some other women's art (for instance, Berthe Morisot's paintings) may not command appropriately broad esteem historically because it has not been widely available for public appreciation (much of Morisot's work has been held privately and until recently has not been available for public exhibition), but these women artists' influence is easily documented without appeal to feminist theory (once one sees Morisot's paintings, it is easy to trace how they influenced very similar, but subsequently executed, work done by the male members of Morisot's circle, such as Manet and Renoir). And, as in her own day Artemisia's work outshone Pietro's, or, to take a more familiar example, as Henry James despaired because Edith Wharton's novels sold so much better than his own, there are others whose initial or continuing fame bears evidence against there being categorical repression of women artists.

In their different ways, these instances all indicate that the underrepresentation of women's works in the canon is not traceable to women's art having been categorically repressed. But in art scholarship—artwriting as distinguished from artviewing, artreading, or even artbuying—it may have been habitually ignored. Having failed to discover what it could be about the political, social, or economic conditions in which art is made that explains women's underrepresentation in the canon, we now turn to whether the cause lies in how art scholarship is conducted.

(How) Should Feminism Reform Artwriting?

Despite the success of some women artists, it is well to consider whether, to the degree feminism accepts the concept of the canon, it will fail because it is contaminated by the very methodological assumptions which caused the problem for women. Some feminists dismiss canon reform as mere methodological minimalism because it adopts, rather than transcends, male-devised and -dominated critical practice. Conceivably, attaining the objective of feminist canon reform demands a theoretical revolution that more thoroughly mutates our conception of art. Whether this is so—that is, whether feminist canon revision requires conceptual transformations more fundamental and radical than, for instance, the aesthetic revaluations occasioned by the Lake Poets or the abstract expressionists—invites examination.

Fortunately, there is no need to belabor the question of what patriarchal presumptions consist in, as these are readily identified in feminist theory. There is enough agreement in feminist scholarship to suppose that obscuring the individuality, let alone the idiosyncrasies, of personal perceptions of art by pretending that some critical judgments are privileged and objective, impersonal and universal, is to be considered typically male. Construing art as autonomously striving for intrinsic value, rather than as valuable in virtue of its place in its group, situation, or context, is also condemned as a male conception. To the rejoinder that these are not gender-related, gender-fueled political presumptions, but instead are definitive of aesthetic evaluation, feminists can reply "just so, this definition is imposed by the men who have dominated us."

But the aspects of critical practice at which this sort of objection aims are unclear. The most obvious objective is that feminists seek to eliminate hierarchical evaluation, including the judgments attendant on there being a canon at all. But to think the canon a masculine device seems misguided on the very criteria given above: the force of canonical judgment, as opposed to assessment directed by aesthetic rules, is precisely to invite comparative valuation which proceeds by focusing on unique individuals, not by subsuming individuals to the strictures of abstract theory.

Canonical judgment elicits assessment based on perceived "matches" between canonical objects and their successors. These comparisons between individuals inform both understanding and appreciation. What the canon is not is the mechanical application of abstracted rules. It takes art to make use of the canon.

That canons are repertoires of individuals, not abstract principles, may be what makes the drive for equitable representation in them so pressing, but that the choice of exemplary works may have been more influenced by, or favor, men does not entail that women's works cannot be models. The question remains as to whether the way canons are formed impedes or precludes this. Must the story of art celebrate heroes only, so that art-historical narrative form is deterred from relating how the work of women artists influenced art unless the women can be cast as heroes?

The Art Hero(ine)'s Story

Like many reformers of the canon, Garrard assumes that the story of art should take the form of heroic narrative. She proposes that Artemisia depicts the biblical Judith as a female hero. As well, she depicts Artemisia herself as an artistic heroine. But in doing so, does she risk substituting biographical scholarship for critical judgment? This is an issue we identified earlier as crucial to revisionist scholarship generally and, as such, to feminist revisionism.

Colin Lyas warns, "historical inquiries typically *follow* the completion of the critic's evaluative task. We do not, e.g., research into Wordsworth's life in order to find out that his poetry was great but because we already know it is."[16] *Contra* Lyas, revisionist practice expects that researching the circumstances of an artist's life reveals rather than reiterates the greatness of the artist's work.

How can this practice elude the defects we have observed in externalism? How can supplying such contextual evidence affect appreciation? What discoveries about an artist are also discoveries about attributes of the artist's art? Citing a well-known motto of the art historian Ernst Gombrich, Richard Wollheim points out that the circumstances of the artist may also be the circumstances of the art and, as we never respond to art with an innocent eye, considering such circumstances enriches or alters how we see the artist's work. And, Wollheim adds, prime candidates for inclusion in the cognitive stock which informs aesthetic appreciation are accounts of how works came to be made.[17]

Although invoking (some part of) the artist's history, Wollheim's method avoids the weaknesses revealed in our earlier analysis of externalist revisionism, for comprehending how a woman artist made her work, and what suppressed her expression in it, might increase our cognitive stock sufficiently to illuminate her art and enhance its value for us. To illustrate, one might demystify Artemisia's unoriginal choice of subjects by casting her painted scenes as ingenious ways of camouflaging the anger and anguish she felt at having been raped, which, in contrast to Pietro's distress at the failure of his ambitions, were feelings impermissible to dwell on in a male-dominated society. Still, this story must be shown to be relevant, for not all the artist's circumstances, just those attendant on the making of the artist's art, are so according to Wollheim's stricture. And an evident asymmetry does exist between Artemisia's rape, which is a documented historical fact, and her purported painted response to rape, which if it is a fact is of quite a different kind.

The difference lies in how these sorts of facts are to be established. Independent of our personal perceptions, the transcript of the trial of her assailant suffices to document the historical event that happened to her person, but only by directly perceiving the evidence of her rage and anguish in her paintings can we become convinced that her rape is a circumstance also of her art.[18] Thus, documentation of her history as an artist, as distinct from her history as a person, lies in her works themselves. Artemisia's rape is relevant to her history just in virtue of its having happened to her, but it is relevant to her art only through the additional demonstration that it is manifest in her paintings. This is the burden of Haskell's argument on disputing that the subjects of her paintings are signs of her painful personal experience by reminding us that these subjects are conventions familiar not only in her art but in that of her male contemporaries.

This discussion suggests a distinction introduced by several contemporary philosophers, notably Kendall Walton[19] and Jenefer Robinson,[20] between historical persons and art-historical persons, a philosophical view that reinforces a thesis proposed early in the 1960s by the literary theorist Wayne Booth.[21] Although we will be oversimplifying the very subtle work of all these scholars, for purposes of comprehending the logic of artwriting we can sort relevant from irrelevant circumstantial historical evidence by treating the artist as a construct, an implied or apparent author. The constructed artist's properties are qualities of art such as expressive attitudes, attributes of mind, character traits, and other aesthetic qualities that also can pertain to real persons, says Robinson.[22] By apprehending the configuration of the features of a work as purposeful rather than accidental, Walton thinks, we view them as the product of an artistic agent.[23]

When these aesthetic attributions compose a coherent and distinctive set, they are treated as constituting a personal style idiosyncratic of their artist. If they are not coherent, they fail to form a hero(ine) whose story can be told; if they are not distinctive, there is no individuated hero(ine). The role of this constructed protagonist is to function within the context of art-historical narration, where what is related is why and how the hero(ine) incorporated valuable properties into the objects (s)he made. Telling the story can promote revaluation by drawing attention to these if they have been neglected.

The properties of the apparent (art-historical) artist are aesthetically relevant because they are qualities discernible in the artist's work. But most properties of the real (historical) artist are indiscernible in the artist's work. So there is no reason to insist that what is true of a historically documented personage and of the artist manifested in that historical person's aesthetic products must be the same, as these are characters situated in different sorts of narratives, discourses with different functions.

From the absence of a necessary identity between real and constructed artist, it follows that persons of the feminine gender who fabricate art are not necessarily identical to women artists. At least theoretically, some may have masculine rather than feminine voices. If this is so, by the way, additional doubt is cast on the propriety of reading deterministically from general sociopolitical forces which operate differentially in respect to gender claims about artistic agents. For feminist theory to pursue its program of canon reformation, it seems prudent to abandon, because insufficiently relevant for its purposes, explaining the obscurity of women's art by reference to the gender of the real persons who crafted it.

Art-Historical and Real Hero(in)es

Let me be clear that this line of argument is not meant to initiate an alternative feminist theory of art. Rather, it reveals constraints which inform art-historical scholarship and which, consequently, need be reflected in pursuing the feminist project of canonical reformation. To summarize, we have discovered so far that, regardless of how satisfying it may be to explain the rarity of great women artists in political rather than aesthetic terms, doing so does not adequately conform to the considerations which appear to impel canonical formation and reformation. But some external circumstances may be linked to properties internal to artworks. To forge the link, we adopted Richard Wollheim's recommendation about focusing on those circumstances in which the work is made. Then, we extended the thought of Jenefer Robinson and Kendall Walton, differentiating between real (historical) artists, who are identified as having fabricated the works, and apparent (art-historical) artists, who are identified in terms of the styles in which the works are made. Features of these styles then can be construed as sufficiently exemplary or influential to qualify the work as canonical.

We thus adopted the thesis that protagonists of stories of art, whether heroes or heroines, are constructs consisting primarily of attributes that are aesthetically relevant because they are distinctive of the artist's art. Although historical and art-historical artwriting both employ narrative, these need not be supposed to be identical, or interchangeable, methods of storytelling. Conceivably, how we construct the apparent (art-historical) artist, the protagonist whose attributes are identified by reference to those discernible in the real (historical) artist's created objects, departs from how we construct the real (historical) artist, as the development of different kinds of narrative characters vary, subject to differences among the rules governing distinct genres or types of discourse. It remains to be seen how circumstance attendant on the real (historical) artist's gender may be imported into the narratives used to relate the (art-historical) story of art.

Supposing no necessary identity between apparent (art-historical) and real (historical) artist, does the history of the real artist nevertheless exercise no constraint over what can be said about the apparent artist, the central character in art-historical narration? This concern is exacerbated by recognizing how weakly art-historical claims need be supported by historical documentation, as the following examples suggest:[24]

> There was, Berenson felt, one artist whose style combined the features of Sandro Botticelli and Filippino Lippi, with a dash of Ghirlandaio; he wasn't any of these, but he leaned most heavily toward Botticelli. Berenson christened him Amico di Sandro and attributed a group of pictures to him. . . . This human artifact of Berenson's was in itself a work of art; it grew in beauty as, over the years, he increased the man's production. . . . But then Berenson began to disapprove of Amico. His patient and laborious studies finally persuaded him that Amico was too good to be true. Nobody, Berenson felt, could be that good—so consistent, so distinctive. In the strong solution of Berenson's scholarship, Amico disintegrated. Berenson divided him into three parts; he gave part of him back to Botticelli, part to Filippino Lippi, and part to Ghirlandaio.[25]

Learning that he owned Botticellis, Lippis, and Ghirlandaios did not console the American collector who wanted to monopolize the acquisition of Amicos and who had not realized the extent to which the methodology of connoisseurship relies on internal evidence.[26]

However, in another instance, Berenson was prevented from retracting all attributions from one of his creations, Alunno di Domenico, when Alunno's birth certificate turned up.[27] It is interesting how this circumstance invigorated Berenson's art-historical account. (This example also illustrates Barthes's contention about the important role proper names play in creating narrative characters.)[28] The example also shows how the intrusion of historical documentation restrains the options available in art-historical narration, for no fiction writer would be similarly impeded in eliminating a character.

To avoid leaving the impression constructing apparent artists is an idiosyncrasy peculiar to Berenson, consider the case of the seventeenth-century painter Georges De La Tour. For many years it was thought that none of his work remained in existence; two paintings signed G. De La Tour in the Nantes museum were attributed to the eighteenth-century painter Quentin De La Tour. Finally, in 1915, Herman Voss, director of the Berlin Museum, began to reconstruct Georges De La Tour. Eventually, additional works were attributed on the basis of stylistic features such as subject matter, facial expression, and the treatment of light and dark. But only one of these was securely dated, so a theory of De La Tour's development, characterized as a movement in the direction of simplicity and reduction, was constructed by comparing and contrasting the undated paintings with dated works by other artists, based on the assumption that the earlier works would be the ones apparently influenced by Caravaggio's followers in the School of Utrecht, and also that De La Tour's artistic development likely resembled that of his contemporary Poussin, since they both were French artists of the same historical period.[29]

From these examples it appears that just as no character in fictional narrative can be composed by relating a single, isolated, disconnected event, so art-historical heroes or heroines are not constructed on the basis of their creating a single work. Art-historical narratives typically trace characters' careers through the production of several works, and the sequence of the works' creation is significant. In fictional narrative, part of the difference between a lifelike, realistic protagonist and a caricatured one lies in whether the narrative permits the character to change, grow, or develop. Similarly, by creating a developmental historical story to relate how an artist came to make successive works, the art historian narrows the gap between apparent (art-historical) and real (historical) artist. But unlike fiction writing, artwriting characteristically is infused with fact.

Though an art-historical character is constituted primarily of presented personal qualities distinctive of the style of her art, the character may be rounded out through reference to supporting environmental historical properties. For instance, by incrementing a critic's perception of the growing explicitness of Artemisia's depiction of male brutality with documentation showing how liberalized social conditions permitted her to be more open, or else by documenting that the aging Artemisia grew careless of social convention, the art-historical account interpreting the artist Artemisia's work as increasingly showing her rage at the events of the historical Artemisia's life grows more plausible. Incremental facts distance stories of art from fiction. References to perceptions of personal properties directly present in a work, converging consistently with references to known historical events, integrate to produce an interpretive pattern which seems to portray both the apparent (art-historical) and the real (historical) artist.

Does documentation of historical properties influence how we see a work's personal qualities? The discovery of Judith Leyster's signature on a work formerly attributed to Hals prompted one critic to discern weakness and lack of vigor in the painting. He insisted no woman could achieve the forceful brushwork of a male painter.[30] But what is remarkable about this case of critical reversal is how decisively its initial plausibility fades. There is nothing extreme in reexamining a work upon learning we had misidentified its maker; we would react similarly should we discover that its date was two hundred years later than was thought, or that it had been made in Japan rather than in Holland. But the objective of looking more carefully in the light of new circumstantial evidence is to perceive, not to impose, previously unacknowledged properties.

Thus, revaluation of art reattributed to Leyster is ultimately unconvincing absent evidence as to why, for so long, the brushstrokes' weakness went unremarked. Art historian Whitney Chadwick observes about this case: "many have looked and have not seen."[31] Nevertheless, although distinct and discrete, historical and art-historical artists cannot diverge too much, for realistic narration recommends that the more the circumstances of the former inform the traits ascribed to the latter, consistent with the pattern of the story, the more convincing the account of the artist's art will be.

Feminist Voices, Weak and Strong

To propose that the properties of the real (historical) fabricator of an artwork are of a different kind from those of its apparent (art-historical) artist challenges the claim that the biological, social, cultural, political, and economic conditions of historically real women artists cannot but have determined the personal qualities of the works they made. The feminist literary scholar Sandra

Gilbert insists, "If a writer is a woman who has been raised as a woman—how can her sexual identity be split off from her literary energy? Even a denial of her femininity would surely be significant to an understanding of the dynamics of her aesthetic creativity?"[32] But this begs the question of how properties of one logical type determine properties of another.

Absent the deterministic hypothesis on which all women's works a priori have similar qualities because art is nothing more than the product of external biological or social forces, and absent convincing causal hypotheses establishing how real (historical) artists cause apparent (art-historical) artists, what could prompt revision of art-historical accounts, integrating previously ignored properties of women's works with environmental evidence into new interpretive patterns sufficiently compelling to reform the canon? What we know of the apparent (art-historical) artist is given to us by the personal stylistic qualities possessed by the works. Narratives about the apparent (art-historical) artist are only rounded out, distanced from being confused with fictional narratives, by reference to circumstantial historical fact. So even supposing all women to have been victimized by masculine social practices, the real (historical) events befalling them only increment rather than cause the apparent (art-historical) events narrated in the art histories about how their art was made.

Accordingly, to reorganize art history to revise the canon requires the revaluation of attributes of art which can be construed as personal feminine qualities appropriate for constructing feminine apparent (art-historical) artists. Nor can we predetermine whether these properties will be found in most women's work, or in the art of only a few, nor can we preclude a priori their occurring in some art made by men. Nor is there reason to suppose the relevant feminine aesthetic attributes to be absent from works now in the canon.

As we have seen in comparing Artemisia and Pietro, gender differences may explain why some expressive themes command more interest from, or better attract, some audiences. But if some women's works are undervalued because their meanings or expressions have seemed less powerful or important than have men's, or men have found them terrifying or offensive, appreciative artwriting conveying the fascination of women's themes can be effective. Indeed, much feminist art scholarship attempts no more than this. If the project to address why women's work is undervalued goes no further, feminism abandons any strong connection with women. Femininity becomes merely a constructed (and deconstructable) attribute of some apparent (art-historical) artists who are not real (historical) persons capable of participating in real (historical) social, political, or economic events.

If this is so, feminism may achieve canonical reform only at the expense of marginalizing women. Is there no way for feminist artwriting to avoid disassociation from women? This depends on whether arts scholarship permits histories of art which do not relate stories of artists, arts scholarship which eschews hero(in)ic narrative form.

Who's Speaking?

As a mode of discourse, art histories which recount individuals' achievements are themselves a Renaissance revival. Familiar in antiquity, they reappear as a mode of artwriting in the fourteenth century when Villani's treatise on famous Florentines includes some painters.[33] Through the next two centuries, from Ghiberti to Vasari, personalist artwriting evolved. When Vasari recommended the imitation of masters as a means to further the development of art, artwriters from other cities hastened to repair the underrepresentation in the canon of their own compatriots by portraying them as also artistically inventive.[34] They wrote of both men and women artists, lavishing anecdotes and even embroidering when the story demanded situational context.[35] Later historians often found themselves subjected to exhaustive archival research in order to document or deny earlier historical commonplaces about which artists had been where at what times. (Cf. Foucault's analysis of the "author-function" as deriving from the Christian tradition of authenticating texts to determine their value by ascertaining the holiness of their authors.)[36]

What about cases where no documentation survives? Can the products of unknown makers have an art history? To propose such a thing departs from the classical and the Romantic traditions which so influence our attitudes toward art. Romanticism recommends appreciating the conveyed emotion peculiar to the individual artist. Classicism credits not artists' personal feelings but instead their singular cognitions as the source of personal style. It is well, though, to remember that there also is precedent for treating art as the expression of groups rather than of individuals. Some nineteenth-century aesthetic theory, for instance, the views of Hegel and the Schlegels, transformed Romantic and classical valuations into attributes of cultural groups.[37] Art historians like Riegl and Wölfflin adapted this approach to direct their research, refining a methodology that has not been absent from visual arts scholarship to this day.[38]

Not all art is equally amenable to being situated in heroic narrative; the makers of some sorts of works, for instance, African carvings, medieval manuscript illuminations, ethnic dance, and quilts, usually go undocumented. Absent the historical record to round out or make lifelike stories of the artists of these objects, heroic histories of them cannot escape appearing elusive, fragmentary, and even fictional. For other kinds of objects, like ceramics or textiles, the canon itself is structured in terms of periods or styles rather than of individual artists or even individual masterworks. Feminist artwriting often finds such media to be inviting subjects, and feminist scholarship examines popular as well as fine arts, revealing how aesthetic virtue occurs in media where it has been common for the makers of objects to go unrecorded.

As with objects whose makers are documented, how an anonymous work appears to be made, that is, what kinds of artistic actions and intentions might have guided its creation, can be manifest in it, although, in accounting for why such works are as they are, artwriters show a somewhat greater tendency to appeal to both cultural and artistic conventions. But here are no historical facts to round out the apparent (art-historical) artist's story and impede its devolving into fiction. Here style attributions tend to shift from personal to general ones, perhaps because the contextual facts available to make the narrative nonfictional are not about particular individuals but instead about types of persons whose existence was contemporaneous with the making of the work. The protagonist of art-historical narrative thus is transformed where situational documentation refers not to the feelings or actions of an individual artist, but rather to sensibilities or practices pertaining to a group of makers, or to a culture.

This suggests that feminism might free itself of methodology that seems to limit it to revising interpretations of personal style by substituting a communal for a heroic individual protagonist in art-historical narratives. Some feminist theory already tries to do so by insisting that the view of the artist as isolated from community, one like Pietro who is beyond or outside of or abstracted from his group, is merely male fantasy. But does submerging individual artists in their communities strengthen, or instead eliminate, the effect of gender?

If feminism substitutes communities for gendered individuals as the protagonists in stories of art, it will find precedents among some of the critical art historians who followed Hegel. These attempted to equalize the value of diverse kinds of art by taking works of different times and cultures to be the expressions of discrete groups, each kind of work being appropriate as an artistic response given the cultural context of the group. By identifying some such groups in terms of gender, strong feminism might recognize general stylistic qualities, distinctive both of female communities and their art, which make the works possessing them sufficiently meaningful to command attention.

Meaningful for whom? This problem was not unfamiliar to nineteenth-century Hegelian art criticism, where it was occasioned by the need to explain how modern audiences can esteem ancient art originated to express more primitive modes of thought. Faced with retrieving the past, that is, explaining how those situated in a culture or historical period can understand art which is relativized to alien circumstance, these theoreticians sought universal aesthetic principles to account for how art could appeal generally to persons foreign to its originating community. In doing so, they evolved precisely the kind of abstraction feminists decry when they (d)emasculate critical practice. Jane Flax, among many others, voices this view: "[F]eminists . . . have begun to suspect that all such transcendental claims reflect and reify the experience of a few persons—mostly white, Western males. These transhistoric claims seem plausible to us in part because they reflect important aspects of the experience of those who dominate our social world."[39]

And so a paradox emerges. Absent aesthetic theorizing of a traditionally general form, celebrating women's art because of, rather than despite, its being relativized to a specialized community depends on an audience which is itself situated in that feminine communal context. Some feminist scholars embrace this. In a 1989 essay, Sandra Gilbert and Susan Gubar, the editors of the *Norton Anthology of Literature By Women*, write:

> Might it happen, though, that even if we defamiliarize the familiar . . . the very nature of institutional structures . . . would force us . . . into situations of cooptation? We want to speculate that a way out of this apparent double bind may be found . . . the community of feminist scholars (was) essentially a utopian imagining. But now that city of ladies has appeared before us in reality, a reality which must inevitably be uncannily transformed by this surfacing of the repressed.[40]

Elaine Showalter, whose 1981 "Feminist Criticism in the Wilderness" is a model for feminist critical theory, now believes that gender theory is the appropriate intellectual vehicle for feminism because "gender theory insists that all writing, not just writing by women, is gendered."[41] Absent transcending theory, it is hard to see how abiding by Showalter's prescription "to transform disciplinary paradigms by adding gender as an analytic category" can avoid segregating audiences by gender into targets for gender-distinct critical discourses with separate canons.[42] But to create a second(ary) canon is neither reformative nor revisionary.

Conclusion

Where weak feminists seek just a room of their own within the canon, strong feminists may set out to immigrate to the city of ladies as a stratagem for keeping women at the center of their scholarship. But it would be well to be sure their destination is more than just a suburb. In an essay on the future of literary theory, having litanized what feminist scholars should not depend on or settle for, Showalter urges: "During a period when many of the meager gains of the civil rights and women's movements are being threatened or undone . . . there is an urgent necessity to affirm the importance of black and female thinkers, speakers, readers, and writers."[43]

As a signpost to the future of feminist artwriting, this advice seems disconcertingly divorced from art. Still seeking freedom in a criticism of their own, but finding that the canon needs a history of its own, feminists need to guard against imagining that egalitarian fervor transfigures commonplace speechwriting into artwriting inspired enough for aesthetic revolution.

More than two decades ago, in "What Is An Author?" Michel Foucault wrote:

> unlike a proper name, which moves from the interior of a discourse to the real person outside who produced it, the name of the author remains at the contours of texts—separating one from the other, defining their form, and characterizing their mode of existence. It points to the existence of certain groups of discourse and refers to the status of this discourse within a society and culture. The author's name is not a function of a man's civil status, nor is it fictional; it is situated in the breach, among the discontinuities, which gives rise to new groups of discourse and their singular modes of existence.[44]

Foucault concludes this essay:

> We can easily imagine a culture where discourse would circulate without any need for an author. New questions will be heard. Behind

all these questions we would hear little more than the murmur of indifference, "What matter who's speaking?"[45]

This murmur echoes uneasily through the city of ladies, for it is not yet clearly and convincingly understood how what befalls real (historical) women is voiced in the art of apparent (art-historical) women artists.

Notes

1. This is all reported in Francis Haskell, "Artemisia's Revenge?" *New York Review of Books* 36 (20 July 1989): 36–38.

2. Mary Garrard, *Artemisia Gentileschi: The Image of the Female Hero in Italian Baroque Art* (Princeton: Princeton University Press, 1989).

3. Haskell, "Artemisia's Revenge?"

4. Ibid., passim.

5. Ibid., 38.

6. Ibid.

7. Ibid.

8. Michel Foucault, "What Is An Author?" in *Language, Counter-Memory, and Practice*, ed. Donald Bouchard (Ithaca: Cornell University Press, 1977), 127. This essay was originally published in France in 1969.

9. It hardly seems necessary here to point out how much feminist arts scholarship over the past twenty years has been devoted to revaluing the work of women writers, artists, and musicians.

10. Nancy Fraser and Linda Nicholson, "Social Criticism Without Philosophy: An Encounter Between Feminism and Postmodernism" in *Feminism/Postmodernism*, ed. Linda Nicholson (New York: Routledge, Chapman, Hall, 1990). Also, Irene Diamond and Lee Quinby, Introduction to *Feminism & Foucault* (Boston: Northeastern University Press, 1988).

11. John Berger, *Ways of Seeing* (New York: Penguin Books, 1977), 83–112.

12. The starving artist, the mentally impaired artist, and the physically impaired artist all are favorite hero figures in the art-historical narratives of the Euro-centered canon.

13. Virginia Woolf, *A Room of One's Own* (New York: Harcourt, Brace and World, 1929). Linda Nochlin, "Why Have There Been No Great Women Artists?" in *Art and Sexual Politics*, ed. Thomas Hess and Elizabeth Baker (New York: Collier, 1971).

14. Frank Stella, *Working Space* (Cambridge: Harvard University Press, 1986).

15. For instance, this is the position adopted in one way or another by most of the writers in the very influential *Critical Inquiry* issue on canons (10 [1983]). When I use the expression "the canon" here and elsewhere, I refer to logical structure and general function, not to any particular set of works. I also sometimes speak of "the canons," the sets of works canonical to each artistic medium.

16. Colin Lyas, "Personal Qualities and the Intentional Fallacy," in *Aesthetics: A Critical Anthology*, 2d ed., ed. George Dickie, Richard J. Sclafani, and Ronald Roblin (New York: St. Martin's, 1989), 449.

17. Richard Wollheim, *Painting as an Art* (Princeton: Princeton University Press, 1987),

16–17. Of course, my treatment of the "apparent artist" here should not be confused with any position taken by Wollheim.

18. Haskell, "Artemisia's Revenge?" points out that it is not altogether certain Artemisia was raped; nevertheless, the transcript of the trial of her accused assailant, including her testimony, is still extant.

19. Kendall Walton, "Style and the Products and Processes of Art," in *The Concept of Style*, ed. Berel Lang (Philadelphia: University of Pennsylvania Press, 1979), 45–66.

20. Jenefer Robinson, "Style and Personality in the Literary Work," in *Aesthetics: A Critical Anthology*, 455–68.

21. Wayne Booth, *The Rhetoric of Fiction* (Chicago: University of Chicago Press, 1961), passim.

22. Robinson, "Style and Personality," 465.

23. Walton, "Style and the Products and Processes of Art," 45–56.

24. I have used some of these examples earlier in related work, particularly in "Once Upon A Time In The Artworld," in *Aesthetics: A Critical Anthology*, 183–95.

25. S. N. Behman, *Duveen* (New York: Random House, 1952), 156–57.

26. Ibid.

27. Ibid.

28. Roland Barthes, *S/Z* (New York: Hill and Wang, 1974), 92 and passim.

29. Mark Roskill, *What Is Art History?* (New York: Harper and Row, 1982), 123–38 and passim.

30. Cited in Rozsika Parker and Griselda Pollock, *Old Mistresses: Women, Art and Ideology* (New York: Pantheon, 1981), 8.

31. Whitney Chadwick, *Woman, Art and Society* (London: Thames and Hudson, 1990), 22.

32. Sandra Gilbert, "Feminist Criticism in the University: An Interview" in *Criticism in the University*, ed. Gerald Graff and Reginald Gibbons (Evanston: Northwestern University Press, 1985), 117.

33. Lionello Venturi, *History of Art Criticism* (New York: Dutton, 1936), 76–81.

34. Ibid., 83–86, 103–9.

35. Ibid., 200–211. See also Chadwick, *Woman, Art and Society*. The second edition of Vasari's *Vite* mentions at least thirteen women painters and sculptors. See Chadwick, 26–30, for a summary of how Renaissance artwriters treated women artists.

36. Foucault, "What Is An Author?" 127.

37. Michael Podro, *The Critical History of Art* (New Haven: Yale University Press, 1982), 71–110.

38. Ibid., 17–22 and 68.

39. Jane Flax, "Postmodernism and Gender Relations," *Signs* 12 (1987): 621–643. See also Nancy Fraser and Linda Nicholson, "Social Criticism Without Philosophy: An Encounter Between Feminism and Postmodernism," in *Feminism/Postmodernism*, ed. Linda Nicholson (New York: Routledge, Chapman and Hall, 1990).

40. Sandra Gilbert and Susan Gubar. "The Mirror and the Vamp: Reflections on Feminine Criticism," in *Future Literary Theory*, ed. Ralph Cohen (New York: Routledge, 1989), 165 and 144–66 passim. See also their *Norton Anthology of Literature By Women* (New York: Norton, 1985).

41. Elaine Showalter, "A Criticism of Our Own: Autonomy and Assimilation in Afro-American and Feminist Literary Theory," in *Future Literary Theory*, 367. Showalter is quoting Joan Scott, "Gender: A Useful Category of Historical Analysis," *American Historical Review* 5 (1986): 1053–75. See also her "The Rise of Gender" in *Speaking of Gender*, ed. Elaine Showalter (New York: Routledge, 1989), 1–16.

42. Ibid., 367.

43. Ibid., 369.

44. Foucault, "What Is An Author?" 123–24.

45. Ibid., 138.

13
Feminist Art History and De Facto Significance

Susan L. Feagin

Much of the work being done by feminist art historians today is given a theoretical underpinning that draws on the work of Foucault, Marx, Lévi-Strauss, as well as Althusser, French psychoanalysts such as Lacan, and even Derrida and poststructuralist literary theory. As someone who has always worked in "traditional," or what is sometimes called "analytic" aesthetics, I have wondered about whether this "Continental" theoretical apparatus was actually necessary to provide a conceptual framework for the trenchant analyses and acute observations that have emerged from feminist art historians. My initial impression was that any intelligent analysis of, for example, representation, expression, style, and "work of art"—the sorts of phenomena central to analytic aesthetics—that sees them as grounded not merely in formal relations or an artist's own storehouse of knowledge and skills, but in cultural and historical realities, would be able to accommodate the kinds of observations feminist art historians were making that I found to be the most compelling.

I now believe that initial impression to be erroneous. However, there are good reasons why I should have been suspicious of that impression from the beginning. It is too easy to miss the most innovative aspects of another's view if one tries to understand it only in terms of one's own theoretical perspective.[1]

In particular, one is likely to fail to understand why one ignored or obscured the points now being emphasized by that other view. What explains why such points have been ignored by one's own perspective may be precisely what one needs to learn from that new view.

Feminists know this well. Feminist art-historical research during its initial stages was concerned with examining the productions of women artists who had not received much, if any, attention, and with recovering *their* histories, which had been ignored for so long. No radical theoretical shift is needed for this kind of enterprise—just the conviction that there's more art history to be told than has been told. But then it became necessary to ask *why* those histories had been submerged: the pattern of exclusion is too clear to see its emergence as a mere oversight. Is it reasonable to believe that there are merely additions or corrections to be made to the standard art-historical story, or is there something inherently exclusionary about the set of concepts and questions that have been used in the pursuit of art-historical knowledge, that explains why women have been glaringly omitted from discussions of artists and the story of art? There is an influential line of thought that the conceptual apparatus which "traditional" art historians use, by its very nature, tends to "marginalize" women artists and their work, and suppress the ways in which women related differently to artistic practices and products of their time.

Thus, a cluster of concepts that have been the primary organizers of art-historical interests (genius, master, canon, aesthetic quality) and a whole range of artist-centered and object-centered concepts (intention, representation, expression, form) have come under attack. These artist- and object-centered concepts have been at the core of traditional aesthetics, and the charge that they inherently "stack the deck" against women accompanies the clarion call for a *new* theoretical framework, one that dismisses this traditional set of concepts and introduces new ones that are not exclusionary in the same ways.

The view that feminist art-historical analyses cannot simply be added to traditional art history, but calls for an overthrow of the conceptual network that is fundamental to traditional ways of doing art history, is what I call an "incompatibilist" view. The incompatibilist believes that feminist art history should supplant art history of the traditional kind because of the inherently biased nature of the orientation toward artist and object of the latter—exactly the orientation that characterizes traditional aesthetics. A pure incompatibilist would believe that *all* of the existing conceptual apparatus must be overthrown; a pure compatibilist that *none* of it needs to be. Mixed views are also possible, and there may be disputes over the specifics of the resulting blend.

I do not wish to reject traditional analyses of individual artists—their abilities and oeuvre, and how they have transmitted their talents, styles, and insights to others within an unfolding history of art—or of individual works, genres, styles, and periods, and the kinds of skills needed to perceive and appreciate their distinctive qualities and merits. But I also believe that an important kind of understanding of artworks is omitted if one adopts these concerns *exclusively*. They do not delineate the only perspectives from which artworks should be seen and understood. We also need to look to the more global *cultural* network and historical situation in which paintings, sculptures, and other things we identify as art are produced, used, and appreciated.

I shall argue that there *is* a bit of conceptual apparatus that traditional aesthetics lacks, but that is necessary to establish a conceptual or philosophical foundation for understanding at least some of the cultural significance of both those things we identify as art and of the kinds of discussions and critiques that feminists, among others, have given of those objects. I will call this bit of conceptual apparatus *de facto significance*. I believe that it is in part because such a conceptual foundation does not exist within "traditional" analytic aesthetics that feminist art historians have needed to look elsewhere for the theoretical underpinnings of their practices.

I begin with an example of *one* kind of contribution made by feminist art historians: how Whitney Chadwick advances on Michael Baxandall's discussion of quattrocento Italian painting, in particular, Piero della Francesca's altarpiece *The Baptism of Christ*.[2] Baxandall explicates the nature of fifteenth-century Florentine painting in light of the economic practices of the day, both with respect to legal contracts and the way paintings functioned as public display and personal glorification. Baxandall is sometimes called a "new art historian" since he presents an understanding of artworks within their social and cultural context, broadly conceived, and not merely within an artistic and *art*-historical context. What Baxandall does not do is explain how paintings relate to women's roles and positions within the cultural and historical context. This is what Chadwick does, and it opens up a whole new dimension for our understanding of these artworks. Though Chadwick does not employ the sort of poststructuralist theoretical apparatus I alluded to above, and is in that sense a relatively conservative feminist art historian, her discussion nevertheless shows it is necessary to introduce a notion that is not within the theoretical repertoire of traditional aesthetics. I call this de facto significance, and it is in light of this notion that we can understand what grounds the relevance and importance of what Chadwick, as opposed to what Baxandall, has done. Thus, my main point concerns the de facto significance of *art-historical writing* about artworks, rather than the de facto significance of the artworks themselves.

I will explain the concept of de facto significance, and how traditional aesthetics already contains a number of notions that approach but do not quite reach it. Returning to the example of Piero's altarpiece, I introduce additional information that reveals the de facto significance of Baxandall's writing about it. I conclude with some remarks about recognizing and taking responsibility for the de facto significance of one's own behavior.

An Example

I begin with an example of the contribution Whitney Chadwick makes to Michael Baxandall's account of how we are to understand fifteenth-century Tuscan painting such as Piero della Francesca's *Baptism of Christ* or his *Annunciation*.[3] First, Baxandall says, a "visual skill" for gauging the size of barrels and packs was used by Piero in the construction of the painting, in a way that emphasized volumes and their geometrical relationships to one another. As he puts it, this "aspect of Piero della Francesca's way of painting represents both a culture making a skill available and an individual electing to take it up" (*PI*, 107).[4] In addition, Piero would have expected viewers of the painting (that is, his clients and those for whom it was made) to have employed this skill when viewing it (*PI*, 107). Baxandall argues that, as an altarpiece, the *Baptism* would have had certain functions: to narrate Scripture, arouse appropriate feelings about the narrated subject matter, and impress it on the memory (*PI*, 106).[5] The visual skill in question facilitates perceivers' following the narrative, responding appropriately, and perceiving it as having a certain unity or integrity that would make it more memorable.

Second, Baxandall points out that an altarpiece such as this would typically have been "furnished by some individual parishioner or family or confraternity," and it would have served to "do the donors proud" (*PI*, 106). Thus, it would have had what one could call the broadly social purpose of aggrandizing those who commissioned it. As Rucellai, a prominent patron of the arts in Florence (where Piero received his training) succinctly and bluntly put it, the paintings he contracted for "serve[d] the glory of God, the honor of the city, and the commemoration of myself" (*PE*, 2).

Baxandall points out that though these aspects of the cultural milieu would have been internalized for those he calls the participants of the culture, they have to be made explicit to those of us who are observers of the culture, those of us who do not automatically employ the requisite visual skill or understanding of the social significance of the painting when perceiving it. *We* do not have the visual skill to gauge irregularly shaped packs and barrels, and even if we did, we would probably not think to use it when viewing the painting unless prompted to do so. The extent to which such things go "without saying" is indicative of the extent to which they are characteristic of a culture, and their having to be pointed out to us is a mark of the distance between us and that set of practices within the culture in question.

There are additional aspects of these practices that Baxandall does not mention, but that Whitney Chadwick reveals in her book *Women, Art, and Society.*[6] Baxandall's first observation concerned the visual skills employed in the construction of the representation, and to be employed in its perception. These skills were developed for commercial purposes, and arithmetical and geometrical elaborations of them were emphasized in public education. As Chadwick puts it, "mathematics [took] precedence [in public education] because of the business orientation of Florentine society" (*WAS*, 65). However, as Chadwick (but not Baxandall) also points out, by the fifteenth century it appears as though *girls* were no longer being sent to public schools. Their education concentrated on Christian virtues and moral education, and was conducted in the home (*WAS*, 65). Insofar as Piero's *Baptism* or *Annunciation* was to be perceived using the visual skills derived from commercial interests in packs and barrels, and a public school education, it was painted for *men*. Women would typically lack the appropriate visual skill; at the very least they would *not* have been spectators "used to measuring and quantifying space" (*WAS*, 66)—the kind of skill Baxandall argues was necessary for the production and appreciation of the painting—and only in rare cases would individual women have found it to be an activity they would "automatically" engage in. They would not have been participants, and were increasingly being excluded from being participants in this aspect of the culture of which this visual skill was allegedly so fundamental a part.

The domestication of education for women also relates importantly to Baxandall's second observation, that such an altarpiece would have served to enhance the reputation and hence status of the patrons. It is in fifteenth-century Florence that we find the origins of modern capitalism and its accompaniment, via labor specialization, the "privatization of the family" (*WAS*, 60). The family, of course, was the sphere for women, whereas men were urged to set aside *private* affairs "in order to assume public roles" (*WAS*, 63). The altarpiece would thus have "commemorated" the patron in the eyes of *other men*: in Baxandall's words, pictures "were designed for the client *and people he esteemed* to look at."[7] Piero's *Baptism* was not a painting made for private devotional purposes in one's own bedchamber, but an altarpiece for display in a church, painted by the town's most successful "native son." It would, of course, have been almost unthinkable for the artist to have been one of the town's native *daughters*. The necessary education, mobility, and prestige would have been virtually impossible for a woman of that place and time.

Thus, I think it fair to say that the *Baptism* was painted by a man, for men, for the glorification of a certain man (or men of the confraternity), in the eyes of other men. When Baxandall writes, for example, that Piero painted such pictures "for men with complicated fifteenth-century needs" (*PI*, 105), I have no doubt that that is quite literally true, and that he is not guilty here, as one reviewer charged, of using "man" and masculine pronouns in the generic sense.[8] However, when Baxandall is talking more generally about an individual and a culture, he is not on such firm ground, for example, when he says, "The participant understands and knows his culture with an immediacy and spontaneity the observer does not share" (*PI*, 109). The men of Florence and Sansepolcro would have viewed Piero's *Baptism* with an immediacy and spontaneity that women, who allegedly also were of the same culture, did not share.[9] Women were typically not participants in this sort of activity: if Baxandall is right, the visual abilities he claims are presupposed by Piero's *Baptism* or *Annunciation* would have been just about as alien to the average fifteenth-century Florentine or Sansepolcran woman as they are to you and me today. Indeed, it is unlikely that *anyone* in a culture will be a participant in *all* of its culturally significant activities. The fact that this fairly obvious point has to be made is reminiscent of feminist objections to taking only those activities in which *men* are participants as defining the values and most important significances of various objects and activities within a culture.

De Facto Significance

Chadwick's observations help us understand the *culture* in which Piero's *Baptism* was produced. They do this by pointing out how certain persons in that culture were quite explicitly excluded from being participants in the kinds of practices that led to the creation, and certain kinds of appreciation, of painted altarpieces. This exclusion manifested itself in part through the differential treatment generally given to boys and girls with respect to their education and responsibilities to the family. Chadwick's observations also help us understand Piero's *Baptism* and *Annunciation* by giving us a better understanding of how they were supposed to function within the culture of quattrocento Italy. They were a part of that culture, and understanding the culture helps us better understand them.

"Culture" is a problematic term. Though there is debate over how to define the term, let us understand culture to be identified in a way that is partly normative in at least three different respects. That is, culture is, at least in part, constituted by (1) people's *beliefs* about what is important and valuable, (2) individual *actions* (and objects produced by actions) that reflect choices made in light of those beliefs,[10] and (3) emergent *patterns* of behavior (exhibited by individuals or groups of individuals) wherein or whereby certain values or significance, advantages, or disadvantages accrue to some individuals or groups of individuals to the general exclusion of others, even if the agents do not make either conscious or unconscious decisions or choices to coordinate their behavior with that of others (or with other behaviors of their own) in such a pattern. (Emergent patterns, it should be noted, may be partially formed not only by actions or behavior but also by objects, because of the properties or characteristics they have.)[11] If the last of these three is admitted to be a component of culture, then a concept that picks out such an emergent pattern will be appropriately employed when describing it. And this will be the case even if individuals within the cultural group were unaware of it at any level, and would not have applied that concept to themselves, perhaps simply because they were unaware of there being other (viable) options. The lack of consciousness of those within the culture that this *is* what they are doing, and that there are other possible ways of doing things will likely itself reflect the extent to which a certain focus of attention or selectivity is culturally embedded.[12]

It is significant that I found myself somewhat strained to describe the last of the three ways listed above in which the normative import of the constituents of culture can be manifested, i.e., by "emergent patterns of behavior (exhibited by individuals or groups of individuals) wherein or whereby certain values or significance, advantages or disadvantages accrue to some individual or groups of individuals to the general exclusion of others, even if individuals do not make either conscious or unconscious decisions or choices to coordinate their behavior with that of others (or with other behaviors of their own) in such a pattern." It would have been much easier to say that a value or significance is "constructed" by behavior, or that various kinds of things are "privileged" or "valorized," while others are "marginalized." That is, it was difficult to describe this phenomenon without lapsing into fashionable vocabulary associated with various contemporary social critiques, the kind of vocabulary sanctioned by a theoretical apparatus whose necessity for feminist art history I am exploring.

Such vocabulary is useful precisely to the extent that we (traditional, "analytic" aestheticians) *lack* the terminology to capture this kind of phenomenon easily. Perhaps it has failed to appear within the vocabulary of traditional aesthetic theory because we have not thought that *this* aspect of culture was especially (or at all) important, at least not for understanding artworks *as* works of art.[13] We have tended to focus on works of art either as "aesthetic objects," removed from their cultural and historical context, or as the products of individuals who, because of their knowledge and experience, desires and intentions, skills and abilities, are responsible for these objects turning out the way they do. Words like "choose" and "select," unlike "privilege" and "valorize," imply that one is *aware* that there are other options and that one makes a choice in light of that awareness, thus depicting the significance of what is done as depending on the intention or decision of the agent.

Nevertheless, things people do and things people make can be given true descriptions when those descriptions apply simply because the action or object partially constitutes—makes some contribution to the formation of—a pattern that emerges out of a whole collection or group of actions or objects in a culture. These descriptions capture the de facto significance of an action or object. "De facto" is opposed to "by design": no person whose actions or productions contribute to this emergent pattern *need* intend, either consciously or unconsciously, that his or her behavior do so. One *may* so intend; the point is that it is not necessary for there to be an individual intent in order for the description to apply. The description applies when the action or object partially constructs the pattern described; the action or object is partially constitutive of it. "Significance" highlights the fact that it's an *important* fact about what people do and make, and hence that it is normatively laden (what I call below a valuative description). Moreover, significance is not the *meaning* of what is done or made.[14] In traditional aesthetics, questions about meaning have dominated discussions about how to interpret or understand paintings and other works of art. It is preferable to use "significance" for the notion I am introducing here in order to make it clear that the deep and intricate debates that have arisen over meaning in analytic philosophy are not relevant to present purposes.[15] Indeed, it is curious that the cultural significance of artworks has (de facto) been taken by analytic aestheticians to be so *insig*nificant.[16]

There is, however, a commonplace of "analytic" action theory that accommodates, to a certain extent, the sort of phenomenon I had difficulty describing. It is well known that there are many true descriptions of what people *do* that are not descriptions under which what they do is intentional. They need not even be descriptions under which one *knows* what one is doing, and they may apply in virtue of unknown or unintended causes or consequences of one's behavior.[17] For example, it may be true of me that I offend someone even though it never occurred to me that saying thus-and-such would indeed offend. I may show myself to be naive and ill-informed in saying what I do, even though it never occurred to me that that is what I would be doing. It is possible to describe a person's behavior truly, even if those descriptions apply in virtue of facts of which the agent is unaware. Let us call these nonintentional descriptions.

There are two ways in which de facto significance descriptions of actions or objects diverge from garden-variety nonintentional descriptions. First, it is not clear to me that descriptions that characterize what was done or made as participating in the *valuing* of or in attributing *importance* or *significance* to a certain sort of thing have typically (or ever) been considered as plausible candidates for nonintentional descriptions. I shall call such descriptions "valuative descriptions"; descriptions of an action or object in terms of its de facto significance are valuative descriptions. This can be seen from the third component of culture cited above, that the behavior described by a de facto significance description is part of a pattern wherein or whereby certain values, advantages, etc., accrue to some individuals or groups and not others. A de facto significance description is therefore to this extent normatively or valuatively laden.

The second way in which de facto significance descriptions differ from typical nonintentional descriptions is that the former apply in virtue of the action's or object's *partially constructing or constituting* the pattern (including valuative patterns) that is described in the description. The action or object does not merely have unintended or unforeseen *effects*, but the action or object at least partially creates the pattern in terms of which it is described. This does not mean the pattern wouldn't be there without that particular action or object, any more than the removal of a single pebble from a pile of pebbles would mean there is no longer a pile of pebbles, or that the removal of a single dot from a connect-the-dots picture would eliminate the picture. Nevertheless, each individual pebble is partially constitutive of, partially constructs, the pile, and each dot partially constructs the picture. A pattern of significance emerges not merely out of a single action or object, but out of the behaviors of a number of people and a number of objects produced.

Putting this second difference together with the first, we can block some of the resistance one might have to giving valuative descriptions of an individual's behavior, or of an object one has produced, even though that individual has not intended or chosen that value or significance. The descriptions require that there be an appropriate *relationship* between what a person does or makes to what others in the culture do. One's behavior (or an object) partially constructs a value by virtue of standing in certain sorts of relationships with other actions and objects. One may or may not be aware of these relationships; that is not important. What is important is that certain patterns emerge out of the objects and activities of a number of people within the culture, and the significance of their activity is described in terms of those culturally emergent patterns, as characteristic of the culture, and not by virtue of the knowledge or intent or choice of any given individual within the culture. Thus, de facto significance descriptions share the theoretical benefits, and difficulties, of other "macro"-level descriptions; what is clear is that they do not depend on intentions or choices of individuals who produce the "micro" components of the "macro"-level pattern.

One very familiar nonintentional description is the accusation of negligence. A comparison of negligence with de facto significance will help to bring out some of the distinguishing features of the latter. One is negligent when one has failed to give due care or regard so as to avoid harmful effects of one's actions. It is interesting to note, however, that, in at least some dictionary definitions, there is an implication that agents are *aware* of, say, the potential for harm, but that they haven't given it *sufficient* attention. However, there seems to be no reason to require that one was even aware of the potential for harm: if one is *extremely* negligent, one might never even bother to think about what harm might possibly be produced.[18] What needs to be asked, of course, is *why* one didn't think of the potential harm one's behavior could produce. We often judge that a person should be held responsible *for* thinking of various things, as well as for forming one's actions with due regard for what one does think of. Interestingly, there are analogies in the epistemic realm as well, in the notion of epistemic responsibility. One's belief may fail to be justified even if one has all sorts of evidence for it and no evidence against it, if the reason one has no evidence against it is that one never bothered seriously to look for any. To get just the evidence you want and then cease the search is, to say the least, epistemically irresponsible.

This brings out two important features of "negligence." It entails (1) an evaluative judgment (in this case, a moral condemnation), (2) of *the person* who produced the object or behavior in question. I will call descriptions that entail (1) "judgmental descriptions," and when the evaluative judgment is made about a *person*, "personal judgmental descriptions." Accusations of negligence are personal judgmental descriptions, and de facto significance descriptions are not. The latter *may* be judgmental, but they do not *entail* a judgment about *the person* who performs the action or produces the object. There is a difference between making an evaluative judgment about an action (as an action of a particular kind), and judging the person who performs that action. Very often a move from the first to the second is justified, but sometimes it is not. It is not part of my purpose here to defend a view about what determines when an *individual* is to be praised or blamed for acting and making things that have a given de facto significance. I am concerned rather with making it clear that descriptions of the de facto significance of a person's actions or objects one produces, even when those descriptions are valuational and judgmental, do not necessarily *entail* a judgment about the person. Under certain circumstances, for example, it may have been supererogatory or just plain impossible for an agent to notice and take steps to avoid engaging in actions that have a given de facto significance. What is important about the concept of de facto significance is its emphasis on what is culturally emergent, and not on the strengths or defects, failures or achievements, of particular individuals.

The terms "privileging" and "marginalizing" have typically been used as terms of condemnation, that is, as (negative) judgmental descriptions. I suspect that those who resist the importation of the terminology of "privileging" and "marginalizing" do so at least in part because they resist the assignment of blame to people who did not *intend* whatever it is that is bad about their behavior by virtue of which it is judged negatively. However, as I argued above, a judgmental description—one that judges a particular act of privileging to be bad—does not *entail* a judgment about the person who engages in that act. For example, there may be factors—such as the need to act quickly—that override the blame which might otherwise be due to the individual. On the other hand, accusations of negligence are sometimes justified, and it is not always the case that lack of harmful intent removes blame.

However, there are also valuative concepts—concepts that characterize a given behavior (or object) as embodying something like a "cultural acceptance" of a value (significance, or differential conveyance of advantage or disadvantage)—that are not themselves judgmental, in that they don't entail a judgment about whether it is good or bad to accept that value, significance, etc. "Valorizing" seems to me to be such a term (which is not to say it is never used with normative force). What one valorizes may or may not deserve to be valorized. This is, I suspect, in part because valorizing does not presuppose a "zero-sum" situation: if something is valorized, it does not follow that something else is devalued or "devalorized." But privileging does imply a "zero-sum" situation: privileging one thing always requires marginalizing or excluding something else. Other value-neutral terms include "foregrounding" and "back-grounding," though these more naturally describe individual actions rather than an action by virtue of its role in an emergent *pattern* of behavior. What occupies the foreground, or the focus of attention, may *and should* shift and change; indeed, it is when only certain kinds of things always or almost always occupy people's attention, or are constantly foregrounded, when other things should at least occasionally also be foregrounded, that *privileging* occurs.

If certain patterns of privileging and marginalizing emerge, it is perfectly reasonable to wonder if there is a psychological explanation for why individuals engage in these behaviors. It will certainly appear as though this cannot simply be an accident, at least to those who *do* notice that something is consistently excluded or marginalized. It is natural to suppose that people engage in this "avoidance behavior" because that is precisely what has been reinforced, but it would require more than a casual analysis to uncover the psychological causes of such fixations, or at least to reveal the pattern of reinforcement that has facilitated the entrenchment of a certain habit of mind in the individuals who compose the group in which the pattern emerges.

Though the pursuit of such explanations is tempting, it is nonetheless a trap. First, note how such explanations focus on what it is about each *individual* that explains why that person did what he or she did. It is thus of a piece with the artist-centered interests of traditional aesthetics, in that it presumes that the normative force of a person's behavior will be explained by the kind of reinforcement or discouragement which that individual has experienced. Second, it is risky for feminists and others to saddle themselves with various psychological theories, especially those that are highly contested and controversial, whose general plausibility as well as application to individual cases will need to be defended. The fact remains that de facto significance descriptions of a person's action, even when they are valuational or judgmental, *do not require* that the action be intentional under that description, or that it be produced under that description by either conscious or unconscious thoughts, motives, or other psychological sources.[19]

Third, there is a difference between explaining why one engages in action *A*, and explaining why one does *not* engage in action *B*. It is true that certain kinds of patterns of attention can be explained by the reinforcement one receives when those things remain salient in one's cognitive arena: there are "rewards" for paying attention to certain kinds of things. But human beings have a well-known disposition to "satisfice"; that is, to satisfy one's desires by doing something that works well *enough*, while sacrificing to the extent that what one does does not work so well as something else would. The reason the phenomenon of satisficing should be kept in mind is because no overt *or covert* intention or desire *to exclude* other possibilities—either behaviors that would work better or even those which would be less effective—is necessarily implicated in this process. Thus, that there are these other possible behaviors—some of which would work even better, and some worse, than what one is doing—does not show that one either consciously or unconsciously excluded them, or that one selected to do what one did from this entire range of alternatives. The phenomenon of satisficing shows that, when giving a *psychological* explanation of the behavior of an *individual*, one may have an explanation for why one pays attention to certain kinds of things, but *not* for why one failed to pay attention to something else (*except* insofar as one has an explanation for why one *did* attend to the original thing). Many feminist art historians have been concerned with the patterns of exclusion and marginalizing of women and their work that have occurred within traditional art history. But there may or may not be any psychological cause (intention, desire) *to exclude* that explains the behavior of any given individual art historian.

Is it legitimate to give valuative descriptions of what a person does, when these are not descriptions under which that person's actions are either intentional, or caused or brought about by some acceptance of the value in question? One might feel a certain resistance to doing this if one is wedded to the belief that values are somehow chosen, and that nothing is accorded value unless it is selected *by that individual* against a set of alternatives. It is at precisely this point that a feminist, seeking a theoretical underpinning of his or her analysis, may appeal to the Althusserian notion of the "myth" of the autonomous self, and hence deny that I can, as an autonomous subject, *choose* what values are created by my actions or what they accord significance. The individual, in this view, is seen as a "construction" of the culture or society, and it is the latter, if anything, that is "real," and the individual is a function of *it*. But it is not necessary to deny that there is a self, or that there is human choice—even free choice. Nevertheless, one does need to countenance nonintentional descriptions of things people do that involve attributing an importance, value, or significance to their behavior (that is, valuative descriptions), and we may as well be explicit about this. People can in fact privilege or valorize certain kinds of things, and marginalize or devalorize others (whether they intend to or not), because their behavior contributes to the formation of a pattern that emerges out of the behaviors of a number of individuals within the culture.

It is important to admit the relevance of de facto significance descriptions of behavior because, for many purposes, *it just doesn't matter* whether there is a psychological cause or source for the emergence of a given pattern of behavior or for an individual's behavior contributing to such a pattern. The fact that individuals don't realize what they're doing, or didn't intend it that way, or even intended the opposite, is irrelevant. If many people in a culture do in fact focus their attention in a given way, so that in fact certain kinds of things are never or only rarely noticed (and when noticed, shrugged off as unimportant), this shows that in fact persons in that culture have certain priorities. (Though notice once again how "having priorities" can also be read as "having chosen" or "intentionally selected," that is, to implicate intent. This again highlights the terminological gap, and the extent to which explanations and descriptions in terms of the personal psychology of an individual are thoroughly entrenched.) What *is* important is that a certain pattern of significance emerges, whether individuals within the culture intend it, are aware of it, or selected it, or not. And, if it really doesn't matter whether there is a psychological cause for the relevant aspect of the focus of attention or pattern of behavior, it is better to recognize the independence of de facto significance from theories about what these causes are and how they operate.

I have given only a sketch of what I mean by de facto significance. In particular, I have not described what form the "patterns of behavior" in a culture must take in order for a bit of behavior to have the de facto significance it has—to be part of a pattern, and to be part of *that* pattern. These are important issues that would have to be addressed in a more detailed analysis of the concept. Indeed, there might well be competing accounts, on the order of competing analyses that have been given of such concepts as representation and expression.

Taking Control of De Facto Significance

In fifteenth-century Florence there was a nonnegligible amount of writing about how women should be excluded from public life and how they should instead concern themselves with domestic virtues. My point is *not* that Florentine painting practices had the de facto significance of excluding women from being painters and sculptors or their clients—*that*, it appears, happened quite by design. Piero's *Baptism* was made by a man, for men, for the valorization of men in the eyes of other men. These are the simple facts of the matter, on which I think Baxandall and Chadwick would both agree. The difference between them is that Chadwick makes these facts *explicit*, and Baxandall doesn't.[20] This changes the de facto significance of what each of *them* does in the writing of art history. In the case of Baxandall, it is his failure to mention these facts about Florentine culture that has de facto significance: he excludes women from the account of what constitutes the particular culture in question. That is, he privileges men and men's activities, according them significance in the very fact of discussing them, and he marginalizes women and women's activities, according them *in*significance in the very fact of not discussing them.

Baxandall writes about the *Baptism* *as* a man, *for* men, or at least for those who are *participants* in the culture where one automatically, without reflection, assumes that what goes on with men will identify the major values and most significant aspects of a culture. How women in fifteenth-century Florence would have related to the artistic activity he discusses, and how they would have responded to Piero's painting, is not mentioned. To the extent that many of us can read Baxandall and not even notice what has been de facto excluded shows something about us. His actions are part of a pattern that exists within our own culture, and it is in relation to that pattern that they may be understood. It shows that *we* privilege men's values and activities as defining or identifying what is of value and significance in a culture—that it "goes without saying" that women's activity will not be discussed because it does not have such significance. There is a continuity of perspective, of what has de facto significance, that has filtered through the centuries as a constituent of what some are fond of calling "Western civilization," and that is a constituent of our own "cultural heritage"—one that many of us are not interested in perpetuating. Baxandall is, at least to this extent, a participant in the same culture, by sharing the same cultural perspective, as fifteenth-century Florentines and Sansepolcrans.

Chadwick not only does not perpetuate this aspect of our culture, but her actions partially construct a new pattern of behavior, where the perspectives and experiences of women are valorized and taken as significant constituents of culture. The exclusion of women is not taken as something unremarkable, but as an important fact about the culture that is worthy of examination and analysis. There are those of us who desire that our actions *not* have the de facto significance that actions of agents in our own culture typically have. One clear way to avoid privileging men and men's activities as defining the most important aspects of a culture is to discuss women and women's roles vis-à-vis the subject in question.

When you look at the categories Baxandall uses to identify possible roles in relation to Piero's altarpieces—client, painter, and those whose beliefs and values were supposed to be affected by them—there appears to be no room for women; they were (apparently) not participants in *those* aspects of the culture. So isn't it possible for a Baxandall to defend himself by saying, "with respect to this sort of quattrocento painting, women didn't *have* a role to play," and this might well seem to follow from the claim advanced above, presumably agreed on by all, that Piero's *Baptism* was painted by a man, for men, to glorify a man in the eyes of other men. If so, the feminist contribution would be merely to point out the extent to which women were excluded from these activities, and how social structures (in this case, often by design) ensured that exclusion.

The word "merely" in the previous sentence should not be read to devalue the significance of this contribution. Even a nuance of detail can have a cascading effect on one's focus of attention and discernment. For example, Baxandall mentions that the *Baptism* was painted for a church in Sansepolcro, Piero's hometown. However, this is slightly misleading. It appears as though the altarpiece was painted for the *priory*—a monastery—of San Giovanni Battista.[21] This would mean, of course, that its typical viewers would not have spent a great deal of time out in the streets sizing up packs and barrels (though its prestige could still derive from the painter's utilization of *en vogue* skills). It would also mean that this altarpiece may indeed have been seen very infrequently by women, at least until after 1808 when it was moved to the Cathedral of Sansepolcro after the suppression of the priory. Moreover, there appears to have been some gender-specialization concerning which saints and stories served moral and religious didactic functions, with Saint John the Baptist one of the most important for men, and the Virgin Mary with scenes from her life for women.[22] Thus, it is likely that women viewing a painting of a baptism would bring rather different attitudes to that experience from the ones they would bring to an annunciation.

However, it doesn't follow from these particulars about the *Baptism* that women didn't have a role to play vis-à-vis altarpieces *in general*. Altarpieces were often located in churches where anyone could go to pray. It's not as though women, especially those of the merchant and professional classes, never *saw* such paintings.[23] Furthermore, given the emphasis on religious virtue for women of these classes in Tuscany in the fifteenth century, it is quite possible that those women who were subject to such influences may well have had a rather rich cognitive and emotional relationship with an altarpiece. They wouldn't have seen it in terms of geometry and the other things that boys were taught, but most likely in terms of the things that they were taught.

We *do know* something about what women of the merchant and professional classes were taught, and one document is even discussed by Baxandall. However, rather predictably, he uses it as evidence for what he thinks is important: how the typical quattrocento *man* would have seen a painting. The document in question is *The Garden of Prayer*, a handbook written *for young girls* in 1454. This handbook instructed young girls to visualize the sequence of events read about in a biblical narrative, filling in one's own city for the location, and people one knew for the central characters, to give it vividness and memorability. Baxandall uses these instructions in the *Garden of Prayer* as evidence that "quattrocento man," when viewing a painting such as Piero's *Baptism*, would already have a visual "image" connected with the depicted event, and that the painting would be like an "overlay" of an existing mental image. The document he cites seems to provide evidence that some *women*— in particular, those who internalized the instructions of the *Garden of Prayer*— would have experienced paintings in this way, but it doesn't strike me as being any evidence *at all* that any *men* would have seen them this way. In fact, it seems implausible to me that such handbooks would have been either read or taken seriously by young boys—they were off at school learning arithmetic and geometry (and, if Baxandall is to be believed, out in the streets sizing up packs and barrels), not at home visualizing Bible stories and meditating on the virtues of chastity, purity, and piety.

Baxandall's using *The Garden of Prayer* in this way is a blatant example of his privileging of men's activities and interests and the marginalizing of women's. It is not merely a failure to point out how a large segment of the population was excluded from being a participant in the part of the culture of which the *Baptism* was a constituent, but a confiscation and appropriation of materials that would have shed light on the activities of that population. It is also precisely the kind of case that leads one to suspect that there is indeed a psychological explanation for Baxandall's behavior in terms of his own biases about what are important constituents of culture. But, once again, it is not necessary to unpack a psychological cause in order to show the significance of what he has done. It is not Baxandall the person we're interested in, but rather what the characteristics of our own culture are, and what sorts of actions and objects construct that culture. What *is* important, or significant, is that what Baxandall did—the art history he wrote—is part of a pattern that marginalizes women's perspectives and experiences, and that Chadwick, even as a relatively conservative feminist art historian, partially constructs a new pattern, one that takes women and women's experiences as important constituents of culture.

Analytic aestheticians, not just art historians, have traditionally been participants in a culture that privileges men and men's activities, and that marginalizes or excludes women and women's activities. Philosophical and art-historical work that pays attention *only* to the traditional conceptual repertoire, which privileges the object, the artist, and the artist's intended audience, rather than the broader social and cultural context of the object's production and reception, is a part of that culture. One way to change the pattern of privileging is to change one's actions so that they no longer play a role in constructing that same pattern. This requires becoming aware of the potential one's own actions have for various kinds of de facto significance, and then changing one's behavior in light of that awareness. It is the sort of thing we call taking responsibility for one's own behavior.

It is therefore *not* open to the traditional aesthetician simply to say, "I shall (continue to) work on representation and expression, and you women (and other marginalized peoples) can talk about de facto significance if you like." That would be to *continue* to act in ways that have the de facto significance they have always had. One's behavior would continue to display the same patterns of privileging and marginalizing precisely because one attends only to those phenomena that in fact exclude or marginalize the activities of women. It is an unfortunate fact that whether a person or group is marginalized depends not only on what that person or group does: it depends in major respects on what *others* do. Thus, the view that the only descriptions of actions and objects that are important are those which see it through the eyes and efforts of the individual agent helps to reinforce the myth that if women are marginalized it's *only* because of what women do. But there are factors that constitute, perpetuate, and reinforce women's marginalization that go far beyond the power of women to control. Indeed, even getting people to admit the cogency of feminist art history is not the hardest part of the project; the hardest part is getting people to alter their actions in ways that change the de facto significance of what they do.

I have argued here that a certain groundwork for the concept of de facto significance exists already within traditional aesthetics. It simply needs to be expanded to include *valuative* nonintentional descriptions, that is, descriptions of the sort that de facto significance descriptions are. Given that any given object or bit of behavior will be meaningful or significant in a variety of ways, de facto significance descriptions need not be seen as inherently incompatible with the artist- and object-centered concepts that have occupied traditional aestheticians' attention. We are all understandably reluctant to allow valuative descriptions of our own actions to apply independently of our own intent, but we must remember that the objective is not to judge individuals but to understand objects and behavior as part of a culture. The fact that traditional aesthetics has failed to employ and examine something like de facto significance, as an important part of understanding the cultural and historical significance of works of art, *itself* has de facto significance. And it has that significance, regardless of what individual practitioners of traditional aesthetics might wish or intend, or what might motivate them to continue to work in ways that do not recognize the importance of such notions. What changes de facto significance is nothing less than a change in a whole cultural pattern of behavior.[24]

Notes

1. In Ivan Karp's words, this would be to strive for assimilation, as opposed to exoticism. See *Exhibiting Cultures: The Poetics and Politics of Museum Displays*, ed. Ivan Karp and Steven D. Lavine (Washington, D.C.: Smithsonian Institution Press, 1991), and "How Museums Define Other Cultures," *American Art* 5 (Winter–Spring 1991): 10. There are interesting analogies between the representation of women, the representation of alien theoretical frameworks, and the representation and display of the artworks of other cultures. See also note 12.

Alasdair MacIntyre and Göran Hermerén have both argued that being reasonable requires that one seriously consider the claims made from alien theoretical frameworks, for these will often reveal inadequacies in one's own point of view that one would otherwise never have seen. MacIntyre argues that alien perspectives are often capable of resolving an "epistemic crisis" within a point of view that the "home tradition" does not have the conceptual resources to solve; see his *Whose Justice? Which Rationality?* (London: Duckworth, 1988), 364. Hermerén argues that it is rationally required of a traditional aesthetician that one consider what these alien theoretical perspectives have to offer, the kinds of things one would be unlikely to recognize as important, given that one is already committed to a set of theoretical options; see his *Art, Reason, and Tradition: On the Role of Rationality in Interpretation and Explanation of Works of Art* (Stockholm: Almquist and Wiskell International, 1991), 100.

2. Other feminist art historians whose work can usefully be understood in terms of de facto significance include, but are certainly not limited to, Griselda Pollock, Rozsika Parker, Estella Lauter, and Kate Linker.

3. My summary of this discussion will of necessity be extremely sketchy, but it is valuable to have an example that gives content to the sorts of theoretical issues that are discussed here. For additional detail, see Michael Baxandall, *Painting and Experience in Fifteenth-Century Italy: A Primer in the Social History of Pictorial Style* (Oxford: Clarendon Press, 1972) (hereafter *PE*), and *Patterns of Intention: On the Historical Explanation of Pictures* (New Haven: Yale University Press, 1985), chap. 4 (hereafter *PI*). Some differences between gender-specific roles of the *Baptism* and *Annunciation* will emerge below.

4. This use of the term "represents" is suggestive. It is not the sense in which aestheticians have traditionally used it, but more akin to senses in which social theorists have used it. Unfortunately, there is not room here to explore this distinction further.

5. This is also discussed by David Summers. See his "Conclusions" in *The Judgment of Sense: Renaissance Naturalism and the Rise of Aesthetics* (New York: Cambridge University Press, 1987).

6. (London: Thames and Hudson, 1990), chap. 2 (hereafter *WAS*).

7. *PE*, 3. My suspicion is that the emphasized passage will de facto exclude virtually all women, with the exception of powerful women of noble families. In characterizing the public role of painting in this way, Baxandall ignores its probable part in reinforcing women's opinions about increasingly gender-defined social roles. Richard C. Trexler paints an uncompromisingly grim picture of the status of women in fifteenth-century Florence, that is, as useful only to reinforce the authority of adult men in the city's most powerful families. See his *Public Life in Renaissance Florence* (New York: Academic Press, 1980), especially 16, 37, 117, 360.

8. J. Rifkin, *Art History* 7 (1984): 247.

9. What constitutes a culture is a disputed issue. Some feminists have argued that women should be seen as having a separate, temporally parallel (though geographically overlapping) culture, and that only on this understanding will it be possible to understand what women do and make. For an analogous move in African American studies, see Anthony Appiah's discussion of the "Black Aesthetic" movement in his contribution, "Race," in *Critical Terms for Literary Study*, ed. Frank Lentricchia and Thomas McLaughlin (Chicago: University of Chicago Press, 1990). In this paper I have assumed a "nonseparatist" account of culture.

10. For individuals to be members of the same culture there must also be appropriate causal connections among individuals in that culture coming to have the beliefs they do. I have not attempted to provide a complete definition of culture here, but only to describe a few constituents of it.

11. Joseph Margolis is well known for his view that art objects are themselves culturally emergent entities. Though my notion of de facto significance has some affinities with his view, I suspect his view is less compatibilist than mine. See especially his *Art and Philosophy* (Atlantic Highlands, N.J.: Humanities Press, 1978).

12. I am arguing here for the importance of at least some holistic descriptions of culturally significant phenomena. This is a rich and controversial topic in many areas, including not only cultural studies and the relation of culture to aesthetics, but also philosophical psychology and philosophy of mind. For an example of an emergent pattern and straightforward discussion of some holistic and reductionist options, see the ". . . And Fugue" segment of "Prelude . . . And Fugue" by Douglas R. Hofstadter, in *The Mind's Eye: Fantasies and Reflections on Self and Soul*, composed and arranged by Douglas R. Hofstadter and Daniel C. Dennett (New York: Bantam Books, 1981), 159–97.

13. There is an enormous amount of literature on what is relevant to understanding works of art, and their history, *as* works of art. Among recent work, Arthur Danto has argued that some intention-independent phenomena are important to understanding history, and in particular the history of art. See his "Narrative and Style," *Journal of Aesthetics and Art Criticism* 49 (Summer 1991): 201–9. See also note 17 below.

14. E. D. Hirsch, *Validity in Interpretation* (New Haven: Yale University Press, 1967), 8, distinguishes between meaning and significance in a way with which I am roughly sympathetic.

15. Gregory Currie (*The Nature of Fiction* [New York: Cambridge University Press, 1990], 109–16) and Jerrold Levinson ("Intention and Interpretation: A Last Look," in *Interpretation and Intention*, ed. Gary Iseminger [Philadelphia: Temple University Press, 1992]: 221–56), argue that the meaning of a work is established by existing, culturally shared conventions, and that this cannot be overriden or undermined by an artist's idiosyncratic intent. It is important to note that their concern is with *meaning*, not significance. De facto significance is important, I am arguing, however one comes down on issues of meaning.

16. Baxandall is sometimes grouped with the "new" art historians, at least in part because he is willing to interpret a work in light of social and economic conditions, whether or not thoughts of them actually informed the artist's work. However, as I read him, this view often seems to be something he resorts to because of the *epistemic* problem of figuring out what indeed did go through the artist's mind. For example, his "legitimacy" requirement for an explanation—i.e., that explanations use only concepts that were available to the artist—signals his attachment to understanding that is constrained by the artist's perspective (*PI*, chap. 1).

17. Arthur Danto has argued for such descriptions of actions for the purposes of writing history; see *Narration and Knowledge* (which includes the text of *Analytic Philosophy of History*) (New York: Columbia University Press, 1985), esp. chap. 8, "Narrative Sentences." Danto emphasizes that future events, events that occur after one acts and that one couldn't reasonably have known would occur, are implicated in narrative descriptions of the events in question. Although my emphasis here is not on temporal relationships, or on narratives, the principle is much the same. My concern is with descriptions of what one does that depend on the relationships of what one does to other aspects of the society or culture in which one lives (rather than in terms of their relationships to future events), that is, with synchronic rather than diachronic relationships.

18. In the United States, an extensive, difficult battle was required to remove the practice of treating drunkenness as an excusing condition, or mitigating circumstance, for causing an automobile accident. The fact that it took such a battle is symptomatic of an inclination to ask only whether one was in control, and not to hold one responsible for *being* in control.

19. The relationship of de facto significance to feminist *psychoanalysis*, however, is more complicated. Not all feminist theories and theoretical uses of psychoanalysis are theories of *individual psychology* per se. Some are theories of the gendered cultural positioning of individuals, and of the cultural determination of the individual or the self. Such views raise issues that challenge the compatibilist position I am pursuing in this paper. I am arguing that one *can* retain a "traditional" concept of the self, but also recognize and accommodate an important kind of significance that is grounded in a network of cultural phenomena that transcend the power of any individual to control. These cultural phenomena will at least sometimes have a gendered quality—as when a particular action has the de facto significance of marginalizing women and women's activities.

20. He does point out in a footnote that Piero was painting for a rather small, elite group of men that excluded peasants and the urban poor (*PE*, 38–39).

21. See Bruce Cole, *Piero della Francesca: Tradition and Innovation in Renaissance Art* (New York: HarperCollins, 1991), 47.

22. Peter Burke, *Culture and Society in Renaissance Italy, 1420–1540* (New York: Scribner, 1972), 113.

23. Burke, 297. Burke does not mention women in particular, but it is clear that a great variety of people roamed around churches at the time.

24. My participation in the NEH Summer Institute, "Aesthetics and the Histories of the Arts," June–July 1991, made possible the development of this essay. I extend special thanks to the faculty of and participants in the Institute, and to Carolyn Korsmeyer and Casey Haskins for comments on earlier drafts of this essay.

14
Leonardo da Vinci and Creative Female Nature

Mary D. Garrard

Possibly the most celebrated artist of all time, Leonardo da Vinci has been examined from every conceivable perspective except a feminist one. A feminist perspective seeks, of course, not only to include women in history but also to expose gender-based conceptual biases that have distorted scholarship. Such a bias has led scholars to ignore an important dimension of Leonardo's art and thought: his unusual valorization of the feminine in a period when the female sex was disparaged, both socially and philosophically. I do not mean "feminine" as a descriptive term, one that might justifiably be connected with Leonardo's very peculiar late paintings. Rather, I speak of the metaphysical "female," understood as a creative and powerful force in the universe. In this essay,* I shall show that Leonardo presented through art a view of the female sex that was culturally abnormal in the patriarchy of his day: woman understood individually as an intelligent being, biologically as an equal half of the human species, and philosophically as the ascendant principle in the cosmos. His position deserves our attention, for it was distinctive in a period when

*This essay is adapted from a longer article that appeared in *The Expanding Discourse: Feminism and Art History*, ed. Norma Broude and Mary D. Garrard (New York: HarperCollins, 1992), chap. 3.

women were neither politically nor socially empowered to make such a case for themselves.

Central to this discussion is the *Mona Lisa*, a painting whose status as a cultural icon obscures to us today its connection with an ancient discourse about the relative powers of nature and art, in which nature is gendered as female. In this painting, as in other works, Leonardo offered a valuable contribution to a philosophical debate of long standing, taking—usually—a positive view of *Natura creatrix*. The artist's exceptional viewpoint on the female sex is manifested, however, at many levels, as may be demonstrated through a brief look at several of his female portraits.

The portrait of *Ginevra de' Benci* in the National Gallery, Washington, D.C. (Fig. 14.1), put forth, in the late 1470s, a fundamentally new female image: posed in a three-quarter view, the sitter confronts the viewer's gaze with an icy stare. In Italy, this revolutionary innovation brought about the replacement of the profile portrait type customary for women in the first three-quarters of the fifteenth century.[1] In the earlier convention, young women were painted in profile, usually at the time of their marriages, presented as beautiful but passive possessions of male heads of household, inert mannequins for the display of family wealth to the gaze of other males.[2] The convention supported patriarchal values, draining the bride of any sign of inner animation or worth, and reifying the inequality of the marital partners. The change initiated by Leonardo gave psychological life to the female sitter, enabling her to confront us on equal terms and form a connection with us personally, in human time.[3]

Ginevra de' Benci, born in 1457 into a wealthy and educated Florentine family, was recognized as a poet, though today we know almost nothing of her literary work.[4] In the Washington picture, long believed to be her marriage portrait, a juniper bush behind the sitter's head, which recurs on the obverse of the panel as a sprig between a laurel and palm branch, has been recognized as an allusion to the name "Ginevra" (the Italian for juniper is *ginepro*).[5] Recent writers have interpreted the image as a Petrarchan emblem of feminine virtue, or else as a portrait of a certain Venetian gentleman's Platonic beloved.[6] The woman herself, the proper and compelling subject of the portrait, is curiously absent from these discussions. Yet every feature of the portrait can be explained by Ginevra's own celebrity as a poet: the honorific form of the bust-length image, the sober, dignified expression, the laurel and palm alluding to poetry and victory.[7] At the compositional heart of the emblematic verso is the subject of its visual sentence: *she* who triumphs in the field of poetry is represented by the sprig of juniper that is Ginevra's personal emblem.

Women in quattrocento Florence were not usually celebrated by men for

Fig. 14.1.   Leonardo da Vinci, *Ginevra de' Benci.* National Gallery of Art, Washington, D.C.; Ailsa Mellon Bruce Fund

their personal achievements. Praised instead in Renaissance literature, quite incessantly, are female modesty and chastity and, above all, female silence, for these qualities are, as Peter Stallybrass has written, "homologous to woman's enclosure within the home," as part of a "property category."[8] Yet culturally prominent women in the Renaissance were sometimes cited for their "manly virtues"[9]—why not Ginevra de' Benci? And since we know that Leonardo enjoyed a personal friendship with the Benci family,[10] is it not logical to speculate that, out of friendship with an unusually talented young woman of his own generation, he painted a portrait that would commemorate her intellectual virtues? It is not my purpose to insist upon this interpretation, but rather to point to the bias that prohibited its ever being considered. Conventional works of art may be satisfactorily explained in terms of the gender conventions of their day, but when both image and sitter are unquestionably unconventional, we should be prepared to recognize gender anomaly.

The unconventionality of the *Ginevra de' Benci* is sustained in two portraits painted by Leonardo at the court of Lodovico Sforza in Milan, where he worked from 1483 to 1499. Most firmly accepted as autograph is the portrait of Cecilia Gallerani, paramour of Duke Lodovico and, like Ginevra de' Benci, a woman of a noble family who wrote poetry. Acclaimed for her incomparable beauty and sparkling intelligence, Gallerani was said to conduct learned discussions with famous theologians and philosophers, and to write epistles in Latin and poems in Italian.[11] Orphaned at about fifteen on her father's death in December 1480, she was taken up by Duke Lodovico, who gave her a residence at Saronno in 1481, and for ten years she was his lover.[12] In 1491, soon after Lodovico's legitimate wife arrived, Cecilia Gallerani married a local count, and set up her own intellectual courts in Milan and in the *campagna* of Cremona. These gatherings attracted celebrated writers, philosophers, musicians, and poets.[13]

Leonardo's portrait of Cecilia Gallerani, *Lady with an Ermine* (Fig. 14.2), painted c. 1484–85, is widely recognized as a major advance in the history of portraiture, introducing, as Martin Kemp describes it, a new "living sense of the sitter's deportment" and "of human communication," an achievement for which "there simply is no equal . . . in contemporary or earlier portraiture."[14] But while Leonardo's portrait projects a vital personality commensurate with the historical identity of an unusual woman, modern art historians have followed Renaissance writers in interpreting Cecilia Gallerani's portrait simply as a model of generic beauty, the plaything of her powerful male patron.[15] The so-called *Belle Ferronnière* (c. 1485–88) in the Louvre, which has been identified as Leonardo's recorded portrait of Lodovico's mistress Lucrezia Crivelli, similarly presents a self-possessed woman with a thoughtful expression who turns her head, engaging the eyes of someone in the viewer's space.[16] Its projection of inner vitality is entirely contrary to a contemporary Latin epigram written in praise of the Lucrezia Crivelli portrait, which asserts: "Vincius might have shown the soul here as he has portrayed everything else. He did not, so that the image might have greater truth, for it is thus: the soul is owned by Maurus [Il Moro] her lover."[17]

We would not know this from the portrait itself. In both the Gallerani

Fig. 14.2. Leonardo da Vinci, *Lady with an Ermine*. Czartoryski Museum, Kraków, Poland

and *Belle Ferronnière* portraits, the sitter's avoidance of the viewer's gaze paradoxically now preserves for the sitter some freedom from patronly possession (even as earlier, Ginevra de' Benci's independent identity is conveyed *through* engagement of the viewer's eyes), for by the 1490s, the direct gaze was already a sign of courtesanal seductiveness in portraits by Leonardo's own followers.[18] By displacing the sitter's attention to an invisible third party, away from the man who paid for the portrait, the artist subtly undermines the man's power and heightens the sitter's. In the discrepancy between these images and what was said about them, we can glimpse a disjunction between the profound originality of Leonardo da Vinci's lifelike and independent images of women and the terms on which they were received in the masculine society of his day.

Of six surviving portraits by Leonardo, five represent women, one a man. This statistic may be accidental, but it is quite unusual in Renaissance Italy, where a far higher percentage of portraits depicted men.[19] Thus, Leonardo's creation of psychologically complex images—speaking likenesses of humans who turn and move in space—appears to have been achieved through the female figure. In direct contrast to the quattrocento situation, the female type now became progressive, for the new cinquecento portrait created by Leonardo was based upon the study of women as prime examples of the human organism. His progressive exploration of human personality through the female was soon subverted by the very circumstances that first sustained it, namely, the flourishing of portraiture within court circles, the rise and increasingly ambiguous status of intellectual courtesans, and the full-blown emergence at the turn of the sixteenth century of the courtesan portrait, recognizable now by her brazenly provocative gaze at the viewer.[20] Such female portraits, though different in appearance from the quattrocento profile type, nevertheless represent a similar form of commodification of the female image: the patron's wife as a particularized material possession now in the new key of the mistress as his ideal amatory possession. From the vantage point of the altered tradition, it is arguable whether Leonardo's *Cecilia Gallerani* and *La Belle Ferronnière* hold their own as autonomous presences or whether, as images of a duke's paramours, they retain a lingering aura of commodification.

The spectacular example of resistance to commodification is the *Mona Lisa*, the world's most famous portrait of a woman, who—whatever else she may be—is no known person's mistress and only conjecturally someone's wife. A host of writers on the *Mona Lisa*, from Walter Pater to Kenneth Clark, have recognized that it is not only, and perhaps not at all, a portrait, but rather an image that conflates portraiture with broader philosophical ideas. The picture may have begun as a Florentine female portrait c. 1503–6,[21] but it is not known to have left Leonardo's hands, and when he went to France for the final three years of his life, he almost certainly took the painting with him. Its only association with any patron is a mention in 1517, by a writer who visited Leonardo in France, that the portrait was "a certain Florentine lady, made from nature at the instigation of the late Magnificent Giuliano de' Medici."[22] It is likely, as Martin Kemp has argued, that Leonardo reworked the painting for Giuliano de' Medici during the period that he was in the *capitano*'s employ (1513–16), and in the intervening years repainted the image along the lines of his own interests.[23] Thus for ten years or longer, this female image seems to have served the artist as a vehicle for private philosophical expression.

Since the nineteenth century, the *Mona Lisa* has frequently been identified as a female archetype. This is typified by Walter Pater's famous description (1869): "She is older than the rocks among which she sits; like the vampire, she has been dead many times, and learned the secrets of the grave."[24] Pater's version of the archetypal female draws heavily upon the nineteenth-century femme fatale, yet he implies an identity between this ancient woman, or Woman, and the cycles of geological time. Similarly, Kenneth Clark noted that the woman's face and the landscape background together express the processes of nature as symbolized by the image of a female, whose connection with human generation links her sex with the creative and destructive powers of nature.[25] The medical historian Kenneth D. Keele at once localized and enlarged this interpretation, identifying in the portrait image unmistakable signs of a woman at an advanced stage of pregnancy, which he understood as a symbol of Genesis, "God-the-Mother . . . enclosed within the body of the earth."[26]

More recently, David Rosand has connected the *Mona Lisa* with the Renaissance concept of the portrait as an image of triumph over mortality and death.[27] Pointing to Leonardo's "preoccupation with transience" and the ravages of time ("Oh Time, who consumes all things!"), Rosand quotes the artist's expressed belief in the competitive edge held by art over destructive nature: "Oh marvelous science [that is, painting], which can preserve alive the transient beauty of mortals and endow it with a permanence greater than the works of nature; for these are subject to the continual changes of time, which leads them to inevitable old age."[28] According to Rosand, the *Mona Lisa* holds in dialectical tension the fluid and changing landscape, subject to endless deformation by water, agent of time and the generative and destructive forces of life, with the contrasting image of perfect human beauty—a figure who, in life, would undergo the same transformations of time but who, as a creation of art, will live forever.[29] In Rosand's view, the beautiful woman is not herself identified with the forces of nature, except as a product of them, subject to their ravages; symbolically, she is allied with the realm of art, as image of perfection and permanent substitute for transitory life. In this interpretation, the *Mona Lisa* is another example of the genre of female portraits in which a beautiful woman's image represents the triumph of art, functioning, in Elizabeth Cropper's words, "as a synecdoche for the beauty of painting itself."[30]

The *Mona Lisa* conspicuously departs from this convention, however, in the very hypnotic strangeness that has made it uniquely famous, in Leonardo's personal stylization of a beauty that is quite different from living or ideal specimens. Moreover, as many writers have observed, she is of a piece with her setting. Laurie Schneider and Jack Flam have pointed to "a system of similes" between figure and landscape, of visual echoes between curved arcs and undulating folds, and to a unity between them expressed through the diffuse lighting and consistent *sfumato*.[31] Martin Kemp has also taken account of the extraordinary geological activity in the background of the *Mona Lisa*, which he sees (as had Keele and Clark) as coextensive with the portrait image, not in dialectical opposition to it. Noting correspondences between the flowing movements and dynamic processes visible in the landscape and the cascading, rippling patterns of the lady's clothing and hair, Kemp describes them as united exempla of the "processes of living nature." For Kemp, the painting expresses Leonardo's idea of the earth as a "living, changing organism," a macrocosm whose mechanisms and circulations of fluids are echoed in the microcosm of human anatomy, and whose fecundity is echoed in "the procreative powers of all living things."[32]

Webster Smith has likewise interpreted the *Mona Lisa* as a micro-macrocosmic commentary on the geological processes of the earth, pointing to Leonardo's comparison of the circulation of blood in the human body with rivers on the earth.[33] In contrast to Schneider and Flam, who consider the painting to be a metaphor or personification of the inner forces of nature, Smith reminds us that for Leonardo this relationship is not merely metaphor, since he describes the earth not as "like a living body" but literally *as* a living body.[34] Smith is hard pressed, however, to explain why this philosophical commentary should be joined with a female portrait (he can adduce only the stock association of female portraiture with Petrarchan beauty and the *paragone* between painting and poetry). Similarly, Kemp, exemplifying Leonardo's micro-macrocosm theory with the *Mona Lisa*, the *Leda* (see Fig. 14.7), and the "Great Lady" drawing (Fig. 14.3), does not comment upon Leonardo's

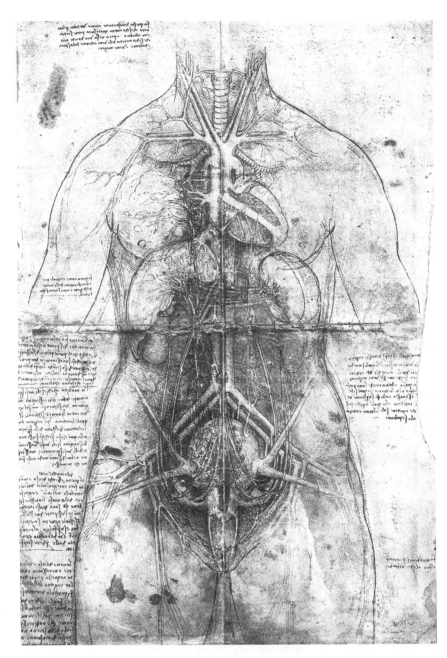

Fig. 14.3.   Leonardo da Vinci, "Anatomical Study." Royal College, Windsor, England

persistent choice of the female figure to illustrate the analogy between "the body of man [*sic*] and the body of the earth."[35]

Missing from these analyses is a framework that would situate in historical perspective the analogy between woman and nature, an analogy already ancient in the Renaissance. The use of a female figure to symbolize the nutritive and generative processes of nature is found in a long line of writers, from Plato, who described the earth metaphorically as "our nurse," to the twelfth-century poet Alain of Lille, who ascribed human and natural generation to a cosmic force personified as the goddess Natura.[36] The figure of *Natura creatrix* had been given impetus by Roman writers such as Lucretius and Cicero, who believed the universe to be ruled by an intelligent and divine female Nature, identical with god yet immanent in the material world. As a deity this figure was exalted in the early Middle Ages by Boethius and Claudian. Claudian describes how "mother Nature made order out of elemental chaos," preserving one of many versions of the creation myth in which the creator of the universe was female. Boethius personifies this Natura as an awesome figure who drives the earth like a charioteer, echoing the Natura of the late antique Orphic hymns, "Physis," the self-engendered and almighty Mother of All.[37]

However, in ancient and medieval philosophy the metaphoric figure of a powerful and creative female Natura coexisted with misogynous beliefs about the deficiency of woman's nature. The key text for the negative gendering of nature is Aristotle's *Generation of Animals*, where it is argued that human procreation is the result of the generative action of masculine form upon inert female matter.[38] This viewpoint provided the philosophical foundation for the Christian view of nature as corrupt and the female as corrupting, epitomized by Saint Augustine's doctrine of original sin, and for the nexus that developed in the Middle Ages between the evil of the flesh, the negativity of matter, and the femaleness of matter.[39] A similar position was taken by the Neoplatonists, particularly Macrobius, in whose Great Chain of Being the phenomena of nature are called "the bottommost dregs," and Chalcidius, who described matter as "insignificant and evil," ugly, lacking in form, like a woman without a husband.[40]

Leonardo entered a discourse to which he made a conscious and original contribution, by affirming to a remarkable extent that the relationship between nature and the female passed beyond the metaphoric, and by presenting evidence in his anatomical studies that directly refuted dominant views about women's deficiencies. Although he had once depicted sexual intercourse in an image that distinctly privileged the male role,[41] reflecting Aristotle's influential dictum that females contributed only passive matter to human procreation while the male played the vitalizing part, he increasingly questioned this theory. Instead, Leonardo drew upon the philosophical opinion of Lucretius and the medical opinion of Galen that both female and male contribute "seed" necessary for conception. In effect, he took one side of a debate ongoing since the fourteenth century among doctors and philosophers over the Aristotelian and Galenist views on procreation, philosophers leaning toward Aristotle and medical practitioners toward the second-century physician Galen. Whereas the Galenic writers shared with the Aristotelians the belief that the female is biologically inferior to the male, they believed that the mother also "seminated," playing a more active role in conception than was accorded by the Aristotelians.[42] During his years in Milan, Leonardo read Galen, Avicenna, and the early fourteenth-century anatomist Mundinus, as well as Lucretius.[43] In this period, he was still aligned with Aristotle, but on his return to Florence, beginning c. 1504–6, he was drawn more and more to Galenist views, becoming stronger in this orientation until c. 1513, when he took the position of independence from authority, basing his conclusions strictly on observation.[44]

About 1509–10, Leonardo obtained a copy of Galen's *De usu partium*, which initiated his period of intense Galenism. The so-called "Great Lady" drawing (see Fig. 14.3), which dates from c. 1510, exemplifies his adoption of a new understanding of human generation. In an annotation on this sheet addressed to Mundinus, Leonardo challenges the Aristotelian view of generation passed by Mundinus, that the "spermatic vessels" (ovaries) do not generate real semen, observing instead that these vessels "derive in the same way in the female as in the male." Here he adopts the Galenic position that both sexes contribute in equal part.[45] Elsewhere, citing the ability of a white mother mating with a black father to produce a child of mixed color, Leonardo concludes that "the semen of the mother has power in the embryo equal to the semen of the father."[46] On the same sheet, he asserts that the mother nourishes the fetus with her life, food, and soul (anima), countering the Aristotelian belief still commonly held then that women, deficient in soul, were mere incubators for gestation: "As one mind governs two bodies . . . likewise the nourishment of the food serves the child, and it is nourished from the same cause as the other members of the mother and the spirits, which are taken from the air—the common soul of the human race and other living things."[47] Leonardo further appears to identify the active power of the womb as generative rather than nutritive, an important distinction within the camp of those who considered the womb to have active power, under which nutritive virtue would generate something joined to it, while the greater virtue, generative, would produce a distinct entity. For he asserts—and illustrates—that there is no continuity between the vascular systems of mother and fetus, as if in response to a standing argument that was to reverberate down to the eighteenth century (when the position taken by Leonardo was finally proved correct).[48]

In the "Great Lady" drawing, Leonardo presents a synthesized image of circulatory, respiratory, and generative processes in the female body. The drawing differs significantly in this respect from his representations of male anatomy, which typically illustrate blood circulation, the genito-urinary system, and other workings in independent images. The distinctive graphic completeness of the drawing expresses Leonardo's precocious awareness that blood flow in the female body is linked with its role in procreation, and implies his comprehension of the systemic order of organic process in the female body, in opposition to the Aristotelian view that menstrual blood was inchoate, given form by sperm, a view that prevailed until William Harvey's discovery of the circulation of blood in the seventeenth century.[49] If we remember Leonardo's preoccupation with the interconnected functions of microcosm and macrocosm, it is a short step from here to a belief that the living earth *is* female, in its regenerative capability and its mysterious life-supporting powers.

For all that Leonardo wrote, it was to his visual explorations that he entrusted the primary task of representing nature: "Painting presents the works of nature to our understanding with more truth and accuracy than do words or letters."[50] Because for Leonardo art was an instrument of discovery, a form of knowing and not merely an illustration of what was already known, the anatomical drawings reveal a process of visual reasoning. The image of an idea *is* the idea, and frequently it tells us something quite different from what the accompanying words say. The words are practical explanations of the matters that preoccupied Leonardo, or they may be the questions that prompted him to the analysis. The drawings, however, reflect an effort to infer a process of nature from a static slice, and for that reason they convey the artist's understanding (or expectation) that form reveals function, just as the functioning of the microcosm is a key to that of the macrocosm—because they are not only metaphorically, but also organically, related to each other.

The well-known drawing of a fetus in the uterus (Fig. 14.4), though not studied from human example and inaccurate in many ways, nevertheless expresses the process of gestation and birth more clearly than a modern textbook. Having promised himself to describe what makes the fetus push out,[51] Leonardo shows this happening, the bursting of the fetus from its uterine container into the world, in the sequential small images that visually

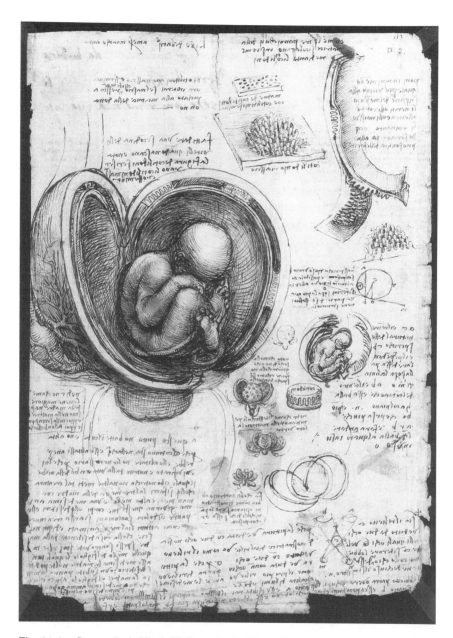

Fig. 14.4. Leonardo da Vinci, "A Fetus in the Womb." The Royal Collection © 1993 Her Majesty Queen Elizabeth II

analogize the process to a nut breaking out of its shell. In the largest image on the sheet, the compact density of the fetus coiled in its umbilicus suggests a seed in a pod (Leonardo had noted that all seeds and nuts have umbilical cords), and the interlocking spirals of its body convey the sense of potential growth and development. Originating in observation but developed under belief in the correspondence between microcosm and macrocosm, this image gives information about human birth that is of a philosophical order, expressing its connection with other forms of birth and growth in the universe. Leonardo found analogy everywhere: the movement of wind currents is like that of water currents, and the trajectories of a bouncing ball are like both. "The earth has a spirit of growth," he said, whose flesh is the soil, whose bones are the mountains, whose blood is its waters.[52]

Leonardo's belief in the interconnection of nature's largest patterns and smallest elements was sharply at odds, however, with prevailing beliefs about nature in the fifteenth century. A medieval distinction that remained in force throughout the quattrocento was that between *natura naturans* and *natura naturata*, between the dynamic creative, generative principle and the inert material result of that creation. For Alberti, Nature was a vestigial female personification (carried over from the medieval allegorical figure Natura), "the wonderful maker of things" who "clearly and openly reveals" such things as the correct proportions of the human body. The principles of Nature's true order—largely mathematical and proportional—might be inferred from disparate imperfect examples by the artist, who could reproduce them in corrected form.[53] In this way of thinking, art was not to imitate the mere phenomena of nature (*natura naturata*) but, rather, its higher invisible principles (*natura naturans*), and by giving them perfected visible form, art could successfully compete with Nature herself.

The strength of this theory, and its intensification under the Neoplatonist doctrines that dominated later fifteenth-century Florence, may be the chief reason why quattrocento art does not display a linear progressive naturalism. The hierarchic distinction between an abstract creative principle and the discredited material forms of the visible world effectively kept intellectually serious painters (such as Piero della Francesca) from too close an involvement with the latter. The hierarchy was reinforced by its gender associations, in that the Aristotelian differentiation of form and matter—the active male principle molding passive and static female matter—supported the binary opposition of, and value distinction between, *natura naturans* and *naturata*. However, creative and material nature were in another sense conflated into a single entity, a female Nature whose creative powers were challenged by the male artist. These overlapping metaphoric structures are most clearly expressed in the model of perspective space construction, in which the artist positions himself *outside* nature, the better to attain mastery over it, and assigns his eye hierarchic priority over the segment of the world that it surveys, symbolically the whole of nature. What is implied in the Albertian perspective diagram is boldly stated in an image by Dürer,[54] where we see the omniscient male eye focused through a framing device upon his subject, a recumbent female form, who is surely a metonymic figure for Nature herself: objectified, passive matter, a mere model, waiting to be given meaningful form in art by the creative powers of the artist.

In the paintings of Botticelli, Leonardo's contemporary, we see an exaggerated separation of the two forms of nature: the elevation of cosmic Nature to the plane of personification, and the demotion of physical nature to the realm of insignificance. A philosophical concept of nature is very much at the core of the *Primavera* and the *Birth of Venus*, closely related paintings that may symbolize respectively earthly and celestial nature, but that in any event present Nature in the figure of Venus, the antique goddess reborn in the Renaissance who, trailing her multiple associations with cosmic and human generation, merged with the Christian Virgin Mary. In the influential Neoplatonism of Marsilio Ficino, the celestial Venus is equated with Mind and divine perfection, while the earthly Venus is conjoined with the sensory realm and with matter.[55] Although both are female, a subtle distinction between them depends upon the lower status of the world of human generation, for Ficino connected the word *materia* (matter) with *mater* (mother) to eulogize the higher celestial Venus as immaterial, born of no mere human mother. Botticelli, accordingly, presents nature's material elements in highly abstracted form, radically suppressing empirical realities in favor of transcendent ones. The solid surfaces of water or grass are presented schematically, rendered as inert. Vitality is exclusively to be found in the contour lines, the most abstract and least material of art's elements. Growth, change, and development are not assigned to the organic world in Botticelli's universe; they belong to the spiritual order, measured in the metamorphic progression of figures across the *Primavera*, or in the transition from that earthly realm to the higher one represented in the *Birth of Venus*.

In Leonardo's contemporaneous painting the *Virgin of the Rocks*, the Louvre version of the 1480s (Fig. 14.5),[56] material nature is described in meticulous detail, but in a form that assures the presence of cosmic nature as well. The distinctive difference lies not in the degree, but in the nature of Leonardo's naturalism. Here, as in numerous independent drawings (Fig. 14.6), Leonardo

Fig. 14.5. Leonardo da Vinci, *Virgin of the Rocks*. Louvre, Paris

Fig. 14.6.   Leonardo da Vinci, "Star of Bethlehem." The Royal Collection © 1993 Her
Majesty Queen Elizabeth II

forms the image of a plant in shapes that emphasize its pattern of growth, implying that the source of change is within matter and not transcendent of it. The arrangement of the leaves at the plant's base evokes the spiral form of generation, now presented as inseparable from matter itself. Whereas Botticelli had symbolized nature as a cosmic power, Leonardo expresses its cosmic operations through its particulars, deriving his understanding of the larger movements from observation of the smaller. The element of movement is critical to their fusion, for it defines their shared participation in time. Thus form and matter are conjoined through motion, just as the barrier between form and space is broken down through the soft-edged *sfumato*. Botticelli and Leonardo both present generative nature as female, but Leonardo's vision of her powers is broader: he conceives her as a dynamic, not static, presence, and he finds her immanent in the entire physical world.

In his visual expression of this idea, Leonardo is most deeply Aristotelian, for Aristotle had defined nature (*physis*) as "the essence of things which have a source of movement in themselves," placing the agent of change within matter, in keeping with his dynamic, teleological vision of nature as matter evolving from inner direction toward its final form.[57] In this, Leonardo has followed an aspect of Aristotle's thought that does not subordinate or denigrate the material world but rather sees it as imbued with the (implicitly female) cosmic power. On the other hand, as we have seen, he rejected Aristotle's model of human biology in favor of one that accorded an active role for the female in generation.

Over and over, in the *Virgin of the Rocks*, the *Mona Lisa*, the surviving designs for the *Leda*, the Burlington House Cartoon, and the *Saint Anne*, Leonardo explicitly associated powerful female images with highly developed, visually extraordinary surrounding landscapes, as if to assert the unity between the physical universe and the female cosmic generative principle as a philosophical claim. The collective impact of this "statement" about the nature of nature may be more pronounced than that of any other single idea in his pictorial oeuvre. The lost painting of *Leda and the Swan* (c. 1506), whose composition is known from surviving studies and copies (Fig. 14.7), has been widely recognized as symbolic of the analogy between female and natural procreation.[58] Leonardo made this connection quite clear through the bursting of Leda's babies from eggs and the adjacent explosion of growing plants. We may further observe that, especially in his first studies for this painting, he converted a lesser character of classical mythology into a more primal figure, not merely one of Jupiter's conquests, but the origin of life itself, both human

Fig. 14.7. Leonardo da Vinci, "Leda and the Swan." Museum Boymans–van Beuningen, Rotterdam

and vegetal, symbolized in the image of the kneeling Leda, who rises in a spiral, self-created, from the earth.

Much earlier, he had essayed a similar image of the generative mother goddess (no other term will do, though he would not have used it) in the *Virgin of the Rocks*. In the Louvre painting (see Fig. 14.5), the Virgin rises from the dark, dense vegetation in a slow spiral turn, hovering over her child, whose tightly curved body and crossed legs anticipate the later drawing of the fetus in the womb. This archetypal mother presides over her son and their solemn attendants in an awesome and mysterious setting of plants, rocks, and a mist-shrouded distance whose remote inaccessibility suggests a recession into time as well as depth, evoking the primeval early life of the planet. The entire painting is already incipiently an image of "formative nature," as Leonardo called her, before whose "various and strange shapes" he described his sensations of fear and curiosity, in the famous passage about a great cavern among some gloomy rocks.[59] The mother in this image, universalized by her conspicuous identification with the natural cosmos, is empowered through movement and gesture as the controlling and motivating agent of the composition. In a sheet that includes studies for the *Virgin of the Rocks*, we see the artist thinking through the female figure to arrive at the monumental pyramidal composition that would later become the emblem of cinquecento pictorial design. It is well known that Leonardo created the innovative pyramidal design that Raphael and others would build on, but it is less often observed that the artist atypically used a female character for the study of the human figure in motion (just as he had for the portrait), and that he was the first to make a variable theme of the active female body.[60]

If the *Virgin of the Rocks* and *Leda* express the cosmic female genesis of human and vegetal life, then the Louvre *Virgin with the Child and Saint Anne* (Fig. 14.8) and the closely related Burlington House Cartoon are clearly meditations on human generation over time. Possibly originating in political circumstance, and certainly displaying advanced notions of *contrapposto* figure composition, the Saint Anne images nevertheless also represent an extension of Leonardo's thinking about the female and nature, now focused upon the cycles of human reproduction.[61] This is suggested in the Louvre painting especially, in the cascading sequence of curved arms that, in conjunction with the glacial and terrestrial landscapes, imply a sequence from geological into human time.[62] The monumental pair of mothers who preside over, or have procreated, the earth's formation and every aspect of life that derives from it might be thought of as a Christian counterpart to the Neoplatonic twin Venuses: Saint Anne representing the remote celestial Venus, and Mary the

Fig. 14.8. Leonardo da Vinci, *The Virgin with the Child and Saint Anne*. Louvre, Paris

more human terrestrial Venus—a polarity that is reinforced by the two-part landscape. Yet in their symbiotic configuration, Leonardo's mothers seem less hierarchically distinguished than causally and generatively connected. They remind us more deeply of the ancient mother-daughter pairing of Demeter–Persephone, who in turn reflect the twin aspects of the even more ancient mother goddess, as she appeared in many pre-Greek images in the Mediterranean world. Leonardo had no special interest in classical myth, and there is no reason to believe he knew any preclassical images. I would suggest instead that in his curious return to, and almost obsessive expression of, the ancient prehistoric identification of the highest cosmic power as female, Leonardo was unusually attuned to, and spontaneously reinvented, a way of thinking periodically voiced in antiquity and the Middle Ages, which would not seem at all strange to us today had it not been consistently subjected to patriarchal distortion.

Leonardo was in many ways a man of his age, for he not only shared but helped define his era's faith in the capacity of art to preserve life and transcend time. In his passionate championing of the art of painting, the artist had no peer, and he proclaimed often in his notebooks what many other quattrocento artists believed, that "the painter strives and competes with nature." However, that was only part of Leonardo's complex understanding of the relationship between nature and art. In both his writings and his art, he demonstrated constantly that nature (mentioned far more frequently than God) is the superior guide, the teacher of all good artists.[63] Implicit in his thinking about art and nature is a recognition of nature's preeminence: "For painting is born of nature—or, to speak more correctly, we shall call it the grandchild of nature; for all visible things were brought forth by nature, and those her children have given birth to painting."[64] In a similar spirit, he announces nature's superiority to technology: "Though human ingenuity may make various inventions which, by the help of various machines, answer the same end, it will never devise any invention more beautiful, nor more simple, nor more to the purpose than Nature does; because in her inventions nothing is wanting and nothing is superfluous."[65]

Clearly, Leonardo shared with other men of his era a number of man-centered presumptions, including the belief that art and technology could in various ways improve upon or control nature for human benefit. This is demonstrated in his many mechanical inventions and designs for water management or urban planning. Yet his faith in human ability to control or direct nature was limited, both by his own pessimism and by his respect for nature's ultimate superiority. This point of view was not common in Renaissance Italy, when the quest to master and dominate nature grew steadily, and such slogans as "art is more powerful than nature" (Titian's motto) were brandished. Leonardo's drawings representing the Deluge may thus be understood as a response to man's dream of mastering nature. In those images of ferociously spiraling explosions of water, a giant apocalyptic flood repeatedly destroys the tiny structures of cities and towns. It is a celebration, rare in Italian Renaissance art, of the superior power of nature over human civilization—implicitly also a gender construct, of the endurance of female generation over male culture.

In defining a pro-female philosophical position for Leonardo, I am not suggesting any real equivalence between his and a woman's viewpoint, for he could never have experienced the world as did Ginevra de' Benci or Cecilia Gallerani, whose perspectives may have been equally interesting. Nor would I propose that Leonardo's vision of woman holds some universal truth-value; indeed, from a modern feminist standpoint, his position might be criticized as romantic and essentialist. [66] Yet if it seems to us today constrictive to identify the female primarily with procreation, it is well to remember that Leonardo's understanding of human generation challenged a descriptive model that was both inaccurate and demeaning to women. Breaking out of the masculinist norm in two directions, he painted revolutionary portraits of culturally distinguished women, presenting them in forceful visual images that fully convey their dignity and intellectual vitality. And he described female-identified nature as the greatest force in the universe, at a time when other men discredited nature's power and sought to control it. By sustaining and rendering concrete the woman-nature metaphor, Leonardo acknowledged and symbolized in positive terms a realm of female power that the majority of men in his era could acknowledge only inversely, through the repressive strategy of declaring women inferior beings.

Notes

1. Full-faced female sitters appeared occasionally in Northern European portraits of the fifteenth century, and in painting Ginevra de' Benci, Leonardo may have followed a Netherlandish type. See Erwin Panofsky, *Early Netherlandish Painting* (Cambridge: Harvard University Press, 1958), pls. 101, 138, 220, 259; Fern R. Shapley, *Catalogue of the Italian Paintings* (Washington, D.C.: National Gallery of Art, 1979), 1:252; and Paul Hills, "Leonardo and Flemish Painting," *Burlington Magazine* 122 (September 1980): 609–15.

2. Patricia Simons, "Women in Frames: The Gaze, the Eye, the Profile in Renaissance

Portraiture," *History Workshop, A Journal of Socialist and Feminist Historians*, no. 25 (Spring 1988): 4–30.

3. The originality of the *Ginevra de' Benci* in this respect has been recognized. John Walker, in his *"Ginevra de' Benci* by Leonardo da Vinci," in *National Gallery of Art. Report and Studies in the History of Art*, vol. 1 (1967) (Washington, D.C.: National Gallery of Art, 1968), 25–26, called this picture "the earliest of all psychological portraits," while John Pope-Hennessy described it as bringing to the history of the portrait "a new sense of the mystery and uniqueness of the human personality"; see his *The Portrait in the Renaissance* (Princeton: Princeton University Press, 1979), 105. Writing in the 1960s, however, these scholars could not fully acknowledge how exceptional it was that the first psychological portrait produced in Renaissance Florence should have depicted a woman and not a man.

4. Ginevra's grandfather, Giovanni de' Benci, was general manager of the Medici bank and an artistic patron in his own right; her father, Amerigo, was patron and friend of the Neoplatonist Marsilio Ficino. (See Walker, *"Ginevra de' Benci,"* 2ff.).

5. The painting was acquired by the National Gallery of Art in 1967; for the provenance, which cannot be traced before the eighteenth century, see Shapley, *Catalogue*, 1:251–55. Leonardo's portrait of Ginevra de' Benci was mentioned in the *Libro* of Antonio Billi (written between 1481 and 1530), in the Anonimo Gaddiano (1542–48), and in Vasari's life of Leonardo (1550). The painting and its juniper attribute are discussed by Kenneth Clark, *Leonardo da Vinci, An Account of His Development as an Artist* (Baltimore: Penguin Books, 1959), 27–29.

6. Elizabeth Cropper has interpreted the portrait as a demonstration of the power of the art of painting, in response to Petrarch's claim that perfect beauty could not be realized in a pictorial image; see her "The Beauty of Woman: Problems in the Rhetoric of Renaissance Portraiture," in *Rewriting the Renaissance: The Discourses of Sexual Difference in Early Modern Europe*, ed. Margaret W. Ferguson, Maureen Quilligan, and Nancy C. Vickers (Chicago: University of Chicago Press, 1986), 175–90. Jennifer Fletcher has argued that the portrait was commissioned by Bernardo Bembo, Venetian ambassador to Florence in 1475–76 and 1478–80, who selected Ginevra de' Benci as the object of his Platonic love and commissioned a set of poems celebrating her beauty from members of the Medici circle; see her "Bernardo Bembo and Leonardo's Portrait of Ginevra de' Benci," *Burlington Magazine* 131 (December 1989): 811–16. For reasons given in the expanded version of this essay, I do not find either of these interpretations convincing.

7. These are the most standard meanings of laurel and palm. Cropper ("The Beauty of Woman," 187) quotes the words of Petrarch's Laura: "The palm is victory . . . the laurel means triumph." Emil Möller ("Leonardos Bildnis der Ginevra dei Benci," *Münchener Jahrbuch der bildenden Kunst* 12 [1937–38]: 191); and Walker (*"Ginevra de' Benci,"* 11) interpreted the laurel and palm as straightforward references to Ginevra's own accomplishments.

8. Peter Stallybrass, "Patriarchal Territories: The Body Enclosed," in *Rewriting the Renaissance: The Discourses of Sexual Difference in Early Modern Europe*, ed. Margaret W. Ferguson, Maureen Quilligan, and Nancy J. Vickers (Chicago: University of Chicago Press, 1986), 127. In Renaissance conduct books, a common admonition was to obedience and silence; characteristic are Juan Luis Vives, *Instruction of a Christian Woman* (1523) and Henry Smith, *A Preparative to Marriage* (1591).

9. On the praise of women for manly virtues, see Ian Maclean, *The Renaissance Notion of Woman* (New York: Cambridge University Press, 1980), 51ff.

10. Leonardo was a close friend of Ginevra's brother, Giovanni, with whom he exchanged books, maps, and precious stones (Möller, "Leonardos Bildnis," 199). According to Vasari, Leonardo's unfinished *Adoration of the Magi* was owned by Amerigo de Benci, Ginevra's nephew (Vasari–Milanesi, 4:27).

11. Information about Cecilia Gallerani comes from Felice Calvi, *Famiglie Notabili Milanesi*, vol. 3 (Milan: Antonio Vallardi, 1884), n.p.; and from Francesco Malaguzzi-Valeri, *La Corte di*

Lodovico il Moro (Milan: V. Hoepli, 1929), 2:465ff. Gallerani's achievements were praised by Francesco Agostino Della Chiesa, *Theatro delle donne letterate* (Mondovi, 1620), 124. None of her writings is known to survive.

12. Tradition has described Cecilia Gallerani as the duke's mistress, but it is difficult to reconcile her high social status and intellectual renown with the previously clandestine and inferior position of mistresses at court. More likely, Gallerani's position at the Sforza court was as an early instance of the courtesan, the new type emerging in the late fifteenth century who—in contrast to the silent, chaste, and obedient wife—was rhetorically celebrated as intelligent, accomplished, outspoken, and sensual. She may herself have been a model for the court lady who would later be celebrated by Castiglione in *The Book of the Courtier*, Book 3 (published in 1528, drafted in 1507).

13. One of these was Matteo Bandello, who dedicated two *novelle* to her and described the "virtuosa signora Cecilia Gallerani" as "one of our two muses," one of "two great lights of the Italian language" (the other was Camilla Scarampa). As with Ginevra de' Benci, however, no one seems to have bothered to preserve a single ray from such a great literary light; see Matteo Bandello, *Le novelle* (Bari, 1910), 1:259; cited by Malaguzzi-Valeri, *La Corte*, 2:470).

14. Martin Kemp, *Leonardo da Vinci: The Marvelous Works of Nature and Man* (London: J. M. Dent & Sons, 1981), 201; Pope-Hennessy, *Portrait*, 101. See also Jaynie Andersen, "The Giorgionesque Portrait: From Likeness to Allegory," in *Giorgione: Atti del convegno internazionale di studio per il 5° centenario della nascita* (Castelfranco, 1979), 153–58. Despite uncertainty by earlier writers, the painting at Cracow has been definitively accepted by recent scholars as Leonardo's autograph portrait of Gallerani.

15. Leonardo's portrait of Cecilia Gallerani is the subject of a sonnet of 1493 by Bernardo Bellincioni, which casts it as the product doubly of nature and of art. The image of Cecilia is praised because she is shown listening rather than speaking (a curious emphasis, given her legendary intellectual brilliance), and because, as the creation of Leonardo's hand, it will keep the sitter's beauty alive for generations to come. In Bellincioni's sonnet Cecilia's personal identity is overshadowed by the artist, by her patron, and by creative nature; the text is given in Jean Paul Richter, *The Literary Works of Leonardo da Vinci*, 3d ed. (London: Phaidon, 1970), 1:77, no. 33. An appalling modern description of Cecilia Gallerani is that of Cecil Gould: "She is of a kind which is familiar to the twentieth century—the highly intelligent, highly sophisticated, attractive, slightly neurotic young woman who holds a responsible job with men as her subordinates. Everyone knows she is the mistress of a prominent statesman or perhaps of an ambassador. She is often to be seen at high-level parties, a glass of champagne in one hand, a cigarette in the other and three or four men round her"; see his *Leonardo, the Artist and the Non-Artist* (London: Weidenfeld and Nicolson, 1975), 72–73.

16. Kenneth Clark (*Leonardo*, 56–57) explains the attribution and identification of the painting, and dates it in the middle to late 1490s. Some writers argue that only the head and shoulders were painted by Leonardo (for example, Pope-Hennessy, *Portrait*, 105).

17. The epigram is quoted by Kemp, *Leonardo*, 199.

18. For example, *A Lady Lutanist* by Bartolommeo Veneto, in the Gardner Museum, Boston, which is an early sixteenth-century variant of a painting by a Leonardesque artist in the Pinacoteca Ambrosiana, Milan, once held to be Cecilia Gallerani herself (for the latter, see Malaguzzi-Valeri, *La Corte*, 2:fig. 537).

19. A contrasting proportion of female to male portraits by Titian is supplied by Harold Wethey in his *The Paintings of Titian*, Vol. 2, *The Portraits* (London: Phaidon, 1971), who counts among 117 autograph portraits only fifteen women, a group that includes six wives of rulers, four images said to be the painter's daughter Lavinia, plus the "portrait" of Flora (cited by Jaynie Andersen, "Giorgionesque Portrait," 156).

20. On the courtesan portrait, see Cropper, "The Beauty of Woman"; Giovanni Pozzi, "Il ritratto della donna nella poesia d'inizio Cinquecento e la pittura di Giorgione," in *Giorgione e*

l'umanesimo veneziano, ed. R. Pallucchini (Florence: Leo S. Olschki, 1981), 1:309–41; and Lynne Lawner, *Lives of the Courtesans: Portraits of the Renaissance* (New York: Rizzoli, 1987).

21. The identification of the portrait with "M/ad/onna Lisa," wife of the Florentine silk merchant Francesco del Giocondo, originates with Vasari, and may result from Vasari's effort to connect the picture with a portrait of Francesco by Leonardo mentioned in earlier sources (see Kemp, *Leonardo*, 268). Other candidates for the lady's identity, none of which has gained acceptance, are listed by Laurie Schneider and Jack D. Flam, "Visual Convention, Simile and Metaphor in the Mona Lisa," *Storia dell'arte* 29 (1977): 15–24, esp. 19. For literature on the picture, see Roy McMullen, *Mona Lisa: The Picture and the Myth* (Boston: Houghton Mifflin, 1975).

22. The description is that of Antonio de Beatis; quoted more fully in Kenneth Clark, "Mona Lisa," *Burlington Magazine* 115 (March 1973): 144–50.

23. Kemp's reconstruction of the dating of this picture is the most plausible so far (*Leonardo*, 268ff.). See also Clark, "Mona Lisa," 146.

24. Pater's essay on Leonardo (1869) was reprinted in 1873 in *The Renaissance* (see Clark, "Mona Lisa," 148). For discussion of similarly mystified interpretations of the image by Théophile Gautier (1858) and other Romantics, in the context of the femme fatale, see George Boas, "The Mona Lisa in the History of Taste," *Journal of the History of Ideas* 1 (1940): 207–24.

25. Clark, "Mona Lisa," 149. See also Charles De Tolnay, "Remarques sur la Joconde," *Revue des arts* 2 (1952): 18–26, who describes the figure as a "personification" of the landscape.

26. Kenneth Keele, M.D., "The Genesis of the Mona Lisa," *Journal of the History of Medicine and Allied Sciences* 14 (1959): 135–39.

27. David Rosand, "The Portrait, the Courtier, and Death," in Robert W. Hanning and David Rosand, eds., *Castiglione: The Ideal and the Real in Renaissance Culture* (New Haven: Yale University Press, 1983), 91–129.

28. Richter, *Literary Works*, 1:77, no. 32.

29. Rosand, "Portrait," 112.

30. Cropper, "The Beauty of Woman," 176.

31. Schneider and Flam, "Visual Convention," 15–24.

32. Kemp, *Leonardo*, 261–65; 275–77.

33. Webster Smith, "Observations on the *Mona Lisa* Landscape," *Art Bulletin* 67 (June 1985): 183–99; esp. 185.

34. Repeating comparisons of the human body and the earth's body written by a thirteenth-century predecessor, Ristoro d'Arezzo, Leonardo "turns them into expressions of his conviction, seemingly not shared by the thirteenth-century writer, that the earth itself is indeed a kind of autonomous and organic body" (Smith, "Observations," 189–90).

35. Kemp, *Leonardo*, 261. For the "Great Lady" drawing and the *Leda* study, see Broude and Garrard, *The Expanding Discourse*, chap. 3, figs. 10 and 16.

36. Plato, *Timaeus*, 32C–34B; 36E and 40C; Alain of Lille, *De planctu naturae* (1160–72).

37. Lucretius, *De rerum natura*; Cicero, *De natura deorum*; Statius, Thebaid; Boethius, *The Consolation of Philosophy*; Claudian, *De raptu Proserpinae*. See also George D. Economou, *The Goddess Natura in Medieval Literature* (Cambridge: Harvard University Press, 1972).

38. Aristotle, *Generation of Animals*, esp. 716a 3–24; 729a 10–15; 729a 28–34; 730a 25–29. See Maryanne Cline Horowitz, "Aristotle and Women," *Journal of the History of Biology* 9, no. 2 (Fall 1976): 183–213.

39. Augustine, *The City of God*, Book 13, chap. 13.

40. Macrobius, *Commentary on the Dream of Scipio*, I.xiv.15; and Chalcidius, CCCXXX, 324–25. See Arthur O. Lovejoy, *The Great Chain of Being, A Study of the History of an Idea* (Cambridge: Harvard University Press, 1936).

41. See Charles D. O'Malley and J. B. de C. M. Saunders, *Leonardo on the Human Body: The Anatomical, Physiological, and Embryological Drawings of Leonardo da Vinci* (New York: Dover reprint, 1983), 460.

42. The Galenic view gained support from Poggio Bracciolini's discovery in 1417 of a manuscript of Lucretius's *De rerum natura*, a text that asserted women's contribution of semen to generation (O'Malley and Saunders, *Leonardo*, 454). See Michael Boylan, "The Galenic and Hippocratic Challenges to Aristotle's Conception Theory," *Journal of the History of Biology* 17 (Spring 1984): 83–112; Helen Rodnite Lemay, "Masculinity and Femininity in Early Renaissance Treatises on Human Reproduction," *Acta Academiae Internationalis Historiae Medicinae* 18, nos. 1–4 (Amsterdam, 1983): 21–31; and also Vern L. Bullough, "Medieval Medical and Scientific Views of Women," *Viator* 4 (1973): 485–501. Also valuable is Thomas Laqueur, "Orgasm, Generation, and the Politics of Reproductive Biology," in *The Making of the Modern Body: Sexuality and Society in the Nineteenth Century*, ed. Catherine Gallagher and Thomas Laqueur (Berkeley and Los Angeles: University of California Press, 1987), 1–41.

43. O'Malley and Saunders, *Leonardo*, 20. (Vasari had noted Leonardo's study of Galen.) Leonardo's familiarity with Lucretius's *De rerum natura* is evident in his writings (for example, Richter, *Literary Works*, 2:373, no. 1492); according to O'Malley and Saunders (*Leonardo*, 454), he was influenced by Lucretius's statement that the fetus "is always fashioned out of the two seeds."

44. O'Malley and Saunders, *Leonardo*, 23.

45. Ibid., 456 (Q 1 12r; written c. 1510). For Galen's text, see *Galen: On the Usefulness of the Parts of the Body (De usu partium)*, translation, introduction, and commentary by Margaret Tallmadge May (Ithaca: Cornell University Press, 1968), 2:Books 14 and 15.

46. O'Malley and Saunders, *Leonardo*, 484 (Q 111 8v; c. 1510–12).

47. Ibid. Leonardo later repeats this important insight; see Richter, *Literary Works*, 1:101, no. 837.

48. O'Malley and Saunders, *Leonardo*, 472 (Q 1 1r; written c. 1504–9).

49. See also sheet Q 111 7v, representing one of Leonardo's few dissections of a human fetus, where he demonstrates the nourishment of the child by the mother's menstrual blood, conveyed through the umbilicus (O'Malley and Saunders, *Leonardo*, 482; dated c. 1510–12).

50. Richter, *Literary Works*, 35, no. 7 (Urb. 2b, 3a, Trat. 7).

51. Ibid., 2:86, no. 797.

52. Leicester 34r, Edward MacCurdy, *The Notebooks of Leonardo da Vinci*, arranged by E. MacCurdy (New York, 1938), 1:91, cited by Keele, "Genesis of the Mona Lisa," 147. On Leonardo's comparison of water and wind currents, see Kemp, *Leonardo*, chap. 2.

53. L. B. Alberti, *De Pictura*, esp. I.37 and III.55, in *Leon Battista Alberti, On Painting and On Sculpture*, ed. and trans., Cecil Grayson (London: Phaidon, 1972), 73–75, 99. Although Alberti does not specifically distinguish *natura naturans* from *natura naturata*, implicit in his argument is a recognition that the source of underlying principles is differentiated from those things in the natural world that artists study.

54. Made for *The Painter's Manual*, published in 1525; see *The Painter's Manual by Albrecht Dürer*, translation and commentary by Walter L. Strauss (New York: Abaris Books, 1977), 435. H. Diane Russell, in *Eva/Ave: Women in Renaissance and Baroque Prints* (Washington, D.C.: National Gallery of Art, 1990), 23, offers a related reading of this print. The print is also illustrated in Broude and Garrard, *Expanding Discourse*, chapter 3, fig. 12.

55. For the connection between the Neoplatonic twin Venuses and Botticelli's *Primavera* and *Birth of Venus*, see especially E. H. Gombrich, "Botticelli's Mythologies; a Study in the Neoplatonic Symbolism of His Circle," *Journal of the Warburg and Courtauld Institutes* 18 (1955): 16ff.; Erwin Panofsky, *Renaissance and Renascences* (Stockholm: Almqvist and Wiksell, 1960), 191–200; and Edgar Wind, *Pagan Mysteries of the Renaissance* (New York: Barnes and Noble, 1968), chaps. 7 and 8.

56. See Kemp, *Leonardo*, 93ff., for a summary of the arguments concerning the relationship between the Paris and London versions and their dating.

57. Aristotle, *Metaphysics*, Book Delta, 1072 a, b; and *Generation of Animals*, A3. See also R. G. Collingwood, *The Idea of Nature* (Oxford: Clarendon Press, 1945), 80–82.

58. For example, Clark, *Leonardo*, 117, and Kemp, *Leonardo*, 270.

59. Describing a rocky landscape, Leonardo wrote: "Drawn by my eager desire, wishing to see the great manifestation of the various and strange shapes made by formative nature, I wandered some way among gloomy rocks, coming to the entrance of a great cavern, in front of which I stood for some time, stupefied and incomprehending such a thing. . . . Suddenly two things arose in me, fear and desire: fear of the menacing darkness of the cavern; desire to see if there was any marvellous thing within it" (B.L.115r; written c. 1480). This passage was also connected with the *Virgin of the Rocks* by Kemp, *Leonardo*, 99.

60. The sheet of studies for the *Virgin of the Rocks*, in the Metropolitan Museum of Art, is reproduced in Broude and Garrard, *Expanding Discourse*, chap. 3, fig. 17. Between 1478 and 1483, Leonardo developed at least five Madonna and Child compositions, only one of which seems to have been prompted by a commission (see Kemp, *Leonardo*, 53).

61. Kemp, *Leonardo*, 226, emphasizes political meaning in the pictures. The Burlington Cartoon and the Louvre painting are usually dated c. 1498 and c. 1508–10, respectively; Kemp suggests a dating of c. 1508 for the Cartoon. Patricia Leighten has located the Burlington Cartoon within a tradition of images that emphasize the physicality of birth and the generative cycle; see her "Leonardo's *Burlington House Cartoon*," *Rutgers Art Review* 2 (1981): 31–42. Meyer Schapiro, in his "Leonardo and Freud: An Art-Historical Study," *Journal of the History of Ideas* 17, no. 2 (1956): 147–178, discusses the Virgin with Saint Anne as a compositional type popular around 1500.

62. Although Leonardo did not invent the Virgin and Saint Anne theme, he concentrated and charged an essentially static and anecdotal pyramidal group with symbolic meaning, through complex formal linkings between figures and landscape. See Alexander Perrig, "Leonardo: Die Anatomie der Erde," *Jahrbuch der Hamburger Kunstsammlungen* 25 (1980): 51–80, who interprets the landscape backgrounds of the *Virgin of the Rocks*, *Mona Lisa*, and *Saint Anne* in conjunction with Leonardo's geological studies, and also as emotional correlatives of the paintings' subjects.

63. Richter, *Literary Works*, 1:371–22, no. 660. For the painter's competition with nature, see the adjacent no. 662.

64. Ibid., 1:367, no. 652; the same text appears in the Trattato (Richter, ibid., 1:38, no. 13).

65. Ibid., 2:100–101, no. 837.

66. For the contemporary debate about essentialism (the belief that there are fixed, unchanging, and "natural" essences of femaleness), see Diana Fuss, *Essentially Speaking: Feminism, Nature and Difference* (New York: Routledge, 1989).

15

Mothers and Daughters: Ancient and Modern Myths

Ellen Handler Spitz

As ivy clings to oak will I clasp her.
—Euripides, *Hecuba*

Psychoanalysis has tended, in its discussions of the entanglements between women, to weight negative aspects—recalcitrant guilt, envy, and rage. This essay seeks to redistribute that balance by adding to the scales a goodly measure of the strength that derives from female-to-female intergenerational bonding. The following pages are dedicated to one regal grandmother, two wise daughters, a stepmother who never quite realized that she had become a real mother, and a very real mother who died too young but whose articulate voice can still be heard, softly modulated, throughout these pages.[1]

Inspired by a small head of Demeter in Sigmund Freud's collection of antiquities, this essay offers a "thematic" reading of the ancient myth of Demeter and Persephone with the interpolation of selected texts of contemporary fiction that also foreground the relations between mothers and daughters.[2] These include: *The Joy Luck Club*,[3] *Annie John*,[4] *Lovingkindness*,[5] *A Raisin in the Sun*,[6] and *The Shawl*.[7] These texts were authored by women of varied racial and ethnic backgrounds, and my aim here is in no way to flatten out the many differences between them nor between them and the ancient texts in which the Demeter–Persephone myth is inscribed. Rather, I have created a bricolage, an intertext, which not only uses but also occasionally challenges psychoanalysis (art always being, as Freud said, in the avant-garde of theory, rather than the other way around) and raises more questions than it answers.[8]

Freud, having read Ovid, clearly knew the story of Demeter and Persephone at least in its Latin version. Yet, although in all its forms it addresses the theme of mother-daughter relations—which Freud eventually came to recognize as central to female development, for he asked "What does the little girl require of her mother?"—he never chose to interrogate this exemplary myth in terms of his own important question.[9] His scattered references to it curiously bypass its central motif. He refers to Demeter only with regard to an incident that occurs in her daughter's absence[10] and to Persephone with no mention of her relationship to her mother.[11] Freud's failure to address the bond between the two women—which is the subject of the myth—suggests that it may yet prove a rich source for the current psychoanalytic exploration of this theme. In this spirit, I offer the following retelling, an amalgam and an abridgement, which draws on two principal sources—the ancient Greek "Homeric Hymn to Demeter" and Ovid's tale, "Calliope tells of the rape of Proserpine," from *The Metamorphoses*.

In relating a mother's search for her lost daughter, the story of Demeter and Persephone gives priority to one role, namely, that of the mother, over that of the daughter. Yet, its fabric importantly suggests that daughter and mother are one and that their experiences both reciprocate and replicate each other. This is a point that pervades Amy Tan's recent best-selling novel, *The Joy Luck Club,* which is dedicated "To my mother and the memory of her mother." A finely brocaded work, this text explores spatiotemporal and cultural continuities and disjunctions between four sets of Chinese-American mothers and daughters, and it offers a moment when one daughter, still a young child, suddenly reencounters the all-but-forgotten mother who had been wrenched from her in her earliest childhood. Despite the years of separation, however, this mother proves to be no stranger. At the moment of meeting, An-Mei Hsu, trying to recapture it years later for her own daughter Rose, says: "I tried to keep very still but my heart felt like crickets scratching to me out of a cage. My mother must have heard [in other words, heard *into* the little girl's heart], because she looked up. And when she did, *I saw my own face looking back at me.*"[12] Later, this same character An-Mei Hsu, describes—again for the benefit of her own daughter—a scene in which she watched transfixed as her mother took a knife and cut a piece of flesh out of her own arm and, bleeding and crying, put it into a soup to feed to her own aged, dying mother in a desperate attempt to prolong her ebbing life.

This focus on the immediacy, intensity, and physicality of identifications is central also to Jamaica Kincaid's *Annie John,* where the title character, growing up on the island of Antigua in the Caribbean, describes her discordant, indissoluble bond with a mother who has exactly the same name as her own:

> Something I could not name just came over us, and suddenly I had never loved anyone so or hated anyone so. But to say hate—what did I mean by that? Before, if I hated someone I simply wished the person dead. But I couldn't wish my *mother* dead. If my *mother* died, what would become of *me?* I couldn't imagine my life without her. Worse than that, if my *mother* died *I* would have to die, too, and even less than I could imagine my mother dead could I imagine *myself* dead."[13]

Such passages, besides scoring deep and ambivalent congruities, also connect, as does the Demeter–Persephone myth, the theme of death with that of the mother-daughter relation—a link with many layers of meaning to which we shall return.

Demeter, goddess of fertility and the harvest, thus a *mother* par excellence, adores her beautiful daughter Persephone who, while gathering flowers with other young girls in an idyllic landscape, plucks a fateful narcissus. This detail, the narcissus flower, is of interest because it recalls another comparable and contrasting myth—namely, that of an ill-fated male adolescent, the youthful Narcissus who fell in love with his own reflection in the water and thereby perished. Thus the flower may be seen as emblematic of self-involvement, of the girl's pleasure in her own loveliness, but also, perhaps, of her desire to add something to it. In evoking its namesake, it alludes both to convergences and to discontinuities between the bodily and developmental experiences of the genders.

According to the text, this sweet-smelling flower, the narcissus, is placed before Persephone as a lure by her father Zeus on behalf of his brother Hades, god of the underworld, who had seen the girl playing and developed a passion for her. As Persephone plucks the flower, the earth gapes open, and grim Hades appears in his golden chariot (the Homeric Hymn) drawn by deathless horses. Panic-stricken, the young girl cries out to her mother (Ovid) and to her father (the Homeric Hymn) to save her. Her entreaties are in vain. Zeus, merely a regal figurehead here, maintains his distance from her throughout the story, and, by staging her ravishment, may in fact be seen as enacting by proxy his own incestuous wishes toward her. Never is he portrayed as having direct contact with her; her entire filiation is bound up with her mother.

Thus, on this "Oedipal" level, the plot follows the paradigm articulated by Lévi-Strauss who, in addition to analyzing the structures of myth, theorized kinship as casting women in the role of a medium of exchange between men—a perspective that Freud himself did not precisely adopt but which might have served him well.[14] (In the Dora case, as has been much remarked, his lack of attention to this dimension of the material caused him to become in fact one of the very men among whom Dora was passed.)[15]

For our purposes here, therefore, it is worthwhile to consider—but to resist overemphasizing—the implicitly triadic structure of the mother-daughter relation. Clearly, initiation into heterosexual relations comes in this myth by means of trickery, violence, and betrayal by the father. But interestingly, this betrayal is considered as such only from the point of view of women. In Ovid, Zeus (or Jupiter as he is there called) protests Demeter's complaints that their child has been pirated. He claims, on the contrary, that his brother's deed "was no crime, but an act of love," and he staunchly upholds the lord of the underworld as a fitting husband for her.[16] According to him, even if Hades has no other qualities to recommend him, he is still, after all, a brother![17] Thus, the father rationalizes and reveals, possibly, his own vicarious pleasure in colluding with the scene of sexual violence.

Demeter's response to Persephone's disappearance has, on the other hand, elements of both narcissistic and object loss: she becomes by turns sorrowful, depressed, and bitterly indignant. Wandering over land and sea in an effort to discover the whereabouts of her beloved child, she enacts a sequence that uncannily prefigures the stages of mourning and melancholia Freud outlined in 1917.[18] Turning aggression inward, she tears the covering on her hair, refuses both food and drink, and ceases to bathe. This self-destructive behavior continues, fascinatingly, for precisely nine days—thus, symbolically, she replicates and magically undoes the nine months of her pregnancy. Upon learning finally that Zeus was party to the rape, her grief reaches fever pitch. Cutting herself off from all company of the gods, disfiguring herself, she assumes the appearance of a decrepit old woman whose childbearing years are over.

Shortly after this, in the course of her wanderings, however, she manages to "adopt," as it were, another woman's child. Partly to deny her loss and symbolically to recover Persephone, she "becomes" a mother again. Yet the child this time is a boy, and the incident has disturbing overtones. That a male child is chosen for the replacement suggests that Demeter, having once been forsaken by a daughter, must now ward off repetition of that loss by acquiring a new child of the opposite sex. She "steals" him, as it were, from his own mother. By breathing on him, clasping him to her bosom, and placing him each night in a fire in order to turn him into a god, she seeks utterly to possess him—and thus to separate him irrevocably from his own mother. In this way, under the guise of beneficence, she gives rein to aggression. Turning passive into active, she relives her own trauma in reverse by inflicting it on another woman.

Ovid, in his more florid Roman style, also dramatizes this cameo. Here, we find Demeter given a sweet barley drink by a woman who takes pity on her in her grief. When, however, this woman's young son taunts the goddess with being greedy (a suggestive detail), Demeter turns on the boy and, enraged at his insult, rewards his mother's kindness to her by hurling the drink into the child's face, thereby setting off in him a grotesque metamorphosis. As his mother watches in horror, her child's skin puckers, spots develop, and legs sprout on him where arms had once been. As she reaches out to touch him, he shrivels up into the form of a loathsome lizard and slithers away to hide, leaving her to tears of grief and astonishment. Thus, here too, Demeter causes another mother to suffer a loss comparable to her own.

It is possible as well to read this incident as revealing by displacement the depths of Demeter's unacknowledged ambivalence toward Persephone—not only, on the Oedipal level, her jealousy toward the girl as the (incestuously) preferred object of the father and her envy for her "flowering," her burgeoning fertility, but also, on a deeper level, Demeter's wish to appropriate unto herself *all* the prerogatives of motherhood. On this reading, the boy child, arriving on scene subsequent to Persephone's abduction, can be seen as representing in Demeter's fantasy her own daughter's future child—a child whom she wishes to appropriate and possess. Furthermore, this boy child may, it has been suggested, represent to her the treacherous male world that has so recently betrayed her.[19]

The intensity of Demeter's comingled sexuality and aggression toward this "new child" are, however, sensed by the boy's real mother, and a confrontation between the two women occurs. This is the sole moment in the narrative where any aggression between women is represented. Direct relations between mother and daughter are, as we have seen, portrayed only as loving while aggression is projected outward onto the predatory males. Here, however, in the frame within the frame, a catalytic moment of open anger toward another woman seems to release Demeter from her depression.[20] She now reveals herself in all her glory as a mighty goddess and, rejecting the substitute child, simultaneously throws off her melancholy disguise. "Thrusting old age away from her," goes the text, "beauty spread round about her and a lovely fragrance was wafted from her sweet-smelling robes . . . golden tresses spread down over her shoulders."[21]

Vehemently now, having regained her royal status, she redirects her wrath outward. In order to punish Zeus, she plays power games with him by withholding her fertility. Permitting nothing to grow on earth, scourging the land with a cruel famine, she coerces him finally into returning Persephone to her. Meanwhile, the girl, pining for her mother among the dark shades of the dead, rejoices when Hermes descends, at the bidding of Zeus, to rescue her. Hades, however, has managed meanwhile to slip some pomegranate seeds into her mouth, the pomegranate being (among its many meanings) redolent of heterosexual union with its seeds and blood-red juice; thus, furtively, he has bound her to him forever.

The myth, as is well known, is resolved by compromise: partially restored to Demeter, Persephone, because she has tasted the fruit, cannot fully sever her ties to her husband. According to different versions, she spends two-thirds or one-half of the year with Demeter and the other half or third in Hades. During the seasons when mother and daughter are reunited, they are portrayed as radiantly happy, and the earth regains its fertility: "So did they then, with hearts at one, greatly cheer each other's soul and spirit with many an embrace: their hearts had relief from their griefs while each took and gave back joyousness."[22] By contrast, when Persephone returns to Hades, "her expression and temperament change instantly: [she becomes] so melancholy as to seem sad to Dis [Hades] himself;" while, in spite of this, she reigns as honored Queen of the Dead.[23]

One further detail must not be allowed to escape notice: Final reconciliation between daughter, mother, and Olympian Zeus is brought about through the agency of another goddess, Rhea, the mother of Demeter and grandmother of Persephone. Rhea's role is to ask her daughter to forgive her husband and to return with her to him and to the other gods at Olympus. For Demeter to acquiesce in this request, therefore, is to obey her own mother. Appearing thus as a crucial agent at the very end of the story, Rhea represents the fertility of the previous generation. Her presence bears special meaning for our theme because it marks a crucial axis of the myth—namely, a powerful matriarchal lineage—an axis of intergenerational gendered bonding—a line that may in fact be read as the spine of the story, etched fossil-like into the softer ground surrounding it. It is a line, moreover, that may easily escape those focused only on an Oedipal reading.

It is the selfsame line, however, evoked by Amy Tan, when she writes as follows in the persona of her character An Mei Hsu: "even though I taught my daughter the opposite, still she came out the same way! Maybe it is because she was born to me and she was born a girl. And I was born to my mother and I was born a girl. All of us are like stairs, one step after another, going up and down, but all going the same way."[24] This wonderful, only apparently paradoxical image from *The Joy Luck Club* uncannily conveys the repetitive perpendicularity of Persephone's movements as she mounts and descends between Hades and Demeter, the worlds of darkness and of light.

This power of a mother's mother over both death and life and her sudden appearance as "dea ex machina" at the end of the myth is a feature also of *Annie John,* where, late in the action, the young protagonist, now entering adolescence, falls ill with a malady that responds neither to conventional nor to island remedies. Unexpectedly, yet as if fated, her grandmother materializes magically from the neighboring island of Dominica and remains with her own daughter and granddaughter on Antigua until the child's recovery is secure: "[she] would come into my bed with me and stay until I was myself . . . again. I would lie on my side, curled up like a little comma, and [the grandmother] would lie next to me, curled up like a bigger comma, into which I fit."[25]

Many questions come to mind at this point, and, as with all art and myth, psychologically valid interpretations may logically contradict one another. How might these texts both illuminate and complicate Freud's own question as to what a little girl requires of her mother (and vice versa)? Does the ancient story represent or teach us anything about what we have come to call normal or pathological relations between a mother and a daughter? Does it offer some layering and combination of these? In celebrating the enduring power of the mother-daughter bond at the apparent expense of joyful heterosexuality, does it endorse its own solution or express wishes and fears—or fears of wishes and denials of fears? Precisely what wishes and fears are at stake? What developmental levels of fantasy are addressed? Does the myth correspond to female or to male fantasies or to both? The aggressive bridegroom figures clinically, for example, in dreams of both genders, and the fear of doing or experiencing damage in the act of intercourse is pervasive.

In order to focus on the mother-daughter dyad, the myth, as we have seen, relegates its male characters to the periphery, and this is likewise a feature of contemporary novels that treat the mother-daughter theme. Take, for example, Anne Roiphe's recent *roman à lettres, Lovingkindness*.[26] Here, a feminist scholar with a name strangely similar to Jamaica Kincaid's heroine (she is called Annie Johnson) struggles with herself over her mothering of a twenty-two-year-old daughter, Andrea, who, when the book begins, has not communicated with her mother for five months. Ideology and intellectualism have long served defensively to hide from this mother her own failure to provide boundaries for a child who now, after years of wild, self-destructive behavior, has suddenly telephoned collect from Jerusalem to announce that she is embracing a new life-style, namely, that of ultra-orthodox Judaism. This choice on her part represents, of course, a rebellious repudiation of her mother's feminist principles, but it also betokens a deeper need—an urgent need for external limits and values that might compensate adaptively for intrapsychic structures that have never fully developed. Fascinating here is the paradox that, because on a deep level, this mother and daughter *are* importantly connected (as in Annie Johnson with her own ambivalently devalued mother), Andrea's rejection of Annie's manifest (feminist) credo is precisely what makes possible at some point in the future (beyond the text of the novel) an identification of the two women *as mothers.* Such an intimation is made explicit by Annie's wishful fantasy in the closing paragraphs that she will one day have a granddaughter who will come from Israel to visit her: a *granddaughter.*

Early on in this book, however, the husband and father of Annie and Andrea is summarily introduced and immediately eliminated. Described as an ineffectual character, he walks out of a penthouse window in a state of extreme inebriation, and, although his ambiguous, surreal demise continues to haunt the text, it works strategically to free the author to treat mother and daughter exclusively as a dyad. Similarly, *Annie John,* while not eliminating its husband/father character totally, relegates him to a clearly subordinate status. Described as shorter than the mother physically, he is of decidedly lesser stature than she in the eyes of their pre-adolescent daughter and plays only a minor role in her life. In her words: "When my eyes rested on my father, I didn't think very much of the way he looked. But when my eyes rested on my mother, I found her beautiful."[27]

Likewise, the death of Lena's husband occurs before any action takes place in Lorraine Hansberry's play, *A Raisin in the Sun,* which is dedicated "To Mama: in gratitude for the dream."[28] The absence of the husband and father here leaves the stage open at the end of scene 1 for a uniquely powerful moment in American theater: Beneatha, fiercely independent, headstrong, and twenty, having just treated her mother to a barrage of typical adolescent jargon on her inalienable right to express herself, culminates with the statement: "God is just one idea I don't accept."[29]

The ensuing stage directions read:

(MAMA *absorbs this speech, studies her daughter and rises slowly and crosses to* BENEATHA *and slaps her powerfully across the face. After, there is only silence and the daughter drops her eyes from her mother's face, and* MAMA *is very tall before her.*)

MAMA: Now—you say after me, in my mother's house there is still God. . . . *In my mother's house* there is still God.[30]

Well acted, this scene conveys the sheer weight of ongoing maternal presence as it shapes the consciousness of a daughter. With keen insight, Lorraine Hansberry crafts Lena's contrasting behavior toward Beneatha and toward her son Walter Lee. Innately in tune with the headstrong young premed student who is obviously a second edition of herself, Lena readily guides, disciplines, supports, *and opposes* her; she knows she can count on Beneatha's strength, just as she can count on her own. With Walter Lee, on the other hand, her inventions falter and misfire, and she comes only painfully, and after loss, to a rapprochement with him.

In marginalizing triadic elements, therefore, both the Demeter–Persephone myth and its modern counterparts force us to recognize the power of *gendered sameness* and of biology—to see, in other words, that, because the girl *is* a second edition of her mother, their object relations are deeply structured by this sameness. Brilliantly, the ancient myth evokes this bodily identification through its cyclical content and its solution—which takes the changing and repeating seasons of the year as a figure for the periodicity of the female reproductive system.

Washing, water, and the female body figure prominently in both ancient and modern myth. Persephone is pictured near a deep lake of gliding waters[31] "playing with the deep-bosomed daughters of Oceanus" when she is abducted; as we have seen, Demeter refuses to bathe when she realizes she has lost her child; she searches over the seas; and (in Ovid) she learns the truth of Persephone's ravishment from a water nymph who has been changed into the water of her own sacred pool.[32] All the contemporary novels cited here take ocean as a metaphor for psychological distance between mothers and daughters (in *The Joy Luck Club*, it is the Pacific; in *Lovingkindness*, the Atlantic;

and in *Annie John* it is both the Caribbean Sea and the Atlantic), and dreamlike mother-daughter scenes of bathing and swimming are likewise featured. In each of these instances, external waters serve both to connect and to divide the women—and thus they serve as metaphors for the inner amniotic waters which originally united and divided the pair.

"My mother and I often took a bath together," writes Jamaica Kincaid in the mesmerizing voice of her young Antiguan heroine. "Sometimes it was just a plain bath, which didn't take very long. Other times, it was a special bath in which the barks and flowers of many different trees, together with all sorts of oils, were boiled in the same caldron. We would then sit in this bath in a darkened room with a strange-smelling candle burning away. As we sat in this bath, my mother would bathe different parts of my body; then she would do the same to herself."[33]

Anne Roiphe begins a passage, "I had been named Annie after my dead grandmother, Ann. My grandmother's picture was in a jade frame near my mother's bed."[34] Thus, she evokes the presence of a matriarchal lineage which itself becomes the frame for a scene in which her protagonist, as a little girl, sits waiting outside her mother's bedroom for her to wake up:

> I would lie on the carpet and put my face next to the crack at the bottom of the door. . . . I could stay in that position a long time. . . . I learned how to float with time as if on a raft in a becalmed sea. My mother's late sleeping habit had the effect of teaching me how to lie like a lizard waiting for a passing fly. It also taught me how to love through a closed door.[35]

Not insignificantly, as we have seen, this same little girl grows up to become a mother who, when *her* own daughter loves *her* through a closed door (by not communicating, for example, for months at a time or by loving through the closed doors of the Yeshiva Rachel), she struggles intellectually to make it somehow all right. The text continues: "Sometimes [my mother] would let me in the bathroom with her. I would sit on the toilet as she soaped in the tub. A small woman with soft folds all over her body."[36]

This passage, by juxtaposing images of grandmother, mother, and daughter with a small girl's feelings of loneliness and ambivalent attachment and the physical intimacy of beholding the mother's naked body (which is, of course, a future version of her own body), overlaid with the rich metaphor of the bath, when read alongside other, similar passages from related texts, seems to tap a kind of organic memory.

And, finally, from *Annie John,* a section that seems designed to tell Persephone's side of the ancient myth:

> The only way I could go into the water was if I was on my mother's back, my arms clasped tightly around her neck. . . . It was only then that I could forget how big the sea was, how far down the bottom could be . . . When we swam around in this way, I would think how much we were like the pictures of sea mammals I had seen, my mother and I, naked in the seawater.[37]

The passage goes on to describe the mother swimming by herself, leaving the little girl to play and watch on shore. Suddenly, however, the child realizes in terror that she has lost sight of her mother:

> My eyes searched the small area of water where she should have been, but I couldn't find her. I stood up and started to call out her name, but no sound would come out of my throat. A huge black space then opened up in front of me and I fell inside it. I couldn't see what was in front of me and I couldn't hear anything around me. I couldn't think of anything except that *my mother was no longer near me.*[38]

This episode, virtually a rewrite of Demeter's mythic loss and separation but from the daughter's viewpoint, ends, as does its prototype, with a reunion that is only partial and with a permanent rift having opened up between mother and daughter. Interestingly, it is at this point that fantasies of *mother and father together* emerge in the text, as do similar fantasies after the comparable bathing passage in Roiphe.

One of the points I stress here is that psychoanalytic theory, by structuring the relationships between women so exclusively around the pivotal figure of a male (or, in some accounts, the male organ) desired by both women (that is, the Oedipal paradigm: mother and daughter vying for the attentions of a husband/father), has tended to miss and to dismiss the intense, ongoing intergenerational relations among women inscribed by the texts I have quoted here—texts written within the past thirty years by gifted women of varied racial and ethnic backgrounds. Each of these texts, by temporarily assigning its male characters to the wings, forces its readers to gaze fixedly and not without discomfort at the female-to-female bond *as a primary structure* placed stage-center and under bright lights.

Classical psychoanalytic theory has posited the little girl as necessarily turning *away* from her mother. While acknowledging the intensity of early ties, Freud states: "[the girl's] attachment is forced away from her mother;"[39] "the turning away from her mother is an extremely important step in the course of a girl's development;"[40] "the attachment to the mother is bound to perish."[41] Our texts, however, indicate that daughter and mother, on the contrary, continue to search for each other throughout their lifetimes.

Current psychoanalytic literature,[42] while it does not deny the centrality of the girl's long dependence on the mother, frequently characterizes it with extreme negativity and expatiates on its "tenacity," "difficulty," "hostility," and "sadism."[43] Its accounts, frequently drawn from the associations of patients who have had "deeply unsatisfying relationship[s] with their actual mother[s] . . . in which the daughter experienced her mother as withholding or withdrawn and as hostile and destructive . . . [yet] found herself, to her continual unpleasant surprise, still seeking her mother's love and approval," tend to disregard the rich preserves of strength, wisdom, self-affirmation, and challenge that inhere in the mother-daughter relation—qualities which, however, in some case histories, are transferred to the patient's new relationship with a female analyst.[44] Without hope, without promise, however, no conflict can maintain its claim; thus, paradoxically, it is precisely the image of *good* mother-daughter relations (inscribed on one level of reading by the Demeter–Persephone myth) that keeps both conflict and communication in play.

Fortunately, adult women, both growing and aging, and young girls in various stages of development can and do cherish ongoing meaningful relations with each other while simultaneously nurturing precious ties to fathers, brothers, male lovers, husbands, and sons. The Demeter–Persephone myth, however, in dramatizing its version of this state of things, ends manifestly in a compromise, but in fact offers a stark either-or solution that can be seen as the simple inverse of the classic psychoanalytic position, which, in its most extreme form, seems equally stark.

Whereas the latter has tended to conceptualize the mother-daughter bond as archaic and atavistic, a stage in female development that must be superseded and "left behind;" the myth, on the other hand, portrays it (manifestly) as ongoing but uncomplicated, as thoroughly tender, loving, and fulfilling. Neither view is adequate, for as our rich literary texts teach, the bond can neither be understood *only* as a positive source of continuing strength nor *only* as a regressive pull or unpleasant site of conflict throughout the individual life history of women. In fact, it is all of the above.

Dreading her loss of self and of object, a mother goes, as we have seen, in search of a daughter whom she must keep. What does this mean? At what price is Persephone rescued from Hades and returned to earth? An all-too-obvious psychoanalytic reading might cast Demeter as an omnipotent *pre-Oedipal* mother, more powerful than all males or perhaps as a narcissistic mother who, under the pretext of salvation, sacrifices her child in order to maintain hegemony and control.[45]

On this reading, Persephone reverts to her mother merely to gratify the latter's need. Not only barred from achieving loving heterosexual relations, she does not within the mythic narrative become herself a (biological) mother. On this moot point, it is possible however to privilege the allegorical nature of the text and interpret Persephone's participation each spring in the refertilization of the earth as a species of symbolic motherhood. In any case, the negative reading offers us a Demeter who only superficially rescues a cherished and victimized child; in fact, she herself becomes the victimizer, using and abusing her daughter for her own ends. By retrieving Persephone and taking her once again to her bosom, she asserts her eternal and *exclusive* prerogative to *be the mother*. (One conjures images here of little girls "playing house," vying with one another as to who will "be the mother.")

To interpret thus, however, is to do so *against the grain* of the manifest content and tone of the myth. It is to deny that Persephone's initiation into heterosexuality comes via rape and perhaps even weakly disguised incest and to misprise the very mood and language of the original texts, which clearly exalt the symmetry, mutuality, and tenderness of the mother-daughter bond. Idealization may, however, serve to defend against underlying pathology, and so-called unconflicted love may cover a tragic inability to separate.

What all these texts teach, however, is that on some level mother and daughter *do not and cannot ever separate*. Rather, they portray deeply felt needs for maintaining ties that the changing conditions of social reality have not significantly altered. Clinical evidence, moreover, reveals that women require not only stable maternal introjects but ongoing contact with primary maternal objects—especially at moments associated with fertility—at menarche, marriage, pregnancy, birth, and the nurturance of children.

The ancient myth, which tells its story manifestly from the mother's side, stresses Demeter's desire to be available as an ongoing presence in Persephone's life, to play an active role and to foster identifications between her daughter and herself, but this is equally true in reverse. It relates the suffering attendant upon their inevitable separations and the gradual acceptance of changes in their relationship. Mothers and daughters who reestablish rapport after the discord of adolescence stand to discover more fully their own unique capacities for nurturance—a point underscored in the myth by the presence in the end of the grandmother, as well as by the closing pages of Anne Roiphe's book where, as we have seen, the mother becomes in fantasy a grandmother herself.

Cynthia Ozick, interviewed recently on the subject of her tragic masterpiece, *The Shawl,* a savage tale of a mother who survives at the price of sanity the murder of her infant daughter in a Polish concentration camp, recalled the memory of her own grandmother.[46] In trying to answer the interviewer's questions about why she, an author who never experienced the Holocaust, chooses to write about it, she evoked an image of her grandmother "weeping and beating her breast" upon learning of the British White Paper in 1939 (an act that cut off, for German Jews, all hope of escape from the Nazi terror). " 'Maybe I was born to be a witness,' she said. 'I got it from my grandmother. I grew up always as a witness'."[47]

The ancient myth associates youthful innocence in an enclosed female space with playfulness and freedom from care; marriage, on the other hand—in the form of Hades—is equated with brutality and death. For Persephone, the joys of marriage and heterosexual love are apparently absent. Despite her restoration to mother, her sacrifice continues, and she fails, as queen of another realm, to establish a satisfying existence there. This dark parallelism of nuptials and death evokes other Greek legends inscribed in the tragedies, such as that of Sophocles' Antigone, who, as she is led to her death in the cave, is said to be marrying somebody in Hades, and Euripides' Iphigenia, the pitiable daughter of Agamemnon and Clytemnestra, whose father, after agreeing to have her throat cut so that the winds may blow as the ships set sail for Troy, laments that Hades will marry her before long.

Thus, sacrifice, marriage, and death are interwoven if not equated in ancient Greek culture, and shards of such beliefs continue even in our time to appear in fantasies and to deform the feminine psyche.[48] Fed by pervasive visual and literary tropes, and simultaneously denied by overidealization in the form of other pervasive myths exemplified by such tales as "Sleeping Beauty" and "Cinderella," where to marry is "to live happily ever after," they deserve to be more widely addressed by contemporary writing on women's anxieties and conflicts.

It would be inaccurate to say that Freud evinced no interest in these complexities. Yet, despite his many references to Greek culture, his theoretical attention remained riveted on the towering figure of Oedipus whose tale, he firmly believed, could stand alone as a paradigm to which all others—even when the protagonists were female—could be referred if not reduced.[49] We have seen here, however, that the image of Demeter, mythical mother, symbol of the harvest, wandering land and sea in search of her daughter (who is also herself), offers another paradigm which cannot be mapped directly onto or equated with the Oedipus myth.

Among the prominent motifs that have emerged in this paper are: (1) the deep bodily identification of mother and daughter, which weaves a cord between them that, though it may at times rip or fray in both pain and anger, can never be completely broken; (2) the importance to a woman of becoming, being, and remaining a mother (a desire that may, in contemporary culture, find many diverse paths of sublimation); (3) the wish to process in perpetuity the power conferred by this role, a power that then encompasses in fantasy both birth and death, which are, in the unconscious, equated (here, on the subject of motherhood and death, I wish to quote a passage by Cynthia Ozick, who writes in *The Shawl*, "Motherhood—I've always known this—is a profound distraction from philosophy, and all philosophy is rooted in suffering over the passage of time. I mean the *fact* of motherhood, the physiological fact. To have the power to create another human being, to be the instrument of such a mystery"—is thus to triumph over death);[50] (4) a recognition of a mourning process on the part of both mother and daughter as they experience the inevitable changes in their relationship; and (5) the significance of intergenerational gendered bonding, of a matrilineal filiation, which deeply etches itself into the lives of women and affects them in ways underexplored by psychoanalysis and structuralism, theories content for so many years to construe women as a variant on, as complementary to, opposite of, even occasionally as inferior to, the male as both model and norm.

Thus, to ponder the myth of Demeter and Persephone in the light of recent literature by and about women is to grasp its significance, longevity, and power and to open rich possibilities for the further elaboration of feminine psychology.

One classicist has written of the myth as encompassing a circularity, a self-containedness that excludes man, and by this, he of course means *mankind* as opposed to the *gods*.[51] But the interpretation of gender works as well. Demeter and Persephone, doubles, mother and maiden—each contains the other within herself. Descending and retreating, the tale moves within a closed system, like the generative earth, with man ploughing and playing in it a crucial rather than a central role.

In closing, I share a more general reflection: psychoanalysis is a study not merely of the ways in which the past constructs the present but of the ways in which the present constructs the past. As such, it offers hypotheses rather than conclusions. Its hypotheses, however, exactly like the great myths, have power to exert far-reaching influence over human lives, both now and in the future. For this, each one of us who works with its ideas must take serious responsibility, and to do so fully means not only to "use" theory but to reflect critically on it, to continue to reinterpret it, to be able both to understand and to imagine alternatives—to exercise that freedom of mind, that openness to possibility which, as I have demonstrated here, is fostered by our contact with the very real, invented worlds of the arts.

Notes

1. A version of this essay was read to the Washington Society for Psychoanalytic Psychology on 24 September 1989. Several sections are adapted from my catalogue essay, "Psychoanalysis and the Legacies of Antiquity" in *Freud and Art: His Personal Collection of Antiquities,* ed. Lynn Gamwell and Richard Wells (New York: Abrams, 1989). A version appears as Chapter 8 of the author's book, *Image and Insight* (New York: Columbia University Press, 1991). Grateful acknowledgment is due the Fund for Psychoanalytic Research of the American Psychoanalytic Association and to the Getty Center for the History of Art and the Humanities. For their thoughtful reading and valuable discussion. I would like to thank Mary Ann Caws, Helene P. Foley, Marilyn Arthur, Muriel Gold Morris, Lisa Burkhalter, Ruth F. Lax, and Joanna Burnstine Strauss.

2. See Ellen Handler Spitz, *Art and Psyche* (New Haven: Yale University Press, 1985).

3. Amy Tan, *The Joy Luck Club* (New York: Putnam, 1989).

4. Jamaica Kincaid, *Annie John* (New York: New American Library, 1983).

5. Anne Roiphe, *Lovingkindness* (New York: Summit Books, 1987).

6. Lorraine Hansberry, *A Raisin in the Sun* (1959, New York: New American Library, 1987).

7. Cynthia Ozick, *The Shawl* (New York: Summit Books, 1987).

8. Sigmund Freud, "Delusions and Dreams in Jensen's *Gradiva,*" in *Standard Edition,* 9:3–95.

9. Sigmund Freud, "Female Sexuality," in *Standard Edition,* 19:225–43.

10. Sigmund Freud, "A Mythological Parallel to a Visual Obsession," in *Standard Edition,* 14:337–38.

11. Sigmund Freud, "The Theme of the Three Caskets," in *Standard Edition,* 12:291–301.

12. Tan, *The Joy Luck Club,* 45, emphasis added.

13. Kincaid, *Annie John,* 88, emphasis added.

14. Claude Lévi-Strauss, *The Elementary Structures of Kinship,* trans. James Harle Bell, Richard von Sturmer, and Rodney Needham (Boston: Beacon, 1969).

15. See Charles Bernheimer and Claire Kahane, eds., *In Dora's Case* (New York: Columbia University Press, 1985).

16. Ovid, *Metamorphoses,* trans. Mary I. Innes (Harmondsworth, Middlesex, England: Penguin, 1955), 130.

17. Ibid.

18. See Sigmund Freud, "Mourning and Melancholia," in *Standard Edition,* 14:239–58.

19. See Marilyn Arthur, "Politics and Pomegranates: An Interpretation of the Homeric Hymn to Demeter," *Arethusa* 10 (1977): 7–47.

20. Ibid.

21. "The Homeric Hymn to Demeter" in *Hesiod, The Homeric Hymns, and Homerica,* trans. H.G. Evelyn-White (Cambridge: Harvard University Press, 1924), 309.

22. Ibid., 321.

23. Ovid, *Metamorphoses,* 131.

24. Tan, *The Joy Luck Club,* 215.

25. Kincaid, *Annie John,* 125, 126.

26. See note 5.

27. Kincaid, *Annie John,* 18.

28. See note 6.

29. Hansberry, *A Raisin in the Sun,* 51.

30. Ibid., emphasis added.

31. Ovid, *Metamorphoses,* 126.

32. *Homeric Hymn,* 289.

33. Kincaid, *Annie John,* 14.

34. Roiphe, *Lovingkindness,* 20.

35. Ibid., 22.

36. Ibid., 23.

37. Kincaid, *Annie John,* 42.

38. Ibid., 43, emphasis added.

39. Freud, "Female Sexuality," 235.

40. Ibid., 239.

41. Ibid., 234.

42. See, for example, Nini Herman, *Too Long a Child: The Mother-Daughter Dyad* (London: Free Association Books, 1989).

43. E. Kirsten Dahl, "Daughters and Mothers: Oedipal Aspects of the Witch-Mother," *Psychoanalytic Study of the Child* 44 (1989): 267–80.

44. Ibid., 268; see also Elizabeth Young-Bruehl, "Looking for Anna Freud's Mother," *Psychoanalytic Study of the Child* 44 (1989): 391–408.

45. See Alice Miller, *The Drama of the Gifted Child* (New York: Basic Books, 1981).

46. See note 7.

47. Quoted in Richard Bernstein, "Being Nice or Rotten in Writing," *New York Times* (2 October 1989), C15 and C21.

48. See Nicole Loraux, *Tragic Ways of Killing a Woman,* trans. Anthony Forster (Cambridge: Harvard University Press, 1987).

49. Freud states: "I should like to insist that . . . the beginnings of religion, morals, society and art converge in the Oedipus complex. This is in complete agreement with the psychoanalytic finding that the same complex constitutes the nucleus of all neuroses, so far as our present knowledge goes. It seems to me a most surprising discovery that the problems of social psychology, too, should prove soluble on the basis of one single concrete point—man's relation to his father" ("Totem and Taboo," *Standard Edition,* 13:156–57).

50. Ozick, *The Shawl,* 41.

51. Walter Burkert, *Structure and History in Greek Mythology and Ritual* (Berkeley and Los Angeles: University of California Press, 1979).

16

The Image of Women in Film: A Defense of a Paradigm

Noël Carroll

Introduction

Feminism is the most visible movement in film criticism today, and the most dominant trend in that movement is psychoanalytically informed. Psychoanalytic feminism came to this position in film studies at the very latest by the early to mid-1980s. Before the consolidation and ascendancy of this particular variety of feminism, earlier approaches to the study of women and film included the search for a suppressed canon of women filmmakers—a feminist version of the auteur theory—and the study of the image of women in films, primarily the image of women in films by men. Neither of these approaches mandated a reliance on psychoanalysis, though, of course, one could pursue these research programs while also embracing psychoanalysis.

My particular interest in this essay is to defend the study of the image of women in film, regarding that project as logically independent from the resort to psychoanalysis. In speaking of this approach to feminist film criticism, I have in mind writing on cinema from the early seventies like Molly Haskell's *From Reverence to Rape* which paralleled research in literary studies such as Kate Millett's *Sexual Politics*.

Work of this sort called to our attention the ways the imagery of women in our culture recurringly portrayed them through a limited, constraining, and ultimately oppressive repertory of characterizations. For example, in film, it was noted that very often the options for depicting were strongly structured by the dichotomy of the mother versus the whore. Insofar as the ways of representing women in popular media in some way influences or reinforces the way real women may be construed, the study of the recurrent imagery of women in film, especially where the relevant options were either impoverished and/or distorting, provided an inroad into one of the sources, or, at least, resources of sexism in the broader society.[1]

Clearly, the study of the image of women in film could proceed without commitment to psychoanalytic theory. However, that is not what happened. As a participant in the evolution of film theory and history, my own sense is that the project of studying the image of women in film was superseded by psychoanalysis due to a feeling that this project, as practiced by early feminists, suffered from being too naively empirical. It appeared to involve meandering from genre to genre, from period to period, and even from film to film, accumulating a mass of observations that, however interesting, were also thought to be theoretically ragtag. Psychoanalysis, in contrast, provided a means to incorporate many of the scattered insights of the image of women in film approach (henceforth, generally called simply "the image approach"), while also sharpening the theoretical direction of feminist research. That is, psychoanalysis could provide not only a theoretical framework with which to organize many of the discoveries of the first wave of film feminism, but also a powerful program for further research.

This, of course, is not the whole story. Many film feminists were also interested in the origins and reinforcement of sexual difference in our culture, and in this respect, psychoanalysis, as a putative scientific discipline, had the advantage of having theories about this, albeit theories whose patriarchal biases would require modifications by feminists.

The purpose of this paper is to attempt to defend feminist film studies of the image of women in film approach, where that is understood as having no necessary commitment to psychoanalysis. In order to carry out this defense, I will sketch some of the shortcomings of the psychoanalytic model, but I will also indicate that the image approach can be supplied with a respectable theoretical basis drawn from the contemporary philosophy of the emotions. My strategy will be to consider psychoanalytic feminism and the image approach as potentially rival research programs; I will show that the psychoanalytic approach has a number of liabilities which can be avoided by the image approach, while also showing that the image of women in film model need not be thought of as irredeemably sunk in atheoretical naïveté.[2]

The first section that follows will outline some of the shortcomings of psychoanalytic feminism in film studies, and the section that follows it will propose some theoretical credentials for the image of women in film model. I will not address the purported advantage of psychoanalysis to provide a theory of sexual differentiation. That would involve a discussion of the adequacy of psychoanalysis as a scientific theory of development, and I obviously do not have the space to enter that issue. Consequently, the objections I raise with respect to psychoanalytic-feminist film criticism will not depend on contesting the scientific pretensions of psychoanalysis, though I should add that I am very skeptical about them. Nevertheless, I shall try to restrict my objections to ones that can be adjudicated within the bounds of film theory.

Furthermore, my opposition to the psychoanalytic model in feminist film criticism in no way implies either logically or as a matter of fact any opposition to feminism as such. The issue is between different models of feminist film criticism. I do not believe that an endorsement of feminism carries with it a theoretical commitment to psychoanalysis.

Mulvey, Psychoanalysis, and Visual Pleasure

At present, as already indicated, it appears fair to say that the most active area in feminist film studies is psychoanalytic in orientation. Moreover, there are subtle differences and debates between the major, feminist-psychoanalytic film critics. As a result, it is impossible in an essay of this scale to chart all the positions that might be correctly identified as feminist-psychoanalytic film criticism, nor could one hope to develop objections to every variation in the field. Consequently, in this section of my essay, selectivity is unavoidable. Specifically, in developing my objections to psychoanalytic feminism in contemporary film studies, I shall focus on Laura Mulvey's seminal essay "Visual Pleasure and Narrative Cinema."[3]

I have chosen this essay for several reasons. First, it can lay claim to being the inaugural polemic of feminist, psychoanalytic film criticism. Second, it is widely reprinted and widely taught. If someone knows just one essay of the psychoanalytic school, it is likely to be this one. And, even though many feminist film critics have registered objections to it and have tried to qualify and expand it, it remains perhaps the major introductory text to the field. One charge that might be made against my choice of this essay for scrutiny might be that it is somewhat dated in its specific claims. However, in response, I would maintain that many of the theoretical tendencies which I intend to criticize in Mulvey's essay continue to plague psychoanalytic film feminism, even in those cases where other psychoanalytically-inclined feminists may explicitly wish to modify Mulvey's approach.[4]

The uncontroversial premise of Mulvey's essay is that the Hollywood cinema's success involves, undoubtedly among other things, the manipulation of the audience's visual pleasure. Moreover, Mulvey hypothesizes that the visual pleasure found in movies reflects patterns of visual fascination in the culture at large, a culture that is patriarchal. And she argues that it is important for feminists to identify those patterns of visual fascination, particularly in order to challenge them. Here it is useful to recall that Mulvey is a leading feminist filmmaker. So her meditations on the resources of visual pleasure in Hollywood film are explicitly motivated by an interest in developing a countercinema, one in which the patriarchal levers of visual fascination exercised by Hollywood will be subverted.

According to Mulvey, one place to look for a theoretical framework that will enable an interrogation of patterns of visual fascination is psychoanalysis. Psychoanalysis has a theory of visual pleasure or scopophilia; so it is at least a candidate for answering questions about cinematic visual pleasure. However, it must be noted that Mulvey's embrace of psychoanalysis seems to be unargued. Rather, she announces the need for theoretical vocabularies and generalizations, and then she endorses psychoanalysis simply because it has them. She does not ask whether there are rival theoretical frameworks to psychoanalysis which might also serve her purposes; she does not consider any problems concerning the scientific status of psychoanalysis; she does not weigh the shortcomings of psychoanalysis against the advantages of competing models. Her acceptance of psychoanalysis appears almost uncritically pragmatic: we need a theory of visual pleasure; psychoanalysis has one, so let's use it.

This unquestioning acceptance of the *scientific* authority of psychoanalysis is a continuing feature of epistemologically dubious merit in contemporary feminist film criticism.[5] Where psychoanalytic hypotheses are not marred by obvious sexism, psychoanalytic feminists tend to be willing to accept them without exploring their possible logical flaws, empirical shortcomings, or relative disadvantages with respect to other theoretical frameworks. In this, they follow Mulvey's lead. However, though I will not dwell on this issue now, I believe that this methodological oversight, in the opening moves of psychoanalytic feminism, with respect to theory choice, compromises feminist-psychoanalytic film criticism fundamentally.[6]

From psychoanalysis, Mulvey inherits the observation that scopophilia is targeted at the human form. To this, then, she adds an empirical generalization, presumably one independent of psychoanalysis, that in film there is a division of labor in terms of the portrayal of the human form.[7] Men are characterized as active agents; women are displayed in order to be looked at. Men do things; women are objects of erotic contemplation—so many pinups or attested images of beauty.

Women are passive; men are active. Men carry the narrative action forward; women are the stuff of ocular spectacle, there to serve as the locus of the male's desire to savor them visually. Indeed, Mulvey maintains, onscreen, women in Hollywood films tend to slow down the narrative or arrest the action, since action must often be frozen, for example, in order to pose female characters so as to afford the opportunity for their erotic contemplation. For example, a female icon, like Raquel Welch before some prehistoric terror, will be posed statuelike so that male viewers can appreciate her beauty. Backstage musical numbers are useful devices for accommodating this narrative exigency, since they allow the narrative to proceed—insofar as the narrative just involves putting on a show—while lavishing attention on the female form.

For Mulvey the female form in Hollywood film becomes a passive spectacle whose function is, first and foremost, to be seen. Here the relevant perceiving subject may be identified as the male viewer, and/or the male character, who, through devices like point-of-view editing, serves as the delegate, in the fiction, for the male audience member (who might be said to identify with the male character in point-of-view editing).[8] This idea may be stated in terms of saying that in Hollywood film, women are the object of the look or the gaze.

What appears to be meant by this is that scenes are blocked, paced, and staged, and the camera is set up relative to that blocking in order to maximize the display potential of the female form. Undoubtedly, as John Berger has argued, many of the schemata for staging the woman as a display object are inherited from the tradition of Western easel painting, where an elaborate scenography for presenting female beauty in frozen moments was developed.[9] Calling this scenography, which *does* function to facilitate male interests in erotic contemplation, "the look" or "the gaze," however, is somewhat misleading since it suggests that the agency is literally located in a perceiving subject, whereas it is literally articulated through blocking, pacing, and staging relative to the camera. What is true, nevertheless, is that this blocking, pacing, and staging is governed by the aim of facilitating the male perceiving subject's erotic interests in the female form, which could be said to be staged in a way that approximates maximally satisfying those interests. And it is this sense—that the image of the woman in Hollywood film is constructed through scenography, blocking, pacing and so on in order to display her for male erotic contemplation—that feminist-psychoanalytic critics invoke when they say that the gaze in Hollywood film is masculine. Indeed, these practices of blocking and staging could be said to impose a male gaze on female spectators of Hollywood film, where that means that female spectators are presented with images of the female form that have been staged functionally in order to enhance male erotic appreciation of the female form. However, as already indicated, this is not simply a matter of camera positioning, and to the extent that talk of the look or the gaze creates that impression, such terminology is unfortunate.

Women in Hollywood film are staged and blocked for the purpose of male erotic contemplation and pleasure. However, at this point, Mulvey hypothesizes that this pleasure for the male spectator is endangered. For the image of the woman, set out for erotic delectation, inevitably invokes castration anxieties in the male spectator. Contemplating the woman's body reminds the male spectator of her lack of a penis, which psychoanalysis tells us the male takes as a sign of castration, the vagina purportedly construed as a bloody wound. Unlike male characters in Hollywood cinema, whom Mulvey says make meaning, female characters are said to be bearers of meaning: specifically, they signify sexual difference, which for the male spectator portends castration.

The male scopophiliac pleasure in the female form, secured by the staging techniques of Hollywood film and often channeled through male characters via point-of-view editing, is at risk in its very moment of success, since the presentation of the female form for contemplation heralds castration anxiety for the male viewer. The question, then, is how the Hollywood system is able to continue to deliver visual pleasure in the face of the threat of castration anxiety. Here, the general answer is derived from psychoanalysis, as was the animating problem of castration anxiety.

Two psychic strategies, indeed perversions, that may be adopted in order to come to terms with castration anxiety in general are fetishism and voyeurism. Similarly, Mulvey wants to argue that there are cinematic strategies that reflect these generic psychic strategies, and that their systematic mobilization in Hollywood films is what sustains the availability of visual pleasure—male scopophiliac pleasure—in the face of castration anxiety.

Fetishism outside of film involves the denial of the female's lack of a penis by, so to speak, fastening on some substitute object, like a woman's foot or shoe, that can stand for the missing penis. Mulvey thinks that in film the female form itself can be turned into a fetish object, a process of fetishization that can be amplified by turning the entire scenography and cinematic image into a fetish object; the elaborate visual compositions of Josef von Sternberg, in Mulvey's view, are an extreme example of a general strategy for containing castration anxiety by fetishization in the Hollywood cinema.

A second option for dealing with male castration anxiety in the context of male scopophilia, Mulvey contends, is voyeurism. Apparently, for Mulvey, this succeeds by reenacting the original traumatic discovery of the supposed castration of the woman—though I must admit that I'm not completely clear on why reenacting the original trauma would help in containing castration anxiety (is it like getting back on a horse after you've been thrown off of it?).

In any case, Mulvey writes:

> The male unconscious has two avenues of escape from this castration anxiety: preoccupation with the re-enactment of the original trauma (investigating the woman, demystifying her mystery), counterbalanced by the devaluation, punishment, or saving the guilty object (an avenue typified by the concerns of the *film noir*); or else complete disavowal of castration by the substitution of a fetish object or turning the represented figure itself into a fetish so that it becomes reassuring rather than dangerous (hence overvaluation, the cult of the female star).[10]

If von Sternberg represents an extreme and clarifying instance of the general strategy of fetishization in Hollywood film, the radical instance of the voyeuristic strategy is located in the cinema of Alfred Hitchcock. Here, one finds cases like *Rear Window,* which other commentators have often described in terms of voyeurism; moreover, Mulvey associates voyeurism with the urge for a sadistic assertion of control and the subjugation of the guilty. And here Hitchcock's *Vertigo* and *Marnie* come particularly to mind, films in which voyeuristic male characters set out to remake "guilty" women characters.

Needless to say, Mulvey's exemplification of the general strategies of fetishism and voyeurism by means of von Sternberg and Hitchcock is persuasive, at least rhetorically, for these are directors whom critics have long discussed in terms of fetishism and voyeurism, albeit using these concepts in a nontechnical sense. What Mulvey effectively did in her essay was to transform those critical terms into psychoanalytic ones, while also implying that cinematic fetishism and voyeurism, represented in the extreme cases of von Sternberg and Hitchcock, were the general strategies through which male visual pleasure in the cinema could be sustained, despite the impending threat of castration anxiety. And, as well, these cinematic strategies—if psychoanalysis is true—reflect patterns of visual fascination in patriarchal culture at large where visual pleasure in the female form depends on either turning her into an object or subjugating her by other means.

In summary, Mulvey situates the visual pleasure in Hollywood cinema in the satisfaction of the male's desire to contemplate the female form erotically. This contemplation itself is potentially unpleasurable, however, since contemplation of the female form raises the prospect of castration anxiety. Cinematic strategies corresponding to fetishism and voyeurism—and emblematized respectively by the practices of von Sternberg and Hitchcock—provide visual and narrative means to protect the structure of male visual pleasure, obsessively opting for cinematic conventions and schemata that are subordinated to the neurotic needs of the male ego. Feminist film practice of the sort Mulvey champions seeks to subvert the conventions that support the system of visual pleasure deployed in Hollywood filmmaking and to depose the hegemony of the male gaze.

I have no doubt that there are conventions of blocking and of posing actresses before the camera that are sexist and that alternative nonsexist styles of composition are worth pursuing. Moreover, as noted earlier, I will not challenge Mulvey's psychoanalytic presuppositions, though I believe that this can and ought to be done. For present purposes, the only comment that I will make about her invocation of psychoanalysis is that, as already noted, it does not seem methodologically sound. For even if psychoanalysis, or specific psychoanalytic hypotheses are genuine scientific conjectures, they need to be tested against countervailing hypotheses. Neither Mulvey nor any other contemporary psychoanalytic feminist has performed this rudimentary exercise of scientific and rational inquiry and, as a result, their theories are epistemically suspect.

Moreover, apart from her psychoanalytic commitments, Mulvey's theory of visual pleasure rests on some highly dubitable empirical suppositions. On Mulvey's account, male characters in cinema are active; females are passive, primarily functioning to be seen. She writes that a male movie star's glamorous characteristics are not those of an erotic object of the gaze.[11] It is hard to see how anyone could come to believe this. In our own time, we have Sylvester Stallone and Arnold Schwarzenegger whose star vehicles slow down and whose scenes are blocked and staged precisely to afford spectacles of bulging pectorals and other parts. Nor are these examples from contemporary film new developments in film history. Before Stallone, there was Steve Reeves and Charles Bronson, and before them, Johnny Weismuller. Indeed, the muscle-bound character of Maciste that Steve Reeves often played originated in the 1913 Italian spectacle *Cabiria*.

Nor is the baring of chests for erotic purposes solely the province of second-string male movie stars. Charlton Heston, Kirk Douglas, Yul Brynner—the list could go on endlessly—all have a beefcake side to their star personae. Obviously, there are entire genres that celebrate male physiques, scantily robed, as sources of visual pleasure: biblical epics, ironically enough, as well as other forms of ancient and exotic epics; jungle films; sea-diving films; boxing films; Tarzan adventures, etc.

Nor are males simply ogled on screen for their bodily beauty. Some are renowned for their great facial good looks, for which the action is slowed down so that the audience may take a gander, often in "glamor" close-ups. One thinks of John Gilbert and Rudolph Valentino in the twenties; of the young Gary Cooper, John Wayne, Henry Fonda, and Laurence Olivier in the thirties; of Gregory Peck in the forties; Montgomery Clift, Marlon Brando, and James Mason in the fifties; Peter O'Toole in the sixties; and so on.[12] Nor is it useful to suggest a constant correlation between male stars and effective activity. Leslie Howard in *Of Human Bondage* and *Gone With the Wind* seems to have succeeded most memorably as a matinee idol when he was staggeringly ineffectual.

If the dichotomy between male/active images versus female/passive images ill-suits the male half of the formula, it is also empirically misguided for the female half. Many of the great female stars were also great doers. Rosalind Russell in *His Girl Friday* and Katharine Hepburn in *Bringing Up Baby* hardly stop moving long enough to permit the kind of visual pleasure Mulvey asserts is the basis of the female image in Hollywood cinema. Moreover, it seems to me question-begging to say that audiences do not derive visual pleasure from these performances. Furthermore, if one complains here that my counterexamples are from comedies, and that certain kinds of comedies present special cases, let us argue about *The Perils of Pauline*.

After hypothesizing that visual pleasure in film is rooted in presenting the woman as passive spectacle through the agencies of conventional stylization, Mulvey claims that this project contains the seeds of its own destruction, for it will raise castration anxieties in male spectators. Whether erotic contemplation of the female form elicits castration anxiety from male viewers is, I suppose, a psychoanalytic claim, and, as such, not immediately a subject for criticism in this essay. However, as we have seen, Mulvey goes on to say that the ways in which Hollywood film deals with this purported problem is through cinematic structures that allow the male spectator two particular avenues of escape: fetishism and voyeurism.

One wonders about the degree to which it is appropriate to describe even male viewers as either fetishists or voyeurs. Indeed, Allen Weiss has remarked that real-world fetishists and voyeurs would have little time for movies, preferring to lavish their attentions on actual boots and furs, on the one hand, and living apartment dwellers on the other.[13] Fetishism and voyeurism are literally perversions—involving regression and fixation at an earlier psychosexual stages—in the Freudian system, whereas deriving visual pleasure from movies would not, I take it, be considered a perversion, *ceteris paribus,* by practicing psychoanalysts. Mulvey can only be speaking of fetishism and voyeurism metaphorically.[14] But it is not clear, from the perspective of film theory, that these metaphors are particularly apt.

In general, the idea of voyeurism as a model for all film viewing does not suit the data. Voyeurs require unwary victims for their intrusive gaze. Films are made to be seen and film actors willingly put themselves on display, and the viewers know this. The fanzine industry would not exist otherwise. Mulvey claims that the conventions of Hollywood film give the spectators the illusion of looking in on a *private* world.[15] But what can be the operative force of *private* here? In what sense is the world of *The Longest Day* private rather than public? Surely the invasion of Normandy was public and it is represented as public in *The Longest Day.* Rather one suspects that the use of the concept of private in this context will turn out, if it can be intelligibly specified at all, to be a question-begging dodge that makes it plausible to regard such events as the reenactment of the battle of Waterloo as a private event.

Also, Mulvey includes under the rubric of voyeurism the sadistic assertion of control and the punishment of the guilty. This will allow her to accommodate a lot more filmic material under the category of voyeurism than one might have originally thought that the concept could bear. But is Lee Marvin's punishment of Gloria Grahame in *The Big Heat* voyeurism? If one answers yes to this, mustn't one also admit that the notion of voyeurism has been expanded quite monumentally?

One is driven toward the same conclusions with respect to Mulvey's usage of the concept of fetishism. Extrapolating from the example of von Sternberg, any case of elaborate scenography is to be counted as a fetishization mobilized in order to deflect anxieties about castration. So the elaborate scenography of a solo song and dance number by a female star functions as a containing fetish for castration anxieties. But, then, what are we to make of the use of elaborate scenography in solo song and dance numbers by male stars? If they are fetishizations, what anxiety are they containing? Or, might not the elaborate scenography have some other function? And if it has some other function with respect to male stars, isn't that function something that should be considered as a candidate in a rival explanation of the function of elaborate scenography in the case of female stars?

In any case, is it plausible to suppose that elaborate composition generally has the function of containing castration anxiety? The multiple seduction jamboree in *Rules of the Game,* initiated by the playing of *Danse Macabre,* is one of the most elaborately composed sequences in film history. It is not about castration anxiety; it is positively priapic. Nor is it clear what textually motivated castration anxiety could underlie the immensely intricate scenography in the nightclub scene of Tati's *Play Time.* That is, there is elaborate scenography in scenes where it seems castration anxiety is not a plausible concern. Why should it function differently in other scenes? If the response is that castration anxiety is always an issue, the hypothesis appears unpersuasive.[16]

Grounding the contrast between fetishistic and voyeuristic strategies of visual pleasure in the contrast between von Sternberg and Hitchcock initially has a strong intuitive appeal because those filmmakers are, pretheoretically, thought to be describable in these terms—indeed, they come pretty close to describing themselves and their interests that way. However, it is important to recall that when commentators speak this way, or even when Hitchcock himself speaks this way, the notions of voyeurism at issue are nontechnical.

Moreover, the question is, even if in some sense these two directors could be interpreted as representing a contrast between cinematic fetishism and voyeurism, does that opposition portend a systematic dichotomy that maps onto all Hollywood cinema?[17] Put bluntly, isn't there a great deal of visual pleasure in Hollywood cinema that doesn't fit into the categories of fetishism and voyeurism, even if those concepts are expanded, metaphorically and otherwise, in the way that Mulvey suggests? Among the things I have in mind here are not only the kind of counterexamples already advanced—male objects of erotic contemplation, female protagonists who are active and triumphant agents, spectacular scenes of the Normandy invasion that are difficult to connect to castration anxieties—but innumerable films that neither have elaborate scenography nor involve male characters as voyeurs, nor subject women characters to male subjugation in a demonstration of sadistic control. One film to start to think about here might be Arthur Penn's *The Miracle*

Worker for which Patty Duke (Astin) received an Academy Award. (After all, a film that receives an Academy Award can't be considered outside the Hollywood system).[18]

Of course, the real problem to be addressed is Mulvey's apparent compulsion to postulate a general theory of visual pleasure for Hollywood cinema. Why should anyone suppose that a unified theory is available, and why would one suppose that it would be founded upon sexual difference, since in the Hollywood cinema there is pleasure—even visual pleasure—that is remote from issues of sexual difference.

It is with respect to these concerns that I think that the limitations of psychoanalytic film criticism become more apparent. For it is that commitment that drives feminist film critics toward generalizations like Mulvey's that are destined for easy refutation. If one accepts a general theory like psychoanalysis, then one is unavoidably tempted to try to apply its categorical framework to the data of a field like film, come what may, irrespective of the fit of the categories to the data. Partial or glancing correlations of the categorical distinctions to the data will be taken as confirmatory, and all the anomalous data will be regarded as at best topics for further research or ignored altogether as theoretically insignificant. Psychoanalytic feminists tend to force their "system" on cinema, and to regard often slim correspondences between films and the system as such that one can make vaulting generalizations about how the Hollywood cinema "really" functions. The overarching propensity to fruitless generalization is virtually inherent in the attempt to apply the purported success of general psychoanalytic hypotheses and distinctions, based on clinical practice, to the local case of film. This makes theoretical conjectures like Mulvey's immediately problematic by even a cursory consideration of film history. One pressing advantage, theoretically, of the image approach is that it provides a way to avoid the tendency of psychoanalytic film feminism to commit itself to unsupportable generalizations in its attempt to read all film history through the categories of psychoanalysis.[19]

The Image of Women in Film

The investigation of the image of women in film begins with the rather commonsensical notion that the recurring images of women in popular media may have some influence on how people think of women in real life. How one is to cash in the notion of "some influence" here, however, will be tricky. In fact, it amounts to finding a theoretical foundation for the image of women in film model. Moreover, there may be more than one way in which such influence is exerted. What I would like to do now is to sketch one answer that specifies one dimension of influence that recurring images of women in film may have on spectators, especially male spectators, in order to give the model some theoretical grounding. However, though I elucidate one strut upon which the model may rest, it is not my intention to deny that there may be others as well.

Recent work on the emotions in the philosophy of mind has proposed that we learn to identify our emotional states in terms of paradigm scenarios, which, in turn, also shape our emotions. Ronald de Sousa claims:

> my hypothesis is this: We are made familiar with the vocabulary of emotion by association with *paradigm scenarios*. These are drawn first from our daily life as small children and later reinforced by the stories, art and culture in which we are exposed. Later still, in literate cultures, they are supplemented and refined by literature. Paradigm scenarios involve two aspects: first, a situation type providing the characteristic *objects* of the specific emotion type, and second, a set of characteristic or "normal" *responses* to the situation, where normality is first a biological matter and then very quickly becomes a cultural one.[20]

Many of the relevant paradigm scenarios are quite primitive, like fear, and some are genetically preprogrammed, though we continue to accumulate paradigm scenarios throughout life and the emotions that they define become more refined and more culturally dependent. Learning to use emotion terms is a matter of acquiring paradigm scenarios for certain situations; that is, matching emotion terms to situations is guided by fitting paradigm scenarios to the situations that confront us. Paradigm scenarios, it might be said, perform the kind of cognitive role attributed to the formal object of the emotion in preceding theories of mind.[21] However, instead of being conceived of in terms of criteria, paradigm scenarios have a dramatic structure. Like formal objects of given emotions, paradigm scenarios define the type of emotional state one is in. They also direct our attention in the situation in such a way that certain elements in it become salient.

Paradigm scenarios enable us to "gestalt" situations, that is, "to attend differentially to certain features of an actual situation, to inquire into the presence of further features of the scenario, and to make inferences that the scenario suggests."[22] Given a situation, an enculturated individual attempts, generally intuitively, to fit a paradigm scenario from her repertoire to it. This does not mean that the individual can fully articulate the content of the scenario, but that, in a broad sense, she can recognize that it fits the situation before her. This recognition enables her to batten on certain features of the situation, to explore the situation for further correlations to the scenario, and to make the inferences and responses the scenario suggests. Among one's repertory of love-scenarios, for example, one might have, so to speak, a "West Side Story" scenario which enables one to organize one's thoughts and feelings about the man one has just met. Furthermore, more than one of our scenarios may fit a given situation. Whether one reacts to a situation of public recrimination with anger, humility, or fortitude depends on the choice of the most appropriate paradigm scenario.[23]

I will not attempt to enumerate the kinds of considerations that make the postulation of paradigm scenarios attractive except to note that it has certain advantages over competing hypotheses about the best way to characterize the cognitive and conative components in emotional states.[24] Rather, I shall presume that the notion of paradigm scenarios has something to tell us about a component of emotional states in order to suggest how recurring images of women in film may have some influence on spectators, which influence is of relevance to feminists.

Clearly, if we accept the notion of paradigm scenarios, we are committed to the notion that the paradigm scenario we apply to a situation shapes the emotional state we are in. Some paradigm scenarios—for example, those pertaining to the relation of an infant to a caretaker—may be such that recognition of them is genetically endowed. But most paradigm scenarios will be acquired, and even those that start out rather primitively, like rage, may be refined over time by the acquisition of further and more complex paradigm scenarios. There will be many sources from which we derive these paradigm scenarios: observation and memory; stories told us on our caretaker's knee; stories told us by friends and schoolteachers; gossip, as well, is a rich source of such scenarios; and, of course, so are newspaper articles, self-help books, TV shows, novels, plays, films, and so on.

These scenarios may influence our emotional behavior. Male emotional responses to women, for example, will be shaped by the paradigm scenarios that they bring to those relations. Such paradigm scenarios may be derived from films, or, more likely, films may reflect, refine, and reinforce paradigm scenarios already abroad in the culture. One way to construe the study of the image of women in film is as an attempt to isolate widely disseminated paradigm scenarios that contribute to the shaping of emotional responses to women.[25]

The recent film *Fatal Attraction,* for example, provides a paradigm scenario for situations in which a married man is confronted by a woman who refuses to consider their affair so easily terminable as he does. Armed with the *Fatal Attraction* scenario, which isn't so different from the *Crimes and Misdemeanors* scenario, a man might "gestalt" a roughly matching, real-life situation, focusing on it in such a way that its object, correlating to Alex (Glenn Close), is, as Dan (Michael Douglas) says, "unreasonable," and "crazy," and, as the film goes on to indicate, pathologically implacable. One might use the scenario to extrapolate other elements of the scenario to the real case; one might leap inductively from Alex's protests that her behavior is justified (you wouldn't accept my calls at the office so I called you at home), which are associated in the film with madness, to the suspicion that a real-life, ex-lover's claims to fair treatment are really insane. Like Dan, one guided by the *Fatal Attraction* scenario may assess his situation as one of paralyzing terror, persecution, and helplessness that only the death of the ex-lover can alleviate.

I am not suggesting that the *Fatal Attraction* scenario causes someone who matches it to a real-life situation to kill his ex-lover, though embracing it may be likely to promote murderous fantasies, in terms of the response component. In any case, matching it to a real-life situation will tend to demote the ex-lover to the status of an irrational creature and to regard her claims as a form of persecution. This construal of the woman as persecutrix, of course, was not invented by the makers of *Fatal Attraction.* It finds precedent in other films, like *Play Misty For Me,* and stories, including folklore told among men in the form of gossip.

Fatal Attraction provides a vivid exemplar for emotional attention that reinforces preexisting paradigm scenarios. However, even if *Fatal Attraction* is not original, studying the image of the woman, Alex, that it portrays is relevant to feminists because it illuminates one pattern of emotional attention toward women that is available to men, which pattern of emotional attention, if made operational in specific cases, can be oppressive to women, by, for example, reducing claims to fair treatment to the status of persecutory, irrational demands.

That a paradigm scenario like *Fatal Attraction* is available in the culture does not imply that every man or even any man mobilizes it. But it does at least present a potential source or resource for sexist behavior. That such a potential even exists provides a reason for feminists to be interested in it. One aspect of the study of the image of women in film is to identify negative, recurring images of women that may have some influence on the emotional response of men to women. Theoretically, this influence can be understood in terms of the negative, recurring images of women in film as supplying paradigm scenarios that may shape the emotional responses of real men to real women.

Recurring, negative images of women in film may warp the emotions of those who deploy them as paradigm scenarios in several different ways. They may distort the way women are attended to emotionally by presenting wildly fallacious images such as the "spider woman" of film noir. Or, the problem may be that the range of images of women available is too impoverished: if the repertoire of images of women is limited in certain cases, for instance, to contraries like mother or whore, then real women who are not perceived via the mother scenario may find themselves abused under the whore scenario. The identification of the range of ways in which negative images of women in film can function cognitively to shape emotional response is a theoretical question that depends on further exploring the variety of logical/functional types of different images of women in film. That is a project that has hardly begun. Nevertheless, it seems a project worth pursuing.

I began by noting that the image approach might appear to some to be without proper theoretical credentials. I have tried to allay that misgiving by suggesting that the program fits nicely with one direction in the theory of the emotions. From that perspective, the study of the image of women in film might be viewed as the search for paradigm scenarios that are available in our culture and that, by being available, may come to shape emotional responses to women. This aspect of the project should be of special interest to feminists with regard to negative imagery since it may illuminate some of the sources or resources that mobilize sexist emotions. Obviously, the theoretical potentials of the image of women in film model need to be developed. What I have tried to establish is the contention that there is at least a theoretical foundation here upon which to build.

This, of course, is not much of a defense of the image approach. So in my concluding remarks I shall sketch some of the advantages of this approach, especially in comparison to some of the disadvantages of the psychoanalytic model discussed earlier.

First, the image of women model seems better suited than the psychoanalytic model for accommodating the rich data that film history has bequeathed us. It allows that there will be lots of images of women and lots of images of men and that these may play a role as paradigm scenarios in lots of emotional reactions of all kinds. One need not attempt to limit the ambit of emotional responses to fetishism or voyeurism.

Of course, the image of women model may take particular interest in negative images of women in film, for obvious strategic purposes, but it can also handle the case of positive images as well. Whereas the Rosalind Russell character in *His Girl Friday* may be an inexplicable anomaly in the psychoanalytic system, she can be comprehended in the image approach. For this model allows that there can be positive images of women in film which may play a role in positive emotional responses to real women.[26] It is hard to see how there can be anything of genuine value in Hollywood film in Mulvey's construction. The image approach can identify the good, while acknowledging and isolating the evil.

The image of women in film model is less likely to lead to unsupportable generalizations. What it looks for are recurring images of women in film. It has no commitments about how women always appear in film.[27] Rather, it targets images that recur with marked frequency. Moreover, it makes no claims about how all viewers or all male viewers respond to those images. It tracks images of women that reappear in film with some significant degree of probability and, where the images are negative, it can elucidate how they may play a constitutive role in the shaping of oppressive emotional responses to women. It is not committed to the kinds of specific causal laws that Mulvey must accept as underlying her account. It can, nevertheless, acknowledge causal efficacy to some paradigm scenarios—indeed, it can acknowledge causal efficacy to paradigm scenarios of all sorts, thereby accommodating the richness of the data.

It is interesting to observe that the image approach can accommodate certain of Mulvey's insights in a way that does not provoke the kind of objections Mulvey's position does. It can acknowledge that it is the case that there is a recurring image, of undoubtedly unnerving statistical frequency, of women in film posed as passive spectacles. Not all images of women in film are of this sort, but many are. Unlike Mulvey, the proponent of the image approach can point to this as a statistical regularity without claiming any overreaching generalizations, and then go on to show how this sort of imagery reinforces a range of paradigm scenarios which mobilize a wide variety of oppressive emotional responses by men toward women, encountered on the beach, on the street, and in more ominous circumstances as well.

One objection that might be raised here, of course, is that I have presented the image approach as a rival to Mulvey's theory. But it might be countered that Mulvey's theory is about the pleasure taken from Hollywood cinema, and the image approach, as described so far, says nothing about pleasure. So though it may be a rival to isolate the way in which Hollywood cinema functions in patriarchal society, it has not answered the question of how it is pleasurable.

One admittedly programmatic response to this objection is to note that insofar as the image approach is connected with engaging emotions, and insofar as indulging emotions in aesthetic contexts is generally thought to be pleasurable, then the proponent of the image approach can explain the pleasure to be derived from Hollywood films in virtue of whatever its defender takes to be the best theory or combination of theories that accounts for the pleasure we take from exercising our emotions in response to artworks, popular or otherwise. That is, where the rivalry between the image approach and Mulvey's approach is about pleasure, the supporter of the image approach has a range of options for developing theories.

On the other hand, I wonder whether the interest on the part of feminists in Mulvey's theory is really in its account of pleasure rather than in the way that it provides a means for analyzing the way film functions in patriarchal society. And if the latter is the real source of interest, two things need to be said: (1) the question of pleasure is only of interest insofar as it illuminates the function of film in abetting sexism, and (2) the image approach is a competing perspective in relation to that question, even if it makes the issue of pleasure less central to feminism than does Mulvey's approach.

Lastly, consonant with the preceding objection, it may be urged that Mulvey's theory is a theory of *visual* pleasure, and though we have spoken of images, even if we could advance a theory of pleasure, it would not be specifically a theory of visual pleasure, for images in the sense we have used it are not essentially or necessarily visual. Here, two points need to be made.

First, it is not clear that Mulvey herself is always talking about uniquely visual pleasure, nor that it is possible, with respect to Hollywood film images, to suppose that we can find some substratum of interests that are exclusively visual in nature.

Second, Mulvey's putative answer to the riddle of how viewers can take visual pleasure in the female form in cinema presupposes that there is a riddle here to be solved, which, in turn, depends upon the conviction that the image of a woman on screen, in some lawlike fashion, provokes castration anxiety in male viewers. There is no problem of visual pleasure without the supposition of regularly recurring male castration anxiety with respect to visual emphasis on female form. So if, like me, you are skeptical about this supposition, then Mulvey has not solved the problem of visual pleasure, for there was no problem to solve in the first place, and, therefore, no pressure on rival theories to address the issue.

Moreover, if, again like me, you are worried about accepting generalizations that are derived from psychoanalysis and treated like laws by film critics, then the image of women in film approach has the virtue of providing means for analyzing the function of film in the service of sexism without necessarily committing one to the still controversial tenets of psychoanalysis. This, of course, is hardly a recommendation that I expect committed psychoanalytic film critics to find moving. I offer it, without further argument, to concerned third parties.[28]

Notes

1. The distinction between *sources* and *resources* above is meant to acknowledge that it is generally the case that popular film more often than not reinforces rather than invents ideology, sexist and otherwise. Thus, film is primarily a *resource* rather than a *source* of ideology. However, at the same time, I have no reason to assert dogmatically that a film could never invent ideology. If this happens, I suspect that it happens very, very rarely. But I have no investment in claiming that it could never happen.

2. I say a "potential rival" because, as already noted, one could marry the study of the image of women in film with a psychoanalytic perspective. Thus, the theoretical rivalry that I envision in this paper is between a study of the image of women in film that is neutral with respect to psychoanalysis and psychoanalytically informed film feminism.

3. This essay first appeared in *Screen* in 1975. It has been reprinted often, most recently, with respect to the writing of this essay, in Laura Mulvey's collection of her own writings entitled *Visual and Other Pleasures* (Bloomington: Indiana University Press, 1989). All page references to this article pertain to that volume.

4. It should also be noted that Mulvey herself has attempted to modify, or, perhaps more accurately, to supplement the theory that she put forward in "Visual Pleasure and Narrative Cinema." See, for example, her "Afterthoughts on 'Visual Pleasure and Narrative Cinema' inspired by King Vidor's *Duel in the Sun*," in *Visual and Other Pleasures*, 29–37. The latter essay, while not denying the analysis of male pleasure in the former essay, offers a supplemental account of female pleasure with respect to narrative film. Space does not allow for criticism of that supplemental account. However, it is interesting that its structure is analogous to the structure of her psychoanalysis of male pleasure insofar as Mulvey attempts to "deduce" female pleasure at the movies from an earlier stage of psychosexual development whose masculine phase film narratives may, supposedly, reactivate.

5. I stress that what is accepted without sufficient critical distance in this matter is the *scientific* viability of psychoanalysis. Feminist film critics, including Mulvey, are aware of and seek to cancel the patriarchal biases of psychoanalysis. But unless the elements of the theory show sexist prejudices, they tend to accept its pronouncements on matters such as psychosexual development and visual pleasure without recourse to weighing psychoanalytic hypotheses against those of competing theories or to considering the often commented upon theoretical flaws and empirical difficulties of psychoanalysis.

6. I have discussed the tendency in contemporary film theory to embrace theoretical frameworks without considering rival views at some length in my *Mystifying Movies: Fads and Fallacies in Contemporary Film Theory* (New York: Columbia University Press, 1988).

7. Indeed, John Berger makes such a distinction—between the male as active and the female as passive—with respect to the iconography of Western easel painting without invoking psychoanalysis. See his *Ways of Seeing* (London: Penguin, 1972), especially chap. 2.

8. Like many contemporary film theorists, Mulvey appears to believe that through point-of-view editing Hollywood film masks two other "looks"—those of the camera on the profilmic event and of the spectator on the finished film. Point-of-view editing, in this respect, functions to abet what contemporary film theorists call "transparency." I have challenged the overall advisability of hypotheses of this sort in my *Mystifying Movies;* see especially the discussion of suture.

9. Berger, *Ways of Seeing.*

10. Mulvey, "Visual Pleasure and Narrative Cinema," 21.

11. Ibid., 20.

12. Other commentators have also questioned Mulvey's generalizations in this regard. See Kristin Thompson, "Closure Within a Dream? Point of View in *Laura,*" in *Breaking the Glass Armor* (Princeton: Princeton University Press, 1988), 185, and Miriam Hansen, "Pleasure, Ambivalence, Identification: Valentino and Female Spectatorship," *Cinema Journal* 25 (1986): 6–32.

13. Allen Weiss in the introduction to his unpublished doctoral dissertation on the films of Hollis Frampton (New York University, 1989).

14. Mulvey may reject this interpretation of her essay. She may think that she is using these psychoanalytic terms literally. In the "Summary" of her essays (26), for example, she speaks of the neurotic needs of the male ego. But this seems tantamount to implying that the male ego is, at least, in our culture, inevitably and essentially neurotic. And I am not convinced that this is the way that clinical psychoanalysts would use the idea of neurosis as a technical classification. Nor would the classification be of much scientific value if it applied so universally. Furthermore, Freud himself, in his study of da Vinci, talks of sublimation as an alternative formation to perversions like fetishism. Why has sublimation dropped out of Mulvey's list of options for visual pleasure?

15. Mulvey, "Visual Pleasure and Narrative Cinema," 17.

16. Christian Metz, perhaps the leading psychoanalytic film theorist, appears to hold such a view. For arguments against this hypothesis, see the second chapter of my *Mystifying Movies.*

17. Here one might object that Mulvey is not committed to regarding the fetishism/voyeurism dichotomy as systematic; so I am attacking a straw position. But I think she is committed to the notion of a systematic dichotomy. For if the problem of castration anxiety with respect to the female form is general, and fetishism and voyeurism are the only responses, then where there is no castration anxiety, won't that have to be a function of strategies of voyeurism and fetishism? Perhaps Mulvey does not believe that there is always castration anxiety in response to the female form. But then we would have to know under what conditions castration anxiety will fail to take hold. Moreover, we will have to ask whether these conditions, once specified, won't undermine Mulvey's theory in other respects. Of course, another reason why one might deny that Mulvey's claims involve a systematic dichotomy between fetishistic and voyeuristic strategies is that she believes that there are other strategies for containing castration anxiety. But then the burden of proof is on her to produce these as yet unmentioned alternatives.

18. This film was, of course, based upon a highly acclaimed Broadway production. So, it is a counterexample that should also be considered by theater critics who wish to apply the generalizations of feminist film critics to the study of their own art form. Likewise, TV critics, with the same ambition, should want to ponder the relevance of this example to the successful remake of the theater and film versions of *The Miracle Worker* for TV in 1979 by Paul Aaron where Patty Duke (Astin) plays the Anne Sullivan role.

Also, it should be obvious, *contra* Mulvey, that not all visual pleasure in film is rooted in sexual difference. Consider the visual pleasure derived from recognition, from detail, from shifts of scale, and, more specifically, from machinery, from casts of thousands, and so on (I owe these examples to Cynthia Baughman).

19. There is another line of argumentation in Mulvey's essay that I have not dealt with above. It involves a general theory of the way in which cinema engages spectators in identification and mobilizes what Lacanians call "the imaginary." The sort of general theory that Mulvey endorses concerning these issues is criticized at length in my *Mystifying Movies*.

20. Ronald de Sousa, *The Rationality of the Emotions* (Cambridge: MIT Press, 1987), 182. The idea of scenarios is also employed by Robert Solomon, "Emotion and Choice," in *Explaining Emotions*, ed. Amelie Rorty (Berkeley and Los Angeles: University of California Press, 1980).

21. For example, Anthony Kenny's *Action, Emotion and Will* (London: Routledge, 1963).

22. Ronald de Sousa, "The Rationality of Emotions," in *Explaining Emotions*, 143.

23. This example comes from Cheshire Calhoun's "Subjectivity & Emotions," *Philosophical Forum* 20 (1989): 206.

24. See the de Sousa citations above for some of the relevant arguments.

25. Of course, there could also be a research program dedicated to studying the image of men in film for the same purposes.

26. Kristin Thompson, in conversation, has stressed that determining whether a paradigm scenario is positive or negative may crucially hinge on contextualizing it historically.

27. Whereas psychoanalytic feminism, given its avowal of the *general* laws of psychoanalysis, is tempted to say how woman must always appear as a result of deducing film theory from a deeper set of "scientific" principles.

28. This paper was read at the 1990 Pacific Division Meetings of the American Philosophical Association where Laurie Shrage provided helpful comments. Other useful criticisms have been offered by Ellen Gainor, Kristin Thompson, David Bordwell, Sally Banes, Peggy Brand, Carolyn Korsmeyer, Sabrina Barton, and Cynthia Baughman.

SELECT BIBLIOGRAPHY TO PART IV

Barnes, Annette. *On Interpretation: A Critical Analysis.* Basil Blackwell, 1988.

Beardsley, Monroe. *Aesthetics: Problems in the Philosophy of Criticism.* 2d ed. Indianapolis: Hackett Publishing Company, Inc., 1981.

Broude, Norma, and Mary Garrard, eds. *The Expanding Discourse: Feminism and Art History.* New York: HarperCollins, 1992.

———. *Feminism and Art History: Questioning the Litany.* New York: Harper and Row, 1982.

Carroll, Noël. *Mystifying Movies: Fads and Fallacies in Contemporary Movie Theory.* New York: Columbia University Press, 1988.

———. *Philosophical Problems of Classical Film Theory.* Princeton: Princeton University Press, 1988.

———. *The Philosophy of Horror.* New York: Routledge, 1990.

Chadwick, Whitney. *Women, Art and Society.* London: Thames and Hudson, 1990.

Clover, Carol J. *Men, Women and Chain Saws: Gender in the Modern Horror Film.* Princeton: Princeton University Press, 1992.

Doane, Mary Ann. *The Desire to Desire: The Woman's Film of the 1940s.* Bloomington: Indiana University Press, 1987.

Fetterley, Judith. *The Resisting Reader: A Feminist Approach to American Fiction.* Bloomington: Indiana University Press, 1978.

Garrard, Mary D. *Artemisia Gentileschi: The Image of the Female Hero in Italian Baroque Art,* Princeton: Princeton University Press, 1989.

Gilbert, Sandra, and Susan Gubar. *The Madwoman in the Attic: The Woman Writer and the Nineteenth-Century Literary Imagination.* New Haven: Yale University Press, 1979.

Gombrich, E. H. *Art and Illusion.* Princeton: Princeton University Press, 1960.

Haskell, Molly. *From Reverence to Rape.* New York: Holt, Rinehart and Winston, 1974.

Hermeren, Goren. *Art, Reason, and Tradition: On the Role of Rationality in Interpretation and Explanation of Works of Art.* Stockholm: Almquist and Wiksell International, 1991.

Higonnet, Anne. *Berthe Morisot.* New York: Harper and Row, 1990.

Kaplan, E. Ann. *Motherhood and Representation.* New York: Routledge, 1992.

———. *Women and Film: Both Sides of the Camera.* New York: Methuen, 1983.

Kristeva, Julia. *Desire in Language: A Semiotic Approach to Literature.* New York: Columbia University Press, 1980.

Kuhn, Annette. *The Power of the Image: Essays on Representation and Sexuality.* London: Routledge and Kegan Paul, 1985.

Lauretis, Teresa de. *Alice Doesn't: Feminism, Semiotics, Cinema.* Bloomington: Indiana University Press, 1984.

Lipton, Eunice. *Looking into Degas: Uneasy Images of Women and Modern Life.* Berkeley and Los Angeles: University of California Press, 1986.

Marcus, Jane. *Art and Anger: Reading Like a Woman.* Columbus: Ohio State University Press, 1988.

Mayne, Judith. *The Woman at the Keyhole: Feminism and Women's Cinema.* Blooming-
      ton: Indiana University Press, 1990.
Miller, Nancy K. *The Poetics of Gender.* New York: Columbia University Press, 1986.
Millett, Kate. *Sexual Politics.* New York: Doubleday, 1970.
Moi, Toril, ed. *The Kristeva Reader.* New York: Columbia University Press, 1986.
Mulvey, Laura. *Visual and Other Pleasures.* Bloomington: Indiana University Press,
      1989.
Nead, Lynda. *The Female Nude: Art, Obscenity and Sexuality.* London: Routledge, 1992.
Nochlin, Linda. *The Politics of Vision: Essays on Nineteenth-Century Art and Society.*
      New York: Harper and Row, 1989.
Shapiro, Gary, ed. *Interpretation and Intention.* Philadelphia: Temple University
      Press, 1992.
Showalter, Elaine, ed. *The New Feminist Criticism: Essays on Women, Literature, and
      Theory.* New York: Pantheon, 1985.
Silvers, Anita. "Pure Historicism and the Heritage of Hero(in)es: Who Grows in Phillis
      Wheatley's Garden?" *Journal of Aesthetics and Art Criticism* 51 (1993): 473–82.
Spitz, Ellen Handler. *Image and Insight: Essays in Psychoanalysis and the Arts.* New
      York: Columbia University Press, 1991.
Wall, Cheryl A., ed. *Changing Our Own Words: Essays on Criticism, Theory, and
      Writing by Black Women.* New Brunswick: Rutgers University Press, 1989.
Zemel, Carol. *Utopian Promises: Themes of Modernity in the Work of Vincent Van Gogh.*
      Berkeley and Los Angeles: University of California Press, forthcoming.

V

Feminism and Aesthetics:
Directions for the Future

The problems discussed in Parts I–IV raise concerns about whether traditional theory is so steeped in bias and resistant to change that it may not be easily amended for feminist purposes. The recent influx of feminist scholarship questions the very foundations of the field of aesthetics, just as it has raised similar questions in other areas of philosophy. Such serious challenges have led a few feminists to abandon philosophy altogether as a hopelessly androcentric quagmire beyond repair. But for those wishing to continue to work within the discipline or to explore previously uncharted terrain in philosophy, these challenges raise the possibility of new forms of conceiving art, perception, culture. This possibility raises at least two questions that are addressed by the essays in this section: What does contemporary philosophy have to offer in response to feminist challenges to established traditions? And in what directions might future thinking proceed? The following four essays grapple with the problem of delineating a new, possibly "feminist" aesthetics that avoids becoming trivialized, essentialized, or marginalized.

Joanne Waugh locates her discussion of feminist aesthetics within the context of "recovery" prescribed for the bleak future of analytic aesthetics generally foreseen at the end of the 1980s. She questions the role analytic aesthetics can play in the future of feminist programs, even for apparently sympathetic varieties of pragmatism such as those advanced by Joseph Margolis and Richard Rorty. Skeptical that their methods of investigation are not "new" enough, she calls for a more severe break with the past in order to escape its covert masculine biases. Rejecting the option of an entirely separate women's discourse, however, she urges vigorous attention to inventing ways of "ironically and critically" using the vocabulary of the past.

In dialectical spirit, Joseph Margolis directly replies to Waugh's concerns. Though he has not previously addressed feminist perspectives in his writing, Margolis claims that he is able to accommodate Waugh's skepticism by offering a vision of aesthetics that not only reconciles analytic and feminist concerns, but is multifaceted enough to be open to many others. His reasoning focuses on the legitimation of philosophical discourse. If he is not wedded to past practice, that is, the tradition of "timeless, ahistorical, exceptionless, apodictic, considerations" for legitimation, but rather to a less conservative view of historical, socially produced, contextualized modes of justification, then, he asks, what is to prevent his framework from reconciling analytic and feminist philosophy? He predicts a healthy outlook for both postanalytic and postfeminist aesthetics.

Bringing Marxist and postmodern theoretical insights into the discussion, Rita Felski suggests that feminist criticism can do without a notion of *an* aesthetic, although it cannot afford to ignore the realm of *the* aesthetic. Resisting the tendency to distill women's experiences to one homogenous type and cautioning that gender does not necessarily ensure works of art that are oppositional to existing male power structures, Felski uses the notion of "paraesthetics" to capture the resistance to definition of what has been posited as a "feminist aesthetic." Assessing artworks in context belies the complexity of any reconciliation of art and politics. Felski urges us to refrain from generalizing across publics and contexts of reception and instead argues for a more diversified model of the relationship between politics and aesthetics.

In the closing essay, Hilde Hein lays some groundwork for future theories by suggesting that feminist aesthetics needs to be at the center of both philosophy and feminist theorizing. An injection of feminism into aesthetics removes it from a marginalized position within Western philosophy and relocates it—as newly constructed "feminist" aesthetics—at the core of the empiricist tradition legitimating *women's* experience in addition to men's. In a similar but more radical move, aesthetics is repositioned from the periphery to the center of feminist theory, placing it within the politicized matrix of claims about women's experiences. Women who have been objectified by the predominantly male discourse about art become the creators of an alternative discourse in which their experiences, as makers, as gazers, take center stage. Just as the relativism of aesthetic judgments defies one, monistic universal standard of taste, aesthetics fits comfortably within the overarching structure of feminism's anti-essentialist, pluralistic nature. Hein's rousing call is for a future of philosophy and aesthetics infused with the energy and vision of feminism.

Each generation must decide what of its past is enabling and what hobbling. Feminist challenges to the foundations of aesthetics have often sought to disrupt the continuity that binds both the present and future to past traditions. If some predictions are correct, the age of postanalysis, postphilosophy, and postfeminism is upon us. If they are not correct, it is still incumbent upon us to pursue certain issues if we remain interested in fundamental questions about the roles that our diverse identities—gender, race, nationality, desire—play in art. Those addressed by this volume concern whether the traditions with which we are familiar are worth retaining, and why, and which are worth replacing, and (the most difficult question) how.

If analysis is passé, what mode of inquiry will take its place? If philosophy generally is no longer useful (as Rorty has suggested), can literary theory or revisionist art theory serve to raise the sorts of deep theoretical questions that still plague us about the nature of art, the limits of interpretation, and the criteria for evaluation? If even feminism's initial vigor is fragmenting into postmodernism, is there another cognitive framework to take its place?

Moveover, if we still see a need for analysis and a use for philosophy, and there are still unanswered questions regarding gender to be pursued, then as we advocated in the Introduction, the intersection of feminism and traditional aesthetics offers opportunities for exploration and investigation that should serve mutual interests.

The legacy of aesthetic theory, once comforting, is behind us; the insight of feminist theory is energizing and still newly upon us; and the future of feminist inquiry in aesthetics is yet to be written.

17

Analytic Aesthetics and Feminist Aesthetics: Neither/Nor?

Joanne B. Waugh

Analytic and feminist philosophers already uncomfortable with the practice of devoting special sessions at meetings and special issues of journals to "feminist aesthetics" may find that this piece adds to their uneasiness. If "feminist aesthetics" is treated as a special topic within aesthetics, then should we infer that the rest of the time we do masculine aesthetics? Some feminists would argue for an affirmative answer to this question; the title acknowledges them in insinuating that if analytic aesthetics is not feminist aesthetics, then it might be (or must be) masculine aesthetics. This essay will consider whether "feminist aesthetics" and analytic aesthetics are congenial, or at least compatible, activities, and in so doing, explore what constitutes "feminist aesthetics."

What constitutes "feminist aesthetics" is not nearly so clear as what constitutes analytic aesthetics, especially to philosophers from the English-language countries. Until very recently, one could hardly deny that feminist concerns have been ignored, for all intents and purposes, in analytic aesthetics. Such neglect is not, of course, unique to analytic aesthetics; it is true of analytic philosophy generally, philosophy generally, and Western intellectual history and culture generally. This is not to say that any or all of these are, or must be, sexist; it does suggest, however, that we should consider the possibility.

The notion of aesthetics is itself a contested one, regardless of the choice of modifier. A certain awkwardness attends talk about aesthetics because it is difficult to specify what entities or properties should be labeled "aesthetic." The disinclination to talk about "the aesthetic" is also a way of responding to a number of recent controversies, which may be summarized in the claims that "the aesthetic" is, at best, an antiquated notion, and at worst, nonsense, or part of a vocabulary of oppression.[1] Works purporting to show how and why these charges are true are among the most interesting and provocative in recent aesthetics, if I may be forgiven the use of the contested term.[2] Common to these works is the claim that whether one focuses on the way we talk about art, as is typical of analytic aesthetics, or on the experience of the aesthetic, it is wrong to do so in a way that ignores or does not fully appreciate the extent to which this talk or this experience is determined by and determines the set of historical, cultural, social, economic, and institutional practices of which aesthetic discourse and experience form a part.[3] Thus we find analytic philosophers talking about the eclipse, if not the end, of analytic aesthetics in ways reminiscent of the critique of analytic aesthetics, or aesthetics generally, offered by "Continental" philosophers, literary theorists, feminists, Marxist critics, and others engaged in the project of culture criticism. These nonanalytic philosophers are not opposed to the fact that analytic aesthetics has focused on talk about art. Indeed, focusing on talk or texts is as much a hallmark of nonanalytic varieties of aesthetic discourse as it is of analytic aesthetics. What separates those who do analytic aesthetics from those doing other varieties is how they focus on such talk. Far too often analytic analyses of the "logic of a concept" proceed without recognizing that this "logic" may be a product of historically specific and contingent factors. As a consequence, these analyses frequently take a universalist tone that suggests the words and concepts under analysis belong not merely to mid-to-late twentieth-century mostly male Britons who received an upper-class education at Oxbridge, or to professional philosophers living in America, but to all people at all times. Conceptual analyses of this sort seem, at least in retrospect, to have too much of a Platonist flavor for those who have rejected the idealist and essentialist tendencies of earlier philosophy. But analytic philosophers' taste for Platonism, their protestations notwithstanding, is not nearly so serious a problem, especially for aesthetics, as is their preference for putting distance between philosophy and the study of culture. To quote Joseph Margolis: "the truth is that the analytic tradition has tended to impoverish itself by a kind of increasing suicidal neglect of the leading themes of cultural life—*a fortiori*, of the leading themes that inform the world of the arts."[4]

Margolis's proposal for the recovery of analytic aesthetics is of particular interest to those considering the possibility of an aesthetics both analytic and feminist, especially in light of his insistence that if analytic aesthetics is to be recovered, it must pursue the following themes:

> the full recovery of intentional phenomena, the irreducibility of culture to nature, the inadequacy of both reductive and non-reductive physicalisms, the admission of emergence, the replacement of the unity-of-science programme, the abandonment of a comprehensive extensionalism, the acknowledgment of the complexities of historicism, the advocacy of ontic indeterminacies, of conceptual incommensurabilities, of divergent pluralisms, of relativistic values, the rejection of closed systems, the insistence on the symbiosis of the psychological and the societal, the symbiosis of realism and idealism, and the constructive nature of selves and world. (185)

Suggesting that we omit the practices of linguistic analyses that ignore the genesis, context, and functions of critical discourse, and in so doing, historicize aesthetics, seems tantamount to proposing that we take the "analytic" out of analytic aesthetics.[5] However, Margolis does not want to replace analytic aesthetics with that currently practiced by nonanalytic philosophers. Rather, he proposes that analytic and Continental philosophy be reconciled; such a reconciliation is necessary, on his view, if "analytic aesthetics is to survive, if analytic philosophy or any philosophy is to survive, if rational inquiry is to survive" (183). The terms of this reconciliation include bridging the difference "between naturalism and phenomenology and deconstruction and genealogy and the like," and providing for "second-order legitimative discourse that does not fail in the 'Kantian' manner that Rorty is at such pains to dismantle" (183). There are, of course, others who wish to dismantle the Kantian-inspired legitimative discourse to which Margolis refers; Nancy Fraser and Linda Nochlin come quickly to mind.[6] Their critique will be discussed below, and the focus here will remain on Margolis and Rorty, since their project of dismantling Kantian-inspired legitimative discourse is one they share with many feminists. Margolis agrees with Rorty that "the metaphysical, transparent, cognitively privileged, essentialist, correspondist, mirrored, objectivist, transcendental, presenced, logocentric idiom of Kant and Descartes is neither necessary nor defensible" (182). But Margolis refuses the options he thinks Rorty leaves us: a source of reasons and arguments for our practices that is "historicized and naturalistic but *not* philosophical or epistemological" (183) or the view that abandons the need for justification by accepting the Quinean point, as stated by Rorty, that "rational behavior is just adaptive behavior of a sort which roughly parallels the behavior, in similar circumstances, of the other members of some relevant community."[7] For Margolis, giving up the "Kantian" position means that "we need second-order legitimative discourse more than ever—not less—because we need the best rational guess about what the conditions of inquiry and truth-claims are by which to guide our practice" (184).

The problem, of course, is that a very important part of our practice consists in making decisions about new cases, for example, how to go on to them, and what to do with them. New cases are a problem because they are new; that is, they are not part of the paradigm learned in learning the practice, and for any "sustained and disciplined inquiry" we need [or want] "rational or critical direction" (183). For Margolis, such direction will be provided by "a foundation-less pragmatism" that asks Kantian-like questions, but does not suppose that its best answers are "either timelessly confirmed, convergent toward some uniquely adequate thesis, powerful enough to disqualify relativistic contenders at every point of contest,—or, of course, secretly assured of some decisive cognitive privilege."[8] The point seems to be that we continue to search for foundations at the same time as we resist foundationalism. Such a search takes the form of "inspecting alternative, *diachronically conservative,* general regularities or conditions that, by arguments to the best explanation . . . are *historically judged to be among the best candidates that have as yet been found for such status.*"[9] In legitimating science, we would proceed by establishing "a minimal realism, by non-epistemic considerations of an *en bloc* sort. And then, on *epistemic* considerations internal to (that is, benignly circular regarding) the putative achievements of science and inquiry—and on the strength of (internally) distributed weightings of reliability, importance, and the like,—*we should continue as before.*"[10]

In legitimating aesthetics, we would proceed in a similar fashion. Since philosophical inquiry about art cannot avoid constative discourse any more than other forms of philosophical inquiry, Margolis argues that for logic's sake, we must concede that there are relatively fixed, stable, and thus individuatable and reidentifiable referents, that is, texts. Before the "eclipse" of analytic aesthetics, these texts constituted a description of the artwork on which interpretation was practiced, and interpretation consisted of making distributed claims about these relatively stable texts, claims which could be assigned truthlike values. But given widespread challenges to the notion of cognitive transparency, and widespread acceptance of the notion of interpretation as a "productive practice by which an entire 'world' or what may be distributively referred to within the world are actually or aptly first constituted *for* certain sorts of further claim or use," the former notion of interpretation requires reinterpretation. [11] The major revision Margolis recommends is that epistemological and metaphysical commitments made in fixing a text, not be seen as privileged, but as "relativized . . . to the mere saliencies or *Erscheinungen* of our shared world."[12] The difference between interpretative discourse and interpreted referent can be viewed, then, as a logical distinction: the referential fixity of a text, what Margolis calls its unicity, can be distinguished from its substantive fixity, that is, its unity. We need only grant that

> the apparent formal fixities of discourse, the fixities of reference or predication, have nothing as such to do with deciding *what* the intrinsic nature of texts or particular texts may or must be—except for the fact (the hardly negligible fact) that whatever we say *is* the nature of a text must be compatible with so saying and with the interpretative discourse it is meant to support. Interpreted texts must have somewhat stable properties but they need not have altogether fixed natures. [13]

That texts have stable properties and responsible readings attests to "socially habituated practices and disciplined options of reading."[14] These, in turn, point to the "preformative historical conditions by which culturally apt individuals become apt. Their world is already culturally preformed *for them;* that is the reason they may be said to learn their native language and their native culture."[15] As culturally apt individuals, they are able to "interpret" the culturally prepared material so as to constitute a text, which permits "interpretation" of the sort that uses constative discourse. For Margolis, the recovery of analytic aesthetics will require a theory of interpretation that explains how texts are constructed so that they can be stable referents for inquiry, and how they may have a fixed and stable reference and yet be open to infinitely many interpretations, any one of which may alter the text of which it is an interpretation so that it is both a new text and yet not numerically different from the text that underwent the altering interpretation. Unlike analytic aesthetics that rests on a "privileged discovery of independently fixed entities," this theory will "secure the stability of texts and interpretation by way of the salient habits of life of a society."[16]

What makes this theory part of a recovery program for analytic aesthetics, and for analytic philosophy generally, is the continuing commitment to disciplined, responsible, stable, rational, truth-seeking, legitimating discourse, that is, philosophical inquiry. Margolis's claim that, given certain concessions, philosophy can and should continue in this role puts him at odds with Rorty and with those feminists who doubt either that philosophy can and should continue this role, or that it should do so in the manner Margolis proposes.

Margolis insists, *contra* Rorty, that our interpretative and descriptive practices must be justified, and that historicized and naturalistic explanations of these practices cannot take the place of philosophical or epistemological ones. Unless Margolis subscribes to some sort of Habermasian capacity for universal reason, or to some Gadamerian-like view of a historically formulated universalist tradition, it is difficult to see why his philosophical and epistemological justifications should not be considered as just another discourse that cannot be justified, but only explained in historicized, naturalistic terms. Margolis might object, in turn, that if one supposes that there is no justification of philosophical and epistemological practices, then not only is there no reason to accept one's own claim about the lack of justification—it is not justified either—but also that we fail to account for the fact that we cannot avoid justificatory language, that it is ineliminable. His pragmatic point is that within our experience, our practices and claims turn out to be justified or unjustified. However, if some group's philosophical and epistemological discourse has no more justification than its being the result of past practice, then how will it accomplish the task that Margolis assigns it—giving rational and critical direction about how to handle those cases that were not part of the paradigm learned in a practice? Unless rational guidance comes from somewhere else, it is not clear how a philosophy based on past practice will deliver any "legitimating" second-order discourse *before* the fact of some legitimating practice. In other words, it is not clear what is rational about a rational criterion, or how one will be devised to handle new cases.

One may have doubts about the role Margolis envisions for philosophy yet concede his point that an explanation of a practice in historicized and naturalistic terms simply sidesteps the question of justification, that such an explanation does not replace a philosophical or epistemological one. Nor need one dispute that philosophical and epistemological explanations aim at something more in the way of justification than appeals to past practice. Positing a norm or limit that transcends current practice, or some external conditions governing human knowledge seems an essential part of the philosophical project; analyses of descriptive and interpretative practices inevitably employ such language: hence philosophy's role, for Margolis, of demonstrating that commitments like minimal realism are reasonable, not merely therapeutic, as Rorty suggests.

Margolis holds that such demonstrations are possible because non-Kantian transcendental arguments are possible, that is, arguments that neither appeal illicitly to external grounds, nor insist on the uniqueness of the conceptual schemes they establish. Non-Kantian transcendental arguments are possible, according to Margolis, as long as we (1) agree that under no circumstances do we possess foundationalist knowledge of the physical world or of our own minds, (2) hold that "relative to a tradition of disciplined speculation about such matters, we simply *propose* conceptual schemes linking our best intuitions about the best work of science . . . with coherent, imaginable conditions deemed necessary to the support of scientific realism," and (3) "legitimate" alternative conceptual schemes as we assess their comparative power "by reference to our developing tradition of what is to count as the kind of (logically informal) rigor that such arguments best exhibit."[17]

Margolis does acknowledge that such arguments are "open to a profound form of rhetorical and diachronic contingency . . . that commits us to an equally deep relativism within philosophical dispute."[18] The contingency of such arguments permits us to reject them, although tradition works in their favor. The weight assigned tradition here accords with the conservative nature of normal scientific practice; successful science is taken as providing criteria, or at least guidance, that increases the likelihood of future success. But the conservatism inherent in the notion that one look to past practice for guidance may inhibit rather than promote success in, at least, some instances, and, perhaps, in many; new cases would be, of course, the most likely examples of such instances.

In many of the arts, the practice of establishing a stable referent for ongoing interpretation, that is, assigning them a nature or features that would make them "conceptually adequated" to making truthlike claims, may be as controversial as any subsequent interpretative claims.[19] The claim that the identification of texts is "a purely logical concession to the minima of discourse," and that any effects these identifications have on the truthlike values of subsequent interpretative claims may be neutralized by "relativizing them to the saliencies of our shared world" may be more problematic than Margolis's discussion admits. To identify a text or artwork as a candidate for interpretation is to constitute it according to the canons held by "culturally apt" individuals; in practice, "culturally apt" readers usually claim more status for their identifications than that of mere stipulations of a logical subject for subsequent predications. Despite the claim that there is no reason to suppose that there is anything illicitly privileged in merely attempting to form an adequational theory, Margolis's reinterpretation of interpretation may not escape Richard

Shusterman's criticism of an earlier formulation of the need for distinguishing between a first-order describing and a second-order interpreting: "it is not that we all agree how to describe the facts and differ only in what interpretations we elaborate from them. It is rather that *the descriptive facts are simply whatever we all strongly agree upon, while interpretations are simply what commands less consensus and displays (and tolerates) wider divergence.*"[20]

Future events may be more contingent than the suggestion that we look for criteria in past practice admits. The guidance provided by the past ill fits less conservative situations, for example, major theory changes in sciences, many episodes of contemporary art in which innovations seem to come at a more furious rate, sudden political and economic events, and the rise of new philosophical movements like feminist aesthetics. These episodes are "thicker" interpretative situations, "new cases" that cannot be accommodated, or at least easily accommodated, in the vocabularies governing current practices. At issue in these situations are substantive changes in vocabulary and questions about the assumptions that have governed past practice, for example, how to distinguish reasons for beliefs from causes for beliefs that are not reasons, or what makes a given choice rational rather than irrational. It is true that we continue to seek legitimating language for the commitments we make in such situations, but seeking is not necessarily finding. More important, legitimating language itself may be at issue in these situations. In cases of major changes in cultural practices or vocabularies, it is not clear how philosophy is to provide a legitimating second-order discourse *before* the fact of the legitimating practice, unless there is something transcendent, or at least, transcultural, to which philosophy may appeal. Margolis's position blocks such appeals.

Philosophy may distill from a practice the justificatory language that governs it, but it is not clear how philosophy can provide theories of legitimation for cases of major cultural change. If philosophy were to provide such theories, it is not clear how they would be adequate to the task of justifying any change except retrospectively, since these episodes nearly always include changes in the languages of legitimation. Episodes of major cultural change are controversial and puzzling because in retrospect we can and do describe them as having occurred for such and such reasons, yet it appears that not all of these reasons were explicitly recognized at the time. Of course, it may be that within the course of such changes some reasons are recognized, and some criteria employed, although the more dramatic and widespread the change, the less likely it is that there will be many. Just because a change does not result from applying some antecedently specified criteria, it does not follow that it must be arbitrary or irrational. Rorty observes that cultural changes of this magnitude "do not result from applying criteria (or from arbitrary decision) any more than individuals become theists or atheists, or shift from one spouse or circle of friends to another, as a result of either applying criteria or of *actes gratuits*."[21]

Rather than assuming that such changes are irrational if we can only give rational accounts of them after the fact, we should ask how such changes occur, and specifically, what role philosophy plays in them. Philosophical debates about legitimation may be an important part of changes in cultural practices, even if they are not resolved or do not yield reasons or criteria that govern such changes. But it is not clear whether this role fits Margolis's notion of disciplined, responsible, stable, rational, truth-seeking, legitimating inquiry, nor is it clear how philosophy of the sort Margolis advocates will be a force *for*, rather than *against* change.

Cultural and individual changes are more likely to occur when there are continuing radical doubts about current practices and their vocabulary, doubts that do not seem resolvable by arguments stated in this vocabulary.[22] Thus Rorty and some feminists claim that such changes are more likely to be generated by poetic or metaphoric discourse, that is, discourse in which words, by standing out as words, get us to see things differently.[23] This discourse stands in contrast to literal discourse in which words do not stand out any longer, but seem to describe or mirror some states of affairs, to make true or false statements about them.[24] In the past, such was the discourse of what Rorty calls "macho metaphysics" in which only inferential connections mattered because the transparency of language was thought to permit an accurate account of the way things are.[25]

Like poetic discourse, utopian politics, and revolutionary science, philosophy can generate a new vocabulary by redescribing "lots and lots of things in new ways" which will appeal to the next generation and which, once adopted, will cause them "to look for new forms of nonlinguistic behavior" which they may incorporate into new practices, e.g., "new social practices or new scientific equipment."[26] Rorty labels this "interesting philosophy" and describes it in terms that apply, appropriately enough, to some recent feminist philosophy.[27]

> This sort of philosophy does not work piece by piece, analyzing concept after concept, or testing thesis after thesis. Rather it works holistically and pragmatically. It says things like "try thinking of it in this way"—or more specifically—"try to ignore the apparently futile traditional questions by substituting the new and possibly interesting questions." It does not pretend to have a better candidate for doing

> the same old things which we did when we spoke in the old way. Rather, it suggests that we might want to stop doing things and do something else. But it does not argue for this suggestion on the basis of antecedent criteria common to the old and new language games. For just insofar as the new language really is new, there will be no such criteria.[28]

Rorty may exaggerate, as do some feminists, the extent to which languages are or can be new, and consequently neglect philosophy's role as second-order legitimating discourse about first-order inquiry. For feminists, the question is which role philosophy should play; for those whose concerns go under the label "feminist aesthetics" the more specific question is whether analytic aesthetics, even a revised analytic aesthetics of the sort Margolis proposes, is compatible with feminist aesthetics.

Attempts to link the future discourse of aesthetics with past practice are viewed with suspicion, or should be, by feminists, who are wary of perpetuating past practice, since ignoring or working against feminist concerns was a part of this practice. Since Margolis does not explicitly address feminist concerns, it is not clear whether or how Margolis's proposals for the recovery of analytic aesthetics can accommodate them. Feminists are apt to have reservations about any project that emphasizes disciplined inquiry, responsible readings, stable referents, and truth-seeking and legitimating discourse—and appeals to culturally apt individuals, the saliencies of our shared world, and diachronically conservative regularities historically judged to be among the best candidates we have found for rational foundations. Disciplined inquiry and responsible reading have yielded theories and texts—instances of truth-seeking and legitimating discourse, in which the subordination of women was implicitly assumed, if not explicitly condoned. These theories and texts were or could have been justified by appealing to culturally apt individuals, the saliencies of our shared world, and diachronically conservative regularities judged to be among the best candidates we have found for rational foundations. It does not follow, of course, that because feminists have these reservations, they must favor undisciplined and irrational inquiry, illegitimate discourse, unstable referents, or irresponsible readings, though some feminists may believe their interests are best served by adopting such practices. Neither does it follow from Margolis's commitments that he does not share the concerns of feminists, deplore the submission of women, or appreciate the project(s) of feminist aesthetics. The question is how Margolis or anyone else, can reconcile all of these commitments, and *whether there is a conservatism inherent in his proposals for the recovery of analytic aesthetics that obstructs the project(s) of feminist aesthetics.* [29]

The key issue for feminists is not simply the vocabulary of his project, but how it would be put into practice. Recently feminists like Nancy Fraser have argued, following Foucault, that attention must be directed to the analysis and critique of social practices rather than ideology: "modern power touches individuals through the various forms of constraint constitutive of their social practices rather than primarily through the distortion of their beliefs." [30] The focus, then, is on the way women are constructed as subjects, how gender functions, in the words of Teresa de Lauretis, "as a socio-cultural construct and a semiotic apparatus," and how gender is constructed by various social techniques and institutionalized discourses, epistemologies, critical practices and practices in daily life. [31] Throughout contemporary feminist theory runs the theme that for women, our languages—the vocabularies we use in daily life, in institutions like the art world, in epistemologies, in critical discourses—are not originally ours, nor of our choosing. [32] Though it is surely also true of men that, as Margolis put it, "their world is already culturally preformed for them," the world is preformed differently for men than it is for women, and languages and cultures are native for men in a way that they are not for women. Historically, men have controlled the sociocultural means of interpretation and communication, and they have taken their descriptive perspective as the truth. [33] They have determined what constitutes disciplined inquiry, responsible readings, rational guidance, and legitimating discourse. Men's control and production of what is observed, examined, and portrayed, means that it is their vocabularies that are internalized by both men and women. Thus women come to see themselves as men see them; often this means that they see themselves as different, as other, as the inferior second sex because that is how men see women in relation to themselves:

> women are . . . defined according to male criteria as regards their characteristics, their behavior, etc. Woman in the male order has learnt to see herself as inferior, inauthentic, incomplete. As the cultural order is ruled by men but women still belong to it, women also use the norms of which they themselves are the object . . . woman in the male order is at once *involved* and *excluded*. This means for woman's self-awareness that she sees herself by seeing *that* and *how* she is seen. She sees the world through male spectacles. . . . She is fixated on self-observation refracted in the critical gaze of man,

having left observation of the external world to his wide-ranging gaze. Thus her self-portrait originates in the distorting patriarchal mirror. In order to find her own image she must liberate the mirror from the *images of woman* painted on it by a male hand.[34]

Thus women's discomfiture at epistemologies using the idioms of mirrors, transparency, and essences, even, perhaps, at those committed to a minimal realism or culturally grounded interpretation, if they are going to harken back to past practices, or take as an unproblematic description *what we all strongly agree upon.* For the cultural order includes women by defining them in a negative opposition to men, and excludes women because of this definition, from evaluative speech on its basis. Their inclusion and exclusion makes the products of this cultural order at once familiar and foreign, since it is a part of this cultural order that women see themselves not simply as they look to themselves, but as men see them.[35]

If women are going to be culturally apt individuals, to the extent that they are permitted to be, then they must learn men's normative standards for evaluation; that is, their legitimating vocabularies, even if according to these standards women must see themselves as less apt. In the past, the degree to which women were permitted to become culturally apt, at least in the sense of high culture, was limited.[36]

Women's opportunities in the arts have been structured by men's domination in the production of art, in the languages of art and art criticism, in the public sector that controls it, and by the fact women have so often been the topic of art. When women become spectators or critics of art, they must adopt the perspective of the male gaze or appear culturally inept.[37] To quote Linda Nochlin:

> the acceptance of women as the object of the desiring male gaze in the visual arts is so universal that for a woman to question, or to draw attention to this fact, is to invite derision, to reveal herself as one who does not understand the sophisticated strategies of high culture and takes art "too literally," and is therefore unable to respond to aesthetic discourse.[38]

Even women who become artists find that the language does not exist for them to be considered just artists. Although permitted to break their silence, they must speak in a different voice. Gisela Breitling, a German artist, observes:

when I say (in German) I'm a painter [*Malerin*] that is not the same as when a man says he is a painter [*Maler*]. If a man wants to convey the same meaning as me then he would have to say that he was a painting man. When I say I'm a painter then the significance of my statement lies primarily in that I'm describing not what I do but in that I do it *as a woman*. With the sentence "I'm a painter [*Malerin*]," I differentiate myself and am differentiated from men who are painters. My vocabulary confines me to the company of women who are painters and thus my painting, too, is primarily considered with this limited context. Language confines women to segregated spaces, denies them any claim to universality which would put them in relation to all human beings. . . . I want to put my painting in a relationship to all painting and that is not just out of personal ambition. It is impossible for someone who is in the art world to have any idea of what being a painter means if she/he does not consider all art which is accessible to her/him or which interests her/him and include it in her/his process of learning, in her/his range of experience which, after all has the conquest of the whole world as its final goal.[39]

When women artists are taken together as a group, their works are taken from their historical context and become less comprehensible as a result: "the ghetto of the feminine presents us with a mixed bag of works, the creators of which usually have nothing more in common with each other than their sex" (166). Breitling's examples of the segregation of women's art—the show of Mexican muralists at the Nationalgalerie in Berlin in which Frida Kahlo's works are not included, but used, instead, in another show with the photographs of Tina Modotti, the placement of Paula Modersohn-Becker's pictures not in the Worpswede room but in a special room of the Kunsthalle in Bremen (167)—have analogues closer to home: the works of Lee Krasner were not shown along with those of Jackson Pollock's, nor were Elaine de Kooning's works shown with Willem de Kooning's, and the women surrealists were routinely excluded from surrealist exhibitions.

Women's works are segregated because the vocabulary and social practice in which women's works are not differentiated from men's do not yet exist. That is why it makes no sense to recommend that if we just give women a chance, they will turn out at least as well as men, that given the chance women can beat men at their own game.[40] If in the vocabulary, social practice, and game, women are seen as *essentially* different from men, women can hardly win the game, that is, turn out to be men, even if they so desired.

The suggestion that women embrace the notion of a separate women's discourse, women's art, feminist aesthetics, is also untenable. It simply inverts and thereby valorizes the oppositional dichotomy that has defined women and their projects as other—speakers of different vocabularies in different voices doing different things—by claiming that this voice, this vocabulary, and these things are not negative in the way that men had thought. But if this were the case, then what would it mean to say that women were oppressed by this dichotomy, and why would women want men to view their vocabulary and their projects positively? One would have thought that as long as women viewed them positively men's evaluation would not matter. If women's viewing these projects positively depends on their valorization by men, then they will not be valuable unless they become men's projects, in which case it is not clear why they should be considered women's special projects at all.[41] If one does regard women as oppressed by past practices, then why would one want to incorporate these practices into women's discourse and women's art and thereby perpetuate them?[42] Separatist solutions contain these ambiguities because they ignore the fact that women's discourse and women's art are still constructed out of existing essentialist vocabularies and existing cultural practices that take men as the standard by which women are judged and defined as other than the norm. Separate spheres for women's art (and feminist aesthetics) are no more equal to, or better than, those of men, than segregated places and institutions for people of color were (or are) equal to those reserved for whites only. For in neither case are they really separate, nor can they become so. The fact that women have been seen and talked about as the other, and that, consequently, they have lived as the other, means that they may see what men have observed and examined and portrayed in a different way. Although women may use the same vocabulary, they may do so in an ironic way that suggests that it is not the One True Vocabulary, that it is relative to the *Erscheinungen* of those who *share* a world. For those whose command of this vocabulary sometimes obscures its historicity and its relativity, such suggestions can be timely reminders. For those who find that their command of this vocabulary does not help in handling a new case, the perspective of those who see things differently might provide needed direction. But these reminders and directions cannot be heard by those who choose to segregate themselves from the other.

It is true, then, that much of what we have done in analytic aesthetics is "masculine aesthetics." It is also true that feminist aesthetics cannot avoid using the vocabulary of the past, although it can use it ironically and critically, and in so doing, prompt its speakers to do the same. One can attempt, as I have attempted in this essay, to show where this vocabulary means something different for women than what it means for men. One may argue that if essentialism is rejected and contingency acknowledged, and if what counts as a reason is grounded in past practice, then there is no reason for women to accept a cultural order that excludes them or treats them differently, no reason to accept a legitimating discourse that does not legitimate them, or a philosophy that has no emotional pertinency for them. If essentialism is rejected and contingency acknowledged, then an aesthetics which does not exclude women is possible. Though it is hard to envision exactly how such an aesthetics might look or what its vocabulary might be, it would seem to require more radical changes in aesthetic discourse than those Margolis proposes for the recovery of analytic aesthetics. Analytic and feminist philosophers interested in generating this discourse will have to engage in processes similar to those that Silvia Bovenschen finds in feminist artistic production: "conquering and reclaiming, appropriating and formulating, forgetting and subverting."[43] It has probably not escaped the reader's notice that this is a somewhat exhausting prospect.

Notes

1. A number of feminist and Marxist critics would be included among those who see "the aesthetic" as part of a vocabulary of oppression; see, for example, Linda Nochlin, *Women, Art, and Power and Other Essays* (New York: Harper and Row, 1988) and Susanne Kappeler, *The Pornography of Representation* (Minneapolis: University of Minnesota Press, 1988). Such a view is also implied by much of what Nancy Fraser writes in *Unruly Practices: Power, Discourse, and Gender in Contemporary Social Theory* (Minneapolis: University of Minnesota Press, 1989). It remains to be seen whether or how the notion of the aesthetic could be part of a vocabulary that was not oppressive.

Analytic philosophers generally resist, or at least claim to resist, any talk that hypostatizes or idealizes concepts in a way that makes them sound as if they were historical individuals, or worse, makes them sound as if they were otherworldly, ahistorical Platonic essences. However, I shall suggest that conceptual analysis of the sort practiced in the heyday of analytic philosophy was, at least in retrospect, pretty Platonic.

2. See, for example, the works by Fraser and Kappeler cited above, and the essays in Richard Shusterman's *Analytic Aesthetics* (New York: Basil Blackwell, 1989), especially Shusterman's "Introduction: Analyzing Analytic Aesthetics," Nicholas Wolterstorff's, "Philosophy of Art after Analysis and Romanticism," and Joseph Margolis's "The Eclipse and Recovery of Analytic Aesthetics."

3. I have not included intellectual practices here because the point of these criticisms is that philosophy in general, and aesthetics in particular, have either ignored historical and contextual factors altogether, or they have constructed internal histories, that is, histories in which

philosophical and aesthetic developments are explained by reference to other earlier philosophical and aesthetic developments, and in which external factors are largely ignored.

4. Joseph Margolis, "Eclipse and Recovery," 162–63. Page numbers for subsequent quotations and references from this work will be given in parentheses following the citation.

5. Margolis concedes that the themes that he suggests analytic aesthetics pursue "go entirely counter to the canonical tendencies of analytic philosophy" but he does not think they are "incompatible with the native discipline of such philosophy," ibid., 185.

6. See note 1 above.

7. The quote from Rorty comes from "Postmodernist Bourgeois Liberalism," *Journal of Philosophy* 80 (1983): 583–89; reprinted in Robert Hollinger, ed., *Hermeneutics and Praxis* (Notre Dame: Notre Dame University Press, 1985), 217. Margolis quotes this statement of Rorty's on p. 183 of "Eclipse and Recovery."

8. Joseph Margolis, *Pragmatism Without Foundations* (New York: Basil Blackwell, 1986), 182.

9. Ibid., emphasis added.

10. Ibid., 158.

11. Joseph Margolis, "Reinterpreting Interpretation," *Journal of Aesthetics and Art Criticism* 47 (1989), 238.

12. Ibid.

13. Ibid., 242. Margolis observes that "in his terribly freewheeling way," Roland Barthes shows us "how to entertain the idea that a text [in Margolis's sense, which he thinks is congruent enough with Barthes] need not be presumed to have a fixed nature throughout a responsible reading [what Margolis is calling interpretation] in spite of the fact that however that nature may change, it remains a changing or changeable nature *assignable to this or that text.*"

14. Ibid.

15. Ibid., 241.

16. Ibid., 249.

17. Margolis, *Pragmatism Without Foundations*, 303.

18. Ibid., 307.

19. Margolis, "Reinterpreting," 238.

20. Richard Shusterman, "Interpretation, Intention, and Truth," *Journal of Aesthetics and Art Criticism* 46 (1988): 403, emphasis added.

21. Richard Rorty, *Contingency, Irony, and Solidarity* (Cambridge: Cambridge University Press, 1989), 9.

22. See Rorty's definition of an ironist in *Contingency*, 73.

23. Richard Rorty, "Deconstruction and Circumvention," *Critical Inquiry* 11 (1984): 4. Rorty borrows the notion of "words standing out as words" from Geoffrey Hartman, *Saving The Text: Literature, Derrida, Philosophy* (Baltimore: Johns Hopkins University Press, 1981), xxi.

24. Of course, all discourse is metaphorical in its origins, if words do not mirror or correspond to reality.

25. Ibid., 2–3, 12.

26. Rorty, *Contingency*, 9.

27. In "Thugs and Theorists: A Reply to Bernstein," *Political Theory* 15 (1987): 577 n. 16, Rorty describes feminism as "one area of *Ideologiekritik* where people are actually having some new ideas, actually unmasking something that hasn't already been unmasked *ad nauseam.*"

28. Rorty, *Contingency*, 9.

29. Feminists might ask whether there is a conservatism inherent in Margolis's talk of scientific realism that works against their efforts to combat sexism in science. For a discussion of how sexism and gender are present in science, see Sandra Harding, *The Science Question in Feminism* (Ithaca: Cornell University Press, 1986).

30. Fraser, *Unruly Practices*, 25.

31. Teresa de Lauretis, *Technologies of Gender: Essays on Theory, Film and Fiction* (Blooming-ton: Indiana University Press, 1987), 2.

32. See, for example, Silvia Bovenschen, "Is There A Feminist Aesthetic?" in *Feminist Aesthetics*, ed., Gisela Ecker, trans., Beth Weckmueller (Boston: Beacon, 1985), 30.

33. This point about men's perspective is made by Silvia Bovenschen in "Is There A Feminist Aesthetic?" 26; she remarks that it was established by Simone de Beauvoir long ago.

34. Sigrid Weigel, "Double Focus: On the History of Women's Writing," in *Feminist Aesthetics*, 61. See also de Lauretis's discussion of the construction of gender. *Technologies*, esp. 14–18.

35. Fraser cites the observation of Phillipe Lacoue-Labarthe and Jean-Luc Nancy that since Aristotle the notion of man as a social and political animal has been based on their sharing in ethical or evaluative speech; *Unruly Practices*, 85. This point neatly connects the denial of women's suffrage with their inability to participate in evaluative speech in the way that men do. For a discussion of how products of this cultural order, especially art, are foreign to women, see Bovenschen, "Is There a Feminist Aesthetic?" p. 28.

36. Cora Kaplan observes that women's limited access to high culture is evident in the "rupture between childhood and adolescence, when in western societies (and in other cultures as well) public speech is a male privilege and women's speech restricted by custom in mixed sex gatherings, or, if permitted, still characterized by its private nature, an extension of the trivial domestic discourse of women"; see her *Sea Changes: Essays on Culture and Feminism* (London: Verso, 1986), 70. Presumably these limitations on public speech are not currently so extensive as they once were.

37. Susanne Kappeler has combined these themes in a blistering attack on how men's control of the creation, content, criticism and production of art has generated a "pornographic" structure of representation in which women, people of color, and the poor are represented as passive objects of domination for the pleasure of white male spectators. Kappeler's approach is not to examine the pros and cons of the thesis; rather, she tries to get the reader to think in a different way by employing various rhetorical strategies. For example, she analyzes the way in which a photograph of a white farmer and the young black man he murdered resembles typical pornographic shots, and she considers how the rhetoric of judgments about art and pornography reflect and reinforce cultural norms.

38. Linda Nochlin, *Women, Art, and Power, and Other Essays*, 29–30.

39. Gisela Breitling, "Speech, Silence and the Discourse of Art," in *Feminist Aesthetics*, 165. Page numbers for further references and quotations from this work will be given in parentheses following the citation.

40. See Bovenschen, "Is There a Feminist Aesthetic?" 29 for some interesting comments on this notion.

41. The obvious exception would be pregnancy and childbirth but this is only one practice that some women can engage in for a given period during their lives. They still must consider the rest of their lives, and other social and cultural practices that structure them.

42. See, Ecker, *Feminist Aesthetics*, 16. See also Teresa de Lauretis, *Technologies*, 1–2 for an interesting perspective on this problem.

43. Bovenschen, "Is There A Feminist Aesthetic?" 47.

18
Reconciling Analytic and Feminist Philosophy and Aesthetics

Joseph Margolis

I have misgivings about any strong presumption regarding the special rigor thought to be conveyed by the attributive use of the term "analytic" in the expression "analytic aesthetics." I don't, of course, deny the admirable rigor of what is fairly collected as analytic aesthetics or analytic philosophy. But I don't think there are any general methods or conceptual preconditions that have the remotest chance of coming close to what is essential to the practice. It proceeds by example. On the contrary, I myself tried to be quite frank in a recent paper, "The Eclipse and Recovery of Analytic Aesthetics," in admitting that certain prejudices about the proper scope and orientation of analytic aesthetics (again, like analytic philosophy) would, if seriously pursued, simply render the entire enterprise irrelevant.[1] The upshot for me was that "analytic" aesthetics was bound to reverse "itself" on a great many substantive issues if it expected to continue to be fruitful at this late date. In particular, it would have to explore more seriously than it ever had, questions of the deep historicity of human existence, the horizontal and preformative conditions of inquiry, the fruitlessness of strongly reductive and extensionalist strategies of analysis, the avoidance of pretended invariances, other supposed ontological fixities, the unlikelihood of theoretical closure, and the impossibility of avoiding the contamination of would-be "objective" analyses in the direction of bias, interest, perspective, *normalization,* power, and sheer domination. Analytic philosophy is not particularly so disposed.

Joanne Waugh's perceptive essay "Analytic and Feminist Aesthetics," discusses some of these views of mine—affords me, therefore, an opportunity to address feminist aesthetics and the relation between the "two" movements.[2] But I must say at once that the grammatical position of "feminist" in the expression "feminist aesthetics" is in even greater danger of generating confusion than the use of "analytic." I have been utterly unable to discern in the feminist literature any homogeneous philosophical practice, substantive claim, or method of working that could, more or less disjunctively, be called feminist, that compared favorably (in the recognitional sense) with the more convergent literature of analytic aesthetics—except, of course, for feminism's decisive emphasis on emancipatory themes and the uncovering of what I hope I may lump together, without explanation, as evidence of the "patriarchal" or "oppressive" structure of Western cultural life.

Of course, if what I have just said about analytic aesthetics is reasonable, then it is entirely consistent with that warning that I take analytic philosophy to have practiced a kind of "patriarchal" oppression on itself. I think I may say that I am recommending that we be forever alert to all sorts of conceptual breaches of *normalization* that may be promising in a subversive and emancipatory way. My only caveat here—hardly advice—is that one cannot really prepare in advance for any particular such promising subversion. One can only be hospitably disposed in general, and then seize as well as one can whatever new currents intuition recommends in time. There is nothing virtuous in mere subversion (*contra* late Foucault); there is no assured subterranean "other" that must be recovered from all our discursive practices (*contra* Lyotard); and there is nothing inherently liberal or emancipatory in a mere consensual impulse to change a practice (*contra* Rorty). We *must* anticipate; but legitimation is inevitably reflexive. Furthermore, we must make room, dialectically, for those who would legitimate resistance to this or that particular revolution or subversion. No one really believes that "anything goes" (not even Feyerabend). To admit that much is not to abandon one's partisan allegiances; it is only to admit that both political and philosophical strength comes from grasping the horizontal limitation of any present outlook.

Without wishing to be falsely compliant, I may say that I am in strong sympathy with what I perceive to be the profound humanity of the feminist movement. But, *whatever* has so far been most visible in the feminist literature in the way of theoretical claims—even to the point of debating whether theory is itself counterfeminist, whether women have a biologically distinct cognitional or affective or effective orientation, whether feminism can afford, conceptually, to *have* a thesis or method, and where, precisely, the difference lies between a feminist philosophy and Marxism or psychoanalysis or deconstruction or genealogy or Lacanian semiotics or liberalism or pragmatism or analytic philosophies of science or the hermeneutics of suspicion or the like—it seems to me impossible to mark off any suitably large theme that has not been soundly trounced within the feminist literature itself or is not sufficiently well formed to count as a fair specimen to be usefully compared, say, with analytic aesthetics (which I concede, is not to endorse the latter either). This is nowhere clearer than in the troubled discussion of the very term "feminist." I find myself pretty well convinced of the need to go beyond "feminist" aesthetics and "feminist" philosophy just as I do of the need to go beyond "analytic" aesthetics and "analytic" philosophy—which, I trust, does not mean merely "masculine" or "patriarchal" philosophy. (Both terms are equivocal and tainted.) I agree, generally, with the way in which "feminist" thought has been problematized in such recent accounts as Toril Moi's *Sexual/Textual Politics: Feminist Literary Theory,*[3] and Rita Felski's *Beyond Feminist Aesthetics: Feminist Literature and Social Change;*[4] and I find myself most in sympathy with the alternative radical treatments of gender identification and domination offered in Nancy Fraser's *Unruly Practices: Power, Discourse and Gender in Contemporary Social Theory*[5] and in Judith Butler's *Gender Trouble and Subversion of Identity.*[6] Well, there you have at least my sympathies.

There *are* some analogies that may be drawn between analytic and feminist aesthetics (and philosophy) that account for their current troubles and strengths, but there are certain decisive differences as well. Analytic aesthetics (and philosophy) is the direct heir to the accumulating practice of the strong empiricism of modern British philosophy, of lessons drawn from logical positivism, from the unity of science movement, from distinctly American currents focused by pragmatism or the analytic model favored by W. V. Quine and his associates, and by whatever might be thought to be congenially recoverable from Kant's aesthetics and general philosophy.

This is an extremely narrow gauge of thought, though its ingenious practitioners have occasionally shown an amplitude that might not otherwise have been thought likely. There is almost no emphasis to be found in it on the complexities of history, the historicizing of cognition and inquiry, the praxical content of judgment, taste, description, explanation, interpretation, the discontinuities of cultural movements, horizontal blindness, and, most particularly, the social forces that form and preform the conceptual orientation of human selves apt for any of the pertinent roles belonging to the world of art.

Feminism is almost completely occupied with just such themes, neglected by the "analytic" crowd: particularly, with assembling evidence of the politically and morally oppressive use of conceptual analysis in situations of gender domination and with recovering a sense of the conditions, existential, historical, political, ideological, educational, or explicitly revolutionary, under which committed feminists *should* engage aesthetics (and philosophy).

Analytic philosophers run the danger of supposing the world is tidier than it really is: they fail to perceive the kind of complexity that feminists excel in uncovering, and they tend to think they can uncover fairly swiftly the universal structures of artworks, objective criticism, aesthetic values, and anything of the sort. They are certainly prone to all the conceptual fixities many critics (not merely feminists) have leveled at them or at the larger company to which they obviously belong—for instance, by Derrida, Foucault, Lyotard and, in a strong pop sense, in the United States, by Richard Rorty.[7]

Feminists, on the other hand, face an unresolved dilemma: they risk being co-opted or challenged *within* the scope of canonical philosophical practice, whenever they formulate a distinctly systematic thesis or method; and they risk being unable to subscribe to *any* large systematic thesis or method, whenever they rally to the patently political or activist concern to dismantle the oppressive practices they mark as their rightful target (which, effectively, leads to contradictions within the movement, or else to a deliberate and canny resistance to familiar ways of speaking that are thought to facilitate being too easily co-opted).[8]

I think the essential problem is this: there is no way to avoid altogether the strictures of enunciative (or constative) discourse, in particular, the resources of reference and predication. But, although the prominent use of those resources may favor the dominance of well-defined social aggregates over others (by class, by color, by race, by sex, by gender, by religion, by ethos, by family), there is no inherently "patriarchal" or similar exploitative function built into them. The disadvantages accrue only historically, only through the habituating function of the practices of this society, or that. But they surely do accrue there. It is, therefore, altogether reasonable that, in the interests of overturning the hegemony of any such socially entrenched use of such resources, feminists and others will improvise new discursive categories favoring their own vision or will subvert the habituated expectations of standard discursive practices—as, for instance, developed in instructively diverse ways by Kierkegaard, Nietzsche, Heidegger, Derrida, Foucault, Lyotard, Deleuze, and, now, Cixous, Irigaray, Kristeva, and Spivak.[9] But the question of the *exploitative use* of whatever is conceptually entrenched in our *enunciative resources* is altogether different from the question of the *cognitively privileged* standing of any of our *metaphysical, epistemological, logical, methodological, or normative categories or theories.*

The uneasy convergence of analytic and feminist views (not altogether consistently managed on either side) lies with the widespread philosophical conviction that reality, including the whole of human culture, is neither invariant in structure nor transparently disclosed to inquiry. But that theme neither requires dismantling enunciative discourse (which seems impossible as well as pointless) nor entails any new fixities of transparency or invariance (on which of course exploitative programs thrive). In my opinion, there is a noticeable backsliding in these regards in both analytic and feminist philosophy and a noticeable extravagance in feminist philosophy meant to avoid just those dangers. But there is a better justification for the latter extreme, simply because feminist concerns *are* primarily political—in the robust sense in which a reading of Virginia Woolf or Samuel Beckett may be made to contribute to an informed feminist intervention.[10] Nevertheless, I must confess in the interests of candor that I cannot see any way of sorting any descriptive, explanatory, or legitimative concerns *of a distinctly philosophical kind* that could be disjunctively marked as feminist; though I hasten to add that I *can* see a distinctive philosophical "program" that *includes* feminism in a favorable and prominent way, and though I can see that feminism's political concerns are more than merely philosophical and should not be expected to rest primarily on the distinction of its philosophical method. I frankly think any other alternative leads to a new "essentializing" that feminists cannot afford. (I take it that Waugh's sympathies for Rorty and Foucault and her uncertainty about my own proposals bear me out.)

What I mean is that feminism has gradually evolved along lines that are best identified with a psychoanalytically informed hermeneutics of suspicion, a Marxist-like emphasis on praxis, a deconstruction of presumed originary and totalizing discourse, genealogies of conceptual discontinuities, contextualized semiotics, and a variety of analytic strategies drawn from many different sources (Kantian, Hegelian, Frankfurt Critical, pragmatist, Heideggerean) opposed to any and all presumptions of ontological invariance or cognitive transparency. Of course, feminism may invent new such strategies, but those strategies could never remain feminist.

My point is simply that feminism has passed through a first confused phase of an exploratory sort and is now pretty well past that threshold. In that sense, it is now no more uncertain, undisciplined, uncharacterizable, uninstructive (or the reverse) than any of the older "schools" that similarly have come to favor a variety of diverging, not always mutually compatible, subcurrents. Nevertheless, it *is* rightly attentive to subversive options, *not* to organizing a new "school"; and analytic aesthetics *is* rightly attentive to the matter of constructing the best conceptual picture of the arts and human culture that it can, though *not* at the expense of what looks promising even if subversive. There is the point of difference and convergence between the two sorts of "presence."

In fact, the dialectical relations that hold between the themes I have specified—(i) the referential and predicative resources of enunciative discourse, and (ii) the disputable status, via (i), of legitimative claims of transparency and/or invariance—are very nicely keyed to clarifying another well-known source of dispute in our own time, namely, the modernist/postmodernist debate. For the modernist typically favors a strong positive commitment on (i) and yields too sanguinely, by a non sequitur, by ineptitude, or by express conviction, to a strong positive commitment on (ii). The best-known example of a failed modernist in this regard is, of course, Jürgen Habermas.[11] On the other hand, the postmodernist strenuously opposes any strong positive presumptions regarding (ii) (for instance, legitimative discourse, standard philosophy) and then, opportunistically, arbitrarily, by way of a non sequitur, either denies the usual features of discourse under (i) (for instance, truth claims) or separates first-order truth claims from second-order legitimative discourse regarding such claims. The best-known examples of a failed postmodernist in this regard are, of course, Jean-François Lyotard and Richard Rorty.[12] It is easy to see the sense in which feminism has been tempted by postmodernism; but it would be a mistake to identify the two, and it would (in my opinion) certainly be a grave mistake if feminism were to adopt the postmodernist's *analytic* stand on legitimation merely to advance its political objectives or to avoid the captured idiom of "patriarchal" discourse.

I can now turn in a useful way to Waugh's remarks. Let me say straight off that Waugh reports my own views quite accurately. I have no complaint. There are a few decisive places where she misunderstands me, I think, or does not quite see the force of the options I recommend. There's a point to explaining all that: I should like to have my views correctly before readers of Waugh's discussion and, more important, I believe the solutions I recommend are entirely compatible with what I take to be the best features of the feminist position—without being, in any sense, feminist solutions themselves. In fact, I honestly believe that there is a natural alliance between Waugh's philosophical critique and my own, that she risks scanting (without actually denying) because of her quite natural attention to the activist implications of accommodating even a more congenial version of "analytic" aesthetics. The solution I offer, therefore, may serve as a clue to what I suggested earlier was the need to go beyond both analytic and feminist philosophy (and other philosophies, of course).

The heart of Waugh's very reasonable challenge to me is in the following passage:

> Margolis insists, *contra* Rorty, that our interpretive and descriptive practices must be justified, and that historicized and naturalistic explanations of these practices cannot take the place of philosophical or epistemological ones. Unless Margolis subscribes to some sort of Habermasian capacity for universal reason, or to some Gadamerian-like view of a historically formulated universalist tradition, it is difficult to see why his philosophical and epistemological justifications should not be considered as just another discourse that cannot be justified, but only explained in historicized, naturalistic terms. (page 404)

Waugh herself refers to *Pragmatism without Foundations,* so she was clearly aware that I rejected both Habermas's and Gadamer's options (just the ones she mentions).[13] The important thing is that the answer to Waugh's question is the very one that, in my view, could advance analytic philosophy beyond its own threatening impasse, could reconcile Anglo-American and Continental European philosophies of the greatest promise, and could provide a bridge between these two undertakings and the work of feminist philosophy (to the extent feminists would be interested). (I myself think that that would be worth a good deal.)

Waugh correctly reports that I hold that "non-Kantian transcendental arguments *are* possible," on conditions she herself details; that shows, of course, that I do *not* subscribe to anything like the Habermasian or Gadamerian line. The result is that she sees that there is no conceptual difficulty to reconciling her view of feminism and her view of my view of analytic aesthetics: she is merely concerned to emphasize a general *political* or activist warning that "the conservatism inherent in the notion that one look to past practice for guidance *may* inhibit rather than promote success" in future science, future philosophy, future accommodations of promising subversions of hidebound practices. I agree, but I see no way to reassure her *philosophically*. Grant only that and the argument sketched regarding the modernism/postmodernism dispute: there remains then no principled dispute between us.

I must, however, accuse Waugh herself of retreating, without grounds, to the canonical view of philosophical legitimation, in challenging my own proposal. Not that she actually subscribes to the canon; but she subscribes to the idea that *if* legitimation were possible, it would (or would have to) be in conformity with something like Kant's or Habermas's (or even Gadamer's) universal claims. *That is just what I deny.* I take the norms of rationality—and of rational philosophical argument in particular—to be normatively projected artifacts *of* and *within* changing human history. I do *not* hold, as Waugh seems to think I must, that legitimation is based on timeless, ahistorical, exceptionless, apodictic considerations *or* on "past practice" alone. Waugh says:

> if some group's philosophical and epistemological discourse has no more justification than its being the result of past practice, then how will it accomplish the task that Margolis assigns it—giving rational and critical direction about how to handle those cases that were not part of the paradigm learned in a practice. Unless rational guidance comes from somewhere else, it is not clear how a philosophy based on past practice will deliver any "legitimating" second-order discourse *before* the fact of some legitimating practice. (page 404)

In short, Waugh offers me the options of the modernist and postmodernist *only*—which I reject. I believe this explains her penchant for Rorty's (failed) repudiation of legitimative philosophy. It manifests itself in a number of ways: notably where she asks, *after* admitting (against Rorty) that "it is true that we continue to seek legitimating language for the commitments we make" (in our various practices)—and concedes that I "block" any appeal to "something transcendent, or at least transcultural" (the "transcultural" needs to be discussed more at length: it is *not* inaccessible, though it is not for that reason changeless or essentialist)—"how [my view of philosophy could] provide a legitimating second-order discourse *before* the fact of the legitimating practice." The answer is: it could not; none is wanted, and none is needed. Legitimation, on my view, is a *rational bet,* made on intransparentist and nonprivileged grounds, subject to revision for cognate reasons as one begins to see the comparative advantages of this way of proceeding and that. That is, in my view transcendental or legitimative arguments have a history and are socially "produced." I do need to explain this third alternative I had in mind; but it is the very one I develop in *Pragmatism without Foundations* and in other places, including "The Eclipse and Recovery" paper Waugh discusses.

I can make my point clear by two brief illustrations. In contemporary physics, there are many puzzles drawn from attempts to interpret the so-called Bell inequalities—which bear on the fortunes of theories of reality favoring quantum-mechanical models but which do not narrowly depend on quantum-mechanical conceptions—that produce apparently insoluble paradoxes for classical physics. Relative to a general realist orientation regarding physics but consistent with a strong commitment to the cognitive intransparency of nature, the predictive power of quantum-mechanical strategies and the relatively independent anomalies for classical physical models resulting from the Bell inequalities oblige us to entertain deep conceptual changes in our very idea of the real structure of physical nature. That issue is at once a first-order (scientific) and a second-order (legitimative) issue. Abner Shimony, for one, speaks instructively here of "experimental metaphysics" as a natural continuation of physics proper.[14] This means that a paradox, a deep conceptual puzzle, a categorical tension, an anomaly, a contradiction, an *aporia,* has spontaneously arisen in the very heart of experimental physics, and there demands a distinct legitimative (second-order, rational "transcendental") argument as to how to go on, given the salient fact, to recommend the most promising line of theorizing about the structure of the real world—which, at the quantum level, possibly affecting all commonsense discourse, does not accord with our most deeply entrenched macroscopic notions of real time and space and physical position.

Our intuitions of conceptual coherence and rationality confront the puzzle, are affected by it, and yield as they must in a variety of ways (including even a deeper entrenching of classical expectations and an insistence on errors of some sort to "explain" away the anomaly). All this is done as a rational bet—under conditions of intransparency, internal to some scientific "ideology" or other, within the terms of historicized change and inquiry, but still legitimatively. So rationality, legitimation, philosophical work in general, is artifactual, emergent, historically horizoned, pluralized, and relativized, contingent, hardly addressed to secure invariances, but not for that reason alone merely "naturalistic" (in Quine's sense) or historicized (in Waugh's).[15]

In a word, it is entirely possible to save the distinction between first- and second-order (legitimative) discourse *under* historical or historicized conditions. The implicit claim or doubt (Waugh's) that that is not possible is either a retreat to the canon or a retreat to Rorty's attack on the canon, which comes to the same thing. But no reason has ever been given for thinking that philosophy (and aesthetics, of course) cannot have learned its lesson well enough to see that it is still necessary to theorize, on *internalist* grounds (on grounds, roughly, within the constraints intended by our distinctions (i)–(ii)), about what the best picture of human knowledge and reality is.

That, at any rate, is the solution I offer. It is one I believe the feminists can accept; but it is the one Waugh does not concede. The evolving practice and its legitimative rationale—each subject, equilibratively, to pressures from the other—explain how it is that, contrary to Waugh's charge, philosophical justification is, can be, and must be made under historically changing circumstances: how it is that legitimation is certainly not based solely on "past practice," and not on the use of any Kantian-like or Platonizing "universalist tradition." I think the solution is a unique one and worth bearing in mind.

Consider a second illustration, this time from the arts. Peter Bürger, assessing Walter Benjamin's justly famous essay, "The Work of Art in the Age of Mechanical Reproduction,"[16] demonstrates with regard to Dada (Duchamp, in particular) that, contrary to Benjamin's "materialist explanation of the changes in modes of [the] reception [of art] as a result of changes in reproduction technique," "the loss of aura [the sacral status of art in traditional societies, which Benjamin links to the analysis of bourgeois art] is not traced to a change in reproduction techniques but [rightly] to an intent on the part of the makers of art [which Benjamin himself admits in a way but downplays]."[17]

What is important here is that Bürger's review of the historical development of Dada (and of other avant-garde movements) uncovers a "contradiction," a dialectical challenge to the seemingly smooth adequacy of Benjamin's first-order explanation of certain bourgeois art currents; and that, in the process of correcting Benjamin's theory and linking it to a stronger theory of avant-garde art, one comes to terms with a historicized view of the legitimation for positing such a change in our understanding. "Critical science," Bürger says—he means both first-order art history and criticism and the second-order conditions of understanding under which first-order theories replace one another—

> differs from traditional science because it reflects the social significance of its [own] activity. . . . Critical science understands itself as part of social praxis, however mediated it may be. It is not "disinterested" [guided by unerring reality] but guided by interest. . . . [It proceeds by a critique of ideology] because [that] permits one to think the *contradictory* relationship of intellectual objectifications and social reality.[18]

Bürger's notion is, precisely, that philosophy is dialectically implicated in the praxis of a society that also permits the development of the particular forms of art that it tries to understand "objectively." Criticism is not detached, not rationally governed by some sort of timeless correspondence between judgment and reality. It is rather "the *production* [the social production] of cognitions."[19] Hence, it faces a distinct (but ubiquitous) problem of objectivity. It is able to function legitimatively only by dialectical means—that is, only in a way internal to its own horizon, critically, in terms of the salient "contradictions" and conceptual tensions it itself encounters. Its best (indeed, its only) rationale regarding "objectivity" depends on systematic resolution (via its own conceptual innovations) of those contradictions and its continued success in resolving further such contradictions. There is no other possibility. There you have another adumbration of the thesis I have tried to put forward.

I have a few final observations to make. In "Reinterpreting Interpretation," which Waugh considers, I show how to construe artworks as (enunciatively) open to reference and predication—that is, to the requirements of reidentification under changing conditions of interpretation—without producing logical paradox, without falling back to a closed or ahistorical picture of interpretable texts, and without abandoning the notion that *what* is interpretable in a text is affected and altered by the very history of its ongoing interpretation.[20] Waugh mentions the point but does not see its importance.

I believe that showing that *that* is possible has never been explicitly attempted in anything like an analytic idiom. It confirms, first of all, that artworks and texts are capable of infinitely many interpretations (also, histories) without generating logical difficulties; second, it advances a purely formal solution, hospitable therefore to any otherwise eligible interpretation; third, it solves the puzzle of how to preserve numerical identity, in intentionally complex contexts, without essentializing art, without insinuating any cognitive privilege, without disallowing divergent, even incompatible, interpretations, without failing to admit the historically open-ended, reflexively changeable significance of particular artworks; and fourth, it shows how to hold such gains while preserving an operative sense of objectivity and resisting privilege. (To say that the solution is "formal" is merely to say that it concerns an apparently minimal structure of all disclosure, and that it is meant to be entirely neutral to all substantive views that themselves need to make use of just that structure.)

The prejudice of the canon is that it is impossible to do all that. It is, apparently, Waugh's opinion as well. When I say that my solution is "diachronically conservative," that we may "continue as before" (as she rightly reports), I mean (and meant) such remarks to be taken only in a formal sense—as permitting the most generous form of "interested" interpretation that anyone

(Marxist, feminist, Heideggerean, Foucauldian, Barthesian) would ever want. I did not intend my remarks to promote any particular "conservative" doctrine (as opposed to radical ones), but only to *conserve,* to save, logically, the least restrictive practice of interpretation imaginable. My objective was, precisely, to show that nothing is lost, as far as coherence and viability are concerned, by admitting a critical practice so clearly at variance with canonical opinions. I honestly think this has never been shown before, but perhaps I'm wrong. What I claim would ensure a viable practice is no more than this: that we sustain the narrative continuity of the history of interpretation of particular texts and artworks. That's all! Those histories will, of course, be similarly affected. But, then, that begins to capture the complexity of the conditions under which I am prepared to claim we live.

On the realism issue that Waugh raises, briefly, I hope my position is entirely clear. I hold, first of all, that realism is initially justified in a holist sense only, without privileged grounds, as an inference to the best explanation of the survival of the race; and that, second, *all* distributed realist claims— whether in physics or art history—are internal to that holism and there legitimated in just the way I have illustrated. It does not bother me at all that there cannot be a uniquely correct or invariant account of reality, whether in physics or art history. Grant that much: the question, What is real? remains important all right, but its usually assigned significance falls away. For instance, the distinction between first- and second-order matters is itself a second-order question embedded in particular forms of life—within which it makes no sense to posit one without the other.

I think a large part of the contribution of feminist philosophy is to inform us of unsuspected *interests* that govern first- and second-order discourse, and that a large part of the contribution of feminist aesthetics is to inform us of just how such interests affect the production and interpretation of artworks and texts. I therefore see no reasons at all for supposing that there is the least conceptual tension between feminist philosophy and what I intend by the "recovery" of analytic philosophy. But I admit the suggestion is hardly orthodox, and I concede the fairness of Waugh's worry that "there is a conservatism inherent in [Margolis's] proposals for the recovery of analytic aesthetics that obstructs the project(s) of feminist aesthetics." It's possible that *I* may be more "conservative" (in Waugh's sense) than the theory I advance. But I don't think even that is true.

Let me add a last word about feminism, philosophically considered. I am persuaded that its strength, at the present time, lies primarily in its conver- gence with poststructuralist tendencies. What I mean by that is that feminism is especially instructive in exposing the protean forms of repressing or suppressing the "other" (*l'autre*) in that sense that has been fairly well standardized in Jean-François Lyotard's account, in the opening passages of *The Différend*.[21]

This is not to endorse Lyotard's resolution of the puzzle regarding the *différend*—which, quite frankly, is a conceptual disaster. But, first of all, feminists (in the strong philosophical sense) are not prepared to confine their analyses narrowly to the repression or suppression of women and feminine interests—in politics or literature or anywhere else; they see the point of isolating the global implications of "hegemonic discourse," although doing that cannot favor any merely abstract function. This is a theme that is bound, I am convinced, to be one of the strongest themes of social, interpretive, and philosophical theory at the end of our century and at the beginning of the next.

Second, however, insofar as the purposive exposure of exploitative practices applied to the "other" cannot fail to be affirmatively connected with corrective public policies—political, moral, economic, educational, artistic, sexual— feminist theory (*any* theory that endorses this much of poststructuralism) must also eclipse poststructuralism itself. For, there are *as yet* no self- consistent policies on political or other practical matters that can rightly be called poststructuralist: there is nothing in Foucault, Lyotard, Deleuze, Baudrillard, Cixous, or Irigaray, for instance, that would suit in this regard; but if there is none, then there is also no sustainable application (no rationale, in that sense) *for* the feminist or post-structuralist critique.

Of course, it would be entirely possible to construe the required practical program as simply liberal rather than as *post*-poststructuralist. But the truth is that the feminist critique finds its opponents among liberals and Marxists and modernists and postmodernists as much as among the champions of estab- lished or privileged canons or authority; there would be no *point*, philosophi- cally speaking, to a critique (whether of art, art criticism, political rights, freedom, history, or anything else) that did not reconcile its practice, or the rationale of its practice, with its philosophical claim.

Feminist criticism and theory are at precisely the same impasse as every other late twentieth-century philosophical program that has tried to come to terms with the same poststructuralist theme the feminists have. I have no tidy solution. But I hold that, with respect to the arts and the interpretation and criticism of the arts, what I have been trying to do—in "recovering" analytic aesthetics—is to explore the possibilities of a post-poststructuralist aesthetics (hence, a postanalytic and a postfeminist aesthetics). I think there are not many who have grasped the problem. But I believe that feminist philosophers should endorse the effort.

Notes

1. Joseph Margolis, "The Eclipse and Recovery of Analytic Aesthetics," in *Analytic Aesthetics*, ed. Richard Shusterman (Oxford: Basil Blackwell, 1989).

2. Joanne Waugh, "Analytic Aesthetics and Feminist Aesthetics: Neither/Nor?" Chapter 17 in this volume.

3. Toril Moi, *Sexual/Textual Politics: Feminist Literary Theory* (London: Routledge, 1985).

4. Rita Felski, *Beyond Feminist Aesthetics: Feminist Literature and Social Change* (Cambridge: Harvard University Press, 1989).

5. Nancy Fraser, *Unruly Practices: Power, Discourse and Gender in Contemporary Social Theory* (Minneapolis: University of Minnesota Press, 1989).

6. Judith Butler, *Gender Trouble and Subversion of Identity* (New York: Routledge, Chapman and Hall, 1989).

7. See Richard Rorty, *Philosophy and the Mirror of Nature* (Princeton: Princeton University Press, 1979). For a fair sense of how Rorty would apply his own philosophical conviction to the arts, see part 3 of his *Contingency, Irony, and Solidarity* (Cambridge: Cambridge University Press, 1989); although part 2 shows, I think, the utter bankruptcy of his sense of politically significant commitment—certainly altogether at odds with the feminist orientation.

8. The treatment of Freudian psychoanalysis is particularly instructive. See, for instance, the early opposed lines of argument favored, discursively, in Kate Millett, *Sexual Politics* (Garden City, N.Y.: Doubleday, 1970) and Juliet Mitchell, *Psychoanalysis and Feminisms* (New York: Pantheon, 1974); and the deliberately innovative idiom intended to stalemate the captured forms of discourse, in Luce Irigaray, *This Sex Which Is Not One*, trans. Catherine Porter (Ithaca: Cornell University Press, 1985), and in Julia Kristeva, *Desire in Language: A Semiotic Approach to Literature*, ed. Leon S. Roudiez, trans. Thomas Gora, Alice Jardine, and Leon S. Roudiez (New York: Columbia University Press, 1980).

9. See, for instance, Elaine Marks and Isabelle de Courtivron, eds., *New French Feminisms* (Amherst: University of Massachusetts Press, 1979).

10. See, for instance, Kristeva, *Desire in Language*, chap. 6; Elaine Showalter, *A Literature of Their Own: British Women Novelists from Brontë to Lessing*, 2d ed. (Princeton: Princeton University Press, 1976), chap. 10; Millett, *Sexual Politics*, part 3.

11. A particularly instructive statement of Habermas's, along these lines, is offered in his "A Review of Gadamer's Truth and Method," in *Understanding and Social Inquiry*, ed. and trans. Fred Dallmayr and Thomas A. McCarthy (Notre Dame: University of Notre Dame Press, 1977).

12. See, for instance, Jean-François Lyotard, *The Postmodern Condition: A Report on Knowledge*, trans. Geoff Bennington and Brian Mussumi (Minneapolis: University of Minnesota Press, 1964).

13. Joseph Margolis, *Pragmatism without Foundations; Reconciling Realism and Relativism* (Oxford: Basil Blackwell, 1986), chaps. 2–3.

14. See Abner Shimony, "Search for a Worldview Which Can Accommodate Our Knowledge of Microphysics," in *Philosophical Consequences of Quantum Theory; Reflections on Bell's Theorem*, ed. James T. Cushing and Ernan McMullin (Notre Dame: University of Notre Dame Press, 1989), 27.

15. See W. V. Quine, "Epistemology Naturalized" in *Ontological Relativity and Other Essays* (New York: Columbia University Press, 1969).

16. Walter Benjamin, "The Work of Art in the Age of Mechanical Reproduction," in *Illuminations,* ed. Hannah Arendt, trans. Harry Zohn (New York: Schocken Books, 1969).

17. Peter Bürger, *Theory of the Avant-Garde,* trans. Michael Shaw (Minneapolis: University of Minnesota Press, 1984), 29.

18. Ibid., 3–6; see also 15–16.

19. Bürger, *Theory of the Avant-Garde.*

20. Joseph Margolis, "Reinterpreting Interpretation," *Journal of Aesthetics and Art Criticism* 47 (1989): 237–51.

21. Jean-François Lyotard, *The Différend: Phrases in Dispute,* trans. George Van Den Abbeele (Minneapolis: University of Minnesota Press, 1988), 12.

19
Why Feminism Doesn't Need an Aesthetic (And Why It Can't Ignore Aesthetics)

Rita Felski

My dissatisfaction with the notion of a feminist aesthetic arises not from any denial of the multifarious connections between art and gender politics, but from a belief that "feminist aesthetics" does not help us to understand adequately the nature and significance of those connections.[1] This conviction is undoubtedly strengthened by a familiarity with the history of Marxist aesthetic theory, which has in recent years been subject to searching critique.[2] "Feminist aesthetics" has by contrast received much less attention as a theoretical problematic, perhaps because feminism's main influence has been within literature departments that are not primarily interested in issues of philosophical aesthetics. Nevertheless, many of the claims made within feminist literary theory, film criticism, and similar fields in fact presuppose a normative aesthetic, even if the term itself is rarely used. In this paper I shall develop further my view that we need to go "beyond feminist aesthetics" by examining some of the difficulties of such a concept, drawing specific examples from the areas of both literature and the fine arts.[3] More controversially, perhaps, I shall suggest that although feminist criticism does not need *an* (autonomous) aesthetic, it cannot afford to ignore the realm of *the* aesthetic, because it is necessarily implicated within and influenced by its institutional and discursive logics.

Feminist Critiques of the Autonomy of Art

As many writers have by now explored the male-dominated history of art institutions, I limit myself to a brief summary of their conclusions.[4] These writers have identified the various material obstacles that have dramatically limited women's participation in art at the level of production: the difficulty of access to education and formal training, a lack of social and economic independence for all but the wealthiest of women, and the difficulty of entry into male-dominated professional elites that play a crucial role in the fostering of both talent and reputation. Nevertheless, this exclusion of women has never been absolute, and its effects have been more pronounced within some cultures, historical periods, and areas of artistic activity than others, so that careful attention needs to be paid to the specific and varying conditions of women's cultural practices. But perhaps more insidious, because less overt, have been the pervasively androcentric metaphors and myths of creativity that have defined "woman" and "artist" as mutually exclusive terms. Such myths reached their apogee in the Romantic celebration of genius, which affirmed the necessary maleness of creativity, even as it paradoxically attributed to the artist "feminine" qualities of emotional receptivity.[5] From Romanticism to modernism and postmodernism, the figure of the artist has become closely identified with an ideal of transgressive masculinity, while women have been seen as at best capable of reproduction and imitation, but not of creative innovation.

This positioning of women at the margins of the aesthetic has been further accentuated in processes of reception, as exemplified in institutional processes of reviewing and canon formation. Within their own time, women's art has been typically read by critics as an expression of the limits of their sex; the transcendent and universal qualities ascribed to great art have remained almost by definition beyond their reach. Those women who did succeed in becoming influential figures in their own time—George Sand is an obvious example—have been frequently rendered invisible by twentieth-century histories of literature and art, which chart an almost exclusively male lineage framed in terms of a grand narrative of cross-generational Oedipal struggle. One striking example of this logic of omission remains Ian Watt's *The Rise of the Novel*, which describes the origins of what was a highly feminized genre in eighteenth-century England through an analysis of the works of three men.[6]

The feminist response to this neglect and trivialization of women's art has included a rediscovery and reevaluation of a tradition of female creativity. One of the most important paradigm shifts of recent history has been effected by the feminist remapping of culture and the consequent revision of prevailing conceptions of styles, genres, and periods within literary and art history. Arguing that women's marginality manifests itself not simply in the sociological fact of their exclusion from art institutions, but in the very criteria and vocabulary of aesthetic evaluation, feminists have shown that a purportedly universal and transcendent canon is dramatically skewed toward masculine norms. In turn, the critique of male-dominated art history has inspired some feminists to conclude that feminism needs to develop an autonomous aesthetic grounded in the distinctive features of women's creativity and the subversive undercurrents of a matrilineal tradition.

Such invocations of a feminist aesthetic can take differing forms, depending on whether the stress is laid on "feminism" or "aesthetics." In *Gender and Genius: Towards a Feminist Aesthetic,* for example, Christine Battersby favors the creation of a canon of great women artists. While she does not spell out the criteria for such a canon, it would presumably require a rethinking of the values and standards by which greatness has been established. For example, women's art that depicts experiences such as domesticity or childbirth has often been taken less seriously than texts that focus on the solitary male subject struggling against nature or society. Feminists can help to debunk such male-centered hierarchies by demonstrating the richness and significance of art by women and by uncovering the distinctive female traditions and genres within which such art acquires much of its meaning. Battersby thus ends her book with a plea for a notion of female genius that can help to frame the discussion of the specificity of women's art.

Such defenses of a female "great tradition" are often used to increase the number of women in literature survey courses or art galleries. Their pragmatic importance should not be underestimated; postmodernism notwithstanding, canons show no sign of disappearing and it thus becomes important, as Battersby argues, to intervene in this arena to give women greater prominence within the institutional cultural domain. Nevertheless, simply to present a woman-centered canon of great texts as the basis for an autonomous feminist aesthetic is surely to leave a number of key questions unanswered. Battersby's own insistence on the fundamentally patriarchal nature of art history and criticism makes it difficult to see how she could disentangle woman-centered criteria of evaluation from what she depicts as a totally compromised tradition. Some feminist theorists might argue in this context that the very notion of a "masterpiece" is the product of phallocentrism; in a secularized society, the work of art takes on the status of sacred artifact, assuming the mantle of transcendental signifier previously assigned to religion. In this light, simply to argue for a countertradition of great female artists is to leave the underlying premises of aesthetic evaluation unexamined.

In a second version of feminist aesthetics, "feminism" takes precedence over "aesthetics" and any appeal to artistic value is read as symptomatic of an elitist and patriarchal worldview. Instead, diverse forms of creativity are celebrated as part of a general affirmation of a woman-centered culture. As a result, the diary, autobiography, or letter becomes as significant as the sonnet or novel and women's traditional crafts such as needlework are considered as important as the paintings of the "great masters." In practice, this populist position often leads to a direct reversal of traditional hierarchies of evaluation. Texts that appear more spontaneous and less obviously crafted are valued highly according to a process-oriented ideal of female creativity, whereas texts that foreground structure, symmetry, and the controlled organization of artistic material are seen to exemplify a masculine, product-oriented aesthetic.

In my view, neither of these positions provides a satisfactory basis for a feminist aesthetic, for a range of reasons. First of all, the legacy of Romanticism reveals itself in a reading of works of art as direct expressions of the gendered psyche of their creator. Not only is female experience often evoked as an unproblematically universal category, but it is assumed that such experience will be visibly reflected in any given work of art. This claim strikes me as a tenuous one on straightforwardly empirical grounds. On visiting the National Museum for Women in the Arts in Washington, D.C., for example, I could not discern any common features among the works on display that bore witness to a shared femininity. If this is true of a relatively narrow sample of contemporary Western women's art, how could one hope to find any common denominators among works by women that span centuries and cultures? Feminist appeals to a substratum of "experience" as the basis for a gendered aesthetic fail to recognize that all artistic creativity is structured by conventions of iconographic or linguistic representation that are by definition intersubjective rather than personal and therefore historically and culturally contingent. It is one thing to argue for a separate artistic space for women on pragmatic grounds, as a means of campaigning against institutionalized forms of sexism; it is quite another to claim that women's art therefore bears witness to some shared essence of femaleness.

Second, one might note that such arguments typically blur the distinction between female and feminist. In those cases where one *can* identify a distinctive body of texts that is produced and consumed primarily by women, it does not follow that such texts thereby form part of an oppositional tradition. Popular romances, for example, are written mainly by women and are read by millions of female readers, yet most feminist critics would be unlikely to affirm such texts as authentic expressions of women's experience or as formally or thematically subversive.[7] Because femininity is always shaped by broader ideological and discursive structures that exceed—and indeed produce—gendered identity, women's representations of the feminine will not automatically carry any critical or oppositional force, though they may acquire such a force under given social conditions. An aesthetic theory grounded in the individual female psyche remains unable to specify what such conditions might be.

Finally, I would suggest that the category of the aesthetic is not adequately addressed in the above-mentioned feminist approaches. Thus critics such as Battersby, in assuming that feminism can generate its own autonomous standards of "great art," do not even begin to address the complex interconnections between discourses of aesthetic value and power-based hierarchies of cultural status and prestige. After Bourdieu it has become difficult to ignore the implication of aesthetics in the social stratification of taste cultures.[8] On the other hand, however, simply to deny the aesthetic as an irrelevant category for feminism is also problematic in denying the existence of real and significant differences between texts, differences constituted as much in the act of reception as in the act of production. A pile of Brillo boxes, after all, acquires a completely different set of meanings and intertextual referents when it is given a signature and exhibited within an art gallery. Such an anti-aesthetic stance tends to result in a condemnation of formally self-conscious and experimental art by women as well as men for its failure to be immediately understandable to a wide audience. In a recent feminist anthology on the visual arts, for example, two writers criticize Mary Kelly's influential gallery installation, *Post-Partum Document* as mystifying and inaccessible, while another contributor argues that avant-garde art is necessarily elitist and patriarchal because of its distance from everyday life.[9] Such accusations of elitism seem unhelpful, however, in denying the value of any feminist intervention in high art and in their largely unexamined nostalgia for a single form of art that would speak to all women everywhere, a nostalgia that denies the fundamental differences between women in terms of education, cultural background, and life-style as well as more commonly cited hierarchies of race, class, and sexuality.

Paraesthetics

How, then, can feminism come to grips with the specificity of the aesthetic without either denying or fetishizing it? An alternative approach to the question of aesthetics has been proposed by David Carroll, whose notion of "paraesthetics" seeks to account for the exemplary status of literature and art in the work of Derrida, Foucault, and Lyotard. For these thinkers, Carroll argues, the value and suggestiveness of art lies in its resistance to conceptual abstraction and theoretical dogmatism, yet they are also deeply critical of traditional philosophical defenses of the aesthetic as a self-contained, transcendental sphere. Hence Carroll's neologism of "paraesthetics," signifying "an aesthetics turned against itself, pushed beyond or beside itself, a faulty, irregular, disordered, improper aesthetic."[10] Poststructuralist theory draws upon a prior tradition of aesthetic discourse in its concern with the figurative, self-reflexive and polysemic qualities of texts rather than their ideological message or pragmatic use value. However, whereas classical aesthetics emphasizes the organic harmony, integrity, and totality of the artwork, paraesthetics by contrast privileges art as a space of contradiction, undecidability, a transgression of boundaries and systems of meaning. The work of art thus comments self-consciously on the rhetorical ambiguity and indeterminacy that ultimately underpins all communication.

A similar "paraesthetic" turn is identifiable among those feminist theorists who emphasize the determining role of representation in the reproduction of hierarchical power relations. A commonsense view of gender as producing different kinds of writing, for example, is replaced by the idea that writing, or more generally textuality, in fact creates our most intimate sense of gendered self. As feminism has taken on board poststructuralist accounts of the discursive construction of reality, so it is argued that there is a preexisting substratum of female experience that precedes signification. Patriarchal power is relocated at the level of semiotic systems, evidenced in the form of binary structures of meaning that position woman in relation to man as both opposite and inferior.

This view of the phallocentric nature of representation engenders a very different feminist aesthetic, or in more fashionable terminology, "textual politics." Such an aesthetic can no longer ground itself in an authentic female identity, for all such notions of a unitary self are now seen as a product of phallogocentrism, a metaphysical illusion generated by a totalizing logic of identity. Instead, it is the experimental text that is valorized because of its potential to transgress the boundaries of signification and to subvert the fixed categories and binary logics of phallocentric thought. *L'écriture féminine* and Julia Kristeva's notion of a revolutionary poetic language have been influential manifestations of such a paraesthetic turn within feminist literary criticism. Similarly, female artists working in visual media have explored a "negative aesthetics" of rupture, fragmentation, and disidentification. Such artists refuse to portray positive images of women on the grounds that all such images remain complicit with a scopophilic culture that positions women as easily consumable objects of the male gaze.[11]

These feminist perspectives take seriously the determining rather than epiphenomenal status of symbolic structures; texts do not simply reflect a pre-given reality but actively *produce* interpretative schemata through which the world is rendered meaningful. Hence the redefined status of the aesthetic within such a framework, given the role of contemporary art in questioning and subverting established conventions of representation. Many twentieth-century artworks have helped to transform irrevocably our commonsense notions of truth and reality; to expose the fiction of a stable, unitary ego; and to explore the opacity and materiality of signification. Such techniques of artistic innovation thus share an elective affinity with a poststructuralist feminism concerned to subvert rather than simply accept dominant definitions of female identity. Similarly, the sensual and libidinal dimensions of aesthetic experience interconnect with the feminist concern with the underside of reason, with the realm of bodies, desire, and pleasure, with that which resists symbolization and conceptual mastery. Thus Ingrid Richardson writes, "feminism has embraced the aesthetic as that one final realm which has not (cannot be) subsumed into reason, as that place which sidesteps-undercuts preoccupations with identity, boundaries, norms, as the space where female desire can finally be written into discourse and spill out new matrices of subjectivity and experience."[12]

The "paraesthetic" turn within feminism, in other words, makes it possible to acknowledge the specificity of the aesthetic as a domain that may possess a resistive and critical rather than purely conservative force. The important value of such an insight, however, coexists with an equally real danger: that of assigning an automatically subversive effect to particular stylistic techniques without paying attention to the discursive, institutional, and material conditions within which they are embedded. This may lead to an exaggerated view of the transgressive implications of avant-garde art at a time when experimental techniques are routinely employed by artists in a variety of media. Thus claims for the radical indeterminacy or subversive negativity of particular art forms typically fail to account for the ways in which meaning is institutionally fixed in the transmission and circulation of texts.

When considered from the standpoint of feminist reception theory, the formalist implications of such a paraesthetics of transgression become acutely apparent. While the multiperspectival, fractured text is often allied to the feminine through the application of a psycholinguistic Lacanian framework, such a theoretical move is typically accompanied by a explicit lack of interest in the social constitution and interpretative practices of actual female publics. The result is a vanguardist aesthetic that elevates a theoretically self-conscious experimental art as the only authentic site of opposition, while disparaging more conventional techniques of representation that have played a historically important role in the emergence of feminist cultures. This is to position the feminist intellectual as the one-who-knows, the one who refuses the passive consumption of meaning promoted by realist genres that lull audiences into an uncritical identification with dominant ideologies. Such elevations of a modernist art practice, I argue, rely on questionable assumptions about the political effects of particular aesthetic techniques, assumptions that in turn rely on a patronizing view of the necessarily naive and conservative reading practices of nonintellectual female readers.[13]

The Institution of Art

In moving toward a different understanding of both the value and the limitations of feminist intervention in contemporary art, I make use of, but also call into question, some recent arguments within the field of postmodern art theory. By drawing attention to the economic and institutional dimensions of the aesthetic, such arguments challenge assumptions about the automatically transgressive effects of textual innovation, pointing out that such innovation may in fact be functional to the ongoing operation of the art institution. On the other hand, however, they typically ignore issues of gender and the different political meanings accruing to the works of female and male artists. In this section, then, I draw on the analytical insights of postmodern art theory while simultaneously questioning its quietistic and apolitical conclusions.

Drawing loosely on Victor Burgin's essay "The End of Art Theory," I shall define the institution of art as consisting of a variety of sites such as publishing houses, galleries, university literature and art departments, academic journals, museums, libraries, etc. These sites are linked together by shared discourses that they in turn replenish and recirculate through such practices as teaching, reviewing, writing, painting, and research.[14] Such a location of the aesthetic within a nexus of diverse social practices and structures is obviously antithetical to any idealist view of art as a transcendental redemptive sphere. At the same time it also differs from the kind of materialist standpoint that regards the aesthetic as nothing more than an illusory fiction cloaking the reality of patriarchal and capitalist oppression. Instead, art is endowed with a relative degree of autonomy as a differentiated domain of discourses and practices shaped by its own logic and history. It thus needs to be situated, in Griselda Pollock's words, in the context of its own distinctive "materials, resources, conditions, constituencies, modes of training, competence, expertise, forms of consumption and related discourses, as well as its own codes and rhetorics."[15]

This domain is clearly shaped by social hierarchies and structures of power, but does not necessarily function as a straightforward reflection of dominant class or gender interests. Some Marxist critics, for example, have argued that the ideology of the aesthetic has had an ambiguous and contradictory history since its emergence in the eighteenth century. While the appeal to the autonomy of art has often served a mystifying function in glossing over the political dimensions of cultural production, it has also embodied a source of resistance to the pervasiveness of economic rationality and the spread of a narrowly utilitarian worldview.[16] Similarly, feminist artists have been drawn to the innovative potential of language, imagery, and form in order to generate new ways of seeing and thereby to disrupt the mono-logic of patriarchal images of the feminine. The flourishing of female creativity across diverse media and genres bears witness to the complexity and sophistication of women's recent engagement with a wide variety of artistic conventions and traditions.

The logic of the aesthetic cannot be defined as inherently conservative; neither, however, is it inherently transgressive. Thus a recurring motif within postmodern thought is a pervasive skepticism regarding the possibility of oppositional art. While an influential strand within Marxism has traditionally valued the avant-garde as a form of resistance to a commercialized and ideologically compromised mass culture, such a distinction, it is argued, may now have lost all meaning. There is no longer any necessary connection between symbolic transgression and political transgression, between stylistic rupture and processes of social change. Even the most outrageous work of art can be turned into a commodity, as "the shock of the new" drives the inflationary spiral of a New York art market that is fueled by media hype and controlled by a managerial elite of dealers and curators. The "death of the avant-garde" is a paradoxical result of the success of the avant-garde, as rampant commercialism deprives artistic experimentation of any critical or oppositional edge.[17] Moreover, the art institution reaches beyond the walls of the gallery to embrace an entire knowledge industry of catalogues, critical discourses, and metacommentaries that governs the interpretative parameters through which texts are rendered meaningful to a larger public. The transgressive gesture of radical art is thus inexorably transformed into part of the cultural capital of educated and professional elites in Western urban societies.

In announcing the powerlessness of art to effect social change in the postmodern era, however, such prognoses rarely pay any attention to gender politics and the differing positions of male and female artists. The campaigns of the Guerilla Girls have drawn attention to the still minimal representation of women in major galleries and exhibitions and their precarious position in the art institution more generally. There are, in fact, effectively no women whose work is endowed with the same economic value or institutional status as the most significant male artists such as Warhol, Johns, Schnabel, Hockney, Kiefer, et al. In such a context, the meanings and associations accruing to works by women will inevitably differ from those of men, not because of the existence of a uniquely feminine aesthetic but simply because of the different conditions under which such art is produced and received. Women's historical marginality within the spheres of high culture and the avant-garde means that their increasing presence within such domains is necessarily charged with political significance. The signature of the female artist does not carry the same meaning as that of the male. When this is coupled with the overtly feminist concerns motivating the work of a number of prominent female artists, it might seem as if, for women, art is in the process of being re- rather than depoliticized. The unprecedented explosion of women's creativity in the last twenty years openly contradicts the prevailing postmodern ennui with the political potential of art.

At the same time, however, the mere fact of their gender does not render female artists immune to the economic and institutional dynamics that I have mentioned above. In contesting the male-dominated structures of the art world, they simultaneously draw upon its professional discourses, skills, and techniques, which help to provide the conditions for their own creative and critical work. Insofar as they have a professional identity as artists as well as women, their own productivity is thus both enabled and constrained by the power/knowledge nexus of the art institution and hence also shaped by its contradictions. For example, feminist artists who seek to *subvert* hierarchy at a textual level, through the creation of multiperspectival, experimental art-works, may paradoxically also *reassert* hierarchy at a social level, in presuming specialized competences in interpretation that are unequally transmitted through the education system. In seeking to transform the male-centered practices of the art institution, in other words, the feminist artist is necessarily implicated within the power relations governing the circulation of particular forms of culture and knowledge. If she is not "inside," neither can she be unproblematically positioned as "outside."[18]

To point this out is not to deny the value of feminist intervention in high art, but to suggest that it needs to be conceptualized more carefully in relation to its particular zone of effectivity. In other words, we cannot afford to valorize experimentation, ambiguity, and complexity at an *aesthetic* level without situating texts *sociologically* in relation to particular publics and contexts of reception. Such a perspective would allow for a more measured assessment of the potential value of particular cultural forms as they relate to the needs, interests, and horizons of expectation of differing female audiences, without invoking abstract oppositions between "masculine" and "feminine," "conservative" and "radical" art forms.

Conclusion

In refusing both a Romantic notion of art as authentic self-expression and a quintessentially modernist belief in the necessarily resistive effects of formal experimentation, postmodern art theory draws attention to the particular social and institutional conditions governing artistic practices. By examining the "site-specific" and power-driven logics of such practices, it challenges the claim of oppositional aesthetic theories to transcend power relations through direct representation of the interests of an oppressed constituency. Such a critique parallels my own skepticism regarding the project of a feminist aesthetic, whether derived from the individual female psyche or from a notion of resistive, feminine textuality. Those artists or critics who seek to ground such an aesthetic in the fact of their own marginality are, in my view, simply denying their own implication in broader discursive and institutional logics.

On the other hand, however, postmodern art theory frequently overemphasizes the fixity of the art institution as a set of autonomous discourses and practices and denies its permeability and openness to the influence of extrainstitutional social forces. Thus feminism, for example, has had a significant impact on both the production and the reception of art, generating interpretative vocabularies that make it possible to read and understand texts in new ways. In this way, the discourses of feminism and aesthetics intersect in the practices of the many women who are also professional artists, critics, teachers, or students, and who work both within and against the institution of art. Such an acknowledgment of the powerful and crucial impact of feminism on prevailing theories and practices in the arts does not require—and indeed is hindered by—a belief in feminist aesthetics. On the contrary, the range of contemporary feminist art practices bears witness to a rich diversity of cultural affiliations that connect in complicated and not always self-evident ways to ethnicity, class, and educational background, age, sexuality, and a multiplicity of other factors. There is no distinctive style, medium, or set of techniques common to the work of all feminist, let alone female, artists. Rather, one can point to a multiplicity of genres and forms that are employed by women across the fields of contemporary art practice.

Furthermore, feminism exemplifies a politics committed to analyzing and combating large-scale structures of gender inequality that cut across and link together specific individuated sites. Inevitably, then, feminist interests and concerns spread far beyond the arena of the art institution, challenging prevailing descriptions of the postmodern era as a period devoid of wide-ranging emancipatory projects. Within this broader context, it becomes clear that the codes and conventions of gallery art or avant-garde literature, which speak to the interests and sensibilities of particular sociologically differentiated publics, may in turn be quite irrelevant to women working with other cultural spaces. It is certainly true, as Burgin points out, that critical art cannot simply transcend institutional logics, which are not simply located in material buildings such as galleries and universities but have also significantly influenced many of the discourses of oppositional criticism. Nevertheless, while feminism cannot lay claim to an uncontaminated authenticity, it has undoubtedly played a crucial role in opening up the category of art to a wider variety of perspectives and in creating alternative locations for artistic practice. Through such initiatives as adult education, community arts projects, alternative publishing, and arts festivals, feminists have brought the issue of women and art to the attention of wider and less specialized publics. Clearly, the practices of representation that are employed in such contexts will need to speak to the particular competences and experiences of their targeted audiences. Rather than criticizing those artists concerned with creating positive images of women for their theoretical naïveté, one can acknowledge the strategic value of such techniques in reaching women who would otherwise have little access to feminist ideas. Popular conventions and forms cannot be simply dismissed as regressive if the feminist critic is to retain a concern with the interests and cultural reference points of ordinary, nonacademic women, and to question, even as she also necessarily works within, existing cultural hierarchies.

Similarly, a feminism concerned with pragmatic questions of accessibility and effecting changes in popular consciousness cannot afford to ignore the power of mass-media forms such as film and television; even the most accessible feminist novel or painting will, after all, only ever reach one particular segment of the population. While the texts of popular culture have not traditionally been included in the domain of aesthetics, cultural studies has helped to undercut such high/mass culture oppositions by foregrounding the semiotically complex structures and intertextual referents of many popular forms and genres. Such popular forms frequently reveal a contradictory intersection of differing and often dissonant ideological strands rather than simply reaffirming and reinforcing the political status quo. In this light, it becomes important to consider how feminist perspectives can interconnect with and gain a voice through the heterogeneous texts that make up the shifting terrain of popular culture. Here again, there can be no single aesthetic strategy, given that the audience of mass culture is neither homogeneous nor monolithic, but is stratified and diversified in complicated ways in terms of affiliations, preferences, and cultural reference points.

To conclude, then, I suggest that the desired reconciliation of art and politics implicit in the category of feminist aesthetics fails to recognize the messy contradictions and tension, as well as the crucial interconnections, between these two terms, Such a category, I have argued, tends either to collapse the aesthetic into an epiphenomenal reflection of a preexisting politics, or to overestimate the political implications of an aesthetics of stylistic experimentation. By contrast, I argue for a more diversified model of the relationship between politics and aesthetics, one that acknowledges the importance of women's visibility within the art institution, while insisting that feminism is also necessarily committed to other, less specialized forms of cultural activity. Thus the production and reception of feminist art and culture bear witness both to shared political and ideological concerns and to specific traditions, vocabularies of interpretation, and cultural preferences that serve to identify and distinguish particular audiences. In this context, the critical potential of para-aesthetic, avant-garde techniques should neither be denied or fetishized but viewed as one significant strand of feminist cultural practice among others. To conclude with a quote from Mary Kelly: "one very important point which applies to all so-called political engaged art is that there's no such thing as a homogeneous mass audience. You can't make art for everyone."[19]

Notes

1. Some of the arguments in this paper were first developed in an earlier piece entitled "Feminist Aesthetics," in *Styles of Cultural Activism,* ed. Philip Goldstein (Wilmington: University of Delaware Press, 1994).

2. The best overview of debates in Marxist aesthetics remains *Aesthetics and Politics*, ed. Fredric Jameson (London: New Left Books, 1977). Recent criticism of the project of a Marxist aesthetics has come from, inter alia, Peter Bürger, *Theory of the Avant-Garde*, trans. Michael Shaw (Minneapolis: University of Minnesota Press, 1984) and Tony Bennett, *Formalism and Marxism* (London: Methuen, 1979).

3. The argument was first made in *Beyond Feminist Aesthetics: Feminist Literature and Social Change* (Cambridge: Harvard University Press, 1989).

4. The following list is necessarily selective. In the area of the fine arts, see, for example, Christine Battersby, *Gender and Genius: Towards a Feminist Aesthetic* (Bloomington: Indiana University Press, 1989); Rozsika Parker and Griselda Pollock, *Old Mistresses: Women, Art, and Ideology* (New York: Pantheon, 1985); Linda Nochlin, *Women, Art, and Power, and Other Essays* (New York: Harper and Row, 1988); Whitney Chadwick, *Women, Art, and Society* (London: Thames and Hudson, 1990). Feminist accounts of gender bias in literary criticism and history include Mary Ellman, *Thinking About Women* (New York: Harcourt Brace Jovanovich, 1968); Joanna Russ, *How to Suppress Women's Writing* (London: Women's Press, 1984); Gaye Tuchman with Nina E. Fortin, *Edging Women Out: Victorian Novelists, Publishers, and Social Change* (New Haven: Yale University Press, 1989).

5. Thus, as Christine Battersby notes in *Gender and Genius*, "the great artist is a *feminine male*" (7).

6. See Ian Watt, *The Rise of the Novel* (London: Chatto and Windus, 1957).

7. It should be noted, nevertheless, that a significant reevaluation of romance fiction has been undertaken in recent years by feminist critics. See, for example, Tania Modleski, *Loving with a Vengeance: Mass-Produced Fantasies for Women* (New York: Methuen, 1984); Janice Radway, *Reading the Romance: Women, Patriarchy, and Popular Literature* (Chapel Hill: University of North Carolina Press, 1984) and Jan Cohn, *Romance and the Erotics of Property* (Durham: Duke University Press, 1988).

8. Pierre Bourdieu, *Distinction* (Cambridge: Harvard University Press, 1984).

9. See Margot Waddell and Michele Wandor, "Mystifying Theory," and Angela Partington, "Art and Avant-Gardism," in *Visibly Female: Feminism and Art Today*, ed. Hilary Robinson (London: Camden, 1987).

10. David Carroll, *Paraesthetics: Foucault, Lyotard, Derrida* (New York: Methuen, 1987), xiv.

11. For an overview of *écriture féminine* and the work of Julia Kristeva, see Toril Moi, *Sexual/ Textual Politics* (London: Methuen, 1985). An aesthetics of disidentification is discussed by Griselda Pollock in "Screening the Seventies: Sexuality and Representation in Feminist Practice—A Brechtian Perspective," in *Vision and Difference: Feminism, Femininity and the Histories of Art* (London: Routledge, 1988), 155–99.

12. Ingrid Richardson, "Feminism and Critical Theory," unpublished manuscript.

13. This would be my main area of disagreement with Griselda Pollock, whose work in most other respects I consider exemplary. For defenses of modernism, see her "Screening the Seventies," and Judith Barry and Sandy Flitterman-Lewis, "Textual Strategies: The Politics of Art-Making," in Robinson, *Visibly Female*.

14. Victor Burgin, *The End of Art Theory: Criticism and Postmodernity* (London: Macmillan, 1986), 181.

15. Pollock, *Vision and Difference*, 9.

16. See, for example, Terry Eagleton, *The Ideology of the Aesthetic* (Oxford: Basil Blackwell, 1990).

17. See Suzi Gablik, *Has Modernism Failed?* (New York: Thames and Hudson, 1984). Gablik's somewhat questionable nostalgia for tradition and a consensus of values does not prevent her from making a number of highly pertinent observations on the current aporias of the avant-garde.

18. For one account of the contradictory relationship between feminism and "official culture," see Griselda Pollock, "Feminism and Modernism," in *Framing Feminism,* ed. Roszika Parker and Griselda Pollock (London: Pandora, 1987), 98–101.

19. Mary Kelly, interview, in Robinson, *Visibly Female,* 79.

20

The Role of Feminist Aesthetics in Feminist Theory

Hilde Hein

Feminism as Theory

"Isms" can be misleading. We tend to think of them as promotional, advancing the cause of or at least foregrounding the subject to which the suffix is attached. Thus nationalism and individualism, respectively, attribute special status to nations or individuals. Those who object to the special designation use the "ism" derogatorily and suggest that anyone who promotes the named cause does so with mindless ideological subservience. Racism is thus a form of advocacy, denoting an attitude, either of deprecation (racial inferiority) or of pride (racial supremacy), applied to persons exclusively on the basis of their race. Those who repudiate racism condemn all mass judgments made according to that stereotype. Whether negatively or positively intended, the terminal identification—the "ism"—bestows significance upon a category that may never have existed as a concept prior to the verbal appendage of its "ism." "Feminism" is a word that expresses such semantic innovation.

Feminism creates new ways of thinking, new meanings, and new categories of critical reflection; it is not merely an extension of old concepts to new domains. Obviously there were women before there was feminism, as well as individuals who loved and hated them both singularly and collectively. However we do not regard womanizers or misogynists as feminists because they love or hate women. The term "feminism" does not pertain to women as the objects of love or hatred, or even of social (in)justice, but fixes upon the perspective that women bring to experience as subjects, a perspective whose existence has heretofore been ignored. This slight but novel twist in point of view is the source of qualitatively new ideas and values identified with women and which may be taken as exemplary. The word "feminism" has associations favorable to women chiefly because it accords subject status to them, but to feminism's detractors it implies only hostility to men. "Feminism" in their lexicon means favoritism that is undeserved and at the expense of men. Oddly, there is no commonly used corresponding word that denotes a converse advocacy.[1] I will use the term "masculinism" in that sense. Feminists claim that this alternative mode of thinking does exist and is in fact the nameless "default mode" of normal thought. It is so pervasive that we fail to recognize it and are oblivious to its influence upon all aspects of intellectual and social operation.

Masculinism is not a position that one "assumes" or can be converted to as one might be to feminism. One becomes a feminist by declaration—not by birth or chance or out of habit. To adopt a feminist attitude is to take an avowedly gendered point of view that is contingently oppositional.[2] Feminism as a way of thinking became a possibility only because gender had already been socially constituted as dual. Feminist scholars in America began seriously exploring the social construction of gender in the 1970s—at first angrily as if discovering a partner *in flagrante,* and then more coolly, observing it as a system of culture and of knowledge to be deconstructed.[3] Feminists accepted gender, not as a metaphysical or biological reality, but as an analytic category like class or race, a tool for understanding complex relations.[4] Initiated at the reputedly deviant pole, the Other, such gendered reflection presupposes a primary role from which it differs asymmetrically, as other, and which it does not define. The primary pole requires the presence of the Other in order to become itself, although it claims both logical and ontological priority to the Other. It depends for its being upon the negatively marked or gendered pole. Born of the Other and known by it, its own gender is invisible, conceptually nonexistent, except in relation to the pole whose opposition and dependency it claims.[5] Feminist theory has made it clear that nonfeminist thinking is also gendered and that we were mistaken in believing that the generic term "man" is gender-neutral. The change in that perception and the now widespread endeavor to replace "sexist" language with "inclusive" words is the result of feminist deconstruction.

One early form that the feminist "discovery" of gender took was the denial of a neutral or generic human being (that comes in two flavors).[6] Some feminists hold that, although individual persons might be blurry in their actual identity, there are two irreducibly different modes of being, male and female. This position had, of course, always been endorsed by certain patriarchal men, many of whom found women sufficiently strange and incomprehensible (all but their wives and mothers) to warrant characterizing them as a biologically aberrant species. Some women, for their own reasons, were equally inclined to defend an essential dualism, and some still do—whether out of feminist or nonfeminist conviction.[7] But many feminists repudiated essentialism as both undemonstrable and politically regressive. The contemporary feminist theory that I discuss rejects metaphysical essentialism, but it does not deny the situational differences that radically separate the lives of men and women and lead to their characteristically different forms of behavior.

Simone de Beauvior, while remaining within the fold of humanism, is undoubtedly the progenitrix of the feminist theory of gender, having said that "[o]ne is not born a woman; one becomes one," and then shown how woman has been constructed as Man's Other.[8] Significant articulators of this theory include other French feminists (notably Hélène Cixous, Luce Irigaray, and Julia Kristeva) as well as British socialist feminists, and many American philosophers, art historians, literary critics, social historians, theorists and philosophers of science. But, remarkably, one is hard-pressed to think of towering heroines. Most ideas seem to be worked out in collaboration and critical communication with others, and certain recurrent themes emerge simultaneously and at many points.[9] Critical ideas are as likely to arise out of political and social practice as from theory, and sometimes the same ideas emerge from both sources, becoming clarified as they converge.[10] The feminist theory that is taking shape maintains with de Beauvoir that gender is socially constructed, but denies its universal overdetermination. Rather, gender must be viewed as a system of human relations that is deeply embedded in all other social relations. This means that one is not a woman *and* white, black, lesbian, heterosexual, Moslem, Jewish, rich, poor, urban, rural, etc., (as descriptive qualifiers), but that gender is complexly and interdependently entwined with all these other features of one's identity. Gender must be thought of adverbially and not as a constant substrate. Women then, are doubly multiple—there is no single explanation of woman as such (no answer to "the woman question") and individual women's subjectivity is also multiple, positionally variable, and contingent.[11] As a result of this plurality, if we are to apply theory to women at all, the traditional notion of theory as unifying principle must give way to something more fluid and multiple. Elizabeth Young-Bruehl proposes that theory become "a process, a constellation of ideas reconfigured and reconfiguring within a myriad of feminist practices."[12]

Feminist theory derives its vitality from feminist practice and its credibility is tested in women's experience. Characterized by a lack even of procedural specificity, it has been called a "musing on the circumference of experience."[13] This experiential reference links feminist theory fundamentally to the aesthetic. Since the aesthetic is the paradigmatic transformation of the immediate, multiple, and qualitatively diverse, even the most monolithic of classical aesthetic theories is obligated to come to terms with multiplicity and sometimes to leave it unreconciled.[14] Given this proximity of feminist theory to the aesthetic, should we not expect of feminists the articulation of feminist aesthetic theory? Feminist aesthetics may well be the prologue of feminist theory understood more broadly. I shall argue that this is the case and that, indeed, feminist theory is at present hindered by the lack of an adequate aesthetic theory. Current discussions of feminist aesthetics tend to be deconstructivist and piecemeal. We have barely begun to consider positively what the prominent features of feminist aesthetics—that is, an aesthetic theory that is feminist—would be. The problem is intensified by its frequent confusion with the quest for *a* feminine aesthetic, a distinction that must be clarified before proceeding further.

The Relation Between Feminist Aesthetics, Feminist Art, and Feminist Theory

The call for feminist aesthetics relies upon a notion of aesthetics that has been randomly aggregated within the historic tradition of philosophies of beauty, the arts, and sensory experience. Whether confined to the post-seventeenth-century discipline for which the term was coined or inclusive of the value theory that precedes it, aesthetics has a place in the matrix of Western philosophy that is consistent with its fundamental logic, metaphysics, and epistemology and with its value commitments. Feminist aesthetics would challenge this entire network, recast and reconceptualize it from its own alternative perspective, much as a feminist focus has unsettled some of the foundations of traditional historiography.[15] This enterprise is independent of and altogether different from the issue of *a* feminine aesthetic. An aesthetic refers to a distinctive style of production. The question whether or not there is a feminine aesthetic—gender characteristic elements, use of imagery (for example, "central core" images), or other gender-specific stylistic devices—has preoccupied art historians and critics as well as artists.[16] It is a matter of controversy because an affirmative answer, especially one that links feminine expression with apparently biomorphic or introjective forms, seems to reinforce essentialistic dualism.[17] The question of feminist aesthetics cannot be divorced entirely from the matter of a feminine aesthetic, but it is not my purpose here to explore their relationship or to enter upon the controversial question of *a* feminine aesthetic.[18] The issue that concerns me is the place of feminist aesthetics in the articulation of feminist theory.

I have suggested that feminism is linked to the aesthetic because of its inherent pluralism and inseparability from experience. Feminist theory cannot arise *de novo* or out of abstract definition. It cannot have the axiomatic purity to which much of classical theorizing aspires. Since feminism presupposes the acknowledgment of gender as socially constituted, the theory that it articulates must be contextualized even as it struggles to overcome the actual context that produces it. Necessarily encountered in context, feminism as doctrine is often challenged as antitheoretical and as polemical, but this begs the very issue that feminists mean to hold up to question—the presumption that theory must be singular, totalizing, and comprehensive. Feminism renounces this monolithic view of theory together with the phallocratic roots from which it springs. Adhering to the view that experience is saturated with theory, feminists are led to the position that theory, likewise, must be saturated with experience.

An antifeminist might happily agree with feminists that women's identity, and therefore their experience, is situationally determined, declaring that women properly derive their being by reflected light and take up whatever coloration is imposed upon them by their particular real-world affiliations together with the prevailing theoretical view of human (that is, masculine) nature. Defined by negation, or in opposition to the male norm, women are then a mystery, sheer potentiality, their being and desire inexpressible in patriarchal terms—and thereby all the more tantalizing. That very unthematized nonidentity that comes into being as the space that the male leaves behind him upon entering the symbolic order is precisely the absence that defines the female. Jacques Derrida and some of his followers have appropriated and romanticized that negative identity as "feminine," making of it a condition to which men might also aspire.

To feminists, however, the feminine negativity left in the wake of male presence is not an absence, but a possible—"what is left of her is unthinkable, unthought." What remains for women is not emptiness, but "the space that can serve as a springboard for subversive thought."[19] The experience perceived to fill that space from a woman's perspective necessarily differs from the pale obverse reflection of "significant" experience that men attribute to women.[20] Thus women are often irreverent toward the rules set by phallocratic reasoning, discounting their intended exclusion as a by-product of a masculine self-confinement that leaves women free to write themselves out of the world that men have constructed and into another one. Not surprisingly, expressive discourse about that world, though employing the familiar vocabulary acquired in the male-centered world, relates only obliquely to that world and strives instead to articulate what is left unsaid.

This observation relates to the fact that feminist *art* often (but not always) concerns and depicts female oppression. Critics of feminism and of feminist art object that such overtly political representations have no place in art. They, however, are failing to grasp the charge implicit in the feminist art that "conventional" art is equally political, the politics being cast in that "neutral" or masculinist mode that appears invisible. Feminist artists face the dilemma that, having been acculturated in a male-dominated artworld, they have imbibed its traditions and values along with their artistic skills and aesthetic sensitivities. Rebelling against those values as women, they confront themselves as artists whose expressive tools remain those of the prevailing order. While striving to express their own perceptions and experience they cannot escape the effect of prior tempering upon those tools and even upon their own critical judgment. Indeed, those tools have not in the past excluded the depiction of women. Far from it! Along with loving and caressive exploration of women in intimate detail, they have been used to represent considerable violence toward and abuse of women. The grand tradition is full of rapes, abductions, mutilations, and hateful degradation of women. But these have not been authentic from a woman's perspective. By and large, they have been viewed through the lascivious, sentimental, or punitive eye of a man. Feminist artists face the challenge of recasting these same experiences *as they are undergone by women,* so as to reveal an aspect of them that has been ignored. In doing so, they expose both the politics and the gender bias of traditional art and risk rejection of their own work on the ground that it is not art within that traditional definition. What is distinctive to feminist art, then, is not that it is "about" women, but that it is so in a way that is new, albeit using the same instruments as before.

Some artists seek to perfect new tools capable of shaping new structures, but here too they face the challenge of a conservative community. They may have recourse to new materials, such as fiber (or to other female-associated objects such as buttons, dolls, and even sanitary napkins) or to new subject matter, such as women's sexuality. Often they seek a new venue in which to present their art. This may not be entirely a matter of choice, but a reaction to rejections and refusals by gallery owners to show work that is not within the prescribed canon. In their search for new methods and media, even where that is undertaken reluctantly, feminist artists nevertheless challenge the tradition of the mainstream. In this respect, feminist art blurs the distinctions between art and criticism, between art and politics, and between theory and practice. The production of such art is at once a theoretical statement and a confrontational act, literally an intervention in the socially produced gender system. It calls attention to that system, displays it in detail and renders it intelligible. Feminist art is thus a means to consciousness raising. When effective, it achieves aesthetically (that is, with felt immediacy) the realization that other feminist theorists strive to convey indirectly and to analyze abstractly. "Art does not just make ideology explicit but can be used, at a particular historic juncture, to rework it."[21] At the same time, feminist art is critical, reflecting upon the artistic tradition that is its point of origin and that it undermines. In this, feminist art is not unlike other examples of modern art, which feed upon their history, borrowing, modifying, transforming, and reversing themselves in order to create a new concept. However, feminist reversals are distinguishable by their ideology. They are not produced simply to be innovative or for the sake of effect. They are more radical in intent and therefore shocking even to would-be innovators. Sometimes these feminist statements appear to violate basic good taste—a taste that feminists had no part in defining.

I have argued that feminist art merges with and commonly expresses a feminist aesthetics. I maintain, moreover, that feminism by its nature depends upon an aesthetics of experience because feminist theory must revert to experience for its formulation. There is nowhere else to go, since theory in its masculinist mold is suspect. But experience is contingent and the language of theory, as we have seen, is inadequate to give expression to women's perspective. If experience is to be more than the inscription of what is momentarily given and gone, it must be aesthetically embodied, that is, given shape through imagery and symbolism. That is how we are carried from experience to reflection. However, the reflection that is evoked by a feminist critique is not universalizing. It does not flee from experience, but stays close to its source and "muses at its edges."

Some Aesthetic Models for Feminist Theory

Feminism is nothing if not complex. Myra Jehlen speaks of the "fruitful complication" of feminist theory and welcomes contradiction not for its irrationality, but in order to tap its energy.[22] Sandra Harding recommends that we abandon the faith that coherent theory is desirable and instead declare our fidelity to "parameters of dissonance within and between assumptions of patriarchal discourses," a route that will enable the creative contribution of a consciousness that is "valuably alienated, bifurcated and oppositional," and whose psychic, intellectual, and political discomfort we should cherish. The offspring of such convoluted consciousness is not a simplifying theory framed from super-Archimedean heights that reduces the world from *this* to *all* in a few neat abstractions. What feminist scholarship should salvage from women's experience and through women's texts is not "issues to be resolved" but "better problems than those with which we started." By expanding the questions instead of reducing the answers, by cultivating instead of suppressing instability, we may find new ways of theorizing that depend less on political repression.[23]

To explore the wealth of women's experience it is necessary to resist the temptation of "privilege-preserving categories." Elizabeth Spelman points out that middle-class white women, who have done much of the talking that is officially preserved, have had little to say about the variety of women's experience simply because they are ignorant of it. "There are no short cuts through women's lives," she says, and if we are to theorize about women, we must know them in all their particularity.[24] This is why the astonishing florescence of literature by and about women all over the world and the explosion of women's production of visual, dramatic, musical, and other art forms is not only illuminating, but vital to theorizing. Only through these works can we come to know ourselves and one another.

There is no lack of works of art to serve as data, and we are not confined to those self-identified as feminist. Feminist critics and theorists often revert to classical works of art, by men as well as women, and to works that have been discarded and neglected in order to find in them insights that will yield new interpretations.[25] They are following the path delineated by Harding for philosophers of science, seeking understanding by probing the interstices and the relations between situations, asking the questions that are not asked and wondering why they were not. This is not simply "busywork" on the part of feminists. They are struggling to engender a new theory that will not be simply a successor drawn in the same mold as the masculinist theories that it replaces. Feminist theory will not be a complement to fill out gaps in the theoretical panoply; neither will it be the coup de grâce that supersedes all other theory in a long line of approximations to truth. Feminist theory is a new approach to theory.

Feminists have found that theorizing is also a gratifying aesthetic experience. Not the first to discover that fact, feminists nonetheless pronounce their pleasure to be different from that of male aesthetes for whom the pleasure of theorizing, like that of most things, is a form of "jouissance," a self-contained entertainment. Pierre Bourdieu, for example, applauds Derrida's examination of Kant's *Critique of Judgment,* as a "skewered" reading in which the treatise is treated as a work of art to be approached disinterestedly, for pure pleasure that is irreducible to pursuit of the profit of distinction. By dramatizing or making a spectacle of the "act" of stating the philosophy, Bourdieu says, the *Critique* draws attention to itself as philosophical gesture. The work itself, as well as the metalevel critique of it are thus bubbles in space, purely playful illustrations of Kant's own analysis—purposive entities without a purpose. Bourdieu goes on to acknowledge that "even in its purest form, when it seems most free of 'worldly' interest, this game is always a 'society' game based . . . on a 'freemasonry of customs and a heritage of traditions.' " In other words there are rules, and they are meant to be exclusive. The pleasure of philosophizing is not for everyone.[26]

Feminists find an altogether different pleasure in theorizing, and it lies precisely in the possibilities that it opens, rather than in those that it seals off. Not at all disinterested, feminist theorists do not divorce themselves from the object of their discourse and have a commitment to drawing it out so that its voices may be heard. Since they treat instability as a fact of life and not as an obstacle to be overcome, feminists do not have the same commitment as masculinist theoreticians to voluntarism, or to the will represented as shaping its environment. Thus, the very features that account for the gender-distinctive pleasure of theorizing reveal the need for a feminist theory of pleasure and with it a feminist aesthetics.

A feminist aesthetics would not resemble the familiar complex of Greek theory of the arts combined with eighteenth-century theory of taste that forms the backbone of academic aesthetics today. Feminist theory regards the dualism defended by classical theories as dogmatic reification and does not consider that authority by one pole of a fantasied reality over another is an issue that merits extensive analysis. Correlatively, feminist theory does not take seriously the claim that manipulation of a medium is a means of self-assertion or a demonstration of power. (Perhaps this is because women have a poorly developed sense of ego-boundaries, or perhaps because the transformation of matter into form is the normal business of motherhood and housekeeping.) If asked, feminists will not hesitate to take a stand on these issues. On the whole, however, neither feminist aestheticians nor feminists more generally have been preoccupied with the subversion of such claims. They simply do not find them interesting.

Seeking to define the area of feminist aesthetics, we have found neither a body of truths nor a central dogma, but an instrument for reframing questions. Some classic questions are ignored or discarded in that process, not because the problems have been solved or because feminist theoreticians are ignorant of the history of attempts to solve them, but because they are not problems within a feminist framework. This list of abandoned problems includes the characterization of aesthetic "disinterest," the distinction between various art forms, as well as differences between craft and art, high art and popular art, useful and decorative arts, the sublime and the beautiful, originality, and many puzzles that have to do with the cognitive versus the affective nature of aesthetic experience.

So far, feminist aesthetic theory has devoted disproportionate attention to deconstruction and critique of phallocratic practice. Theory is invoked in a partial, piecemeal fashion, and only when the context of experience or aesthetic discourse allows it. There is no single, totalizing feminist aesthetic theory and none is sought. Nonetheless, I believe that, rudimentary as it is, feminist aesthetic theory serves both as a model and a point of departure for feminist theory more broadly understood. Clearly addressed to the works of art and phenomena that are its data, there is no question that feminist aesthetic theory is experientially grounded. And open to the new data that are constantly proposed to it, feminist aesthetic theory has no alternative but to be a "musing on the circumference." With the help of a feminist aesthetics we are able to appreciate old things in new ways and to assimilate new things that would be excluded by traditional aesthetic theory. Solely that it makes the world more fascinating would suffice as reason enough to find merit in feminist aesthetic theory. I believe, however, that feminist aesthetic theorizing also promises to yield positive and practical consequences in nonaesthetic dimensions because it illuminates and *corrects* certain imagery that has exerted a powerful influence upon our conventional understanding of the world. I will conclude with two examples that illustrate how feminist aesthetic theory can affect ordinary thought about nonaesthetic matters.

Feminist Reconstructions of Vision and Creation

In her essay "Visual Pleasure and Narrative Cinema," Laura Mulvey makes her own theoretical objective very clear. The point of theory is not to understand the world, but to change it:

> The satisfaction and reinforcement of the ego that represent the high point of film history hitherto must be attacked. Not in favor of a reconstructed new pleasure, which cannot exist in the abstract, nor of intellectualized unpleasure, but to make way for a total negation of the ease and plenitude of the narrative fiction film. The alternative is the thrill that comes from leaving the past behind without rejecting it, transcending outworn or oppressive forms, or daring to break with normal pleasurable expectations in order to conceive a new language of desire.[27]

Possibly with excessive help from psychoanalytic theory, Mulvey examines the "magic" of mainstream Hollywood films and exposes their exploitation of women by gratifying unconscious male scopophilia. The eye of the camera, the eye of the actor-protagonist and the eye of the audience—all are male, and it is with the erotic pleasure of that eye that any viewer of the film, regardless of gender, must identify. In the world that the film creates, the image of woman is as (passive) raw material for the (active) gaze of men, and the voyeuristic conventions of cinema determine the conditions of its pleasure.[28] Mulvey intends her deconstruction of this practice as a political assault, and she notes that radical filmmakers, especially women, are already developing a new film language. But the implications of Mulvey's attack go beyond the critique of film to a reflection upon the concept of theory in general.[29] For theory, like film, is specular.

Since Plato's glorification of the "eye of the mind," vision has been regarded as the noblest and most theoretical of the senses, and indeed the propaedeutic to the highest form of "seeing," which is nonphysical. Because vision is mediated by light and therefore does not have the direct intimacy of touch or taste or smell, it is less primitive than they are and more philosophical. Thus legitimized by distance, vision is epistemologically privileged. It is lawfully permitted where other forms of perception are not, even though it may be injurious to the object seen. (You can look, but don't touch!)[30] Especially where the theatrics of distance and indirection are enhanced (as in a medical examination) there are virtually no constraints on intrusiveness. In the area of aesthetics, Stanley Cavell problematizes the alienation of the absent film-viewer, but at the same time indulges him with the ultimate voyeuristic triumph: "How do movies reproduce the world magically? Not by literally presenting us with the world, but by permitting us to view it unseen. This is not a wish for power over creation (as Pygmalion's was), but a wish not to need power, not to have to bear its burdens."[31] The theorymaker, likewise, sits comfortably, anonymous and invisible, and fiddles with his machine.

Mulvey exposes this glorification of vision and points to the injury that it does to women. Of greater theoretical interest is her observation that the presumption of truth borne by the image of distance is a non sequitur. We do not know a subject better as a result of mediation; and there is no reason to believe that distance (any more than proximity), whether physical or psychic is conducive to greater objectivity or better understanding. Why should one suppose that a distant observer would be less partisan than a close one? The mythology remains, and Mulvey analyzes its persistence in terms of psychoanalytic theory (male castration anxiety). Whatever its origin, it is undoubtedly reinforced by a genderized social history, transubstantiated in art and culture. Invariably, a (masculinized) seer is glorified at the expense of a (feminized) seen. In science as in art, the prize is possession, and it is awarded to the strangely inactive interventionist who causes the entrapment of the ever-enticing, yet elusive object. This, in turn, manages somehow to be both self-exposing and passive.

Using the critique of an aesthetic genre as her point of entry, Mulvey obliquely indicts an entire epistemological structure. By no means alone in her attack on subject/object dualism or on the conquest model of knowledge, she nevertheless expresses it in a manner that emphasizes the concrete consequences of these apparent abstractions.[32] She makes the gendered object intuitively accessible, so that it is seen as both object and gendered.[33] Her contribution to aesthetic theory is thus as well a contribution of feminist theory.

A second example of an aesthetic art of feminist protest casts light upon another prominent misperception. Susan Stanford Friedman has examined the use of the "childbirth metaphor" to yoke artistic creativity and human procreativity, and she reveals some gross distortions.[34] She deconstructs the model of creativity that the metaphor of giving birth represents to both male and female interpreters, highlighting the fact that different concepts of creativity are encoded into the metaphor depending upon the gender of both readers and writers of a text. Friedman discovers in the literature a sustained and "subversive" inscription of women's (pro)creativity that has existed for centuries. However, the dominant representations of both childbirth and creativity have not been rendered by women, but by men. Ironically, the language of procreation, commonly used to describe the activity of the artist, has been used in a manner that excludes women from that activity. Insemination, fertilization, conception, gestation, incubation, pregnancy, parturition—all parts of the birth process—are invoked to denote an activity that is also theologized as the paradigmatic male act of will, the imposition of form upon inchoate matter. Yet women, whose experience provides the source for all this linguistic speculation, have historically been found unfit for the creative act.[35] The actual birthing of infants has been conceptually demoted to a form of natural secretion, while the willful production of art has been reserved for the male. Friedman points out the contradiction between vehicle (procreation) and tenor (creation) of the metaphor, leading to the characterization of artistic creation as an archetypically paradoxical and therefore heroic act. Men create by overcoming the impossible—that which women are by nature fitted to do. Thus women, designed to follow the natural course, are precluded from the acrobatics of transcendence. Confined to procreation, they cannot create. But seen through women's eyes, procreation has an altogether different quality, one not opposed to creativity.

Babies are never reduced to books, nor books to babies. Women do not lose sight of the literal falsity of the metaphor, but the incongruity of its terms is worked through, yielding a range of complex fusions and integrations that differently affect how women understand their own creativity. One suggested application of the experience of motherhood, extended not alone to the creation of art, but to social engagement and specifically to maintaining the peace, comes from Sara Ruddick.[36] Ruddick borrows a notion from Iris Murdoch *(The Sovereignty of Good),* which is taken in turn from Simone Weil, who advocates a particular form of "attention" that is loving and careful as well as acute. Indeed works of art are not more "dropped" than babies. Nor are they launched into space and disowned. The author is not released with the pain of birth (a "plop" and then it's over) but is unalterably affected by and connected with the fate of her offspring, albeit that does not remain entirely under her control. Friedman speaks of a "female metaphor" that expresses a "defiant reunion of what patriarchal culture has kept mutually exclusive—'this unwearying maternal love, this habit of creation.' "

Unlike Mulvey, Friedman is not interested in psychoanalytic explorations of men's reasons for appropriating the childbirth metaphor. Her avowed purpose is to display how gender "informs and complicates the reading and writing of texts," and she takes the childbirth metaphor for creativity as illustration. She finds that male use of the metaphor intensifies "difference and collision," while females tend to "enhance sameness and collusion."[37] I am taking her analysis one step further to observe that the male representations of both creativity and procreativity have been normative. Just as the feminist deconstruction of vision by Mulvey took an aesthetic form as a wedge into a larger theoretical issue (effectively an assault on traditional theory), so does Friedman's examination of the birth metaphor unearth some fundamental inadequacies of "mainstream" metaphysics. Essentially it reveals a primitive understanding of creation as a willful and incoherent act, often an act of violence—the author drops his load and moves irresponsibly on to new territory.[38] Is it any wonder that we are beset with monumental ethical and social problems of pollution, overpopulation, and environmental destruction?

These two cases illustrate how aesthetic analysis is a tool for feminist theory. Concentrating upon the deconstruction of a deceptively minor detail, such criticism serves as an entry into a thicket of unexamined philosophical presumptions. As layer upon layer of error and incongruity is revealed cleansed of its cover of familiarity, we are compelled—by fascination as well as need—to push on to greater understanding. Perhaps there is also a sense of embarrassment that we have stood by for so long, allowing our lives to be dictated in such a bungling fashion and for such unworthy ends. Whatever the reasons, there seems now to be some hope of recovery.

Conclusion

Feminist theory is still in its infancy, and feminist aesthetic theory is only beginning to find itself. I am suggesting that aesthetic theorizing provides a key to the development of feminist theory because of its intrinsic adherence to the immediate and the experiential on the one hand and its dedication to the communion of form on the other. That combination does not guarantee success, but it allows us to proceed bit by bit, checking along the way that neither content nor order are sacrificed, and that we remain close to our base in experience even as we reframe our ways of thinking about it. Since feminist theory abjures the all-consuming totalizing format that is our patriarchal heritage, it must devise new modes of theorizing that will permit sustained attention to the minutiae of difference without loss of intelligibility. Failing that, we fall back on anecdote and trivia that quickly lose both aesthetic and intellectual interest.

Another caveat is that feminists must avoid disingenuous pluralism. The pronouncement that if we are not infallible there can be no truth is not a genuine acknowledgment of difference, but only a grudging sacrifice of sameness. Feminists should find it easier than traditional philosophers to live without overarching truths or ultimate legitimization because we have always been contingent. This is not a case of making virtue out of necessity, but rather a recognition that what was seen as a mark of deviancy is in fact the norm. We are not in search of a soul, nor of a leader, and the absence of both would be no tragedy. Feminists must define themselves and their own world without succumbing to the arrogant presumption that they are choosing for all, yet being prepared to undertake the responsibility that they are choosing for some. It is possible to opt for pluralism without abandoning either rationality or idealism and certainly without giving in to despair. As I have shown, the pleasure of theorizing should spare us from that. I have argued that feminist theory is radically innovative in its philosophical approach and that aesthetics is at its center. Traditionally, Western philosophy places aesthetics at its periphery, where it recapitulates the paradoxes of metaphysics and epistemology. In reversing that pattern, feminist theory discovers new areas for exploration. Asking new questions, forging a new language, meeting new counterparts likewise drawn in from the margins, we meet ourselves with new faces, and that is surely enlivening.[39]

Notes

1. Iris Marion Young uses the word "masculinism" or "masculinist" in her essay "Humanism, Gynocentrism and Feminist Politics," *Hypatia: A Journal of Feminist Philosophy,* special issue of *Women's Studies International Quarterly* 8 (1985): 173–83. She uses it in polar correspondence with "gynocentrism," a form of feminism that focuses on gender differences in values and language and brings the distinctively feminine critique to the masculinist values and language that are dominant in the world. A more commonly used word introduced by French feminists influenced by the psychoanalytic reflections of Jacques Lacan and the philosophy of Jacques Derrida is "phallocratic" or "phallogocratic." However, these terms, in their etymology, refer more restrictively to the issue of power and political dominance. The more ambiguous word "masculinist" is gender-specific while leaving open the issue of power distribution.

2. Contrary to a commonly held belief, feminism comes no more naturally to women than to men. Women are normally socialized to experience the world in accordance with male-determined categories. Knowing themselves to be female, they nevertheless understand what that means in male terms, unless they explicitly take an oppositional stand and declare their right to self-determination. This is why feminism entails the forging of a new vocabulary and new conceptual framework.

3. See Micheline R. Malson, Jean F. O'Barr, Sarah Westphal-Wihl and Mary Wyer, eds., *Feminist Theory in Practice and Process* (Chicago: University of Chicago Press, 1989).

4. Some feminists do believe in the metaphysical or biological reality of gender and in the absolute distinctness of the sexes. I will not dispute the feminism of that position. However, since it can be maintained equally plausibly by nonfeminists and antifeminists, it is not a distinctively feminist position. I am arguing that feminism entails the deliberate adoption of a gendered-feminine perspective as a critical stance. This may be done compatibly with both essentialism and its denial.

5. As early as the Pythagorean Table of Opposites and perhaps even earlier the same paradox of knowledge and ontology affirms that the engendered has epistemic priority over the engendering principle. Darkness begat light, but is known only in relation to it. The same is true of the infinite and the bounded, the female and the male. That which is born defines itself in opposition to and knows the other only by negation.

6. Humanistic or liberal feminism does claim the generic unicity of human being. Perhaps the earliest expression of feminism, dating back at least to Mary Wollstonecraft's *A Vindication of the Rights of Woman,* and classically defended by John Stuart Mill in "The Subjection of Women," this philosophical doctrine is primarily political in purpose. It declares that the obstacles to women's equality are external to their nature as human and calls for the removal of all those impediments that interfere with women's full self-realization as human. Libertarian feminism can be radical in its solutions. Proponents have advocated the replacement of natural childbirth with extrauterine fertilization and gestation (see Shulamith Firestone, *The Dialectic of Sex* [New York: Bantam Books, 1970]) and various forms of androgyny (see Carolyn G. Heilbrun, *Towards the Promise of Androgyny* [New York: Knopf, 1973]). See also Mary Vetterling-Braggin, ed., *"Femininity," "Masculinity" and "Androgyny"* (Totowa, N.J.: Rowman and Littlefield, 1982). The theory of liberal feminism is essentially that of liberalism with special attention to the equality of women.

7. An outstanding proponent of gender dualism is Mary Daly, author of *Gyn/Ecology* (Boston: Beacon, 1978). In her view the essential woman is in transformative process, coming to be—"sparking" and "spinning" and en-spiriting herself. Susan Griffin in *Woman and Nature: The Roaring Inside Her* (New York: Harper and Row, 1978) likewise affirms the essence of women in contradistinction to male-determined culture.

8. With this phrase Beauvoir opens Book 2 of *The Second Sex.* See discussion in Young, "Humanism, Gynocentrism," 174.

9. Collaboration itself has been defended as a characteristically feminist mode of interaction, but it is not without its difficulties. Women have been forced to acknowledge among themselves the presence of once tabooed competition. The issue is explored in an (ironically) coauthored and coedited text, *Competition: A Feminist Taboo,* ed. Valerie Miner and Helen E. Longino (New York: Feminist Press, 1987).

10. An example of such convergence would be the current celebration of the idea of *difference.* Early in the second wave of the North American women's movement (that is, in the 1970s) working-class women and women of color repeatedly reminded white middle-class women that they were no more entitled to define the norm of women's identity than men were entitled to represent the human norm. Thus chastened, white women did begin listening to their sisters, hearing with difficulty and not without conflicts (see bell hooks, *Feminist Theory: From Margin to Center* [Boston: South End Press, 1984]). Dialogue did occur, and with it some movement toward mutual understanding and respect for diversity. Similar rapprochements took place in political environments between lesbian women and heterosexuals, between young and aging women, and between intellectuals and others. At the same time, within academe, postmodernist theory has glorified multiplicity, diversity, and profusion. Where difference had been suppressed in the interest of unity, it now became fashionable to find opportunity in difference. It remains to be seen whether this is a genuine convergence that will be productive either theoretically or practically, but it has led to the breaking down of cultural myths and conventional hierarchies so that already it is possible to experience the world in new ways.

11. While men are also contextually gendered, their gender is represented as the paradigm and thus is not contingent upon that of women. Relatively speaking, male identity is more uniform.

12. Elizabeth Young-Bruehl, "The Education of Women as Philosophers," in *Feminist Theory in Practice and Process*, 35–49.

13. Jeffner Allen and Iris Marion Young, eds. *The Thinking Muse* (Bloomington: Indiana University Press, 1989), introduction.

14. Theories that elaborate unity in diversity, organic unity, and especially those that focus upon "open texture" in aesthetic theory are seeking ways to accommodate real and potential variety. Though wedded to synthesis, aestheticians perhaps beyond all other theoreticians, must affirm the unprecedented and original and cannot deny their infinite variety. Thus aesthetic theory is closer in spirit to feminist theory than any other model of theory.

15. Joan Kelly, *Women, History and Theory* (Chicago: University of Chicago Press, 1984).

16. The confusion is compounded by misleading titles, such as *Feminist Aesthetics*, ed. Gisela Ecker (Boston: Beacon, 1986). This book begins with an essay by Silvia Bovenschen, "Is There a Feminine Aesthetic?" which is followed by a series of affirmative and negative answers given by women interested in the distinctively feminine contribution that women have made in a number of fields of artistic endeavor. See also Teresa de Lauretis, "Rethinking Women's Cinema: Aesthetics and Feminist Theory," in *Technologies of Gender* (Bloomington: Indiana University Press, 1987).

17. Authors responding to a call for papers on Feminism and Aesthetics for *Hypatia* 5 (1990) were preeminently concerned with the issue of a feminine aesthetic. Disagreeing among themselves regarding its fixity or necessary gender specificity, they were, by and large, in agreement that style and gender correlates are contingently real.

18. Note the difference between the adjective "feminine" and the word "feminist," which may be a noun, adjective, or adverb. The former purports to describe behavior by females and carries the covert, if not explicit implication that such behavior is certainly proper and probably natural to females. The latter term refers to the political conviction that advocates the assumption of the woman's perspective. Feminists are not always feminine, although they may be, and feminine behavior may or may not be compatible with feminism.

19. Hélène Cixous and Catherine Clément, "Sorties," in *The Newly Born Woman*, trans. Betsy Wing (Minneapolis: University of Minnesota Press, 1986), cited in Rosemary Tong, *Feminist Thought: A Comprehensive Introduction* (Boulder: Westview, 1989), 224, 225.

20. Space, including absence and negativity have generally played an important part in defining the female. A famous statement by Erik Erikson is in "The Inner and the Outer Space: Reflections on Womanhood," *Daedalus* 93 (1964): 582–606. Reasoning by anatomical analogy, Erikson concludes that woman experiences an "emptiness" that is fulfilled by motherhood. Feminists are inclined to take a larger view of the negativities of their role. They concentrate upon women as potentiators, creators of time and space—as they are frequently called upon to do in their personal and social relations. See R. Perry and M. Watson Brownley, eds., *Mothering the Mind* (New York: Holmes and Meier, 1987). A crucial element of the contemporary women's movement has been the creation of spaces by women for themselves—refuges for battered women, workplaces, centers for study, alternative arts spaces, crisis referral places, and health resources.

21. Lisa Tickner, "The Body Politic: Female Sexuality and Women Artists Since 1970," in *Framing Feminism: Art and the Women's Movement, 1970–1985* (New York: Pandora, 1987), 273.

22. "Literary criticism especially, because it addresses the best this thinking has produced, exposes this paradox in all its painful complexity—while also revealing the extraordinary possibility of our seeing the old world from a genuinely new perspective," Myra Jehlen, "Archimedes and the Paradox of Feminist Criticism," *The Signs Reader: Women, Gender and Scholarship*, ed. Elizabeth Abel and Emily K. Abel (Chicago: University of Chicago Press, 1981).

23. Sandra Harding, "The Instability of the Analytical Categories of Feminist Theory," in *Feminist Theory in Practice and Process*, 19, 20.

24. Elizabeth Spelman, *Inessential Woman: Problems of Exclusion in Feminist Thought* (Boston: Beacon, 1988), 161, 162, 187.

25. See *Hypatia* 5 (1990), especially the essays by French, Barwell, Schrage, and Robinson and Ross.

26. Pierre Bourdieu, *Distinction: A Social Critique of the Judgment of Taste,* trans. R. Nice (Cambridge: Cambridge University Press, 1984), 496.

27. In Constance Penley, ed., *Feminism and Film Theory* (New York: Routledge, 1988), 59.

28. Ibid., 67.

29. Mulvey explicitly appropriates Freudian psychoanalytic theory as a political weapon to unmask the working of the "magic" of cinema. While she does not give explicit acknowledgment to Sartre's elaboration of the (male) gaze, his discussion in part 3 of *Being and Nothingness* (trans. Hazel Barnes [New York: Philosophical Library, 1956]) is an exemplary account of a perceptual reduction of ontology. The perceived object, aware of herself perceived, finds herself coerced to self-awareness as through the eyes of another, thus ceasing to be for herself.

30. Technologies of surveillance have given a new dimension to this privilege and complicated its legality, but generally the principle holds that indirection confers immunity.

31. Stanley Cavell, *The World Viewed: Reflections on the Ontology of Film* (New York: Viking, 1971), chap. 6.

32. See for example Evelyn Fox Keller, *Reflections on Gender and Science* (New Haven: Yale University Press, 1985) or such prefeminist critiques as William Leiss, *The Domination of Nature* (New York: George Braziller, 1972).

33. Admittedly one must wade through her ponderous prose style to get there, but once arrived, one cannot but see films with an altered awareness, much like that induced by John Berger's influential pictorial essay on women in *Ways of Seeing* (New York: Viking, 1973).

34. Susan Stanford Friedman, "Creativity and the Childbirth Metaphor: Gender Difference in Literary Discourse," *Feminist Studies* 13 (1987): 49–82.

35. From Aristotle's *Generation of Animals* to De Beauvoir's *The Second Sex,* procreation has been viewed as an essentially passive process, something that happens to the individual, rather than a project that she undertakes. Only recently, thanks to both feminist awareness and the possibility of control, has there been serious exploration of the extent to which reproduction is a spiritual as well as physical activity.

36. Sara Ruddick, "Maternal Thinking" and "Preservative Love and Military Destruction: Some Reflections on Mothering and Peace," *Mothering: Essays in Feminist Theory,* ed. Joyce Tribilcot, (Totowa, N.J.: Rowman and Allenheld, 1983).

37. Friedman, "Creativity and the Childbirth Metaphor," 75.

38. Feminist authors frequently and incredulously call attention to the insulting use of reproductive metaphors in the context of militarism. "Oppenheimer's baby" to refer to the atom bomb is only the most obvious. See Carol Cohn, "Sex and Death in the Rational World of Defense Intellectuals," in *Feminist Theory in Practice and Process.*

39. In using this figure of speech, I have inadvertently adapted the title of bell hooks, *Feminist Theory: From Margin to Center* (Boston: South End Press, 1984) and also agreed with its thesis.

SELECT BIBLIOGRAPHY TO PART V

Allen, Jeffner, and Iris Marion Young, eds. *The Thinking Muse: Feminism and Modern French Philosophy*. Bloomington: Indiana University Press, 1989.

Barrett, Michele. *Women's Oppression Today: Problems in Marxist Feminist Analysis*. London: Verso, 1990.

Beauvoir, Simone de. *The Second Sex*. New York: Vintage Books, 1989.

Benjamin, Andrew, and Peter Osborne, eds. *Thinking Art: Beyond Traditional Aesthetics*. London: Institute of Contemporary Arts, 1991.

Bigwood, Carol. *Earth Muse: Feminism, Nature, and Art*. Philadelphia: Temple University Press, 1993.

Bovenschen, Silvia. "Is There a Feminine Aesthetic?" In *Feminist Aesthetics*, edited by Gisela Ecker. Boston: Beacon, 1986.

Cixous, Hélène, and Catherine Clément. *The Newly Born Woman*. Minneapolis: University of Minnesota Press, 1986.

Ecker, Gisela, ed. *Feminist Aesthetics*. Boston: Beacon, 1986.

Felski, Rita. *Beyond Feminist Aesthetics: Feminist Literature and Social Change*. Cambridge: Harvard University Press: 1989.

———. *The Gender of Modernity*. Harvard University Press, forthcoming.

Fraser, Nancy, and Sandra Lee Bartky, eds. *Revaluing French Feminism: Critical Essays on Difference, Agency and Culture*. Bloomington: Indiana University Press, 1992.

French, Marilyn. "Is There a Feminist Aesthetic?" In *Aesthetics in Feminist Perspective*, edited by Hilde Hein and Carolyn Korsmeyer. Bloomington: Indiana University Press, 1993.

Gablik, Suzi. *Has Modernism Failed?* New York: Thames and Hudson, 1984.

———. *The Reenchantment of Art*. New York: Thames and Hudson, 1991.

Hein, Hilde. *The Exploratorium: The Museum as Laboratory*. Washington, D.C.: Smithsonian Institution Press, 1990.

———, and Carolyn Korsmeyer, eds. *Aesthetics in Feminist Perspective*. Bloomington: Indiana University Press, 1993.

Holland, Nancy J. *Is Women's Philosophy Possible?* Totowa, N.J.: Rowman and Littlefield, 1990.

Irigaray, Luce. *This Sex Which Is Not One*. Translated by Catherine Porter. Ithaca: Cornell University Press, 1985.

Jardine, Alice. *Gynesis: Configurations of Women and Modernity*. Ithaca: Cornell University Press, 1985.

Kruger, Barbara, and Phil Mariani, eds. *Remaking History*. Seattle: Seattle Bay Press, 1989.

Le Doeff, Michele. *Hipparchia's Choice: An Essay Concerning Women, Philosophy, etc.* Translated by Trista Selous. Oxford: Basil Blackwell, 1991.

Margolis, Joseph. *Art and Philosophy*. Atlantic Highlands, N.J.: Humanities Press, 1978.

————. *The Flux of History and the Flux of Science*. Berkeley and Los Angeles: University of California Press, 1993.

Moi, Toril. *Feminist Theory and Simone de Beauvoir*. London: Basil Blackwell, 1990.

————. *French Feminist Thought: a Reader*. London: Basil Blackwell, 1987.

————. *Sexual/Textual Politics: Feminist Literary Theory*. New York: Methuen, 1985.

Nicholson, Linda, ed. *Feminism/Postmodernism*. New York: Routledge, 1990.

Robinson, Hilary, ed. *Visibly Female: Feminism and Art Today*. London: Camden, 1987.

Scheman, Naomi. *Engenderings: Constructions of Knowledge, Authority, and Privilege*. New York: Routledge, 1993.

Showalter, Elaine. *Speaking of Gender*. New York: Routledge, 1989.

Shusterman, Richard. *Pragmatist Aesthetics: Living Beauty, Rethinking Art*. Oxford: Cambridge University Press, 1992.

————, ed. *Analytic Aesthetics*. Oxford: Basil Blackwell, 1989.

Tuana, Nancy. *Woman and the History of Philosophy*. New York: Paragon House, 1992.

Whitford, Margaret. *Luce Irigaray: Philosophy in the Feminine*. London: Routledge, 1991.

Wolff, Janet. *Feminine Sentences: Essays on Women and Culture*. Berkeley and Los Angeles: University of California Press, 1990.

Contributors

CHRISTINE BATTERSBY is senior lecturer in philosophy and contributes to the Centre for the Study of Women and Gender at the University of Warwick. She works in an interdisciplinary manner, producing numerous essays on feminist philosophy, cultural history and aesthetics, and women in literature and the visual arts. Her *Gender and Genius: Towards a Feminist Aesthetics* was first published by The Women's Press and Indiana University Press in 1989. She is currently working on a monograph on feminist metaphysics and the sublime.

PEGGY ZEGLIN BRAND is assistant professor of philosophy at Indiana University, coeditor (with Carolyn Korsmeyer) of the special issue of the *Journal of Aesthetics and Art Criticism*, "Feminism and Traditional Aesthetics" (1990), and author of various essays in feminism and aesthetics. Her current interests include women's humor, particularly parody.

NOËL CARROLL is professor of philosophy at the University of Wisconsin–Madison. He has written widely on the field of art and aesthetics, and his most recent book is *The Philosophy of Horror.*

MARY DEVEREAUX is an associate professor at Bucknell University, working on topics in aesthetics, film theory, and feminist theory. She has published articles and reviews in the *Journal of Aesthetics and Art Criticism, Philosophy and Literature, Art Journal,* the *Philosophical Review,* and *Ethics.* She is currently working on the topic of art and censorship.

ELIZABETH ANN DOBIE is a graduate student in philosophy at the University of Connecticut. She is currently completing her dissertation on interpreting visual works of art. She plans to continue her research in the areas of aesthetics and feminism.

SUSAN L. FEAGIN is associate professor of philosophy at the University of Missouri–Kansas City. She was book review editor of the *Journal of Aesthetics and Art Criticism* from 1988 to 1993, and her publications have appeared in such journals as the *Journal of Aesthetics and Art Criticism*, the *British Journal of Aesthetics*, the *American Philosophical Quarterly*, and *Philosophical Studies*.

RITA FELSKI is professor of English at the University of Virginia and the author of *Beyond Feminist Aesthetics* (Harvard University Press, 1989). Her *Gender of Modernity* is forthcoming from Harvard University Press.

MARY D. GARRARD is professor of art history in the Department of Art, American University, Washington, D.C. She is the author of *Artemisia Gentileschi: The Image of the Female Hero in Italian Baroque Art* (Princeton University Press, 1989). She coedited (with Norma Broude) *Feminism and Art History: Questioning the Litany* (Harper and Row, 1982), and its sequel *The Expanding Discourse: Feminism and Art History* (HarperCollins, 1992). She has also published articles and reviews on Renaissance art and feminist theory. Her current work includes a book on the American feminist art movement of the 1970s, coedited with Norma Broude (1994). The Leonardo essay reprinted here forms part of a book in progress, *Nature, Art, and Gender in Renaissance Italy*.

TIMOTHY GOULD teaches at Metropolitan State College in Denver and writes about the persistence of Romanticism in contemporary culture and criticism. He has recently completed a book entitled *Traces of Freedom: An Archeology of Kant's Aesthetics*.

HILDE HEIN teaches philosophy, aesthetics, and feminist theory at Holy Cross College and is the author of *The Exploratorium: The Museum as Laboratory* (Smithsonian Institution Press, 1990) and co-editor (with Carolyn Korsmeyer) of *Aesthetics in Feminist Perspective* (Indiana University Press, 1993).

BELL HOOKS is a cultural critic, feminist theorist, writer, and the author of seven books published by South End Press, most recently *Black Looks: Race and Representation* (1991) and *Sisters of the Yam: Black Women and Self-Recovery* (1993).

CAROLYN KORSMEYER teaches philosophy at the State University of New York–Buffalo. In addition to her published work in aesthetics, she is coauthor of *Feminist Scholarship: Kindling in the Groves of Academe* (University of Illinois Press, 1985) and coeditor (with Hilde Hein) of *Aesthetics in Feminist Perspective* (Indiana University Press, 1993).

RENÉE LORRAINE is a professor at the University of Tennessee–Chattanooga, where she teaches in the music, philosophy, and humanities departments. She is the author of various articles on music, aesthetics, and feminist theory, and teaches music history, aesthetics, feminist theory, and double bass. She is at present serving as a trustee of the American Society for Aesthetics.

JOSEPH MARGOLIS is currently the Laura H. Carnell Professor of Philosophy at Temple University and is a past president of the American Society for Aesthetics. His most recent book is *The Flux of History and the Flux of Science* (University of California Press, 1993).

PAUL MATTICK, JR., teaches philosophy at Adelphi University and is the author of *Social Knowledge* (M. E. Sharpe, 1986) and editor of *Eighteenth-Century Aesthetics and the Reconstruction of Art* (Cambridge University Press, 1993). He has written criticism for *The Nation, Arts Magazine,* and *Art in America.*

TRINH T. MINH-HA is professor of Women's Studies and Film at the University of California–Berkeley, and is a writer, filmmaker, and composer. Her recent works include the books *Framer Framed* (Routledge, 1992), *When the Moon Waxes Red* (Routledge, 1991), and *Woman, Native, Other* (Indiana University Press, 1989); and the films *Reassemblage* (1982), *Naked Spaces—Living is Round* (1985), *Surname Viet Given Name Nam* (1989), and *Shoot for the Contents* (1991).

ADRIAN PIPER is professor of philosophy at Wellesley College and a conceptual artist whose work in a variety of media has focused on racism, racial stereotyping, and xenophobia for more than two decades. A recipient of Guggenheim, AVA, and several NEA fellowships, her work has been internationally exhibited since 1968; a conference on her contributions to art and philosophy was held at New York University in October 1992.

ANITA SILVERS is professor of philosophy at San Francisco State University and codirected the 1991 NEH Summer Institute for College Teachers on Philosophy and the Histories of the Arts. She is the author of many articles, including a series that explores how the hero(in)ic figure of the artist integrates tradition and innovation in the arts. Her most recent work includes a series of essays comparing how the ethics of equality (or justice) and the ethics of vulnerability (or caring) treat the figure of the defective agent.

ELLEN HANDLER SPITZ is lecturer on aesthetics in psychiatry at the Cornell University Medical Center and was a Getty Scholar in 1989–90. She is the author of *Art and Psyche* (Yale University Press, 1985) and *Image and Insight* (Columbia University Press, 1991) and the coeditor with Peter L. Rudrytsky of *Freud and Forbidden Knowledge* (New York and London: New York University Press, 1994).

JOANNE B. WAUGH is associate professor of philosophy at the University of South Florida. She writes on issues involving art, ethics, and society.

Index